TEN YEARS
IN JAPAN

A Contemporary Record
Drawn from the
Diaries and Private and Official
Papers of

JOSEPH C. GREW

United States Ambassador
to Japan
1932–1942

19 44

SIMON AND SCHUSTER
NEW YORK

About the Appearance of Books in Wartime

A recent ruling by the War Production Board has curtailed the use of paper by book publishers in 1944.

In line with this ruling and in order to conserve materials and manpower, we are co-operating by:

1. Using lighter-weight paper, which reduces the bulk of our books substantially.
2. Printing books with smaller margins and with more words to each page. Result: fewer pages per book.

Slimmer and smaller books will save paper and plate metal and labor. We are sure that readers will understand the publishers' desire to co-operate as fully as possible with the objectives of the War Production Board and our government.

MANUFACTURED IN THE UNITED STATES OF AMERICA
BY AMERICAN BOOK—STRATFORD PRESS, INC., NEW YORK

To Alice, My Teammate

who, by her wise advice and encouragement
through difficult years, was a solid rock of support

CONTENTS

1

Ambassador and Mrs. Grew, with Bishop James De Wolfe Perry, before the memorial to Commodore Nathaniel G. Perry at Shimoda, Japan. (See p. 93.)

2

Along the coast of the Izu Peninsula, near where Commodore Perry landed.

3

Dedicating the monument to Townsend Harris at the Zempukuji (a Shinto temple), site of the first American Legation in Japan. Left to right: Mr. Houston, Commissioner of the New York World's Fair; Mr. Fujihara, now Minister of Commerce; Baron Masuda, who, as a boy, served in Harris' household; and Ambassador Grew.

4

5

A tank passing through the street
outside the Embassy.

Sandbags in front of the American
Embassy.

6

A barricade in front of the Embassy.

7

Admiral Viscount Saito, assassinated in the February 26 Incident,
and his granddaughter. (See p. 171.)

8

Justice Frank Murphy, then High Commissioner to the Philippines, stands at the center of this picture. Foreign Minister Hirota stands between him and Ambassador Grew. At the extreme right stands Shigemitsu, former ambassador to Britain and Russia, subsequently Foreign Minister in Tojo's war cabinet. Eiji Amau, Foreign Office spokesman who later became wartime Minister to Switzerland, stands behind and just to the left of Mr. Grew. Second from the left is Saburu Kurusu of the infamous mission who later became Ambassador to Germany, and just in front of him and to his right is Debuchi, former Ambassador to the United States. Horinouchi, another former Japanese Ambassador to the United States, stands just behind Hirota. (See p. 93.)

9

Admiral Murfin, former Commander in Chief of the United States Asiatic Fleet; Admiral Nagano, Navy Minister, and Ambassador Grew. Admiral Shimada, present commander of the Japanese Fleet in China, is second from right.

10

Manuel Quezon, then President of the Philippine Islands, arrives in Tokyo, 1937.
(See p. 204.)

11

Helen Keller visits the Embassy garden. Left to right: Foreign Minister Hirota,
Mrs. Grew, Helen Keller and her companion, and Ambassador Grew. (See p. 207.)

12

13

Imperial Duck Hunt. (See p. 82.)

14

Babe Ruth and "Lefty" O'Doul stare at Ambassador Grew's method of putting.
(See p. 144.)

15

The Ambassador attends the Tokyo Golf Club's annual luncheon for the winners of the women's tournament.

16

The Ambassador attends a geisha dinner. (See p. 93.)

17

Ambassador and Mrs. Grew offer their condolences to Mrs. Hiroshi Saito and her daughters while awaiting the landing of the ashes of the late Ambassador Saito, who died in the United States. (See p. 275.)

18

A dinner gathering at the American Embassy in honor of Captain Turner and the officers of the U.S.S. *Astoria,* including (second from left) the late Mr. Iwanaga, director of the Domei news service; Captain Turner; War Minister General Itagaki; Foreign Minister Arita; Ambassador Grew; Imperial Household Minister Matsudaira; Navy Minister Admiral Yonai; former Foreign Minister Yoshizawa. Former Foreign Minister Admiral Nomura is directly behind Yoshizawa. (See p. 275.)

19

A meeting with prominent Japanese. Front row, left to right: Mr. Shigemitsu, former Ambassador to the Court of St. James's; Ambassador Grew; Prince Chichibu,
the Emperor's brother; Mr. Hirota, former Foreign Minister; Count Kabayama.
Second row: Mr. Kishi, private secretary to Hirota; Mr. Horinouchi, former Ambassador to the United States; Prince Konoye, former Prime Minister; Count Maeda,
secretary to Prince Chichibu; Baron Harada, secretary to the Genro; Prince Saionji.

20

Meeting with Townsend Harris' houseboy. Front row, left to right: Captain Martin,
Mrs. Crane, Ambassador Grew, Baron Masuda, who served Townsend Harris dur-
ing his mission to Japan in 1859, Colonel Crane, and Mrs. Masuda. Standing:
Miss Konda, Miss Masuda, Lieutenant Smith-Hutton, Mr. Fukukita. Back row:
Count Kabayama, Mrs. Grew, Admiral Uriu, who attended Annapolis in his youth,
and unknown woman.

21

The Ambassador and staff of the American Embassy enjoy a Japanese dinner.

22

Office building and apartment houses of the American Embassy. The Imperial Diet building is in the background.

23

A Japanese country villa.

24

A view of the rooftops of Tokyo, taken from the American Embassy. The prominent building in the background is the Imperial Diet.

Foreword

THIS BOOK has a method and a purpose, both of which require a word of explanation.

First for the method. Convinced that the accurate recording of history depends upon frank contemporary comment, I have followed the practice during my thirty-nine years in the foreign service of the United States of jotting down day by day the information, impressions, and thoughts of the moment. The resulting written record has the defects of its qualities—and vice versa. Only in the pages of an honest and candid diary can we find set down the convictions and assumptions on which our decisions and actions have been based. No one at any time can aspire to infallibility, but anyone can at all times set down his honest opinions. These opinions, of course, change—partly because circumstances change and partly also because we keep acquiring new information that causes us to modify our views.

The diary entries during my ten years in Japan suffer from the shortcomings of any such record, but if occasion has more than once occurred to revise my judgments, the record has been scrupulously kept from day to day. Not only that, but I believe that this strictly contemporary record has a value that has no relationship to the wisdom or unwisdom of the various judgments in records. Opinions are therefore here reproduced that were later revised as new facts came to my attention. Views and prognostications that were later shown to be wrong have herein been set down quite as frankly as those which time proved to be right. In keeping the diary there was never a thought of eventual publication. Furthermore it was impossible, especially in a post like Tokyo, during the difficult years before Pearl Harbor, for us to have exactly the same global perspective that obtained in Washington. Perspectives develop from what one knows, and additional knowledge broadens and deepens and sharpens one's understanding.

In spite of all discouragements that I experienced, especially when periods of hopeful labor with peace-minded and constructive-minded Japanese governments were terminated by their downfall and were succeeded by reactionary cabinets, the results of

that labor having been wiped out as if by a typhoon, I worked for
peace up to the end. An ambassador who on taking a foreign post
throws up his hands and says "War is inevitable" might just as well
pack up and come home. Our foreign service is our first line of
national defense. It must hold that line if possible, and work to
hold it. In the case of Japan, once the war had broken out in Europe
and the initial German victories had gone to the heads of the Japanese militarists like strong wine, the outlook was ominous and I so
informed our Government, warning of possible action by Japan of
dangerous and dramatic suddenness. But I never wholly abandoned
hope or stopped working for peace. To have done so would have
been to discredit the service of which I am a member.

Here is another point to bear in mind. This book contains only
a small fraction of the original diary which, for the past ten years,
fills thirteen large typewritten volumes quite apart from many other
volumes of my letters, speeches, records of conversations, and pertinent press clippings. Many of the items in the original possess no
permanent historic value. Others overlap. Still others cannot properly be published now. And since this is an intimate off-the-record
journal I have also had to keep confidential the identity of many
living colleagues and other individuals who might be embarrassed
or suffer some personal consequences if their names were made
known. The main story has, however, not been injured by these
omissions. I have avoided cluttering up the text with asterisks and
footnotes but have selected and arranged the original diary entries
together with other contemporary material in such a way as to present a smooth-flowing chronological narrative. While it has obviously
been impractical to include in the diary all of the texts of the
official documents pertaining to the story, many of these texts are
available to the public in two volumes published in 1943 by the
United States Government Printing Office entitled *Foreign Relations of the United States, Japan, 1931–1941.*

And now a word about the purpose of this narrative. This book
aims to present to our people and, I hope, to the people of all the
United Nations, a more accurately focused view of Japan than is
now widely held, for only through a correct conception of that
country and its people can we approach with intelligence the difficult problems which will have to be solved after our military victory
is complete. My last book, *Report from Tokyo*, was aimed primarily
at acquainting the people of the United States with the formidable
character of the Japanese military machine and to correct some of

the fallacious thinking which has widely persisted throughout our country, underrating the stamina, fighting-power, and staying-power of the Japanese enemy. Knowing that enemy through ten long years of close observation, I fear that we may have a long, hard road ahead before complete victory can be attained. Wishful thinking and complacency are dangerous. To achieve that victory and to bring about the ultimate unconditional surrender of the enemy, our united war effort must be constantly intensified and accelerated, never for a moment relaxed.

We have been presented for some years past with cumulative evidence of unmitigated subtleties, trickery, brutality, and cynical faithlessness on the part of the Japanese military caste and machine, and there is presented in my story fresh evidence of the medieval character of the Japanese military mind and temperament. A primary axiom of war is to "know your enemy." In my former book and in many speeches and broadcasts throughout our country I have tried to set forth the great strength and fanatical determination, the utter cruelty and brutality, of the Japanese military.

The present book will not have served one of its purposes, however, if it does not bring home to my readers the fact that there are many Japanese today who did not want war, who realized the stupidity of attacking the United States, Great Britain and other United Nations, and who did everything in their power to restrain the military extremists from their headlong and suicidal aggressions. In the heat and prejudice of war some will deny that there can be any good elements among the Japanese people. Yet those critics, in all likelihood, will not have known personally and directly those Japanese who were bitterly opposed to war with the United States—men who courageously but futilely gave all that was in them and ran the gravest dangers of imprisonment if not of assassination—indeed several were assassinated—in their efforts to stem the tide or, let us say, to halt the tidal wave of insane military megalomania and expansionist ambition.

Those people must and will loyally support their leaders in war; those who have to fight must and will fight to the end. But we shall need to know and to weigh all factors in approaching the difficult postwar problems. It is my hope that these intimate, day-to-day records may serve to produce for the future a wider and more helpful picture of those people as a people.

First, however, Japan's power to wage war must be wholly destroyed; the decision must be complete and irrevocable if our sons and grandsons are not to fight this war over again in the next generation. Japan, no less than Germany, must never again be allowed to threaten world peace. Aggressive militarism must be *permanently* eradicated.

In completing this book I cannot omit an expression to three persons of my full appreciation of their helpfulness in connection with its preparation: to Eugene H. Dooman, Counselor of the American Embassy in Tokyo during the critical years before Pearl Harbor, my *fidus Achates* on whose long experience in Japan, mature advice, and incisive diagnosis of political developments I counted greatly in the formulation through those years of the views herein set forth; and to Miss Marion Arnold (now Mrs. Dana W. Johnston) and Nelson Newton, my secretaries, who gave a great deal of their time, their interest, and their devoted care to the preparation of the diary on which this book is based.

JOSEPH C. GREW

Washington
January, 1944

I

THE ASSASSIN'S SHADOW LIES ACROSS JAPAN

(May 14, 1932–February 15, 1933)

THE TEN years that this narrative covers witnessed a series of explosive crises in the internal and external affairs of Japan. Some of these crises remained confined to the political sphere. Others took the form of assassination and military attack. The year 1932 opened with a series of political assassinations, culminating in the murder of Premier Inukai on May 15. The first section of this narrative therefore covers the period of surface calm that, for once, did not end in violence but merely in Japan's recognition of the state of Manchukuo and her decision to quit the League of Nations.

n in the late afternoon after two or three hard sets of deck
his, thus keeping wonderfully fit, and the talkies on alternate
hts.

May 26, 1932. Honolulu

A great big red-letter day, our first in Honolulu. Was up at 5:30,
eminding me of the occasions on which my daughter Anita and I
ad often risen early to watch our entrance into the lovely Bay of
Naples. Soon after 6, we docked to the welcoming strains of *Aloha*
played by a band on shore, which effectually awakened the rest of
the family. Major Ross, Sheriff of Honolulu and aide to Governor
Judd, came on board with the pilot, welcomed us in the Governor's
name, and decorated us with the usual floral leis. Indeed, by evening we must have had a dozen or more leis around our necks, shed-
ding them from time to time to make room for more—all woven
with deliciously smelling flowers of different sorts.

During the day, the commanding naval officer, Admiral Yates
Stirling, invited us to visit the naval station and take a ride in one
of the navy hydroplanes, but we were far too busy to accept. The
commanding general sent his aide to welcome us with leis. The
Japanese Consul General likewise called and sent flowers. I radioed
our thanks later.

The ten days from Honolulu to Yokohama were calm, warm, and
pleasant, with the exception of one or two days of rain and fog.
This ship could do the whole voyage from San Francisco to Yokohama via Honolulu in three or four days less than we actually take,
but she has to adjust her speed to the speed of the other ships on
the line.

ARRIVAL AT TOKYO

June 6, 1932. Tokyo

By golly, what a day! It is seldom that days which one has anticipated in imagination for weeks or months ever measure up to one's
expectations, but this one has gone far beyond. I was up at the
absurd hour of 4:45 A.M., hating to miss a trick. Thick fog and only
the shadowy form of other ships to be seen. We had skirted along
the coast of Japan last evening and had anchored in the roads of
Yokohama sometime during the night after the foghorn had wailed
drearily for an hour or more. Then, at 5:30, pandemonium: the
stewards banging with full force at every cabin door and shouting
in raucous voices for us to get up and meet the quarantine officer,

THE MISSION BEGINS

May 14-18, 1932. On the Overland Limited, Chicago to San Francisco

We're off. A new adventure in this kaleidoscopic life of ours—our
fourteenth post and our fourth mission, and it promises to be the
most adventurous of all. For five years we've watched the Turkish
Republic digging out from the ruins of the defunct Ottoman Empire and hewing its way, painfully, to a new salvation. Now we enter
a much bigger arena, on which the attention of the world is going
to be centered for many years, perhaps for many decades, to come.
Almost anything may happen except one thing: the abandonment
by Japan of her investments, her property, her nationals, and her
vital interests in Manchuria. She is there to stay, unless conquered
in war, and the interesting question is the policy and methods she
will pursue to meet international susceptibilities and what camouflage she will employ to cover uncomfortable facts.

Indeed, many interesting questions present themselves. Will
Japan be content with safeguarding her present rights in Manchuria
or, as some would have it, does her program include ideas of far-
flung empire throughout Asia, with Korea the first step and Manchuria the second? Can she avoid a clash with Soviet Russia, with
America? The big issue is whether this irresistible Japanese impulse
is eventually going to come up against an immovable object in
world opposition and, if so, what form the resultant conflagration
will take, whether internal revolution or external war. It will
depend largely upon how Japan plays her cards, and this is the
problem which we are going to be privileged to watch from the
inside, I hope for a long time to come.

I shall do my utmost to keep a detached and balanced point of
view. An ambassador who starts prejudiced against the country to
which he is accredited might just as well pack up and go home, because his bias is bound to make itself felt sooner or later and render
impossible the creation of a basis of mutual confidence upon which
alone he can accomplish constructive work. On the other hand,
there is always the danger of becoming too much imbued with the
local atmosphere. However, I know the minds of the President, the
Secretary, and the Department pretty well, and that should help to
keep a straight course. To begin with, I have a great deal of sym-

pathy with Japan's legitimate aspirations in Manchuria, but no sympathy at all with the illegitimate way in which Japan has been carrying them out.

One can have little sympathy with the Twenty-one Demands, formulated when the world was busy with the Great War, or with the typically Prussian methods pursued in Manchuria and Shanghai since September 18, 1931, in the face of the Kellogg Pact, the Nine-Power Treaty, and the Covenant of the League of Nations. The purely Sino-Japanese problem has so many complicated features—the interpretation of treaties, what treaties were valid, and who broke the valid treaties first—that one can regard that phase of the situation only as a technically insoluble puzzle. But fortunately our position is clear as crystal: we hold no brief for either side in the Sino-Japanese dispute; we hold a brief for the inviolability of the international peace treaties and the Open Door, and on that issue we have carefully registered our opinion and position before the world and will continue to do so when necessary. So much by way of preface to what may come.

At the very start the pot begins to boil. A correspondent of the *Herald-Examiner* met us at the station in Chicago with the Sunday-evening paper of May 15 bearing flaring headlines: JAPANESE PREMIER SLAIN; SERIOUS REVOLT; PALACE IN PERIL. This is the fourth important assassination. The military are simply taking the bit in their teeth and running away with it, evidently with a Fascist regime in view. But in spite of the press reports, I can't believe the Emperor is threatened, considering the supposedly universal veneration for the throne. There must be something wrong there. If this latest demonstration of terrorism—the murder of Premier Inukai and the exploding of bombs in various public buildings—is the work of a group of fanatics, I wonder whether such extremes may not possibly have a steadying effect on the military themselves. We shall see in due course.

At the principal stops along the way—Chicago, Omaha, and San Francisco—photographers and correspondents met us and solicited interviews, but naturally I have refused to say a word about Japan or Japanese problems or the problems of my mission; a few words about Turkey have generally sufficed to send them away in a friendly mood, which is much better than refusing to talk at all. We were highly amused by one paper in Honolulu which said:

Ambassador Grew is a man of polish, combining an alert

American aggressiveness with the cautious re͏͏ pean. He is tall, possesses an engaging smile, a͏͏ a drawl that is not Bostonian, nor is it English, mixture of the two.

Sort of a general mixture, it appears.

At Omaha one correspondent asked what I consi͏ standing world diplomatic problem which has develop͏ last thirty years, to which I promptly replied: "Unques͏ building up of an international peace structure." I decli͏ ment on his observation that the principal danger elem͏ world today are Germany and a Russo-Japanese war.

ACROSS THE PACIFIC

May 20, 1932. *San Francisco*

Gave a luncheon for Consul General Garrels of Tokyo and͏ sul General Lockhart of Tientsin and their wives and J. Gra͏ Parsons, Jr. Parsons comes as my private secretary, a Groton a͏ Yale man, highly recommended by Mr. Peabody, our former hea͏ master at Groton, and others. Phi Beta Kappa. He promises we͏ and seems eager to learn and to be helpful.

Sailed at 4 on the *President Coolidge* of the Dollar Line, the͏ Japanese Consul General, as well as Garrels and Lockhart, coming down to see us off. Confetti and cheers. Never in my life saw so many or such beautiful flowers as were sent us.

May 20–June 6, 1932. On Board the S.S. *President Coolidge*

The voyage was comparatively uneventful, cold at first with a deep swell, then gradually warmer and calmer as we sagged to the south. This swell apparently always lasts for the first four hundred miles from San Francisco. The big ship is almost empty as far as first-cabin passengers are concerned—only fifty or sixty. On the 23rd there were suddenly six blasts of the siren, the ship stopped, and a boat was lowered. A Chinese woman in the steerage had jumped overboard, leaving three small children. She was never seen again, although we circled around for an hour or so.

I wrote fifteen letters in the first few days of the voyage and am rapidly catching up to date. Also writing speeches for Japan and reading much on Japan and Manchuria. It is at least a profitable if not an exciting voyage. The two chief distractions, besides work, are the open-air swimming pool, where we swim before breakfast and

and five minutes later repeating the performance. Those stewards certainly know how to carry out their orders with the utmost thoroughness, but I wonder if others don't get the same results without making you want to punch them on the nose for the way they do it.

Anyway, we did meet the quarantine officer at 6 A.M., although it was quite unnecessary for Alice and our daughter Elsie (who had slept for only two hours) to have dressed so early, as a special Japanese officer had been deputed to look after us and he went through our passports with Parsons without seeing us at all. Another Japanese officer examined our police dog, Kim, and issued a special health certificate, while still a third man took charge of our baggage. It was all done with quiet efficiency and the least possible bother.

Then, even before we docked at 7, the reception began. Yesterday there had been a flight of welcoming radiograms. This morning one deputation after another came on board and to our cabins. These visitors included half a dozen Japanese newspaper correspondents and photographers, and finally the good Edwin Neville, Counselor of the Embassy, and his wife. We posed for photographs and were asked questions by the press; naturally I refused to say a word about politics, but my answers to their innocent questions were later adroitly manipulated into a quoted interview, the *Japan Times* bearing headlines, MR. GREW GIVES AN INTERVIEW, which began out of a clear sky: "I have written a book called *Sport and Travel in the Far East* but I know hardly anything about the present Japan. I hope to get down to serious study when I'm settled in my new post. Mrs. Grew's mother, who was a *daughter* of Commodore Perry . . ." etc., etc. Some mother-in-law!_

Well, we took leave of Captain Ahlin of the *President Coolidge* and motored to Tokyo in a drizzling rain, but the ugliness of the route was lost on me as Neville and I, who drove together, had too many interesting things to talk about. Then the Embassy. Big bushes, smooth green lawns, flowers, fountains, tessellated pools, and the buildings themselves, four of them, white with black ironwork trimmings, already framed in luxuriant trees—a real oasis in the more or less ugly surroundings of the new-grown city. The residence is on the crest of a hill looking down on the chancery and the dormitories, to which one descends on little steppingstones through a thick grove of leafy woods. As for the interior of the residence, when we had explored it with the Nevilles, examined the furniture and curtains and the thick luxurious carpets in the big salon and the little

salon and the still littler salon, the smoking room with its wonderful wainscoting, its many bookshelves and abundant deep cupboards (where at least I shall have space enough to file and store,
separate and catalogue, to my heart's content), the loggia, the banquet hall, the private dining room, the cloakroom, and the seven
bedrooms and the four bathrooms, the ironing room, sewing room,
and storerooms—while Elsie emitted little shrieks of delight and Kim
wagged his entire acceptance of the new situation—I asked Alice
how many cons she found, and she answered: "Not a single con;
they're all pros."

We all went to the chancery, passing the swimming pool on the
way. I met all the staff and then received the principal American
correspondents: Babb, of the Associated Press; Byas, of *The New
York Times;* Vaughn, of the United Press; Fleisher, of the *Japan
Advertiser.* We chatted, and I spoke of my hope for the closest
co-operation which would be of mutual benefit and urged them to
drop in often. Colonel McIlroy and Captain Johnson, the Military
and Naval Attachés, told Neville that their regulations required
them to call on me in full uniform, but I sent back word I hoped
they would forget their regulations, as we could have a much pleasanter and more satisfactory chat if they would cut out the gold lace
which would undoubtedly leave me tongue-tied.

Maya Lindsley Poole and Parsons came to lunch. I didn't know
Maya until she introduced herself at table. It was amusing to remember that when she was pointed out to me at the Copley Hall
dance in January, 1904, as the girl who had just returned from
Japan, and later when I asked to be introduced to "the girl who
had just returned from Japan," I was led up to Alice instead.

At 3 Neville came to take me to the Diet to call on Viscount Saito,
who could not leave the session to receive me at the Gaimusho, or
Foreign Office. He is old—over seventy, I believe—and looks old and
tired. Conversation was halting, and he seemed to have too much on
his mind to concentrate, but he is decidedly distinguished; he was
formerly an admiral in the Navy and Governor General of Korea
and has now stepped into the breach as Prime Minister and Minister for Foreign Affairs to tide over, with his personal prestige, and
probably temporarily, a difficult cabinet situation. I stayed a very
short time, knowing that he was busy in the session and that we
could talk only platitudes; left with him notes asking for audiences
with the Emperor and Empress, copies of my letters of credence and
the letters of recall of Cameron Forbes, my predecessor, and a copy

THE MISSION BEGINS

May 14-18, 1932. *On the Overland Limited, Chicago to San Francisco*

We're off. A new adventure in this kaleidoscopic life of ours—our fourteenth post and our fourth mission, and it promises to be the most adventurous of all. For five years we've watched the Turkish Republic digging out from the ruins of the defunct Ottoman Empire and hewing its way, painfully, to a new salvation. Now we enter a much bigger arena, on which the attention of the world is going to be centered for many years, perhaps for many decades, to come. Almost anything may happen except one thing: the abandonment by Japan of her investments, her property, her nationals, and her vital interests in Manchuria. She is there to stay, unless conquered in war, and the interesting question is the policy and methods she will pursue to meet international susceptibilities and what camouflage she will employ to cover uncomfortable facts.

Indeed, many interesting questions present themselves. Will Japan be content with safeguarding her present rights in Manchuria or, as some would have it, does her program include ideas of far-flung empire throughout Asia, with Korea the first step and Manchuria the second? Can she avoid a clash with Soviet Russia, with America? The big issue is whether this irresistible Japanese impulse is eventually going to come up against an immovable object in world opposition and, if so, what form the resultant conflagration will take, whether internal revolution or external war. It will depend largely upon how Japan plays her cards, and this is the problem which we are going to be privileged to watch from the inside, I hope for a long time to come.

I shall do my utmost to keep a detached and balanced point of view. An ambassador who starts prejudiced against the country to which he is accredited might just as well pack up and go home, because his bias is bound to make itself felt sooner or later and render impossible the creation of a basis of mutual confidence upon which alone he can accomplish constructive work. On the other hand, there is always the danger of becoming too much imbued with the local atmosphere. However, I know the minds of the President, the Secretary, and the Department pretty well, and that should help to keep a straight course. To begin with, I have a great deal of sym-

3

pathy with Japan's legitimate aspirations in Manchuria, but no sympathy at all with the illegitimate way in which Japan has been carrying them out.

One can have little sympathy with the Twenty-one Demands, formulated when the world was busy with the Great War, or with the typically Prussian methods pursued in Manchuria and Shanghai since September 18, 1931, in the face of the Kellogg Pact, the Nine-Power Treaty, and the Covenant of the League of Nations. The purely Sino-Japanese problem has so many complicated features— the interpretation of treaties, what treaties were valid, and who broke the valid treaties first—that one can regard that phase of the situation only as a technically insoluble puzzle. But fortunately our position is clear as crystal: we hold no brief for either side in the Sino-Japanese dispute; we hold a brief for the inviolability of the international peace treaties and the Open Door, and on that issue we have carefully registered our opinion and position before the world and will continue to do so when necessary. So much by way of preface to what may come.

At the very start the pot begins to boil. A correspondent of the *Herald-Examiner* met us at the station in Chicago with the Sunday-evening paper of May 15 bearing flaring headlines: JAPANESE PREMIER SLAIN; SERIOUS REVOLT; PALACE IN PERIL. This is the fourth important assassination. The military are simply taking the bit in their teeth and running away with it, evidently with a Fascist regime in view. But in spite of the press reports, I can't believe the Emperor is threatened, considering the supposedly universal veneration for the throne. There must be something wrong there. If this latest demonstration of terrorism—the murder of Premier Inukai and the exploding of bombs in various public buildings—is the work of a group of fanatics, I wonder whether such extremes may not possibly have a steadying effect on the military themselves. We shall see in due course.

At the principal stops along the way—Chicago, Omaha, and San Francisco—photographers and correspondents met us and solicited interviews, but naturally I have refused to say a word about Japan or Japanese problems or the problems of my mission; a few words about Turkey have generally sufficed to send them away in a friendly mood, which is much better than refusing to talk at all. We were highly amused by one paper in Honolulu which said:

Ambassador Grew is a man of polish, combining an alert

American aggressiveness with the cautious reserve of the European. He is tall, possesses an engaging smile, and he speaks with a drawl that is not Bostonian, nor is it English, but is a pleasing mixture of the two.

Sort of a general mixture, it appears.

At Omaha one correspondent asked what I considered the outstanding world diplomatic problem which has developed during the last thirty years, to which I promptly replied: "Unquestionably, the building up of an international peace structure." I declined to comment on his observation that the principal danger elements of the world today are Germany and a Russo-Japanese war.

ACROSS THE PACIFIC

May 20, 1932. San Francisco

Gave a luncheon for Consul General Garrels of Tokyo and Consul General Lockhart of Tientsin and their wives and J. Graham Parsons, Jr. Parsons comes as my private secretary, a Groton and Yale man, highly recommended by Mr. Peabody, our former headmaster at Groton, and others. Phi Beta Kappa. He promises well and seems eager to learn and to be helpful.

Sailed at 4 on the *President Coolidge* of the Dollar Line, the Japanese Consul General, as well as Garrels and Lockhart, coming down to see us off. Confetti and cheers. Never in my life saw so many or such beautiful flowers as were sent us.

May 20–June 6, 1932. On Board the S.S. President Coolidge

The voyage was comparatively uneventful, cold at first with a deep swell, then gradually warmer and calmer as we sagged to the south. This swell apparently always lasts for the first four hundred miles from San Francisco. The big ship is almost empty as far as first-cabin passengers are concerned—only fifty or sixty. On the 23rd there were suddenly six blasts of the siren, the ship stopped, and a boat was lowered. A Chinese woman in the steerage had jumped overboard, leaving three small children. She was never seen again, although we circled around for an hour or so.

I wrote fifteen letters in the first few days of the voyage and am rapidly catching up to date. Also writing speeches for Japan and reading much on Japan and Manchuria. It is at least a profitable if not an exciting voyage. The two chief distractions, besides work, are the open-air swimming pool, where we swim before breakfast and

again in the late afternoon after two or three hard sets of deck
tennis, thus keeping wonderfully fit, and the talkies on alternate
nights.

May 26, 1932. *Honolulu*

A great big red-letter day, our first in Honolulu. Was up at 5:30,
reminding me of the occasions on which my daughter Anita and I
had often risen early to watch our entrance into the lovely Bay of
Naples. Soon after 6, we docked to the welcoming strains of *Aloha*
played by a band on shore, which effectually awakened the rest of
the family. Major Ross, Sheriff of Honolulu and aide to Governor
Judd, came on board with the pilot, welcomed us in the Governor's
name, and decorated us with the usual floral leis. Indeed, by evening we must have had a dozen or more leis around our necks, shed-
ding them from time to time to make room for more—all woven
with deliciously smelling flowers of different sorts.

During the day, the commanding naval officer, Admiral Yates
Stirling, invited us to visit the naval station and take a ride in one
of the navy hydroplanes, but we were far too busy to accept. The
commanding general sent his aide to welcome us with leis. The
Japanese Consul General likewise called and sent flowers. I radioed
our thanks later.

The ten days from Honolulu to Yokohama were calm, warm, and
pleasant, with the exception of one or two days of rain and fog.
This ship could do the whole voyage from San Francisco to Yokohama via Honolulu in three or four days less than we actually take,
but she has to adjust her speed to the speed of the other ships on
the line.

ARRIVAL AT TOKYO

June 6, 1932. *Tokyo*

By golly, what a day! It is seldom that days which one has anticipated in imagination for weeks or months ever measure up to one's
expectations, but this one has gone far beyond. I was up at the
absurd hour of 4:45 A.M., hating to miss a trick. Thick fog and only
the shadowy form of other ships to be seen. We had skirted along
the coast of Japan last evening and had anchored in the roads of
Yokohama sometime during the night after the foghorn had wailed
drearily for an hour or more. Then, at 5:30, pandemonium: the
stewards banging with full force at every cabin door and shouting
in raucous voices for us to get up and meet the quarantine officer,

and five minutes later repeating the performance. Those stewards certainly know how to carry out their orders with the utmost thoroug'ness, but I wonder if others don't get the same results without mak.ng you want to punch them on the nose for the way they do it.

Anyway, we did meet the quarantine officer at 6 A.M., although it was quite unnecessary for Alice and our daughter Elsie (who had slept for only two hours) to have dressed so early, as a special Japanese officer had been deputed to look after us and he went through our passports with Parsons without seeing us at all. Another Japanese officer examined our police dog, Kim, and issued a special health certificate, while still a third man took charge of our baggage. It was all done with quiet efficiency and the least possible bother.

Then, even before we docked at 7, the reception began. Yesterday there had been a flight of welcoming radiograms. This morning one deputation after another came on board and to our cabins. These visitors included half a dozen Japanese newspaper correspondents and photographers, and finally the good Edwin Neville, Counselor of the Embassy, and his wife. We posed for photographs and were asked questions by the press; naturally I refused to say a word about politics, but my answers to their innocent questions were later adroitly manipulated into a quoted interview, the *Japan Times* bearing headlines, MR. GREW GIVES AN INTERVIEW, which began out of a clear sky: "I have written a book called *Sport and Travel in the Far East* but I know hardly anything about the present Japan. I hope to get down to serious study when I'm settled in my new post. Mrs. Grew's mother, who was a *daughter* of Commodore Perry . . ." etc., etc. Some mother-in-law!

Well, we took leave of Captain Ahlin of the *President Coolidge* and motored to Tokyo in a drizzling rain, but the ugliness of the route was lost on me as Neville and I, who drove together, had too many interesting things to talk about. Then the Embassy. Big bushes, smooth green lawns, flowers, fountains, tessellated pools, and the buildings themselves, four of them, white with black ironwork trimmings, already framed in luxuriant trees—a real oasis in the more or less ugly surroundings of the new-grown city. The residence is on the crest of a hill looking down on the chancery and the dormitories, to which one descends on little steppingstones through a thick grove of leafy woods. As for the interior of the residence, when we had explored it with the Nevilles, examined the furniture and curtains and the thick luxurious carpets in the big salon and the little salon and the still littler salon, the smoking room with its wonderful wainscoting, its many bookshelves and abundant deep cupboards (where at least I shall have space enough to file and store, separate and catalogue, to my heart's content), the loggia, the banquet hall, the private dining room, the cloakroom, and the seven bedrooms and the four bathrooms, the ironing room, sewing room, and storerooms—while Elsie emitted little shrieks of delight and Kim wagged his entire acceptance of the new situation—I asked Alice how many cons she found, and she answered: "Not a single con; they're all pros."

We all went to the chancery, passing the swimming pool on the way. I met all the staff and then received the principal American correspondents: Babb, of the Associated Press; Byas, of *The New York Times;* Vaughn, of the United Press; Fleisher, of the *Japan Advertiser*. We chatted, and I spoke of my hope for the closest co-operation which would be of mutual benefit and urged them to drop in often. Colonel McIlroy and Captain Johnson, the Military and Naval Attachés, told Neville that their regulations required them to call on me in full uniform, but I sent back word I hoped they would forget their regulations, as we could have a much pleasanter and more satisfactory chat if they would cut out the gold lace which would undoubtedly leave me tongue-tied.

Maya Lindsley Poole and Parsons came to lunch. I didn't know Maya until she introduced herself at table. It was amusing to remember that when she was pointed out to me at the Copley Hall dance in January, 1904, as the girl who had just returned from Japan, and later when I asked to be introduced to "the girl who had just returned from Japan," I was led up to Alice instead.

At 3 Neville came to take me to the Diet to call on Viscount Saito, who could not leave the session to receive me at the Gaimusho, or Foreign Office. He is old—over seventy, I believe—and looks old and tired. Conversation was halting, and he seemed to have too much on his mind to concentrate, but he is decidedly distinguished; he was formerly an admiral in the Navy and Governor General of Korea and has now stepped into the breach as Prime Minister and Minister for Foreign Affairs to tide over, with his personal prestige, and probably temporarily, a difficult cabinet situation. I stayed a very short time, knowing that he was busy in the session and that we could talk only platitudes; left with him notes asking for audiences with the Emperor and Empress, copies of my letters of credence and the letters of recall of Cameron Forbes, my predecessor, and a copy of my proposed speech to the Emperor. As Neville liked it, we sent it in. Afterward I called on Baron de Bassompierre, the Belgian Ambassador and Dean of the Diplomatic Corps—very pleasant.

Then, at 5, Alice had the entire staff with wives and daughters to tea—sixty-five people. What a staff! And what a situation that enabled us to give a reception, with buffet, for sixty-five people on the very day of our arrival! Cam Forbes' Japanese servants are all on the job and functioning like clockwork; I suppose we shall keep them all.

Bingham and Parsons came to dinner. The latter is to stay with us until he can get his apartment in one of the dormitories into shape. I have written up the day while the initial impressions are still fresh, and now, thank heaven, I shall hit the hay at 10:30 and hit it hard.

PRESS COMMENTS ON THE NEW AMBASSADOR

June 7, 1932

The press gives me much amusement. Yesterday the *Japan Times* quoted me as saying that I knew hardly anything about the present Japan but that I hoped to get down to serious study, which I didn't say at all, although I may have remarked that I had much to learn here. Anyway, this evening's militaristic and anti-American *Times* built its whole column-and-a-half editorial around that alleged remark, referring in complimentary terms to my "modesty" and the fact that I had come here with an open mind and was willing to learn. Some of the other papers, published in Japanese, have taken still further liberties. The *Tokyo Jiji* observes:

> Mrs. Grew is a most fitting consort of the new Ambassador who is a diplomat for the promotion of peace. Interviewed by the *Jiji* on board the liner, the new Ambassador said *in a mild and soft tone of voice that the situation is serious indeed* and that as to conditions in Japan he has no sufficient knowledge. . . . His Excellency has written a pamphlet, the title of which is *Exploitation and Travel in the Far East.* The mother of Mrs. Grew has drawn many oil paintings representing the scenic views of Japan and through these pictures the new Ambassador and Mrs. Grew have been so influenced as to entertain favorable sentiments toward Japan. [The italics are mine.—J. C. G.]

Chugai Shogyo says:

> The new Ambassador is a great sportsman. He is a tall gentleman and his thick eyebrows show his characteristics. He has a manly appearance. He diplomatically said that except Mt. Fuji,

which represents Japan's scenic view, he has no sufficient knowledge about Japan, so he is unable to answer all questions. Apparently the new Ambassador is a talented diplomat.

Tokyo Asahi observes, among other comments:

The new Ambassador is a tall gentleman, full of vigor, being as high as six feet. His long and thick eyebrows indicate that he is a gentleman of quick decision. He has written a pamphlet called *Athletic Sports and Travel in the Far East*. As regards Japan, which has attained a marvelous development unprecedented the world over, his knowledge about Japan may be as imperfect as a fairy tale. Mrs. Grew had once visited Japan a long time ago and she is in possession of many oil paintings representing the scenic views of Japan which she has drawn herself. She is more delighted in coming to Japan than the Ambassador himself. The daughter of the Ambassador was seen walking actively on board the liner in spite of rainfall.

As for *Nichi Nichi:*

Interviewed by a representative of *Nichi Nichi* on board the liner, the new Ambassador said: "It is quite perplexing for me to discuss such current topics as the Manchurian question, the Round-Table Conference, etc., at this moment. Both Japan and the United States are at present showing such a tension as to sting their nerves even by a slight touch of a tiny needle. Instead of talking over such a question I would say that the Olympic games to be held in the United States are attracting a worldwide attention. I understand that Japan is sending thither a party of strong champions who will play splendidly. Troublesome diplomacy is necessary for the promotion and maintenance of friendly relations among nations but the exchange of sports is more essential and greater diplomacy at the present time than ordinary diplomacy." . . . The new Ambassador is accompanied by his fourth and final daughter.

Considering that I never mentioned and that my dull imagination never even thought of the Olympic games as a useful topic of conversation, the Japanese press is clearly more diplomatic than I am. Of course I didn't say a single word about the "tense situation," or about my "final daughter."

PREPARATIONS TO MEET THE EMPEROR

June 7, 1932

I thought it was going to be possible to mark time until presenting my letters of credence. Not so, for today has been about as hectic a day as I have experienced anywhere. I fortunately got an early start before 7 and was at my desk in the chancery at 9, which I expect to do regularly because the staff decidedly needs jacking up in the matter of office hours.

At 11 came Takeo Yamagata, a chief of section under the Master of Ceremonies in the Imperial Household Department. Mr. Yamagata said that the Emperor would receive me in audience on June 14 and that the Empress would also receive Alice and Elsie and that after the audience we would return to change clothes and then would all three lunch with both the Emperor and Empress. He was very neat and very cordial.

At 7 Neville brought me his telegram to the Department reporting the talk which the British, French, and Italian Ambassadors and Neville had had with Viscount Saito this afternoon after they had held a preliminary conference at our Embassy, it being nearest to the Foreign Office. The Italian, being the senior, acted as spokesman and told the Minister, in which the others concurred, that owing to the publicity given to Yoshizawa's * proposal for a Round-Table Conference in Tokyo, the Chinese were already prejudiced against the proposal and that it was therefore felt that such a meeting in Tokyo, omitting the Chinese, would be unprofitable.

The four powers, however, desired to co-operate and suggested that further proposals should be broached through the Japanese ambassadors in their respective capitals. Saito replied that he himself thought the conference ought to take place in Shanghai with the Chinese present but that he didn't want to make commitments before the new Japanese Minister for Foreign Affairs should be appointed, which he hoped would take place next week, and that the matter would therefore be left open for the present. Cabled that I had authorized Neville to attend the meeting as I had not yet presented my credentials. Saito's remarks make it look as if Count Uchida, president of the South Manchuria Railway, were going to be appointed Foreign Minister.

June 9, 1932

Sir Francis Lindley, the British Ambassador, called for Alice and me at 11 and motored us down to Hayama while Elsie went by train with the Nevilles. There we lunched at their little bungalow, a Japa-

* Former Japanese Foreign Minister.

nese house, on the shore with Lady Lindley, the Nevilles, and Mrs. Kennedy, wife of the correspondent of the London *Times*.

INSTRUCTIONS TO THE EMBASSY STAFF

June 13, 1932

Called a meeting of the staff at 10, including the Counselor, Secretaries, Military, Naval, and Commercial Attachés and their assistants, and the two Consuls, and told them that I wanted to bring our little group into the closest possible co-operation, that my door would always be open to any of them, and that I wanted them to drop in whenever they had any information, views, or suggestions which they thought would be helpful to me. I also wanted them to send me confidential memorandums whenever they picked up any significant opinions or information, especially of a political nature, and that these memorandums would be kept in utmost confidence and would be very helpful to me in piecing out the general picture, particularly as they would undoubtedly be in touch with individuals and classes that I myself might find it difficult to get in touch with. I wanted all shades of opinions. I also told them that I was not in the habit of holding regular meetings of the staff at stated times because such meetings generally were rather forced and seldom useful, but that I would call meetings whenever there was some specific subject to discuss, as, for instance, a telegram to the Department commenting on the general situation, or some development upon which I wished elucidation.

Count Kuroda, one of the Vice-Masters of Ceremony, called to go over the protocol for tomorrow's presentation of my credentials to the Emperor. Then came Mr. ———, a correspondent of the *Jiji*, who had been in Manchuria and with whom I had an interesting talk. He said that the Japanese officials of the new "Manchukuo" state were not at all inclined to see things from the point of view of the Japanese Government and not at all inclined to be dictated to from Tokyo. The International Commission had been very discreet and had thus far given no indication whatever of their attitude. Later came Babb, the A.P. correspondent, whom I had asked to come to see me because I wanted a newspaperman's opinion on my speech for the America-Japan Society, especially whether there was anything in it which might be magnified out of proportion by the press. He read it carefully and made two or three minor suggestions but said that otherwise he could find no fault with it and that he thought it good. Butts, the Commercial Attaché, also read it and gave the same opinion. Bingham has made some excellent suggestions. It's an awfully difficult thing to put meat into a speech when you have to avoid every subject which would really interest your audience but which at the same time would stir up a lot of undesirable comment and controversy in the press, such as our precise attitude toward the Sino-Japanese dispute, Manchuria, the Nine-Power Treaty, the Round-Table Conference, the Hoover Doctrine, and all the rest of it. I can't see anything to be gained by ramming our policy down their throats in my first speech, but I am going to emphasize the universal interest and concern throughout the United States in Far Eastern problems and hope that this will sink in.

One of Japan's leading statesmen asked for an appointment before my audience with the Emperor tomorrow and told me that before he went to the United States last winter the Emperor and the Japanese public believed that the notes written by Mr. Stimson at the time of the Manchurian crisis represented only Mr. Stimson's own point of view and had been drafted on his own initiative. When this Japanese diplomat returned from the United States he told the Emperor that quite the contrary was the case and that the notes to the Japanese Government had been written under pressure from American public opinion, particularly that of the church, the educational institutions, and the women's clubs and societies. The feeling of these organizations, and indeed of public opinion generally, was engendered by the memory of the Great War, which was still fresh in people's minds. There was still another reason for the American attitude. America had created and was sponsor for the League of Nations and, while not a member, the American institutions mentioned above felt a moral responsibility for the League, and this feeling of moral responsibility had been stimulated by European nations, which had tried to throw the burden on American shoulders. The Stimson notes were therefore based more on a social than on a political ground. He had told the Emperor that the church and the universities in America were really tantamount to the Court in Japan and wielded great influence. He had had all of the foregoing facts confirmed, he said, by a considerable number of prominent men, all of whom said the same thing about American public opinion, men such as Mr. Hughes, Mr. Coolidge, Mr. Castle, Mr. Charles Francis Adams, various university presidents, and others.

This Japanese gentleman said he thought it would be helpful for me to know before my audience that the Emperor knew these facts, as the subject might possibly be touched upon in conversation, and that it might likewise be helpful to my wife in case the Empress should talk with her about women's organizations in the United States and their public influence.

I thanked my Japanese informant for his thoughtfulness in telling me this and I said that what he had told the Emperor about American public opinion was quite correct as far as it went, but that the feeling of moral responsibility of the United States in this question was not so much centered on the League of Nations as on the Kellogg-Briand Pact and the Nine-Power Treaty.

At 7 I called Neville to the Embassy because it seemed to me wise to send the Department a telegram about the possible early recognition by Japan of the "Manchukuo" state and the imminent appointment of Count Uchida as Foreign Minister of Japan. There are a good many conflicting rumors, and public opinion is split on the subject of recognizing Manchukuo now, but Uchida is in conference with General Araki, the Minister of War, and it is clear that if Uchida does accept the job he will be doing it with the full approval of the military.

Whatever way it falls out, one thing is certain and that is that the military are distinctly running the Government and that no step can be taken without their approval.

AUDIENCE WITH THE EMPEROR

June 14, 1932

This has been a terrific day. After all, life is a succession of hurdles and once over them they look a great deal easier to negotiate than before one took off. Most of our troubles—the kind that will wear us out if we let them—are based on totally unnecessary apprehension.

The Imperial coaches came to the chancery, where it was easier for them and the attendant company of cavalry to maneuver than at the Embassy, at 10:20. The Embassy staff, all in immaculate dress suits, had been photographed and were still in solid phalanx when Count Kuroda, Vice-Master of Ceremonies, came to get us. It was pouring rain, and the plumes of the coachman's hat and on the cap of the captain of the convoying lancers were sadly wilted, but not even the rain could dull the birthday-cake effect of the coach. We set off at 10:35. Cavalry in front, cavalry behind, and then the other coaches conveying the staff. The Ambassador of the United States of America sat in state alone on the back seat, with Count Kuroda facing; all traffic had been held up by the efficient police, and whenever somebody in the trams or taxis or on the street bowed, which was seldom, the Ambassador doffed his hat.

We solemnly entered the very beautiful palace grounds, where a guard of honor stood at attention and the bugler gave a fanfare, and precisely at 10:50 drew up at the entrance. Baron Hayashi, Grand Master of Ceremonies, whom I had met at the Lausanne Conference when he was Ambassador in London, received and led the way to the big reception room where a lot of officials were gathered, Viscount Saito, of course, and many others. Soon afterward came Alice and Elsie and the ladies of the Embassy. We sat around for ten or fifteen minutes and admired the really marvelous room, especially its screens and lacquered doors, and then I was summoned to the Emperor. A bow at the door, a second bow halfway, and a third bow on reaching him.

I read my speech; it was translated into Japanese by the interpreter, the well-known Shiratori, "spokesman of the Foreign Office" who has spoken quite a mouthful from time to time; I presented my letter of credence and my predecessor's letter of recall; the Emperor read his speech in Japanese in a high singsong voice, which was translated into English by Shiratori; then, according to the protocol, "shake hands," and the Emperor asked two or three of the usual formal questions, which I did my best to answer intelligently in spite of hearing only one word in four of Shiratori's translation (he had been told that I heard badly but simply couldn't raise his voice in the Imperial presence). When the Emperor said that he would see me again, I asked permission to present the staff, and they came in one by one, each making the regulation three bows and backing out with three more bows: Neville, Dickover, Turner, Washington, Bingham, McIlroy, Johnson, Roberts, Butts, and Dowd. I myself successfully negotiated the backward retreat, and that was over. The whole thing was done with clockwork precision and solemnity.

The Emperor Hirohito is young—thirty-one, I believe; he has a small mustache and glasses and smiles pleasantly when talking. Of course, he received in military uniform. There is a marked resemblance between the three brothers, the Emperor, Prince Chichibu, and Prince Takamatsu.

Immediately after the audience with the Emperor, Alice, Elsie, and I went in to the Empress, where the same thing was repeated—of course, without the speeches and presentation of letters—and to

Her Majesty I presented the staff and their wives. The Empress looks more like a charming Japanese doll than any of the other women; she is not so pretty as the really lovely Princess Chichibu, but she has a nice expression and she does smile delightfully. Madame Takagi did the interpreting but much too low for me to hear, and it was fortunate that Alice was there to reinterpret to me everything that was said, for otherwise I could never have answered the Empress' questions. I suppose that sooner or later they will find out that they simply have to speak up if they expect me to reply intelligently. It's an awful bore to be deaf—especially at the Japanese Court.

Then we returned to the Embassy as we had come; I invited Count Kuroda, the captain of the escort, and the staff to my office in the chancery for a glass of champagne, but it had to be snappy because I had just seven minutes to get up to the Embassy, change into a morning coat, and start again for the palace in our own car for lunch. We arrived at the palace again at 12:20 and stood around talking with Prince and Princess Chichibu, the Saitos, Count Makino, Baron Hayashi, Count and Countess Matsudaira, and the other officials of the Court, until the Emperor and Empress entered. I presented Alice and Elsie to the Emperor, and soon we all went in to luncheon.

The luncheon was far less formidable than I had imagined; it was quiet and stately, of course, but both the Emperor and Empress talked with us almost steadily and without any formality except that they spoke only Japanese and everything had to be interpreted by the guest on our other side. As we came into the magnificent dining room, the servants bowed low, as indeed everybody did when the Imperial couple appeared—much lower than in Europe, and they stay bowed for an appreciable time. There were about twenty-four or twenty-six at table. The Chichibus, of course, occupied the seats on the right. Alice was on the Emperor's left with Count Makino, Lord Keeper of the Privy Seal and an adviser to the Throne, next her; I was on the Empress' left with Madame Takagi next to me. Elsie sat between two of the Vice-Masters of Ceremony.

The food and wines were perfectly delicious, and an orchestra concealed behind a screen played softly. I said that the room was magnificent and it was, but not so beautiful as the big reception room; there were too much rather unattractive woodwork and heavy draperies; but one could hardly take one's eyes off the really magnificent gold screens with stunted pine trees and flowers, beautifully arranged, in front of them, or the glorious flowers on the table. Alice found Count Makino congenial and the Emperor most pleasant and easy to talk to, of course, through Makino. The latter is really a great gentleman, but so were they all. Of course with Makino we talked much of Bill Castle, who had preceded Cameron Forbes as our Ambassador to Japan.

I talked almost steadily with the Empress through Madame Takagi, who finally got her voice up to the necessary pitch for me to hear; the Empress seemed interested in everything and little by little extracted pretty nearly the whole story of our lives, including my travels, our various posts, our interests in sport, the family, and of course Anita's nineteen-mile swim, the whole length of the Bosporus, from the Sea of Marmora to the Black Sea. After luncheon we separated into groups; the Emperor chatted with me through Shiratori, asking me much about Turkey, and the Empress with Alice and Elsie. At 2 o'clock precisely, Baron Hayashi came up, we bowed and curtsied, and the thing was over.

It was, perhaps, a satisfaction to have it all over and my letters safely presented; being a hardened soldier I don't sweat the way I used to before such things, but still it was a hurdle just the same.

Returning to the chancery, I signed the notes to all the diplomatic colleagues, but insisted on changing the note to the German because I declined to subscribe to the phrase "the happy relations which have always existed between our two missions." To be consistent I also altered the note to the Spaniard. Neville asked why not the Englishman, but I said that we didn't have diplomatic missions here in 1812.

THE AMBASSADOR GETS INTO HARNESS

June 15, 1932

Herzel and Tait, President and Vice-President respectively of the American Association, called to say that the Association wanted to give me a dinner and when would I come. Neville had told me that he thought that this affair could be put off until autumn, but they seemed to want to hold it now before the Americans leave town for the summer, so I agreed to July 1. Another speech, of course. Incidentally, Mr. Tait offered us a big new Lincoln car until our Cadillac arrives; it was ordered for the late Prime Minister Inukai, who was assassinated before he could take delivery.

Then came Mr. Happer, Secretary of the American Merchants'

Association, who wants to give a luncheon. Another speech. This is a terrible life, considering that apart from the American Association, the American Merchants' Association, the American School, and the America-Japan Society I am booked for three separate speeches in connection with the departure of the Japanese Olympic team—one for Fox Movietone at a reception at the Embassy, another at the farewell Japanese dinner, and still a third, over the radio, at the reception to be given for the team by the Japanese press; I suppose there will be many others in due course. Happer is a connoisseur and collector of Japanese prints, which we are keen to see, and he will soon arrange to get his best ones together.

Later I received Mr. Otani, President of the Shojiku Cinema Company and of the Shojiku Theatrical Corporation, and Mr. Mishima, Director. The former controls most of the principal theaters in Japan, and he came to invite us to a representation on Friday, which we have accepted. It will be fun to see our first Japanese play. Then came Waugh, Manager of the National City Bank.

At noon I called on the French Ambassador, de Martel, who struck me as intelligent and sane in his views about the general situation in the Far East, which we discussed at length. He has spent much of his career in China. Then to the palace to sign in the books of the Emperor and Empress and to the Chichibus' to sign in their book too. At 2:30 I made my formal call on Viscount Saito after presenting my letters—he received me in the building of the Prime Minister, a magnificent house with a lovely garden; he said that he had nothing further to tell me since he had talked with Neville and the other ambassadors but that he expected a new Foreign Minister to be appointed very shortly. At 3 to the Italian Ambassador, Majoni, whose Embassy is in a very ugly house in a perfectly lovely garden completely shut off from the outside world by big trees and bushes. I liked him immediately, and we had a good long talk. He thinks, as does nearly everyone, that anything can happen at any time. At 4:30 I called on the Brazilian Ambassador, Amaral; he said: "When I came to your palace the other day you called it a bungalow; now, in welcoming you to my bungalow, I must call it a palace."

That finishes my formal calls on the ambassadors, except on Lindley, when he returns from his fishing trip, as the German is away, but now I shall have to receive the ministers and chargés and then go to see them. As there are thirty-two missions besides the Russian and ourselves, that means sixty-four calls in all, and they all have to be made by appointment and in person, a thoroughly cruel infliction.

Thus does an ambassador get into harness—by the sweat of his brow. The only interlude in the whole day was a cocktail at the Tokyo Club before lunch with Neville, Raymond, of the firm of architects who built the Embassy, and Akimoto, treasurer of the club. If the job keeps up at this pace I shall need one every day.

Confidential memorandums from the staff are already beginning to come in as a result of my request at the meeting the other day. Here is the gist of some of the more significant items:

At luncheon, the Counselor of another Embassy made the interesting statement that he believed future co-operation between Russia and Japan to be much more probable than a war between the two countries. He indicated that his own, and presumably his Embassy's, line of thought is that a radical revolution in Japan is very much within the realm of possibility and from the point of view of international politics he dreads the power of an alliance between Russia and Japan.

The same informant also stated that handbills urging the assassination of Premier Saito had been circulated recently. As he put it, plenty of people were hot on the trail of the Premier. He also expressed the belief that there were elements not averse to taking action against the Emperor, possibly assassination but more likely a desire to relegate the Imperial family to Kyoto once more. He feels that the inability of the last Diet to accomplish very much may be capitalized by the reactionary and extremist elements, and while nothing may happen it is perfectly possible that the lid may blow off in the very near future.

Colonel —— stated that in previous years when the sons of wealthy men had been drafted into the army it was quite usual for them to be assigned to duty with the Imperial Guard, especially if trouble were brewing. In 1932, however, the sons of farmers had been appointed for duty of this kind and the sons of the wealthy had received no preferred treatment. He had this on good authority and believes it highly significant. He also places significance in the evident desire of the Mitsui to play safe by increasing all salaries and making large contributions personally for emergency relief. He intimated that it was something new for the Mitsui to do anything at variance with pretty tight-fisted business principles.

AN EVENING IN THE JAPANESE THEATER

June 17, 1932

In the evening at 6 we went to the Kabuki-Zu Theater, with Bingham and Parsons, as guests of Mr. Otani, who is president of the biggest theater corporation in Japan and controls over thirty theaters and 450 cinemas throughout the country. There we saw two plays, *Kiri-Hitoha* and *Kagami-Jishi,* the former featuring the celebrated actor Utaemon, whom Alice had seen in the old days. In tonight's play Utaemon took the part of an old woman. The other play featured the outstanding dancer-actor of Japan, Kikugoro, in his marvelous Lion Dance.

We were tremendously impressed; this was the best theater in Japan and the best classical drama and dancing. The theater is very large, every single seat was filled, and the stage as large as I have seen anywhere. The scenery and costumes were simply magnificent. All the women's parts were taken by men, and they did it extraordinarily well. There is almost a national veneration for Kikugoro and for the Lion Dance which is supposedly his masterpiece. He learned it from his teacher, the famous Danjuro, and is said to have improved upon his master. Danjuro used to say that it was the most difficult dance he had known. Most of these great actors inherit their art from many generations of forebears, Kikugoro being the fifth of his line. During the Lion Dance there was not a flicker of expression on his face, the entire significance of the dance being expressed by the movement of his head, his hands, and his body; the head movements, when he was representing a beautiful young girl, were amazingly graceful. The classical conventions of these Japanese dances are so totally different from ours that one cannot immediately appreciate the great art displayed, but it grows on one gradually. To the Japanese it is almost sacred.

The story of the Lion Dance is quite simple: the beautiful chambermaid who has been chosen to perform the annual Lion Dance before the castle of the shoguns is timid before the crowd and it is only after some time of urging that she begins to dance. She dances gracefully, the head of a lion in her hand, surrounded by two butterflies who come to dance with her, but gradually the butterflies, who in the first scene are merely mechanical butterflies on long poles but later two beautiful dancers, stir her into a frenzy until she actually becomes possessed by the spirit of the lion and changes into the lion himself. At this point she comes on to the stage from behind the audience by a sort of bridge in a marvelous golden robe and long white mane and then begins the wild and final Lion Dance, while the Nagauta orchestra eggs her on with still wilder music. This orchestra, composed of about eighteen men in kimonos, sits at the back of the stage facing the audience; about a third of them sing or chant while the rest play instruments and drums. It is, to our Western ears, sheer cacophony, especially when a shrill fife continually runs totally counter to the theme or air of the Japanese guitars and voices, and after an hour of it I had a good old-fashioned headache, but it certainly added to the impressiveness of the dance. The audience was wild with enthusiasm, and I could perfectly understand it. The fife, by the way, is supposed to announce that the principal actor is about to come on the stage or to leave the stage, or that a climax in the plot is impending.

Between the acts Mr. Otani took us behind the wings, where we were solemnly introduced to the great Kikugoro in all his robes and photographed with him, and later Otani, entirely unexpectedly by us, entertained us at dinner in the theater restaurant, together with two of his codirectors, at a table decorated with Japanese and American flags. I cannot imagine a newly arrived Ambassador in Washington being entertained thus by a prominent theater magnate, but it appears to be quite the custom here, and in America there is nothing that approaches or can be compared with the nationally venerated classical acting and dancing or such nationally venerated exponents as Utaemon and Kikugoro. These programs include a whole series of six separate plays and they run from 3 P.M. until 9 or 10, but we saw the best and most popular two of them, lasting about two hours. I can readily see how they appeal to the public, and even we, as initiates, went home thoroughly enthusiastic.

In reply to my telegram regarding the possible impending recognition of the Manchukuo regime, the Department today inquired whether we could confirm or deny the press reports that the Diet had passed the resolution favoring recognition. I replied that the House of Representatives had passed the resolution but that there was no indication that it was more than political ebullition or that the Government had engineered it or would be guided by it. I added the substance of an informal talk which Neville had had with Arita, in which Arita had said that the Government would not act precipitately and that Count Uchida, who would not take office until July as he was returning to Manchuria to wind up some affairs with the railway, would certainly not act hastily.

I do not think it would be wise for me myself to discuss this question with the Foreign Office, at least at present. We ought not to acknowledge officially that there is even a possibility of Japan's recognizing Manchukuo, because such action would seem effectively to nullify all the assurances given to us concerning ultimate withdrawal. But at the same time I must know what is going on and I asked Neville to do it casually and informally while discussing other matters, in connection with the conflicting reports in the press.

ADDRESS BEFORE THE AMERICA-JAPAN SOCIETY

June 21, 1932. *Tokyo*
Your Excellencies, Ladies and Gentlemen:

If any of you have been alpinists or mountaineers you will understand a little how I feel today, for you will have known the exhilaration of reaching some long-hoped-for height at sunrise and of gazing through new eyes and under new auspices at the scene which lies about you. I think of sunrise in this connection because your beautiful national emblem has turned my thoughts to those alpine dawns experienced in bygone days. The scene and the auspices indeed are new since my last visit to Japan nearly thirty years ago. The vantage point is unquestionably one of the highest in the gift of my Government, and the satisfaction of having come to this particular post after twenty-eight years in the Foreign Service is deeper than I am able to express.

I wish I could find words to tell you of my full appreciation of your welcome. It gives me great courage in undertaking this important mission. I particularly appreciate the presence of His Excellency Prince Tokugawa and the other high officials of the Government who have courteously and hospitably honored this occasion with their presence. May I also express to you thanks on behalf of my wife and daughter for the welcome you have extended to us? Japan has a wonderful reputation for generous and kindhearted hospitality of which we have seen abundant proof during our first few days here. Sometimes our language—indeed, all spoken languages—seems thin and superficial. We have to depend, in such cases, on a sort of X-ray language which vibrates underneath the spoken words and is often more effective than anything we can say. Your welcome justifies my hope that as we come to know each other better, this other inaudible language, which perhaps extends less from mind to mind than from heart to heart, will prove to be an effective interpreter supplementing the often inadequate written or spoken word, whether in your tongue or mine.

Now let us look at the situation. It would be foolish to assert that no important problems beset us. We must recognize that they exist and do our best to solve them. Many of the complicated international problems with which we are faced today are urgently in need of settlement during the next few months. The outlook might be discouraging if it were not for the hundreds of men in Japan, in America, and in all countries who are devoting their full time and energy to solving the world's difficulties. Gradually men are learning to co-operate with each other, to talk matters over, to discuss things openly and frankly at conferences, and to share their wisdom and knowledge with each other for the good of all. I am convinced that in this direction lies eventual success. I cannot go into any of those problems in detail tonight; it would be presumptuous to do so before even taking root in your soil. But let me assure you of the deep and universal interest in Japan throughout the United States. Let me assure you that few if any problems today concern the people of the United States as a whole more deeply than the problems of the Far East.

This interest is not limited to Washington or New York or California. It is universal. After talking with the President and the Secretary of State, and with my good friends Mr. Forbes and Mr. Castle and many others, I traveled across the entire continent, and everywhere, with everyone I felt a keen desire to understand Japan, her thoughts, her aims, her underlying motives. I believe that the people of Japan have an equally keen interest in really knowing the United States, and in really understanding her thoughts and aims and motives. My principal role here, as I conceive it, is going to be that of interpreter, and I shall hope to be able to interpret each country to the other in a way which will redound to the steadily increased mutual confidence of both. It seems to me that my chief problem will be in explaining your country to mine. You Japanese have been studying us assiduously for years, whereas we as a nation have much to learn of your manners, customs, history, and marvelously developed culture. The fact that you use our language is only one proof of this.

As for the American people, if I were asked what is the subject in world affairs which interests and concerns them most today—the subject to which in the past fifteen years they have given most thought and most discussion—I would unhesitatingly say the efforts of the nations to build up a durable structure of international peace. The interest in this subject is not confined to the so-called intellectual classes—the church, the universities, the various societies of men and women which aim to educate and to form public opinion, although these organizations wield great influence; this interest extends from the highest official to the lowest laborer in the land; it is universal and fundamental, and while the memory of the dark days of 1914 to 1918 may gradually, with time, become less acute, the experiences of those years have instilled into the people of the United States, as well as into the people of other nations who have shared the same grim experiences, a will to solidify, both in spirit and in fact, that structure of international peace which neither time nor circumstances can ever destroy.

As for the world situation at large, its seriousness cannot be denied. All countries, including Turkey, from which I have just come, and the United States, are feeling the stresses and strains of the economic depression. Countries are made up of individuals, and it is always possible that countries, as people, may react differently under conditions of stress than they would react under normal conditions. This infuses an added element of uncertainty and one for which allowance must be made. But I am not an alarmist. There are far too many of them in the world today. I am an optimist both by nature and conviction and I firmly believe in the ability and the intelligence of man to overcome and master the difficulties which are now besetting the world, of which Japan, and my country too, are shouldering their heavy share.

Calmness, serenity, and philosophy, essentially Oriental virtues, are particularly needed while our problems are being solved. This takes time. No country can expect to regain prosperity overnight. We are all more or less in the same boat and we know that we are so interdependent that what happens in one country intimately affects its neighbors. After all, we are all imprisoned, as it were, on this tiny planet floating in a space filled with stellar bodies much larger than our little earth. We can't get away from it so we might just as well learn to get along together as well as we can.

This is only one of the many reasons why the United States has a very real interest in Japan and is anxious to see her succeed in pulling through this period of depression. Consider our trade relations alone. The United States alone takes forty per cent of Japanese exports and contributes thirty per cent of her imports. These figures are worthy of thought.

So far as my own sympathy and good will are concerned, I should like in due course to be able to translate them into something tangible, into constructive work of benefit to both our countries. Otherwise the mere expression of such sentiments is of little value. That constructive work can be accomplished only by straightforward speaking leading to a perfectly clear conception of each other's points of view. After all, what is friendship? What is it built upon? Surely not upon empty phrases. Surely not upon the desire to please and to acquire popularity at the expense of honest opinion. The only friend who counts—who can count in any walk of life—is the friend who says exactly what he thinks. Sometimes what he says is pleasant to hear, sometimes it is not. But then one knows where one stands. Nowadays indirectness is a weakness, not a strength. Nowadays he who indulges in false phrases is discredited, and he who indulges in expressions of genuine good will must prove it in his dealings. That is the only kind of diplomacy, the only kind of friendship that I know.

When I arrived in Japan two weeks ago, the correspondents of various newspapers very kindly met me on the ship and asked me a number of questions. I answered as many of those questions as I could, but I fear there were misunderstandings because I was quoted as saying a good many surprising things, among others that I knew nothing about present-day Japan. It is true that I have much, very much, to learn; it is true that I come with an open and unprejudiced mind; it is true that I wish to study Japan and her problems with all the zeal that I possess. But it is hardly true to say that I know nothing about present-day Japan. On the contrary, I have read much and thought much and talked much, not only with the high officials of my Government but with many men prominent in the life of our country and of other countries who know Japan, and I have also talked with many representatives of the Japanese Government abroad, whose opinion I value and whose information I trust. With such a background one cannot be totally devoid of knowledge. It is my earnest hope that so long as I have the good fortune to be with you I may constantly add to that knowledge; if in some respects it is inaccurate, I wish, by sympathetic observation and study, to correct it.

I have other bonds with Japan too. On my visit here many, many years ago, I aimed to learn as much as possible, stopping at a Japanese hotel in Tokyo and trying to enter in every way into the life of your country. But what changes since then! Wide streets and avenues, great modern buildings, luxuriant parks and gardens. The city is going ahead so fast that it is almost impossible for an ancient visitor like myself to catch up with it. Also, I think I owe to Japan my wife. She lived here for three years as a girl, and when she returned to America I am perfectly sure that what really bowled me over and caused me to ask her to marry me was the vision of her standing on her hearth at home in a gaily colored Japanese kimono with obi and all. May I add that one of our most treasured possessions, which we cherish with pride and profound respect, is the autographs, courteously given to me personally at the Paris Peace Conference, of Prince Saionji, Count Makino, and the other Japanese delegates to that historic conference. For whatever picture may now be painted, that general background offers a useful and workable canvas.

Patience, and lots of it, in solving our problems is essential, and there must be faith in leadership. I find myself in a position of great responsibility. If I am to be of practical service, I must have the faith and confidence, so long as it is justified, not only of the Japanese Government but also of my fellow countrymen here. I want them to feel, as I want my Japanese friends to feel, that my door is always open; that I shall welcome their constant co-operation, their suggestions and their advice, at all times and under all circumstances. And I wish with all my heart that my mission to your country may be productive of practical and permanent benefit to both of our great nations.

In closing I should like once more to refer to Mr. Castle, with whom I have been in intimate association since we were both young students at Harvard University. He is a sincere friend and admirer of your country. I mention him now because I recently came across the speech which he made at the laying of the cornerstone of the new American Embassy in Tokyo, and there are certain passages in that speech which I think should never be forgotten. I should like to adopt those passages as my watchword while in Japan because they typify exactly what I want our Embassy to be, and I cannot do better than to repeat them on this to me, important occasion:

We hope that the new buildings may be an ornament to reconstructed Tokyo. But an embassy fails if it is only a shell, no matter how attractive. It fails if it merely keeps the rain from spoiling a multiplicity of papers, merely houses men and women who carry on routine work. It must be the habitation of a spirit of service both to America and Japan. It must be a center of

understanding. Those who work within its walls must consecrate their lives to the fulfillment of this great purpose. . . .
I hope that this stone, impervious to attacks of the elements,
may in a material sense typify that spiritual friendship between
our two countries which will withstand eternally the attacks of
slanderers and mischief-makers. In this continued understanding and friendship is enshrined our confidence of future happiness and peace.

To the development of that understanding and confidence, while
depending much on the co-operation of this public-spirited society,
I pledge my every effort.

"THE SITUATION IN JAPAN IS VERY SERIOUS"

June 29, 1932

The following statement was made to one of my staff by a Japanese, a member of the Metropolitan Police Board. As this visitor
generally talks about the weather, his remarks on this occasion are
significant:

The situation in Japan is very serious. It appears quiet on
the surface, but underneath there is great discontent among the
people. Wherever a few get together, their brains start to work
and they try to solve their difficulties and to see a way out of
them. We are continually hearing reports of probable actions
on the part of various groups of people. We raid them, take
their papers, and arrest a few of them and so try to keep down
any outbreaks. But when something serious will occur it is very
hard to say. It may happen at any time. The young Army officers are out of hand; they have their own ideas of what should
be done. The whole place is full of malcontents.

As for the cabinet—Viscount Saito is an honest man and there
are a few others in the cabinet who are trying to do their best
for the country. But most of them are still the same old politicians, working for themselves and for the good of their parties.
Look at the trouble about the governors of the prefectures. This
man Adachi is not to be depended upon to do anything for the
good of his country. He is just an old politician, working out
his own political schemes.

Many people have been trying to get together and find a man
who could lead and form a new party based on honest principles, but such a man is difficult to find; as far as I know, they
have not gone very far with this scheme.

Yes, I think it is very possible that there will be some more assassinations. It is very difficult to prevent them with the people in their present mood.

The politicians talk about saving money for the Government by having reduced all of the officials' salaries but at the same time they have appointed various political friends to positions that are quite unnecessary, such as, for instance, the parliamentary secretaries to the ministries. These secretaries have nothing to do. The people know these things and it makes them quite angry.

A GLORIOUS FOURTH

July 4. *Independence Day*

The day began early as I had to attend the opening of the Oriental Culture College at 9 o'clock and make a short speech. Saito and two other members of the cabinet were scheduled to attend but did not come.

Then at 12:15 to the Tokyo Club, where, according to custom, the American Ambassador proposes the health of the President of the United States to the assembled members (they included Lindley, British Ambassador, Marler, Canadian Minister, the Persian Minister, Baron Hayashi, Viscount Ishii, and a great many Japanese and others) and then the same thing at the American Club at 12:30. The ceremony at both clubs took place in the bar, but far be it from me to interfere with long-hallowed custom.

From 4:30 to 7 Alice and I were at home to all and sundry. We had invited all Americans by inserting a notice in the press and had telephoned to each diplomatic mission and to the Foreign Office that everybody would be welcome, although a good many had announced that they intended to come anyway. I wore formal clothes and had the Military and Naval Attachés in uniform. Foreigners are not usually asked to the diplomatic missions on their respective national holidays here, but Alice and I felt that with our new big Embassy we might as well set the precedent and make it a sort of *ricevimento*. Nearly all the diplomatic and Foreign Office people and many Americans came, about 350 altogether, commencing with Viscount Saito himself. Alice had the Embassy beautifully arranged, and as it was fortunately clear the guests could circulate on the terraces and the lawn. The buffet, champagne, and punch were in the big banquet hall and there was dancing in the ballroom, but the music wasn't very good, as the leader and pianist of the Japanese orchestra failed to turn up, and while his four colleagues did their best they were so ashamed that they absolutely refused to be paid. Still, it was a very successful afternoon and nearly everybody stayed right through and seemed to enjoy it.

Afterward we had a buffet supper on the terrace overlooking the swimming pool and the chancery. Alice had had special Japanese lanterns made with the name of the Embassy in Japanese characters and big sailing junks in yellow (I understand that this touch was a special tribute to my love of ships) and the terrace was furnished with cane chairs, straw matting and a great many pillows, and with the big trees hanging overhead it was really a beautiful spot for supper, lighted only by the lanterns and the moon. Those who stayed for supper were General and Mrs. Frank McCoy with Dr. Blakeslee and Lieutenant Biddle of his staff (McCoy arrived this morning with the League of Nations Commission and called on me in the forenoon), the de Vaults, Captain Johnson, Colonel McIlroy, the Nevilles, Mildred Teusler and her married sister Mrs. Funsten, Lieutenant Dusenbury, Washington, Parsons, and some other members of the younger set who later took Elsie down to Yokohama for the Fourth-of-July dance, where she had a magnificent time.

I forgot to say that all the members of the League of Nations Commission except Lord Lytton, who is ill, came to our reception, including General Claudel, Aldrovandi, and Dr. Schnee. Young Astor, Nancy Astor's son, who is acting as aide to Lord Lytton, expressed his chief's regret that he couldn't come and his appreciation of my having sent Colonel McIlroy to the station to welcome the Commission and to offer the Embassy's co-operation in its work. Lytton is really very ill with intestinal trouble and a temperature of 105 and Lindley is much worried. I told McCoy that we would have been delighted to have had Mrs. McCoy and himself stay at the Embassy were I not uncertain how the Japanese would take it; it might look a little like tampering with the jury. McCoy said that he could not have accepted as he had consistently avoided staying with any of our diplomatic or consular representatives and that he had declined to stay with Forbes when they were here before.

Thus was the glorious Fourth fitly celebrated.

MANCHURIA TO "MANCHUKUO"

July 5, 1932

Fleisher, who is the only American correspondent who has followed my invitation to drop in often and does so every day or two, told me the source from which he had picked up the material for his article this morning on certain points of view of the League of Nations Commission which had aroused a howl of protest. He also told me that he had cabled the *New York Herald Tribune* that Lindley had made representations to the Foreign Office against Japanese recognition of Manchukuo and that Arita, Vice-Minister for Foreign Affairs, had told Lindley that recognition would not take place at least until the Commission had submitted its report to Geneva. This also later aroused a storm of protest in the Japanese press against Arita, who squirmed out of it by saying that he was only giving his personal opinion.

Incidentally, Fleisher told me that Ting Chien-hsiu, the Manchukuo Minister of Communications, at present visiting Tokyo, yesterday received the correspondents. To the great amusement of the latter, Ting, when he came into the room, was immediately surrounded by about seven Japanese officials. A correspondent said: "Do you favor the complete independence of Manchukuo?" to which the Chinese replied in the affirmative, whereupon one of the Japanese officials whispered something in his ear, and he added: "In accordance with the self-determination of the Manchurian people." Another correspondent asked something about Japanese recognition, to whch Ting replied. Again the Japanese official got up and whispered in his ear, and Ting added: "And we likewise hope for recognition by the United States." Fleisher said the correspondents could hardly keep from laughing out loud it was so ludicrous.

July 6, 1932

I went to see Martel to find out if he too had made representations concerning the recognition of Manchukuo by Japan. He told me that he had had no instructions to do so but that yesterday, in a conversation with Arita, he had urged against precipitancy on the ground that such action would complicate the whole situation. Martel believes that the public statements of Araki and others expressing a determination for early recognition are purely for home consumption and that the Government will not act hastily.

Uchida was today formally installed as Minister for Foreign Affairs and he gave an interview to the Japanese press correspondents in which he said that Japan's foreign policy would remain unchanged and that while Japan will claim what is due, Japan dislikes to act unnecessarily against the interests of other powers; that the misunderstandings of the other powers will eventually be dispelled but that any blunder on Japan's part may lead to grave consequences. The term "grave consequences" as published in the *Japan Times* naturally caught my eye, and I had Dickover call up Shiratori and ask him if this was an accurate translation of Uchida's remarks. Shiratori replied that the rendering in English sounded somewhat more forcible than in Japanese but that the statement as we had it was substantially correct.

OFF ON THE RIGHT FOOT

July 9, 1932

With regard to informative contacts, it is not going to be very easy to make many of them this summer because so many people go away and there is practically no social entertaining to give one a chance to get in touch with informed Japanese. A pleasant initial basis appears to have been laid, but the question is how best to make use of it. Some foreign diplomat told me the other day that his Japanese dentist remarked to him that the new American Ambassador had started "on the right foot," while Count Makino told General Frank McCoy, American representative on the Lytton Commission, that we were going to have great influence here and could accomplish a lot. The question is: how.

The Japanese Government knows the point of view of the United States perfectly, and I believe that in the present very restive state of public opinion, more is to be lost than gained by rubbing it in. Any publicity to the effect that the American Ambassador was trying to prevent the Government from recognizing Manchukuo would result in a howl from the public and in the press which might force the Government into earlier action than it intended, and the press at present represents the military point of view. A big mass meeting has just been held, attended by some of the highest officers including one or more lieutenant generals, and passed a resolution demanding the immediate recognition of Manchukuo.

Today I wrote to Count Makino to ask if I might come to see him to pay my respects. I hope that we can have a very frank discussion and that he may perhaps give me some useful suggestions. I want to go over the situation with him along the lines of Mr. Stimson's recent talk with Nitobé, in the hope that our conversation will be reported to the Emperor, and I want to find out, indirectly, whether Makino's remarks to McCoy merely mean that he thinks we can accomplish a lot by explaining the Japanese point of view to Washington or whether he thinks we can bring influence to bear at present by more clearly explaining the American point of view to Tokyo. There's a great difference in meaning there. Just at present I can see no avenues for useful work opening up and am very much hoping that my talk with Makino may reveal them. From the foregoing it may be surmised that diaries are as useful for clearing one's thoughts as for recording events.

COUNT MAKINO SAYS THE YOUNGER GENERATION HAS TAKEN OVER

July 13, 1932

At 11, I went to call on Count Makino by appointment. He received me in his Japanese house in Japanese dress and I had a long and intimate talk with him. I went over the ground of our attitude about Manchuria with reference to the treaties and along the lines of Mr. Stimson's recent talk with Dr. Nitobé, and said that I earnestly hoped Japan would not extend recognition without the most careful deliberation. He listened to my presentation of the matter in the most courteous and kindly way and said that the younger generation were running things now; he traced Japanese history since the Restoration and said that the elder statesmen who had carefully controlled the policy of the country had now mostly gone and that a sort of interim was taking place before the younger generation had developed its own statesmen, but that this would come about in time. He said that he was an optimist as to the future. His talk was very similar to that which I had with Ambassador Matsudaira in London with regard to the swing of the pendulum.

We then discussed the great importance of education and the prominent part which the universities played in American national life, and I told him how university graduates were more and more taking part in our public affairs. He described his own visit to America when on his way to the Paris Peace Conference after a lapse of just half a century since his last visit. In the course of our talk Count Makino referred to certain passages of my speech before the America-Japan Society in very pleasant terms and said that a translation of it had been made for the Emperor. He spoke of Bill Castle and of the constructive work he had done here. At the end I said that if Count Makino should ever see specific ways in which he thought I could be of service I hoped he would feel free to make suggestions to me in an informal and personal way, as I would greatly value his advice.

In every nation great gentlemen stand out, and during our entire conversation, which was by all odds the pleasantest I've had here, Count Makino impressed me as a really great gentleman. He is close to the Emperor but he doesn't, alas, carry much weight in these days of military domination. He referred, as nearly everyone does here, to the sentiment of the Japanese for Alice as a Perry; he had spoken of this to Frank McCoy in even more expansive terms. As for the net result of my talk with Makino, I didn't learn very much of a concrete nature, it is true, and of course he is not in a position to reveal to the American Ambassador his precise attitude toward Japanese policy, but I could read between the lines and believe he is going to be a sympathetic and possibly a helpful friend.

To turn to an entirely different subject, I was astonished after our Fourth-of-July reception to find that all the candies on our buffet table bore the legend "Moscow, made in U.S.S.R. (Russia)." I learn that the Soviets are flooding the Far East with these candies, which sell for less than the price of raw sugar and, incidentally, are delicious.

"DANGEROUS THOUGHTS"—AN ANTI-FASCIST MONOPOLY

July 15, 1932

Two hundred alleged Communists are undergoing trial in the Tokyo courts. They are those who have been taken in police raids since April of last year. Hardly a week passes that the papers do not tell of the arrest of radicals somewhere in Japan, but needless to say, none of the raids has been on the military extremists or other reactionaries. They usually involve comparatively harmless students and clerks. The movement does not appear to be widespread—in fact, it has been practically stamped out—but the publicity attendant on these raids is for the purpose of deterring others of the same persuasion, as well as to provide a cloak for the military extremists.

COMPROMISE OR QUIBBLE?

July 16, 1932

Fleisher came to tell me that at this morning's press conference Shiratori had told the correspondents that the Japanese Government, in trying to meet the point of view of the League Commission, was trying the possibility of recognizing Manchukuo as a "government" and delaying recognition as a "state" until it should have proved its qualifications for the latter status. It is not clear whether this proposition is intended to preserve the territorial integrity and the sovereignty of China over Manchuria or not, but whatever it means it is the very first indication of a possible compromise. Either it must mean preserving China's sovereignty or it is a pure quibble of words.

WHY JAPAN HEDGED ON MANCHUKUO

July 18, 1932

Fleisher came in this morning to tell me that Shiratori had again talked to the foreign correspondents about Manchukuo along the same lines as on Saturday, indicating clearly that full recognition might be delayed for some time out of deference to the recommendation of the League Commission. As Shiratori's remarks were open to various interpretations, especially involving the question of the continued sovereignty of China over Manchuria, I asked Neville to have an informal talk with Arita and to be sure to say that he had no instructions whatever but merely wanted to know what Shiratori's comments meant. I particularly did not want to prejudice the situation in any way by seeing Uchida and asking for an official interpretation.

Neville talked to Arita for nearly an hour and on his own initiative told him a lot of good, homely truths, which, since he knows Arita intimately, he could do. Arita said that Shiratori must be "crazy," as there had been no change whatever in the intention of the Government to recognize Manchukuo and that recognition, when it was accorded, would involve complete sovereignty.

I sent a long telegram to the Secretary reporting both Shiratori's and Arita's remarks and stating that the former's statements might well be in the nature of a trial balloon to gauge foreign reaction, for I could not believe that he had talked without at least the knowledge of his superiors, especially as he had substantially repeated his remarks after an interval of two days. Arita also told Neville that he thought Uchida would send for me shortly in order to go over the whole situation. I felt a lot better when I had got that telegram to the Secretary off my chest, for the situation, with its cross currents of contradictory announcements, press statements, and ordinary gossip, is bothersome and I want at least to keep Washington informed as to what is really happening. I dare say

the Japanese don't yet know themselves what they are going to do
and that the tone of Shiratori's statements was carefully studied in
order to create a favorable impression abroad until they decide
what to do.

July 20, 1932

I picked up the morning paper and saw that Neville's call on
Arita day before yesterday was published in headlines with the
statement that now Great Britain and America had both taken up
the question of the recognition of Manchukuo but that it wasn't
known whether Neville had acted on instructions from Washington
or not. This, of course, is the irrepressible Shiratori, as Fleisher
confirmed to me later in the morning, for Neville very carefully
told Arita that he was merely asking for a clarification of certain press reports and that he was *not* acting under instructions or
making any representations, which could of course be done only by
the Ambassador. I don't see what the Foreign Office expects to gain
by this system of wholesale publicity. It simply means that I can't
drop in to discuss matters informally, as every visit to the Foreign
Office is bound to be told the press, including what was said, and
to raise publicity out of all proportion to its significance. When
Japan's Ambassador Debuchi comes to the State Department, it is
true that the correspondents may see him and ask questions, but at
least the Department itself doesn't reveal the nature of the conversation unless there is some good reason for it, or if they do reveal it,
they take care to give it out correctly. Not so in Tokyo.

On going to the chancery at 9 I found a confidential telegram
from the Secretary anent the subject of the recognition of Manchukuo, which gave me great satisfaction. I think he is following
exactly the right policy. He said that he had read my reports with
interest and "solicitude"—defined by Webster as "with fear and
anxiety."

The new Chinese Minister, General Tsiang Tso-ping, made his
formal call this morning. He has me stumped as to dress (that all-
important element of diplomacy) because he came in a short black
coat and a top hat. If I return his call correctly clad in a tail coat
and top hat I shall be exceeding his procedure, whereas if I wear a
short coat and a bowler I shall clearly be jeopardizing the good
relations between China and the United States. In any case, I refuse
to commit so heinous a breach of sartorial convention as that of

which the Minister was guilty. This is a real problem with which I shall have to wrestle during the next few days, for of such stuff is diplomacy made.

To luncheon came the Italian Ambassador, the Canadian Minister and Mrs. Marler, who are leaving this week for a short leave of absence in Canada, and Mr. and Mrs. Arita, Vice-Minister of Foreign Affairs. After luncheon I told Arita of my surprise at seeing Neville's informal talk with him published in the press because Neville had carefully told Arita that he, Neville, was not acting under instructions and was not making official representations but only seeking a clarification of certain press reports. I also said that I had noted Arita's remark to Neville that Uchida would probably send for me in a few days to go over the situation. Arita replied that the British and Italian Ambassadors had asked to see Uchida this week and he thought it would be better if I, also, would apply for an interview. I said that I had no particular reason to bother Count Uchida with a request for such an interview at the present moment, although I might perhaps wish to do so later. The matter was left on that basis.

SOME DIPLOMATIC USES OF THE PRESS

July 22, 1932

Another scorcher, the glass at 86 in our breakfast room at 8 o'clock in the morning.

I sent a telegram regarding the military situation in Jehol and another confidential one to the Secretary concerning my not asking for an interview with Uchida. I told him that it was going to be very difficult to maintain close relations with the Foreign Office and to discuss matters informally from time to time because such conversations were almost always given to the press, generally inaccurately, and were likely to stir up undesirable and sometimes inflammatory comment in the local press. Shiratori, as the Department is aware, seems to act independently of his superiors and seems to enjoy giving sensational impressions. I added, however, that I hoped to be able to work this problem out in time. Shiratori, indeed, is quite an enigma; Shidehara tried to get rid of him and couldn't, as he is apparently supported by the military, with whom he seems to be in entire sympathy. He is also a nephew of Viscount Ishii and is closely connected with Hiranuma, President of the

Privy Council and chief of the Kokuhonsha reactionary society, which of course renders him impregnable at the Foreign Office. Furthermore he is very thick with Tani,* Chief of the Asiatic Bureau of the Foreign Office, who is a brother of General Tani of the Army, and thus both have close relations with the military.

Fleisher came in to say good-by before departing for two weeks' vacation in Karuizawa. I shall miss him, as he is my regular link with the press, but he has promised that Don Brown, of his staff, will keep me *au courant* of any interesting disclosures by Shiratori in the daily press conferences. The other correspondents apparently are going on the old assumption that the American Embassy never knows anything and never gives anything and they haven't bothered to find out whether there is any change in that situation. Fleisher profits because I frequently tell him current bits of information which he didn't know himself. You can't cultivate useful relations with the press unless they are reciprocally useful.

GOLF FOR GOOD WILL

August 4, 1932

Warner, an importer of American films, had offered to show the new Bobbie Jones golf films at the Embassy before release to the public and I thought it a pleasant way to get in touch with the Japanese golfing world. Through the presidents of the various golf clubs near Tokyo, invitations were extended and about eighty Japanese golfers came, as well as a smattering of Americans and others. The thing was very well done: both movie and talking machines were set up behind curtains in the big ballroom so that they were hardly visible; Bobbie Jones' voice, when explaining his shots, was as clear as if he were speaking in the room. Unfortunately, only four of the series of twelve films had arrived in Japan, showing the use of the putter, niblick, mashie-niblick, and mashie, but these were intensely interesting and afterward I noticed many of the Japanese practicing their grip and swing with imaginary clubs during the excellent buffet supper. The golf films were sandwiched between the usual silly musical cartoons, but the Japanese seemed to enjoy them. They were expressively appreciative of the party.

* Successor to Togo as Foreign Minister in 1942. Replaced in 1943 by Shigemitsu.

SECRETARY STIMSON'S "VILE, PROVOCATIVE" SPEECH

August 15, 1932

The next event, which called me from a few days of refreshment at Karuizawa back to Tokyo, from August 10 till the 13th, was the outburst in the Japanese press against Mr. Stimson's speech before the Council on Foreign Relations. Neville went down too. At this writing I have not yet seen the text of the speech, which I believe was delivered on August 7, so that I don't yet know just what was said, but so far as can be gathered from the latest press dispatches, the Secretary spoke of the application of the Kellogg Pact to the Far Eastern situation in an academic way and did not directly charge Japan as the aggressor. However that may be, the dynamic Mr. Shiratori told the Japanese press that all Japan was indignant at Mr. Stimson's charges and the newspapers came out with such slurring comments as "malicious propaganda," "highly improper," "imprudent utterance," "vile and provocative," and so on. For two days the vernacular press was full of it, and the tone was not a bit conducive to good relations between Japan and the United States. The text, when it finally came to me after the incident was closed, showed that the speech contained nothing whatever at which Japan had any good reason to take offense. Japan has consistently maintained that she acted in self-defense in Manchuria, and the public reaction of the Foreign Office to the speech was a surprising indication of the guilty conscience.

JAPAN'S PRO-WAR, ANTI-LEAGUE PROPAGANDA

September 1, 1932

When the Commission of Inquiry of the League of Nations visited Tokyo in July, 1932, the Japanese press published concerted and inspired articles affirming Japan's determination to pursue its "fixed policy." This was partly for the benefit of the Commission, but also partly to inspire the people to defy the League if necessary. The Foreign Office spokesman, Mr. T. Shiratori, as already stated in the diary, released to the Japanese press on August 9 an entirely uncalled-for, inaccurate, and provocative interpretation of the speech of the Secretary of State before the Council for Foreign Relations. This was obviously released for the purpose of arousing nationalistic and anti-American feeling.

The people throughout Japan (even school children) are being

urged to subscribe to funds for purchasing and presenting to the
Army "patriotism" airplanes, tanks, passenger motorcars, armored
motorcars, and antiaircraft equipment. This is partly for the purpose of conserving Army funds and partly to encourage war fever.

ONLY FORCE CAN STOP JAPAN

September 3, 1932

I had a conference of the staff, including the Military and Naval
Attachés, and read to them my telegram to Mr. Stimson, redrafted
after we had slept on it. They all concurred. I don't want to be
sensational, but I do want to go on record—continually—that the
Japanese Government intends to proceed with its program in Manchuria unless prevented by superior physical force. The telegram
said that I could not too strongly impress on the Secretary the certainty that the Japanese Government firmly intends to carry out its
Manchuria program unless prevented by superior force; furthermore, that the elements who now control the Government believe
that their cause is just and that this gives added strength to their
determination. Liberal statesmen carry little or no weight; the
military preparations are going forward steadily. They expect an
unfavorable report from the League of Nations but regard America
as their greatest stumbling block; little is being said of friction
with Soviet Russia just now.

I said that it was difficult to believe that the Japanese, as intelligent people, could really give credence to the obviously false
premise of self-determination for Manchuria, but they regard their
whole course of action as one of supreme and vital national interest,
if not one of self-defense, and on that basis they are prepared to
fight if necessary. All of these opinions have been confirmed with
increasing intensity, especially during the past few weeks. After a
careful study of the situation I can find no approach by which the
present Japanese intransigeance might be overcome or modified.
Japanese policy may, in time, be compelled to modify owing to
foreign moral and internal financial pressure, but for the present
we must inevitably continue to face openly conflicting policies and
principles between our two countries.

I was very glad to get that telegram off and to have placed the situation squarely on record. American policy should be framed with
a precise knowledge of these facts.

It gives one a strange sensation to live in a country where individually everyone is thoroughly friendly and where one's personal relations are of the best, but where collectively one is constantly aware of a deep distrust of and animosity against one's own nation. This animosity doesn't seem to apply to individual Americans at all, except Mr. Stimson, upon whom the whole Japanese animus is concentrated. Indeed, one often gets the impression from the press that the Japanese doubt if Mr. Stimson really represents American public opinion regarding Japan. Many seem to think that his various notes protesting against Japanese action in Manchuria represent only his own personal point of view and they talk freely of an altered situation when Mr. Stimson finally leaves the State Department. But for any American, the Japanese press is not agreeable reading. They steadily slam the United States, and the editorials and articles concerning Manchuria are built, quite simply, on muddy thinking. All their arguments—to the effect that Japan has not violated the Nine-Power Treaty and all the rest of it—are erected on two false premises, the arguments of self-defense and self-determination. Their legal argument of self-defense is fallacious. But when the Japanese advance the argument of self-determination for Manchuria and blandly assert that the 27,000,000 Chinese inhabitants of Manchuria have broken loose from their mother country in a bona-fide revolution and that they, the Chinese inhabitants, have themselves set up this *opéra-bouffe* state of Manchuria, the Japanese become simply puerile and insult one's intelligence. Yet this argument is constantly advanced as an accepted premise which is not open to question, and the case for Japan is constantly and carefully argued out in the press on this false basis.

This is where their muddy thinking comes in and where their whole case falls like a house of cards. I do not see how the Lytton Commission can fail to explode these two false premises of the entire Japanese position, although I suppose it will be done with plenty of soothing sirup if only to please the French. There are rumors and Japanese press reports that General Claudel received instructions to tone down the findings of the report as much as possible.

There was a long article published in the *Advertiser* on September 3, by one Shin-Ichiro Fujita, comparing Japan's action in Manchuria with the action of the United States in Panama. Indeed, this is a favorite thesis of Japanese editorial writers. I was therefore very glad to see that Fleisher published side by side with the Japanese article his own editorial reciting all the facts concerning the creation of the state of Panama and terminating:

> The foregoing are the facts. That there is a similarity in the policies pursued by the United States in Panama and by Japan in Manchuria none will deny. But there is one essential difference, which is generally overlooked by Japanese writers, and that is the factor of time. American intervention in Panama took place thirty years ago. When American warships supported the revolution of 1903 in Panama which brought into being the administration which signed over the Canal rights to the United States, there were no international commitments to stand in the way of the American Government.
>
> The Covenant of the League of Nations, the Nine-Power Treaty, and the Kellogg Pact are products of the era which has followed upon the close of the World War. Formerly nations worked out their destiny by the rule of force, using war as an instrument of their national policy. Today the peoples of the world have set their faith in a new order of which the treaties are a symbol.

This was just about as far as the *Advertiser* could go without being confiscated and it showed a certain amount of courage on the part of Fleisher, who has to watch his step pretty carefully.

These comments are not, currently, particularly interesting, but I think a diary should set forth, more or less, what one is thinking at the time it is written. History is a continuous unfolding panorama, and in later years it may be valuable to be able to furnish a little color and atmosphere to a particular scene of the past.

THE NATIONAL CITY BANK AFFAIR

September 10, 1932

Today was largely taken up with the National City Bank affair. The matter would be ludicrous if it were not serious. The bank in New York had instructed its various branches throughout the Far East—in China, Manila, Singapore, etc., quite as much as in Japan—to forward photographs of the business sections in their respective cities in order to indicate the modern building progress in those cities. In Osaka the Japanese gendarmes suddenly asked the local branch of the bank to stop taking these photographs and shortly thereafter the Japanese press, not only in Osaka but throughout the entire country, carried sensational headlines and many columns of print charging the bank with taking these photographs (although in strict accord with Japanese laws and regulations) for the purpose of furnishing the United States Government with plans for bombing these districts in case of war. The matter on the face of it was absurd because these photographs of these same spots can be bought in the open shops, and the Japanese Chamber of Commerce in Yokohama had recently circulated in the United States a pamphlet containing similar photographs for purposes of business propaganda. The action of the bank was in fact in the interests of the Japanese themselves. But the poison immediately worked its course: at least one Japanese member of the staff of the bank has resigned, threatening letters and visits from patriotic societies calling for wholesale resignations are being received, so that the bank's prestige and business will inevitably suffer, even if its personnel and property undergo no damage.

Shiratori as usual indulged in some high-flown language to the newspaper correspondents. I sent Colonel McIlroy yesterday to see some high officers in the War Office, since that ministry is in charge of the gendarmerie which apparently started the trouble, and to ask that an official statement be issued absolving the bank from blame, but the officers seemed merely amused and refused to take the matter seriously. Yesterday, also, Curtis of the bank had a long talk with Arita, who seemed sympathetic, but when he asked that an official statement be issued, Arita remained silent for about three minutes and finally said: "Well, how can we prove to our satisfaction that the action of the bank was not open to suspicion?" The press campaign had, however, died down and Curtis thought that no further action was necessary on my part, but today he telephoned me that the Osaka papers had broken out again with inflammatory headlines, that the matter had been publicly broadcast over the radio, and that patriotic societies were causing trouble. I therefore decided to call on Count Uchida and lay the case before him.

Conversation No. 2   September 10, 1932

COUNT YASUYA UCHIDA,
MINISTER FOR FOREIGN AFFAIRS
Affair of the National City Bank of New York

Called at 3 o'clock by appointment on Count Uchida, who smilingly observed that he hadn't seen me for a long time. Replied that

I had tried to bother him as little as possible since he took office.

I laid before him in detail the case of the Osaka Branch of the National City Bank of New York, which had ordered the taking of certain photographs of the business sections of the city under the instructions from their head office in New York.

I told Count Uchida that the Japanese gendarmerie at Osaka had asked the bank to stop taking these pictures, even although there were no laws or regulations against such action, and that immediately thereafter practically the entire Japanese press had come out with sensational headlines charging the bank with taking these photographs to send to the United States Government in order to assist bombing operations in case of war. I described in detail the harm that was being done to the bank's prestige and business by this campaign and asked (1) that an official investigation be instituted, (2) that on receipt of the report an official statement be issued to the press absolving the bank from blame with a view to partially rectifying the harm already done, and (3) that steps be taken to stop the press campaign.

Count Uchida listened carefully to my presentation and then remarked that it was difficult in Japan to interfere with the press but that an investigation was already under way as a result of Mr. Curtis' call on Mr. Arita, and that when the report was received he would give it full consideration in the light of my representations.

DOUGLAS FAIRBANKS FOR THE WEEK END

September 11, 1932

There followed a delightful few days in Karuizawa, our last for the summer. Douglas Fairbanks was a most acceptable guest, full of fun, a born entertainer, but surprisingly modest and appreciative. I had written him on his arrival in Tokyo inviting him to Karuizawa (had met him many years ago in Washington) but explaining the simplicity of our surroundings. He had another engagement to spend Sunday with Lieutenant Baron Nishi, the hero of the equestrian steeplechase at the Olympic games, but was so keen to come to us that he got his other engagement postponed. We began Sunday with a swim in the icy pool and then thirty-six holes of golf in pouring rain, Fairbanks shooting consistent 43's. He is a crack golfer and plays scratch in England. Another eighteen holes on Monday before he returned to Tokyo in the afternoon.

We had a lot of young people in the house—in fact, nearly all our friends—for lunch, tea, and dinner, and Fairbanks kept them amused with all sorts of tricks, stories, anecdotes, and reminiscences. He took quite a shine to Elsie and gave her a wonderful time. On Monday after lunch we all called on Marquis and Marchioness Tokugawa, who had asked us to lunch, but we couldn't make it on account of golf. They had once met Fairbanks on a cross-channel boat and wanted to see him again.

Of course the penalty of publicity could not be entirely avoided even in peaceful Karuizawa: he was continually recognized and pointed out; had to spend most of his time signing autographs, which he always did with excellent grace, beginning with the two small Moss boys at 7:30 in the morning; and, of course, the Golf Club was thoroughly stirred, having its best caddies ready and a big group of onlookers at the first tee. I introduced him to everyone, and he was invariably cordial and jolly. Every day he sent his daily cablegram to Mary, who is to join him in Tokyo in a couple of months; he is taking a house there for the time being as he wants to get to know the Japanese and have a lot of golf. In one autograph book he wrote his name, and when the possessor asked for more he added, "Mary Pickford's husband." He has recently completed a film in the South Seas and is going to let us have its first showing in the Embassy.

After he left he telegraphed us: "Had a most delightful week end; enjoyed every minute; many, many thanks." I really believe he did, and certainly he gave us all a most amusing time. We now know more about the making of movies, Hollywood, and the cinema world than we ever did before. He explained clearly every detail of his films that we wanted to know about—the Indian tricks in *Around the World in 80 Minutes*, etc.—and was not in the slightest degree reticent or pompous. The sensational trick of the Indian boy who climbs up a rope thrown into the air is managed by the simple expedient of taking the photograph upside down, the rope hanging down, not up.

On Monday, September 12, the press carried a dispatch from Washington telling of my representations to Count Uchida in the National City Bank affair on Saturday and quoting textually my entire telegram, pretty quick work. I suppose my telegram must have arrived in time for the Department's Saturday press conference as I hoped it would do, knowing that the Department would be besieged with questions, as the affair may well have been served up somewhat sensationally in the American press. I had coined the phrase "photographic espionage" in my telegram, and of course the press adopted it. After all, that is exactly what the charges amounted to. The day after the telegram was published in the *Japan Advertiser* an editorial appeared in *Jiji* saying that too much had been made of the affair and that it regretted that I had made a diplomatic incident of the matter by taking it up with Count Uchida, which was considered an unfortunate indiscretion on the part of the American Ambassador. Shiratori at first told the correspondents that Count Uchida's promise to me to conduct an investigation was merely the usual polite diplomatic reply to representations by an ambassador and that no investigation would be made, but two days later, evidently under instructions, he altered his tone and said that Count Uchida would shortly reply to my representations and would say that "the Japanese Government sees no irregularity, nor does it attribute any impure motives to the action of the American bank. Count Uchida is expected to inform the American Ambassador that he sees no objection to having this information released to the American press, but it is unlikely that he will make any statement to the press in Japan." I presume that someone may have advised the Foreign Office to watch its step a little with the American public, but so far as the Japanese press is concerned, I am convinced that the Foreign Office cannot control it and doesn't care to try. This lies with the military who, in all probability, engineered the whole campaign against the bank as another opportunity for stirring up anti-American feeling in the country.

LEGITIMACY IN JAPAN—MARITAL AND POLITICAL

September 20, 1932

The following memorandum comes from a member of the Embassy staff:

The Japanese laws and customs governing the legitimating of children born out of wedlock are much more lenient than those of most countries of the world. In European countries and in most states of the United States, an illegitimate child can only be legitimated by the subsequent marriage of the parents, and even in such cases there are usually obstructive conditions, such as that both parents have been in a legal position to marry at the time of the birth of the child. In Japan, a child of unmarried parents at birth is a member of the mother's family;

upon recognition by the father, however (whether the father be married or not), the child enters the father's family as a *shoshi,* or legitimated child, and takes the father's name. He can succeed to the headship of the house and inherit the family property—in fact, he becomes a full-fledged member of society, with practically no stigma attached to him because of his origin. Recognition by the father is accomplished by the simple process of notifying the local registrar that the child is one's own—in other words, by acknowledgment before an authorized official.

So thoroughly accustomed are the Japanese people to this practice of easily legitimating an illegitimate child that they see no reason why it should not be applied to international affairs. Manchukuo, conceived in dishonor and born in disgrace, is to be made a full-fledged, respectable member of the family of nations by the simple process of recognition by the father!

Diaries to me are a great blessing, for the spice of life is its details, and letters seldom paint more than an impressionistic picture; even a regular correspondent seldom takes up the tale just where it was left off, and individual lives, especially of those who are close to us, furnish the most absorbing of all stories. The inimitable letters of my father-in-law, Thomas Sergeant Perry, were the nearest approach to a diary of any correspondent, and I always miss them. My daughters Lilla and Anita, in their letters, are very faithful, too. Diaries, to be human, must inevitably be indiscreet. Through nearly thirty years my own literary indiscretions have never come back to plague us.

I return to political questions. The Japanese press, probably on the principle that the wish is father to the thought, predicts the early dissolution of the League of Nations, for the following reasons:

(1) The United States and Russia have not joined the League and there is no prospect of the former doing so. Therefore Great Britain and France are in favor of dissolution and the establishment of another international organ in which the United States will participate.

(2) Great Britain has shown lack of zeal in supporting the League, and Ramsay MacDonald believes that international problems should be settled by direct negotiation.

(3) The activities of the League regarding Far Eastern questions are worthless, and Japan threatens to withdraw if the League tries to enforce its Covenant upon her.

(4) If France should bring pressure on Germany through the

League, the latter would withdraw. Italy would follow suit in sympathy with Germany, followed by Hungary, Austria, and Bulgaria.

(5) The League has shown weakness in the Chaco question between Bolivia and Paraguay.

(6) The impending resignation of Sir Eric Drummond and the question of expenditures are contributary causes.

This is an interesting discussion and furnishes food for thought. I do not know whether the dissolution of the League is being seriously considered, but much water has flowed over the dam since the Covenant was adopted; its weaknesses and disadvantages have been shown up by practical experience. Today, with the existence of the Kellogg Pact, a general revamping, to which the United States and perhaps Soviet Russia could subscribe, might well be feasible and to the better interest of all concerned. As a great international clearinghouse the League is a world necessity in which we ourselves must and do co-operate; the Kellogg Pact has rendered certain articles of the Covenant theoretically obsolete. Why not reorganize the whole show, while retaining the existing machinery; redraft the Covenant with reference to the Kellogg Pact in a form to which the United States could and would subscribe, and begin again on a new footing, having profited by the practical experience of these thirteen years?

A MEMBER OF THE GERMAN EMBASSY DISCUSSES JAPAN

September 27, 1932

In conversation today, a member of the German Embassy staff expressed doubts concerning current newspaper reports of an understanding between Japan and the Soviets. Koiso (Chief of Staff to General Muto), however, did seek out Soviet Ambassador Troyanovsky before leaving for Manchuria and conferred with him unofficially. Troyanovsky states that there is no agreement but he is satisfied that Russia is safe from Japanese attacks for the immediate future. The present Japanese cabinet does not want trouble with Russia, and Koiso will hold the Army in check. While the present cabinet lasts, therefore, all will be quiet, but the cabinet is not expected to last beyond January of next year, and what will happen then no one knows.

I asked whether the Russians believe that the military preparations now going on are directed against them.

The answer was: they do not know. My German informant had been making a study of this matter for a report to his Government and did not believe that the preparations were on such a very large scale. The situation, as he described it, is this. The Wakatsuki Ministry (which fell in December, 1931), especially Wakatsuki and Finance Minister Inouye, wanted to stay on the gold standard, and to do so had to save as much from the government expenditures as possible. They were planning to save money by reducing the Army, entirely independent of any disarmament proposals. The Army had to do something or lose all its influence in Japan. The Wakatsuki government wanted to run the country with the capitalists, not with the bureaucrats or the military. So the Army started the Manchurian affair and assassinated Inouye and Dan. When the nation got the war fever, the Army used this to get as much money as possible, for the purpose of bringing its equipment up to date. They do not need all the money which has been appropriated already to keep the five divisions in Manchuria. They are using the money to buy equipment. Also they are playing up future dangers, such as war with the United States, in order to get more money.

LETTER FROM A JAPANESE SCHOOLBOY

September 20, 1932

The following letter received from a Japanese schoolboy is worth recording:

DEAR MY SIR

How do you do?

I am a young boys of eighteen years old but I am so very like of Aeoroplane that of cause most like of aeoroplane. As only a photograph to amuse me. Japan have not only slightly aeroplane photograph and it is high price and value. I am a want of good beautiful Aeroplane photograph.

Please no laugh. Please no laugh of my convenience demand.

If you have photograph of aeroplane now please give me one peace or two peace curtiss all right bouwing all right moth all right.

If you give me it how a joyful and happy and you have not now please teach me address your country of famous Aeroplane company.

Sir please allow my convenience demand. Please Please

Good by Sir

YONG BOY

"LIKE IT OR FIGHT"

October 7, 1932

We hear a good deal to the effect that the liberal elements in Japan are steadily working beneath the surface and that they will eventually be heard from. Of this there is little concrete evidence, although the decision to send Ambassador Debuchi back to Washington in spite of military opposition may be a good sign. I rather think that the Emperor had a hand in that. Anyway, somebody has been sensible enough to see that it would be fatal to send a blatant type to Washington at this juncture, just as it would be fatal for America to have a blatant type here. Secretary Hurley summed up the situation in a nutshell when I saw him in Washington last May: "Like it or fight."

In the afternoon Fleisher called to discuss an article he was sending to the *Herald Tribune,* and then came ―― for an hour's talk. He said that he had been making speeches steadily, one of them to three hundred military officers, and had clearly explained the position of the United States. He has had two hours and ten minutes with the Emperor in the presence of Count Makino and others and was surprised and immensely pleased by the Emperor's keen interest in all he told him. He says that the Emperor understands our position perfectly and is anxious to stop the anti-American press campaign and the chauvinistic war talk. ―― then said that he wished to impress on me two points, first, that if the Young Marshal, Chang Hsueh-liang, will only keep quiet, there will be no question of Japanese troops going to Peiping and that this all depends on Chang's movements; and, second, he expressed the hope that after the maneuvers of our Atlantic fleet in the Pacific it will return to the Atlantic next winter, because its presence on the west coast furnished an excuse for much of the chauvinistic war talk and military and naval preparations here. ―― continually repeated that the domestic political situation is now well in hand and that the more chauvinistic military people are being compelled to moderate their views. Of the truth of the latter assertion I have yet to be convinced.

―― can do what I cannot do, and, as I wrote to Mr. Stimson, this is a time when, on the part of the American Ambassador, silence on political matters in public speeches is golden. I can show the American point of view in private conversations, but the moment I should try to do it in public speeches—and practically all speeches are liable to get to the press even in spite of assurances to the contrary—a public debate would be precipitated and the chauvinists would take good care that my remarks should leave anything but a favorable impression on the mind of the public. Later, if and when the United States takes action in connection with the Lytton Report, a public speech may be timely. The Department recently formulated in an admirably clear manner, for the information of the ambassadors in Europe, our attitude and policy regarding disarmament, the German claim for equality in armament, and the sacredness of the treaties, and it was repeated to me in view of its indirect application to the situation here. Part of that statement, together with parts of some of the Secretary's speeches, might form the basis for a speech here, but not until it is called for by developments.

——— told me that public sympathy was with me because I had been patient in the face of attacks, and he intimated that my influence would be much greater when the time should come to use it than if I had followed a different policy.

As a little humor is here needed I quote the card of a Japanese reporter which was handed in to me at the chancery the other day, applying for an interview:

> Please show me on the Litton Commission Report, your american people's views coincide with Lord Stimson?

He deserved the interview but didn't get it because interviews are just as dangerous as speeches.

NOTE ON DINING OUT IN JAPAN

October 10, 1932

Dinner at Prince Tokugawa's, including the Debuchis, Aritas, Takeda, McIlroys, and so on. The daughter-in-law, also a Tokugawa, acted as hostess. The food, wines, flowers, table, and service were as near perfection as I have seen anywhere, but the whole effect was ruined by the blinding glare of unshaded electric lights. It is strange that advancing civilization in some countries cannot get away from the idea that the degree of one's hospitality is measured by the volume of electric light turned on the scene. It hurts the eyes, irritates the senses, and robs the women of whatever beauty they possess. As usual I had terribly uphill work in dinner talk because the Japanese women, with few exceptions, won't help to keep the ball of conversation rolling; it dies after each remark, and even when they make an observation it is whispered and I have to get my ear down into their plates to hear; besides, the strain of trying to hear is very bad for the digestion. I always feel like saying to those who won't speak up: "If anything has to be strained, it's much easier to strain the voice than the ear"—but I never do say it. As for dinner conversation, Alice gets the best of it because she sits between men and I between women. Anyway, it was a pleasure to dine with nice old Prince Tokugawa and to remember that his family once ruled Japan.

THE OTHER JAPAN SPEAKS

October 18, 1932

In the afternoon ——— came to see me by appointment. He said he wished merely to thank me for our dinner, but that is generally done by merely leaving cards, and it was obvious that he wanted to talk. He said a good deal to the effect that the moderate element in Japan is stronger and more widespread than is generally known, because their views do not get into the press or public speeches; the people who do the most talking and writing in the newspapers are not always the ones who carry most weight, and that the moderate thinkers will be heard from in due course.

This is the refrain that they are all trying to convey to me, but naturally I want some material evidence and want to know just how this alleged moderate movement is going to register in practical policy if it does eventually make itself felt. Now that Japan has formally recognized Manchukuo it is not evident how any Japanese Government could disavow that step or acknowledge even nominal Chinese sovereignty over Manchuria, which seems to be the crux of the whole problem. For my part I talked to ——— very frankly and told him of the exact position of the American Government in the issue. I am told that he is going to be a strong force here and am very glad because he is anything but a chauvinistic fire-eater.

Dinner at the Uchidas', including Mrs. Woodrow Wilson, the Debuchis, Count Makino, Count Kabayama, Prince Tokugawa, the Aritas, the McIlroys, and so on. Both before and after dinner I had long talks with Count Makino, who spoke very much along the lines of ———'s talks this afternoon, emphasizing the existing "undercurrent" of moderate thought, and then we talked of the results of the Versailles Peace Treaty. Later I sat down with ———, who spoke along precisely the same lines as Makino. They are all trying to get this idea across to me.

The only possible indications I can yet see which might point to a slight lessening of military prestige is the fact that Debuchi is to return to Washington in spite of presumed military opposition, and the fact that the *Jiji* this morning published a statement that General Ugaki, Governor General of Korea, might succeed Saito as he is the only man who, it is felt, can control Araki, being his superior officer in the Army. The fact that this article was allowed to appear at all may be significant, although I do not attach much importance to the prediction as yet.

If anything can undermine the military element, it will be the heavy budgetary expenditures for prosecuting the Manchurian campaign and that is certainly an item which will have to be reckoned with. The "bandit" menace in Manchuria seems to be growing rather than lessening, and although we hear of bandit strongholds being captured, we do not hear that any appreciable number of "bandits" have been put out of action. Meanwhile there are reports of disaffection among the Manchukuo troops. There is also a healthy anxiety as to what Soviet Russia may eventually do, this anxiety being strengthened by the fact that most of the Manchurian railways are more or less out of commission owing to "bandit" depredations. With their lines of communication disorganized, the Japanese Army cannot view the hypothetical Russian menace with equanimity. Herein lies the danger that the Japanese will eventually feel it essential to occupy Peiping and all of northern China. They will probably keep out of Jehol until the League of Nations has acted on the Lytton Report, but Chang Hsueh-liang is always busy and something is going on in that part of the world which disturbs McIlroy but which he cannot at present diagnose. Things are too nebulous for my liking.

DINNER WITH MRS. WOODROW WILSON

October 24, 1932

Alice took Mrs. Woodrow Wilson for a motor drive and walk in the Meiji Shrine Park and had an interesting talk with her. Mrs. Wilson said one significant thing—that a smile goes a long way in Japan. It is perfectly true, and from the policemen at our gates to the mothers and babies on the route where Alice exercises Kim she has made many "smiling" friends.

Dinner at the house of Dr. Teusler, the head of the local American hospital, St. Luke's, with Mrs. Woodrow Wilson, Count Kabayama, and others. Mrs. Wilson, next to whom I sat at table, told me the following very interesting account of the way in which President Wilson learned of his re-election in 1916. He did not think it proper to conduct his campaign from the White House and therefore took a house in New Jersey not far from Asbury Park but was kept busy in Washington all summer and did not move down until a few days before the election, which took place, of course, on a Tuesday. Those were the days before the radio and President Wilson did not want the "special privilege" of having the telegraph company install a special wire in the house, so they decided to have Tumulty, the President's secretary, telephone the result of the election from the office in Asbury Park.

The only call on Tuesday night was from a friend of Margaret Wilson in New York who rang up to express sympathy because the Times Building had just flashed a red instead of a white signal, indicating that Hughes had won. Margaret Wilson replied that she refused to concede until further evidence came in, but the President thought it was all over and, remarking that he was happy to be relieved of the cares of office (Mrs. Wilson observed that he would probably be here now if he had been relieved), took a glass of milk and went to bed, although the others sat up and talked most of the night. No news came on Wednesday, except that Vance McCormick telephoned at 4 A.M. that he refused to concede the election until the returns from the West were in.

On Thursday night, the second day after the election, having still heard nothing, President and Mrs. Wilson started for Williamstown to be present at the christening of one of the Sayre children, and it was on the station platform at the little town of Weehawken, where they had to change trains, that an unknown woman gave Mrs. Wilson a bunch of flowers and congratulated her on her husband's victory. That was the first they heard of it, still thinking that he had been defeated. The news was known in Washington at least twenty-four hours earlier, but nobody had sent word because everybody thought that of course they knew. I asked what Tumulty was doing all this time. Mrs. Wilson said she guessed he was merely overcome by the reports. Thus the person most concerned, the President himself, was one of the last people in the country to hear that he had been re-elected.

TEMPLES OF JAPAN

October 27, 1932

Another perfect day at Nikko. In the morning we went out with Lilian Miller to see the temples, of which there are a great many, both Shinto and Buddhist, in memory of the founder of the Tokugawa dynasty and his grandsons, Iyeyasu and Iyemitsu. There is no use attempting to describe them, their amazing richness of architectural design and detail or the wealth of color in their lacquer work and woodcarving. Miss Miller said that when Lindbergh saw them he uttered not a word until he had gone through the lot, and then he merely remarked: "They should all be kept under glass." That about sizes it up. Of course I was particularly interested in the world-famous design of the three monkeys, hearing, seeing, and speaking no evil, and of course the sacred bridge in red and gold. But what adds immeasurably to the effect is that the temples (I believe there are some sixty of them) are buried in an immense grove of huge cryptomerias, some of them said to be a thousand years old according to their rings. These trees are of the sequoia family and are called the "little brothers" of the California redwoods. They stand like stalwart guardians of the temples and the vista from some of the long flights of moss-covered stone steps, with trickles of sunlight falling through their shade on the vivid red and green and gold of the temples, is a sight never to be forgotten.

VISIT TO A JAPANESE SILK FACTORY

November 2, 1932

This morning Alice, Elsie and I, accompanied by Butts, our Commercial Attaché, and his wife, drove to Omiya, an hour and a quarter away, to see the Katakura silk factory. The visit had been long arranged and they made much of it, the Mayor and Chief of Police of Omiya and the high officials of the company, including old Mr. Imai, the Vice-President, receiving us in state. We saw the whole process including the development of the cocoons, the soaking in hot water, the unwinding of the silk threads from the cocoons, the weaving into skeins, and finally the packing in "books" for shipment, ninety-two per cent of all the silk in Japan going to the United States. The unwinding from the cocoons was much the most interesting procedure—long lines of machines where hundreds of Japanese girls watch twenty separate machines at the same time, the thread of five cocoons passing through one eye to form a single strand, the thread itself being too fine for the naked eye to see—at least for the untrained naked eye.

The girls have to dip their hands into water at 150 degrees Fahrenheit to change the cocoons when they are finished or to mend the thread when broken and their poor fingers are pretty raw, but they work so fast that the untutored spectator can't possibly follow just what they are doing. There are loud-speakers in the workrooms and the girls are continually given concerts to make their hard work pleasanter. While we were there the loud-speakers suddenly thundered out *The Star-Spangled Banner* in our honor; of course we stopped in our tracks and stood at attention, but the trouble was that it must have been an enormous record because that noble tune was played about three times in succession and I couldn't move until it was over.

ROOSEVELT ELECTED

November 9, 1932

My own reaction to the results of the election are those of "watchful waiting" because I have very little knowledge of Frank Roosevelt's potential capabilities. Some men, when they get to the presidency, acquire greatness, and Frank at least has the background. I know very little of his grasp of foreign affairs, but he has a fine panel from which to pick his Secretary of State. As to the effect on our own fortunes, of course I haven't the slightest idea and probably shall not have until after March 4 because, while there will be all sorts of cogitations and predictions in the press (one Japanese correspondent in New York has already cabled that the Dean of the School of Journalism of the University of Missouri, Dr. David Williams, will probably be appointed Ambassador to Japan), they will all be guesswork and nothing else. Naturally I should like to see this job through but shall count no chickens until they are hatched.

The Japanese press is unanimously pleased with the election result, first because they foresee a tariff policy more favorable for them, and second because it means the passing of Mr. Stimson, whom they consider personally responsible for most of their troubles with the world over Manchuria. It is significant that even the Japanese servants—Parsons' maid and Johnson's chauffeur—were in high glee at the news and both said, "No more Stimson." Few of them realize that the American people as a whole are solidly behind the

administration in its attitude toward the peace treaties and not a
bit inclined to sympathize with Japan.

DINNER À LA JAPONAISE

November 25, 1932. *Kyoto*

Tonight we had another great treat—how many treats seem to
come our way in Japan, for life has much to offer here. We dined
entirely *à la japonaise* in the lovely home of the Osawas. The father
is a businessman, representative in Kyoto of General Motors and
President of the Kyoto Chamber of Commerce, but of an old samurai family; one of the sons, the one who looked after us when we
arrived, is a graduate of Princeton, and his wife is very lovely. The
mother, another daughter, and another son were present at the
dinner, as well as our entire party and Mr. Takino. I wonder if I
can describe the dinner—difficult to do because the beauty and gracefulness of it all must be experienced to be appreciated.

We enter the house, leaving our shoes at the door, and are greeted
by the family, all but the sons in Japanese dress, the young women
in gaily colored kimonos. After a few minutes of general conversation the host leads the way to the ceremonial tearoom where we
kneel or sit, each on a cushion, along the walls. The room is built
of the usual square-latticed screens and spotless straw matting, not
a single piece of furniture marring its perfect simplicity. There is,
however, customarily one object of art, either a *kakemono* or a
flower arrangement, which the guests are supposed to admire in order
to get into the proper frame of mind for the ceremony. At one corner a hot-water urn is sunk in the floor, reposing on charcoal which
of course is invisible. The daughter of the house comes to the entrance, prostrates herself, and then, assisted by her sister-in-law,
brings one by one the articles for the ceremony—a wooden stand, a
light wooden ladle, the tea box, a rest for the ladle when not in use,
a bowl, a brush, and a scarlet towel in her belt. When all are in
order and ready, the sister-in-law brings in the first teacup, a beautiful little china bowl, all of which are placed in particular positions
on the clean straw matting.

Then begins the ceremony. First a sweet called *manju,* made out
of a sort of paste of beans and barley sugar, is placed before each
guest with a little stick with which to eat it. Then the daughter,
kneeling, dips the ladle in the sunken urn and fills the bowl with
hot water; the scarlet towel is unfolded and refolded with three or

four precise motions, the teacup is washed, the green tea is ladled into it, hot water ladled into it likewise and then stirred with three motions of the brush which is clicked against its side at the end of each motion. Now the first tea is ready; the sister-in-law rises in one sinuous motion, comes to the first guest, prostrates herself, and places the cup before him. The guest bows low in acknowledgment, offers the cup to his right-hand neighbor, who courteously refuses it, offers it to his left-hand neighbor, who likewise refuses it, then bows low again and drinks, being careful to hold the cup with his left hand underneath and his right hand covering it, and being careful also to turn the cup half around in order not to drink from the spot which has been presented. After drinking, the guest places the cup on the floor in front of him and, leaning forward, admires the cup and comments to his host on its beauty. Precisely the same ceremony is carried out for each guest until all have been served. It was my first tea ceremony and I found it delightfully graceful and impressive, an almost solemn national rite.

The tea ceremony being over, we repaired to the adjoining room, where again we knelt or sat on cushions in a square and waitresses in lovely kimonos and old-fashioned headdress brought in the usual little lacquered dinner trays on legs, prostrating themselves as each was placed before a guest. Then hot sake was served and two or three of the tiny cups were emptied and refilled before we began on the first round of the dinner—delicious boiled fish in soup, another fried fish, a shrimp salad, and one or two other dishes, eaten of course with chopsticks. I finished most of them, but it was dangerous because sukiyaki was coming.

After the first trays were removed, two large round low tables were brought in, with a charcoal *hibachi* on each, a dish with a raw egg in it for each guest and bowls and bowls of raw beef, onions, and all the other ingredients for cooking this most delicious of all dishes. Needless to say, we were replete long before the end of it, and then came fruit and two successive cups of tea. But during the meal I could hardly take my eyes from the perfect symmetry and gracefulness of the room itself—a large square chamber, framed with the usual simple square-latticed screens, flanked by an open corridor with big windows looking out on the Japanese garden, spotless straw matting, and only three articles in it: one, a lovely *kakemono* of a blossoming cherry tree; two, a flower arrangement (three roses and a big cherry branch in an urn), and three, a lacquered stand bearing a china lion and below a simple lacquered box. That was all, and yet the room, from the Japanese point of view, was perfectly furnished. Well, we almost waddled like hibernating bears on taking leave, but it was another evening that we shall long remember.

THE AMBASSADOR RELAXES

December 29, 1932

We had a bully game of poker at the Embassy in which I took much pleasure in badly rooking Shiratori; there's nothing like the poker table for getting to know people and it was not alone the pleasures of the game that led me to organize the party. We began at 5, had dinner at 7:30—a mighty good dinner—and played until 10. The players were the Norwegian Minister Aubert, Shiratori, Kaneko, Ohashi,* Le Gallais,† Alice, and myself. Shiratori was the biggest loser and I the biggest winner, which perhaps, after all, was not so very diplomatic on my part—but poker is poker. I showed him conclusively that I can bluff as well as he, but that I generally had the cards.

SOVIET RUSSIA: A FOOTNOTE ON DIPLOMATIC PROTOCOL

I had always taken the position in Turkey that I could not recognize the Soviet Ambassador as Dean of the Diplomatic Corps and that the German Ambassador, who was next in line, was the acting Dean for those countries which didn't recognize Soviet Russia. But in Turkey there never arose a situation where I had to place this attitude on record. Now, however, when Troyanovsky became Dean ad interim during the absence of Bassompierre, I was suddenly called upon to sign or to refuse to sign one of the Dean's circulated announcements, requesting approval of the speech which he proposes to make to the Emperor at the Imperial banquet on January 5. I refused to sign it, as did the Dutch Minister, who is guided by the attitude of the late Baron Rengers in Turkey, as well as the Rumanian Chargé d'Affaires and certain other colleagues, but I asked Voretzsch ‡ to say to Troyanovsky that this did not imply any intentional discourtesy on my part but was purely a technical matter. Troyanovsky replied to Voretzsch that he felt that recognition

---

* Subsequently Vice-Minister for Foreign Affairs.
† A Luxembourg businessman, now his country's Minister to Washington.
‡ German Ambassador.

of himself as Dean would not imply recognition of his country and that he would like to discuss the point with me when next we met. So I took the precaution of telegraphing to the Department to ask for instructions, believing it would support my attitude.

To my great surprise, and indeed to the surprise of Neville and all of us, the Department replied that there was no objection to my carrying on with Troyanovsky all relations of a social and ceremonial character which usually exist between the Dean and the Diplomatic Corps; that I should receive him if he called on me and could exchange cards as long as mine was labeled "To the Dean of the Diplomatic Corps" and that in all subsequent exchanges of cards I should use personal ones. In effect, I could do anything which did not make it appear that I was entering into relations with him officially in his capacity as representing the Soviet regime.

Anyway, no harm was done. I promptly called on the Dutch Minister, General Pabst, to tell him of my altered decision—he was very appreciative of my doing so—and asked the Rumanian Chargé d'Affaires, Stoïcesco, to call so that I could tell him too. I then had Neville ask the Soviet Embassy to send the circular around again and promptly signed it.

WHY THE JAPANESE PLAY BAD POKER

January 24, 1933

At 5:30 I went to the house of a Japanese friend for poker, stayed to dinner, and played until 10. I was the only foreigner with six Japanese. It was a very pleasant evening and my presence didn't seem to detract from the informality, for they spoke Japanese or English among themselves as they pleased. Shiratori said that the Japanese are not good poker players because they are too honest, but I observed several occasions when they failed to live up to this reputation. However, I won.

DIPLOMATIC SYMPOSIUM

February 14, 1933

Yesterday and today I had conversations with the German Ambassador, on whom I called, and with the Dutch Minister and the Italian and French Chargé d'Affaires, who called on me to find out what I was thinking about the general situation. Voretzsch calls the situation more dangerous than at any time since the Sino-Japanese dispute began. Weillschott, the Italian Chargé d'Affaires, is even more inflammatory and confidently predicts a world war within two years. He and the German, Voretzsch, both foresee the eventual application of sanctions under Article XVI of the Covenant and the withdrawal of Japan from the League. Pabst and I see eye to eye in the whole business.

When they ask me my own views, I carefully preface them by saying that these views are purely personal; first, because not being a member of the League of Nations we have nothing to say about the League's procedure; and second, because I cannot speak officially for the incoming administration in the United States, except to quote Roosevelt's public statement about supporting the treaties, and that there is nothing to add to the attitude of the present administration which has repeatedly been made perfectly clear.

With this preface I am always willing to say that in my personal opinion I cannot see the League or anyone else applying active sanctions under Article XVI (in connection with the Manchukuo issue) and while the smaller powers who have nothing to lose are inclined to regard the prestige of the League as more important than any other consideration, I do not believe that the powers who have interests in the Far East will readily let matters get to that stage. I therefore do not believe that the League will go beyond moral sanctions.

The Japanese love nothing so much as allegedly heroic fighting against overwhelming odds; coercive measures would weld them together even more completely than they are welded now, and it is doubtful if any action which the nations would be willing to take would ever smoke them out. I have also doubted whether Japan would withdraw from the League. The military and the chauvinists want to withdraw now, but the liberals are fighting hard against it. Shidehara went down to see Prince Saionji, the last Genro or Elder Statesman, today. Weillschott assures me that he went to pledge his support of the Government in any steps it might take, but —— told me definitely that he went, as I supposed, to plead against leaving the League. Others are working hard too.

Of course I may be proved to be wrong, because one can never be sure of the strength of the military, but withdrawal from the League would first have to be approved by the cabinet, the Privy Council, and the Emperor, and with such outstanding men as Saito, Takahashi, and Makino fighting against it, as I know they are, the step will at least not be taken without counting the cost. Whatever the views of my colleagues, they all agree that coercive measures would be attended by the utmost danger to world peace.

JAPANESE TRAFFIC REGULATIONS

February 15, 1933

There being nothing further to report today, I take refuge in the following "Rules of the Road in English" as allegedly posted in the Central Police Station in Tokyo:

1. At the rise of the hand policeman, stop rapidly.
2. Do not pass him by or otherwise disrespect him.
3. When a passenger of the foot heave in sight, tootle the horn. Trumpet at him. Melodiously at first, but if he still obstacles your passage, tootle him with vigour, express by word of mouth the warning "Hi Hi."
4. Beware the wandering horse that he shall not take fright as you pass him by. Do not explode the exhaust box at him as you pass him by. Go soothingly by.
5. Give big space to the festive dog that shall sport in the roadway.
6. Go soothingly in the grease mud, as there lurks the skid demon.
7. Avoid tanglement of dog with your wheel spokes.
8. Press the braking of the foot as you roll round the corner to save collapse and tie up.

LETTERS TO SECRETARY OF STATE STIMSON

THE LYTTON COMMITTEE'S
CONCLUSIONS ON MANCHURIA

Tokyo, July 16, 1932

Strictly Confidential

Dear Mr. Secretary:

If a brief résumé of the situation as we see it here would be helpful to you from time to time, I will send you such a statement by the fortnightly pouch when there is anything to report.

The important event during the past two weeks was, of course, the visit of the League of Nations Commission which has just ended. . . .

In a nutshell the commissioners are unanimous in finding that Japan's action in Manchuria is based on two false premises: (1) the

argument of self-defense and (2) the argument of self-determination
for Manchuria. Neither argument is considered sound. The commissioners have proved to their satisfaction that the blowing up of
the railway and every subsequent incident in Manchuria since September 18, 1931, were carefully planned and carried out by the
Japanese themselves. They consider that the setting up of this puppet state, far from tending to pacify the Far East, will result in a
festering sore which will inevitably lead to future wars with China
and Russia and a case of irredentism much worse than that of
Alsace-Lorraine. They realize that the Japanese may supply a more
efficient government in Manchuria than did the Chinese but that
this fact in no way weakens the element of irredentism. They consider that the action of Japan runs directly counter to the provisions
of the Nine-Power Treaty, the Kellogg Pact, and the Covenant of
the League of Nations and that discussions with the other signatories
should have been held before action was taken. They still recommend such discussions and delay in extending recognition to the
Manchukuo regime. They feel that the case against Japan was made
perfectly clear in their conferences with the Japanese themselves,
even if they had talked with no Chinese at all. All of the foregoing,
with the exception of the last sentence, was made clear to Count
Uchida in their two interviews with him. Count Uchida, on his side,
stated unequivocally that Japan had made up its mind to recognize
Manchukuo and that he could not consider any counterarguments
nor enter into any discussion of the matter.

I do not of course know whether the report of the Commission to
the League will clearly embody the foregoing points nor what its
tone will be, but there seems to be no doubt that the five commissioners are unanimous in their findings.

As regards the Japanese now carrying on the Manchukuo regime,
I understand that all of the commissioners feel that these officials
are in fact directly subservient to the Japanese Government and that
any evidence to the contrary is "window dressing." Some members
of the Commission's staff are, however, inclined to believe the contrary and feel that these officials are "feeling their oats" and decline
to be dictated to by Tokyo.

Whether the findings and opinions of the Commission, as expressed to Count Uchida, will have any influence on the Japanese
Government and will lead to any modification of its attitude, it is
impossible to predict. Probably not. At present it looks as if recognition would be extended to Manchukuo in the not very distant

future, but if the step is taken, the Japanese Government will be doing it with their eyes fully open to Western opinion.

In my telegram of July 7, I said that from the point of view of purely practical results, as distinguished from the legal aspects of the matter, I believed that American representations against Japanese recognition of Manchukuo at the present time would be unwise. The press, which at present largely represents the point of view of the military, would under present circumstances be quite capable of magnifying such representations by the United States in a manner out of all proportion to their significance and an outburst might well occur which would afford the military a pretext for earlier action than the more conservative members of the Government may desire. That this risk exists is the opinion of every member of my staff. Naturally it is not for me to determine the wisdom of such representations from the legal point of view, or from the point of view of world public opinion and history. Apropos of this, a prominent peer recently said to a member of my staff, referring to the military: "I hope they will change their minds before they wreck the country."

Respectfully yours,

HOW JAPAN APED GERMANY

Tokyo, August 13, 1932

Strictly Confidential

Dear Mr. Secretary:

The outburst in Japan against your speech before the Council on Foreign Relations savors distinctly of a tempest in a teapot if not of a guilty conscience on the part of the Japanese, for we now understand that the speech was merely an academic discussion of a hypothetical case, while the Japanese took it as a specific charge of guilt. Unfortunately I was unable to take any steps to mitigate the effect here, because neither the text of the speech nor a résumé of its substance and intentions has reached me, and by the time the text arrives from Shanghai the incident will presumably be closed. However that may be, the Foreign Office has used the speech deliberately to pour fuel on the temporarily quiescent flames of public animosity against the United States. I say deliberately, because the violent Japanese press reaction was based not on the press dispatches from the United States but on the Foreign Office's inflammatory interpretation of Japanese Ambassador Debuchi's cabled account, and this interpretation was given to the Japanese press a day before it was released to the foreign correspondents.

This situation reminds me strongly of the efforts of the German Government, by calumniating foreign nations, to build up a public war psychology in 1914, the effort being repeated whenever some new venture, such as the indiscriminate submarine warfare, was about to be launched. Here in Japan the deliberate building up of public animosity against foreign nations in general and the United States in particular has doubtless a similar purpose—to strengthen the hand of the military in its Manchurian venture in the face of foreign, and especially American, opposition.

I believe that on the part of the Japanese it is a sign of weakness, not of strength. The internal economic and financial situation in Japan is serious and may become desperate. The plight of the farmers is very bad, many industries are at low ebb, unemployment is steadily increasing. The yen is falling and prices have not yet risen proportionately. Money cannot be obtained from abroad; I was recently told, although I cannot vouch for the reliability of the information, that the Government had tried without success to obtain loans from England, France, and Holland in turn. It will become increasingly difficult to obtain domestic loans. This situation is not critical, but it may become so when the ability of the National Bank of Japan to absorb domestic bonds comes to an end.

Meanwhile millions of yen are being squandered to support the Manchurian venture, of which the eventual economic advantage is highly problematical, and when the full purport of these expenses becomes known to the people, in their own serious deprivation, there is no telling what effect it will create. I believe that a steadily increasing anxiety exists among the Government and the thinking men of the country outside of the hotheaded military clique which refuses to face these facts. It seems to be primarily this military element—vocalized by such men as Shiratori—who believe that the best way to obscure these facts is to work the public into a patriotic and nationalistic fervor by representing foreign nations, particularly the United States, as trying to thwart Japan's efforts for alleged self-preservation.

Such a national temper is always dangerous. The German military machine, supported by a carefully nurtured public war psychology, took the bit in its teeth and overrode all restraining influences in 1914. The Japanese military machine is not dissimilar. It has been built for war, feels prepared for war, and would welcome war. It has never yet been beaten and possesses unlimited self-confidence. I am not an alarmist but I believe that we should have our eyes open to all possible future contingencies. The facts of history would render it criminal to close them.

Respectfully yours,

MANCHURIA AND THE LYTTON REPORT

Tokyo, October 8, 1932

Strictly Confidential

Dear Mr. Secretary:

Since my last letter to you the two outstanding events in Japan have been the recognition of Manchukuo and the publication of the Lytton Report. The hastiness of the Government's action in recognizing Manchukuo had a twofold purpose: to confront the League of Nations and the United States with an accomplished fact before the Lytton Report could be acted upon, and to afford a sop to the Army to prevent their wrecking the present Saito Government and perhaps setting up a military dictatorship. The net result has been the internal pacification of the country, which is a great deal less restive than before the step was taken.

The Japanese were apparently surprised when no action was taken by the United States at the moment of recognition and that the step caused so comparatively little repercussion in the world at large. This feeling may have been one of relief, but I am inclined to believe that the relief was tinged with a measure of disappointment, because in the present temper of the country the last thing the Japanese really want is to be ignored by the nations. They prefer dramatics.

The reaction to the Lytton Report here has been just what was expected—a general condemnation of the findings and an outburst of self-righteous indignation, but without any serious attempt to refute the findings save by blunt denials of their accuracy. This public bluster is, however, not shared by the saner and more moderate thinkers, of whom one, Baron Hayashi, Master of the Emperor's Household and a thoroughly outspoken man, recently observed to a group of friends that he considered the Report an admirable and well-balanced document, especially Chapter 6 indicating that the Manchukuo regime had been set up by the Japanese military. There are plenty of people in Japan who have serious misgivings as to where the Manchurian venture is going to lead the country, but the press does not dare to publish their views. The military are still completely in control.

In explaining the present psychology of the Japanese, two recent conversations are significant. Recently Prince Chichibu invited to dinner Frederick Moore, who has just come from the United States and is to act as a Counselor to the Japanese Delegation at the forthcoming meeting of the Assembly of the League of Nations, and questioned him for over an hour as to public opinion in America, finally asking him point-blank whether it is true that the United States is actively preparing for war with Japan. Such a question from the Emperor's brother is highly significant of the present nervousness of the country. The other conversation was with a friendly Japanese whose comments seem to me to size up the situation as well as anything I have heard, and I therefore append a brief résumé of them. The kernel of his remarks lies in the statement that the Army undertook the Manchurian venture because it felt that it would lose all influence if it did not do something "for the good of the country." Whatever developments may occur in the future, there will therefore enter into the problem the important element of "saving face," so essential in Oriental countries. Here, I think, is the most dangerous factor in the whole situation. If the fanatical military clique finds that its program is being impeded and is likely to fail, whether from internal or external influences, it is quite capable of plunging the country into any kind of disaster rather than give in to the saner and more moderate elements in the country and acknowledging the defeat of their plans.

.   .   .   .

The anti-American press campaign is subsiding, although the military will probably not permit it to cease altogether. Several rather friendly articles have recently appeared and the President's message of sympathy in the apparent loss of the Japanese fliers who were trying to win the prize offered by the newspaper, *Hochi*, will have an excellent effect. A prominent American journalist told me the other day that he had spoken to Shiratori of the absurdity of the fear of the Japanese that the United States was preparing for war with Japan, to which Shiratori replied: "Of course it's absurd; do you think we would have dared to attack Mr. Stimson the way we have done if we thought there was any real danger of war?"

The new Manchukuo envoy, Pao, is truculently asserting to all and sundry that Manchukuo proposes to escape from Japanese tutelage at the earliest possible moment, that most of the Chinese ministers in Changchun are in the pay of the Japanese but that he himself is "fairly independent," et cetera, but I am inclined to doubt his sincerity. He has also expressed his opinion that Henry Pu-yi will soon become Emperor of a North China State, embracing Manchuria, with his capital in Peiping. Some of my diplomatic colleagues and foreign press correspondents seem to attach importance to his remarks, but neither Lindley nor I am impressed. The diminutive Pao, who looks like a child, will probably continue to "talk big."

As for our own future policy, it seems to me more than ever wise, while firmly maintaining our position with regard to the Kellogg Pact, the Nine-Power Treaty, and the Open Door, to avoid any unessential steps which might tend to reinflame public opinion and give the military further strength. Friendly gestures such as the comments about Japan in your recent speech in Philadelphia, the friendly nature of which was finally acknowledged even by Shiratori, and the President's message of sympathy concerning the *Hochi* fliers, tend to help the hand of the moderate elements in the country. This, I gather, is your own feeling. It seems to me that the more the League's action on the Lytton Report can be tempered with friendly and constructive suggestions, the more we shall gain rather than lose in the long run. Our only hope of the eventual enforcement of the peace treaties in the Far East lies in encouraging the moderate elements in Japan.

In this connection, a remark made to the Military Attaché by a Japanese member of the General Staff is significant. The officer said: "We are working overtime nowadays from 8 till 6 because we have to run two separate departments, the War Ministry and the Foreign Office."

Respectfully yours,

A JAPANESE FRIEND EXPLAINS THE ARMY'S
FEAR OF RUSSIA

A Japanese friend states that, when the Army first started on its Manchurian adventure, the people of Japan looked doubtfully at the matter. Later, when the League and the United States started to condemn the Japanese for their actions, the people rallied behind the Army, like all members of a family will stand behind one member who is being attacked from outside. Just now they will not admit that the Army was wrong, but, just like a family, eventually they will admit that maybe the person who was attacked was in the wrong. Any violent move against Japan now will strengthen this family feeling and keep the Army in power, but if everyone stays quiet for a while, there will be a feeling arising against the Army and maybe the Shidehara diplomacy will return. Nations are like people; they do not like to be disliked.

The Army is trying very hard to keep in power, and they are trying to keep the people aroused. They are trying to show the people that the Army is necessary to the country. That was one of the reasons why they started the Manchurian affair. There was a feeling in Japan that the country had to have an economic outlet, but also the Army felt that it would lose all influence if it did not do something for the good of the country. If disarmament was successful, the Army would not amount to anything in the future, so they had to act to save their position.

The Japanese people are very nervous. They are like a boy who has hit another boy and is looking around fearfully, expecting someone to punish them. They will be nervous until after the League meets to discuss the Manchurian affair.

The Japanese Army's operations are really aimed at Russia—not at present, but at some time in the future. Japan is afraid of Bolshevism and feels that it must drive Bolshevism out of Asia.

WHEN JAPAN PIPED DOWN

December 3, 1932

Strictly Confidential

Dear Mr. Secretary:

The political situation here is very quiet, except for one significant factor, which is that the powers that be, including General Araki himself, seem to think that political assassinations in Japan have gone far enough and have determined to put a stop to them by striking at the soul of the whole movement, namely, old Mitsuru Toyama of the Black Dragon Society himself. His house was recently raided and searched by the police and his son arrested. Hitherto Toyama has been immune, but recent rumors of plans to kill Saito, Makino, Ikki, and Takahashi—after the political murder of four of the best men in the country (Hamaguchi, Inukai, Inouye, and Dan)—determined the Government that it was time to take drastic measures to put an end to assassination. The fact that the Government dared to take these steps—Toyama having been looked upon by a large section of the public, including the military, as a sort of superpatriot—is significant of its growing confidence and authority. This does not mean that the Saito cabinet will necessarily last beyond the next session of the Diet, for it very likely will not. But it does mean that the chauvinistic military hotheads and the so-called patriotic societies, who were directly or indirectly responsible for the former political terrorism, are less firmly intrenched and are, it is hoped, giving way to a more constructive statesmanship.

The anti-American press campaign has, for the present, practically ceased. I am inclined to think that ——— had something to do with this and I dare say that some order to that effect may have come from the Emperor himself. It is significant that the personnel of the press bureau of the Ministry of War has recently been completely changed. One of the new officers assigned to the bureau had been transferred from the Japanese Legation in Mexico, and when our Military Attaché smilingly expressed to him the hope that he was going to put a stop to the anti-American press campaign, he replied that this was exactly what he was going to do. General Araki has recently been unexpectedly cordial in his meetings with our Military Attaché, as he has with me. Shiratori has lost much of his influence: his intimate contacts in the Army have been transferred, and his political ally, Kaku Mori, the Seiyukai * schemer, is ill and temporarily out of the picture. Shiratori has been singing on a much lower note in his press conferences. In my telegram of November 28, I gave further reasons for the present quiescence of the anti-American feeling in the country. But of course this feeling is always present and would rapidly be fanned into flame by any untoward incident.

With regard to the forthcoming meeting of the Assembly in Geneva, after talking with many diplomatic colleagues, foreign press correspondents, and American residents who know Japan, I find no one who believes that Japan will make substantial concessions, certainly none that would alter or modify Japan's recognition of Manchukuo. On the other hand, I think it possible that Japan may have something in reserve to bring forward at the last moment.

I base my supposition on three reasons. One is the unlikelihood that Japan will be so rash as to attempt to face the moral condemnation of the whole world, in spite of all the brave talk which is

* The more conservative of the two chief political parties in Japan, the Minseito being the more liberal.

now taking place. It seems possible that they may have some plan by which they hope to forestall a vote of censure. The second is that Japan is arguing its case at Geneva. If the nation is as sure of its ground as it claims, why argue? In the third place it is becoming increasingly evident that the recent drastic decline in the yen exchange and consequent further impairment of the country's credit abroad are to be traced largely to a lack of confidence in Japan's political relations with the world at large. Until this feeling is liquidated, the danger of financial and social dislocation through the collapse of the currency is ever present, while foreign capital markets cannot be counted on to come to her aid.

It seems to me that the Japanese are trying to ameliorate the feeling aroused by the Lytton Report against their actions, and that having put the best face possible on their behavior they may possibly come forward at the last moment, before any action is taken against them, with some suggestions looking toward an eventual settlement some years hence. I do not for a moment believe, however, that any suggestions which they may make will contemplate the relinquishment of their recognition of Manchukuo as an "independent state." The members of my staff and I have been endeavoring for the past week to obtain some inkling of what the suggestions, if any, will consist of, but we have had no success. It is probable that the discussions in the Assembly of the League will continue for some time, and if I succeed in obtaining any idea as to Japan's intentions, I shall inform you immediately by cable.

In my cablegram of November 28, I suggested that restraint be exercised in handling the Sino-Japanese dispute, because coercive measures would undoubtedly result in more firmly welding the Japanese nation together in opposition to the League and the United States. Any hint of force, either military or economic, I believe, would result in the uniting of the nation behind the military and would completely overwhelm the more moderate influences which are working beneath the surface to restore Japan to its former high place in the councils of nations. Moral pressure, however, I think, can be exerted without this danger and might tend to widen the rift now beginning to be noticed between the military and the moderate elements. Eventually the force of public opinion throughout the world, coupled with the difficulty and overburdening expense of pacifying Manchuria, might cause Japan to change its attitude toward the problem. Anyway, as I see it, it is our only chance, as the threat of material pressure would almost certainly have the opposite effect from that desired. Thus the time factor is important, and a gradual rather than an immediate solution of the problem indicated.

My speech in Osaka appears to have been helpful. Its main purpose was to correct the general belief here that the American people are not behind you in your active support of the peace treaties. The contrary was clearly brought out by the words:

> As for the American people, they are heart and soul behind this [peace] movement and behind those who have labored to bring about a situation where warfare between civilized nations will be as extinct as human slavery in civilized nations is today. This peace movement represents a fundamental, united, and unanimous desire of the American people as a whole. The position of the United States in this issue is clear-cut and unambiguous. It has repeatedly been made clear.

On the other hand, the speech was eminently friendly in tone and substance, so that the pill was administered without causing irritation. The Minister for Foreign Affairs last night expressed to me personally his appreciation of the address.

May I take this occasion to say that I think your instructions to Norman Davis and Hugh Wilson relating to the Manchurian issue meet the situation exactly?

Respectfully yours,

SECRETARY STIMSON REPLIES

January 21, 1933

The fortnightly pouch came in late last night with a very pleasant personal letter from Mr. Stimson in which he says, among other things:

> The picture which you give of the situation is substantially in accord with ours, and our line of procedure has been substantially in accord with that which you suggest.
>
> I note with special interest the effort which you have been making to explain to the Japanese the feeling of the American people and my position in support of the peace treaties. The paragraph which you quote from your recent address states our position exactly. I am sure that what you are doing will be very helpful.

Thus the Embassy appears to be in the clear up to date.

2

THREE YEARS OF CALM BEFORE THE STORM

(February 20, 1933–February 11, 1936)

NOBODY could miss the political significance of Japan's decision to quit the League of Nations. It marked a clear break with the Western powers and prepared the way for Japan's later adherence to the Axis. But the immediate consequence of Japan's departure from the League was not a swing toward extremism either in domestic or foreign affairs. Quite the opposite. Having made their hostile political gesture toward the Western powers, the leaders of Japan took a line that looked almost like appeasement —at any rate as far as the United States was concerned. But in spite of its apparent moderation, Japanese foreign policy remained unyielding on essentials: the Naval Limitation Treaties were not renewed, more Japanese troops poured into China. But events did not move fast enough to suit the militarists. The longer the period of calm, the more intense the storm.

JAPAN DECIDES TO QUIT THE LEAGUE

February 20, 1933

The cabinet today voted to secede from the League of Nations as soon as the Assembly adopts the Report and Recommendations of the Committee of Nineteen. It is therefore evident that the opposition of Saito, Takahashi, and others has been definitely overcome, and the haste with which the cabinet acted indicates that the step was taken as a threat in the hope of preventing the Assembly from adopting the Report and as another gesture of chauvinistic independence. The step will have to receive the sanction of the Emperor and the Privy Council, and it is not made clear how and when the secession will take place, but there now seems little doubt that it will go through.

My own guess was wrong; until recently I did not think they would do it, and yet it is right in line with everything that they have done so far, the hasty recognition of Manchukuo and all the rest of it. Their policy is to face the world with one *fait accompli* after another. The military are still supreme and still form a dictatorship of terrorism. There seems little doubt that Saito was told to fall into line or else there would be an internal crack-up in the country commencing with the assassination of himself and others who had opposed withdrawal. The Genro himself is practically helpless before the military clique and will presumably be overridden right along. The saner heads in the Government are in just the same position as they were at the time of the organization of the Saito cabinet; from patriotic motives they give in to the violent elements, always hoping in vain that later they will get control and that in the meantime it is best for the country to avoid further affairs like that of May 15. In the meantime, Shiratori announces that the advance into Jehol may be expected to start any day. If Japan does go on to Peiping there will be great risk of a general war. The outlook could hardly be blacker than it is.

Anyway, I am entirely in accord with the League's action and with the Report and Recommendations. Now that Japan has finally determined to defy the world and to isolate herself, putting into practice the "Back to Asia" movement and with the probable intention of eventually formulating a Monroe Doctrine for the Far

75

East, there seems to be no further purpose in trying to humor her by patience. I am afraid that we are in for a very bad time ahead.

LET THE PEOPLE KNOW

February 21, 1933

Fleisher came in to ask my opinion of a rather sensational dispatch which he was about to cable to the *New York Herald Tribune* setting forth the dangers of the present situation and the general talk of the possibility of war. I said that in my personal opinion it was well to let the public at home realize the potential dangers ahead, and since his dispatch would be published in Paris it might likewise have a salutary effect in Geneva. I told him that I saw no reason for camouflaging the gravity of the situation.

JAPAN'S BREAK WITH THE WEST AND WHAT IT MEANS

February 23, 1933

After several days of thought and consultation I have tried to bring my thoughts into focus with the following result:

In any estimate of the situation in the Far East, full consideration should be given to the following points:

(1) By the cabinet's decision to secede from the League of Nations, Japan has taken steps to burn her most important bridge with the outside world. This step represents a fundamental defeat for the moderate elements in the country and the complete supremacy of the military. Since the beginning of the Sino-Japanese dispute, every important action of the League of Nations has been forestalled or succeeded by a *fait accompli* here, so that Japan's independence of the West, and her disregard of Western interference in her affairs and with what she believes to be her vital interests, might be clearly demonstrated. There will be no surrender to moral or other pressure from the West. The military clique and, as a result of military propaganda, the public are fully prepared to fight rather than give in. At present the moral obloquy of the world is a negligible force in Japan. Far from serving to modify the determination of the Japanese, it merely tends to strengthen it. Were the Government to show any inclination to temporize or compromise with the League of Nations, further assassinations if not internal revolution would almost certainly result.

(2) This national temper is based on many factors, of which the following are important:

(a) The military are determined to maintain their prestige and to permit no interference whatsoever.

(b) The essentially important element of "saving face" permits no backward step.

(c) The belief that Manchuria is the "life line" of Japan has been carefully inculcated among the people.

(d) Future financial difficulties due to the huge expenses of the Manchurian campaign are totally disregarded by the military, which simply refuses to be bothered with ideas of retrenchment in matters touching their province.

(e) The Japanese are fundamentally incapable of comprehending the sanctity of contractual obligations when such obligations conflict with what they conceive to be their own interests.

(3) As for the incursion into Jehol, I have reason to believe that the Japanese are taking special precautions to avoid crossing the Great Wall, even although the campaign may be rendered considerably more costly and difficult by this decision. It would be unwise, however, to overlook the risk that developments or incidents, now unforeseen, may lead to the taking of Peiping and Tientsin, which would of course immediately bring foreign interests into direct clash with Japan. Japan is perfectly capable of replying to any action of the League in applying active sanctions by promptly occupying North China. This really constitutes the greatest potential danger for the future.

(4) Finally we must bear in mind the fact that a considerable section of the public and the Army, influenced by military propaganda, believes that eventual war between either the United States or Russia, or both, and Japan is inevitable. The military machine, already in a high state of efficiency, is steadily and rapidly being strengthened and its arrogance and self-confidence are complete. The Navy is becoming increasingly bellicose. With this temper present in the Army, the Navy, and the public, the risk is always present that any incident tending to inflame public opinion might lead Japan to take radical steps without counting the cost thereof.

The foregoing diagnosis represents the opinion not only of the principal members of the Embassy staff but of most of my diplomatic colleagues and other foreigners in Tokyo. These facts and views are of course reflected in my frequent reports to the Secretary of State.

COMIC RELIEF

In these politically dark days in Washington it must have brought joy to the heart of the Department when it recently received a telegram from one of my distinguished colleagues in a European capital: "The Queen has given birth to a daughter. I have congratulated the Prime Minister."

CAN ANY PEACE PACT KEEP THE PEACE?

February 23, 1933

In the diary I recently said that I was in accord with the Report and Recommendations of the League of Nations in the Sino-Japanese dispute. This statement must be modified, as indeed many of the statements in this diary, in which I am merely thinking aloud, are modified from time to time on maturer thought and consideration. The recommendations may be all right in theory, but the trouble is that they are ineffective in practice because they don't fit the facts and at least at present are unworkable. No doubt, from the League's point of view, it could hardly have acted otherwise, and once having become involved, spurred on by our own Government, it has at least shown patience and restraint. Yet the more one mulls over the whole problem, the more one is inclined to question whether the peace machinery which the world has been trying so earnestly and painstakingly to erect these last fourteen years is basically sound, or rather whether it is basically practical.

To let one's imagination rove a bit—compare the Manchurian situation in 1931 with the Cuban situation in 1898. If the latter crisis had developed subsequent to the conclusion of the Kellogg Pact, and if the *Maine* had been blown up in Havana Harbor, resulting in a war psychology sweeping over our country like a forest fire and the words "Remember the *Maine*" on the lips of every man, woman, and child in the land, could our Government ever have prevented hostilities with Spain? McKinley wanted to avoid war in 1898 but couldn't. Even if the Kellogg Pact had existed at that date, might we also not have occupied Cuba without declaring war, on the grounds of self-defense, forced by public opinion to do so? The public guesses but does not *know* today who blew up the *Maine*. The public guesses but does not *know* today who engineered the incidents which led to the Japanese attack of September 18, 1931. Of course the Cuban situation was very different from the Manchurian situation in many respects, for our action was basically humanitarian while Japan's action was expediency pure and simple. Yet the force of the war psychology was equally potent in both cases. There are many who are convinced that Japan had long intended to take Manchuria, just as she took Korea, and was merely awaiting a favorable opportunity. Very likely they are right.

My point is not to excuse Japan but to question whether the peace machinery is sufficient to deter *any* country, even our own, from hostilities if the urge is sufficiently strong. Could the Kellogg Pact, for instance, conceivably have prevented the South African War? ————, of the British Embassy, tells me that his father was literally stoned in his own village for advocating peace at that time. The Jameson Raid was quite as outrageous a procedure as the Japanese action of September 18, 1931, and the British themselves would have condemned it if it hadn't been for the Kaiser's telegram to Kruger. That telegram, trivial incident as it was, furnished the match that set the war fever ablaze. These things will always create in every country a war psychology, tending to override all other considerations and needing no military propaganda to inflame it.

Situations and circumstances similar or analogous to those mentioned will with almost mathematical certainty arise in future. Hostilities are steadily occurring and will continue to occur in spite of the Kellogg Pact, the Covenant of the League of Nations, and all the rest of the machinery so laboriously and studiously created. If the world allows Japan to break those covenants with impunity, not only will the peace covenants themselves lose their force and sanctity but the stability of treaties everywhere will inevitably suffer. They are suffering already in many parts of the world as a more or less direct result of the failure or inability of the world to call Japan to account. What are we going to do about it?

Moral sanctions? When a nation is beset with a war psychology, the moral obloquy of the rest of the world is a negligible force, except that it tends to strengthen, not to weaken, that nation's warlike temper, as witness the situation in Japan today. It will always be questionable, furthermore, how long the unanimous moral obloquy of the world can continue, for eventual breaks in the solid front are practically certain, induced by self-interest.

Then if moral ostracism is ineffective, or likely to be ineffective, what more can we do? How can we implement the Kellogg Pact? Certainly not by force of arms, which would be contrary to the very principle for which the Kellogg Pact stands. The great war to end wars has signally failed in that particular purpose. If other world wars are the only method of protecting our peace structure, then we had better abandon that structure here and now, because civilization itself will be in jeopardy. Severance of diplomatic relations would be futile unless followed by other steps. Arms embargoes are generally ineffective in practice. In the present case they would simply aid the aggressor. There remains an economic and financial boycott. Probably futile in practice. In the present case, an economic boycott would simply cause Japan to occupy those parts of China whence needed supplies could be obtained, with the resultant risk of a general world conflagration. Financially Japan cannot even now obtain a loan abroad; she has tried and failed, but she still carries on.

Clearly, then, our peace machinery while magnificent in theory is ineffective in practice. It is ineffective because it is superficial. It is like a poultice prescribed for cancer by the surgeon long after the cancer has been allowed to develop. Most of our international ills closely resemble the ravages of cancer. They generally begin on a small scale as a result of long irritation on a given spot. Even the most skillful physician may not be able to sense the irritation in advance, but the moment the obvious symptoms appear, he seeks to eradicate the disease by treatment long before operation becomes necessary.

The future peace machinery of the world must go one step further than the physician. It must sense the spots of irritation and diagnose the future potentialities of disease and attempt treatment long before the disease itself materializes. This, of course, is pure theory. How it can ever be worked out in practice is the real problem which ought to be studied by our usually ineffective peace organizations precisely as the Rockefeller Foundation and other similar bodies are constantly conducting their research for the elimination of cancer today. To put the matter in a nutshell, the peace machinery of the world must be far more radical, far more prescient, far more concerned with facts, conditions, and circumstances than with theories than it is today, if it is ever to succeed in abolishing war.

A DIPLOMAT'S WORK AND PLAY

March 14, 1933

Lunched at Hodogaya Country Club and played golf with Goold and Dennison, two Standard Oil men, and Parsons, my private secretary. A most dramatic match. On the eighteenth, a par-4 hole, Dennison, who is a star player, and I needed both best-ball and aggregate to win the nine. Parsons went down in a birdie 3. Dennison was fully thirty yards from the green, chipped, hit the bamboo flagpole, and dropped straight into the hole for an eagle 2. That gave us best-ball, but we still needed aggregate. Goold and I had both had trouble; he was on the green in four while I was several feet off the green in the same number. Amazingly my twenty-foot approach over a rough winter green went in for a 5 while Goold was down in 5 also, and thus we saved the day, to the perfect disgust of our opponents, by what can only be called two miraculous shots at the critical moment. Such incidents are half the fun of golf.

Speaking of golf, I remember that in Constantinople some of the hard-boiled businessmen used to chaff the Embassy people rather disagreeably because we didn't sit at our desks daily from 9 till 6 the way the businessmen did and therefore were unaccustomed to a real day's work. But what they forgot is that we, the much-maligned diplomats, are really on the job throughout the twenty-four hours. I arise at 6:30 and get to work at 7:15. If we play golf from 2 till 5, it means, for me, almost invariable work from 5 o'clock up to any hour. Three times last week Alice and I were awakened from "the first sweet sleep of night" about midnight by telephone calls from the chancery to read incoming telegrams, some of which had to be acted upon immediately. During our free evenings at home I have to read a vast amount of literature which I should never think of reading if it wasn't in connection with the job, and on many of the other evenings we have to attend official dinners which are generally a great deal less amusing than sitting at one's desk watching the hands of the clock get around to 6. I doubt if the working hours of the average businessman abroad total anything like ours.

Speaking further of golf, I remember a rule printed in all seriousness on the score cards of the Constantinople Golf Club, to wit: "A ball found in a sun crack, hoof mark, or rut on the putting green may be removed without penalty." The Turkish cavalry and field artillery, which maneuver in that region, resented the golf course and in spite of barbed wire protecting it used to gallop across the links, often when the ground was soft from rain, always concentrating on the putting greens. Encouraging for the golfer!

IMPERIAL DUCK HUNT

March 23, 1933

Alice, Elsie, and I started out in a dismal downpour of rain for the Imperial Duck Hunt.* These hunts occur at intervals throughout the winter and every embassy and legation is invited to one of them, including the chief of mission, the counselor, and the military, naval, and commercial attachés with wives and daughters. One of the Imperial princes also attends, and we were delighted when we found that the Chichibus had chosen to come today because they liked the crowd, which included several of the other Embassy staffs. We met at the Asakusa Kaminari Mon Station at 9:15 A.M. and went by special electric train to Bashu Osawa, about fifty minutes' ride, and then a walk across the fields of some fifteen minutes (some went by automobiles) to the Imperial hunting lodge. The wild ducks, of which there are thousands in the vicinity, settle in canals attracted by tame decoys. For each "hunt" ten guests are selected and are given great nets, like butterfly nets although much larger and broader at the mouth. Each guest has a number, and at a given signal he runs to a marked station, five guests on each side of the canal, behind parapets which are built on both sides of the narrow but deep canals. The wild ducks, as soon as they hear the "hunters," rise from the canals and the "sport" is to catch them in the nets as they rise. It isn't sport at all because it is almost impossible not to catch those that fly up within reach of one's net, unless they escape because two nets clash. Four came my way and I easily caught them all. It is all a matter of luck how many come one's way—or ill luck, for there is no pleasure in catching the helpless creatures. Lindley caught ten during the day, most of the guests one or two, some none. Elsie caught one, much against her will. Alice did not participate. If a duck flies up and escapes, a falcon is sent after it to bring it down. Today was bad, for there was no wind and many of the ducks wouldn't rise. I was twice asked by attendants to scoop them out of the water but absolutely refused to do so, although others did. They want to get all the ducks possible, because, after giving six to each ambassador and relative quotas to the guests of lesser rank, the remainder are used by the Imperial household.

The real amusement of the day, which turned out to be a delicious, clear, sunny spring day after the rain ceased, was in the minor sports which were carried on in front of the lodge—a baby golf

* See photographs Nos. 12 and 13.

course, a clock putting green, ping-pong, quoits, battledore and shuttlecock—and a delicious luncheon. We were with the Chichibus most of the time—I beat him in the ping-pong tournament, but the Princess finally won the tournament. They are perfectly informal and very congenial personally, and we thanked our stars that it wasn't one of the other princes because most of them are stiff and out of their element with foreigners. Elsie, especially, had a grand time. The Chichibus say that they enjoyed the dinner and movie at our Embassy so much that they want us to ask them again soon; I think the truth is that it is the only way in which they can see a good movie, and we shall arrange it after Easter. Prince Chichibu is a brother of the Emperor, and his lovely wife was the daughter of Tsuneo Matsudaira, formerly Ambassador in Washington, where she went to school.

GOOD NEWS FROM SECRETARY HULL

March 23, 1933

Returned at 5 and found a very pleasant telegram from Secretary Hull, referring to my resignation, which I had placed in the President's hands by letter of December 5, and stating that he was happy to inform me that as the President was satisfied with my services here, he desired me to continue as Ambassador to Japan. This is very gratifying. I hadn't expected such a message, having supposed that if the President wished me to remain he would simply not appoint a successor. This is really tantamount to a definite appointment under the new administration and it makes us very happy to know definitely that we are to carry on.

JAPAN QUITS THE LEAGUE

March 27, 1933

Japan's formal withdrawal from the League of Nations was passed by the Privy Council and the Emperor and cabled to Geneva today, while an Imperial Rescript by the Emperor and a statement by Saito were published here. These and other similar documents talk much about all Japan's actions being aimed at the preservation of peace, but the trouble is that the Japanese interpretation of that phrase is diametrically different from our own and the League's interpretation. By the preservation of peace Japan means the cleaning up of Manchuria by force of arms until no opponent is left to challenge her control and a peaceful situation will have been brought about, with Japan in command.

If I remember correctly, the document by which Japan announced her entry into the World War with the Allies stated that she did so for the purpose of preserving peace in the Orient and then, quite properly, she proceeded to clean the Germans out of China. But the term "preservation of peace" was just as inappropriate then as it is now. And yet I doubt if one Japanese in a hundred really believes that they have actually broken the Kellogg Pact, the Nine-Power Treaty, and the Covenant of the League. A comparatively few thinking men are capable of frankly facing the facts, and one Japanese said to me: "Yes, we've broken every one of these instruments; we've waged open war; the arguments of 'self-defense' and 'self-determination for Manchuria' are rot; but we needed Manchuria, and that's that." But such men are in the minority. The great majority of Japanese are astonishingly capable of really fooling themselves; they really believe that everything they have done is right, that the Lytton Commission was misled by Chinese propaganda and that the foreign powers and the League of Nations have likewise been misled into entirely false conceptions of the facts.

Such a mentality is a great deal harder to deal with than a mentality which, however brazen, knows that it is in the wrong. The great majority of Japanese—and I include intelligent Japanese—do not know that they are in the wrong, and therefore their determination to resist foreign interference is doubly resolute and strong. Their mental processes and methods of reaching conclusions are radically different from ours; the more one associates with them the more one realizes it; this is one of the great cleavages between the East and the West. The Westerner believes that because the Japanese has adopted Western dress, language, and customs he must think like a Westerner. No greater error can be made. This is one of the reasons why treaty commitments between the West and the East will always be open to misinterpretation and subject to controversy. It isn't that the Japanese necessarily has his tongue in his cheek when he signs the obligation. It merely means that when that obligation runs counter to his own interests, as he conceives them, he will interpret the obligation to suit himself and, according to his own lights and mentality, he will very likely be perfectly honest in so doing. This, in fact, is the situation in the Sino-Japanese dispute today. No wonder that a solution is difficult if not impossible.

As for Japan's action in fortifying Yap and the other mandated islands in contravention to express treaty stipulations, of which we have abundant firsthand evidence, it is perhaps difficult to see how even Japanese mentality can square this with their solemn undertakings and contractual obligations, but here again there enters the unquestioned fact that the Oriental conception of such obligations is not our conception. This whole question of the mandated islands is full of potential dynamite and may yet cause as much trouble as Manchuria. This post is not likely to be a quiescent one for some time to come, but I am not grousing.

Incidentally, the Japanese Government has solved with the wisdom of Solomon the awkward question of permitting foreign astronomical expeditions to visit these very islands for the total eclipse of the sun next year. They have decided to send them all down on a Japanese warship as the guests of Japan! They will be honored guests but mighty carefully chaperoned guests too. The invitation, or order—as you will—was conveyed to us officially in reply to our application on behalf of an American expedition for permission to visit the islands.

JAPANESE AID CALIFORNIA EARTHQUAKE VICTIMS

Nine small Japanese boys in a Sunday school at Meguro have sent me 96 sen (about 20 cents) of their weekly pocket money for the sufferers in the California earthquake in recognition of American help to Japan after the great Japanese earthquake in 1923. I have answered their letter with appreciation, have given both their letter and my reply to the press, and shall send the money to the American Red Cross through the State Department in an official dispatch, just as if the little gift had been a large one. The principle is the same.

Incidentally, the Japanese Red Cross did subscribe 10,000 yen for our earthquake sufferers, half of which was given by the city of Tokyo, but this gift, considering the millions of dollars that we sent to Japan in 1923, impressed me far less than the 96 sen given by the boys.

P. S. SHE DIDN'T GET THE JOB

The following translation of a letter just received is quite delightful:

SIR:

With the advent of the spring season, we feel very pleasant

in and outside our houses. Are you and members of your family enjoying sound health at this season of the year? I am happy to say that I am in excellent health. Is the capital of Tokyo undergoing a change in all spheres of activity?

I am quite willing to come and reside in Tokyo as soon as possible. While serving in your household years ago, I felt as if I was at my home.

Will you be so kind as to find a job for me in Tokyo? I beg you will be so good as to let me know your present address.

Trusting to be favored with a reply soon.

Your obedient servant,

MATSUOKA REPORTS ON GENEVA AND POINTS WEST

May 1, 1933

The really interesting event was my talk with Matsuoka, just returned from Geneva and the United States; as a matter of fact, he did nearly all the talking. His use of English is perfect but he gives an impression of great self-assurance and conceit. Judging from some of his published interviews and speeches I should say that he is capable of expressing a wide range of opinions and sentiments, according to the nature of his audience. Today he told me of his endeavors in the United States to improve American-Japanese relations and of his speeches to American-born Japanese on the Pacific Coast to the effect that they must be loyal Americans. He told me that in his opinion the development of good relations between Japan and the United States should be the cornerstone of Japanese policy and that he had preached this to the cabinet this morning and was going to work for it here.

From the way he talked I gather that he addressed them like a group of schoolboys. I spoke to him of the harm done by the anti-American propaganda in the press. Recently he said to someone that if he were the next Foreign Minister he would do thus and so. Obviously his head is badly swelled by the adulation of the Japanese public and by his reception as a hero on his return from Geneva.

•

THE BURDENS OF SPEECHMAKING

May 21, 1933

Worked all day writing a speech for the dedication of the new St. Luke's Hospital building and finished it. Last Sunday I completed two speeches, for Memorial Day at Yokohama and for the commencement exercises of the American School. The difficulty in all these speeches is to get started on a theme, but once started the rest is easy. For Memorial Day and the American School it was simple to draw on former speeches made in Turkey, but St. Luke's required an entirely new approach. I profoundly hope that these three will suffice until autumn, but one can never tell. These speeches are really millstones; they are inseparable from the job, but I am getting harder boiled about accepting invitations as time goes on. I have made thirty-five speeches since our arrival in Japan a year ago.

MORE TROUBLE IN NORTH CHINA

May 23, 1933

On the basis of a note sent me hurriedly at 6 P.M. by a Japanese friend of the Embassy, I cabled the Department that the Japanese Army had received explicit instructions not to enter Peiping, and that if there should be any tendency to break in, further more drastic instructions were in readiness. It looks as if our diagnosis sent last week, that the Japanese would merely "invest" Peiping and then negotiate with the Chinese to withdraw in return for assurances that the Chinese would cease attacking them at the Wall, were correct. But there is evidence that the Japanese want to set up a buffer state in North China and they may be successful. This military activity around Peiping on the eve of Viscount Ishii's conversation in Washington * doesn't look any too well. The lack of co-ordination between Japan's military and diplomatic actions and policies is very unfortunate; just when the Manchurian situation was fading out of the picture with every probability of ultimate tacit acceptance by the world, the Japanese Army gets itself on the front page again and creates the impression abroad that it is still running amok (which it is), and at just the moment when the nations are really trying— or at least going through the motions of trying—to get together on some practical disarmament, security, and nonaggression agreement, I know that many of our Japanese friends here are really writhing at the situation but are powerless to influence it.

KURUSU ON STIMSON

My secretary, J. G. Parsons, writes: "Last evening Mr. Kurusu and I were fingering the last number of *Foreign Affairs* and, referring to

* This took place while Viscount Ishii was en route to the 1933 World Economic Conference in London.

Stimson's article, I ventured the remark that Stimson was a great and sincere idealist. Kurusu's answering remark was, 'It's easy to be an idealist when you're not in trouble.' This to me was a perfect example of the essentially *defensive* psychology entertained by many Japanese of influence which has promoted their *aggressive* action. I sincerely believe it is no stretch of the imagination for even educated Japanese to believe the dogma of 'self-defense' of which we heard so much last summer. It seems to me that until this notion that the Japanese are 'in trouble' is dispelled there will be no halt in the somewhat misnamed 'expansionist' movement of the Army. While I do not dispute that the military entertains visions of Asiatic hegemony, I feel that its strength is rooted in a defensive attitude, a fear of Russia, of Japan's security. Therefore it is 'Conquer or die.' "

FOR A "FACULTY OF INTERNATIONAL POLITICAL HEALTH"

Address at the Opening of the New Unit of St. Luke's
Medical Center, Tokyo, June 5, 1933

The truth which men of vision of all ages have felt is that the human family is a unit. Yet the practical consummation of this fundamental truth is inevitably a slow and gradual process. The thought has been cradled in the past, as it will be fostered in the future, by individuals in every nation who insist on looking about them and whose interests are not confined to their own home or to their own creed or to their own country.

In this philosophy of the unity of the human family, no element makes a stronger appeal to our common humanity than physical suffering, for in the relief of disease and pain a broader and deeper significance than mere utilitarianism is involved: our hospitals teach compassion, and the veneration which they invoke is fundamentally due to the fact that they stand for love and the responsibility of mankind as a whole for the welfare of humanity.

It was this enlightened philosophy that led thousands of parishes of the Episcopal Church in America, the Rockefeller Foundation, and many progressive and public-spirited individuals to contribute to the erection and operation of this noble building which we open today. That the establishment of St. Luke's Hospital in Tokyo was a joint and co-operative undertaking is forcefully attested by the openhearted and munificent gift from His Imperial Majesty, the

late Emperor of Japan, and by most generous contributions from
the Imperial household, the Department of Home Affairs, the city
of Tokyo, and other organizations, and by a group of prominent
Japanese gentlemen including Count Goto, Marquis Okuma, Viscount Shibusawa, and many others. The assistance given by the
Japanese Council, who, in co-operation with the American Council,
have been most generous and helpful in giving advice and assistance
when most needed, has played a prominent part in the development
of this whole great organization, while the success of St. Luke's Hospital and its affiliated activities is due in great measure to the vision
and faith and untiring energy of one man, Dr. Rudolph Bolling
Teusler, ably supported by his efficient associates representing both
of our nations. I heartily associate myself with the well-deserved
tributes that have been paid today and congratulate the dreamer
of a dream that has come true.

It is not my purpose today to describe in detail the background
and history of the hospital. Others who have been more intimately
associated with its development have dealt with this aspect far more
effectively. My own thoughts may find expression—inadequate, I
fear, but not the less earnest—in the broad significance of this building and all it stands for.

Far above national statecraft and politics stands that noble philosophy, of which I have spoken, that the human family is a unit. It
is a sublime conception of mankind, a conception toward which the
forces of nature must inevitably exert their impelling influence,
gradual perhaps but not the less certain of eventual realization. Has
not the whole tendency of civilization been in that direction? The
prehistoric family found that its better interests lay in tribal association. The tribe developed gradually into the nation. Today the
nations of the world are steadily moving toward a more intimate
and enlightened co-operation because they have come to realize that
only thus can the greatest good of the greatest number be attained.
Thus the co-ordination of the human family is gradually but surely
in the making. When we pass through eras of discouragement, let
us look back on the road that has already been traversed and the
progress already made, even in our own generation. The eventual
triumph of the movement is not a matter of opinion, tinged either
with optimism or pessimism according to the times or the individual; it is a matter of mathematical certainty, because mankind as a
whole, in spite of all the discouragements and obstacles and delays
which it is bound to meet, will always work toward its greatest good

and its greatest happiness, and with that instinct inherent in the human race, eventual success is as inevitable as the fulfillment of the laws of creation. If I am called a visionary, let those who doubt merely trace the facts, the development, and the fundamental tendencies of history and then apply the rules of mathematical analogy to the future.

I speak of this movement today for two reasons. First, because the establishment of this great medical center in Japan, representing in concrete form the principle of international co-operation, is a material manifestation of that fundamental truth that the human family is in spirit, and by the nature of things eventually must become in practice, a unit. I speak of it secondly because the principles of medicine apply so aptly to the ills from which the world has suffered, is suffering, and will assuredly continue to suffer before that millennium of world unity can, by gradual development, experience, and the wisdom of its leaders, be attained.

Most of our international ills closely resemble insidious disease. Like cancer, they generally begin on a small scale as a result of long irritation on a given spot. If that irritation can be sensed in advance and dealt with promptly, the disease can perhaps be avoided. Even the most skillful physician may not be able, or may not be given an opportunity, to sense the irritation in advance, but the moment the obvious symptoms appear, he seeks to eradicate the disease by curative treatment long before operation becomes unavoidable.

Someday in the distant future we shall have, perhaps, a sort of Faculty of International Political Health who will study international relationships from every point of view, much as the family physician studies, or should study, the mental, physical, and moral conditions of his individual charges. When sources of potential danger to international health are perceived, the Faculty will prescribe, long before the actual illness occurs, in order to eliminate the causes of potential friction, the sources of infection. The curative measures must be taken long, long before the disease has been given an opportunity to grow. In international affairs, once the fever of animosity has appeared, avoidance of the disease is uncertain; it may be too late. The prophylactic steps must be taken in time. Much can be done around a green table in a definite case by the sober judgment of a few farsighted statesmen long before public opinion has had a chance to become inflamed and their own saner judgment warped by the course of events and by the heat of international animosity.

This Faculty of International Political Health—a vision of the future (and let me label it as purely a fantasy of my own mind)— must sit constantly, conducting research as in any laboratory, precisely as the Rockefeller Foundation and other similar bodies are constantly conducting their research for the elimination of cancer today. Its members will not be prime ministers or other prominent officials but nonpolitical technical experts in the many branches of life's activities. Their findings, their warnings, their recommendations must be made in time for the prophylactic measures to be effective.

We have come a long way since the First Hague Peace Conference of 1899; we still have a long way to go. But need we be discouraged? This movement toward international co-operation did not spring, like Athena from the brow of Zeus, full-grown from birth; it must develop gradually, profiting like any infant from its lessons and experience. It *will* grow to full maturity, just as the potentialities of this great hospital for public service will grow with experience, invention, and discovery in the realm of medical science.

And so, my friends, I have ventured to indulge in flights of fancy, inspired by the significance of today's event. My Faculty of International Political Health is but a figment of the mind, a chimera perhaps. I have used the term but figuratively and the conception merely as an illustration induced by the thought of what *this* faculty of medicine will accomplish for the individual and the community in its enlightened mission. Perhaps even daydreams sometimes do no harm. They at least set our minds working in profitable channels. I see in this great building and the organization whose activities it will nobly house, a practical manifestation of the fundamental unity of the human family. Let us then find in the principles for which it stands a practical analogy in the efforts that are being made today to bring that family into closer co-operation, and apply also to that broader cause this great hospital's demonstration of international friendship, its alleviation of disease and suffering, and its embodiment of the spirit and precepts of the Cross.

WHEN JAPANESE-AMERICAN RELATIONS IMPROVED

June 8, 1933

Went to Yokohama and was received on the *Houston* * with the

* The *Houston* was the flagship of the American Asiatic fleet and visited Japan as part of its regular round of duties.

usual honors; spent an hour going all over her and then received with Admiral Taylor a large number of guests from Yokohama and Tokyo. She is a splendid ship, clean as a whistle, and has twice won the Navy championship in gunnery and once in communications, so that she now holds both shields for this year. The antiaircraft guns and fire control stations were of course carefully concealed.

I asked Captain Bagley if the Japanese naval officers had asked to inspect the ship when they came on board, but he said they had not done so, presumably because they would not be willing to return the courtesy when the American admiral visits Yokosuka. However, planes were observed taking photographs from above the ship. *The Star-Spangled Banner* was played at 6 to close the reception, at which the Japanese girls, at least, had had a very good time. Elsie had asked Sumako Uchida to go as her guest, but neither she nor her mother had dared ask Count Uchida's permission because he had "let her do so much lately." However, Countess Uchida suggested that Elsie approach the Minister directly. She took her courage in her hands and did so after the Minister's luncheon for the Perrys. At first he said no, but later relented and Sumako had a grand time, chaperoned of course by Alice, and was very grateful to Elsie. It reminds me a little of the old Turkish pashas who did not encourage their families to ask for favors.

Sent a long telegram to the Department with regard to the noticeable improvement in American-Japanese relations. This is due to a variety of causes. First and foremost the fact that Japan's relations with England have entered upon a very unfavorable state owing primarily to the abrogation of the trade agreement with India, which is a heavy blow to the Japanese cotton industry. The Army has obtained the appropriations which it desired, the Chinese situation is less acute, while Japan has withdrawn from the League of Nations, all without a clash with Western nations. It cannot, of course, be said that the war spirit has died out, but the obviously inspired anti-American propaganda is not now in evidence.

This improved feeling toward the United States is markedly shown by the favorable and prominent press comment concerning (1) Viscount Ishii's conversation with President Roosevelt and the general belief that the President listened sympathetically to Ishii's exposition of Japan's problems. There is a feeling that the new administration in America is a great deal more friendly to Japan than the last one; (2) the visit of Admiral Taylor, which has been an unqualified success; Admiral Taylor's helpful co-operation with

Admiral Nomura at Shanghai last year is generally appreciated and the American admiral has been given a most cordial reception here; (3) the brief visit of the new Governor General of the Philippines; * his calls on the high Japanese officials made a favorable impression; (4) the visit of Bishop Perry and particularly his visit to the Perry monument at Uraga, which was given wide publicity; † (5) the opening of St. Luke's new medical center in the presence of the Emperor's brother, and a distinguished Japanese representation.

Of course it is quite possible that the military clique may in due course maneuver to undermine this wave of good feeling by continuing to fill the press with anti-American propaganda, but I feel that constructive and probably lasting headway has been made. Shiratori's removal from the Foreign Office and his appointment as Minister to Sweden is a further hopeful factor. Incidentally, I hear that up to the last minute Shiratori fought against his transfer.

This new friendly feeling for America is shown even in our personal relationships here. Captain Johnson, for instance, tells me that some of his best Japanese friends who were formerly most cordial have hardly dared be seen with him during the past year, especially one in particular, who was thought by the military to be too fond of foreigners. The other day both he and Viscount Inouye joined Johnson and myself at our table at the golf club on their own initiative, beaming and very genial, a move which they would not have dared to make during the past year. I am glad to have remained here long enough to see this improvement come and shall be mighty happy if it lasts; I think it will last unless unforeseen incidents or developments occur to injure it. Certainly there is a very great change since a year ago.

GEISHA EVENING ‡

June 29, 1933

Horrid, sweaty Nyubai weather. Spent the day in shirt sleeves in my study.

Captain Johnson gave a geisha dinner at the Koyokan for the high admirals of the Japanese Navy and most of our staff, thirty-two in all. We sat on the floor in two long rows, while the girls plied us with hot sake and the courses of an excellent Japanese dinner were gradually served. After an hour or so the dinner began to warm up

* See photograph No. 8.
† See photograph No. 1.
‡ See photograph No. 16.

and after two hours the "Yo, yo, ye" game was in fast and furious swing and the ceremonial visiting had begun.

The "Yo, yo, ye" game is as follows: the geisha who happens to be serving you for the moment (they continually shift places) proposes the game, which is the old time-honored one of scissors cut paper, paper wraps rock, rock break scissors; if she wins you have to drink to her, if you win she has to drink to you. The girls at this famous teahouse are much more lively than most of them and full of fun. Meanwhile your neighbors are continually proposing toasts, as well as the visitors who slip along the floor to drink every other guest's health in turn, and then you return their visits. So, all in all, a good deal of sake is consumed during the evening, although the sake cups are very tiny and thus a mere thimbleful is taken at a time. It made me enjoy the evening thoroughly, and there are no uncomfortable effects whatever in the morning—if you don't put whisky on top of it, as most of the Japanese do; the Japanese food is wholesome and easily digestible, which probably helps, and the vapors of the hot sake wear off very quickly. It certainly helps to make a gay and highly amusing party that was convivial but never obstreperous, intimate yet always dignified, formal, and restrained.

Between the courses there were Japanese music and fan dancing, and later, when we arose after almost three hours on the floor and got our cramped leg muscles straightened out, a gramophone was turned on and the geishas proved themselves as good at Western dances as they are at their own. Admiral Takahashi, who sat next me, observed that if international conferences could take place in such an atmosphere there would never be the slightest difficulty in reaching agreements. I concurred.

ROMANCE IN THE EMBASSY

By the time that this mail reaches the family, Elsie's good news will be no longer a secret to them, although it must be kept confidential until announced sometime in August. On June 30 she became engaged to Cecil Lyon. He had been here hardly a month and when he came to me to ask my permission to marry Elsie I remarked that he was a quick worker; he replied, "Can you blame me?"—to which, of course, there was nothing more to be said. We are all very happy about it; he's a fine, upstanding young man, twenty-nine years old, and in height at least he measures up to the standard set by our other sons-in-law. I will let Elsie deal with his other qualifications. Apart from our eminent approval of her choice from the point of view of character and personality, I am naturally glad that she is marrying into the service; to have given three daughters to the service must, I should think, constitute a record. That thought goes far to compensate for the sad prospect of losing her from our midst, where she has brought nothing but gaiety, music, and sunshine. Now she is at least bringing another son of whom Alice and I are going to be very fond indeed. They plan to be married on our own twenty-eighth wedding anniversary, October 7.

RUSSIAN-JAPANESE TENSION GROWS

July 18, 1933

Informal dinner at the Prime Minister's for Bishop and Mrs. Welch, whom they had known for years in Korea. Had a long talk with Viscount Saito after dinner; he said he wished that America could help China to get on its feet; I replied that the problem was one that no single power could solve alone. He was very affable and the next day sent me an American flag woven from Japanese silk. There must have been more than a dozen police around the entrance to the official residence where the dinner was held. Some excitement occurred at the moment of our arrival as the alarm went off by mistake and the police rushed about with drawn swords and cocked revolvers, looking for some uninvited guest. There is naturally a tense atmosphere about that mansion, considering the constant threats of assassination. Viscountess Saito seemed terribly depressed throughout the evening.

After a month or so with hardly a telegram out or in, I sent a very long cablegram to the Department concerning the tense situation between Japan and Soviet Russia, itemizing the various incidents that have occurred and the reasons for regarding the situation as potentially serious. The incidents may well be regarded as of a provocative nature, somewhat similar to those which occurred before the Manchurian affair. The intentions of the Japanese military clique cannot be measured by Occidental standards; if they foresee an eventual clash as inevitable, it is quite possible that they may intend to strike before Soviet Russia gets stronger—and the time element is all in favor of the latter. Therefore, while I do not consider war imminent, I do believe that the situation is potentially dangerous and bears careful watching. We had written all this in a dispatch by the last pouch, but it won't reach Washington for another ten days, and while not wishing to be unduly jumpy or sensational, I don't want to be caught napping if anything breaks. In this part of the world it is unwise to take anything for granted, even the avoidance of a provocative war.

THE REVOLUTION IN DIPLOMACY AND
JAPANESE-AMERICAN RELATIONS

Article for the Japan-America Issue of the Japan Times

During thirty years in the diplomatic service of the United States, I have watched a gradual but nevertheless well-defined change take place in the character of the work of the diplomatic agents of the various countries of the world. Formerly, each nation, through its diplomatic agents, sought to outwit other countries and to conclude bilateral treaties or agreements, open or secret, which would give the country seeking the treaty or agreement some definite political or commercial advantage over other countries. Stories of diplomatic life are filled with purely imaginary instances of the conclusion of such treaties. Usually the hero, the young and handsome Minister of Ruritania, let us say, through his special friendship with the Queen of Erethria, concludes a secret treaty with Erethria, thereby outwitting the villain, the Ambassador of Lithia. Treaties were once concluded more or less in this manner, and continued to be so concluded up to the end of the last century, but the writers and readers of such tales of diplomatic life probably little realize the change which has come over our international relations and over the business of treaty-making since the beginning of this century.

If you examine the treaties and international agreements in force today—the treaties governing the external relations of the participating states and to some extent their internal administration and policies—you will note that a considerable proportion of them are the result, not of secret negotiations between two countries, but of open international conferences. Even bilateral treaties of commerce and navigation, or of arbitration, are usually parts of a series of identical treaties negotiated with all interested nations. Diplomatic agents nowadays rarely endeavor to negotiate secret agreements—the world has progressed beyond that stage of international political relations.

We do not have to look far to find the reason. Today the world has become so small, with the development of communications, and there is such a constant interchange of peoples, and such close com-

mercial and financial relations between states, that the relations of
any one nation with another are of deep concern to all nations. This
development greatly resembles the development of our community
life in the United States. In the old frontier days, when the settlers
upon the land lived far apart, each man was a law unto himself. He
was his own policeman, judge, and executioner. But as the land
gradually became more closely settled, as communications developed, and as organized communities grew up, the pioneer settlers no
longer were able to act only in the light of their own interests or
desires; they were compelled to consider as well the interests of the
community. The relations between any two members of the community, whether of enmity or friendship, became a matter of concern to all members of the community. So it is with international
relations today. Our various interests—political, economic, and military—are so closely interwoven and interrelated that a disturbance
in the relations between any two countries, instead of being a matter
of interest only to the two countries concerned (as was the case
until fairly recent times), now inevitably reacts upon the interests
and relations of many other countries.

It is in this light that our two countries should regard Japanese-
American relations. Here we are, two politically and economically
powerful nations, one on each side of the broad Pacific Ocean, and
holding largely in our hands the destiny of that ocean—holding
largely the power to determine whether the Pacific shall in the
future be the scene of interminable jealousy, suspicion, and dissen-
sion, or shall be a broad, peaceful highway for the friendly interchange of culture and commodities and a medium for friendly and
sincere co-operation in the advancement of the welfare of the world.

Our policies and actions will have immense repercussions upon
the future course of international relations throughout the world.
The future of American-Japanese relations, therefore, is not a matter of concern only to our two countries. For our own welfare, peace,
and prosperity we must certainly strive to ensure the continuance
of the friendly relations between Japan and the United States, but
in addition we have a larger duty—a duty which we owe to all the
nations of the world. This duty is to develop the coming Pacific Era
as an era of peace and friendly co-operation, rather than one of
bitterness and strife—such bitterness and strife as were evidenced,
for example, in the Mediterranean Era of international relations.

It should not be at all difficult for our two nations to live in peace
and harmony and to co-operate. Economic interests, which in the

past history of the world have been the cause of many great con-
flicts, are, in our case, complementary rather than antagonistic. We
are both suppliers of raw materials, but of raw materials which do
not compete with each other. Likewise, we both supply manufactured goods to the markets of the world, but again these goods are
of different, noncompeting categories. Japan supplies manufactured
goods based primarily on the manual skill and dexterity for which
this nation is famous, while the United States supplies goods such
as can be manufactured in immense quantities by automatic machinery. Our economic interests, therefore, do not necessarily clash,
and thus the principal basis of conflict among other nations is eliminated from our relations. Other interests, which jingoists in both
Japan and the United States are constantly bringing forward as
possible causes of conflict, can undoubtedly be reconciled by patient
study and a mutual spirit of helpfulness.

I can see no reason why the coming Pacific Era, whose destiny lies
so largely in our hands, should not be one of peace and friendliness,
consecrated to the promotion of the welfare of the world, and it is
in our combined power to make it so.

MORE RUSSIAN-JAPANESE WAR RUMORS

September 7, 1933

The Rumanian Chargé d'Affaires, Stoïcesco, called to discuss
Japanese-Soviet relations. I showed him in confidence my last telegram on the subject, with which he said he entirely concurred. One
of our assistant military attachés says that he and his colleagues consider war absolutely inevitable and predict it for the spring of 1935,
although some believe that it may come much sooner. Much comment has been aroused by the remarks of the Soviet Ambassador at
a dinner which he gave recently to the foreign newspaper correspondents. He was apparently stung beyond endurance at the actual
and implied accusations being cast on his country and people by the
Japanese press, and at the dinner he denounced Japanese "defense
propaganda" in no uncertain terms, assuring his hearers that the
U.S.S.R. was nearing the limit of its patience and forbearance. He
stated further that Soviet Russia is not only able to meet any overt
act of aggression by the Japanese Army, but is well prepared on
land and in the air to take the offensive across the border into Manchuria if such a step becomes necessary—pretty plain speaking.

Of course, this must have leaked out to the Japanese. As the Russians have observed that in case of war they would completely destroy both Tokyo and Osaka from the air, I imagine that Tokyo will be a somewhat active spot in such an eventuality. The recent Japanese air maneuvers, when for three consecutive evenings the entire city of Tokyo was kept in complete darkness, during the raids, not even reading lamps being allowed, were clearly held with the Russian threat in mind.

FIRST INTERVIEW WITH FOREIGN MINISTER HIROTA

September 18, 1933

Received by Hirota, the new Minister for Foreign Affairs, at 2. Amaral of Brazil was the only other ambassador there, Yurenev, the Russian, and Auriti, the Italian, being either absent or late. Hirota received me with warmth, clasping my hands in both of his and in the course of our short talk he said that the cornerstone of his policy would be the development of better relations with the United States and that this, in fact, was the primary reason why he had accepted the appointment which had come to him as a complete surprise. I am convinced from his manner that he meant it. I said that so far as I could see, one of the chief impediments to good relations between our countries was the press, which constantly stirred up distrust and suspicion on totally illusory grounds. He replied, "We shall talk all that over together."

My brief impressions of him were favorable; he certainly has far more warmth and resiliency than the austere Count Uchida possessed; I believe that it will now be a pleasure to go to the Foreign Office, which it never has been before, and that he may be a man with whom one can sit down and really talk things out. Count Uchida, aside from being very deaf, was never willing to talk, and on the few occasions on which I have gone to him on special cases he never appeared to know anything about them and merely said that he would take the matter under consideration. He has never been able or willing really to discuss matters in general.

One of the first things I want to take up with Hirota is the unfortunate and irritating publicity which attends our calls at the Gaimusho, as the Japanese Foreign Office is called. The other day I wanted to discuss a purely routine matter, the question of a Standard Oil tank near Kobe which, after a lot of expense in its construction, carried out with a definite permit from the Government, could not be used on account of the alleged and absurd fears of the inhabitants of the village of the danger of fire. I had taken the case up with Arita last spring but without results. However, knowing the undesirable publicity which would attend a visit on my part to the Foreign Office, I asked Neville to go and see Shige-mitsu. An hour later *Nichi Nichi* came out with a definite state-ment, under Neville's picture, that he had started negotiations with Shigemitsu for putting a stop to the race in naval armaments be-tween the two countries. Not a word was said by the Foreign Office in denial. Byas, Babb, Vaughn, Fleisher, and others called up in turn to find out if the report were true before cabling it to America, but of course they all dropped it promptly on hearing our reply. That sort of thing is positively disgusting, but it has gone on con-sistently throughout Uchida's regime without any apparent effort on his part to stop it.

A really amusing point about the matter is that in Neville's talk with Shigemitsu the latter brought up this very matter of publicity on his own initiative and inveighed against the irresponsibility of the Japanese press; an hour later this ridiculous canard was out. Of course, it may conceivably be a heavy-footed method of floating a *ballon d'essai*. Perhaps Hirota will be the man to stop it and make it possible for me to go to the Foreign Office without apprehension as to the results, but, on the other hand, he may find himself as impotent as his predecessor.

THE LOW-DOWN ON MANCHURIA

The following interesting statement was recently written in con-fidence by an American newspaperman, whom I know. He men-tions a Japanese businessman whom he got to know in Tokyo and quotes this Japanese as "opening up" one night as follows:

I am going to tell you the real truth about Manchuria. It was a War College plan of long standing; but with no imme-diate prospects of fulfillment. The Chinese in Manchuria ex-asperated the Army beyond endurance. They suddenly went off half-cocked and decided to punish them. The Army ex-pected resistance, but got none. The Chinese ran away. We chased them all over Manchuria. In the course of the chase we felt something heavy on one of our feet. We looked down to see what was sticking to our shoe. To our amazement, we found it was Manchuria.

They will tell you at the Foreign Office and War Department that they are now going to work on this and that enlightened plan. To tell the truth, they haven't any more idea than the man in the moon what to do. They are completely bewildered and dismayed. It is just beginning to dawn on everybody except the Army that we have made the most tragic blunder of which any modern nation has ever been guilty. For instance, if they develop the Manchurian copper mines, all the Japanese copper mines will have to close down, throwing thousands of men out of work. The Japanese Government realizes perfectly well that, as an outlet for overcrowded Japan, Manchuria is just a dream. The most we can possibly hope for in the way of immigration from Japan to Manchuria is about 20,000 a year. To a nation increasing at the rate of 900,000 a year, this is no solution.

The American newspaperman continues:

——, as you know, is one of the intellectual leaders of Japan. He narrowly escaped assassination at the time of the Manchurian Incident, having rashly raised his voiced against the military party. His friends took him to a hospital and sneaked him out of a second-story window at night. He came to the United States; publicly yelled banzai all over the place to save his life; then told me privately what he really thought.

He too believed that Manchuria is a tragic blunder. I asked him what he thought of General Araki; he replied: "Like all soldiers, General Araki is a fool."

He said that the policy toward which his party is working is to recognize the Chinese ownership of Manchuria; but to extend the Liaotung lease over the whole of Manchuria for ninety-nine years. He said that war with Russia was almost certain at the end of the next Five-Year Plan. To avert this, he thought Japan should grant Russia free access to the sea at some port in Manchuria and try to persuade Europe to open the Dardanelles to Russia.

After —— came back to Japan, the Emperor summoned him to describe to him the condition of American public opinion. Obviously the real reason was to save him from assassination. After the interview —— told me what happened. He said that the Emperor was much distressed at the Manchurian Incident, of which he disapproved. He (the Emperor) said that Japan's greatest peril was chauvinism. Too much nationalism. —— said that the Emperor had ordered the Army on no account to take Peking.

(All this time General Araki was publicly shouting: "Shall

the Army turn back when our Emperor orders us to carry the colors of the Rising Sun onward," etc., etc.)

I had an interview with Viscount Saito which I am sure was censored and stopped. He was very bitter and sad.

He said that the Manchurian Incident should never have happened. That the same result could have been achieved without offending the world. I asked him what could be done about it now. He said: "Mr. ——, I have no doubt that the little chicken often thinks back to the egg—how warm and comfortable it was; but once pecked out, there is no egg to which he can go back. We only go ahead now and hope for the best."

I asked him about the rumors of war between the United States and Japan. I told him both navies seemed to have the jitters but I couldn't see any prospects of war. He said: "Don't be too sure of that, Mr. ——. Always remember that those whose careers depend upon war always want war."

I asked him: "Do you mean the Navy, Your Excellency?"

"Oh no, no, no," he said. "The Navy is all right; but the Army knows very little about the world."

THE GREAT PACIFIC LABORATORY

The Ambassador's Address at the Luncheon of the Pan Pacific Association and the Pan Pacific Club in Commemoration of Balboa Day, Tokyo, September 25, 1933

Mr. Chairman, Your Excellencies, Ladies and Gentlemen:

When we picture Balboa standing, over four hundred years ago, on that mountain chain in Darién and gazing for the first time on the broad expanse of the Pacific, we inevitably wonder whether he was gifted with imaginative foresight and could visualize that this great ocean would someday become not only a mighty commercial clearinghouse for the exchange of many of the world's essential products, but that it would develop also into the greatest experimental laboratory in history. For on the shores of that ocean a number of great and smaller powers are working out their respective destinies under radically different systems of government, the outcome of racial, historical, or geographic factors or, in some cases, as the result of a break with the past and the adoption of a new orientation.

Among other nations of the Pacific, Japan, with her vast background of Oriental culture combined with the energy and initiative of a virile people, absorbed the civilization of the Occident, and yet

came through the process—a process of abnormal rapidity—strong
in her own personality and national character, in which centraliza-
tion of authority and the pre-eminence of the Throne are the outstanding elements.

The British Commonwealth of Nations, which spreading round
the world keeps its far-flung units in vital intercourse by protected
maritime traffic and by periodical conferences that decide how they
can assist and guard one another's freedom and interests, owes its
strength to the elasticity and resiliency of the system.

The contribution of the United States is a federal organization
that permits of the freest intercourse between its component states,
each of which possesses and enjoys its own legislative individuality
in matters not essentially of national concern.

And finally Russia, embarked on an untried course, has coined a
new word, sovietism, in the dictionary of government, while the
world looks on with interest at the development of still another
experiment in this laboratory of political science.

Now in looking into the future, we must picture as best we may
the tremendous developments which are bound to take place in
international relationships and contacts. With expansion and advancement in aviation, and invention in the realm of electricity
and other fields, it is not difficult to foresee the day when the nations
of the world, in matters of communication and transit, will be
physically linked in far greater intimacy than now. A century ago
the steam engine and steamship were in their infancy; the telegraph
and telephone unknown in general application; the radio and airplane unconceived. At the present rate of progress in invention and
development, progressively accelerated during the past few generations, what may we not expect in the century to come, and the next,
and the next? What may we not expect in the development of the
international structure of commerce and finance, and indeed in
many other fields, if world progress maintains, as it surely will, its
ever-increasing velocity? The day will surely come when international frontiers will lose much or all of their present physical
restraint, and with these physical restraints crumbled or vanished,
who shall say to what degree the world's eventual community of
interests will bring about a political intimacy among the nations
which we, in our present stage of development, can but dimly
visualize?

I have spoken of the Pacific as a mighty experimental laboratory.
In the old days, the chemists strove to discover and to blend the

necessary elements which would produce the elixir of life. Letting our imagination rove into the impenetrable mists of the future, may we not wonder whether at some future epoch there will emerge from these various experiments and experiences a system or a combination of systems, best adapted to universal acceptance and to world unity? That goal, if goal it be, can exist today only in our castle-building imagination. Yet castle-building and daydreams are not always futile and not always so fantastic as they seem. Perhaps Balboa dreamed, yet it is inconceivable that he could have foreseen, even with the most fertile imagination, the developments to which his discovery has already led.

Before that epoch comes, human outlook may have undergone many a change. But always this great laboratory of the Pacific—where the racial types which have shown high capacity for advance in civilization have been brought face to face—will be at work, developing, experimenting, learning, perhaps perfecting, against the day when frontiers, which seem natural today, can no longer physically exist; when neither oceans nor mountains can longer maintain their character as barriers to international intimacy; when the whole structure of world relationships will have assumed so intricate, delicate, and universal a nature that the general community of interests will far exceed in importance the interests of any one group or nation. When that day comes, if the machinery for meeting it is wisely conceived and intelligently built from one generation to another—and if it is solidly founded upon the enlightened viewpoint recently expressed by Prince Tokugawa that "the future happiness and welfare of all mankind will in no small degree depend on the promotion of good understanding and mutual helpfulness among the nations surrounding the Pacific"—who shall say that the world will not achieve a happier and more enlightened destiny than our forefathers could have visualized?

Then may Balboa look down on the great arena to which he initiated world access, and smile with gratification at his contribution to the working out of the mightiest problem in history.

WEDDING DAY

October 7, 1933

Elsie's wedding day is over; the captains and the kings and the bride and groom have departed.

It was not the crisp autumnal day of October 7, 1905, but at least
the rain was driven away by a high wind, and the weather was
warm and not unpleasant. At 10 we all filed in to the Consulate
General and appeared before Consul Spamer, where papers were
signed, Neville and I acting as witnesses; then to the municipal
office of Kojimachi Ward, which is always used for American wed-
dings because the officials there are familiar with American legal
procedure and it avoids having to answer innumerable questions,
even though it necessitates the bride and groom giving the Imperial
Hotel as their residence, a fiction accepted by the authorities as the
hotel is in that district. The premature demise of the bride and
groom was avoided by a hairbreadth when the press photographers,
fiddling with the window curtains, brought down the heavy wooden
contraption over the windows within an inch of their heads in a
cloud of prehistoric dust. Of course we all laughed, but it would
have been no joke had it hit them, and the Mayor, or whatever he
is called, was much upset, muttering to Neville in Japanese: "I have
been exceedingly rude." That ceremony over (it cost the munificent
sum of fifteen sen—about three cents), we returned to the Consulate,
where Spamer issued the certificate that he had witnessed the civil
marriage and Mr. and Mrs. Lyon, according to American law, were
man and wife.

The religious ceremony at 3 and the official reception at 4 are
best described by Esther Crane in the *Advertiser* and by Chiyo
Hirose in the *Times*. I cannot do more than say that the bride was
as lovely as they make them, that the groom did credit to his nation,
and that Fay van Rechteren, the matron of honor, added much
to the picture. We had invited only 65 people to the ceremony,
as friends of Elsie, but some 400 came to the reception. Alice and I
had to look after the Chichibus, who are not a bit stiff, but I can't
say that I ever feel very comfortable entertaining royalty, especially
in Japan, where they are surrounded by the many drastic rules and
customs of the Imperial Household. However, I had taken the
precaution of carefully writing out our proposed procedure and
submitting it in advance to Count Maeda, who approved. I did
invite the diplomatic Ministers to the terrace, where the Chichibus
had tea, and Marler afterward observed that the Ministers would
never forget their gratitude.

Hitherto Japanese etiquette had permitted only Ambassadors to
talk with members of the Imperial family during entertainments in

foreign houses. However, I cut the Gordian knot by insisting that the Canadian and other Ministers should be present.

Elsie and Cecil drove to Yokohama and thence took the train to Gotemba, on the slopes of Fujiyama, where Count Kabayama had placed his villa at their disposal. Father and mother resume their daily rounds and try to smile in spite of the empty nursery upstairs, for the nursery to them has been the most important part of life.

A DIPLOMAT DISCUSSES PAN-ASIA

November 13, 1933

One of my diplomatic colleagues told me that ever since last March when a meeting had been held, attended by General Araki, Yoshizawa, Hirota, *et al.*, the idea of revising the Pan-Asiatic movement, or Great Asiatic Association, was being pushed in Japan. He believes that Hirota, in spite of his policy of improving relations with foreign countries, is a stanch supporter of the movement and that he is in sympathy with Japan's expansionist ambitions. But my colleague had no precise evidence to support this theory. The idea, as he understands it, is to form an Asiatic League of Nations composed of Japan as the leader, and Manchukuo, China, and Siam; in other words, a bloc of the yellow races against the white. He said that he had just been looking at a new textbook for the primary Japanese schools in which is included a large map of the Far East, comprising Japan, Manchukuo, China, French Cochin China, Siam, the Straits Settlements, the Philippines, and the Dutch East Indies, and that on this map there are three flags— the Japanese, Chinese, and Manchukuoan. The American, French, British, and Dutch flags are absent. He thought this significant, adding that he had observed a significant thing at the funeral of Princess Asaka yesterday, namely, that in the row of funeral wreaths the place of honor was given to the wreath from President Pu-yi. The second place of honor was given to that of General Tinge, the Minister of Manchukuo to Japan, while the wreath from the Diplomatic Corps was in the third place. His interpreter who was with him had read the inscriptions.

My colleague thinks the Soviet-Japanese situation very tense and that any serious incident might precipitate a conflict. He considers that the Russians have become much less yielding in their attitude and that the Japanese are genuinely afraid of air raids from Vladivostok. He had not heard of the United Press dispatch from

Moscow yesterday reporting the shooting down of Japanese air-planes over Soviet territory and the sinking of Japanese auxiliary warships off Kamchatka. I have summarized this conversation in a confidential dispatch to the State Department.

THE SOVIET AMBASSADOR PAYS HIS RESPECTS

November 20, 1933

At 11 Yurenev, the Soviet Ambassador, made his official call after our recognition of the Soviet Union. I received him in my study at the Residence and we pledged each other's healths in some excellent sherry. I believe he played a prominent part in the revolt of the Russian Navy at the very beginning of the Revolution. He has been Ambassador to Italy and Minister both to Persia and Austria, so must have accumulated considerable diplomatic experience. He says that Russia will not cede an inch on the Chinese Eastern Railway, and gives an impression of pessimism as to the future relations of the two countries. He is clearly overjoyed at our recognition and very, very friendly.

I returned his call within the hour and was regaled at the Soviet Embassy with a wineglass full of cherry brandy and delicious caviar sandwiches. The Embassy is a new and ultramodern building and with its large bright rooms it might be made very attractive. Incidentally, I profit by the recognition of Soviet Russia to the extent of a large tin of fresh delicious caviar. Can't think what to send him in return, as he doesn't smoke cigars.

Troyanovsky's appointment to Washington is an excellent selection. The fact that they picked their principal Japanese expert for Washington is regarded here as intensely significant.

WHY THE JAPANESE RESPECTED ROOSEVELT

November 30, Thanksgiving Day, 1933

Read the President's Proclamation in church. There was a fine turnout of Americans, including most of the Embassy, and the clergy was well represented by Bishop Reifsnider, Father Burton, Dr. Gowan, Dr. Evans, and another clergyman from the Union Church.

There was a significant allusion in the Proclamation to "a clearer knowledge by all nations that we seek no conquests and ask only honorable engagements by all peoples to respect the lands and rights of their neighbors." The Proclamation was published in the *Advertiser* and will certainly prick the conscience of a few of those Japanese who read it. It will make some of the Japanese liberals writhe, I should say. The President has played his cards well: he said not a word about Manchuria but started building up the fleet and recognized Soviet Russia; as a result he gets an entirely new and more friendly orientation of Japanese policy toward the United States. Hoover and Stimson had to go on record, and the present administration is profiting by that record having been made. All Roosevelt had to do was to announce at the start of his administration that there would be no change of policy, and then to keep quiet, which he has done with entire success, and to act instead of talking or writing, using an unwritten language which the Japanese thoroughly understand.

ADVERTISING—JAPANESE STYLE

December 7, 1933

The mail having come in at this moment, I have before me a typically delicious circular from the Ginza Columbia Retail Store wherein it is stated:

> Modern living conditions—strain, noise, haste—have made human irritable. Music is a only medium to help overcome and to console this unpleasant and unhealthy state of heart and mind.
>
> Our store requests the honour of your visit to enjoy the record music in sucking a cup of tea offering by us without obligation. You can hear music, modern and classical, European, American and Japanese, what you like. . . . Apply us anything you want with regard to the musical discus and talking machine by lines. Just try and get a good information. English speaking stuffs are in keen attention to serve on you. You cannot doubt the value of devoting part of your leisure to hear various music in our office.

TRIBUTE TO F. D. R.

December 9, 1933

In the pouch which came yesterday was a splendid letter from the President, signed by himself, conveying his greetings and good wishes for Christmas and the New Year to our personal and official families and to all the Foreign Service staffs in Japan and saying some very pleasant things about our helpful co-operation. I have never seen this done before and it is certainly typical of F. D. R. that he should have given the thought and taken the trouble to sign, presumably, some fifty such letters to all American chiefs of mission. We have never had a President who has taken so direct an interest in the Foreign Service; in spite of tremendous political pressure from hungry Democrats after sixteen years on the side lines, he didn't throw overboard a single career chief of mission.

THE EMPRESS BEARS A SON

December 23, 1933

Alice awoke me punctually at 7, saying "It's the siren." Sure enough, the siren was blowing to announce the birth of the Imperial babe, one minute if a girl, and two minutes, with a ten-second interval, if a boy. I waited eagerly through that ten-second interval, and when the second blast shrieked out, we were happy, for only those who have lived in Japan can realize all that this means.

PORTRAIT OF A NAZI DIPLOMAT

December 28, 1933

The new German Ambassador came to call. He arrives fresh from Moscow, where he seems to have heard of us from the Polychroniades. He is very tall, with a high bald dome of a head and a hatchet-shaped face, the typical Junker, so that one expects the customary stentorian voice and is surprised at his effeminate handshake and high, gentle tone. With typical Prussian methods he started off by sending Knoll, of the German Embassy, to *The Japan Advertiser* to say that he didn't like the tone of some of their articles about Germany and that this must change. As a matter of fact, Fleisher has carefully avoided all editorial comment on Hitlerism, because he didn't want to cause ructions in the German element of the rather compact foreign community here, and has confined himself to publishing merely the press telegrams, which are not always very complimentary to Hitler. When he asked Knoll what the Ambassador would do if the *Advertiser* didn't change its tone, Knoll replied that the Ambassador would report it to Berlin. Horrible threat!

Wilfrid Fleisher told me that when he described the incident to his father and asked him what he would have done, the latter replied that he would have thrown Knoll out of the office. In her initial press interview in the *Advertiser,* which all newly arrived *chefesses de mission* are accustomed to give to Esther Crane, the Ambassadress is reported to have said that she expected very quickly to understand the Japanese "because we Germans are unusually sensitive to foreign psychology." Alas, that is one of their greatest weaknesses, as witness their misjudgment of Belgian, British, and finally of American psychology during the last war. Among the messages given to *Nichi Nichi* by the various ambassadors and ministers on the birth of the Crown Prince, the Ambassador is quoted as saying: "Upon hearing the news of the birth of the Crown Prince, I wish to express my hearty congratulations. So soon upon my arrival at my post, *I consider it a personal honor to me."* It really was very kind of the Empress to welcome him so cordially.

JAPANESE WRESTLING—SUMO STYLE

January 15, 1934

This afternoon we went to the Japanese Sumo wrestling tournament in the big arena. No form of sport that I can imagine could be more boring. The wrestling is not at all like ours. The wrestlers are a caste by themselves, chosen in youth for their height and then stuffed like turkeys to make them enormously fat and heavy; they appear on the scene stark naked save for a loincloth and with tremendous bulging bellies. In each match the opponents face one another, after various lengthy ceremonial gestures, precisely like cocks in a ring, stooping and with their fists on the floor; they spring simultaneously and the stronger one almost always throws his adversary out of the ring with one shove and the match is over. The longest match we saw didn't last more than ten or fifteen seconds. When any part of the body touches the floor outside the small ring the bout is finished. There is no rolling on the floor, merely shoving. There are said to be forty-eight different holds.

But the ludicrous element is that when the bout is called and the wrestlers crouch for the spring, they survey each other for a few seconds and then, generally six or eight times or more, they rise and saunter out of the ring, swabbing themselves and drinking water as if they had undergone tremendous exertion; they then throw a handful of salt into the ring and repeat the same performance. Thus the spectators have to wait for ten or fifteen minutes for a few seconds of actual combat.

I am told that the purpose of the repeated failures to spring is that each combatant desires to hypnotize the other by simply glaring at him and by keeping him waiting as long as possible before the actual fight. Once in a while one of them actually barks at the other. Sometimes, also, one will spring while the other remains crouching, constituting a false start and a repetition of the process. It is entirely ludicrous. But these wrestlers are the idols of the public; there were, I should say, well over a thousand spectators in the arena, camped there for the day with their *hibachis* for warmth and food. The papers report every match and the champions rival Babe Ruth in public estimation, especially the fattest ones. The sport is carried on as a Shinto rite, a priest being in the ring for every bout and striking a dramatic attitude when the contestants crouch; the throwing of salt is also part of the rite, and the announcer of each match carries a fan and declaims in a high sort of chant. We were glad to have seen it, once.

WHEN JAPAN SUSPECTED LINDBERGH

January 16, 1934

The press during the past few days has been full of Admiral Suetsugu's article in the magazine *Gendai,* a pretty jingoistic utterance in which the warlike intentions of the United States are more than hinted at. He says that Japan fought the Sino-Japanese and the Russo-Japanese wars and took over Manchuria in order to maintain peace in the Far East—which to every Japanese, of course, means simply Japanese dominance, yet they say it with apparently genuine sincerity. Among other comments he observes:

> They [the Americans] are now bringing airplanes to Canton in large numbers; they are reinforcing the air lines at Shanghai, Hankow, etc. At the present moment they are bringing more to Canton and then to Amoy and Foochow, constructing air bases along the coast up to Shanghai. Now in the north we remember that Americans several times attempted to cross the Pacific via Alaska and repeatedly failed. Viewed from our military point of view, their frustrated attempts were simply reconnoitering. They were purposeful, but the Japanese, being a race of good-natured men, showed unstinted kindness to them, especially the country people were kindly disposed to them, acting as if they were their own sons who were trying to fly across the big sea.
>
> A certain lieutenant made a strange flight and returned. Then what happened, do you think? The Lindberghs came,

and they delayed in the Kurile Islands for a week, saying it was bad weather yesterday, and again today. They flew and again returned. It may be imagination of course, but it is equally possible that they reconnoitered in that part of the country. What are the Americans doing now? They are continuing since then surveying along the Aleutians, on a large scale making use of survey corps, telegraph corps, and aviation corps, etc. What does all this point to? Then they have resumed diplomatic relations with Soviet Russia.

Of course we can see economic motives in this, but it is possible to say that they may have had in view the possibility of surrounding Japan in all directions with their warlike preparations. Soviet Russia is concentrating efficient bombing planes and making war preparations in the Far East. In case of an outbreak, from Formosa, from the North, and from the Soviet territory, they would surround Japan by air raids in three directions. We must expect a large air force will be brought by the large fleet across the Pacific. We are preparing for such an eventuality.

The allegations of Lindbergh's spying seem to me to be going pretty strong.

THREE JAPANESE RESCUE ONE EMBASSY DOG

January 19, 1934

Elsie and I were taking a last walk with our dogs, Kim and Sambo, along the palace moat this morning when suddenly looking back we found that Sambo had disappeared. Elsie said, "Do you think he could have fallen into the moat?" We looked over the edge and there, at least thirty feet below, was poor Sambo struggling in the ice and water with only his head showing, like a drowned rat. The wall was perfectly vertical and I could see not the slightest possibility of climbing down it. I ran back to see if a rowboat was available anywhere, but the policeman on duty at the palace entrance shook his head and didn't seem in the slightest degree interested. There didn't seem to be a place anywhere where I could climb into the moat and swim to the dog, and at that moment I saw no chance whatever of saving him. But when I got back to the spot, there was Sambo, shivering in the midst of a large crowd of people and motors who had stopped to look on or to help.

It appears that Motosawa, our chauffeur, a passing taxi driver, and a delivery boy had managed to climb down that perfectly sheer wall of the moat with the aid of a rope, and by digging their fingers and toes into the cracks had rescued the poor little animal, who had somehow climbed into a small crevice. It was a courageous thing for them to do because a single slip would have meant a serious drop onto the ice below, and it was a big drop; Sambo was very lucky not to have been killed outright by the fall. I tried to get the names of the man and the boy who had helped, but the taxi had gone and the delivery boy absolutely declined to tell his name or to accept a present, and I could only shake him by the hand. Anyway, we got Sambo home and after half an hour in front of an electric heater and some warm milk he was as fit and frisky as ever.

Count Kabayama, to whom I told the tale after lunch, said it would make a good story for the press and asked if he might send me a correspondent from the *Asahi*. I received him and told him of the appreciation of the help given and my desire to get in touch with the two anonymous rescuers. The next day the story, with Sambo's picture, was nicely spread in the *Asahi* and also in the *Advertiser*, so that Sambo is now a well-known public character, and when Alice takes him out driving she sees people pointing to him as he stands on his hind paws looking out of the window. The episode was a nasty shock to Elsie and me. I suppose that Sambo had either frisked over the edge of the moat or that Kim had unwittingly brushed him off. We certainly love those dogs, both of them.

JAPANESE FAMILY EVENING—WITH MUSIC

January 20, 1934

Dined at the Azabukis', who do things extremely well, a lovely table, beautiful old plates, and a perfectly delicious dinner, the best we have had in any Japanese house. It began with the head of a wild boar served as hors d'œuvres with the cocktails and included a delicious salmon and a Manchurian wild turkey, the meat of which is the color of venison and even more gamy. After dinner one of the sons played the xylophone, accompanied on the piano by Miss Fumicko Ikeda. There are seven children, each of whom plays a different instrument, forming a family orchestra. I have often heard them practicing when passing their big house near the Nevilles' in Karuizawa. For a mother of seven children Mrs. Azabuki's youth and beauty are amazing.

ARAKI RESIGNS—HAYASHI TAKES OVER

January 21, 1934

General Araki resigned as War Minister today, and I had to draft a long telegram to the Department which went out on the 23rd, trying to interpret it after talking with a great many people. One can get interpretations all the way from *A* to *Z* and from white to black. Of course, his present illness is the main reason; the War Ministry needs a representative in the coming debates in the Diet and there is no telling how long Araki's convalescence will take. But I think the opportunity was gladly seized by those who wanted to get him out. As ——— said to me, "Araki talked too much." He certainly both talked and wrote too much and he was a symbol before the world of military aggressiveness. I hear on fairly good authority that Wakatsuki of the Minseito and Suzuki of the Seiyukai had threatened to make a scandal and seriously to embarrass the Army by interpellations in the Diet, and agreed to refrain only if Araki resigned.

In the Army itself, Araki is not overpopular with the younger officers. Strangely enough, they consider him too moderate and not sufficiently forceful to suit their views; he is a kindhearted man and has hesitated to retire the old generals to make way for younger men, and they believe he has compromised too much in the cabinet. As a matter of fact, Araki stands about halfway between the liberal Ugaki and the young hotheaded chauvinists. General Hayashi, his successor, is a leader of troops rather than a staff officer. He has the reputation of being a silent man, but cold and hard, self-willed and impetuous, and capable of taking rapid decisions as when he moved the troops from Korea to Manchuria on his own responsibility in 1931 in spite of Shidehara's opposition. It is said that he considers that the Army should keep out of politics, mind its own business and not make speeches, particularly inflammatory ones. The majority of observers therefore feel that his appointment presages an improvement in Japan's foreign relations. There are others, however, who see in his appointment a definite step in preparation for possible war, because he is a leader of troops, is not conciliatory and is less likely to compromise than Araki. I discussed these various factors with opinions in my telegram to the Department and said that I at present believed Hayashi's appointment would have a favorable effect on the political situation and on Japan's foreign

relations rather than the reverse but that the coming debates in the
Diet might give enlightenment.

CALM BEFORE THE STORM

January 23, 1934

Surveying the general political situation:

(1) Hirota is genuinely doing his best to improve Japan's relations with foreign countries all along the line. He has succeeded
in creating a better atmosphere with the United States, mainly
through keeping the military comparatively quiet and by exerting a
calming influence on the press. Relations with Great Britain have
been improved by the agreement with India but are subject to
fluctuation through many economic and commercial difficulties.
There is no evidence of improved relations with China; very likely
an effort is being made to buy off some of the northern leaders, and
there is a general feeling that North China will sooner or later be
incorporated into Manchukuo or else will become an autonomous
buffer state. With Soviet Russia the relations are about as bad as
they can be, for in spite of the attempt to reopen the negotiations
for the sale of the Chinese Eastern Railway to Japan, the Soviet
press and the Japanese reactions to its fulminations are openly bitter
and provocative. The risk of an eventual conflict is always present.
Germany, having left the League of Nations, is beginning already
to flirt with Manchukuo.

(2) The political parties are heckling the Government in the Diet
as they have not for long dared to do. This indicates increasing
strength and confidence on their part, and a belief that the country
as a whole is getting tired of the vast military and naval expenditures. But they run the risk of overplaying their hand and bringing
about renewed terroristic activities by the younger military and
naval officers from whom angry reverberations are already being
heard.

(3) It is generally felt that Araki's retirement as War Minister
represents a victory for the liberals and the political parties, and it
seems probable that there will be less public rattling of the saber
than heretofore. But Hayashi is still an unknown quantity; still
waters run deep, and he is firm and forceful. The Army, as well as
the Navy, must cultivate the war psychology if they are to continue
to get the enormous appropriations at which they aim.

(4) If there is any real improvement in the general political situation, it probably represents the calm before the storm. Whatever may happen with regard to the Naval Conference in 1935, whether it takes place or not and whether an agreement is reached or not, it will inevitably subject Japan's relations with the United States, and perhaps also with Great Britain in less degree, to a more or less serious strain, with loud and angry vituperations against us for keeping Japan an "inferior nation." The outburst will subside but it will leave another scar, if not an open wound. Every effort that can be made to create a friendly atmosphere in anticipation of that storm will be constructive work.

(5) The Japanese do not expect us to recognize Manchukuo in the near future. They know our policy and there is no need to reiterate it, unnecessarily arousing new antagonism. We sacrifice no principle by silently maintaining our position.

January 24, 1934

Dinner at the Embassy for the Foreign Minister.

Hirota was very friendly as usual but also evidently very tired from the strain of the opening of the Diet and of answering interpellations. Said it was an entirely new and difficult experience for him. Our dinner was unusually delicious, beginning with thick pheasant cream soup, which drew forth many comments, and ending with hot maple sirup on ice cream; there were also trout and quails. It's easy to dish out good chow in Japan.

SEQUEL ON SAMBO

January 25, 1934

Today I was informed that the taxi driver who had rescued Sambo and who had been discovered by the *Asahi* had come to receive my thanks and a present in answer to our wish published in the press. There was some delay while Alice wrapped up and sent down to the chancery the wrist watch which she had bought for that purpose. When finally I asked to have the man brought in, there was a further delay and after twenty minutes or so Neville and Jeff came in with somewhat sheepish expressions which finally ended in guffaws. It appears that while waiting for the present, the taxi driver had been assaulted outside of the Embassy by another taxi driver whose taxi he had stolen to come to the Embassy, and that

in the ensuing fight both taxi drivers had been carried off to the
police station, where it was discovered that the alleged rescuer of
Sambo was merely an impostor who had seen the publicity and
thought he could wangle the present. Old Neville rocked with
merriment. I put the present back in a drawer and locked it up.

January 30, 1934

The *Asahi* man came in today with the bona fide taxi driver
who did rescue Sambo; we had him come up to the residence,
where Alice gave him the wrist watch, and a photograph was duly
taken, which appeared the next day in the *Asahi*, of Alice handing
the package to the chauffeur while Sambo looked on. The chauffeur
was a nice-looking boy and very, very shy and modest. I was glad
to have him get the deserved and probably helpful publicity.

RUSSO-JAPANESE TENSION BEGINS TO EASE

February 8, 1934

The chances of war between Russia and Japan continue to agitate
most well-informed persons here. Barring incidents of a provocative
nature, such a conflict might occur in 1935, but the outlook for
peace has improved slightly during the past six months. These are
the chief factors now working against a Russo-Japanese war:

(1) There has been in recent months a noticeable reaction against
the military and especially against the vast military expenditures
and demands in the budget. This reaction has manifested itself in
the cabinet, in the press, and especially in the Diet. The recent
attacks on the Army and Navy through interpellations in the Diet
have been the most direct and forcible antimilitary manifestations
that have occurred in Japan since the Manchurian adventure began
in 1931.

(2) The forcible nature of these interpellations in the Diet indicate a growing strength and confidence of the political leaders. The
military have overplayed their hand. It now remains to be seen
whether these political elements, with their increasing confidence,
will in turn overplay their hand. If they do so, there will be the risk
of further terroristic activities. Angry reverberations have already
been heard from the Navy. Once the Diet is adjourned, however,
there will be less opportunity for the politicians to express their
views in public, although they will have had full opportunity to

register their concern at the dangerous situation into which military aggressiveness has been leading the country.

(3) Public feeling against the Army has been accentuated by the light sentences given to the officers concerned in the assassination of Premier Inukai on May 15, 1932, compared to the heavy sentences meted out to the civilians, although the latter were involved to a lesser degree. General Araki, it has been reliably reported to me, remarked not long ago that the military court-martial in determining the military sentences made a serious mistake, having totally misjudged the force of public opinion. He added that if the officers who assassinated Premier Inukai had committed hara-kiri on his doorstep instead, there would have been an immediate revolution, but they adopted the wrong method of gaining their ends.

(4) It is generally felt that General Araki's resignation, actually due to his illness—which many feel to have been providential dispensation—has relieved the situation of an inflammatory element. While his successor's attitude toward a Soviet-Japanese war is not known, it can at least be said that there will now be less public rattling of the saber and fewer provocative utterances from the military. This should exert a calming influence.

(5) The middle classes, including the liberal professions, merchants, industrialists, landlords, have changed their mentality during the past year, and in the face of the economic prosperity caused by increasing exports, they desire a continuation of the *status quo* and dread the upsets which a war would bring. The rural population has not shared fully in the prosperity which has fallen to the industrial and merchant classes. In the face of constantly rising living costs, the farmer's income has remained stationary, or nearly so. In addition, the modern urge for improved living conditions has affected rural areas, and the people there are no longer content with the simple hard life of their ancestors. These factors, added to the heavy taxation which rural communities have to bear, have caused a great deal of unrest in the country districts. They naturally desire relief, and are showing more interest in, and opposition to, heavy military expenditures than they have ever done before.

(6) The highest influences in the country are pacific. The Emperor is a man of mild and peaceful character. The era of his reign is characterized by the word "showa," which he himself chose and which means "enlightened peace." There is no reason to believe that he approved of the Manchurian adventure, for the matter did not lie in his decision. Prince Saionji, the Genro, and Count Makino

are profoundly imbued with the horrors of war. Since 1931 they have not been able to make their view publicly felt, but they are constantly working behind the scenes and it is believed that their influence is gradually increasing.

The Prime Minister is personally an influence more peaceful than bellicose. Hirota, the Minister for Foreign Affairs, has displayed unexpected strength and is personally largely responsible for the comparatively milder tone of the press since he took office and for a new orientation in endeavoring to develop better relations with foreign countries. A strong group of liberals in the country have been steadily working behind the scenes and are, it is believed, developing more strength than they formerly possessed. At a recent dinner at the Tokyo Club in honor of Sir Francis Lindley, the British Ambassador, and Ambassador Debuchi, Baron Hayashi, the chairman, in introducing the speakers, said slowly and with firmness, in a tone nearly menacing and emphasizing his remark with a bang of his fist on the table: "We want peace!" This is a small detail, but Baron Hayashi is Grand Master of Ceremonies of the Imperial Court and one of the Emperor's favorites.

(7) From the point of view of the Army itself—for in the last analysis the Army is likely to have the last word as to whether it shall be peace or war—new factors may exert a restraining influence. Even in the Army itself there are not lacking sane elements who are aware of the seriousness of a Japanese-Soviet conflict and who question whether the end to be attained would justify the risks run—whether the game would be worth the candle.

Undoubtedly the Army has complete confidence as to its ability to take Vladivostok and the Maritime Provinces and probably all of the territory up to Lake Baikal, for the Russians, separated by several thousand kilometers from their home base of supplies, will always be in a strategically hazardous position. But their defenses in the East have been materially strengthened, and their air forces in Vladivostok and elsewhere along the frontier constitute a serious threat to Tokyo and other important Japanese cities. Furthermore, American recognition of Soviet Russia has injected an important psychological element into the situation and gives pause to those in authority in Japan, for regardless of the pacific policy of the United States, American action in the event of a Japanese-Soviet conflict would be to the Japanese an unknown and disturbing factor, necessarily to be taken into consideration. Military plans may be regarded as infallible; but the attitude and possible action of the United States constitute the element of uncertainty and therefore an unknown hazard. American recognition has increased self-confidence in Moscow, but no one believes that the Soviet Union will commence hostilities. I therefore believe that our recognition of the Soviet Union has injected into the situation a restraining influence, probably of greater effect than any other single integral.

(8) The opinion among the military attachés in Tokyo is that the Japanese Army will reach the zenith of combat efficiency in 1935, and that after that period, time will tell in favor of Soviet Russia in point of lines of communication, organized man power, fortification, and equipment. The hypothesis was advanced, and is firmly held by the majority of foreign observers, that in the general scheme of Japanese expansionist ambitions the Maritime Provinces and eastern Siberia occupy an important position, and that in those ambitions the Soviet Union constitutes an obstacle which must be removed at a favorable moment. Granting that this is true, I nevertheless believe that an increasingly influential body of opinion in Japan recognizes the importance of consolidating gains already made before embarking on further military adventures. The creation of the "Manchukuo Empire" is a step toward that consolidation. This school of thought feels that Manchukuo must first justify itself before the world as a stable and progressive political unit before further expansionist plans should be put into operation. There seems at present to be greater hope that the influence of this saner element in the country may predominate over those who are less amenable to reason.

In spite of the foregoing tendencies and considerations, the course of future events is subject to incidents and uncertainties which no one can predict. The foreign military attachés are, I believe, unanimously pessimistic. It is certain that an important faction of the armed forces of the Empire, especially the younger elements, earnestly desire a conflict with the Soviet Union, for the primary purpose of which all the energies of the Army and Navy are united in an intense and unanimous effort of preparation. I have once before drawn the parallel of the intensively trained football team which, being convinced of its superiority and dissatisfied with mere practice, desires a game. This is precisely the attitude of a considerable element of the Army, just as it was the attitude of the German Army in 1914. If this element has its way, there will be war, and there will always exist the hazard that this element will work to create a situation where war will be unavoidable.

As an illustration of this hazard I have been told the following incident by Mr. J. B. Powell, editor of the *China Weekly Review*. He was dining with a young Japanese officer in Mukden who pointed out a small table in his apartment which he said was historical. "On that table," he remarked, "were worked out the plans for bombing Chingchow. There was a difference of opinion, and I myself voted against it, but the majority of my friends voted in the affirmative and the bombing was therefore carried out as planned." The implication was that the step was taken without higher instructions. I cannot of course guarantee the accuracy of the story, but Mr. Powell was convinced of its truth. It is in line with other incidents of the 1931 campaign in Manchuria. We must not close our eyes to the fact that similar incidents may occur in future, regardless of the views and policies of those in authority either in Tokyo or at the front, and that any one serious incident might create a situation where war with Soviet Russia would become unavoidable.

To sum up, the pacifist tendencies latent in Japan have in the past few months been able to make themselves felt and heard to a greater degree than at any time since September 18, 1931. If the proponents of these tendencies do not overplay their hand, they may be expected to gather strength and influence, and they may, in the long run, effectively guide the country into saner and less aggressively militaristic channels. The possibility of avoiding a conflict with the Soviet Union depends to some degree upon the continued strengthening of these newly manifested tendencies, for which, at the present moment, there appear to be reasonable grounds for optimism.

THE JAPANESE COURT CELEBRATES

February 23, 1934

Court mourning was raised for three days to celebrate the birth of the Crown Prince, and for three days all Japanese officials of certain rank are to be entertained in turn at the palace—on the third day 7000 of them. Today the Imperial princes and princesses, the Diplomatic Chiefs of Mission, and the Members of the Cabinet and their wives were invited to luncheon with the Emperor and Empress, all seated at one big table. First Amaral, as Acting Dean in

the absence of Bassompierre, presented the Emperor with a tremendous silver bowl and a silver-bound book containing the signa-
tures of the members of the Diplomatic Corps, on behalf of the
Corps, with an appropriate speech, and the Emperor replied, subsequently shaking hands with each of us.

The luncheon was magnificently done. Alice, being acting Doyenne, sat between two of the princes. The Emperor and Empress
were in the middle. Special crimson sake cups with the Imperial
crest in gold, and small silver samurai helmets, were presented to
each guest. Prince Ri, whom I do not know, suddenly leaned across
Mrs. Hultman, and said to me in German: "Where is the most
beautiful spot in the world?" Without thinking I quickly replied:
"The Scheidegg, under the Jungfrau." He seemed satisfied and said,
"I shall go there."

That terminated the conversation. Afterward each chief of
mission and his wife were asked in to the room where the Emperor
and Empress were sitting, sat down with each in turn, and had a
talk of five minutes or so, of course through interpreters. The
Emperor said he was glad to see a distinct improvement in Japanese-
American relations. I expressed American congratulations on the
birth of the Crown Prince and then, to our surprise, he said, "How's
Sambo?" or words to that effect. He had evidently read all about
the dog's falling into the palace moat and subsequent rescue. The
Emperor seemed to me exceedingly cordial, and the Empress was
beaming; she wanted to know all about Elsie. Alice told her how
Elsie had not dared to take the Empress' wedding present to
Peking lest it should be lost because it was her most valued treasure.
I also had a long talk with Shidehara. The wives of the members
of the cabinet and of a few other high officials were dressed in
costumes of some 1000 years ago—magnificent brocades, red shoes,
hair down their backs plaited with sticks. It was a great party,
never to be forgotten; we were there from 12 till after 3.

THE SOVIET AMBASSADOR SEES THE
SPRING OF 1934 AS DECISIVE

March 9, 1934

During a long conversation today with the Soviet Ambassador,
Mr. Yurenev, he first told me the present status of the negotiations
for the sale of the Chinese Eastern Railway; these negotiations are
still confined to *pourparlers* between the Minister for Foreign Affairs

and himself, the general conference not having yet reconvened. These *pourparlers* have taken the form of bargaining pure and simple, each side naturally wishing to win a success—especially Mr. Hirota, who will have difficulty in satisfying Japanese public opinion. In brief the situation is as follows:

The Soviet Government places the negotiations in two categories, the first comprising (1) replacement of the Russian personnel of the railway and (2) Manchukuo assumption of the railway's debt, and the second category comprising the actual sale of the railway itself. For the compensation of the personnel the Soviet Government will expect an amount of between nine and ten million yen. The approximate amount of the debt he did not tell me. With regard to the price for the railway, the Manchukuo authorities have not moved from their original offer of fifty million yen. The Soviet demand which was originally placed at two hundred and fifty million rubles was later reduced to two hundred million rubles. In order to convenience the Japanese, the Soviet Government had subsequently agreed to receive 50% of the total amount in merchandise and of the other 50%, 15% would be paid in yen immediately on signature and the remaining 35% would be paid within three years by the Manchukuo Government. The final figure to be agreed upon would be a global amount. Bargaining with regard to the type of merchandise to be received is now going on, the Japanese desiring to make as favorable a deal in this respect as possible.

I asked the Ambassador whether he was optimistic as to an eventual favorable outcome of the negotiations. In reply he made the significant remark: "An agreement will be reached if the Japanese wish to avoid war with Soviet Russia." I said to him: "That remark could be interpreted as meaning that if the Japanese do not come to terms the Soviet Union will declare war." He replied that this was not his meaning and that what he wished to convey was that if an agreement for the sale of the railway should not be reached, this fact would be a significant indication that the Japanese intended to bring about a war and would use the failure of the negotiations as an excuse to satisfy public opinion in Japan as to the reasons for such a war. They had already given their hand away in the documents published, to the effect that they would take the railway anyway, whether the negotiations succeeded or not.

I then asked Mr. Yurenev whether he was optimistic that war would be avoided. He said that it was important to be optimistic and implied that he had to be very careful to take such a position because at a given moment the Japanese Government might make public his *pourparlers* with Hirota over the railroad and that his attitude as then revealed might be an important element in the situation. In spite of this statement he gave me the distinct impression that he was far from optimistic with regard to the future. He said that a meeting of the principal generals of division will take place in Tokyo sometime this month * and that the pros and cons of an attack on Soviet Russia will be thoroughly discussed at that time. He alluded to the significant fact that a similar meeting of generals had taken place shortly before the outbreak of the Manchurian adventure in September, 1931. He said that Hayashi has constantly worked against Soviet Russia, particularly in Sinkiang, and that while it is very difficult to get a precise line on his present attitude, there seems to be no good reason to credit him with peaceful intentions.

Mr. Yurenev repeated what he has frequently said to me before that the Soviet Union is fully prepared for all eventualities and is strongly fortified both in Vladivostok and along the Siberian border. The double-tracking of the Trans-Siberian Railway has been carried on steadily throughout the winter in spite of the intense cold. If the Japanese should attack, they could of course pour immense forces into Manchuria and might be able to take Vladivostok and the adjacent portion of eastern Siberia, but further operations would entail extending and weakening their lines of communication, and little by little the Soviets could pour more and more troops into that region. If war should commence, it would not stop until one side or the other was completely exhausted, and it would take a long time to exhaust the almost unlimited power of the Soviets. Japan's Navy, he said, is of course incomparably stronger than the Russian Navy but the Russian fleet of submarines at Vladivostok is very strong and the sinking of a Japanese battleship or two would have immense significance and would alter the whole situation in the Far East. He said furthermore that while the Soviet measures were now purely defensive in character, if war should break out these measures would immediately become offensive, and unless Japan should quickly win an outstanding victory the Soviets would be able to occupy part or all of Manchuria, especially, he said, as at

* This meeting of division commanders is scheduled to meet in Tokyo on March 26 and to last for five days. It is not an annual meeting but is said to be customarily held after the appointment of a new Minister of War.

least 100,000 of the present troops of Manchukuo would support the Soviet arms and might turn the whole tide of the operations.

I said to the Ambassador that most of the foreign military experts in Tokyo believe that the Japanese Army will reach the zenith of its combat efficiency in 1935 and that if war is intended, the spring of 1935 will be the most likely moment for attack. The Ambassador replied that while nobody could foresee a precise date, he thought it more likely that such an attack would occur this spring, at any time after the coming meeting of Japanese generals, because they realize that time is constantly telling in favor of the Russian forces. He seems firmly convinced that the final decision will be taken at this coming meeting of high Japanese military officers. He agreed with me that important pacific influences are at work in Japan, including the Emperor, Prince Saionji, Count Makino, a considerable body of liberal opinion, and especially Hirota, but he added that in the last analysis the decision would lie with the military.

In further conversation Mr. Yurenev spoke of the situation in Sinkiang, where the Chinese troops which had been repatriated by Soviet Russia had been victorious over other troops. He believes that the Japanese are steadily working in China to foment further disruption. He thinks that the Japanese are convinced that the United States is backing China, especially in its aircraft development. He asked me many questions with regard to our intentions concerning the further fortification of the Philippines, Guam, etc. He also said that according to his information England is showing a distinct pro-Japanese tendency. England, he said, is in a very difficult position because she has good reason to be afraid of Japan becoming too strong. On the whole he agreed that the political situation is rather nebulous, although he finds that international intrigue is constantly working throughout the Far East.

CELEBRATING JAPANESE-AMERICAN FRIENDSHIP

April 22, 1934

A grand red-letter day. Alice and I were up at 6 and boarded the Japanese destroyer *Shimakaze* at Yokohama at 7:45. I had asked the Department if they saw any objection to our going down to Shimoda on an American destroyer, but they disapproved the suggestion as Shimoda is technically a closed port—unless the Japanese should themselves propose it, which they didn't. However, they did take us down on one of their own destroyers, together with Debuchi,

Admiral Nomura, Count Kabayama, the Rogers, Cranes, Dickovers, and Goolds, several other prominent Japanese and a raft of press and cameramen. This was to be the main celebration of the eightieth anniversary of the signing of Japan's first treaty by Commodore Perry, at the spot where the "black ships" made their principal stay.

The trip to Shimoda lasted three hours and a half, going at a speed of twenty-five knots. The day was lovely and the sea quite smooth, thank heaven (yesterday the trip would have been appalling), but even so, there was a marked swell when we got out of Tokyo Bay and some of the ladies looked rather green, while Debuchi and Kabayama passed out completely. (Which reminds me that the Japanese press solemnly spoke of the ceremonies that were to be held at the graves of five sailors of Perry's expedition who had "passed out"—not "passed on"!) Fuji, which was constantly in sight, was crystal clear and remarkably impressive.

The little harbor of Shimoda is lovely—high, thickly wooded shores and pretty little islands, one of which was not so pretty when a Russian warship was later wrecked on it in a fog. In those days the Japanese intended it to be the main post for foreign commerce, and in Perry's treaty only Shimoda and Hakodate were opened, but later of course it proved to be impractical and Yokohama was opened instead.

We landed first at the little village of Kakizaka on the other side of the harbor from Shimoda, where Townsend Harris lived in his Gyokusen-ji ("ji" means temple) for four years before going to Yedo—with Okichi, the geisha, who deserted family and friends to nurse and cook for Harris and was consequently regarded at the time as a social outcast and was denied decent burial, but was later almost sainted in Japanese estimation for her unselfish service to the then hated foreigner. Her memory lives in verse and song today. The original temple was destroyed but an exact replica now stands on the same spot and we were met and escorted to it by the chief priest, with whom I have already had much correspondence.

Alice and I first burned incense before each of the graves of the five American sailors, and then to the memory of Townsend Harris himself within the temple. We were profoundly moved by the significance and solemnity of it all. After pausing before the shrine we examined the various relics of Harris which are reverently kept in the temple, including some of his personal articles and the suit of his Dutch interpreter, Heusken, who was later assassinated. On a monument to Harris near the temple is engraved the following excerpt from his diary on the day that he raised the first consular flag in Japan:

Thursday, September 4, 1856. Slept very little from excitement and mosquitoes,—the latter enormous in size. Men on shore to put up my flagstaff. Heavy job. Slow work. Spar falls; break crosstrees; fortunately no one hurt. At last get a reinforcement from the ship. Flagstaff erected; men form a ring around it, and, at two and half P.M. of this day, I hoist the "First Consular Flag" ever seen in this Empire. Grim reflections—ominous of change—undoubted beginning of the end. Query,—if for the real good of Japan?

Admiral Nomura asked me what he meant by "Undoubted beginning of the end." I said he must have meant that this was to be the end of Japanese isolation (I wonder) and that his final observation "Query,—if for the real good of Japan?" showed that he was thinking of the interests of Japan quite as much as of the interests of his own country.

Then we motored a mile or more to Shimoda, through almost unbroken rows of Japanese school children, both girls and boys, hundreds and hundreds of them gathered from towns and cities as far away as Nagoya, all waving Japanese and American flags and shouting "Banzai!" with a heartiness which could hardly have been simulated. This was really very moving too. At length we came to the town school where the exercises were to take place in the open air. A shrine had been erected for the occasion and a Shinto service was held in memory of Perry and Harris, with music, several priests, and the usual banquet heaped up on tables; the evil spirits were driven away by waving *sakaki* branches, the audience was purified with sacred water, and then the chief priest was in a position to ask the gods to descend and to listen to our petition for the repose of the souls of the two heroes which he read from a parchment. Thereafter we all came up and offered *sakaki* branches and finally the little door in the shrine was closed, indicating that the gods might now retire.

There followed speeches, many of them—from the Governor, the Mayor, the chairman of the celebration committee, Debuchi on behalf of Hirota, Kabayama, Admiral Nomura, Yamada, a descendant of the famous Egawa Hidetatsu, and myself. Yamada, who is reputed as an orator, spoke very frankly and said that the next twenty years of Japanese-American friendship were going to be much more important (and impliedly critical) than the past eighty years, and that the centennial of Perry's treaty would be a far more significant observance than the present one.

The speeches had lasted so long that a visit to another temple and a town luncheon had to be abandoned and we departed at 3, having been there for three hours and a half, through the same rows of cheering children, accompanied out of the harbor, just as we had been received, by many decorated boats and among them an old steam trawler painted to represent one of the "black ships," with side paddles and all, and prominently labeled on the stern *Powhatan*. The trip back was smoother and very pleasant, with much fraternizing over refreshments in the wardroom. It was a really grand day.

RUSSIAN FABLE

Troyanovsky is reported to have related in his speech before the American Society of International Law the Russian fable of a cook who, upon discovering a cat eating meat, lectured to it. Though the animal listened it continued eating. "I guess this fable was written with international relations in view, for it raises the question of what is to be done when a cat listens but continues to eat."

THE SITUATION FLARES UP AGAIN

April 28, 1934

These are days of political intensity. Indeed, in our job the interesting situations and work come in cycles; we pass through periods of comparative calm, with more or less routine duties to perform, and then quite suddenly something breaks and we are busier than bees. Ever since the statement of Foreign Office spokesman Eiji Amau on April 17, the political pot has been boiling; long telegrams out and in; ambassadors, ministers, chargés d'affaires, press correspondents constantly coming in for information or diagnosis of events; there is little rest. Amau at least has given the press correspondents plenty of occupation while the diplomats have been spending thousands of dollars on telegrams. I told Amau at a dinner the other night that we were all going to send our telegraph bills to him, to which he replied that that would be all right because he would naturally get a rake-off from the Ministry of Communications for stimulating the telegraph service. It is difficult these days to judge whether Amau is regarded in Japan as an *enfant terrible* or a hero; it rather depends on whether you seek opinions from the camp of the moderates or that of the chauvinists.

The first reaction of the Japanese press to Amau's original statement was one of unqualified approval, but when the unfavorable repercussion began to come back from abroad, some of the papers, while approving without qualification the doctrine that Japan has the sole responsibility for the "preservation of peace in the Far East," agreed that the wording of the statement was a little awkward. It will be noted that the statement given me by Hirota on the 26th differed from Amau's statement. According to the unofficial translation of the statement of the 17th, Amau said:

> . . . This country considers it only natural that, to keep peace and order in East Asia, it must act singlehanded and upon its own responsibility. In order to be able to fulfill this obligation, Japan must expect its neighbor countries to share the responsibility of maintaining peace in East Asia, but Japan does not consider any other country, except China, to be in a position to share that responsibility with Japan.

In the official translation of the 26th the wording is modified:

> However, Japan cannot remain indifferent to anyone's taking action under any pretext which is prejudicial to the maintenance of law and order in East Asia for which she, if only in view of her geographical position, has a most vital concern. Consequently, she cannot afford to have questions of China exploited by any third party for the execution of a selfish policy which does not take into consideration the above-mentioned circumstances.

Amau, in his statement of the 17th, is further reported to have said:

> Japan will oppose any attempt of China to avail herself of the influence of some other country with the idea of repelling Japan, as this would jeopardize the peace in East Asia; and it will also oppose resort by China to any measure intended to "resist foreigners by bringing other foreigners to bear against them." Japan expects foreign nations to give consideration to the special situation created by the recent Manchurian and Shanghai incidents, and to realize that the undertaking of joint operations in regard to China, even if they be in regard to technical or financial assistance, must eventually attain political significance for China. Undertakings entailing such significance, if carried through to the end, must give rise to complications

that might even necessitate discussion of problems like fixing zones of interest or even international control or division of China, which would be the greatest possible misfortune for China and at the same time would have the most serious effects upon East Asia and, ultimately, Japan.

Japan therefore must object to such undertakings as a matter of principle, although it will not find it necessary to interfere with any foreign country negotiating individually with China in regard to propositions of finance or trade, as long as those propositions are beneficial to China and are not likely to threaten the maintenance of order in East Asia. If such negotiations are of a nature that might disturb peace and order in East Asia, Japan will be obliged to oppose them.

For example, supplying China with warplanes, building aerodromes in China, and detailing military instructors or military advisers to China, or contracting a loan to provide funds for political uses, would obviously tend to separate Japan and other countries from China and ultimately would prove prejudicial to the peace of East Asia. Japan will oppose such projects.

The foregoing attitude should be made clear by the policies followed by Japan in the past. But, due to the fact that gestures for joint assistance to China and for other aggressive assistance, by foreign countries, are becoming too conspicuous, it is deemed advisable to make known the foregoing policies.

There has been much conjecture regarding the reasons for the issuance of Amau's statement of April 17. I endeavored to define those reasons in our telegrams and in our last dispatch to the Department, based chiefly on the theory that Japan was becoming restive at the cumulative evidence of foreign activities in China. Furthermore, approval of the doctrine that Japan alone is responsible for the maintenance of peace in the Far East would give Japan added claims to naval parity in the forthcoming naval conference, and would also enable her to dominate China. Amau had been pressed by the Japanese newspaper correspondents for comment on these various matters and Shigemitsu finally agreed to his giving out the substance of an instruction already sent to Ariyoshi, Minister to China.

Whether or not Hirota approved the issuance of the statement is unessential, for the statement accurately expresses the policy which Japan would like to pursue. While there has been criticism of the phraseology, the substance of the statement seems to have the unqualified approval of practically all Japanese, and Hirota, in the present state of public opinion, could not repudiate the statement and remain in office. The net result of the statement will probably be: (1) an intensification of the feeling of isolation that has prevailed since the Manchurian campaign; (2) a furtherance of the Army and Navy campaign to prepare for the "crisis" of 1935–36, and (3) the development of patriotic feeling to such an extent that no Japanese Government will be able to compromise with the powers in case of decided differences in viewpoint regarding policies toward China or with respect to naval ratios.

Saw Sir Francis Lindley off at the station, Hirota and most of the colleagues being there.

With deep regret I saw Lindley go. We were colleagues in Cairo thirty years ago, and Alice and I have always had sincere affection for him and his wife. He has been a good colleague and perfectly frank and free in imparting even confidential information.

Another colleague of mine recently read to me a dispatch he had sent his Government and later, at my request, sent me a copy in confidence. Among other things he says:

> It is true, as —— said (after a conversation with Ambassador Dodd in Berlin), that the attitude of America toward Manchukuo has not changed up to the present. I have given you my opinion, namely, that the day when the United States sees an advantage in it, she will not hesitate to abandon the Stimson Doctrine which she is bound to no one to uphold. She did not hesitate in 1920 to abandon the League of Nations notwithstanding the fact that the Covenant was the work of her President.

This comparison shows a complete lack of familiarity with our system of government. The so-called Stimson Doctrine is an executive policy, and the recognition or nonrecognition of foreign states is an executive prerogative. Congress can pass resolutions but it cannot send ambassadors without the approval and action of the executive. Congress, however, was competent to refuse its approval of the Treaty of Versailles comprising the Covenant of the League of Nations.

This same foreign diplomat went on to say that he continues to believe that the Kellogg Pact should not have been considered as applicable to the events in Manchuria, and he raises the point:

> By virtue of the protocol of Peking of September 1, 1901, the United States (as well as France, England, Italy, and Belgium)

had the right to maintain garrisons in China—at Peking, Tientsin, Shanhaikwan, and other points. Supposing that the American garrison at Tientsin, which exists at present, which is numerous and well equipped with modern armaments, should be led by circumstances to use force to fulfill its normal mission and one envisaged by the treaties; for example, to prevent a massacre of American missionaries at 20 or even 100 kilometers from the city. In such a case would Mr. Stimson maintain that the Chinese frontier or the Kellogg Pact were violated? No, because it would be absurd. Nevertheless, he did maintain this in the case of the Japanese military action in Manchuria, which was an absolutely analogous case. Strict legality pushed to a certain point risks becoming a challenge to elementary common sense.

The argument is weak and the analogy false. For a local foreign garrison to make a sortie to protect life can hardly be held as analogous to the action of a country in pouring tens of thousands of troops into a foreign area, and conducting large-scale military operations with the purpose and result of separating that area permanently from its owner. I said so to my colleague, but he refused to agree. He continues in his dispatch to argue that as long as America and the League of Nations persist in their present attitude, a situation pregnant with the danger of war will continue to exist in Eastern Asia.

My colleague's attitude toward the Nine-Power Treaty is this: being unwilling to acknowledge that Japan violated the provisions of Article I he won't acknowledge that she violated the provisions of Article II. Yet the contracting powers, having agreed in Article I "to respect the sovereignty, independence, and the territorial and administrative integrity of China," proceed in Article II to agree *"not to enter into any treaty,* agreement, arrangement, or understanding, either with one another, or, individually or collectively, *with any Power* or Powers, *which would infringe or impair the principles stated in Article I."* Even those who are able to accept the patently illusory theory of "self-determination" in Manchuria, and who can therefore persuade themselves that Japan did not violate Article I, can hardly, with any intelligence or intellectual honesty, hold that Japan did not violate Article II. She most certainly did violate that Article when she concluded her treaty with Manchukuo. We hear much talk about changed conditions superseding legalistic obligations, yet if that perfectly clear violation is con-

doned and accepted, we might as well regard all treaties as "scraps
of paper" to be torn up when they become inconvenient to an individual nation, precisely as when Germany violated Belgium in 1914.
Mr. Hull, in his recent *aide-mémoire,* made clear the fact that there
are accepted means for modifying or terminating treaty obligations,
but only by processes prescribed or recognized or agreed upon by
the signatories. I hope that I shall not see a day when the United
States recognizes Manchukuo.

SECRETARY HULL STANDS FIRM

April 29, 1934

Fortunately I was at home when Mr. Hull's *aide-mémoire* on the
question of foreign assistance to China came in. It was decoded at 5
and typed at about 5:30. In spite of its being Sunday and the Emperor's birthday I immediately wrote a personal letter to Hirota
asking if he could see me urgently. He replied by telephone setting
the hour at 6:30 and I was therefore able to deliver the document
without delay. He read it slowly and carefully and then asked me
what portion or portions I considered the most important. I replied
that I did not feel that I ought to try to interpret it and that the
text seemed to me to be quite clear. He merely remarked that
Amau's statement had caused "great misunderstanding" and said
that he would reply after studying our *aide-mémoire* in due course.
He was perfectly friendly and showed no surprise or disapproval.
In my opinion the *aide-mémoire* is wholly admirable, absolutely
called for by the circumstances, drafted in masterly fashion, perfectly
clear in substance, moderate and friendly in tone.

It seems to me that after all that has passed, Sir John Simon appears to have accepted a little too readily Hirota's assurances that
Japan intended to respect the Nine-Power Treaty, and his statement
to the House of Commons to the effect that he was satisfied with
those assurances may cause certain elements of the British public to
feel that something more was called for and desired. At any rate,
we have registered our own position with complete clarity. I think
that the Department's "rush" instruction to me to present the *aide-
mémoire* at the earliest possible moment was probably to forestall
another pious statement which it was reported that the Foreign
Office would issue to the press tomorrow. Evidently it did forestall
it because the following day Amau announced to the press that
there would be no further statement for the present. Whatever the

other nations may think or do, we shall have their (perhaps grudging) respect. I am very happy about it.

JAPANESE PATRIOTS THREATEN
THE NETHERLANDS INDIES

May 14, 1934

Pabst came in for one of our periodical talks. He said that a delegation from the Japanese patriotic society "Meirinkai," including a retired admiral and a retired general, recently called on him and presented a memorandum drawn up by the society with reference to the forthcoming Japanese-Netherlands East Indies trade conference, shortly to meet at Batavia, Java, in which the society somewhat aggressively urged the Netherlands Government to ensure a successful outcome of the negotiations. Among other comments, the memorandum referred to the oppression of the natives of the Dutch East Indies by the Netherlands Government and observed that failure of that Government to come to terms with the Japanese would cause "dark clouds" to arise in the relations between the two countries.

General Pabst said that he raised two points: (1) that dealings between his Government and the natives of the Dutch East Indies were matters of purely domestic concern in which his Government could not tolerate interference by others, and (2) that the observation concerning "dark clouds" was in the nature of a threat which likewise was not acceptable, and that these two points must be withdrawn if he, the Minister, were to receive the memorandum. The Japanese delegation bowed in apparent acquiescence; the Minister said: "May I take your bow as an apology?" whereupon they bowed again.

The Minister further informed me that he had learned that the above-mentioned society has recommended to the Japanese Government the severance of diplomatic relations with Holland if the forthcoming negotiations do not prove successful.

The Netherlands Minister requested information as to the customary procedure of this Embassy in regard to the reception of such delegations and the acceptance of their communications. He was informed that the delegations are usually received with courtesy, but that the Embassy has consistently refused to accept, on behalf of the United States, any memorandums, protests, or other communications addressed to the Government or to officials of the United

States, maintaining that such communications, coming as they do from Japanese sources, must pass through the usual and proper channels, namely, the Japanese Foreign Office and the Japanese Embassy at Washington.

Persistent adherence of our Embassy to this procedure apparently has succeeded in discouraging attempts by patriotic and other societies to put their ideas before us, as no attempts to present communications to the American Government through the Embassy have been made by these societies since my arrival, although at several periods such attempts might have been expected.

THE POLICY OF APPEASEMENT: JAPANESE STYLE

(Mr. Grew to Mr. Prentiss B. Gilbert, American Consul, Geneva, Switzerland)

Tokyo, May 17, 1934

Confidential

Dear Mr. Gilbert:

I acknowledge with thanks the receipt of your letter of April 5. In answer to your letter and in compliance with the suggestion contained therein I shall endeavor to outline briefly the present political situation here with particular reference to the Japanese attitude toward international co-operation both at present and in relation to the basic Japanese policy of dominating East Asia.

In your letter you remark that "one gains the distinct impression that having achieved to such a large degree their objective in Manchuria, the Japanese are now endeavoring to effect an appeasement of the feeling against them in every direction possible." That is, in fact, the specific task which Hirota has set himself as Foreign Minister. Accordingly—to use the phrases current in the Japanese press—for the "desperate diplomacy" of Count Uchida there has been substituted the "national defense by diplomacy" of Mr. Hirota.

In promoting his policy of conciliation Hirota has shown force and ability. He came into office last September at a moment when the pendulum of public feeling was tending to resume the norm. Already Shiratori, the aggressive spokesman of the Foreign Office, had been forced out. The resignation of Count Uchida was in itself a blow to military influence. Within a few weeks commenced the momentous "Five Ministers' Conference" at which Hirota by confronting Araki with pure common sense is believed to have won his pledge not to interfere in matters of foreign policy. And then in January, Araki himself, the high priest of the military cult, found he could not redeem the pledges he had made to the Army and resigned.

Furthermore, through public utterances and in the Diet, the voice of public opinion revealed dismay at the size of the military budgets and an inclination to blame the Army for the unnecessary and dangerous state of agitation into which the nation as a whole had been led. Businessmen and capitalists wished to be free to reap the profits of the export boom.

During all these months Hirota worked steadily, and I believe sincerely, to create a friendly basis upon which to deal with China, Soviet Russia, Great Britain, and the United States. His hand was manifest in an immediate toning down of antiforeignism in the press; it was revealed in the renewed efforts to solve the current problems between Japan and Soviet Russia one by one; and it was emphasized to me in conversation in which Hirota showed an eagerness to explore any possible avenue which would lead to an improvement in American-Japanese relations. Certain people considered him a genuine liberal and the strongest Foreign Minister since Komura and Kato.

Nevertheless, many believe Hirota's moderation to be one of manner and strategy rather than substance. Certainly no one could have come into office last year unless he was pledged to support Japan's continental adventure and unless he profoundly believed in Japan's "mission to preserve the peace of East Asia." It is precisely here that we find a deep-rooted antithesis. The Japanese Government is at present struggling to escape from the dangers of international isolation and yet substantially every Japanese—in the Government and out—is determined that their nation must realize its long-cherished ambition, hegemony over East Asia.

It is for this reason that the Japanese Government finds it difficult to beg for the world's friendship with anything more tangible than words. One cannot avoid the suspicion that at heart a great many here—we might even say a majority—view the treaties and international commitments to which Japan is a party as just so many obstacles in the path to empire. Of course there are reasonableminded elements, and the older statesmen, Saionji, Makino, and others who influence the Throne, do not share these somewhat unscrupulous views without many reservations, but they are old men and we cannot count on their restraining influence much longer. It is simply that the nation, with the goal in sight, is reluctant to admit that the period of consolidation, customary after each wave of Japanese expansion, is now in the best interests of the country.

It immediately comes to mind that this incompatibility between the desire of Hirota to win friends for Japan and the fundamental ambitions of the nation has already been illustrated by the justly famous "Amau Statement" of Japan's policy toward foreign assistance to China. It has already proved a source of great embarrassment to Hirota's policy of friendship on the one hand, and yet, on the other hand, no one, no government official even, has publicly denied that this statement represents the genuine policy of the Government. It happens, as a matter of fact, that the original Amau statement was an instruction to Japan's diplomatic representatives abroad and that its public announcement did not have the approval of the Foreign Minister, but this circumstance is beside the point. Japan has revealed herself as firmly opposed—say what she may—to the objects and purposes of the Nine-Power Treaty and the efforts of the League of Nations to extend international (and Occidental) assistance to China. . . .

With Soviet Russia Japan is trying to keep the peace at present. Viewing the situation from Tokyo, neither side has now any stomach for war, nor are there indications in Japan or Manchuria of preparations pointing to imminent warfare. For the time being at least we need only fear a frontier incident of unusual gravity. Although Hirota has taken up the Chinese Eastern Railway question, the yen-ruble exchange question, the fisheries dispute, and the boundary problems one by one with an evidently genuine desire to remove them from the slate, progress has been very halting and bids fair to continue so.

The rumors that the U.S.S.R. is contemplating joining the League have not aroused great attention here although such comments as have come to light interpret the step as prompted by considerations of national safety. Undoubtedly the Japanese realize that the League's influence in the Far East would be strengthened by the entry of the Soviets, but the possibility seems too remote to have aroused any great degree of apprehension as yet. Incidentally, the Soviet Ambassador recently told me that he had no reason to believe that Soviet Russia was about to join the League but that he did not know what might come about in future.

So far as the question of a nonaggression pact between the U.S.S.R. and Japan is concerned, Hirota has stated that it is his policy first to remove the specific points of conflict between the two nations before taking up the question of a general pact. It is believed that a strong minority, notably the Army, opposes such a pact and that to ignore this minority would court the risk of reversing the present trend toward a more normal national psychology. After these specific points of conflict have been removed, the minority would retain no valid reason for continuing their opposition.

In concluding this letter I refer to the portion of your dispatch outlining the position which Japan is taking at the present time in Geneva, namely, the wish to be represented on League bodies in return for Japanese co-operation, the alternative being withdrawal from all League treaties. Writing from Tokyo I should be inclined to question the value of Japanese co-operation in the first place (except in social matters such as narcotics control) owing to the exclusive character of Japanese ambitions in the Far East, and in the second place I should question whether withdrawal from all League treaties would create a situation entirely distasteful to the majority of the Japanese people. That the technical and political difficulties involved in securing acceptance of the Japanese reservation should be envisaged in Tokyo as providing plausible reasons for not withdrawing from the League next year, I am inclined to doubt. Japan has burned her bridges behind her so far as the League is concerned. The Government has repeatedly indicated that Japan's withdrawal from the League was necessitated by a fundamental divergence of views and, only two weeks ago, the Foreign Minister —the spearhead of the conciliatory forces now articulate—said publicly:

> Our proposition having been rejected by the powers, we were compelled to serve notice of withdrawal from the League of Nations, with which we had maintained close co-operation for so many years. However, that step was one which Japan perforce had to make in order that we might fulfill our mission and responsibilities in East Asia.

Any Japanese Government which attempted to retain Japan's membership in the League would court the danger of denying Japan's "mission and responsibilities in East Asia"—one of the terms in which the conviction of Japan's "Manifest Destiny" is expressed. If, then, Japan's secession from the League and League activities should be definite, it would of course carry with it the inevitable corollary that Japan would be estopped from making use of the

League as a medium for the manipulation of the balance of power.

The arguments of the foregoing pages indicate the nature of the problem which confronts the present "Cabinet of Old Men." The Saito Government is trying, so to speak, to keep the brakes on. Furthermore, having survived recent political crises with increasing difficulty, the cabinet is racing against time. Will the common sense of the nation reassert itself with sufficient celerity or will the Government succumb to death by attrition before the forces of moderation have gained the upper hand? At the present time it is only the liberal, super-party advisers to the Throne who are keeping the Government in power in the face of dissatisfaction in many quarters. Should they fail in the near future the succeeding Government would almost inevitably be more reactionary. For the real good of the country they must hold on as long as possible. In any event, the mantle of government will not again fall on the generation which was at the helm when Japan rose to the position of a world power. We shall sooner or later be seriously concerned as to whether the new generation will acquit itself successfully of the gigantic task to which the nation seems committed, because American and Japanese policy in the Far East will directly conflict—unless someone puts the helm over hard.

With kind personal regards,

                                        Yours very sincerely,

On July 3, the cabinet of Premier Saito resigned and a new cabinet, headed by Admiral Okada, took office.

ESTIMATING THE OKADA CABINET

July 6, 1934

Cabled the Department an extensive estimate of the new cabinet given me by an eminent Japanese liberal. He regards it as an outstanding victory for the moderates, as indeed it is, because the chauvinists were pressing hard for an ultranationalist line-up. Saionji, Makino, and their group are clearly in the saddle. Foreign Minister Hirota and War Minister Hayashi are to stay, and Finance Minister Takahashi for a while, although he will probably later be succeeded by the Vice-Minister of Finance, Fujii. My informant told me that the decision had come like a "thunder clap" and that if the United States had had the privilege of choosing the cabinet in its own interests, it could not have done better. The new cabinet, he said, would follow precisely the policy of the Saito cabinet but with more driving force and initiative, which Saito lacked. I told the Department that while I was not yet in a position to subscribe to the foregoing estimate in its entirety, I did believe that the moderates had come out on top. My source of information had already shown that his opinion was worthy of consideration because he had predicted Admiral Okada's appointment some time before the latter's name had even been mentioned publicly.

A HELPFUL TALK WITH THE SOVIET AMBASSADOR

September 7, 1934

Called on the Soviet Ambassador and asked him if there were any particular developments or facts concerning the negotiations for the sale of the Chinese Eastern Railway other than those which had appeared in the press which he might be willing to tell me. Mr. Yurenev replied that in spite of the Japanese statement that the negotiations had only been adjourned, they were in fact broken off *de facto*. He said that the termination of the negotiations had at least eliminated from the scene Mr. Ohashi, who was an ignorant and obstructive element and had been brought into the negotiations only at the insistence of the Japanese military in Manchuria. He thought that Mr. Hirota was equally glad to be rid of him.

I asked Mr. Yurenev whether the failure to come to terms on the sale of the railway was not more a question of prestige and a desire to achieve a moral victory than a mere question of price because the Soviet demand and the Manchukuo offer were now separated only by the comparatively trivial difference of ¥40,000,000. The Ambassador replied that the Japanese were great bargainers where money was concerned and that Mr. Hirota when Ambassador in Moscow had haggled for a long time with the Soviet Government over a matter of a mere ¥500. I asked the Ambassador if there was any indication as to which party would take the next step in reopening the negotiations, to which he only replied that this could not at present be foreseen.

In this connection Mr. Yurenev expressed a high opinion of Mr. Hirota, for whom he said he had genuine admiration. He said he considered him a very able and shrewd negotiator but a great deal pleasanter to deal with than Count Uchida, who was merely a mouthpiece of the Japanese military.

General Relations

The Ambassador said that he thought there was little danger of a Soviet-Japanese conflict at the present time. The Soviets were very strong in Siberia and Vladivostok and were prepared for any eventuality. Even if some inflammatory incident should occur, he thought it could be localized, especially because the Japanese Army in Manchuria was by no means in condition to take the offensive at present. He said he also considered Japan's military were much more in hand than during the regime of General Araki and that the Emperor and his entourage were very much stronger and much more able to dictate a sane policy for the nation. He thought that the recent withdrawal of Admiral Suetsugu from the command of the fleet and his replacement by Admiral Nagano was a very important indication of this strength and presaged a desire for a conciliatory policy in the coming naval negotiations. Mr. Yurenev did not seem to know whether Admiral Suetsugu was to be given another assignment or not.

While the Ambassador avoided saying that he was either pessimistic or optimistic about the general situation, his remarks gave me the impression that he was not particularly anxious as to the outlook at the present time but rather that he thought matters were improving.

Arrest of the C.E.R. Employees

Asked about the significance of the arrest of a large number of the Soviet employees on the C.E.R., Mr. Yurenev did not seem to attach any great importance to the incident. He of course said that they were absolutely innocent of the charges against them and that on the contrary there was definite evidence that the sabotage complained of had been carried out from other quarters. He said it was particularly significant that the railroad cars carrying Japanese guns and other military equipment had suffered no damage.

Eastern Locarno Pact

The Ambassador then turned to the situation in Europe and said that the Eastern Locarno Pact would undoubtedly go through but that it was not at all sure that Germany and Poland would participate therein.

Anglo-Japanese Alliance

The Ambassador asked me what I thought about the rumors of

an Anglo-Japanese alliance. I told him what I knew about the rumors and said that while it was easy to build up an academic case to justify the rumors I had nevertheless no evidence whatever that they had any foundations in fact and that on the contrary I doubted if any definite negotiations for a rapprochement had taken place. The Ambassador said he agreed with me and that he also had no information but he thought that England's situation in the Far East at the present time might well give her cause for concern. He asked me if I knew anything definite about the British Industrial Mission to Manchukuo, to which I replied that I had no reason to believe that it had any political significance whatever. The Ambassador concurred.

HIROTA ON THE 1934 NAVAL CONFERENCE

Leave of Absence

I called on the Minister of Foreign Affairs to take leave of him before departing on a month's leave of absence to Peiping and told him that if any questions should arise during my absence which he wished to discuss with the Embassy Mr. Neville would be in charge and would be glad to be helpful at any time.

Naval Conference

The Minister, on his own initiative, approached the question of the Naval Conference and said that Japan had definitely decided to abrogate the Washington Treaties toward the end of 1934. Many elements in the Navy wished to abrogate immediately, but Mr. Hirota had insisted on waiting until after the London conversations in October because as soon as one signatory had abrogated, the Washington Treaty would become null and void as regards all the other signatories and Mr. Hirota intended to discuss the matter with the other parties before abrogation in order not to give offense to the other signatories and also in order to avoid, prior to the next naval conference, unfavorable atmosphere which might be created if the abrogation should take place without some preliminary mutual understanding. The Minister said that the discussions concerning abrogation would be conducted with the various powers separately and that owing to Ambassador Saito's absence from Washington the matter is to be taken up with the American delegation to the preliminary conversations in London by Ambassador Matsudaira.

Mr. Hirota said that while the difficulties of solving the naval problem with foreign powers were no doubt considerable, they were not so difficult as the domestic problem which he had to face in dealing with the chauvinists. He said he had great hopes of some solution of the naval problem which would avoid saddling the various countries with future heavy building programs, especially because the younger officers of the Japanese Navy were definitely opposed to the building of big ships and were in favor of small ones.

"THE IMPERIAL NAVY MUST BE AVENGED"

November 2, 1934

We have a firsthand report of a meeting at the Young Men's and Ex-Soldiers' Association in Kobe, where a Lieutenant-Colonel Matsumoto, a member of the staff of the Commander of the Fourth Division of the Army, made an inflammatory address of which the gist was as follows:

1. The outcome of the Naval Conference is immaterial in that Japan now has a preponderance of warships of the class desired, and will continue to maintain this advantage. Japan is in a position to defeat America at any time, and, in fact, any other country or combination of countries.

2. American duplicity during former naval conferences degraded Japan, and this insult to the Imperial Navy must be *avenged*.

3. After all, America is the one nation that stands in the way of justice, and the long list of insults from that country must be wiped out, and to establish Japan as the just ruler of the world America must be crushed.

4. America, formerly the richest and most opulent nation in the world, has become weak and flabby through dissipation and now is the time for Japan to prove the worth of her inheritance of the *Yamato Damashii*.

5. War is surely coming and all must be prepared so that a successful outcome may be assured. The Japanese Army is now waiting for the time to act, and the ex-service men and reserves must be prepared at any time to be called to the colors, which will probably be by the end of this year, or early next year. No ex-service man should leave his district unless on very urgent business, and then only for a very short time.

6. Japan has never lost a war and never will.

When one considers the impressionable age and somewhat limited outlook of the young persons who usually attend these meetings, speeches of the type reported seem dangerous and may easily lead to incidents, particularly at this time when there is more or less excitement over the London naval conversations. I shall bring the matter informally to Hirota's attention.

ENTERTAINING BABE RUTH

November 6, 1934

Motored Babe Ruth, Lefty O'Doul, and Shiro Akaboshi, champion of the Tokyo Golf Club, to Asaka for golf, where we managed to finish about fourteen holes in spite of the cameramen who pursued the Babe over the course. The Babe hits a tremendous ball, as does O'Doul, and both of them play sound golf but both were out of practice and their shots were not always straight. It amused me to hear the Bambino observe, when he said I was trying to hit the ball * too hard (my usual weakness), that it was precisely the same principle in baseball and that if one tried to hit too hard (listen to the King of Swat) one was bound to take one's eyes off the ball. I haven't noticed the Babe letting up any at the home plate.

But the real kick of the day for me was to listen to the Babe and Lefty discussing a hundred subjects in the baseball world while we motored out and in. Wish I had had a stenographer present. After the game we had to sit on the steps of the Club, with our caddies behind us, and talk for the newsreels. Suddenly and unexpectedly told to say something I observed, so far as I can remember: "Well, Babe, it's fine to see you in Tokyo. I don't know if you realize what distinguished company you are in today: Mr. Akaboshi, champion of the Tokyo Golf Club, and—the worst golfer in the world—myself."

The Babe responded nobly that he must dispute that title with me as he had been in every blankety-blank trap on the course. He had. But he always got out with his first explosion shot, while I didn't. Of course the personnel and caddies at the Club were thrilled to the core, and I presented the Babe to such players as we met on the course; "Pleased to know you," said the Bambino. Of course all Japan has gone wild over him. He is a great deal more effective Ambassador than I could ever be.

* See photograph No. 14.

WHY AMERICA MUST STAND FIRM IN THE FAR EAST

December 27, 1934

In the London naval conversations the firm stand of our Government and delegation to maintain the present naval ratios intact in the face of Japanese intransigeance, as well as their decision that the action of the Japanese Government in denouncing the Washington Naval Treaty automatically created a new situation in which the conversations must be suspended sine die, leaving the Japanese to return home empty-handed, were especially gratifying to those of us who have watched the development in London from this angle.

The thought which is uppermost in my mind is that the United States is faced, and will be faced in future, with two main alternatives. One is to be prepared to withdraw from the Far East, gracefully and gradually perhaps, but not the less effectively in the long run, permitting our treaty rights to be nullified, the Open Door to be closed, our vested economic interests to be dissolved, and our commerce to operate unprotected. There are those who advocate this course, and who have advocated it to me personally, on the ground that any other policy will entail the risk of eventual war with Japan. Frank Simonds has emphasized that risk as almost a certainty. In their opinion, "the game is not worth the candle" because the United States can continue to subsist comfortably even after relinquishing its varied interests in the Far East, thereby eliminating the risk of future war.

The other main alternative is to insist, and to continue to insist, not aggressively yet not the less firmly, on the maintenance of our legitimate rights and interests in this part of the world and, so far as practicable, to support the normal development of those interests constructively and progressively.

There has already been abundant indication that the present administration in Washington proposes to follow the second of these alternatives. We may therefore, I assume, discard the hypothesis of withdrawal and examine the future outlook with the assurance that our Government has not the slightest intention of relinquishing the legitimate rights, vested interests, nondiscriminatory privileges for equal opportunity and healthful commercial development of the United States in the Far East.

In following this second and logical course, there should be and need be nothing inconsistent, so far as our own attitude is concerned, with the policy of the good neighbor. The determination to support and protect our legitimate interests in the Far East can and should be carried out in a way which, while sacrificing no point of principle, will aim to restrict to a minimum the friction between the United States and Japan inevitably arising from time to time as a result of that determination.

The administration of that policy from day to day becomes a matter of diplomacy, sometimes delicate, always important, for much depends on the method and manner of approach to the various problems with which we have been, are, and will continue to be faced. With the ultrasensitiveness of the Japanese, arising out of a marked inferiority complex which manifests itself in the garb of an equally marked superiority complex, with all its attendant bluster, chauvinism, xenophobia, and organized national propaganda, the method and manner of dealing with current controversies assume a significance and importance often out of all proportion to the nature of the controversy. That our Government fully appreciates this fact has been amply demonstrated by the instructions issued to this Embassy since the present administration took office, and we have tried to carry out those instructions or to act on our own initiative when such action was called for, with the foregoing considerations constantly in view.

But behind our day-to-day diplomacy lies a factor of prime importance, namely national support, demonstrated and reinforced by national preparedness. I believe that a fundamental element of that preparedness should be the maintenance of the present naval ratios in principle and the eventual achievement and maintenance of those ratios, so far as they apply to Japan, in fact. With such a background, and only with such a background, can we pursue our diplomacy with any confidence that our representations will be listened to or that they will lead to favorable results. General Douglas MacArthur, Chief of Staff of the United States Army, was recently reported in the press as saying: "Armies and navies, in being efficient, give weight to the peaceful words of statesmen, but a feverish effort to create them when once a crisis is imminent simply provokes attack." We need thorough preparedness not in the interests of war but of peace.

It is difficult for those who do not live in Japan to appraise the present temper of the country. An American Senator is reported to have recommended recently that we should accord parity to Japan in order to avoid future war. Whatever the Senator's views may be concerning the general policy that we should follow in the Far East, he probably does not realize what harm that sort of public statement does in strengthening the Japanese stand and in reinforcing the aggressive ambitions of the expansionists. The Japanese press of course picks out such statements by prominent Americans and publishes them far and wide, thus confirming the general belief in Japan that the pacifist element in the United States is preponderantly strong and in the last analysis will control the policy and action of our Government. Under such circumstances there is a general tendency to characterize our diplomatic representations as bluff and to believe that they can safely be disregarded without fear of implementation.

It would be helpful if those who share the Senator's views could hear and read some of the things that are constantly being said and written in Japan, to the effect that Japan's destiny is to subjugate and rule the world (*sic*), and could realize the expansionist ambitions which lie not far from the surface in the minds of certain elements in the Army and Navy, the patriotic societies, and the intense nationalists throughout the country. Their aim is to obtain trade control and eventually predominant political influence in China, the Philippines, the Straits Settlements, Siam and the Dutch East Indies, the Maritime Provinces and Vladivostok, one step at a time, as in Korea and Manchuria, pausing intermittently to consolidate and then continuing as soon as the intervening obstacles can be overcome by diplomacy or force. With such dreams of empire cherished by many, and with an army and navy capable of taking the bit in their own teeth and running away with it regardless of the restraining influence of the saner heads of the Government in Tokyo (a risk which unquestionably exists and of which we have already had ample evidence in the Manchurian affair), we would be reprehensibly somnolent if we were to trust to the security of treaty restraints or international comity to safeguard our own interests or, indeed, our own property.

In a confidential conversation with the Netherlands Minister, General Pabst, a shrewd and rational colleague with long experience in Japan, he said that in his opinion the Japanese Navy, imbued as it is with patriotic and chauvinistic fervor and with a desire to emulate the deeds of the Army in order not to lose caste with the public, would be perfectly capable of descending upon and occupying Guam at a moment of crisis or, indeed, at any other moment, regardless of the ulterior consequences.

I do not think that such an insane step is likely now, yet the action of the Army in Manchuria, judged from the point of view of treaty rights and international comity, might also have been judged as insensate. The important fact is that under present circumstances, and indeed under circumstances which may continue in future (although the pendulum of chauvinism throughout Japanese history has swung to and fro in periodic cycles of intensity and temporary relaxation), the armed forces of the country are perfectly capable of overriding the restraining control of the Government and of committing what might well amount to national hara-kiri in a mistaken conception of patriotism.

When Japanese speak of Japan's being the "stabilizing factor" and the "guardian of peace" of East Asia, what they have in mind is a *Pax Japonica* with eventual complete commercial control and, in the minds of some, eventual complete political control of East Asia. While Ambassador Saito may have been misquoted in a recent issue of the *Philadelphia Bulletin* as saying that Japan will be prepared to fight to maintain that conception of peace, nevertheless that is precisely what is in the minds of many Japanese today. There is a swashbuckling temper in the country, largely developed by military propaganda, which can lead Japan during the next few years, or in the next few generations, to any extremes unless the saner minds in the Government prove able to cope with it and to restrain the country from national suicide.

The efficacy of such restraint is always problematical. Plots against the Government are constantly being hatched. We hear, for instance, that a number of young officers of the 3rd Infantry Regiment and students from the Military Academy in Tokyo were found on November 22 to have planned to assassinate various high members of the Government, including Count Makino, and that students of the Military Academy were confined to the school area for a few days after the discovery of that plot. A similar alleged plot to attack the politicians at the opening of the extraordinary session of the Diet—another May 15 incident—is also said to have been discovered and nipped in the bud. Such plots aim to form a military dictatorship. It is of course impossible to substantiate these rumors, but they are much talked about and it is unlikely that so much smoke would materialize without some fire.

I wish that more Americans would come out here and live here and gradually come to sense the real potential risks and dangers of the situation instead of speaking and writing academically on a subject which they know nothing whatever about, thereby contributing ammunition to the Japanese military and extremists who are stronger than they have been for many a day. The idea that a great body of liberal thought lying just beneath the surface since 1931 would be sufficiently strong to emerge and assume control with a little foreign encouragement is thoroughly mistaken. The liberal thought is there, but it is inarticulate and largely impotent, and in all probability will remain so for some time to come.

Perhaps this gives the impression that we at the Embassy are developing something of an "anti-Japanese" complex. This is not the case. One can dislike and disagree with certain members of a family without necessarily feeling hostility to the family itself. For me there are no finer people in the world than the best type of Japanese. I am rather inclined to place Hirota among them; if he could have his way unhampered by the military I believe that he would steer the country into safer and saner channels.

One of these friends once sadly remarked to us: "We Japanese are always putting our worst foot foremost, and we are too proud to explain ourselves." Theirs has been and is a "bungling diplomacy." They habitually play their cards badly. While it is true that the military and the extremists are primarily responsible for the "bungling diplomacy" of Japan, the Japanese as a race tend to be inarticulate, more at home in action than with words. But the military and the extremists know little and care little about Japan's relations with other countries, and it is the desire of people like Shiratori, Amau, and other Government officials to enhance their own prestige at home and to safeguard their future careers by standing in well with the military that brings about much of the trouble. Perhaps we should be grateful that they so often give their hand away in advance.

But all this does not make us less sympathetic to the better elements in Japanese life or in any sense "anti-Japanese." Japan is a country of paradoxes and extremes, of great wisdom and of great stupidity, an apt illustration of which may be found in connection with the naval conversations; while the naval authorities and the press have been stoutly maintaining that Japan cannot adequately defend her shores with less than parity, the press and the public, in articles, speeches, and interviews, have at the same time been valiantly boasting that the Japanese Navy is today stronger than the American Navy and could easily defeat us in case of war. In such an atmosphere it is difficult, very difficult, for a foreigner to keep a detached and balanced point of view. We in the Embassy are making that effort, I hope with success, and in the meantime about all we can do is to keep the boat from rocking dangerously. Constructive work is at present impossible. Our efforts are concentrated on the thwarting of destructive influences.

In view of all these considerations, I have little hesitation in reiterating and emphasizing the potential dangers of the situation and the prime importance of American national preparedness to meet it. As a nation we have taken the lead in international efforts toward the restriction and reduction of armaments. We have had hopes that the movement would be progressive, but the conditions of world affairs as they have developed during the past twelve years since the Washington Conference have not afforded fruitful ground for such progress. Unless we are prepared to subscribe to a *Pax Japonica* in the Far East, with all that this movement, as conceived and interpreted by Japan, is bound to entail, we should rapidly build up our Navy to treaty strength, and if and when the Washington Naval Treaty expires we should continue to maintain the present ratio with Japan regardless of cost, a peacetime insurance both to cover and to reduce the risk of war. In the meantime every proper step should be taken to avoid or to offset the belligerent utterances of jingoes no less than the defeatist statements of pacifists in the United States, many of which find their way into the Japanese press, because the utterances of the former tend to inflame public sentiment against our country, while the statements of the latter convey an impression of American weakness, irresolution, and bluff.

My own opinion, although it can be but guesswork, is that Japan will under no circumstances invite a race in naval armaments, and that having found our position on the ratios to be adamant, further propositions will be forthcoming within the next two years before the Washington Treaty expires, or before our present building program is fully completed. When the United States has actually completed its naval-building program to treaty limits, then, it is believed, and probably not before then, Japan will realize that we are in earnest and will seek a compromise. We believe that Japan's naval policy has been formulated on the premises that the United States would never build up to treaty strength, a premise which has been strengthened in the past by the naval policy of the past two administrations, by the apparent strength of the pacifist element in the United States, and more recently by the effects of the depression.

While it is true that Japan, by sedulously forming and stimulating public opinion to demand parity with the United States in principle if not in fact, has burned her bridges behind her, nevertheless the Japanese leaders are past masters at remolding public opinion in the country by skillful propaganda to suit new conditions. Once Japan is convinced that parity is impossible, it is difficult to believe that she will allow matters to come to a point where competitive building becomes unavoidable. With a national budget for 1935–1936 totaling 2,193,414,289 yen, of which about 47% is for the Army and Navy, and with an estimated national debt in 1936 of 9,880,000,000 yen, nearly equal to the Cabinet Bureau of Statistics estimate of the national income for 1930, namely, 10,635,000,000 yen; with her vast outlay in Manchuria, her already heavily taxed population, and the crying need of large sections of her people for relief funds, it is difficult to see how Japan could afford to embark upon a program of maintaining naval parity with the United States and Great Britain.

Once we have registered our position firmly and unequivocally, we can then afford to await the next move on the part of Japan. I believe that it will come.

So far as we can evaluate here the proceedings of the recent preliminary naval conversations in London, I am of the opinion that the most important and the most valuable result issuing therefrom has been the apparent tendency toward closer Anglo-American co-operation in the Far East. If we can count in future—again as a direct result of Japan's "bungling diplomacy"—on a solid and united front between the United States and Great Britain in meeting Japan's flaunting of treaty rights and her unrestrained ambitions to control East Asia, the future may well assume a brighter aspect for all of us.

Theodore Roosevelt enunciated the policy "Speak softly and carry a big stick." If our diplomacy in the Far East is to achieve favorable results, and if we are to reduce the risk of an eventual war with Japan to a minimum, that is the only way to proceed. Such a war may be unthinkable, and so it is, but the specter of it is always present and will be present for some time to come. It would be criminally shortsighted to discard it from our calculations, and the best possible way to avoid it is to be adequately prepared, for preparedness is a cold fact which even the chauvinists, the military, the patriots, and the ultranationalists in Japan, for all their bluster concerning "provocative measures" in the United States, can grasp and understand. The Soviet Ambassador recently told me that a prominent Japanese had said to him that the most important factor in avoiding a Japanese attack on the Maritime Provinces was the intensive Soviet military preparations in Siberia and Vladivostok. I believe this to be true, and again, and yet again, I urge that our own country be adequately prepared to meet all eventualities in the Far East.

Of course I have conveyed these views to our Government.

EXPLAINING THE DIARIES AND DISPATCHES

January 22, 1935

On reading back over this diary I really wonder how I have the courage to send it to anyone, it is such a patchwork and crazy quilt and so many of the comments so rapidly set down require further elucidation or discussion. The field of Japanese-American relations, for instance, is so broad and so impossible to cover in a running document of this kind that my day-to-day comment, hastily expressed, might well give erroneous impressions. Our official dispatches, taken as a whole, probably cover the field fairly well, and from the point of view of history they must furnish the criterion. The only thing the diary can do is to supply a few illustrations to the text, but these illustrations, historically, should never be considered without the text. They are too likely to give one-sided and inadequate impressions.

Our dispatches, also, must be read as a whole and over a period of time to get the correct picture. Some of our dispatches, for instance, might be regarded as inconsistent. For instance, one of our dispatches on the naval conversations (No. 1087), which I am told was sent to the President, was based on the idea that the Japanese as a whole are absolutely intransigent regarding the question of naval parity and that there is complete solidarity in the country on that issue. That is absolutely true at present, but a fortnight later I wrote another dispatch (No. 1102) conveying the idea—though only as guesswork and so stated—that when the Japanese eventually find that we mean business in maintaining the present ratios, and that we intend to build and do build up to treaty strength, and propose to continue that policy even if it means a naval race, they, the Japanese, will seek a compromise rather than face such a naval race, and that although they have burned their bridges behind them, they are capable of remolding public opinion and policy over a period of time—even during the two years elapsing before the treaty expires. This, as I said, can be but guesswork, but everybody in the Embassy, including the Counselor and the Naval and Military Attachés, agrees that it is a sound guess. So the two dispatches were not actually inconsistent: the first dealt with the present, while the second had to do with the future if certain things happen, namely, the clear and factual demonstration of our determination to construct and maintain our navy on a 5–3 proportion. I only hope that the President, if he saw both dispatches, will get this point.

WHY AMERICA SHOULD NOT REPEAL
THE EXCLUSION ACT

January 27, 1935

The Bishop Reifsniders, just returned from America, and the Walter Edges, on their way around the world, came to tea. Reifsnider told me of his talks with Hull, Castle, and others, chiefly with regard to a repeal of the discriminatory provisions of the Exclusion Act of 1924. He tried to see Hearst in California to ascertain his attitude, but Hearst was ill and couldn't see him. I do not think that this is the time to approach the question; of course the Act always rankles and always will, but to repeal the discriminatory provisions now would be interpreted by many as an indication of weakness and as a desire to placate the martial spirit of Japan, and while lovely editorials would be written about our graceful action in recognizing Japan as an equal, it would not in the slightest degree alter Japanese policy or tone down the military propaganda. On the contrary I can see some Japanese writers arguing that having recognized Japan as an equal on the immigration issue, it would now be all the more appropriate and logical for us to recognize her as an equal on the naval issue. Besides, who can ever predict with certainty that any bill will pass the Senate? We thought our Lausanne Treaty with Turkey secure, and, so far as I am aware, the administration thought the World Court Protocol would pass, yet both were defeated. To bring up the repeal of the discriminatory provisions of the Exclusion Act and to have the effort fail would be disastrous. Better let things lie for the present.

WHY OUR FLEET MANEUVERS IN THE
PACIFIC OCEAN AIDED PEACE

April 1, 1935

Dr. Ivan Lee Holt, recently elected President of the Federal

Council of the Churches of Christ in America, came to see me on his way home from Shanghai. I had arranged an interview for him with Hirota, to whom he merely wishes to deliver a message of good will. He asked me what position I thought he ought to take as regards the efforts of the churches at home to have the scheduled naval maneuvers in the Pacific canceled on the ground that they would constitute a provocation and threat to Japan.

I went to the bat hard on this issue and told him that I thought the movement against the maneuvers was both nefarious and actually dangerous. The maneuvers, which were purely routine and had been arranged some two years ago, would not come within 1500 miles of the shores of Japan; we have two oceans to protect and it would be not only the height of absurdity but a confession of weakness and fear of Japan if we were to cancel them. If we are to shape our policies and actions solely with a view to pleasing the Japanese, it will make them more cocky than ever and simply invite aggressive tactics on their part and will give them the impression that the so-called pacifist element in our country is so strong that they, the Japanese, can do whatever they please and ride roughshod over our rightful and reasonable interests without any concern whatever as to protective action on our part—a distinctly unhealthy impression to convey.

We want peace, not war, but the surest way to court war is to follow the weak and defeatist policy advocated by some of the churches, and the best way to ensure peace is to follow the wise policy of our Government, preparedness without aggressiveness, and protection of our rightful interests interpreted in the spirit of the good neighbor. If Japan sees fit to interpret our routine naval maneuvers as saber-rattling she has only herself to thank, for it was certainly Japan which began the rattling, and the more we adopt a spineless attitude, the more will Japan be tempted to unsheathe the sword. There is nothing that the Oriental respects so much as strength, and nothing that conduces to his aggressiveness so much as weakness.

I didn't say all this in precisely these words, but I did talk with the utmost frankness because the attitude of some of the churches at home disturbs me greatly and Dr. Holt probably has a good deal of influence as President of the Federal Council. He looked mildly surprised at my attitude because he had told me that I am regarded as a stanch supporter of church interests, but I think he got the point and when he left he at least implied that he would be guided by what I had said. If I do possess the reputation of being a good

friend and supporter of the church workers out here—which I am—
my advice on this point may be listened to with more respect than
otherwise.

HOW GERMANY'S REARMAMENT HELPED JAPAN

April 2, 1935

Stoïcesco, the Rumanian Chargé d'Affaires, and later Pabst came
in for political talks. The German declaration of rearmament has
certainly brought about a sort of *bouleversement* in the general situation, all in favor of Japanese interests. The increased tension in
Europe absorbs most of the available attention of the foreign powers,
with the exception of the United States, which are interested in the
Far East. Japan can feel safer from foreign interference than at any
time since the termination of the Anglo-Japanese Alliance and
therefore has a distinct advantage in political negotiations with
other countries. Amau denied yesterday that any steps had been
taken for a Soviet-Japanese nonaggression pact. Indeed, under
present circumstances, Japan has no need for one., Developments
are playing directly into Japanese hands. Amau said that Japan has
no alliance or ententes except the more or less defunct sort of informal understanding that exists with Poland, and we have indications that there is an intimate exchange of views and information
going on between Japan and Germany. But all this is nebulous, and
the main fact is that Japan can now "sit pretty" and carry on more
or less as she wishes, with the assurance that the European powers
are much too busy at home to bother very much about the Far East.
This situation is not going to make our diplomacy any easier.

A GREAT JAPANESE GENTLEMAN ON JAPAN

May 22, 1935

Big Japanese dinner given by the Grand Master of Ceremonies
and Viscountess Matsudaira at the Maple Club, including Count
Makino, Baron Hayashi, members of the Imperial Household Ministry, and all the chiefs of mission and their wives, with the exception of the chargés d'affaires ad interim. The chargé d'affaires *en
titre* were there. It was a brilliant function.

After dinner I sat with Count Makino and had an interesting
talk, in the course of which he told me of a conversation he had
just had with Dubosc, editor of the Paris *Temps,* who has been

traveling in Japan. Dubosc apparently told Count Makino that he considered the political situation in Japan as "dangerous" owing to the strife and corruption among the political parties and the risk of military Fascism on the one hand and of Communism on the other.

Makino said to Dubosc (as the former repeated the conversation to me), "When you return to Paris and make your report or write your editorials on the domestic situation in Japan, cut out the word 'danger' from your vocabulary. We have a safeguard in Japan which other countries do not possess in the same degree, namely the Imperial Household. There will never be 'danger' from military Fascism or Communism or from any other kind of 'ism' simply because the Emperor is supreme and will *always* have the last word."

I have never heard the old man speak so emphatically or exhibit so much patriotic emotion; his eyes filled with tears and he had to wipe his glasses. The manner in which he talked tonight—his emphasis and emotion—gave a momentary revelation of the intensity of their devotion to the Throne, and I think that the force of that devotion throughout the nation—in spite of all the bickerings and political agitations and even the assassinations—or perhaps because of them—is stronger, much stronger, than foreigners generally appreciate. At any rate, I was greatly impressed tonight by this momentary glimpse into the mind of the usually suave, courteous, and eminently gentle Count Makino, whom I shall always regard as one of the world's greatest gentlemen.

MR. AND MRS. AMERICA VISIT JAPAN

June 20, 1935

Mr. and Mrs. America called at the Embassy this morning in the course of their round of official visits. They are two life-size American dolls, sent over to Japan on a "good-will mission" by the Mayor of New York. They are not only life size but amazingly lifelike. After looking into the young lady's lovely eyes, Alice said it was astonishing not to find a soul behind them. The visit has stirred up quite a lot of controversy which has taken the form of open letters to the *Advertiser,* one correspondent asserting that the whole thing is silly and undignified and that the reception of the dolls by the Prime Minister and the American Ambassador—who allegedly served the dolls with iced tea—was absurd and placed both Japanese and Americans in a ridiculous light. Other correspondents disagreed with that view.

What happened is that the Board of Tourist Industry of the Japanese Railways suggested to the Mayor of New York that a "goodwill mission" of two American dolls would be warmly welcomed in Japan and Mayor LaGuardia took it up and the dolls were dispatched after appropriate ceremonies in New York. They were given, according to the press, the suite de luxe on the Japanese liner which brought them over and they are being taken all over Japan by train, bus, airplane, ferry, and every other means of transportation. Of course, the thing is merely propaganda for the Japanese Tourist Bureau—a publicity stunt pure and simple—but when informed that the dolls would call on us at the Embassy I could not possibly have refused to receive them without giving unnecessary offense and creating an unpleasant impression. However, I did take the precaution of consulting a Japanese officer of the America-Japan Society, and he, after investigation, advised me to go ahead.

There were several reasons for doing so: first, the dolls were to be received by the Prime Minister and several members of the cabinet and by the Mayor of Tokyo; second, the sentiment for dolls in Japan is deep and universal, arising no doubt from the Japanese devotion to children; there are annual doll festivals and doll societies; third, I believe in supporting American tourism in Japan; the more Americans who come and travel in Japan, the better, barring certain exceptional incidents and cases, for Japanese-American relations. So Alice and I received the dolls on the back terrace, with most of our staff there to see the fun; although Mrs. America's arm dropped off as she entered, the accident was quickly repaired and they were seated in two chairs while we shook hands with them in front of a battery of press cameras. Iced tea was served, as customarily, to the Japanese who accompanied the dolls. The whole thing didn't last ten minutes.

Later there was a big public meeting in Hibiya Hall, attended largely by children, at which the Mayor of Tokyo personally appeared and made a welcoming speech, and the least I could do was to send Andrews, a Third Secretary, to read a speech for me in which I said that I was glad to support the visit. My speech was given a light touch by the remark: "Mr. and Mrs. America have one advantage over other visitors to Japan: they speak and understand Japanese precisely as well as they speak and understand English." The Japanese press unfortunately failed to catch the point of this intended delicate humor and quoted me as saying that the dolls spoke and understood Japanese perfectly.

Letters to the *Advertiser* are still continuing daily, some very nice and others very horrid. The incident really hasn't deserved so much attention. The Japanese, I am sure, were glad that I entered into the fun of the thing and respected the sentiment for the doll in this country.

RUSSIA'S AMBASSADOR SEES TROUBLE
AHEAD FOR AMERICA AND JAPAN

July 17, 1935

I called today on Soviet Ambassador Yurenev, who is departing soon on leave of absence, and our conversation opened with a discussion of Russian-Japanese relations. The Ambassador said that while certain difficult questions were at issue between the two countries he was not at all anxious concerning the outcome because the Japanese did not want war and were not prepared for war. He thought the questions which I had to handle between Japan and the United States were much more difficult than his own questions and that the outlook for Japanese-American relations was much less favorable than that of Japanese-Soviet relations. He implied that he thought the future relations between Japan and the United States were ominous. I took issue with the Ambassador on this point and after enumerating and dealing briefly with each of the important issues between Japan and the United States, I said that I was convinced that they could be amicably solved or, if not solved, they could at least remain in abeyance.

Mr. Yurenev said that the situation regarding the Soviet-Manchukuo frontier dispute had somewhat altered since our last conversation. The present intention is to set up a commission which will deal not with the delimitation of the frontier but only with the specific controversies arising therefrom. He had first taken the position, as he told me in our last talk, that the Soviets would be willing to deal either with the Japanese or the Manchukuoans on the commission but not with both. His Government has now, however, agreed to meet representatives both of Japan and Manchukuo on the basis of parity. In other words, there would be as many Soviet delegates as there were delegates from Japan and Manchukuo together. Mr. Hirota has not yet accepted this proposal and he expected that the negotiations would continue over a considerable period, particularly as the Japanese military were very hard to please in the matter. He thought there would be a lot of discussion and negotiation concerning the agenda, place of meeting, et cetera, before the commission could be set up and he himself would have to conduct these negotiations, so that he saw not much hope of getting away to Karuizawa this summer.

FAREWELL TALK WITH HIROTA

July 18, 1935

I called on the Minister for Foreign Affairs this morning and told him that having been more than three years in Japan my Government had accorded me a leave of absence and that I was sailing for the United States tomorrow. Said that I expected to return to Tokyo sometime in the late autumn. The Minister was good enough to say that he hoped I would return without fail because changing ambassadors always caused a certain amount of disturbance and an undesirable interim during which the new ambassador and the government to which he was accredited had to get used to each other. He thought it most important that no change should be made especially at the present time. I replied that so far as I was aware there was no intention to make a change at present and I fully expected to return to Tokyo.

I said that on arriving in Washington I would of course report directly to the President and to the Secretary of State and tell them of my observations and impressions concerning the situation in Japan and the situation between our two countries. If the Minister should desire to express any views, I would be only too happy to communicate them to the President and to Mr. Hull. Mr. Hirota replied by reminding me of the statement he had made to me when he first took office, to the effect that he considered good relations between the United States and Japan to be of paramount importance and that he intended to make the improvement of those relations the cornerstone of his policy. He said that while our relations had been difficult two years ago he felt that they were now distinctly good and he saw no reason whatever why they should not remain good. It was his purpose to do everything in his power to contribute to that most desirable result. He added that in his opinion the relations between Japan and certain other countries were very much more difficult and less satisfactory than the present relations between Japan and the United States.

In this connection he mentioned the naval situation and said that unless there was some prospect of coming to an agreement and concluding a treaty this year, he thought it much better to leave matters in abeyance and to maintain the present "peaceful" situation. He said he thought the most important thing to avoid was the bringing of pressure by one country on another, which could only cause irritation. The Japanese Navy had no plan at present and was content to let things remain as they are for the time being. He thought that a conference would have to be held before the end of the year but it could be a purely formal meeting and could adjourn for a year or two without necessarily stirring up controversies. Mr. Hirota gave me the impression that the Japanese Navy was in a less exacting frame of mind than it has been but he did not say this in so many words. The idea expressed was that if given sufficient time a good many difficult problems could be smoothed out.

A five months' leave after three years in Japan interrupts the diary at this point, but the following item seems worth including for the record:

REPORT TO THE WHITE HOUSE

August 4-5, 1935. Washington

We were met by most of the Far Eastern Division, all of whom, especially Hornbeck, their chief, were exceptionally cordial and helpful during my three visits to Washington. Met Billy Phillips at the Carlton and had a long talk with Secretary Hull, whom I had not known before. Saw the President, who was quite affectionate. He indicated complete optimism, cheerfulness, and energy. During my three talks with him I was astonished by his power of concentration in the midst of intensely busy days and his detailed grasp of the problems of my post. He said that the fact that he had not written me very often was a compliment as it meant that no mistakes had been made. Saw nearly everybody in the Department and did a great many jobs. Went to two of the open-air concerts on the Potomac.

BACK IN TOKYO

December 17, 1935

Here beginneth the second lesson—the first having extended from June 6, 1932, to July 19, 1935.

I have neither the time nor the intention to mention or to discuss at the start the various new or old problems facing us on our return from five months' leave of absence, save to say that there are plenty of them and that comment thereon will crop up from time to time.

Went to see Baron de Bassompierre, the Belgian Ambassador. He broke the unwelcome news that I would be acting Dean of the Diplomatic Corps from now until next September because he was at present in official mourning for the late Queen and in January would go on a long leave of absence. That means that I must make the periodical speeches before the Emperor four times a year and attend to lots of other official ceremonies at this exacting Court. In fact, the text of the speeches for January 5 has already been circulated to the colleagues with the notation that I, as Vice-Doyen, would deliver it, a rather terrifying task.

In the afternoon I called on Hirota at the Gaimusho merely to report my return, and in our brief conversation nothing of interest came up except that Hirota observed with a twinkle in his eye that the Japanese press had recently shifted its customary broadsides of vituperation from the United States to England. He didn't use just those words but that is precisely what he meant. Sir Frederick Leith Ross, chairman of the British Financial Mission to China, is the nigger in the woodpile and is generally regarded here as responsible for the financial and political machinations in China which have led to the recent troubles in the north—in other words, tampering with Japan's "stabilizing influence" in that allegedly misguided country.

A YEAR OF WRATH BEGINS

New Year's Day, 1936

Life has taught me a good many things but nothing more definite than the fallacy of making New Year's resolutions. If you know you're going to break a treaty, it's much better not to sign one, and as I know by long experience that I am most certainly going to break all the nice resolutions made on January 1, philosophy now dictates the unwisdom of making them at all. So I no longer prepare the old charts (à la Benjamin Franklin) of just how many hours shall be spent in educational reading, piano practice, exercise, limitation of drinks and smokes, etc., but shamble across the threshold into the new year with a carefree thumb-nose at my New England conscience, which it has taken me all of half a century to conquer. I shall in all probability waste valuable time even more in 1936 than in 1935—and why worry? Life is good, but only if you don't take it too seriously, and those good old New England forebears of ours (bless their memory) certainly did their best to make it hell. Yet in such a job as mine, how can life be other than serious?

For the first time since 1933 the Emperor held Court, although the Empress, having recently given birth to her second son, did not appear. However, this did not exclude the ladies, who came in their court trains and swept past the Imperial presence with the required three curtsies, in all their glory. As acting Dean of the Diplomatic Corps I had to lead the long line, and I must say that the extent of our own Embassy was rather staggering. Our commissioned personnel and wives totals thirty-five persons and most of them were there.

One's march across the big throne room is too brief really to size up the spectacle, but it is a gorgeous one just the same—the Emperor standing before the throne, the solid phalanx of Imperial princes to the Emperor's right and the princesses on his left, and behind them the line of high court officials in all the glittering splendor of their gold-encrusted uniforms. Some of the colleagues groused because they and their ladies have to get all dressed up merely to file past the Emperor with no opportunity either before or afterward to mingle with the Court, a procedure which they say exists in no other Court in the world. I still maintain that the unhurried dignity of the Japanese Court is unsurpassed anywhere, but it seems to me that at the last Court in 1933 we were at least offered a champagne buffet afterward; this year there was not even that. I myself had to be received by the Grand Master of Ceremonies of the Empress in order to request him to express to Her Majesty the New Year's good wishes of the Diplomatic Corps, but that was all and we were out of the palace in record time.

HOW ROOSEVELT'S NEW YEAR WARNING STRUCK JAPAN

January 5, 1936

The President's message to Congress was published here in extensive summary with long quotations but without any editorial comment whatever in the vernacular press; I rather think that the Foreign Office has passed out word to stay off it in order to avoid the vituperative reaction in which some of the papers would surely have indulged. Amau and other officials took refuge in the statement that they hadn't read the address. The President's remark that any nation which chose to do so might fit the shoe to its own foot was a masterly stroke.

There was some pretty plain speaking, directed obviously at Italy, Germany, and Japan, with such comments as: "A point has been reached where the peoples of America must take cognizance of the growing ill-will and marked trends toward aggression, increasing armaments, and shortening tempers—a situation which has in it many elements leading to the tragedy of war." "Nations seeking expansion, seeking rectification of injustices springing from former wars, and seeking outlets for trade, population, and even their own peaceful contributions to the progress of civilization fail to demonstrate the patience necessary to attain reasonable and legitimate objectives by peaceful negotiations and by appeal to the finer instincts of world justice. They have hitherto impatiently reverted to the old belief in the law of the sword or to the fantastic conception that they alone are chosen to fulfill a mission and that all others must and shall learn from and be subject to them. I recognize that these words, which I have chosen with deliberation, will not be popular among any nation that chooses to fit this shoe to its foot. . . . I emphasize on you the gravity of the situation confronting the people of the world. Peace is jeopardized by the few, not the many, and is threatened by those who are seeking selfish power."

This I call courageous statesmanship, and whether or not it will have any real effect, except to help pass the neutrality legislation and armament budgets which the President desires, it will inevitably sink deep into the consciousness and conscience of those at whom it is directed. It won't stop the Japanese push into China— for nothing can stop that except defeat in war—but it may conceivably exert a moderating influence on their methods and tactics; it may possibly tend to slow up the movement temporarily. The Japanese didn't like Stimson, but knowing Roosevelt's predilections as a big-Navy man, and with this public warning—"A point has been reached where the peoples of America must take cognizance"— on top of it, I rather think that they will pray for a Republican victory at the next election.

HIROTA ANSWERS ROOSEVELT

January 21, 1936

Cabled about Hirota's speech before the Diet. He made a sort of reply to the President's speech before Congress, mentioning no names, but criticizing "foreign statesmen" who lay down the law about foreign countries without knowing the facts. Of course the Japanese will give him a high mark for allegedly outsmarting the Americans. The pertinent remarks of Hirota were:

> It is to be regretted that there are abroad statesmen of repute who seem determined to impose upon others their private convictions as to how the world should be ordered, and who are apt to denounce those who oppose their dictates as if they were disturbers of peace. No one is qualified to talk world peace unless he not only knows the national aspirations and obligations of his country but also understands and appreciates the standpoints of other countries. The understanding and appreciation of another country's standpoint is often attainable through the understanding and appreciation of that country's culture and civilization. We have succeeded in building up our national strength and prestige by adding and adapting to our civilization Occidental art and science, which we have imported during the past years. Now it is time for us, I believe, to try to introduce our arts and culture to other lands, and thus contribute toward international good understanding and to the enrichment of the world civilization and the promotion of the peace and happiness of mankind.

SENATOR PITTMAN TELLS OFF JAPAN

February 11, 1936

Received from the Department a cablegram quoting the comments of the Secretary on Senator Pittman's inflammatory speech in the Senate about the danger to the United States of Japanese aggression. Mr. Hull said that he had not been consulted about the speech and had had no hand in its preparation—of course. These telegrams from the Department are very helpful to us in checking up on press reports. Of course the Pittman speech was utterly jingoistic and it is quite right that the American press editorials should excoriate it as they appear to have done. But just the same I personally and unofficially am not sorry that it was delivered and believe that its net result will be helpful rather than harmful—or rather that its advantages will outweigh its disadvantages.

From the American point of view it should serve to modify the outcry which will be raised by the pacifists against our big military and naval budgets. In Japan it should tend to indicate to the Government and public that we are not, as many believe here, a country ruled by our peace organizations and women pacifists, and that when slapped in the face often and hard enough a time might come when we wouldn't turn the other cheek. The Japanese, I think, tend to forget history, which shows that the American people are among the most inflammable in the world; they forget the sudden wave of anger which swept over our country like a forest fire almost overnight in 1898 and brought on the war with Spain against the wishes and intentions of the Government, Congress, and the great majority of the public, and there has been so much peace talk and activity since the Great War that they seem to regard our action in 1917 as in a forgotten era. I am therefore not at all sure but that an occasional speech like Pittman's is useful in making the Japanese at least stop to think; it may penetrate to the extent of making them realize that there is a point beyond which they cannot interfere with our rights and interests in the Far East in general and in China in particular without risk of retaliation.

Let the executive branch of our Government continue the eminently wise policy which it has followed in recent years of avoiding unnecessary friction and irritation while recording its position at every step, but meanwhile let American public opinion, whether in Congress or in the press, convey the idea that we have not the slightest intention of pulling out of the Far East and that we have every intention of protecting our commercial and industrial and other interests even in the face of Japan's so-called "stabilizing influence" in East Asia, which means, in effect, a *Pax Japonica*—East Asia for the Japanese exclusively. We have allowed the door to be closed on our nose in Manchuria; perhaps we couldn't have avoided it without war; we shall no doubt allow further encroachments in other parts of China, but the time is likely to come when the American people will begin to get just a little impatient, and if at that time some incident should occur (as is always possible), even an incident less dramatic than the blowing up of the *Maine,* the fat might well be in the fire overnight.

I can't help feeling that just once in a while it is healthy to let the Japanese know that fire still exists in what they may believe to be an extinct volcano. It may tend to slow down their acquisitive program and somewhat to implement our diplomacy. Therefore I am not at all so angry with Pittman as I probably ought to be.

3

FROM ABORTIVE REVOLUTION TO OPEN WAR

(February 26, 1936–July 13, 1937)

JAPAN'S DRIVE for world power began at home. Ever since the onset of the world depression, successive Japanese governments had failed to provide an outlet for the energies of the same elements in the younger generation who had followed Hitler in Germany. Only the Army offered these young men their chance—but the civil authorities kept trying to hold the Army in check. In 1932, rebellious young officers assassinated some of Japan's leading statesmen but never came close to gaining power themselves. In 1936, they struck again. This time they attempted a revolution of sorts and though their bid for power failed and some of their leaders were sentenced to death and executed, their failure served only to inspire them with dreams of foreign conquest more dazzling than their plans for domestic revolt.

THE LIGHTNING STRIKES:
TWO TELEGRAMS THAT MADE HISTORY

Telegram Sent

To: Secstate Washington
36 February 26, 10 A.M. 1936

The military took partial possession of the Government and city early this morning and it is reported have assassinated several prominent men. It is impossible as yet to confirm anything. The news correspondents are not permitted to send telegrams or to telephone abroad.

This telegram is being sent primarily as a test message, to ascertain if our code telegrams will be transmitted. Code room please acknowledge immediately upon receipt.

GREW

Telegram Sent

To: Secstate Washington
RUSH
37 February 26, noon. 1936. Section 1.
Embassy's 36 February 26, 10 A.M.

1. It now appears fairly certain that former Premier Admiral Saito, former Lord Keeper of the Privy Seal Count Makino, Grand Chamberlain Admiral Suzuki, and General Watanabe, Inspector General of Military Education, have been assassinated. It is also reported that Finance Minister Takahashi and the Chief of the Metropolitan Police Board have been wounded.*

2. The military have established a cordon around the district containing the Government administration offices and the Imperial palace and do not permit ingress without Army passes. Telephonic communication with the administrative offices has also been stopped. The stock exchange has been closed.

Section 2.

3. It is now reported that Premier Okada, Home Minister Goto, and former War Minister Hayashi were also assassinated and that Finance Minister Takahashi has died of his wounds. The Embassy cannot confirm any of these rumors.

* See photographs Nos. 4, 5, 6, and 7.

4. So far there has been no disorder and no street fighting, as far as the Embassy is aware. The troops taking part in the uprising appear to be under perfect discipline and are not interfering with the normal affairs of the people. Until the nature and probable results of the uprising are better understood by the Embassy, however, the Embassy is advising those who ask to remain at home. There appears to be absolutely no antiforeign feeling involved in the affair.

Section 3.

5. A mimeographed statement was left by groups of soldiers at each of the principal newspaper offices this morning. The statement alleged that the present Government has been drifting away from the true spirit of Japan and that it had usurped the prerogatives of the Emperor. As evidence of this the statement cited the signing of the London Naval Treaty and the dismissal of General Mazaki. It continued rather vaguely with an expression translated by the U.P. about as follows: "If this condition is permitted to continue, the relations of Japan to China, Russia, Britain, and the United States will become 'explosive in nature.'" The statement was signed by Captain Nonaka and Captain Ando, both of the Third Infantry Regiment stationed in Tokyo. According to the soldiers who delivered this statement, another announcement will be made at five o'clock this evening and at that time "a new law of state" will be promulgated. The Embassy's informant believes that certain constitutional prerogatives will be suspended. He likened the existing situation to the Batista *coup d'état* in Cuba.

Section 4. [Paraphrase]

6. The uprising, as far as can be ascertained by the Embassy, is in the nature of a *coup d'état* engineered by the young Fascist element in the Army and intended to destroy the entire group of elder statesmen who have been advisers to the Throne and thereby effect the so-called "Showa Restoration." Presumably to prevent anyone from obtaining access and securing an Imperial Mandate which would interfere with the plans of the Army group, the Emperor himself is apparently being held in the palace incommunicado. The trial of Aizawa, murderer of General Nagata, which has excited the feelings of the Fascist element in the Army, and the recent election which returned an unexpectedly large number of more candidates who are liberal, appear to be the immediate causes of the uprising. Latest reports indicate that Admiral Osumi, Minister of the Navy, has assumed the position of Acting Prime Minister and that General

Mazaki is the leading spirit in the affair. The movement, down to the last detail, appears to have been thoroughly organized in advance. [End of paraphrase]

7. The Embassy has just learned from a fairly reliable source that Count Makino is safe.

GREW

THE MURDER OF VISCOUNT SAITO

February 27, 1936

This is a dreadful time and I have just returned from a harrowing experience—calling at the Saito * house, the very one where he was murdered yesterday, being ushered up to the little room where his body lay on the floor under a sheet, probably the same room where he was killed, kneeling to burn incense and then turning to the mourning family and finding myself face to face with dear Viscountess Saito herself. Yesterday she was in the hospital, recovering from the wounds inflicted on herself; she must have dragged herself out, her arm in a sling, to be with the body of her beloved husband.

She asked if I wished to see his face and then removed the sheet; there was a bullet wound visible (only one of his thirty-six wounds), but he looked peaceful enough. How we loved him and admired and respected him. He had a winning smile, always, and his white hair gave him a distinction quite apart from the distinction he had won in his many high posts and useful life. Only a few hours before the assassinations he sat at our table beside Alice, jolly and gay, and his wife next to me, and opposite me was Admiral Suzuki, who lies at the point of death from his own wounds.

Today, when I had paid my respects, Viscountess Saito said to me while we were both still kneeling in front of each other beside the body that her husband had never before seen the sound films and that he had loved the picture at our Embassy and that she knew he would wish her to thank us for having given him such a happy last evening. I was really too much moved to do more in reply than to convey Alice's sympathy too. Who could have foreseen that he was leaving our Embassy that night, and probably Admiral Suzuki too, to go straight to his death by bullet and bayonet in his own peaceful little Japanese home?

These assassinations have stirred us terribly—Saito, Takahashi, Watanabe dead and Suzuki probably fatally wounded. Thank heaven that Count Makino escaped; he was warned in time and

* See photograph No. 7.

managed to leave the hot-spring hotel where he was staying and find some refuge just before a gang of the insurgents broke in with the intention of killing him in cold blood. Kabayama has talked with him since and telephoned from Miyanoshita to tell me so. Prince Saionji, in the country at Okitsu, also escaped in time, but those in Tokyo seem to have had no warning whatever.

It is significant that somebody telephoned to our servants during dinner asking that they be informed the moment Saito left our Embassy and when we looked up the number later it was found to be the local police station; they may have had some special warning or it may have been merely the usual precautionary protection, probably the latter. At any rate, Saito's presence under our roof that night made no difference one way or the other; he left well before midnight and was not killed until 5 or 6 o'clock the next morning. It would have been doubly horrible if the murderers had invaded our Embassy, as they could easily have done so far as their force was concerned, and bayoneted him at our table; the international aspects of such a move would probably have weighed little with those young hotheads if they had felt that it would facilitate their object; some and perhaps all of their groups were armed with machine guns; in the case of the Prime Minister several police were mowed down before the building was entered, and at the Watanabe house his entire family and servants were wiped out.

PIECING TOGETHER THE COURSE OF THE TRAGEDY

March 1, 1936

Everything that happened before the revolt now seems so trivial in comparison with the events of the past four days that there is no incentive to record the earlier daily notes. Little by little I shall have to try to piece out all that took place between February 26 and 29. The final denouement, namely the sudden reappearance of Prime Minister Okada, alive and uninjured, after we and nearly everybody else believed him to have been assassinated, savors of the most intense melodrama and it has certainly made the insurgents the laughingstock of Japan if not of the world, which is a very healthy thing. Yet sorrow and anger overcome the humor of it.

To begin the story we have to go back to our dinner for the Saitos on the evening of February 25. We sat down to two tables, thirty-six in number, and wishing to give the old gentleman and our other guests something out of the ordinary in the matter of entertainment I had seen several films at the Metro-Goldwyn-Mayer studio during the past few days. On the last afternoon, Shathin showed me *Naughty Marietta,* with Jeanette MacDonald and Nelson Eddy and I decided at once that the ideal picture had been found, for it was full of lovely old Victor Herbert music, beautiful scenes, a pretty, romantic story and no vulgarity whatever, almost as good a film as *One Night of Love.*

Almost immediately after dinner the film began. We put Viscount Saito in a comfortable armchair, knowing that if he was bored with a film he could comfortably sleep because he had told Neville that he had learned in the Navy to catch a nap at any time and under any circumstances. But I think he enjoyed it too much to sleep. We had a pause with refreshments halfway through and then continued, nearly two hours of film. Betsy Neville said that the Japanese ladies' eyes were distinctly red at the end of it, so I think they were moved by the romantic story. There was supper afterward, but the Saitos left at about 11:30, pretty late for them because they generally leave dinners punctually at 10. I saw the old gentleman out and that was the end of a friendship which began when I made my first call on him as Prime Minister and Acting Minister for Foreign Affairs in June, 1932.

It is interesting to think that he began his great career with Americans—with Admiral Schley and at the Naval Academy at Annapolis—and finished it at the American Embassy. He was a lovable character, gentle, charming, courtly, but with great wisdom and broad liberal views in an age of chauvinistic strife. I had hopes that he would be able to use his influence in settling the school crisis in Korea, arising out of the demand of the petty authorities that both Christian pupils and teachers worship at the Shinto shrines—a demand which may result in the closing of all our mission schools if persisted in. He always supported our missionaries. But now his wise influence has gone and who knows what the future will bring?

The telephone rang early on the 26th—it was Neville, I think— who broke the news of the assassinations during the early morning —wild rumors that the insurgents had taken over the Government and parts of the city—no one knowing who had been killed and who survived or how intensive the insurrection might be. Our first telegram was sent in the morning and was acknowledged by the Department, six hours in transmission. During the four days of revolution we had scouts constantly moving about the city, especially our Military Attaché, Colonel Carey Crane, and his language officers, observing developments to the best of their ability. On the very first morning Neville quietly walked through the lines of troops, politely telling the soldiers in Japanese that he wanted to go to the Foreign Office and being passed through with equal courtesy; I think he was probably the only foreigner who got to the Gaimusho that first day—and he did it twice.

That night Alice was nervous lest the American Ambassador might be included in a sort of supplementary program of the revolutionists and insisted on our sleeping in an unusual room and nearer to the baby; I fear she didn't sleep very much at all but I laughed at her fears, well knowing that the last thing the insurgents wanted was trouble with the United States at this particular juncture. The next day our Embassy was heavily guarded with troops, outposts, and sandbag barricades below the chancery, as well as three detectives (including our friend Iida from the police station) and two soldiers inside the house, and whenever I descended to the chancery they insisted on coming too.

The Mexican Minister came into town from the country the first day and couldn't even get into his Legation and telephoned to me for help; I did my best through Horinouchi, but the Foreign Office was completely powerless and the Minister seemed to be satisfied with my efforts, unavailing as they were. The rebels were situated in the official residence of the Prime Minister and the Sanno Hotel, very near us, and their banners floated from both buildings; we watched developments through glasses from our roof.

The Japanese Government quietly made all military preparations to capture or kill the rebels, meantime maintaining the most perfect discipline and order in the city, and then waited for two days until they surrendered little by little, in small groups, as a result of broadcasts, leaflets dropped from airplanes into the grounds of the Prime Minister's residence and the Sanno Hotel, and a big streamer attached to a balloon, all stating that the Emperor called on the men to return to their barracks, where they would be pardoned because they had been misled, that their parents and brothers and sisters were weeping at the thought of their disobeying the Emperor, and that unless they disbanded they would be shot. This had precisely the desired effect and the whole thing was settled with very little, if any, shooting except for the original assassinations. I should call this anything but barbarism.

We now know that when the last soldiers had left the Prime Minister's residence and the Sanno Hotel, the officers who had engineered the revolt finally surrendered after four days and that the Government gave them two hours to commit hara-kiri. But they didn't commit hara-kiri because they expected civil trials as in the case of former assassins and they fully intended to use the court-room as a forum to stir up the people against the Government. It must have been a great shock to them when they were tried by court-martial and several of them sentenced to death and shot.

The story of one incident, that of the attempt to kill Count Makino, is deeply moving. The old gentleman was staying at a hot-spring hotel in the country when an officer and several soldiers arrived in the middle of the night to assassinate him. According to the story which reached me, and I believe it to be true, Count Makino's guard shot and killed the officer and was himself killed by the soldiers, who then set fire to the hotel with the intention of forcing Count Makino into the open. Behind the hotel was a precipitous cliff and the old gentleman was led by his granddaughter Kazuko and trained nurse up onto a ledge on the cliff from which they could climb no higher. They were shortly lit up by the fire as if a flood light had been turned on them and the soldiers raised their guns. At just that moment, however, the little granddaughter, who was a lovely girl and a great friend of our daughter Elsie, spread her own kimono in front of her grandfather and the soldiers, being deeply moved by this heroic gesture, dropped their guns and did not shoot. I have always felt that little Kazuko was one of the real heroines of the February 26 incident and she certainly saved her grandfather from death.

JAPAN'S NEW ERA BEGINS

March 1, 1936

The period of the insurrection lasted only four days and yet we in the Embassy feel as if an era had passed since that happy evening when we had the Saitos and Suzukis under our roof last Tuesday. If time is measured by events, certainly an age has gone by since then. Such things are occurring in many parts of the world from time to time, disasters of one kind or another whether caused by the forces of nature or by the hand of man, and the rest of us look on objectively. We read the morning paper and say "What an awful catastrophe" and pass on to our daily tasks and thoughts, not greatly moved. It is only when such things occur in one's midst and when violent death and heroic action take place among one's friends and almost at one's door that the shock really comes home and remains.

Gradually, from the accounts of friends, we can now reconstruct the way the assassinations took place, and not only do the stories redound to the credit of the men but they show the true stuff of Japanese womanhood—how Viscountess Saito placed herself in front of her husband, said, "Kill me instead; my husband cannot be spared by the country," and actually put her hand on the mouth of the machine gun until her wounds forced her aside, and how Mrs. Watanabe lay down with her husband in her arms so that the assassins had to force the gun underneath her body.

The story of Admiral Suzuki should live in history; Captain Ando, pointing his revolver, discussed the situation with him for ten minutes and when the discussion faltered, Suzuki asked: "Have you anything more to say?" Ando replied: "No, sir." "Then shoot," said Suzuki, and Ando fired the three shots. One grazed his skull but failed to penetrate the brain, one went through the chest and lungs, and the third lodged in the leg. The chest wound was the serious one and the Admiral lost so much blood that only blood transfusions could save his life. It looks now as if he might pull through. Takahashi's murder was the really brutal one: not content with shooting, the rebel officer hacked him with his sword—and then apologized to the household for the "annoyance" caused.

Well, we must carry on and try to see what it is all going to mean. One thing emerges as absolute certainty: there must be a "New Deal" in Japan or the same thing will happen—as predicted by the defense counsel in the Aizawa trial—again and again. I have confidence in Hirota, but he is saddled with one of the most difficult problems which any man ever faced. He has a tremendous opportunity, in some ways the same opportunity which confronted Franklin Roosevelt when he took office, and if he can deal effectively and successfully with the problem he should go down in history as a very great statesman.

It is easier to understand how such things as the incident of February 26 can occur in Japan if one stops to think that the history books upon which the Japanese youth is brought up are full of the records of just such deeds from the earliest times—assassinations or suicides for motives of revenge or loyalty to one's chief or the assumption of responsibility for a given situation. Paradoxically— and Japan is a country of paradoxes—these young officers held that they were acting in the interests of the Emperor, ridding him of the alleged nefarious influences around the Throne, men whom the Emperor himself had chosen. And there was no personal animosity involved. When they had killed Saito and Watanabe and Matsuo (mistaken for his brother-in-law, the Prime Minister), they called for incense to burn beside the bodies; in the Takahashi house no incense could be found, so they insisted on placing lighted candles beside the murdered statesman. If these things are to be prevented in future, not only will a social and economic New Deal have to be brought about within the country, but Japanese education in the schools and in the Army will have to undergo a radical alteration.

One of the pleasant things which emerged from the incident was the absolute unity of the Embassy staff as a single team both in action and spirit. This included the Naval, Military, and Commercial Attachés, and their several assistants who worked with the rest of us, hour by hour, in the closest co-operation, pooling their observations and information for the good of the whole, without any special thought of their own departments. Although all our nerves had been pretty well tried by the end of the four days, there was never a sign of irritation or friction on the part of anyone. Of course it is easier to weld such a group into a unit in a place like Tokyo than in London or Paris, and we certainly have unity here. Our staff is made up of all sorts of heterogeneous types and characters, yet no club membership could be more congenial. One of the secrets, I think, lies in the fact that any group of men who play together a lot will almost certainly work well together too.

HOW PREMIER OKADA ESCAPED ASSASSINATION

March 2, 1936

The facts concerning the escape of the Prime Minister now seem to be fairly well established. Early in the morning of February 26 the alarm bells in the official residence rang (as they once rang by mistake when Alice and I were dining with Viscount Saito when Prime Minister some four years ago and the report got around that we were being assassinated). Admiral Okada looked at his watch and remarked to his brother-in-law, Matsuo, who was sleeping in the same room: "Well, my last hour has come but I won't die in pajamas." Matsuo replied: "Your life is too valuable to be spared," and while Okada dressed, Matsuo ran downstairs and into the garden, shouting "Banzai," where he was pursued and promptly killed, being mistaken for Okada in the early-morning light.

Five of the police guards were shot and killed at the entrance and one wounded. Okada was pushed into the servants' quarters and shut in a closet. There he remained until the next night, when Matsuo's body was removed and Okada, disguised, simply walked out with the mourners. I should say that Matsuo was the real hero of the whole rebellion because, while there were plenty of brave and loyal police who met death in trying to protect their charges, they were acting in line of duty and Matsuo's action was spontaneous altruism.

HIROTA REORGANIZES

March 5, 1936

Cabled to the Department that Hirota has been commanded by the Emperor to form a cabinet. I am very much pleased because I believe that Hirota is a strong, safe man and that while he will have to play ball with the Army to a certain extent, I think that he will handle foreign affairs as wisely as they can be handled, given the domestic elements which he will have to conciliate. I think too that he wants good relations with the United States and will do what he is able to do in that direction—in other words, as much as any Japanese Minister could do. If I had had the pick myself, I know of nobody whom I would have more gladly chosen to head the Government, with American interests in view. To have chosen an out-and-out liberal would have been fatal because any Prime Minister at this juncture must absolutely possess the confidence of the Army and Navy if he is not to be hamstrung at the start.

To our astonishment, Hirota immediately announced the make-up of his new cabinet, including Yoshida as Minister for Foreign Affairs, and the press said that Yoshida was acting as his chief of staff in choosing the various Ministers. This seemed to us precisely like waving a red flag at a bull because not only is Yoshida a pronounced liberal but he is the son-in-law of Count Makino. But naturally the Army wouldn't accept him for a moment, and it was soon announced that Hirota had run into hot water and was having difficulty in forming his cabinet and that General Terauchi, his choice for Minister of War, would not serve unless a radical alteration were made in Hirota's slate.

I can't imagine why Hirota made the announcement because he surely must have known that Yoshida would be impossible and it would seem to put him, Hirota, in a weak position to have to throw

Yoshida overboard and revamp his cabinet at the Army's dictation. There must have been some deep-seated purpose in the maneuver, possibly to place squarely on the Army the responsibility for tampering with Hirota's foreign policy. To anticipate a little, it took Hirota four days to smooth out his differences of opinion with the Army and to submit to the Emperor his final slate in which he himself is to keep the portfolio of Foreign Affairs for the time being. Throughout all this time very little if anything has been heard from the Navy, publicly that is. It is said that no love is lost between the two forces and that during the uprising the Navy, which brought several ships up to Tokyo, said to the Army: "Settle the affair quickly or we will either settle it for you or pull out," and they did pull out almost immediately. I am told that they are, in fact, thoroughly ashamed of the Army's responsibility for the whole business. The story of Admiral Osumi's going to the palace the first day of the uprising surrounded by a large body of bluejackets and with two machine guns is perhaps significant.

HIROTA DEFINES "POSITIVE DIPLOMACY"

March 13, 1936

At 3 o'clock Mr. Hirota received me in the Prime Minister's official residence and while I was waiting to go in, Kishi, who has now been appointed Private Secretary to the Prime Minister, showed me the room where Okada slept and from which Matsuo ran out into the garden to his death. Hirota saw me alone without an interpreter. He said at the start that the policy which he has been following as Minister for Foreign Affairs would continue unchanged and that now that he was at the head of the Government this policy would always prevail. He said that he had the support of all members of the cabinet and that eventually he would select a Minister for Foreign Affairs upon whom he could count equally to support his policy.

I asked Hirota if he would define the term "positive diplomacy" which was now being aired in the press as the program of the new Government. Hirota said that this term applied only to China and Soviet Russia and it simply meant a general speeding up of the policy already followed. So far as Soviet Russia was concerned, the Army is dissatisfied with the great difference between the Soviet forces in Siberia and the Japanese forces in Manchuria and they wish the latter—referred to as "defensive forces"—to be built up to a point more nearly approximating the Soviet forces across the border. He said, however, that a Soviet-Japanese war would be stupid because neither party could be expected to accomplish concrete results and he assured me that there would be no war so long as he is in office.

With regard to China, Hirota said that the three points already enunciated would form the basis for future Sino-Japanese negotiations and that these points had already been accepted by the Chinese Government in principle. At my request he defined these points as follows:

a. A stop must be put to anti-Japanese activities and propaganda in China.

b. It is understood that de jure recognition of Manchukuo by China at present would be difficult and it is not demanded, but what is desired is recognition of the existence of Manchukuo and regularization of such factual relations as customs, communications, transit, et cetera.

c. Sino-Japanese co-operation is desired to combat the spread of Communism.

I told Hirota that it would be helpful if he could authorize me to reassure my Government that the pursuance of Japan's policy in China would not interfere with foreign rights and interests, including the principle of the Open Door. The Prime Minister said that there would be no tampering with the principle of the Open Door by Japan and that, so far as he could see, the only possible way in which foreign rights and interests might be indirectly affected by Japan's policy would be through the possible relinquishment by Japan of her extraterritorial rights some time in the future.

Before leaving I took occasion to speak to the Prime Minister, on my own initiative and not under instructions, about the difficulties which the Government in Washington is encountering through the increasing flow of cheap Japanese goods into the United States; I spoke of the co-operative efforts which were being made between the Department of State and the Japanese Embassy in Washington to solve these difficulties on a practical and equitable basis, but said that in spite of all efforts in this direction, our domestic industrial interests were bringing greater and greater pressure to bear on our Government and it might become necessary eventually to ask for more restrictive efforts by the Japanese Government.

Incidentally Hirota said during our conversation that, as he had told me at our first interview, good relations between Japan and the

United States were the cornerstone of his policy and would continue
to be so.

ROYAL FUNERAL SHINTO STYLE

March 26, 1936

Attended with Alice the Shinto funeral of the Dowager Princess
Kitashirakawa, precisely similar to that of Princess Asaka, which we
attended in 1933. Had to go in a dress suit, out-of-doors, on a cold,
windy day, with overcoat prohibited, so took the precaution of wearing two sets of underwear and socks plus a sweater under my boiled
shirt; felt like a stuffed boa constrictor but did keep warm.

The Shinto service is in three parts, first the placing before the
shrine of a complete repast including the *mochi* or rice cakes, a big
fish, vegetables, fruit, tea, etc., and then a trunk containing wearing
apparel for the deceased, all most reverently carried out by five or
six priests; then the reading by the chief priest of a message to the
spirit of the departed, and finally the laying of *sakaki* branches first
by the representatives of the Emperor, the Empress, and the Empress
Dowager in turn, then by each of the Imperial princes and princesses and finally by each member of the Diplomatic Corps, the
Prime Minister, and the rest of the Government. These things are
tremendously moving and carried out with an unhurried precision
and reverence which are really impressive. There is never any scur-
rying at the Japanese Court; things simply don't go wrong because
every step is so precisely planned in advance, and everyone knows
just what to do and when to do it.

TWO LETTERS TO THE EMBASSY

1. "I WANT AT 60 YEN ON SALARYED"

U. S. Ambasyder.

Dear Sirs

Excuse me to tell like this. I know so much that way never good.
but I can't any way. I worship to America very very like. and I
wanted liveing in the freedom U. S. A. but Another tene years I live
at the Tokyo City of Japan. Becouse. I study Japan thing. please
your ears I say in the now I tell about my tragic lot. I was born 30th
Sept 1914 in Tokio. My mother and father divorced owing to the
discord. when I was fifteen years old. He had to miss of the work
and to fall flat. lost the estate. Mother took her childs to leave with-

out me. and go out my father very degraded and not love me. what-
never. I still on the his family relation for the Japanese low father's
Another Wife before got married with my mother. and also her
childs a several. they all unlucky. My father not fit father. Father now
got step wife. he love her more than I and they go away. I never
life so that heard father. but I alone. my father 61 years old. my
mother 45 years old. I have six sister and brother than I watched
mothers poor family. I understand tutelary their at heart. I was just
at one of the taxie driver. but I dislike that groups.
I wish employment with some American by moter car driver. Well
I can drive very safely. and I am very health. please have a heart.
will you kindly introduce me. some American.
I want at 60 yen on salaryed.
Please your word write to me.

Sincerely yours

Junichiro ———

2. A SECRET AGENT PRESENTS HIS CREDENTIALS TO MR. NEVILLE, COUNSELOR OF THE EMBASSY

[Address on the envelope]
To Sir Nuviel, Esq.
Chief Superintendent of Rep. U.S.A. Government
in Tokyo,
Tokyo, Japan.

To
Sir, Nevil Esq.
Rep. Chief Magistrade of U.S.A.
in Tokyo.

Dear Sir:
Pardon me writing to you such a letter as circumstances compels
me to do so.
I am an American Citizen, thirty eight years of age.
I am here for finding out some secret affairs in Japan.
I speak English, German, Japanese and several Chinese dialects
fluently.
I have been here in Japan now about an year and been working
all kinds of works since.
And found nearly all about Japans opinions and the truth about
Japanese war mind & secrete places.

I am ready now to send the map of the principle places Japan's navy & army.

But I am stand in knot now, over here, as I am broked up, as I lost my money.

I am staying in a small Japanese Hotel privately by Japanese name as I can't give my real name.

Now Sir! please keep this secretely by yourself or General Luit! Standley of U.S. otherwise. I'll be kaptured by Japanese Army Corps.

I beg to ask if you could be so kind as to help me by lending me some money to fix up everything to send to U.S.A.

I need here now at present, two hundred dollars gold at once, and to get back to Shanghai and send the news & etc. through Consul General at Shanghai to U.S., as it will be save, I must do all the work secretely & very carefully.

So I am sorry as I can't send to you for U.S. as it mite be found by some Japanese on the way by mail.

Please lend me the amount two hundred dollars gold at least.

I'll certainly return to you as soon as I get to Shanghai.

I can come to interview with you privately if you need.

Please reply me as soon as possible, as I can't stay here too long.

I'll close for this time, as I can't write anything secrite on this letter so long, but will give you a good news when interview.

Please do me this favor as I'll be awaiting for it and I can't move at presend as I'm no mor money.

Please write my Japanese name when you reply.

A good health & a kind regards to you.

Awaiting for your favorable reply.

Thanking you in anticipation

I remain
Dear Sir
Yours Sincerely

State Nick name! H. Tanaka in Japan when reply.

HOLLAND'S MINISTER FORESEES JAPAN'S SOUTHWARD THRUST

April 25, 1936

The Dutch Minister came in to see if I knew of any developments concerning recent statements that the scope and field of activity of the Japanese Navy would be extended to include the area of the South Sea islands. Dickover had recently asked Admiral Hasegawa, Vice-Minister of the Navy, about it and Hasegawa said frankly that it simply meant an effort to extend Japanese trade to the south and the natural protection by the Navy of the new trade routes.

Without mentioning names or countries, I told General Pabst of a remark made by a highly placed Japanese during the Washington Conference of 1921–22: "There is absolute unanimity in Japan on the proposition that we must expand; but there are two schools of thought as to where we should expand: the first is the Continental school, the second is called Blue-water school. For the moment, the Continental school has the upper hand and probably will for years to come, but if ever it should be blocked or thwarted, then——"

This first school of thought is obviously military and the second school, naval. General Pabst was perfectly familiar with this situation but he said that in view of recent talk in Japanese naval circles with regard to expansion toward the south, he believed that, if conditions in Europe remained in the present state, compelling the British fleet to stay in or near home waters, there was a fifty-fifty chance that the Japanese Navy would attempt a *coup de main* within six months, with the objective of taking possession of New Guinea or Borneo or some part of the Netherlands Indies producing petroleum.

As I have often said, General Pabst is essentially a pessimist and as a Dutchman interested in the protection of the Dutch East Indies he can hardly afford to be otherwise. It was he who told me two years ago that he thought a Japanese naval descent on Guam was by no means beyond the bounds of possibility. He seems to like the phrase "a fifty-fifty chance" and recently used it with regard to the possibility of a Japanese-Soviet war this summer. From all I see of the general reaction in Japan to the incident of February 26 and the real anger which has developed in many circles against the direct actionists, I do not look for a *coup de main* by either Japanese Navy or Army in the South Seas or in any other part of the world in the near future, always qualifying such opinions with the observation that it is dangerous ever to predict anything precisely in this part of the world.

THE ITALIAN AMBASSADOR CELEBRATES
THE NEW ROMAN EMPIRE

May 9, 1936

Dined with Auriti, the Italian Ambassador, at the Tokyo Kaikan; he had invited most of the members of the American and German Embassies because, as he told us, he wanted to begin his official dinners with the representatives of the countries which had not declared sanctions! It was, incidentally, a rather horrible evening with heavy food, poor Italian wines, an ugly room and a blinding glare of electric light, but Italy evidently can't afford just at present to spend money on such details as putting her dilapidated Embassy in condition. Auriti after dinner spoke volubly to me on the crimes of the League of Nations and their net results; they had driven Japan to declare the independence of Manchukuo and Italy to make Abyssinia an Italian colony whereas if the League had kept its finger out of things Italy in all probability would merely have taken an Abyssinian mandate. Furthermore, the League had embittered Anglo-Italian and French-Italian relations, had brought Europe nearer to war, and had practically ruined its own prestige.

Seldom have I seen in any man such a transformation as in Auriti since Italy's victory in Abyssinia. A few months ago he seemed crushed and despondent; now he is on the crest of the wave, gay, talkative, and almost flaunting the Italian flag in our faces. At a party at our Embassy I found him after dinner playfully embracing Mrs. Stoïcesco and I naturally commented to Stoi, who was looking on, on the outrageous behavior of Italy, which, not content with Abyssinia, was now going after Rumania. Stoi loved it. But I wonder whether my silly quip was really so farfetched and whether dreams of a revived Holy Roman Empire may not be lurking in the background of Mussolini's political megalomania. Who can tell whether friction with Yugoslavia might not eventually lead to war, and with Yugoslavia conquered, where would the Roman chariots stop?

JAPAN FORBIDS OUR NAVY TO VISIT HER
MANDATED ISLANDS

The Secretary of State to the Ambassador in Japan
(Paraphrase)

Washington, June 13, 1936

For several years now the Government of Japan has requested.

each year, that the American Government extend facilities in its territorial waters off the Alaskan coasts to two Japanese Government ships and permit their entry into harbors in Alaska and in the Aleutian Islands that are not open, ordinarily, to foreign commerce. In the case of one of the vessels in question it was stated that its purpose in visiting these waters and harbors was the making of studies in connection with protection of fur-bearing seals; in the case of the second vessel, however, it was not suggested that the visits would be made on basis of any treaty or formal arrangement between the American Government and the Government of Japan. The Government of the United States has acceded, nevertheless, to the requests of the Government of Japan in this regard.

A strong undercurrent of suspicion and conjecture has existed for some time past over harbor developments or fortifications in possessions which both Japan and the United States have in the Pacific. No objection to the visits of Japanese Government vessels to the territorial waters and closed harbors of Alaska has been made by this Government, as it was believed that the opportunities which were open in this way for observation by Japanese vessels would serve to remove any suspicion which the Government of Japan might hold that any improvements have been made of such a nature as would violate either the letter or the spirit of the naval treaty signed on February 6, 1922.

In our view it is unfortunate that the Government of Japan so far has not adopted an attitude similarly liberal in the face of allegations that in the Japanese mandated islands of the Pacific improvements are being carried out which are irreconcilable with Japan's treaty obligations not to fortify these islands. We can understand that the Government of Japan should be reluctant to give any countenance to irresponsible allegations but nevertheless the Government undoubtedly shares with the Government of the United States the view that persistent suspicion with regard to this matter is provocative of mutual distrust, and that such suspicion, therefore, should be dispelled.

The American destroyer *Alden* will be sent shortly to the Asiatic Station according to the Navy Department plans. The Japanese Government will thus have presented to it an opportunity to extend to a vessel of this Government courtesies at the larger unopened ports of the Pacific mandated islands, as well as at the open ports. An invitation by the Government of Japan for the *Alden* to visit these ports would have, in our opinion, highly beneficial results from the point of view of relations between the two nations.

Please consider carefully and attentively our views as we have sketched them. If no objection is perceived, please present these views informally and orally to the Minister for Foreign Affairs, putting forward the suggestion outlined in the foregoing paragraph as on your own initiative.

Inform the Department currently by telegraph.

HULL

The Ambassador in Japan to the Secretary of State
(Paraphrase)

Tokyo, July 8, 1936

Today I made suggestion, as on my own initiative, to the Minister for Foreign Affairs with regard to an invitation to the *Alden* to visit open and unopened ports in the Pacific islands under Japanese mandate.

Marked interest was shown by the Minister in the situation as I described it, but he professed not to know anything at all about the subject. He told me that he would see what there was that could be done and that he would try to give me, before July 20, the results of his inquiries.

GREW

The Ambassador in Japan to the Secretary of State
(Paraphrase)

Tokyo, July 28, 1936

At the request of the Vice-Minister for Foreign Affairs, the Counselor of the Embassy called on the Vice-Minister to discuss certain questions that had been broached by the Ambassador to the Minister for Foreign Affairs. One of these questions related to the possibility of the visit by the *Alden* to ports in the Japanese mandated islands. This call was the only opportunity that presented itself for discussion of the matter since the visit of the Ambassador on July 8.

The Vice-Minister stated that the suggestion of the Ambassador had been referred to the Ministry of Overseas Affairs but that no reply had been received. He further stated that there would probably be a consultation with other government departments. In response to a query by the Counselor, he expressed the fear that the Foreign Office had no way of expediting the reply.

The manner of the Vice-Minister was friendly, but it indicated that the Foreign Office could do nothing further.

GREW

The Acting Secretary of State to the Ambassador in Japan
(Paraphrase)

Washington, August 7, 1936

Embassy's telegram No. 163, July 28, 1 P.M. With regard to the suggestion made relative to the *Alden,* the Department assumes that there is no prospect that the Japanese authorities will take favorable action. In reply to a communication from the Japanese Embassy here, the Department is today returning an adverse answer to that Embassy's request that the Japanese Government training ship *Shintoku Maru* be permitted to enter a Hawaiian harbor which is not listed as a port of entry.

PHILLIPS

GERMANY MAKES FRICTION BETWEEN
RUSSIA AND JAPAN

June 18, 1936

In conversation today ——— told me confidentially that he was aware of the fact that all German newspaper correspondents in Japan had been instructed from Berlin to use every effort not only in their written dispatches but also by direct and indirect intrigue to embroil Japan with Soviet Russia since it accords with German interests that Soviet Russia should have its hands full in the Far East and therefore be less free to cause trouble for Germany in Europe. ——— said he was also aware that the French Ambassador in Moscow was taking precisely the contrary action by endeavoring to calm Soviet-Japanese relations, so that in case of a German attack on France, Soviet Russia would be in a strong position to come to France's rescue.

DEATH SENTENCE TO THE FEBRUARY REBELS

July 6, 1936

Telegraphed the Department that the War Office had announced at 2 o'clock this morning that of nineteen officers, seventy-five non-commissioned officers, nineteen privates, and ten civilians indicted and tried for complicity in the incident of February 26, the following sentences have been given:

13 officers and 4 civilians to death;
5 officers to life imprisonment;
1 officer, 17 noncommissioned officers, and 6 civilians to imprisonment of from 2 to 15 years;
27 noncommissioned officers and 3 privates to imprisonment of from 18 months to 2 years but with stay of execution for 3 years (meaning probation).

Nothing is said in the sentences concerning the guilt of assassination; the punishments are based exclusively on the fact that the officers were guilty of employing the Imperial Army without Imperial sanction. Some of the noncommissioned officers and privates were found to have participated knowingly in the incident while others were acquitted because they had only obeyed the orders of their superior officers. No appeal will be granted and the executions will be carried out by shooting.

Meanwhile the press publishes the complete details of the incident, the ban having been lifted, and they are extraordinarily interesting reading. These sentences of Army officers to death are, so far as we can ascertain, unprecedented in Japan. It is impossible to foresee just what effect this severity will entail; the press, no doubt taking its cue from the Government, is practically unanimously in favor of the sentences; on the other hand, the guilty officers, when executed, will have become martyrs to many of their fellow officers in the Army, and revenge in Japan is a traditional virtue. I think that further "incidents" are more than likely.

A visit to the United States to attend the Harvard Tercentenary celebration interrupts the diary and correspondence at this point.

BACK IN TOKYO

November 27, 1936. Tokyo

And here we are, picking up the threads again, all too many of them, but after a vacation like that, one feels ready for anything. In fact, I am more than happy to be back in harness, and Dickover said that *he* was more than happy to unload the responsibility, a feeling which we've all many a time experienced. So on with the dance—and, incidentally, the diary.

CHECKING IN WITH HIROTA

November 30, 1936

During my call today on the Prime Minister to pay my respects on returning from leave of absence, the conversation at first entered upon the recent election in the United States and the assurance that the general foreign policy of the present administration, including the policy of the good neighbor, would be continued for another four years. I spoke also of the Harvard Tercentenary celebration and the Japanese art exhibition in Boston.

When I asked Mr. Hirota how things were going in Japan, he replied that his greatest difficulty at present had to do with taxation. He said that the Japanese Army and Navy were seriously disturbed at the great increase of armaments in Soviet Russia which exceeded even the military organization of the czarist regime, and it was largely owing to these increasingly heavy Soviet armaments that the Japanese Army and Navy were calling for greater increases of armaments in Japan, which in turn led to the necessity for higher taxation.

Since Mr. Hirota on his own initiative had touched upon foreign affairs, I then asked him concerning the reports in the press about an agreement between Japan and Italy. He replied that no agreement existed. The simple facts were that Italy was going to open a consular office in Manchukuo and Japan would eventually do the same in Abyssinia and that this was all there was to it.

The Prime Minister then said that as regards China the negotiations were proceeding very slowly and that they were still based on the three points which he had formerly enunciated, particularly the demand that anti-Japanese activity in China should cease and that steps would be taken to combat Communism. I asked him about the reports to the effect that the Japanese demands included tariff questions and also the appointment of Japanese advisers. Mr. Hirota said that these points had also come up; that the question of the tariff had already been settled and that as regards Japanese advisers, the simple fact was that other countries had many advisers in China whereas Japan had none and that the Japanese merchants in China were pressing for the appointment of such advisers. Mr. Hirota said definitely that such advisers would be purely economic and not political or military. He said that obviously the Chinese Government was in a difficult position regarding the Bolshevist menace because there were so many Communists in China itself.

AN AMBASSADOR DETECTS A GERMAN-JAPANESE ALLIANCE

December 3, 1936

An ambassadorial colleague told me today that there is no doubt in his mind that the German-Japanese treaty includes a secret military agreement. His appraisal of the matter is that the negotiations have been conducted through Major General Oshima, Japanese Military Attaché in Berlin, without the knowledge of the Foreign Office here, and very likely without the knowledge of the German Foreign Office. In other words, the negotiations had been conducted entirely through military channels.

This theory is given weight, he said, by the fact that Colonel Ott, the German Military Attaché in Tokyo, was suddenly called to Berlin last autumn during the presence there of the German Ambassador to Japan and that Colonel Ott had returned to Tokyo just before the signing of the agreement. He thought that Shiratori, Japanese Minister to Sweden, who is very close to the Japanese military, may also have had a hand in the affair. The Ambassador said he thought it quite possible that in view of the lack of success in trying out the German trade agreement with Manchukuo, negotiated last year, this secret pact might well envisage the shipment of German arms to Manchuria to pay for Manchurian soya beans and other commodities.

THE SOVIET AMBASSADOR ON THE GERMAN-JAPANESE AGREEMENT

December 3, 1936

In my talk today with the Soviet Ambassador he spoke with considerable heat concerning the Japanese-German agreement and said that his Government possessed definite evidence that a secret military pact existed. He said that the military pact was undoubtedly directed against Great Britain and on my inquiring how the pact worked in that direction, he said that it envisaged the division of various British overseas possessions and the Dutch East Indies between Japan and Germany in case of war. He said that this was directly in line with the Japanese program for southern expansion as well as for Germany's need for colonies. He spoke ironically regarding the anti-Comintern agreement. The Ambassador emphasized the fact that Soviet-Japanese relations had suffered a severe setback as a result of the German-Japanese agreement.

AS JAPAN PREPARED TO FIGHT THE WORLD

January 1, 1937

The New Year for Japan, so far as her international relations are concerned, opens in an ominous key. Not only has her reputation in the world suffered an important deterioration during the past year, but her relations with Great Britain, Soviet Russia, and China are on a far from satisfactory footing and recently have been growing worse. With the Dutch East Indies relations have improved. Only with the United States, among her nearer neighbors, can it be said that the *status quo* has been maintained, but with the expiration of the Washington Naval Treaty, due to Japan's intransigeance, and the risk of a race in sea power and fortifications, the long future as contrasted with the immediate present holds out no evident grounds for optimism.

For this unhappy situation Japan herself is primarily to blame, for she has played her cards unwisely and is now reaping the logical results. It is the old story of the defects arising out of a dual control of foreign policy wherein the civil authorities of the Government, including the Prime Minister and the Foreign Office, are overridden by the military and are subject to the behests of the Army and Navy, which know or care little about developing good relations with foreign countries but without whose support the cabinet could not long survive. We saw very much the same thing working out in Germany in 1914.

United States

General Araki observed to the British Ambassador a year or two ago that if it were not for the exclusion clause of the Immigration Act of 1924, the relations between Japan and the United States might be considered as thoroughly satisfactory. While it is true that no current controversies of prime importance are at present sufficiently acute seriously to disturb those relations, nevertheless we should not close our eyes to the fact that several current issues may in due course become acute and are potentially hazardous.

First and foremost is the naval issue which has automatically arisen with the termination of the Washington Naval Treaty. How the future will shape up in this respect we cannot yet foresee, but it is safe to say that if a race in naval building and in the construction of fortifications results, the suspicion and uneasiness engendered will inevitably make for tenseness in those relations. Other issues which appear to be potentially disturbing are Japan's aggressive policy in China, with the possibility of that policy eventually interfering with American interests, and the flooding of American markets with Japanese low-priced goods against which we may ultimately be obliged to protect ourselves with resultant international friction and irritation.

The Philippine Islands also remain as a potential, although not an immediate, source of danger to the relations between Japan and the United States.

China

It does not appear necessary to deal extensively or in detail with Japan's diplomacy and activities in China during the past year. Sufficient to say that the overt intention and efforts of the Japanese military to detach the five northern provinces from the jurisdiction of Nanking largely miscarried; that the support of the Japanese military of the widespread smuggling operations not only became an international scandal but went far to bring down on Japan the censure of foreign countries including the United States and Great Britain; and that, far from co-operating with Nanking in an effort to control the anti-Japanese sentiment rapidly developing throughout China, the Japanese have constantly intensified that sentiment by their truculent and aggressive attitude and tactics.

Now, at the opening of the New Year, the Japanese program in China, whatever it may be, appears to have come to a temporary halt owing to the new developments arising out of the capture and subsequent release of Chiang Kai-shek by Marshal Chang Hsueh-liang. The Japanese are clearly marking time. Whether these developments will lead to an intensification of the anti-Japanese movement in China and whether, and to what extent, they will induce a stiffening of the future policy of Nanking remain to be seen.

The Japanese nation seems to be somewhat thunderstruck by the sudden and unexpected determination of China to yield no more to Japanese pressure. The nation is, figuratively, scratching its head and wondering what it should do next. There has been some discussion in the newspapers of a reorientation of policy toward China, but there has been no indication as yet of the direction which that reorientation will take. It is strange but true that Japan appears to have been the last to appreciate the changed conditions in China.

Now that Japan realizes that its bluff of military pressure no longer works, some other aggressive method of dominating North China may be tried. Economic co-operation, with emphasis on its aim being "improvement of the conditions of the people," is an old Army plan that is being advocated increasingly by Army spokesmen which might be an outlet for Japanese expansionist activities, not too objectionable to the Nanking Government. For the present it appears that Japan is not attracted by the thought of a frontal attack, on her own volition, against Nanking. More probable is the method of peripheral penetration and digging in in North China and along the Mongolian frontier.

There can be no doubt as to the soundness of my survey of the general situation facing Japan at the commencement of the last year, which said, in relation to Japan's policy with China:

> The procedure to be followed and the methods to be pursued are open to influence by many factors, but the expansionist urge is fundamental, and I think there is no doubt that whether quietly and gradually or openly and aggressively Japanese energies will be found, from now on, steadily directed towards consolidating Japan's control in North China and Mongolia.

Soviet Russia

Good relations between Japan and Soviet Russia in the present political era are an anachronism. Apart from frontier incidents and other minor troubles it is perfectly obvious that Russia's well-justified fears of eventual Japanese expansion into Mongolia and Siberia on the one hand, coupled with Japan's fear of the spread of Communism in neighboring territory on the other hand, are in themselves sufficient to prevent the development of any basis of mutual confidence. Nevertheless, up to the month of last November, diplomatic efforts had succeeded in elaborating a fair *modus vivendi* under which Soviet-Japanese relations might be carried along for the time being without too great risk of critical developments. The appointment of a mixed commission to consider frontier questions had been accepted in principle and a fisheries treaty, distinctly favorable to Japan, had been initialed and was ready to be signed on November 20. The Soviet defenses in Siberia and Vladivostok, coupled with the double-tracking of the Siberian Railway, had been brought to a point of effectiveness where Moscow could afford to regard the bluster and saber-rattling of the Kwantung Army with a degree of cynical tolerance, while the Japanese on the other hand were too busy modernizing their army and aiming to strengthen their forces in Manchuria to a point of reasonable balance with the Soviet forces to the north to seek further grounds for early conflict.

This temporary amelioration in Soviet-Japanese relations, however, was rudely shattered by the conclusion by Japan of the anti-Comintern pact with Germany. While ostensibly the pact aims only at co-operation in combating the activities of the Comintern in spreading Communistic propaganda and practice abroad and is therefore not openly directed against the Soviet Government, nevertheless the existence of a secret understanding or agreement between the General Staffs of the two countries is generally accepted as fact, and the Soviet Ambassador in Tokyo asserts that Moscow is in possession of precise evidence to that effect. Political opponents of the cabinet in Japan maintain that if the news of this pact had not been permitted to leak out before November 20, the Soviet-Japanese fisheries treaty would have been signed and all would have been well and they therefore charge the Foreign Minister with a grave blunder in allowing this leakage. But it is inconceivable that Moscow was not well aware, long before that date, of what was going on in Berlin, and the blunder, if such it was, would seem to lie not with the leakage before a certain date but in entering into any such pact at all.

The explanation is simple. The pact and whatever secret agreement may be attached to it were concluded by the Japanese military, the negotiations with Germany having been largely carried on by Major General Oshima, the Japanese Military Attaché in Berlin. We do not know whether these negotiations were conducted with the blessing of the Japanese Foreign Office, but since the Foreign Office has long been assiduously working to improve and stabilize Japan's relations with the USSR as a matter of major policy, it is reasonable to question whether the shattering effect on those relations of a pact with Germany would not have been abundantly clear in advance and whether the civil Government in Tokyo could have been in sympathy with so sharp a divergence in the political orientation of Japan's diplomacy. Certainly the pact has called forth widespread criticism throughout Japan.

Here again the dual system of policy control in Japan would seem to have manifested itself. At any rate, the die is now cast and it is obvious that Japan's relations with Soviet Russia have suffered a rude setback which is not likely to be overcome in the near future. Moreover, we may be sure that the Soviet Government will continue to act on the principle that the only language understood by the Japanese is force, and that when struck, whether by a minor frontier incursion or by some broader form of aggression, the wisest policy to follow is promptly to strike back with double force.

Germany

That the treaty between Japan and Germany envisages anything in the nature of a pact of military mutual assistance in case of war seems highly unlikely. It is said that Japan did her best to get Poland to participate in the arrangement with Germany but without success, and with Poland independent of commitments, and with France at Germany's back, it is hardly likely that Germany would undertake to attack Russia in case of a Soviet war with Japan. Nevertheless, the existence of an agreement for an exchange of military information and for the supply of arms and ammunition and technical aid to Japan in return for commercial commodities from Manchuria is a reasonable hypothesis. Whatever the precise nature of the agreement concluded, it is evident that a new orientation has arisen in Japan's policy, that her relations with Germany are likely to be strengthened as time goes on and that this new orientation is bound, whether intentionally or otherwise, to react unfavorably on any improvement of Japan's relations not only with Soviet Russia but with Great Britain and other democracies as well.

Italy

While there is no good reason to believe that Japan is purposely aligning herself with a Fascist bloc, nevertheless her recent almost simultaneous pacts with both Germany and Italy have naturally given rise to such a theory. In actual fact, the agreements by which Japan will withdraw her Legation from Addis Ababa and substitute therefor a Consulate, while Italy opens a Consulate General in Mukden, thereby implying de facto recognition respectively of the Italian acquisition of Ethiopia and of the "independence" of Manchukuo, would appear to envisage reciprocally privileged trade relations rather than to have any important political bearing.

Great Britain

Japan would like good relations with Great Britain but, as the British Ambassador recently said to me, she would like them on the basis of "all take and no give." Japanese cordiality is but skin deep and is induced solely by the consideration that the Japanese Army has at last awakened to the fact that in the event of a Japanese war with Soviet Russia, Britain might not preserve even a benevolent neutrality. This fact gives the Japanese pause. A large element of the British people today are anti-Japanese in sentiment as a result of the Manchurian episode, Japan's aggressiveness in China, trade questions, and other controversies.

In the meantime no serious setbacks in Great Britain's relations with Soviet Russia have occurred during the past three years. These relations are not cordial but they are at least satisfactory. The Soviets know that Communistic propaganda in Great Britain will not be tolerated. Naval and trade agreements have been concluded. Thus the former enmity of the two countries is largely evaporating while Britain's relations with Japan have steadily grown worse, and the Japanese Army has at last grasped the possible future implications of these developments which are beginning to cause anxiety. Under these circumstances it is not surprising that Japanese Army officers should go out of their way to be cordial to their British confreres.

Potentially serious is the Japanese program of control in various parts of China because such control is certain, sooner or later, to interfere with British interests in that country. The notorious Amau Statement and other pronouncements of Japanese policy relating to China have not served to render any less determined Great Britain's intention to support and develop those interests, and it is reasonable to surmise that, if carried to their logical conclusion, the respective policies of Great Britain and Japan in China are bound to clash.

In the meantime Anglo-Japanese relations have been rendered difficult by trade controversies in India, Australia, and elsewhere, and by the oil question, while the Keelung incident, wherein British naval seamen are alleged to have been assaulted and injured by Japanese police in Formosa, has further embittered these relations. As the Japanese Government has, up to the present, refused to make adequate amends for this incident, the situation has come to an impasse. The Commander-in-Chief of the British East Asiatic Fleet has postponed his official scheduled visit to Japan while embarrassing questions have been asked and resolutions introduced in the British Parliament. Although Prince Chichibu, the Emperor's brother, is to represent the Emperor at the forthcoming Coronation in London in May, it would appear, under present circumstances, that he may not receive so warm a welcome as would have been the case a few years ago.

In Japan itself, much outspoken criticism is heard by those who dislike the agreement with Germany and who would prefer to strengthen the old Anglo-Japanese friendship, a friendship which at present is distinctly on the decline.

DOMESTIC

Protest from the people is the significant new factor in Japanese politics. As the year 1937 opens, popular opposition to the Government's policies is making itself felt with greater emphasis than at any time since before 1931. Cabinets in the past have been subjected to opposition pressure, but for many years no opposition has so directly derived from the people themselves.

This does not mean that public opinion is even approaching control. Far from it. There is, however, an encouraging growth of popular sentiment that the people should have a voice in current discussion of political questions. This sentiment, growing by reason of the economic and political difficulties brought on the nation by the military, lacks unification and leadership; but there is in the movement some prospect of its eventually developing into a check on the belligerent attitude of the country now dictated by the military who are still in the saddle. Observers have often felt that the greatest international danger from Japan is the vulnerability of her system of government to the provoking of a war not initiated by the desires of the people. Any tendency for the people to demand the right to be consulted is salutary. It is a long road to a mature appreciation on the part of any population, no matter how advanced in political experience, of the cost of war; but the first stretches of that road—possibly to be abandoned later—have at least appeared in the virulence of recent protest against the secret diplomacy which faced the country with an accomplished fact. The country has recognized the agreement with Germany as holding serious dangers to Japan's position in the world. The protest has rapidly spread to other subjects also. Public opinion in Japan has a way of dissipating itself ineffectually, and that may be the upshot of the present protest, but as the year opens it is conspicuous and real.

In addition to the disapproval of the agreement with Germany, of the failure of negotiations with Nanking, and of the miscarriage of relations with the Soviet Union, there are domestic factors contributing to the insecurity of the Hirota cabinet. When Hirota formed the cabinet after the incident of February 26, 1936, the military apparently exacted from him a promise of action on clarification of the national policy, improvement of the livelihood of the people, strengthening of national defense, and the adoption of a positive foreign policy. On the latter two points Hirota has been obliging: the military budget is sharply increased, and the Army-favored anti-Communism agreement is certainly a concession to a "positive" foreign policy. On the other two points, however, Hirota has temporized. Certain of the military were pushing, under the first point, various proposals of administrative and Diet reform, which Hirota effectively side-stepped by endless reference to special commissions and committees. Playing for time, he was finally aided by other and more pressing political problems to distract attention. The second point, improvement of the livelihood of the people, has not been accorded even the pretense of fulfillment. Rising prices, rising debt, and rising taxes contradict the commitment; and what has been done in the direction of control of the electric-power industry is poorly comprehended by and of doubtful advantage to the people.

The military appear to be in a position to oust the Hirota cabinet whenever desired, explaining their action, when they decide to take it, on the ground of the cabinet's failure to execute the platform; but thus far there is no indication that the military agree that any other cabinet could do better. The military are still the dominant influence in control of the Government and may continue to be so during 1937, but as evils caused by military domination continue to accumulate, sentiment against the domination increases in volume and force. One field of notable opposition is in financial and industrial circles, where business is more and more openly resentful of fascist tendencies of control by the Government.

Meantime the Diet will meet with 44 per cent of the seats of the lower house held by the Minseito, 36 per cent by the Seiyukai, and the remaining 20 per cent divided among Labor, other small parties, and independents. The Minseito are represented in the Hirota cabinet by the Minister of Communications and the Minister of Commerce and Industry, the Seiyukai by the Minister of Railways and the Minister of Agriculture and Forestry. The most important ministers of the Hirota cabinet do not have party connections.

At the opening of 1937, to recapitulate, domestic politics in Japan are characterized by popular criticism of the Government (particularly for its foreign policy), and public dissatisfaction with the mounting cost of living, budget increase, and pressure of taxes. Against this opposition the advantages enjoyed by the Hirota cabinet in its effort to stay in office are, first, that the military (still in control) are not yet determined that a change would be an improvement, and second, that the political parties still lack unity of attack.

MILITARY

While there is no doubt that the Japanese Army suffered a severe setback in public estimation as a result of the incident of February 26 last, nevertheless subsequent developments have served to offset this unfavorable opinion and to bring the Army back to a position of strength and popularity in public opinion to a degree even greater than formerly. The quick and bloodless suppression of the insurrection and the efficient manner in which order was restored by the Army authorities met with public approval. In addition, the resignation of the generals who held themselves responsible for the incident, the drastic punishment of the officers convicted of direct responsibility, and the announced determination of the military to purge the Army of the "direct actionists" and to exact discipline throughout all ranks created a very favorable impression on the public at large. General Terauchi, the War Minister, has undoubtedly gone a long way toward the suppression of the "direct action" elements and the establishment of stricter discipline in the Army and has also had a large measure of success in curbing the political activities of officers on the active list. Furthermore, the Army is credited with the definite intention of forcing reorganization of the Government and of effecting various social measures for the good of the farming community and other elements of the people, all of which has served to enhance its popularity.

While there is a current outcry in the press against various blunders and failures in Japanese diplomacy, for which the military are largely responsible, most of this publicity comes from the politicians who are threatening dire attacks on the cabinet in the coming session of the Diet. With the public at large, however, these politicians are in general discredited, as is the Diet as a whole, owing to the many scandals arising out of individual corruption and the fact that few deputies after election make any effort whatever to carry out their election promises. The fact that these parliamentarians are at present allowed to attack the cabinet in the press in unbridled terms is in itself an indication that the military have full confidence in their strength and popularity and there is every probability that a good deal of the present fire and slaughter aired in the press by these politicians will peter out when it comes to actual debate in the Diet.

Past experience with the Diet has shown that the attacks against the military made in that body by isolated though courageous liberals are apt to have little or no effect on the policy of the Government.

The people in general are inclined to hold the Foreign Office rather than the Army responsible for the patent failures in diplomacy which have occurred in various directions. On the other hand, the enlightened minority feels perhaps more than ever that the Army is responsible for the unpleasant diplomatic situation with which Japan is now faced.

The important fact should not be overlooked that the cabinet's approval has been secured of military appropriations in the 1937–38 budget of ¥727,965,556, the largest Army appropriations in the history of Japan and an increase of ¥219,648,856 over the 1936–37 figure. There is very little likelihood that this amount will be materially reduced by the Diet.

In conclusion, there seems to be no diminution in the Army's influence on both the domestic and foreign policies of Japan.

NAVAL

With the expiration on December 31, 1936, of the Washington Naval Treaty of 1921–22 and of the London Naval Treaty of 1930, Japan enters the new year in a nontreaty status vis-à-vis the major naval powers of the world. She faces the possibility of unlimited competition in naval construction from the United States and Great Britain and she is confronted with the possibility of greatly increased fortification by these two powers of their Pacific and Far Eastern possessions. This situation has been, of course, brought about by the action of Japan (1) in giving notice in December, 1934, of her intention to abrogate the naval treaties; (2) in withdrawing from the London Naval Conference of 1936 and refusing thereafter to adhere to the Three-Power Treaty; and (3) in permitting the treaties to lapse on December 31, 1936, without entering into any agreement with the other naval powers either with respect to quantitative or qualitative restrictions or with respect to the restrictions of fortifications in the Pacific and Far East.

The main reason which impelled Japan to withdraw from the

naval treaties and to refuse to enter into further commitments was, and is, her passionate unwillingness to bind herself legally and contractually to a position of inferiority; in short, the 5–5–3 ratio had, in the minds of the Japanese, so humiliated this country and had so wounded its *amour-propre* as to have become intolerable and the nation made up its mind, probably shortly after the signature of the London Treaty of 1930, to pay whatever price might be necessary to rid herself of the stigma of inferiority.

Another, and perhaps no less cogent reason, was the conviction that the Washington ratios no longer provided Japan with the measure of security which she felt she enjoyed at the time the treaties were signed. It cannot be denied that conditions have greatly changed since 1922 and, especially with regard to aviation, developments have undoubtedly reduced Japan's security from attack. Furthermore, the adoption in recent years by Japan of a role of stabilizing factor in East Asia has rendered it necessary that this country free itself of restrictions which might hamper the effectiveness of this new policy.

In appraising the results of Japan's action in casting the naval treaties overboard and choosing to remain in a nontreaty status with the other powers, the following may be listed among the possible benefits to Japan: (1) due to her geographic position and her natural defenses arising from the insular character of her possessions and mainland, with the many harbors, inland waterways, and so forth, Japan feels that even with her relatively slender resources she is in a position, if free from both quantitative and qualitative restrictions, to build a navy of such a kind as to render her secure from attack; (2) Japan feels that her position in the Orient, especially vis-à-vis China, will be immeasurably strengthened by this evidence of her unwillingness to submit to restrictions imposed by Western powers; in short, she hopes to gain "face" with the Chinese; (3) Japanese naval experts are confident, and there is some evidence to support this view, that they can attain a measure of parity by the qualitative method, that is, by building vessels of new design, or great size (45,000 tons to 60,000 tons), with high gun calibers, thus rendering existing battleships obsolete. They recall that Germany vastly improved her relative naval position vis-à-vis Great Britain when the British brought out the *Dreadnought* class in 1906, thus rendering obsolete all her own pre-*Dreadnought* battleships.

The disadvantages to Japan of the nontreaty status may, however, prove to outweigh the benefits. In the first place, the Washington

Naval Treaty was an integral part of a political group of treaties, and the Japanese by abrogating these have destroyed the collective system of security which has governed the Pacific and Far Eastern area since 1922. In order to correct this situation she may be forced to seek security through new political agreements, perhaps of a bilateral character. But the former Anglo-Japanese Alliance is probably forever lost to her and there appears on the horizon at present to be no political arrangement which can possibly replace either that alliance or the collective system which she has just abandoned.

Furthermore, Japan's actions in respect to the naval treaties has completed her isolation, an isolation which was begun with her withdrawal from the League of Nations in March, 1934. In addition to this, Japan will now be faced with the threat of a possible increase in Pacific and Far Eastern fortifications of American and British possessions and territories, a threat which, if not immediate or actual, at least will prove a costly bargaining point in any negotiations for naval or other political agreements which Japan might be in the future forced to seek.

As far as the acquisition of "face" vis-à-vis China is concerned, recent events have proven that expectations on this score have abjectly failed to materialize. Japan was not only checkmated in her negotiations at Nanking last fall, but she is at present faced with a stiffer resistance and a more united China than she has ever before encountered.

Other results have not been happy. The realization that isolation constitutes a real danger to a country, especially in time of war, has made itself keenly felt during the past year, and Japan has consequently made real efforts during the past six months to emerge from this condition. In November the Japanese Government announced the anti-Comintern agreement with Germany, the arrangements with Italy involving at least *de facto* recognition of territory brought by extralegal methods under the domination of the other, and shortly thereafter the agreement with Poland for the increase of cultural relations with that strategically important buffer state between Germany and Russia. The reaction in Moscow was immediate and vigorous, with the result that relations with that heavily armed neighbor have been badly strained.

In the light of evidence now available it therefore may be argued that in a political sense Japan has not improved her position by failing to renew or to enter into new naval agreements with the great powers; in the technical naval sense, however, bearing in mind chiefly considerations of defense, it is quite possible to believe that Japan may have been the gainer, although this remains to be seen.

QUEZON AND MACARTHUR VISIT TOKYO

February 1, 1937

Last night President Quezon * of the Philippine Commonwealth arrived in Tokyo on his way to the United States. I met him at the station and motored him and General MacArthur to the Embassy, where they will be our guests for a night. We welcomed Quezon and MacArthur at an informal dinner.

This morning I presented President Quezon to the Emperor and after the audience we remained to luncheon, at which were present Prince Takamatsu, the two Matsudairas, and a distinguished gathering. The Emperor talked freely with Quezon, discussing the Davao land question and other issues. In my own talk with the Emperor at luncheon I told him a good deal about the Tercentenary celebration at Harvard and the Japanese art exhibit in Boston, in which he appeared greatly interested. We also thoroughly discussed golf and he seemed much impressed when I told him that I had played on twenty-four different golf links in Japan, which I considered a golfers' paradise. I have seldom seen the Emperor so affable. Owing to the political crisis and not knowing who was going to be in office at the time of President Quezon's visit, I had not arranged an official reception, but we did have a fairly large informal tea this afternoon. In the evening Quezon dined with Foreign Minister Arita.

The speeches at the dinner were very significant because Arita in his welcoming speech to Quezon made no mention whatever of the United States, but Quezon in his reply talked of the United States all the way through his speech and very gracefully spoke of the gratitude which the Philippines owed to America for all we had done for them. In replying to Arita's suggestion that Japan and the Philippines should in future develop the closest cultural and economic relations Quezon said that of course in any future relationship of that kind the first duty and interest of the Philippine Commonwealth would be to include the United States but he saw no reason why there should not be a three-cornered understanding which would be helpful to everybody. That is not precisely the way he phrased it but that is what he meant. His speech when published the next day filled me with delight. I doubt if the Japanese will have

* See photograph No. 10.

realized what a definite rebuff was contained in his phraseology, especially when he said that so far as the future relations between Japan and the Philippines were concerned, "deeds speak louder than words." General MacArthur told us that he considers Quezon one of the five great statesmen of the world, and I dare say he is right. I found him thoroughly stimulating and was very glad to have had him under our roof.

WHEN JAPANESE-AMERICAN RELATIONS
WERE NEVER BETTER

February 12, 1937

This afternoon Alice, having a cold and feeling poorly, stayed at home while I did the family duty by going to a reception at the Chinese Embassy, and it was worth while because it gave me an opportunity for a long and intimate conversation with Amau. Amau said that he thought that Japanese-American relations had undergone a great change in the last two or three years and that Japan's attitude toward America was very different from that of three years ago. He said that there were really no important issues pending between us at the present time and he thought it very significant that the speech which the Minister for Foreign Affairs is about to make in a few days is going to state that Japan desires the most friendly relations with both the United States and Great Britain; so far as the United States is concerned he will stop right there, but so far as Great Britain is concerned he will continue to the effect that current controversies can be settled by diplomatic negotiations. In other words, said Amau, the absence of comment with regard to the United States would indicate that there are no prime issues worth mentioning.

I said I thought that this situation was in large measure due to Mr. Hirota and his efforts in curbing the Japanese press, which had caused so much trouble in times past in its bitter comment about the United States; these comments were repeated by correspondents to America and of course the American press took them up there, causing a vicious circle all around. Amau then told me of his own efforts in this direction and how in the weekly meetings with representatives of Japanese journals he had tried to influence the editorial writers to lay off bickering with the United States. In this respect he had been rather successful. I told Amau that although I had ascribed the credit for our improved relations to Hirota I knew very well that he himself had had an important hand in this development. I mentioned the press report about Shiratori as possible Vice-Minister, but Amau brushed Shiratori aside, saying that he wanted war with Soviet Russia and would therefore certainly not fit into the present regime. I said I thought that Japan was at present in a very critical position and that she really stood at the parting of the ways; Amau agreed with me and said that this was why a moderate cabinet had been appointed at the present time. On the whole this conversation seemed to me significant because Amau emphasized so distinctly the fact that the present cabinet is moderate and it looks at present very much as if this might prove to be the case.

WARNING AGAINST THE CALM BEFORE THE STORM

March 19, 1937

The past month has been especially interesting politically owing to the strong attack on the Government in the Diet by Hamada, Ozaki, and other interpellators, as well as to the comparatively gentle replies of the Prime Minister and other members of the cabinet, and particularly to the indications that the Government really intends at least for the present to follow a more moderate policy in its relations with other countries, especially with China. How long it will or can follow this policy is an open question. There is no doubt that a certain degree of discipline has been instilled into the Army so that military officers are being very careful what they write and what they say. It is generally understood among the younger officers that those who are reported as talking politics or criticizing the Government's policy are more than likely to be shipped to undesirable posts in the next general shakeup, so they are carefully watching their step. For the moment it might almost appear that there was a tendency to revert to the "Shidehara diplomacy" and that the moderate influences in the country are becoming more articulate and possibly more influential than they have been for a long time.

I do not for a moment, however, delude myself by believing that this new orientation is likely to last very long. This in all probability is merely an interlude or one of the periodic waves of retrocession in the expansionist movement of which I have often spoken and have compared it precisely to the waves on the seashore, being firmly convinced that the tide is coming in and not going out and that recurrent waves of aggressiveness and forward movement are perfectly certain to go farther ahead than their predecessors. Therefore, in shaping our policy toward Japan we should be very careful not to be led astray by appearances of any permanent change of heart in policy and tactics on the part of the Japanese Government. The military are too firmly in the saddle and will continue to remain there. Now the Diet has been dissolved because it refused to pass a good many of the bills desired by the Government, and the cabinet has no intention of continuing to bicker with the political parties, and we shall have to watch carefully to see just how the ship of state is steered during the coming months, which, as always in Japan, are bound to be interesting ones. One feels a little like living on a volcano here, never knowing when an explosion is going to occur, and I am quite sure that the day of possible explosions is by no means past.

JAPAN GREETS HELEN KELLER

April 18, 1937

This afternoon a large meeting followed by a "banquet" was held at the Tokyo Kaikan to honor Helen Keller.* The meeting showed, better than anything else could do, the real sentiment that lies deep in the character of the Japanese people. Their traditional politeness is generally but a veneer, save in the case of the well-bred families; that politeness does not comprise thoughtful consideration of others in any degree. But sentiment is another matter. Here is a woman of no official standing who, by her own efforts, having overcome her terrible handicap of total loss of sight, speech, and hearing, has devoted her life to constructive work for the blind and now comes to Japan to spread her gospel and her assistance here. This appeals to the Japanese more deeply than any case that I have seen during our five years' stay here.

On the platform at the meeting were the Prime Minister, perhaps in his capacity as Minister of Education, the Foreign Minister, the Home Minister, the Governor of the Prefecture, the Mayor of Tokyo, Prince Tokugawa, and Marquis Okubo, President of the Foundation for the Blind. The great hall was literally packed with five or six hundred people, every last seat taken, among whom I noticed Baron Shidehara, Mr. Yoshizawa, and many of the highest people in the country. Each of the high officials made a brief speech extolling Miss Keller's work; she replied through Miss Thom-

* See photograph No. 11.

son and was then presented with a beautiful Japanese incense burner.

When it came my turn to speak at the end I was so deeply moved that I dropped my text and tried to tell the meeting how I really felt about it all, thanking them on Miss Keller's behalf. Alice, who with several guests at the Embassy, heard my speech on the radio, said there was no doubt about my feelings. Indeed, it was a meeting that I shall never forget. I am sure that Miss Keller must have been equally moved. But *Asahi* said: "Had they [the Government and the people] devoted a fraction of the attention they have paid to the reception of Miss Keller to the promotion of the welfare of the blind, deaf, and dumb, that would have pleased her much more than the greetings extended her by the Premier, the cabinet members, and the other leaders of the nation. But her visit to these shores has been the occasion for the awakening of the people to the condition of private institutions devoted to the promotion of the welfare of the blind, deaf, and dumb. . . . Let us hope that the Government will fix a definite policy and carry it out. . . ."

4

CHINA INCIDENT

(July 8, 1937–October 10, 1939)

THWARTED in their attempts to seize power inside Japan, the military extremists committed
their country to large-scale war in China. This
war not only rallied the people to the support of
the extremists; it committed the whole country
to a military adventure of world-wide scope.
The Japanese militarists had originally hoped
that their occupation of all the main China
ports would give them control of the entire
country, but these calculations proved mistaken.
Then, the Nazi-Soviet Pact of August, 1939,
which set the stage for Hitler's attack on Poland,
caused almost as much consternation in Japan
as it had in Europe. Even the most fanatical
militarists had not expected the Germans to
enter into any kind of deal with the Soviet
Union, for the strongest bond holding Germany and Japan together at this time was the
Anti-Comintern Pact. Thus, the outbreak of
war in Europe did not prove an unmixed blessing to the Japanese military. It gave them a
freer hand to the south, but it created new
anxieties to the east.

THE CHINA INCIDENT BEGINS

July 8, 1937

Fighting has broken out at the Marco Polo bridge not far from Peiping between Chinese and Japanese troops. Not clear who started the trouble, but Nelson Johnson says that considering the fact that the Japanese conduct maneuvers close to a Chinese garrison it is only surprising that such an incident had not occurred long ago.

A UNIFIED JAPAN EMBARKS ON WAR

July 13, 1937

Cabled the Department that in the present crisis there seems to be complete unanimity of opinion between the cabinet, the military, the Foreign Office, the press, and the businessmen to resist any weakening of Japan's position in North China. Of course it might readily be said that when the Prime Minister consulted the various politicians, financiers, and business leaders and asked them if they were behind the Government they could hardly have said no, but in the present situation we sense a greater unanimity than was ever present in the Manchurian issue.

AMERICAN AND BRITISH REPRESENTATIONS

July 14, 1937

The Japanese and Chinese representatives in Washington yesterday called at the Department and the opportunity was taken to express our hope that both sides would exercise restraint. The British Government was informed of our action and the following press release was issued by the Department:

> The Japanese Ambassador and the Counselor of the Chinese Embassy each called at the Department this morning and communicated information in regard to events in North China. In the course of the conversations which ensued both were given expression of the view that an armed conflict between Japan and China would be a great blow to the cause of peace and world progress.

No reinforcements have yet left Japan.

"ASK THE TOURISTS"

July 17, 1937

The following well-known story is applicable to the present situation. During a Far Eastern crisis an American businessman asked an old resident in Japan what was at the bottom of it all and what was going to happen. The resident replied: "I don't know." "What, you've lived here thirty-five years and you don't know?" "No," said the old resident, "I don't know. But ask any of the tourists out here. They'll tell you." There are plenty of people in Japan today who are firmly convinced that the present crisis is a put-up, predetermined job on the part of the Japanese, engineered with the definite purpose and intention of taking over North China. They adduce plenty of evidence: the smoothness with which the Konoye cabinet came in, the various developments during the past year or two leading up to the final stroke; the theory that Soviet Russia has been weakened by internal dissensions and would be incapable of intervention; the hazardous position of Great Britain in Europe preventing the use of her fleet in the Far East; the understanding with Germany. But in spite of all this, I have to align myself with the old residents. I don't know. Ask the tourists. It's all guesswork, and all we can do is to watch developments, gather facts, and try to the best of our ability to analyze them from day to day.

Mr. Hull has made an admirable public statement in Washington. It is perfectly balanced; it accuses nobody; mentions no names, but it leaves no doubt as to our policy toward the maintenance of peace, the sanctity of treaties and the orderly modification thereof, respect for international law, American economic policy, disarmament, and co-operation without entangling alliances. Whether it helps the situation or not, it is a great deal wiser than direct representations, which not only would not help but would harm by engendering irritation. The Japanese won't like it because they will know it is directed at them, but the form of the statement absolutely precludes their taking umbrage.

CHINA'S REPLY TO JAPAN'S AGGRESSION

July 20, 1937

The Chinese Government has delivered an *aide-mémoire* to the Japanese Embassy in Nanking, covering four points:

1. The two countries should agree on a date when movements of their military forces would cease and they would be recalled to their original positions.

2. Diplomatic negotiations for the settlement of the dispute.

3. The authorization of the Nanking Government is essential for any agreement concluded on the spot.

4. China is willing to accept any means of settlement recognized by international law and treaties.

Apparently the Japanese want to know if this is intended to be a reply to their own note and, if so, why their various points were not answered. The Japanese press of course characterizes the Chinese note as "insincere" and this evening's papers indicate that the situation is hopeless. It seems to me that when Nanking has offered Japan an armistice and proposed a settlement by diplomatic negotiations, the Japanese are not going to have a very good case to present to the world if they now go to war. Nevertheless, it would, from their point of view, be inconsistent to agree to diplomatic negotiations when they have insisted that the matter is a local issue to be settled locally.

It is reported this morning that Soviet forces have again attacked on the Manchurian frontier. I should think that the unknown factor of Soviet action in case of war would at least enter into Japanese calculations.

"HOW CAN WE COMPROMISE WHEN YOU REFUSE TO ACCEPT OUR VIEWS?"

July 21, 1937

An officer of the Military Affairs Bureau of the War Ministry told Carey Crane that Suma's * conversation with Hornbeck yesterday revealed our pro-Chinese attitude and the fact that we don't understand the situation in North China at all. That is precisely the impression which would inevitably be created in Japanese minds by the carefully balanced observations which Hornbeck undoubtedly would have made to Suma. It reminds me of the naïve remark made by the Japanese delegation in the Dutch-Japanese shipping conference: "How can we compromise when you refuse to accept our views?"

* Then Counselor to the Japanese Embassy in Washington; in 1940 he became spokesman for the Japanese Foreign Office.

TROOP ACTIVITIES EVERYWHERE

July 31, 1937

Somebody told me today a delicious story, and a true one, which can only be appreciated if recounted in a rich Oxford drawl. An English lady, rather high and mighty, was recently passing through Japan, and on landing she said to her host: "Ah, so this is Kobe. Tell me, who is our Governor General here?"

Cabled the Department today that the Japanese determination to use decisive force against any Chinese military advance into North China would appear to be increasingly firm. After a five-minister conference yesterday, Prince Konoye went to see the Emperor, and a press report said that a decision of the greatest importance had been taken, a "second step" in Japan's program in China. Troop activities are everywhere evident here.

AMERICA STILL TRIES TO KEEP THE PEACE

August 6, 1937

The British Government, repeating suggestions made to our London Ambassador on July 28, now proposes an Anglo-American offer of good offices to both the Japanese and the Chinese in providing neutral ground where plenipotentiaries could meet and in helping to smooth out such difficulties as might occur in the negotiations, arrangements for withdrawing the troops to follow, but before acting they wanted Dodds' * and my opinion as to the probable reaction in Japan to such an offer.

After a long conference in my study tonight with Dodds and Sansom of the British Embassy and Dooman, who has succeeded Neville as our Counselor, I have come to the following conclusions:

1. We feel that there is no discernible enthusiasm among the Japanese Government or people for war with China, although we must obviously omit the military machine from this characterization. The prevailing feeling among the Japanese is that Chinese manifestations of enmity toward Japan brought about the present situation and that while the Japanese Government and people would still be glad to avoid a general war, they will support whatever military or other measures the Government decides to take. A powerful and practical argument for peace is involved in the appropriations of four hundred million yen for military operations on the continent,

* British Chargé d'Affaires in Tokyo.

together with the assurance of steadily mounting costs in the event of an extensive campaign.

2. The Japanese insist that the initiative for either peace or war must now come from China. On the other hand, although I defer to Johnson's opinion in this respect, it does not now look as if the Chinese, considering that Chinese authority in the Peiping area has now been virtually eliminated, would take any initiative toward peace. If the Chinese forces continue to move toward Hopeh it seems inevitable that a general clash is bound to occur.

3. It seems to me of the utmost importance that we should leave no stone unturned to prevent war, and I therefore cannot conscientiously recommend against a final effort by the American and the British Governments by offering good offices on the basis of the British Government's practical proposal, although it should be made abundantly clear that such action would in no sense constitute intervention. We feel that in Tokyo the chances of acceptance are small but not necessarily hopeless. Publicity should be carefully avoided and much would depend on the manner and method of approach. If the two Governments should decide to proceed, I feel that Dodds and I, separately, should ask to see Hirota at his residence, not at the Foreign Office, and should present the offer in complete confidence, asking whether the Minister thought that the suggested plan would, from the Japanese point of view, serve a useful purpose. If it should be considered undesirable to sound out one Government before the other, a similar and simultaneous approach might be made in Nanking.

4. As for the probable reception in Tokyo I believe that the best prospects of forestalling any possible resentment would be a confidential and exploratory approach such as I have outlined. Indications could be given that these channels for good offices would be open now or later if desired.

5. My careful judgment is that an oral, exploratory, semi-informal, and confidential talk with Hirota along the lines of the British proposal would be more likely to avoid any possible resentment of "interference" and more likely to bring favorable results than would a formal "diplomatic *démarche*." In any case, publicity should be most carefully avoided.

6. While fully aware that I have previously expressed the opinion that we have left nothing undone which could favorably affect developments, nevertheless I should like to feel that history will regard the record of America's action in this most pregnant and critical

period in Far Eastern affairs as exhaustive, impartially correct, and unstintedly helpful.

Dodds and Sansom said that they agreed with my views.

CHINESE BOMBS ON SHANGHAI HURT CHINA'S CAUSE ABROAD

August 29, 1937

It seems to me that nowadays the diary is generally written on hot Sunday mornings and today, August 29, is no exception to the rule. Everyone else, or nearly everyone, has gone off to the hills for the week end. Alice and Elsie are in Karuizawa and the rest of the staff divided between Karuizawa and Chuzenji. Only Crocker, who is on duty this week end, the clerical staff, and I remain. Dooman proposed that he and I take alternate week ends off, but I don't like to be away at such a time; things happen too fast, and sometimes something happens which only the Ambassador can handle, or ought to handle. We diplomats have plenty of easy periods with plenty of play; our intensive work comes in cycles and I heartily welcome such work when it does come, for every professional man likes an opportunity to function at top speed once in a while. So I'm not easing up just now. Alice rather went to pieces on account of the heat and I bundled her off, with Elsie, to Karuizawa, the children being already parked there in Carey Crane's house. Personally I thrive on heat and am fit as a fiddle. So on with the—no, I've used that phrase too often. What I mean to say is that we'll keep going, regardless.

The bombing in Shanghai on August 14 was one of the most horrible episodes in modern times. The bombs fell indiscriminately, hitting the Cathay and Palace Hotels and killing hundreds of Chinese civilians gathered on the Bund and elsewhere. Bob Reischauer, the son of an American missionary, was fatally injured at the entrance to the Cathay and other Americans may have been killed or injured. I wrote to Dr. and Mrs. Reischauer in Karuizawa. Subsequently we received the most heart-rending firsthand accounts from refugees.

FIRST CONVERSATION WITH SIR ROBERT CRAIGIE, BRITAIN'S NEW AMBASSADOR TO JAPAN

September 8, 1937

The new British Ambassador, Sir Robert Craigie, came to call, although he will not present his credentials until Saturday. We had a pleasant talk which gave me the impression that he desires the closest co-operative relations between us. He had talked with Clive * and I suppose that this initial frankness and friendliness may be due to what Clive said to him of our own relations.

WARNING TO HIROTA

September 20, 1937. Kawana

Eighteen more holes of golf, sixty-three holes in the three days. I ended in a blaze of glory with a birdie 3 on the sixty-third hole. Sunburnt and physically tired but psychologically rested, and that meant much.

Dooman had telephoned that it would probably be necessary for me to see Hirota today, so we hurried back after lunch and I found that the Japanese plans to bomb Nanking called for immediate representations. I saw the Minister at 6 and talked to him in much stronger terms than I had yet employed, feeling that the time had come for the most emphatic language. In the course of my remarks I said that we must not forget history; that neither the American Government nor the American people had wanted war with Spain in 1898, but when the *Maine* was blown up nothing could prevent war. The American people are the most pacific and patient people in the world; we lead the world in matters of international peace and disarmament and the maintenance of the sanctity of treaties. But under provocation we can become the most inflammable people in the world. It is well not to forget history.

Evidently these representations made an impression because Hirota went to see the Emperor early the next morning and later we began to notice concrete indications that the Government was getting disturbed about the effects of the indiscriminate bombings and were taking steps to control the aviators. Of course it is these young hotheads who cause the trouble; having once smelled blood they simply fly amok and "don't give a damn" whom or what they hit. Probably as a result of our representations and of the reactions they are getting from abroad, the Government later sent an admiral down to Shanghai to discuss this situation with Hasegawa, the Commander in Chief, and word was sent out that there would be no further bombing of Nanking after September 25. This of course was

* Sir Robert Clive had been replaced as British Ambassador by Sir Robert Craigie.

after they had destroyed about everything they wanted to destroy in that city. Meanwhile Moore, who was Acting Secretary of State, likewise talked to Saito, and later, under instructions, I filed a strong note here. This is no time for pussyfooting.

STRONG WORDS TO A HELPLESS GOVERNMENT

September 20, 1937

My conversation with the Minister for Foreign Affairs at his official residence at 6 o'clock this evening was prefaced by a word of appreciation from me with regard to the arrangements made by the Japanese authorities to avoid bombing the Hankow-Canton railway during the evacuation of Americans on September 22 and 26. The Minister inquired if I had received his note concerning the bombing of the American missionary hospital at Waichow, to which I replied in the affirmative and expressed further appreciation of the Minister's expressions of regret and the offer to consider indemnification.

I then turned to the announced plans of the Japanese naval forces to bomb Nanking commencing tomorrow at noon, and I made to the Minister the most emphatic and earnest representations with regard to the serious danger to which foreign diplomatic establishments and personnel, as well as other noncombatants, would inevitably be subjected if such a course is pursued. I spoke of the very serious effect which would be produced in the United States on the American Government and people if some accident should occur in connection with those operations, and I then spoke of the steadily mounting feeling which is developing in the United States and in other countries against Japan, which by her course of action is laying up for herself among the peoples of the world a liability of distrust and suspicion, popular antipathy, and the possibility of Japan's becoming ostracized from the family of nations. I said to the Minister that the good will between our countries which he and I had been building up during these past years was rapidly dissolving as a result of Japan's action in China and that while the American people are patient they are nevertheless easily aroused by some serious incident involving their legitimate interests abroad, and that I am constantly dreading the effects in my country which would undoubtedly be called forth if as a result of Japanese operations in China some serious incident should occur which the American people would feel had touched their honor.

I then spoke earnestly of the Minister's own responsibility for guiding Japan's foreign relations and for restraining the Japanese naval and military forces in China from their course of action which is rapidly causing Japan to lose the world's good will and is building up abroad an almost universal sentiment of antagonism against his country. I said that the military and naval forces did not understand and appeared not to care about Japan's foreign relations and her position in the world and it was therefore his own responsibility to guide the course of action which is now being pursued in China. The force and directness of my statements and appeal left nothing whatever to Mr. Hirota's imagination. I tried to bring home to the Minister with maximum effect the certain repercussion which would occur in the United States if some serious accident involving American interests were to happen in connection with the proposed bombing of Nanking.

Mr. Hirota made no effort to counter my observations, but listened gravely and silently throughout my talk. When I had finished he observed that four hours ago from Tokyo he had ordered the naval command in China to make every effort to avoid injury to the foreign diplomatic establishments or to noncombatants in Nanking in connection with the proposed bombing operations. I said that the afternoon press had reported that certain bombing operations in Nanking had already occurred yesterday, but the Minister said that these were unimportant and far away from the diplomatic establishments. With regard to the warning by the Japanese Navy that the bombing operations would commence at noon on September 21, the Minister volunteered the opinion that the warning was "too short."

Although I talked to the Minister today with an emphasis and directness unprecedented since my arrival in Japan, he gave no indication of resentment. His demeanor was naturally graver than usual and he appeared to me to receive my observations rather sadly but without any effort whatever at rebuttal. While recent developments indicate that he has made and is making efforts to avoid antagonizing the United States by cautioning the military and naval forces in individual local issues, we must reluctantly face the fact that the civil government in Tokyo has very little influence with these forces where their general objectives are concerned.

"GOOD-WILL ENVOYS"

October 5, 1937

Kojiro Matsukata came in for a talk before departing for the United States. In spite of my informal recommendations to Kabayama, Soyeshima, and others against sending so-called good-will envoys to America, a whole flock of them are going out: Matsukata, Ashida, Takeishi, and Bunjiro Suzuki to the United States, Viscount Ishii to England and France, Admiral Godo to Germany, Baron Okura to Italy, etc. In America they will get nowhere.

Their fundamental theme is that they are fighting China in self-defense, and no American will listen to such rot, however presented. The American is *a priori* sympathetic to China and always has been, and he is furthermore almost always sympathetic to the underdog. Japan is fighting on Chinese soil. What more need be said? These envoys will receive a rude shock if I am not greatly mistaken.

But Matsukata says that he is not going as a good-will envoy but simply to make business contacts and to buy needed commodities such as oil, scrap iron, and trucks. I warned him that he would find public opinion in the United States inhospitable to Japanese claims that China is responsible for the present conflict, that Japan has recently done much to render difficult the continued application of the good-neighbor policy, and that in shaping its own policy and action the American Government must listen to public opinion at home. He claims that American influence is today paramount in Japan and can play a prominent part in helping to stop the warfare.

On October 5, President Roosevelt delivered his famous "Chicago speech" calling for a "quarantine" of aggressor nations. Shortly thereafter, the Belgian Government invited the signatories of the Nine-Power Treaty of 1922, promising to respect the political and administrative integrity of China, to attend a conference at Brussels.

WHAT CAN THE NINE-POWER CONFERENCE ACCOMPLISH?

October 9, 1937

As for the military and political situation, the Japanese are making a big drive around Shanghai, doubtless with the purpose of impressing the Nine-Power Conference. They appear to have cleaned up a good deal of ground. But what we ask ourselves is this: assuming that the Japanese Army is able to occupy and control all the territory it wishes; supposing that the Chinese forces are partly annihilated, wholly disorganized, disrupted, scattered. What then? Can they or anyone else force China to make peace? And if peace is not made, can the Japanese afford to withdraw any substantial number of their troops?

They must hold the ground already won. Their lines of supply are becoming more and more attenuated. How long can they afford to maintain this great force in China with constant guerrilla warfare seeking to harry and deplete their strength? And what about Soviet Russia—*after* the Japanese forces are thus thoroughly involved and correspondingly weakened? That, it seems to me, is the big imponderable factor in the situation. But, in the meantime, will China collapse, morally disintegrate and descend into utter chaos? That, of course, is what the Japanese are aiming at; it explains their constant bombing of defenseless cities. These are just a few of the headaches that confront us.

Meanwhile, what can the Nine-Power Conference accomplish? Press the combatants to negotiate for peace—and get thoroughly rebuffed? Try economic sanctions and ignominiously fail as they did in the case of Abyssinia? Or content themselves with moral thunderbolts which would have about as much effect in Japan as a mild hailstorm in the country?

Perhaps the answer to some or all of these questions will be clearer by the time that this inadequate soliloquy reaches American shores.

JAPAN REFUSES TO ATTEND THE BRUSSELS CONFERENCE

October 21, 1937

A diplomatic colleague said that he had yesterday made renewed representations to Hirota, repeating the representations made on October 15, in an effort to persuade the Japanese Government to participate in the Nine-Power Conference at Brussels. He advanced the argument that the Japanese case had gone by default at Geneva and that Brussels would offer a further opportunity to present Japan's case, which would be carefully considered by the assembled powers who wished above all to be helpful toward arriving at a peaceful settlement of the Sino-Japanese hostilities. The Minister replied that since his last talk with the Ambassador

he had consulted a great number of prominent people here and that
the sentiment against participation in the conference, especially
among the leaders of the political parties, was practically unanimous. However, as no invitation had yet been received, no final
decision had yet been reached.

October 22, 1937

Yoshizawa told Dooman yesterday that so far as the Foreign Office
was concerned, the Nine-Power Conference invitation would definitely be declined, and that a favorable reply could not be expected
so long as the invitation did not specify that the Conference does
not arise out of the League of Nations resolution and the American
Government's announcement of October 6.

RUMORS OF PEACE, BUT JAPAN'S WAR
SPIRIT GROWS

October 30, 1937

Today came three telegrams from the Department indicating interest in press rumors that Japan is ready to discuss peace terms and
desiring our comments and estimate of the situation. They included
a rumor that the German Ambassador in China, Trautmann, was
actually negotiating as a mediator with Kawagoe in Shanghai. We
nailed this rumor to the mast by talking it over frankly with Noebel,
German Counselor, who said that the German Embassy here knew
nothing of such negotiations, that the relations between Kawagoe
and Trautmann had not been very satisfactory owing to Japanese
suspicion that the latter is pro-Chinese and owing also to the employment in China of German military instructors, and that Trautmann had taken advantage of a recent visit to Shanghai to get on
better terms with Kawagoe.

I told the Department about the general press comment here,
which concentrated on the idea that Japan will tolerate no outside
interference when the time comes to talk terms with China, and I
then said that the only way really to ascertain the mind of the
Japanese Government would be for me to go to Hirota and
"explore." I said that I could best do this by asking to see Hirota
at his residence to avoid publicity and to open the conversation by
referring to a remark which I had made to him on August 6 to the
effect that I hoped he would let me know if he ever saw ways in
which I could personally be of help, and then to lead up to the

Brussels Nine-Power Conference, making it clear that I was acting on my own initiative and without instructions. Thus nothing that transpired would commit or involve the American Government, and it might possibly elicit some suggestions from Hirota, who might welcome the opening thus afforded in order to mobilize elements in Japan which do not favor war to the bitter end. In any case, I don't believe in using "go-betweens" in such important matters, for they are too liable to mess things up or to get things twisted.

Hitherto the only Japanese terms known to us are Hirota's famous "three points" and these are open to such broad interpretation that they can mean almost anything at a given moment that the Japanese want them to mean. It will be remembered that the three points envisage Chinese factual recognition of Manchukuo, cessation of anti-Japanese activities and propaganda, and the suppression of Communism. Whatever the final terms may be, it is safe to say that they will undoubtedly involve practically complete Japanese political and economic control in North China, whatever else they may include. I am rather skeptical of Hirota's committing himself to me even informally to anything more specific than his nebulous three points, but it might do no harm to try to create an opening for negotiations. I once helped to stave off war between Turkey and Greece; it would be a tremendous satisfaction to help to stop the war between Japan and China.

The Department replied immediately, leaving to my discretion the action proposed but suggesting that it might be well not to make the approach specifically for the purpose stated but to utilize some opportunity to broach the subject when I was seeing Hirota about something else. I certainly appreciate the latitude the Department allows me and the fact that it almost always "suggests" rather than "directs."

Having got that particular telegram off, I then held a series of conferences with Craigie, both at our Embassy and his, with Dooman participating in the final drafting of a telegram which, it was suggested, we should send identically to our respective Governments to help the Brussels Conference. In brief, the idea is that if good offices or mediation are to result from the Conference, the Conference must take care not to go beyond its mandate of attempting "to promote peace by agreement" and it should avoid expressing judgment as to the origins of the conflict or the responsibilities involved. The more the Conference can maintain impartiality, the better will be the prospect of eventually successful mediation.

Furthermore, mediation, if undertaken at all, should be entrusted to one power, preferably to the United States or Great Britain, and not to a group of powers or to America and Great Britain acting together, for this would imply an element of pressure, and foreign pressure, or any semblance of it, would be resisted to the last ditch. The Conference, too, should carefully consider the possible effects of its proceedings on the internal situation here. Hirota's position is shaky; the military and the chauvinists want Matsuoka to take his place, and if that should happen, not only would we have to expect even greater ruthlessness in China, but American and British interests here would inevitably suffer. The war spirit here is noticeably growing.

We were able to subscribe to the essential part of the proposed identic telegram and the final draft, which was satisfactory to both Craigie and myself, was dispatched about 7 in the evening and I hope it will be sent on to Norman Davis and Eden in Brussels and that it may influence the tactics of the Conference. Our French colleagues agreed to telegraph in the same general sense to Paris. I felt that we had done a good day's work.

Craigie was very much perturbed today; Anglo-Japanese relations are about as bad as they can be; three more British soldiers have been killed in Shanghai, probably by Japanese shells, and the anti-Japanese feeling in England is steadily growing. He is worrying too about the organization of a new Japanese fleet, the Fourth Fleet, and is fearful lest its main object may be effectually to blockade Hong Kong. I think he really fears the possibility that the Japanese Navy will intentionally provoke war with England. At any rate, we now know that the animus of the Navy has definitely turned from the United States toward Great Britain and we also know that the Navy hates to have the Army steal the whole show and is chafing for action. Pabst is equally worried that this new fleet may have designs along the lines of the "southward advance," involving the Dutch East Indies. And both he and Craigie are worried about the possibility of another February 26 incident and think it may be possible.

But what, we ask ourselves, can the military elements and the chauvinists be grousing about? Certainly it looks as if the Army and Navy were having their way, with very little interference on the part of the Government or the Old Guard elements. Saionji, Makino, Yuasa, and Matsudaira don't seem to come into the picture at all nowadays. What would be the use of further assassinations? But the Japanese military and chauvinists, with their samurai traditions and

swashbuckling ideas, are always an unpredictable element in the
political arena here. Almost anything can happen.

HIROTA ACCUSES AMERICA OF INITIATING
AN ANTI-JAPANESE FRONT

November 16, 1937

Hirota's talk with me was along the following lines: according to
reports received from Brussels it appears that the draft final resolution contemplates united action against Japan; the Minister has
seen only the original draft and doesn't know if it was passed without alteration or amendment, but if it does call for united action he
fears that a very unfortunate effect on Japanese public opinion will
be created; "united action" would appear to imply some sort of
sanctions, such as an economic boycott, and far from helping to stop
the hostilities, such action would merely encourage the Chinese and
would result in indefinitely prolonging them. According to information received through the diplomatic representative of "a certain
power," the United States not only took the initiative in proposing
the Brussels Conference but is also taking the active leadership
there.

Hirota said that these rumors were sure to appear soon in the
Japanese press and that they would have a very unfortunate effect.
Hitherto the Japanese public have felt that the country foremost in
developing a solid front against Japan was Great Britain, but if the
press were now to report that the leadership at Brussels was being
taken by the United States, the onus would be largely shifted to
American shoulders. As the Minister had often told me, good relations with the United States were his fundamental policy and he
greatly "feared" the results of the possible developments which he
had described. Up to recently the Japanese felt that America was the
only country whose impartiality during the Sino-Japanese hostilities
had been genuine; the impartiality of all of the other countries was
doubted, owing to their special interest in China, but owing to the
position taken by the United States it was felt that we might play
an important role in helping to bring about peace just as we had
done in the Russo-Japanese War, as being the most impartial of all
the friends of Japan. This situation had been somewhat altered by
the speech of the President in Chicago, but in the President's
address to Congress he had omitted mention of the Far East and
this had given the Japanese public the impression that the attitude

of the United States was perhaps not quite so "strict" as had at first been feared.

Hirota then went on to say that the Japanese campaign in China is going along smoothly and although the Army can carry on if they consider it necessary, it will probably not be necessary for them to go much farther than they have already gone. It would be in China's own interest to bring about a peaceful settlement now. If the Chinese Government evacuates Nanking it will be a very foolish move; some of the generals are already forming an opposition to Chiang Kai-shek and his position is not too secure. The Japanese terms, if peace were made now, would be "reasonable" and not a foot of Chinese territory would be kept by Japan, but if the hostilities are long continued, this attitude might change and in view of the increased sacrifices involved, more drastic terms might result. The way in which the United States could best help would be to persuade Chiang Kai-shek to negotiate for peace. If a willingness to negotiate were indicated by the Chinese Government, Hirota would send a representative to Shanghai to talk, either publicly or privately, with a representative of China.

At the end of Hirota's remarks I repeated them point by point and asked if I had correctly understood everything that he had said, to which he answered in the affirmative. I told him that I would repeat his observations to my Government and in the meantime I hoped he would do everything in his power to prevent the Japanese press from publishing unconfirmed reports with regard to the attitude of the United States. I told him of what Eden had actually said in the House of Commons and of the definite denials of the State Department that our Government had taken the initiative in connection with the calling of the Brussels Conference and I told him once more just how its convocation had come about. Hirota said that he agreed with me as to the importance of keeping the Japanese press quiet and that he would do his best. I also pointed out that the Chinese Ambassador was still in Tokyo and that diplomatic channels for peace overtures appeared still to exist. Hirota assented but made no comment.

It was significant that Hirota's comments about the part we had played in the Russo-Japanese War and the implication that Chiang Kai-shek's withdrawal from Nanking would render peace conversations more difficult were two of the points which Dooman had mentioned to Yoshizawa last night. The latter must have passed them on immediately to the Minister.

HULL DENIES HIROTA'S CHARGES

November 17, 1937

The Department cabled us the full text of the Declaration adopted by the Brussels Conference on November 15.

The Embassy in Rome reports that a Havas dispatch from Tokyo gives the purported terms which Japan intends to impose on China and asks for our comment. We replied to the Department that the Foreign Office spokesman on November 15 described the reports as "entirely groundless."

Referring to my talk with Hirota, the Secretary cabled me that the words "united action" nowhere appear in the Declaration adopted by the Brussels Conference. Mr. Hull assumes that Hirota may have had in mind the last paragraph of that Declaration, which was phrased as follows:

> Though hoping that Japan will not adhere to her refusal, the States represented at Brussels must consider what is to be their *common attitude* in a situation where one party to an international treaty maintains against the views of all the other parties that the action which it has taken does not come within the scope of that treaty, and sets aside the provisions of the treaty which the other parties hold to be operative in the circumstances.

The Secretary also authorized me to tell Hirota from him that there is *not an atom of truth* in any report that we took the initiative in calling the Conference. Mr. Hull also understands that no Government at the Conference has done more than to assume its share of the common responsibility for an exchange of views and is astonished that any Foreign Office with the information publicly available could have any misunderstanding with regard to these facts. He asked me to tell Hirota of his appreciation of the latter's wish to maintain good relations with the United States, for which he, Mr. Hull, has constantly worked during the past five years, but that he must frankly and in all friendliness express his apprehension lest the cause of developing and fostering these good relations, which both have always in mind, should be injured by the present situation in the Far East.

WHY HIROTA MISUNDERSTOOD HULL

November 20, 1937

Yoshizawa, Chief of the American Bureau of the Foreign Office, told me in private that there had been some misunderstanding about the phraseology and substance of Mr. Hull's message to Mr. Hirota, which I had communicated to the latter on November 18. What happened was this. In order to be sure of conveying Mr. Hull's message precisely as cabled, I had written it down before going to see Hirota and actually read it to him, taking no chances on a casual oral communication. The message said that Mr. Hull sincerely appreciated Mr. Hirota's desire to maintain good relations with the United States; that during the past five years Mr. Hull had constantly striven to that end; and that in all friendliness and frankness Mr. Hull must express his apprehension lest the cause of fostering and developing those good relations which they both have in mind be injured by the present situation in the Far East (paraphrase).

In view of the implied sting in the tail of the message I was a little surprised when Mr. Hirota expressed great pleasure at receiving it and asked me to thank Mr. Hull. Hirota asked me if I would leave with him the message as I had written and read it to him, but I pleaded that the piece of paper was merely a rough record and that I would send him a neater transcription as soon as I returned to the Embassy. The reason for this was that I could not leave with him the true reading because it had come in confidential code and also because there were other notes on the paper which I didn't want to give him. As soon as I had returned to the chancery I sent him a personal letter with a close paraphrase of the message.

When I saw him at the time of my call with MacMurray * this morning I asked if he had received my letter. He said no and that he had thought of telephoning me to ask for it. I said that I had sent it two days ago, immediately after our interview and that I would investigate. Just as we came out of Hirota's office we met Yoshizawa going in with my letter. He said that it had gone first to the Archive Bureau and had thus been delayed. Yoshizawa asked Dooman to come to see him this afternoon and said that Mr. Hirota had understood the message quite differently; he thought that Mr. Hull was saying that he was working for good relations with Japan

* Former American Minister to China, at this time Ambassador to Turkey.

in spite of the situation in the Far East. Apparently Hirota had misunderstood the significance of the word "apprehension."

Hirota was so pleased with the message, as he had understood it, that he had cabled it to the Japanese diplomatic missions in several capitals abroad. Now that he had received my letter he saw the marked discrepancy between his understanding and the actual meaning of the message and he found himself in something of a dilemma as to whether to correct the misunderstanding by sending a revised version abroad. Yoshizawa thought that it would probably be better to leave the matter as it is. All this arose through Mr. Hirota's inadequate grasp of English and goes to indicate that one can never rely on purely oral communications. I am glad at least that the misunderstanding cannot be attributed to any carelessness on my part because I read to Hirota the actual message from the original text.

LETTER TO A JAPANESE LIBERAL

Tokyo, December 3, 1937

Personal and *Confidential*

Dear ——

Your circular letter of November 11 to friends in England, a copy of which you were good enough to send me with your letter of November 19, has been read with great care and interest. It is full of valuable and significant material and I thank you for it.

A great deal of material, "explanatory" of Japan's attitude and actions, comes to me nowadays in the form of letters, memorandums, and other documents from many sources. A very small portion of this material is worth reading, being objective and representing an honest effort to get at facts and to weigh them, but most of it is not worth reading because it is based on ex parte, unconfirmed assertions, with no evidence to test the accuracy of those assertions. In these days of international troubles it seems to me of prime importance that we should all of us take an objective attitude and should be perfectly sure of the accuracy of our information before arriving at judgments, recommendations, or decisions. Otherwise our estimates are not worth very much and unless we are sure of the soundness of our *premises,* the world is very likely to class our appraisals as biased or as outright propaganda.

It is because you yourself preserve an enlightened, courageous attitude and are a searcher after truth, and because at the same time you are a patriot and have the best interests of your country constantly at heart, that I venture to make a few comments on your circular letter. Please be sure that I do so as a warm friend, not only of yours but also of Japan. I have always felt that a friend who is unwilling to speak frankly for friendship's sake is not a real friend. I said this in my initial speech before the America-Japan Society in 1932 and have always tried to follow that course. But sometimes a friend may speak when the diplomatist may not, and it is in the former capacity that I am writing this letter.

On page 16 of your circular letter you say: ". . . it was China that provoked Japan, after having consummated a carefully arranged plan." And on page 18: ". . . a strong Chinese force, without rhyme or reason, fired upon a small unit of our garrison who were carrying out maneuvers." Obviously each side would charge the other side with having commenced the hostilities, but the general opinion of neutral observers is that the evidence of Chinese aggression is not sufficient to prove the point. No one seems to *know* who started the trouble, but there is a general consensus that with the Japanese frequently holding maneuvers in such close proximity to a Chinese garrison on Chinese soil, it is only a wonder that the trouble did not start long ago. If you have any reliable evidence to support your point, other than the ex parte assertion of the Japanese military, it would interest me very much indeed to know of it. This, it seems to me, is a case where purely ex parte statements are insufficient.

Secondly, I know as a definite fact (firsthand, not secondhand information) that the Chinese Government proposed to the Japanese Government an armistice on July 17 and expressed its readiness to withdraw its troops to their positions prior to the incident at the Marco Polo Bridge and to terminate all troop movements in the affected area if similar action were taken by the Japanese Government. No effort to occupy strategic positions was to be attempted by either side in the meantime; in other words, a gentleman's agreement under which there would be no advantage taken of the intervening period of the armistice, until a settlement could be reached. This proposal was conveyed to the Japanese Government on July 16 but it was ignored. I greatly fear that this fact will not look well on the historical record, and this is fact, not rumor.

Thirdly, on page 19 you mention only one instance of Japanese bombing (in Canton) in which noncombatants (a very small number, you say) were killed through an accident. We have a great deal of absolutely reliable evidence, based on the direct observation of neutral observers, of many instances of Japanese bombing of undefended cities, towns, hospitals, missionary and educational establishments, in which great masses of bombs were dropped by Japanese planes many miles from any Chinese military establishments, and therefore not accidental, and in which a very large number of noncombatant civilians were killed. Very few, if any, of these bombings were reported in the Japanese press. They were reported, on the basis of absolutely reliable neutral observation, in the American press and these reports are largely responsible for the wave of indignation which swept over my country from coast to coast. I enclose, for your own personal and *confidential* information, a list of some of these incidents of which we are officially aware.

I readily grant that the Chinese propaganda abroad has been more effective than the Japanese propaganda, but these points which I have mentioned are not based on propaganda but on reliable neutral evidence. Japan has a substantial case to present to the world if one goes back into the history of the past many years, but her case is not strong if based on the current hostilities and the way in which they have been carried out. I think the term "self-defense" which has been constantly used by Japanese propagandists in my country was unfortunate. The average American will listen politely but will merely ask: "Well, you are fighting on Chinese soil, aren't you?" It needs a lot of historical background to attempt to justify that charge, and the term "self-defense" was not well chosen.

I am sure you will appreciate from all this that quite apart from propaganda there has been a great deal of ground to explain and to justify the feeling against Japan which has arisen in my country. My constant and earnest prayer is that in spite of all that has happened and is still happening, the old friendship between our two countries will emerge unscathed. I think you know how hard I have been working to that end.

This letter is, as I have emphasized, personal and confidential and I beg you so to consider it. But you, who are a searcher after truth, have a right, I think, to know these things.

Very cordially yours,
JOSEPH C. GREW

LETTER FROM A JAPANESE EXTREMIST

December 4, 1937

The following letter received today is significant of the general feeling here:

[Translation] December 2, 1937

H. E. Joseph Clark Grew,
American Ambassador to Japan

Down with Great Britain!

Due to Great Britain's instigation, China has assumed a challenging attitude against Japan and the consequence was the issue of the present Japan-China conflict. With the progress of military operations in China, Hong Kong has now become the center of anti-Japanese movements. The Japanese Navy insists that Hong Kong should be taken possession of by Japan, otherwise the blockading of the Chinese coast line will be useless.

We hold that Japan should occupy Hong Kong and Singapore first of all and thereby eliminate the fundamental cause of the Japan-China conflict. Despite Great Britain's assistance rendered to China, Japan has already occupied five provinces in South China, namely Kiangsu, Chekiang, and Anhwei provinces. A million Japanese should henceforth be stationed in China forever with a view to maintaining peace in East Asia.

Lessons in English in middle and other schools in Japan should hereafter be lessened. Only those who desire to study English specially should do so.

The above statements were presented to the Japanese Army and Navy on November 15.

[Signed] ——— ———
(Commander of Japanese Navy Retired)

WE RECEIVE THE NEWS OF THE *PANAY* SINKING

December 13, 1937

This was a black day indeed. As Mondays are generally easy days, owing to the comparative Sunday rest in Washington, we had planned a golfing day at Takenodai with several foreign colleagues and others, but as soon as I saw the morning flight of telegrams from China I gave up all thought of an outing, changed my clothes, and went to see Hirota at 11:30. The Japanese military were shelling the retreating remnants of the Chinese troops fleeing from Nanking by way of the Yangtze and indiscriminately firing on all ships whether native or foreign, having reportedly been instructed by the military command to do so.

The U.S.S. *Panay*, with members of our Embassy staff, and three Standard Oil boats bearing American refugees were moving up river from Nanking and were being followed by shellfire for at least two miles, according to our information. Shells were falling all around them. I reminded Hirota of my note of December 1 about the *Panay* and gave him all the facts as received by the Embassy, leaving with him an *aide-mémoire* as well as excerpts from four of Johnson's telegrams, in one of which it was made clear that the Japanese batteries had received orders to fire on all ships indiscriminately. I appealed to the Minister to take steps to restrain this indiscriminate shelling of our ships and pointed out the deplorable and serious effect which would be caused in the United States if an incident should occur involving injury to American nationals. Hirota merely observed that all foreigners had been warned to evacuate the area of hostilities around Nanking but that he would bring my representations to the attention of the military authorities. This action was taken on my own initiative and without instructions and later I was very glad to have done it, if only for the record.

I also took occasion to thank Hirota for the action of the Japanese Government in sending a cruiser, a destroyer, and a merchant ship to assist the *President Hoover*, which went on the rocks off Formosa and may be a total loss. I also asked permission for the *Augusta* to go there too. The Minister said he thought there would be no trouble about that and that he would let me know if they wanted a formal note on the subject.

Nothing more appeared until 3 o'clock, when Alice told me that Hirota had just telephoned that he was coming to see me at the Embassy. I said to her at once that if the Minister for Foreign Affairs was coming in person to the chancery, an unprecedented step, something terrible had happened, and of course I immediately thought of the *Panay*. Hirota was in my office when I got down there and he at once told me of the reports of the sinking of the *Panay* and the Standard Oil ships by bombing by Japanese planes. He made no effort whatever to pretend that it might have been caused by Chinese planes and he expressed "the profound apologies and regrets" of the Japanese Government. Hirota seemed as genuinely moved as any Japanese is capable of registering emotion; he said, "I can't tell you how badly we feel about this." I went down-stairs with him and saw him off in his car.

The account of my call on Hirota this morning was cabled to the Department at noon and I reported Hirota's call on me at 3 P.M. The telegram added that both the Navy and War Ministers had likewise expressed regrets through the respective attachés.

In the meantime the Department had cabled me (December 12, 11:45 P.M.—received at the Embassy December 13, 9:15 P.M.), "triple priority," that reports of the incident had been received from Han-kow and directed me to call on the Minister, ask for information, request that the Japanese immediately take appropriate action, and impress upon Hirota the gravity of the situation and the imperative need to take every precaution against further attacks on American vessels or personnel. I replied at 9:45 P.M. that the Department's in-structions had been anticipated and acted upon this morning; that we had as yet received no word of the sinking of the *Panay* from American official sources, and that as the Department's telegram had taken nine hours in transmission I suggested that all urgent messages be sent by radio instead of by cable via Manila and Shanghai.

At first a press ban was placed on the publication of the news in Japan, but this was shortly withdrawn and the Foreign Office gave out an official statement implying that the *Panay* and the Standard Oil ships were mixed up with a lot of Chinese ships conveying the fleeing remnants of the Chinese forces in Nanking and that the incident was therefore purely accidental. Morin of the A.P., Thomp-son of the U.P., and Fleisher of the *New York Herald Tribune* all came in to find out what we knew. I told them, off the record, that I had been working for five years to build up Japanese-American friendship and that this incident seemed to me to risk shattering the whole structure. Indeed, at the moment, I seriously feared a breach of relations and already began to plan the details of hurried packing in case we had to leave—precisely as we began to pack in Berlin after the sinking of the *Lusitania* in 1915. I could not then foresee whether the patience of the American Government and people would stand the strain of this apparently gratuitous, if not intentional, insult.

AFTER THE *PANAY* SINKING

December 20, 1937

Once again the diary has fallen badly behind and I find it difficult in these days of stress and strain to keep it up to date. We have been working very hard, night and day and Sundays, and the crisis arising from the incident of the *Panay* has tended to exacerbate our nerves and feelings. That incident does seem really incredible. War never is and never can be a humane pursuit, but the action of the Japanese naval and military elements first in bombing the *Panay* and then in machine-gunning at close range and attempting to exterminate the wounded and other survivors even after they had crawled into the thicket on the shore is almost past comprehension.

Hitherto the Japanese have pleaded "poor visibility" and error as an excuse for their various air bombings of nonmilitary objectives, including hospitals, missionary institutions, and universities, but no such plea can be advanced with any weight in the case of the *Panay*. It looks very much as if, having sunk the ship by bombing from a height, either knowing or not knowing that it was an American gunboat (although the American flag was clearly painted or stretched on the awnings), the planes dived low and Army launches approached to machine-gun the survivors. There could then have been no possibility whatsoever of failure to see the American flag. It looks very much as if the intention was to exterminate the witnesses to the original bombing. We hear on good authority that at least the military, and probably the Navy too, had given orders that every boat on the Yangtze was to be attacked, although they had been definitely informed and knew very well that our ships were there—knew, in fact, their precise positions.

My first thought was that this might result in a breach of diplomatic relations and that Saito would be given his passports and that I would be recalled, for I "remembered the *Maine*." As the details come out at home and the country begins to realize the incredible brutality of the attack I still believe that this may happen. It certainly must happen if further incidents of that kind occur. But the fact that Hirota called on me immediately in person to express "the profound apology and regrets" of the Japanese Government, and the Japanese Navy took similar steps, an unprecedented action, and that no effort was made to deny responsibility for the bombing, seems for the moment to have calmed public susceptibilities. In this respect the Japanese Government was eminently wise. But there is a tendency in the local press at least to deny the possibility of the machine-gun attacks; the spokesman of the Foreign Office has done so. Meanwhile the evidence is being assembled by Admiral Yarnell in Shanghai and the War Ministry here has sent a special officer to Shanghai to investigate. An American naval court of investigations will be held, witnesses heard, and affidavits taken. The Japanese Navy meanwhile, we learn, has recalled and retired the admiral responsible for the airplane bombing. It is a tense and critical moment.

But never before has the fact that there are "two Japans" been more clearly emphasized. Ever since the first news of the *Panay* disaster came, we have been deluged by delegations, visitors, letters, and contributions of money—people from all walks of life, from high officials, doctors, professors, businessmen down to school children, trying to express their shame, apologies, and regrets for the action of their own Navy. One well-dressed Japanese woman stepped behind a door in the chancery and cut off a big strand of her hair and gave it to us with a carnation—the old-fashioned gesture of mourning for the loss of a husband. Another Japanese broke down and cried at his country's shame. Wherever we go, people try to express their apologies. Highly placed women, the wives of officials, have called on Alice without the knowledge of their husbands. That side of the incident, at least, is profoundly touching and shows that at heart the Japanese are still a chivalrous people.

We cannot yet foresee whither the incident may lead. As the details become known at home and Congress and the public become more and more exacerbated, we may be forced into a breach of diplomatic relations. But if we can weather the storm, it seems just possible that the net result of the incident will be to jolt the Japanese Government into the realization that unless it exerts control over the Army and Navy, such a breach is inevitable—and they certainly don't want that, with all it would imply. The net result may therefore just possibly be salutary. But the question exists, *can* they exert control? If repressive measures are taken, another February 26 incident may well occur in Tokyo. The Government itself is between the devil and the deep sea. We know, however, that the Emperor himself desires to take a hand in the situation, but will he be permitted to do so? Here we have one of the many paradoxes of Japan: the Army and Navy are the Emperor's "children," faithfully serving him, subject to his every wish and order—yet arbitrarily taking the bit in their teeth, running amok, and perpetrating atrocities which the Emperor himself cannot possibly desire or sanction.

The British are in the same boat with us, for their ships on the Yangtze have also been attacked and Englishmen killed.

EMBASSY STATEMENT TO JAPAN'S INVESTIGATORS
OF THE *PANAY* SINKING

December 22, 1937

Landon's letter promising the President his support in matters of foreign policy is published. I only wish that certain others would board the same boat, but I should guess that their advocacy of our scrapping our interests, national dignity, and prestige—if not our national honor—in the Far East does not represent a majority of American opinion. I should not think that the G.O.P. could make much political capital out of the administration's policy and action in this part of the world.

Today's conference at the Embassy with Admiral Yamamoto and other officers concerning the *Panay* incident took place in my study, with the floor strewn with maps, and the group sitting around in a circle included the Vice-Minister of the Navy, Admiral Yamamoto, Commander Takada, Colonel Shibayama, Lieutenant Colonel Nishi, Mr. Yoshizawa, Mr. Dooman, Captain Bemis, our new Naval Attaché, and Major Creswell, our new Military Attaché, and it lasted for more than three hours. We were all impressed with the apparently genuine desire and efforts of both Army and Navy to get at the undistorted facts, but for a good many reasons this has not been easy. I closed the conference with the following remarks:

May I make a very brief statement? Do these officers understand English? [The Ambassador was told by the interpreter that the officers did understand English and that interpretation was unnecessary.]

I appreciate very much your coming here today and your telling me all that you have told me. I appreciate the efforts which have been made to get at the facts of this whole incident, and I appreciate also the direct reports of Commander Takada and Lieutenant Colonel Nishi, which I have listened to with great interest. There is being held a board of inquiry, a Naval Court of Inquiry, by our Commander in Chief in Shanghai, Admiral Yarnell. I have not yet received the findings of that court, nor have I received the final report of the evidence which that court has gathered. I know that it has been hearing witnesses of the incident, among others the survivors, and has gone into the matter as fully as possible. I hope shortly to have that report. I have, however, received some of the evidence and that evidence as gathered by our Court of Inquiry coincides with many of the facts presented by these two officers today, but that evidence does not coincide with their evidence in all respects and there are still certain discrepancies. A good deal has been said about rumors. I am perfectly ready to grant that some rumors have been passed around which may not have substantial basis, but I also think the final evidence will show that some of these rumors are based on fact.

Now to go back I will just tell you very briefly the attitude of our Government—what we have done.

I first took up the matter the first of December, telling the Foreign Minister about the fact that the *Panay* was there and that members of our Embassy would be on board and asked that measures be taken to avoid jeopardizing the ship. Then on the morning of the 13th at 11:30, having received reports from Nanking and Shanghai that shells were falling around the *Panay*, I called on the Minister for Foreign Affairs and told him of these reports and asked that measures be taken to avoid jeopardizing American life and property. At 3 o'clock the same day Mr. Hirota came to see me, informed me of the incident of the bombing of the *Panay*, and expressed deep apologies and the regret of the Japanese Government, and the War and Navy Ministers did the same.

Subsequent expressions which have been conveyed to me from Japanese people in all walks of life, who have come to see me or who have written letters, have gone a long way to calm the feelings of the American people, which were deeply stirred by the incident. On the 14th I received instructions to present a note setting forth the attitude of my Government and at 4 o'clock I asked for an appointment with the Foreign Minister, who was occupied. I was unable to see him until 8:30 o'clock, when I presented the note.

In the meantime, at 5 o'clock, Mr. Yoshizawa brought me the Japanese note which was responsive to some of the points in our note but not to all the points, so we are still awaiting a further communication.

On the 17th we had information which indicated that the incident was even more serious than we first thought because evidence was coming in from Shanghai and the most important piece of evidence was that after the ship had been bombed it was machine-gunned at close range, as well as the survivors who were taking refuge in the reeds. At least one airplane came down low and machine-gunned them. There was also the statement made that the *Panay* was machine-gunned by Army launches. These statements added to others presented to the Shanghai Court of Inquiry made the incident appear very much worse than we had first thought.

That is the situation at present. My Government does not want to enter into controversy with the Japanese Government over the details because such controversy would tend merely to obscure the main issues and on those issues the substantial facts are clear and undisputed and about them there can be no doubt whatsoever. There can be no doubt that our ships were on the river by right; that the fact that they were there and their approximate location were known by the Japanese military authorities; the ships were clearly marked with American flags both in vertical and horizontal positions; the ships were bombed by Japanese naval planes at low altitude; they were approached by Japanese surface crafts, fired upon, and the *Panay* was boarded but had already been abandoned; and the survivors were machine-gunned by Japanese planes; there can be no doubt but that the Japanese armed forces have committed offenses which have fully warranted the representations made by our Government and for our expectations that full amends will be made.

I should like to say once again that I appreciate very much the apologies that have been made, the expressions of regret, the efforts to get at the facts, the reports that have been made to me, and the assurance as to indemnities. I think that the most important thing, however, is that the most drastic measures shall be taken to make it utterly impossible for this sort of thing to happen again. I am terribly afraid that another similar incident would bring about the most serious results. So now the next step is that we shall await a reply to our formal note as well as the findings and evidence of the Court of Inquiry in Shanghai, and after that we shall be able to see our way clear.

THE *PANAY* INCIDENT IS CLOSED

December 26, 1937

This was an eminently happy day and it showed that wisdom and good sense of two Governments which refused to be stampeded into potential war in spite of the tendency of the one side to "save face" at almost all costs, and in spite of an outrageous affront offered to the other. The Japanese Government had expressed the most abject apologies for the sinking of the *Panay* and we, without a moment's delay, accepted those apologies. I thought that our Government's note was a masterpiece; we had observed with satisfaction the promptness with which the Japanese Government had admitted responsibility, expressed regret, and offered amends; we accept the Japanese action as responsive to our requests and expectations; we each reply on our own evidence and conclusions as to the details; we express the earnest hope that the steps taken by the Japanese Government will prove effective toward preventing any further attacks or unlawful interference by Japanese authorities or forces with American nationals, interests, or property in China.

Equally masterly was the Japanese arrangement that its note should get to Washington on Christmas Eve and should be dealt with by our Government on Christmas Day (our reply was dispatched from Washington at 3 o'clock on Christmas afternoon). The Japanese could hardly have failed to realize that the Christmas spirit is strong in our country and that the thought "Peace on earth, good will toward men" must inevitably color and influence our decision. Anyway, I was so profoundly happy at the outcome that when I called on Hirota at noon I entered his room wreathed in smiles (a very different attitude from my call on him on December 17) and told him that I brought good news. When I had finished reading our note to him, his eyes were really filled with tears and he showed as much emotion as any Japanese is capable of showing; he said: "I heartily thank your Government and you yourself for this decision. I am very, very happy. You have brought me a splendid Christmas present." I think his relief must have been tremendous, as was mine. We have, for the moment, safely passed a difficult, a very difficult, hurdle.

Yet I cannot look into the future with any feeling of serenity. Other hurdles, perhaps even more difficult ones, are almost certain to present themselves, and the patience of the American people is not inexhaustible. War between Japan and the United States will not come through mere interference with or even destruction of our tangible interests in China, or yet from the breach of treaty rights, or the breaking down of principles for which we stand, but war may very easily come from some further act in derogation of American sovereignty or from an accumulation of open affronts. Therein lies the danger, and it is a real danger which no one with knowledge of the irresponsibility of the Japanese military as distinguished from the Japanese Government can eliminate from the future picture. I left the Minister's house realizing only too clearly that our satisfaction at the settlement of the *Panay* incident may be but temporary and that the rock upon which for five years I have been trying to build a substantial edifice of Japanese-American relations has broken down into treacherous sand.

LETTERS AND POEMS FROM JAPAN'S
TEACHERS AND CHILDREN

Dear Sirs:

I hasten to offer you my profound sympathy for the great grief that has fallen upon the great battleship, and also for your countrymen.

News has rendered me of the disastrous accident and you cannot know how enraptured in sorrow we Japanese are.

You must know that we had not the slightest intention to do harm, and the great damage done came from pure accident.

Please be kind enough to extend our heartfelt sympathy and condolence to the bereaved family, who had lost their dear ones.

I wish you to accept this humble mourning song which I have written in Japanese.

When the Chinese conflict occurred my brother was killed at Tsushu, in a village between Peking and Tsienting. He was staying at Kinsuiro Hotel when the protective military force there suddenly fired to us Japanese who were all unarmed.

We could not get despatches concerning, whether he was alive or not for several months.

The anxiety which overtook us made our hearts in great grief.

Friends—unknown—from across the oceans gave us words of courage and people offered services who were near us.

It was all a great comfort to me in my unhappiness to receive kind words.

Though our situation is very difficult, I deeply express my heartfelt sympathy and condolence.

My best wishes to all friends of the United States of America.

Yours cordially,

IN MEMORY OF THE ILL-FATED CRAFT
PANAY AND HER CREW

(A Japanese poem by ———)

Beguiled by the rough mischievous waves
And amid the din and turmoil of the battle,
The heroes of the air, eager to chase the fleeing foe.
Bombed, alas! by mistake, a ship not of the enemy,

But of the friendly neighbor country, which sank with a few sailors
  aboard.
The source of the nation-wide grief, which knows no bounds,
  That fatal missile was.

(Note: The original with play upon words defies a literal translation into any alien language. The above version is a mere representation of the meaning the poem conveys.—Translator Mogami.)

[Translation]
                                                        Tokyo, December 12, 1937
His Excellency
  American Ambassador
My dear Ambassador:
  The Japanese air force has dropped bombs by mistake on a man-
of-war of your country, the United States of America! I was taken
aback at being told so by mamma. Indeed, I was dumfounded at the
news. I am sure that the mistake was due to a dense mist that hung
over the river. There can be no reason why the Japanese air force
would have aimed at an American man-of-war in dropping bombs
if the airmen had been aware that it was an American ship. My great
concern is that the mishap may have caused some casualties among
the officers and sailors on board the ship, and I hope that nobody
was injured in the unhappy accident.
  My dear Ambassador, I sincerely wish that you would not take
the matter so seriously but be generous enough to forgive the Japanese Navy airmen, who are not to be blamed after all. It is my sincere wish that I may be allowed to apologize to you for the grave
mistake of the Japanese air force. I like your country so much.
"Banzai" for America! "Sayonara."

                                    ———

                                    Fifth year class,
                                    Moriyama Primary School,
                                    Setagaya-ku, Tokyo

                    JAPAN BEGINS TO SEE WHAT THE CHINA
                              INCIDENT IMPLIES

February 10, 1938
  The year opened on an ominous note, for although in the true
Christmas and Christian spirit which applies so seldom to interna-

tional affairs, and with admirable good sense on the part of the American Government and people, the *Panay* incident had been provisionally settled, nevertheless the future outlook for further dangerous incidents was anything but serene. On the one hand, the ability of the Tokyo Government to control the action of the Japanese forces in China in jeopardizing American life, interests, and property is negative. On the other hand, I cannot conceive that with all our pacifist tendencies and longing for peace the patience of our people under cumulative insult is inexhaustible.

Granted the accuracy of those two premises, there seems to be plenty of ground for concern and very little ground for assurance. My own concern can perhaps best be illustrated by the fact that I have lately measured the bound volumes of this diary and of my personal letters since coming to Japan five and a half years ago and have ordered two or three leather containers in the shape of book suitcases so that the diaries can be packed at a moment's notice and easily transported by hand to the ship in case we have to leave Japan suddenly. I do not think that such a contingency is by any means unlikely.

Hardly had the reverberations of the *Panay* incident begun to die down when news came of the utter ruthlessness of the invading Japanese forces in Nanking and their wanton violation of American rights, including the looting of American homes and the desecration of the American flag, which, in numerous cases, was torn down, burned, and otherwise mutilated. Chinese were apparently murdered more or less indiscriminately, while many Chinese women were raped. Of course the Japanese have an answer for everything. With regard to the desecration of the American flag they say that the Chinese were themselves using it to protect their property, but that does not explain why no attention was paid to the certificates in the Japanese language signed by our Consul General and posted on bona fide American property. As for the cases of rape, they say that hundreds of professional Chinese women had fled from the public houses of prostitution and that the soldiers were merely bringing them back to carry on their usual commerce, and, anyway, that the reports which we had received came through missionaries who were merely quoting their Chinese employees and had not themselves witnessed the incidents of which they complained.

I was told that what the Japanese really wanted was that the Chinese families and shopkeepers who had fled should return and settle down peacefully to their customary occupations, but my informant was somewhat at a loss for a reply to my observation that in the face of the reports of wholesale executions, murders, and cases of rape it was perhaps not surprising that the Chinese inhabitants, especially those who had daughters, should be a little chary about returning. In fact, my informant went so far as to say that he could understand their attitude.

JAPAN OPPOSES BRITAIN AND APPRAISES AMERICA

March 31, 1938

Life to us in the Embassy under present circumstances represents a cinder track with a series of hurdles. There is a good deal of satisfaction as each is surmounted, but we do not delude ourselves by supposing that the final hurdle will ever be reached. New ones are constantly appearing. Under ordinary conditions these hurdles would be far more difficult than they are, simply because the Japanese Government at present has the urge to avoid unnecessary friction with our Government and people; it knows that it has and will probably continue to have plenty of trouble on its hands and it is not deliberately courting more trouble than the military machine presents it with. We therefore enjoy at present a certain degree of leverage in our diplomatic negotiations, arising out of the desire of the Japanese Government to keep Japanese-American relations on an even keel.

No sentiment is involved in this attitude; far from it. The urge is purely common political sense. They know that they are bound to antagonize Great Britain constantly and progressively; in fact, one of the things they are, without public announcement, fighting for is to supersede British interests in China, gradually perhaps, but none the less surely in the long run. The last thing they want is to stir up the United States to a point of irritation where we will make common cause to the extent of an active united front with Great Britain in the Far East. They don't think we will do this because they believe the pacifist and isolationist sentiment in America is too strong to permit it, but they, the Government, are taking no chances more than the military machine obliges them to take. To that situation I attribute the settlement of most of our troubles as they arise, and there is every probability that this situation will continue. So while this cannot by any stretch of the imagination be called an easy post under present conditions, nevertheless it might be a great deal more difficult if we didn't enjoy the leverage just mentioned. Our diplomatic successes, if such they can be called, are due to this situation plus the very sensible attitude of our own Government in handling the various issues that arise.

The domestic political situation in Japan has been far from serene. The Government has been badly heckled in the Diet by the political parties, and the National Mobilization Bill and Electric Power Control Bill, which smack considerably of Fascist regimentation, have aroused a great deal of opposition. But the Government will in the end have its way in the Diet, as usual. There also appears to be a difference of opinion within the Government itself as to the strategy of the campaign in China: one school of thought believes in pushing through to Hankow and bringing the warfare to an end by sheer military force; the other school favors less drastic methods and prefers to consolidate the ground already occupied, relying on time and economic and financial strain to bring the Chinese Government to terms. Strange to say, it is understood to be the civilian element, led by the Prime Minister and Hirota, which prefers the former method, while the Army leaders favor the latter on the ground that insufficient troops are available to conquer and hold a greater extent of territory.

At the end of March there is no indication of a march on Hankow. Japanese forces are "mopping up" in Shantung and Shansi and according to the radio news reports from abroad they are not having too easy a time of it. In fact, recent reports come in of Chinese victories. Of course no word of any Japanese setbacks is ever allowed to appear in the local press, but when we read that the Japanese have occupied a certain town, and when several weeks later we again read that the same town has been occupied, it is not difficult to draw conclusions. Colored pins on the wall map in the office of the Military Attaché show fairly clearly what is happening.

Meanwhile we have the *Anschluss,* apprehension in Czechoslovakia, marked progress by Franco in Spain, the Anglo-Italian conversations, Chamberlain sitting on the fence. Maybe his policy has relieved the imminent danger of war, but viewing the arena from afar I can see little ground for optimism for the future. Everyone, especially Great Britain and Germany, is simply getting ready once again for *Der Tag.* As for the *Anschluss,* those of us who sentimentally loved our old *gemütliche Wien* deplore the thought of the Nazification of that lovely city and that once smiling, happy land. Can anyone under the Nazi system be really happy?

MEMORIES OF PADEREWSKI

May 15, 1938

An incident in the Paderewski film shown recently reminded me of a very similar incident in my own relations with the maestro. I first knew Paderewski by name when I was a child, because his name (of course wrongly pronounced) was then a household word in America as the greatest living pianist; Alice remembers seeing him at the Hotel Brunswick in Boston and being impressed by his aureole of then golden hair. My first personal contact with him was during the war in 1917 and 1918, when I was Chief of Western Europe in the Department and had charge of controlling the relief funds which Americans wanted to send to their friends or coreligionists in the enemy countries. Of course these had to be restricted to a minimum in order to avoid giving "help and comfort" to the enemy.

Paderewski used to come down with money for the Poles in Germany, generally comparatively small sums of fifty or sixty thousand dollars; he would plead as only a man like Paderewski could plead, with the tears running down his face. The Poles had the ideal attorney to plead their case.

My next contact with Paderewski was at the Peace Conference, when again I heard him plead for the Poles, but this time for their political independence, and again he was successful. Later he became the first Prime Minister of Poland, the perfect figurehead for the new nation, but in that capacity he was not successful, for his great heart was not adapted to the political arena; he couldn't get on with Pilsudski and resigned at the end of 1919.

Then in 1924, when Minister to Switzerland, I went down with Alice to Paderewski's annual birthday party at Morges. Generally he had fireworks, but it rained that evening and supper was served inside. When the champagne was passed I proposed the birthday toast, making a little speech about how greatly the maestro was beloved in America and then said that I had known him as a great patriot, a great philanthropist, and a great orator but had never known him as a musician because, while he played chiefly in America, our life had been lived abroad and we had therefore always missed his concerts. Paderewski got up to reply, with the tears as usual coursing down his cheeks in emotion at my little tribute; he called his wife over and said to her: "The very next evening when we are free we are going to invite Mr. and Mrs. Grew to spend the evening with us alone and I shall play for them all the evening!"

That was a wonderful thought and I'm sure he meant it at the time. But soon afterward I was transferred to Washington as Under Secretary of State and had to leave before the promised evening at Morges materialized. Then our eldest daughter, Edith, died, and Alice, after closing the house in Berne, sailed for home with the other girls—a sorrowful voyage. The night before their arrival I went down to New York and, seeing in the paper that Paderewski had also arrived and was giving a recital in Carnegie Hall that evening, I took a single seat. At the end of the recital I moved up under the piano, just as the couple in the film *Moonlight Sonata* did, to hear the encores. Paderewski saw me there; he must have known of our bereavement; perhaps he remembered his promise. At any rate he played encores for the better part of an hour—and he played them to me. That was an evening that I can never forget.

FIRST INTERVIEW WITH FOREIGN MINISTER
GENERAL UGAKI

May 31, 1938

General Ugaki,* the new Minister for Foreign Affairs, received the diplomatic chiefs of mission individually today. Apparently without knowledge of English, he spoke through an interpreter.

He said that he desired to do his utmost to develop good relations with the United States, adding that having had no experience in diplomacy he is unused to the intricacies of that profession and that therefore he will always speak frankly. I replied that with thirty-four years of experience in diplomacy I had become steadily more convinced of the stupidity of indirection and that he could always count on complete frankness from me in our relations. We had therefore mutually arrived at the same conception by different roads.

I said that it would be helpful if I might report to my government about his attitude toward the protection of American interests in China. The Minister replied definitely that he would guarantee the protection of American interests in China and that if questions should arise in connection therewith he wished me to inform him of them.

* An officer of liberal leanings who, when later the Emperor chose him as Prime Minister and directed him to form a cabinet, failed to do so because the Army regarded him as too liberal and refused to nominate a Minister of War.

WHY FOREIGN MINISTER HIROTA LOST HIS JOB

June 21, 1938

A prominent member of the Japanese Government, speaking with full knowledge of the situation, has given the following picture of the purposes of the recent change in the cabinet and the intentions of the Government as they shape up at present. Prince Konoye and other members of the Government realized that if progress were to be made in consolidating Japan's position in China and in avoiding serious friction with Great Britain and the United States the conduct of everything except purely military affairs must be taken out of the hands of the Army and lodged in the civil part of the Government. Hirota had fallen because he was too weak in opposing the Army while at the same time insisting that the Foreign Office has control of Japan's foreign relations in China. This the Army would not tolerate, and it was for this reason that they were now setting up the so-called "China Organ" to deal exclusively with questions relating to China.

General Ugaki and Finance Minister Ikeda had accepted office only on condition that political and economic affairs in China should be taken out of the hands of the military, and this explains the appointment of General Itagaki as Minister of War, because he has the confidence of the younger officers in the Army and at the same time believes that the Army should stay out of politics and should limit itself to its duties as an efficient fighting machine. Both Ugaki and Ikeda realize that the solution of Japan's problem in China will be impossible unless good relations are maintained with Great Britain and the United States and Ugaki therefore proposes to do everything possible to see that their respective interests are protected. Obviously it is not going to be easy to take these matters out of the hands of the military and to persuade them to follow policies laid down by the civil elements in the Government, and whether they can succeed is an open question. At the same time the purpose of setting up the North China Development Company and the Central China Renovation Company is to take economic affairs in China out of the hands of the Army. In all these questions "the Big Five" see eye to eye. The foregoing statement of the Government's position "came straight from the horse's mouth" and is considered entirely reliable.

THE CHINA INCIDENT BECOMES THE CHINA WAR

July 1, 1938

June brought chiefly the fearful bombings of Canton and Japanese preparations to advance on Hankow, which had to be materially altered owing to the cutting of the dikes by the Chinese and the consequent floods. Furthermore, the remodeling of the Japanese cabinet.

The bombings of Canton have been one of the worst episodes in modern warfare and added to the appalling atrocities in Nanking have blemished the Japanese escutcheon in a way which has given foreign nations a new conception of the traditional *Bushido* and honor of Japan. Japan's reputation can never recover from these things.

Following the bombings of Canton, the British and French Ambassadors and the Apostolic Delegate made formal representations to the Minister for Foreign Affairs. We chose a different method and expressed our well-justified denunciation at home through public statements by the Secretary and the Under Secretary of State. On June 9 I took the occasion of my call on Horinouchi, the Japanese Vice-Minister for Foreign Affairs, in connection with the Scovell case (an American missionary shot by a drunken Japanese soldier) to say that I wished to speak informally with regard to the bombing by Japanese forces of civilian populations in China. I said distinctly that I was not making official representations and that in fact I had no instructions to do so, and that I was acting on my own initiative and from the point of view of Japanese-American relations. I said that having worked steadily during the past six years for the maintenance and development of good relations between our two countries I always felt constrained to point out to the Japanese Government, at least informally, issues and developments which in my opinion were likely to injure these relations.

I said that I did not wish today to go into the technical aspects of these bombing operations or of fortified or unfortified areas. What I did wish to do was to point out the deplorable effect on American public opinion when large numbers of civilian populations were killed or injured by large bombing operations anywhere and to raise the question whether the military advantage to be gained from such operations was sufficiently important to justify the inevitable harm such wholesale slaughter must have on Japan's reputation abroad, especially in the United States. I said that this seemed to me to be an aspect of the problem which chiefly concerned the Ministry of Foreign Affairs, responsible as that Ministry is for Japan's foreign relations. It seemed to me of the utmost importance that the Japanese Government should constantly bear in mind the deep humanitarian interest of the American Government and of the American people in the bombings of civilian populations wherever and however carried out.

The Vice-Minister expressed appreciation of the friendly way in which I had approached the subject and said that General Ugaki would be equally appreciative. He said that full consideration would be given to my observations and that in fact the Foreign Minister was now negotiating with the military authorities in connection with this problem.

This method of approach seems to have carried some weight. At any rate, we later heard that the Government had sent a liaison officer to the front to try to control these indiscriminate bombing operations, and we were told from various sources (it was even being discussed at the Tokyo Club) that it was our representations, on account of the method used, that had impressed the Government. The Japanese, with all their military ruthlessness, are a sensitive people and there can be no doubt that methods of approach are more important here than in any Western country. These things have to be learned by experience, long experience. Table-thumping is absolutely useless here and would defeat its own object.

We have analyzed the changes in the cabinet. They indicate a realization that Japan is in for a long pull, and for the first time since the beginning of the hostilities a wartime psychology and economy are being created which remind us of the old war days in Germany. Food is not yet much interfered with but many materials are now to be taboo to the public, including leather, so that shoes will no longer be made and the people will be encouraged to return to the old wooden geta. At last they are really digging in. Golf balls, being made of rubber, are prohibited, and I foresee a dwindling if not a termination of golf in the not distant future, with probably all or most of the courses eventually closed. That, if anything, will bring home to many Japanese that their country is really at war.

JAPAN AND RUSSIA CLASH, BUT AVOID WAR

August 1, 1938

The chief development in July was the Soviet-Japanese fracas at

Changkufeng on the Soviet-Manchukuo border, in which the Soviet forces occupied a strategic hill in disputed territory and, according to local reports, the Japanese drove them back again with considerable casualties on both sides. Similar incidents have been occurring in that general region periodically during the past six years, ever since we came to Japan, but this particular incident seems to have been more serious than usual and reminded us of the trouble over the islands in the Amur River last year, when the Japanese appeared to be trying out the Soviet strength. In the present case it may be that the Russians were testing the Japanese strength and determination, or they may have staged the incident in order to draw Japanese troops away from the drive on Hankow, with a view to co-operating with the Chinese. If this was their purpose, they seem to have been at least partially successful, for considerable troop movements to the north are reported, and Japan can now hardly afford to omit preparation for any eventuality in that area.

Being convinced that the Soviets do not want war with Japan at present, and equally convinced that the Japanese cannot now afford any such venture, I was not greatly perturbed by the incident and felt from the beginning that it would be localized. General Ott, the German Ambassador, who has close relations with the highest Japanese military officers, told me that these high officers had said to him that they want no trouble with Russia at present because they are far too much occupied in China and that they would therefore not allow the incident to develop. I knew that Ott would not mislead me, because our personal relations are of the friendliest, and that barring unexpected developments the incident would soon be settled. Fortunately, it was settled, in the shape of an armistice, and while the germs of conflict are always present there, the probabilities are that the Changkufeng incident will take its place with the many other incidents which have caused momentary excitement and then have petered out.

Otherwise the month has been marked by our constant efforts to obtain Japanese respect for our various interests in China, with some slight success, but only slight. I have had three long interviews with General Ugaki and asked for a fourth appointment which he could not grant at the moment, so I saw Horinouchi. The first interview, which, appropriately, took place on the Fourth of July, lasted for nearly two hours and a half, and I went over with the Foreign Minister the entire field of American interests in China. Nothing was left to chance in that interview and several days were spent in

intensive study of every subject to be discussed so that every wrinkle
would be at my finger tips. The Minister might well have bridled
at some of the things I said and the forcefulness with which they
were said, and I expected that he would do so. But he didn't. He
actually thanked me for my sympathetic approach to the situation,
and this was after he had been told in no uncertain terms just how
the American Government and people felt about the hostilities in
China in general and their abhorrence of the bombing of civilian
populations in particular.

I don't know whether that conversation will help or not. It may
help, in spots. But unless or until the Japanese have reason to feel
that the United States will *do* something about it, we can expect
few constructive results. Assurances they will give, in plenty, but
they will always say: "Be patient; the military situation prevents
fulfillment just now." The British are in the same boat but in a
worse situation than we are because their interests are far more extensive than ours and the Japanese are rapidly crowding them out.
There are signs that the British Government is getting pretty well
fed up and wants to show its teeth, but just as long as the Japanese
know that Great Britain cannot afford to fight, on account of her
troubles in Europe, just so long will they continue to snap their
fingers in Great Britain's face—in moderately polite language.

JAPAN ON THE EVE OF MUNICH

September 30, 1938

September 28 was a busy and important day. Europe was trembling on the brink of war. We gathered around the radio for the
afternoon and evening news from London, Hong Kong, and Sydney
but received little enlightenment, only reports of general mobilization, of Chamberlain's final message to Hitler assuring him that
Great Britain and France would guarantee the obligation undertaken by Czechoslovakia to surrender the Sudeten territory, and of
President Roosevelt's second appeal for peace addressed directly to
Hitler himself, a powerful and enlightened document. But, of
course, none of these appeals was allowed to be published in Germany.

I have not lost hope that war will be avoided and unless Hitler
is utterly insane, some agreement may be reached at the eleventh
hour. But that Hitler may be insane I readily grant. Hitler has now

gone so far in his public speeches in Germany that it would be very difficult to recede without serious loss of prestige.

Then came a triple-priority telegram from Washington instructing me to see the Foreign Minister, or some other official of the Foreign Office, and to suggest that Japan follow the President's initiative in appealing to Germany and Czechoslovakia for peace. The telegram was decoded and typed at 1, and realizing that minutes might count in the present crisis I had Dooman take it over to the Foreign Office and place the message in the hands of a responsible official at 1:05 in anticipation of my appointment with General Ugaki at 2:50. When I asked for an appointment, Kishi said that both the Minister and the Vice-Minister were tied up all day and could not receive me, but I told him that my business was of the utmost importance and urgency and that I definitely must see the Minister himself; hence the arrangement. Cabot Coville, a secretary in our Embassy, went with me to check the interpretation of Tsuchiya of the Foreign Office; it was entirely accurate. I opened the conversation by saying to the Minister that this was a moment of the utmost gravity in the history of civilization and a moment at which decisions and actions may fundamentally influence the future course of civilization. The message of the American Government was then presented both orally and in an informal paper so that the text would be clear on the record, accompanied by a written transcription of the text of the President's appeal to the Chancellor of the German Reich, the President of Czechoslovakia, and the Prime Ministers of Great Britain and France.

After listening to the interpreting of the message into Japanese, carefully followed by Coville, the Minister replied substantially as follows: "I would express on behalf of the Japanese Government full agreement with the action taken by the President of the United States in the controversy between Germany and Czechoslovakia. As you are aware, Japan is always desirous of peace, and although unfortunately engaged at the present time in hostilities in China, Japan hopes to establish there conditions of peace. We also seek a peaceful settlement between Germany and Czechoslovakia; but there is a question whether action by Japan similar to that taken by the President would be efficacious. We must give careful consideration to what action we, in Japan, may best take, from the point of view of our own position. At the same time we firmly share the convictions expressed by the President."

Later in the afternoon Yoshizawa suggested that it might be a good thing if the Foreign Office were to publish our message and Ugaki's reply; I immediately agreed and he obtained Ugaki's authorization to do so. I had no authority from the Department to do this, but the Foreign Office might readily have done so without inquiring, and, anyway, it would have almost certainly leaked, perhaps in inaccurate form. Besides, it seemed to me distinctly useful to have Japan go on public record as approving the President's action, even if they could not see their way to take similar action. As Horinouchi said to Craigie later in the day, the fact that they themselves were conducting hostilities made it rather embarrassing for them to appeal to others to avoid hostilities. The Foreign Office communiqué was given out at 10 in the evening; I was a little disappointed in its form because it did not go quite so far as Ugaki had gone with me in expressing approval both of the President's attitude and action, subscribing only to his "wishes," but it was better than nothing. I guess Kawai, the chauvinistic spokesman, toned it down after Yoshizawa had drafted it; such things often happen.

Craigie came to see me at 7:15 and we had a long talk about the situation.

Then, toward midnight, I was awakened by a message that the Hamburg American Line had ordered its ships to remain in Japanese waters, and that the British P. & O. had ordered its ships to leave Japanese waters within twenty-four hours, an ominous development. This was promptly cabled to Washington, which must be flooded with similar messages just now.

Dooman, Coville, Valenza, our code clerk, and I spent an hour or so in the late evening going over the various telegrams I had drafted and listening to the late radio news in my study. Even after the midnight call about the ships I couldn't sleep.

On the 29th Dr. Goodsell, American Congregational missionary, came in to tell me the result of his interview with the Foreign Minister. He had expected but five minutes, merely to express his thanks for the letters Ugaki had given him to Japanese officials in China, but the Minister kept him for an hour and a half and wanted to know every last detail of his observations of the way the Japanese military treated the American missionaries and their establishments. Goodsell got right down to brass tacks, told the Minister frankly of atrocities, murder, rape, truculence, cruelty, and left with him a long list of notes which Goodsell had prepared. The Minister received it all in good part and forestalled Goodsell's repeated efforts to give him a chance to terminate the interview if he wished. For the Minister for Foreign Affairs to do this on the day before his resignation was certainly worthy of note. Goodsell actually told Ugaki the story of the inscription in large Chinese letters on the wall of a town adjoining the Marco Polo Bridge where the "China Incident" began, which Goodsell himself saw. It read: "Birthplace of Peace in East Asia." The Minister, said Goodsell, loved the story and chuckled over it.

At luncheon at the Bassompierres' with many colleagues, the Vellosos (Brazilian Ambassador), Thurnheers (Swiss Minister), Pabst, etc., to meet Madame Peltzer, widow of our former Belgian colleague in Berlin and Berne, who was later in Brazil, there was little note of optimism about the European crisis. Alice and I stayed around the radio until about midnight, getting no news of importance because the Munich conference was not to start till 11 P.M. here, and then we were up at 6:30 the next morning, the 30th, to find that there was real hope in the situation. At 10:45 in the morning the welcome news came through, "Agreement reached."

So we fare forth into October in a far happier spirit than has been ours for many days.

TWO INTERVIEWS WITH FOREIGN MINISTER ARITA

November 7, 1938

My initial interview today with Mr. Arita,* the new Minister for Foreign Affairs, assumed on his part a negative and therefore unsatisfactory character. After the amenities as between two old friends I referred to the assurances expressed to me by Mr. Arita's three predecessors in turn to the effect that the foreign policy of the Japanese Government would undergo no change during their respective administrations and that American rights and interests in China would be respected and the Open Door and equal opportunity supported. I then inquired whether the new Minister would renew those assurances.

Mr. Arita replied that when he was formerly Foreign Minister the attitude of the Japanese people toward the United States was particularly friendly and that it is still friendly today, but that in the meantime the attitude of the United States toward Japan has considerably altered due to things that have occurred in China. He supposed that by reading recent comments in the Japanese press I must have gleaned some comprehension of the present attitude of

* Former Vice-Foreign Minister. Appointed Foreign Minister October 29, 1938.

the Japanese people in that connection. The Minister said that in estimating opinion in his own country he must proceed slowly and "with great prudence."

The Minister referred to the public address of the Prime Minister on November 3 as an indication of Japanese policy. I immediately replied that we had carefully studied that address but that portions of it required interpretation and I asked specifically whether he was in a position to interpret the following excerpt:

> Japan does not reject co-operation with other powers, neither intends to damage the interests of third powers. If such nations understand the true intention of Japan and adopt policies suitable for the new conditions, Japan does not hesitate to co-operate with them for the sake of peace in the Orient.

I asked what policies "suitable for the new conditions" the Prime Minister had in mind. Mr. Arita replied that he thought it important that we should have a long talk concerning all these matters and that he would be better prepared for such a talk after he had been a little longer in office. He repeated the view that he must proceed slowly and that the situation is "very difficult." I asked whether he would see me as soon as he returns from reporting at the national shrine at Ise, whither he proceeds tonight. The Minister replied that he needed a little more time but hoped that we could have the talk some time next week.

On my stating that these matters are urgent and that they are so regarded by my Government, Mr. Arita counseled patience and added that if we should press for an immediate reply to our note of October 6 he was afraid that the Japanese reply would not be satisfactory. He repeated and emphasized the word "patience."

I thereupon informed the Minister that I must bring specifically and urgently to his attention the question of free navigation on the Yangtze River between Shanghai and Hankow, and after vigorous oral representations I left with him my note of today's date. I told the Minister that my Government would not be satisfied with an indefinite reply and I pressed him for a favorable answer, including the naming of an early date for the withdrawal of restrictions on freedom of navigation on the Yangtze River below Hankow. The Minister was noncommittal.

November 21, 1938

In a long conversation this afternoon with the Minister for Foreign Affairs I said I felt sure that the Minister would agree with me that the historical record shows clearly that the United States has never attempted to "exploit" China or to acquire any sphere of influence whatever in that country. Our desire always has been and is today to avoid spheres of influence and exploitation. Our interpretation of the Open Door is totally contrary to those principles. With these remarks the Minister expressed agreement.

I then turned from questions of principle to matters of fact, pointing out that the Minister had asked for patience but that for our part the·patience of the American people is not inexhaustible and that my Government must listen to public opinion in the United States. I said that there could be no doubt that owing to Japan's policies and actions in China there was good reason why the Minister and I should be disturbed with regard to the developing situation in Japanese-American relations and that I for my part was more disturbed than I had been for a long time. I felt that it was of the utmost importance in stemming this tide that the Japanese Government should forthwith take some of the more obvious steps to show the American Government and people that there is no truth in the repeated allegations reaching us from various Japanese sources that all foreign interests are to be gradually turned out of China.

I said that one obvious step of prime importance would be the immediate cessation of bombing and otherwise interfering with American missions and other American property in areas far removed from military or naval operations. Such unwarrantable acts are taking place constantly, as daily reports pouring into our Embassy clearly show. Moreover, the plea that these outrages are accidental is obviously untenable in view of the volume and constancy of these depredations, which recently have involved not only the loss of American property but the loss of American life and the desecration of our flag.

I also brought out an oral rejoinder to the Japanese note of November 14 concerning navigation on the Yangtze River.

I furthermore again asked for an interpretation of Prince Konoye's observation in his broadcast of November 3 that Japan will co-operate with foreign nations so long as they understand the true intention of Japan and adopt policies suitable for the new conditions. I said I would be glad to learn how this proposed co-operation is expected to work out in actual practice. For instance, Americans have continually been told in recent months by Japanese nationals in China that American trade with China will be tolerated only if American interests deal through Japanese middlemen. I asked whether the Minister envisaged such "co-operation" in that light since this practice is progressively being put into effect in China today.

The Minister in reply thanked me for my frankness. He agreed with me that complete frankness between us was most desirable even if unpalatable truths had to be expressed. With regard to the allegation that Americans would in future be expected to deal only through Japanese middlemen he authorized me to give the Secretary a categorical denial. He said that Japan desired and intended to assure for herself certain raw materials but that there would be a very large and probably increasing field for American trade and other enterprise which would be welcomed.

I once again appealed for immediate measures to meet our desiderata, again emphasizing their great importance in meeting American public opinion, and the formal part of our conversation terminated.

I left with the Minister an informal record of my representations, marked "oral," and said that this was in no respect a diplomatic document but merely an aid to him in accurately recording what I had said. The Minister expressed appreciation of this procedure and said that he himself would follow it in his future talks with me. We agreed that it would be mutually helpful to meet often.

REPLYING TO JAPAN'S OBJECTIONS TO OUR
OPEN DOOR POLICY

(Written summary of oral report made to Foreign Minister Arita and left with him after our conversation.)

November 21, 1938

I wish to say at the outset that I am very glad that Your Excellency was good enough to receive Mr. Dooman on Saturday and to explain at least part of Japan's point of view regarding the new situation created in China. I have been apprised of everything that you said to Mr. Dooman, so, if you wish, we may proceed on the assumption that I am familiar with that conversation.

I was very glad to note your wish expressed to Mr. Dooman to have several future conversations with me with a view to smoothing out so far as possible the present discrepancies between the points of view of our respective Governments and I shall do my very best correctly to interpret to my Government Japan's point of view as it may be set forth to me from time to time.

On the other hand you will realize that I must as clearly as possible set forth the point of view of my own Government because future adjustments cannot take place unless we understand each other with complete clarity.

I believe that our conversation today will be purely exploratory and I wish to make clear to you the fact that I am not at this time attempting any reply to the Japanese note of November 18, because my Government will need time to study it carefully and in detail and I shall expect to receive my Government's observations in due course thereafter.

There are a few points, however, which I would like to bring up at once.

Your Excellency has discussed the question of the "exploitation" of China and spheres of influence therein. I think you will agree with me that the historical record shows clearly that the United States of America has never attempted to "exploit" China or to acquire any "sphere of influence" whatever in that country. Our desire always has been and is today to avoid spheres of influence and exploitation by or in any one country.

Our interpretation of the Open Door is totally contrary to those principles. The principle of equality of commercial opportunity has been a fundamental principle of the foreign policy of the United States ever since our country came into existence. The treaties relating to the Far East to which the United States is a party and in which provisions relating to that principle appear were in all instances concluded with a view to decreasing and avoiding frictions which had developed in or which might develop in international contacts in that area.

We feel that respect for an observance of those principles and provisions will make for peace and general prosperity whereas contrary courses would inevitably make for friction and consequences injurious to all countries including those which pursue such courses. The American Government and people believe with conviction that those principles and provisions are in the interests of all concerned.

My Government is anxious to take steps to arrest the present trend toward international anarchy and to contribute toward an improvement of international relations and restoration of international order. The adjustment of problems in international relations by peaceful negotiation and agreement and the faithful observance of international agreements are advocated by my Government.

My Government has pursued a trade policy whose object is to induce the removal and reduction of restrictions upon the exchange of goods in international trade in the belief that living standards would be raised and enriched and more harmonious relations promoted among nations as a result of a normal expansion of foreign commerce.

The principle of equality of commercial opportunity has always been the belief and guiding principle of the people and the Government of the United States, and American opinion believes it to be incompatible with the establishment and maintenance of American and world prosperity that any country should endeavor to establish a preferred position for itself in another country.

My Government also feels that no one Government can properly expect throughout an extensive and important area of the world to make its wishes and its will conclusive and exclusive, and that whatever may be the motives, the attempt on the part of any Government to do that will inevitably result in injuries to its own country and itself and to other countries.

In my last talk with Your Excellency I asked for an interpretation of Prince Konoye's observation on November 3 that Japan will *co-operate* with foreign nations so long as they understand the true intention of Japan and adopt policies suitable for the new conditions.

I would be very glad to learn how this proposed co-operation is expected to work out in actual practice. For instance, Americans have constantly been told in recent months by Japanese nationals in China that American trade with China will be tolerated only if American interests deal through Japanese middlemen. Do you envisage such "co-operation" in that light? This practice is progressively being put into effect in China today.

Your Excellency has asked for patience on the part of the American Government but it is obviously my duty to point out that whatever the attitude of the American Government the patience of the American people is not inexhaustible and my Government is obliged to listen to public opinion in the United States.

There can be no doubt that owing to Japan's actions and policies in China there is good reason why both you and I should be disturbed with regard to the developing situation in Japanese-American relations. For my part I am more disturbed at present than I have been for a long time and it seems to me that whatever may result from our future conversations and negotiations Japan should now without further delay proceed to take the obvious steps to prevent those relations from steadily deteriorating.

One of the first steps would be to open up the lower stretches of the Yangtze River to American shipping and commerce. We know as a fact that quite apart from provisioning the Japanese forces Japanese trade is proceeding both up and down the river at the present time in regular and openly advertised commerce, so that we are totally unable to accept the reasons advanced by the Japanese Government for preventing such American trade.

My Government takes note of the recent assurance that the Japanese Government has no intention whatever to hinder willfully navigation and commerce on the Yangtze River and that the Japanese Government is now engaged in particular efforts in order to bring about at the earliest possible moment a return of normal conditions; but at the same time the American Government is of the opinion that with every day's delay in rectifying the present state of affairs the seriousness of this discrimination against foreign rights and interests is intensified.

Another obvious step of prime importance on the part of the Japanese authorities would be forthwith to cease the bombings of and other interference with American mission and other property in areas far removed from military or naval operations. Such unwarrantable acts are taking place constantly, the reports of which are daily pouring into our Embassy. The plea that these outrages are accidental is obviously untenable in view of the volume and constancy of these depredations which recently have involved not only the loss of American property but the loss of American life and the desecration of our flag.

Other points brought forth in our note and in the Japanese reply of November 18 I shall reserve for future discussion.

THE KERNEL OF DIPLOMACY

(From an Address Delivered at the Farewell Dinner of the America-Japan Society on November 22, 1938, for Mr. Horinouchi, Newly Appointed Japanese Ambassador to the United States)

Here, I think, lies the kernel of diplomacy. It seems to me that a very minor part of diplomacy is or can be conducted by the written word. What really counts is the interpretation of the written word and of the spirit that lies behind it. And above all this, in our present world, is the tremendous force of public opinion. Written documents may reflect public opinion but they can never fully and accurately interpret it or convey the real spirit which prompts the formulation of those documents.

Here, then, lies the supreme purpose and duty of an ambassador. He must be, first and foremost, an interpreter, and this function of interpreting acts both ways. First of all he tries to understand the country where he serves—its conditions, its mentality, its actions, and its underlying motives—and to explain these things clearly to his own Government. And then, contrariwise, he seeks means of making known to the Government and the people of the country to which he is accredited the purposes and hopes and desires of his native land. He is an agent of mutual adjustment between the ideas and forces upon which nations act. International friction, indeed, is often based not so much on radical disagreement as on nebulous misunderstanding and doubt. How little of all this can be done by the written word without oral discussion is patent to anyone in our profession. I remember saying at the welcoming dinner which this society was good enough to tender to my wife and myself on our arrival in Japan six and a half years ago that sometimes our language —indeed, all spoken and written languages—seems thin and superficial. We have to depend in such cases on a sort of X-ray language which vibrates underneath the surface and is often more effective than anything we can write or say. That comes, and comes only, from personal contacts.

Thus, in effect, an ambassador's potentialities for creating harm and danger through misinterpretation are tremendous; his opportunities for constructive good are absolutely incalculable.

AN ITALIAN INFORMANT FORESEES JAPAN'S NAVAL CHALLENGE

November 27, 1938

In strictest secrecy, I was informed yesterday by a prominent member of the Italian Embassy who is in close and cordial personal relations with me that the Japanese Navy had definitely decided to declare war, presumably in the near future, as the first step toward war with Soviet Russia.

My informant emphasized his opinion that he "wouldn't give a nickel for Hong Kong." His explanation is that the Navy feels it has been merely a beast of burden for the Army, which has had all the glory since 1931; it is becoming restive in this role and has decided to take advantage of the present war pitch of the nation to remove Japan's opponents in East Asia and so complete her absolute domination in this sphere. England, as a result of the lag in her armament program during the past fifteen years, is helpless, it is felt. The only fear which has so far deterred the Navy is what the United States fleet might do, but this has been removed within the last week since it is evident that the United States is determined at any cost not to become involved in the Far East.

Although my informant is perhaps prone to exaggeration, the assumption may be made that he is in a position favorable to access to information the sources of which are not available to others. My opinion is that he may reflect the wishful thinking of the younger naval officers.

PRESIDENT ROOSEVELT TAKES A HAND

November 30, 1938

In September the emphasis was all on the European crisis. Now, so far as we are concerned, it has shifted back to Japan, but I am writing this at the very end of November and so much has taken place since then that it is difficult to remember just what took place in October and what in November. The principal events of course were the fall of Hankow and the fall of Canton. The Japanese suddenly landed in Bias Bay and pushed on into Canton with astonishing rapidity, practically unopposed. Of course the Japanese public assumes that the war is now practically at an end, and carefully regimented lantern parades by way of celebrating took place in Tokyo for several days. But the authorities have told them that they have a long way to go still. Of course there is no telling how long Chiang can hold his forces together, but at least they are still there, some of them, withdrawn but not annihilated, and so long as those forces exist at all, I don't see how Japan can risk weakening her lines and her forces of occupation.

The most important diplomatic *démarche* took place at the very beginning of October. It began with a long telegram from the Department, dated October 1, authorizing me in my discretion to present a long note to the Foreign Office covering pretty much the whole field of Japanese interference with American interests in

China, including such subjects as the Open Door and equal opportunity, monopolies, exchange control, custom tariff, telephone and telegraph communications, wharves and shipping, trade on the Yangtze, restrictions on Americans desiring to return to their property, Japanese interference with railway traffic, censorship of mail and telegrams, etc., etc.

The text of the telegram, as it was laid on my desk, said that the President, in the light of the situation herein reviewed, asks that the Japanese Government forthwith implement its assurances already given with regard to the Open Door and to noninterference with American rights by taking prompt measures, and adding that the Government of the United States believes that in the interest of relations between the United States and Japan an early reply would be helpful. I had no reason whatever to doubt that the President had sent this message. He had done so once before in another matter, and the importance of the representations now to be made fully justified, in my opinion, the use and force of his name; in fact, I recognized at once the important opening which it gave me to ask for an immediate interview with the Prime Minister, who was still acting as Minister for Foreign Affairs ad interim but was not yet receiving the diplomats.

As a matter of fact, the President sent no such message. The word "President" was purely and simply a code garble.

Nevertheless, I immediately asked for an interview with the Prime Minister on the ground that I desired to communicate to him a message from the President of the United States. Of course Prince Konoye could not refuse, and I was thus able to lay before him as Prime Minister, without going over the head of any Foreign Minister, the whole situation that confronts us in China, of which he very likely had little comprehension. At first they said that the Prime Minister didn't have a moment free all day, but I insisted and finally got a half-hour between 1 and 1:30, just before he went to see the Emperor on another matter, which was all to the good. In order to avoid any publicity they sent me the Prime Minister's own car with an ordinary license plate and I was taken in through the garden of the residence and up the private stairs at the back of the house to his office.

Prince Konoye listened to my full oral representations, which I said would be embodied in a note to be delivered shortly to the Foreign Office, and as usual I left an informal record of my remarks for the sake of accuracy. At the end of these representations Prince

Konoye said that he was honored by the message from the President. He said that in spite of the change of Foreign Ministers there would be no change in Japan's policy toward affairs in China or toward other nations, and that the assurances already given us concerning the Open Door and equal opportunity in China would be steadfastly maintained. (Strange that a month later, on November 3, he did adopt a new policy and went back on all his assurances. So much for international commitments.)

The Prime Minister said that the military situation in China might cause delay in meeting all of our desiderata but he gave explicit assurances that this delay would be but temporary. He said that he wished and intended to continue to do everything in his power to improve relations between Japan and the United States as he had in the past and that he highly valued these relations. He also observed that he was not familiar with many of the points which I had raised (of course not) but that he would study them. I learned later that after my talk with him, Prince Konoye had called on the Foreign Office for a report on each of the points and issues which I had raised.

In my report to the Department I said that the Department's telegram had come at a very favorable moment and explained why. It was something of a jolt when three days later another "rush" telegram came from the Department saying that the President had sent no message whatever. The Department assumed, however, that its telegram had been received in garbled form, that it would naturally not wish to impair any advantages which had resulted, that the matter had been laid before the President and that he had ratified the use which I had made of his name. I hate to think of my position if he hadn't ratified it. But I think that the President may have had a merry little twinkle in his eye when he heard the story. As for the Japanese Foreign Office, I believe they still think there was something suspicious about that interview, especially as Yoshizawa once said to Dooman in informal talk: "We can't quite make out why the Ambassador's oral representations were labeled as from the President while the supporting note of October 6 did not mention the President at all"! As for our code clerk who had accepted the word "President" without further exploration, I said to him: "God bless you, but don't do it again."

In connection with the note, we made one suggestion to the Department to the effect that its references to the monopolies in Manchukuo should be used merely as illustration instead of conveying the possible implication that we were reopening the whole Man-churian controversy at just the moment when the League of Nations had invoked against Japan the sanction clause of the Covenant; in other words, to make clear that we feared the same things might happen in North China that had happened in Manchuria. The Department said that it had meant the comment to be purely illus-trative, authorized the change, and the note was sent in on October 6. That note has now become a document of world importance be-cause the other interested nations realized that it involved a show-down with regard to the Open Door in China, and several of my colleagues were very complimentary about its contents and admira-ble phraseology which was drafted in the Department, not by me. The Japanese reply, for which the British and the French were waiting as impatiently as we were, didn't come in until November.

As early as October 4 I told the Department to be ready for a move on the part of the Japanese to take Canton prior to the fall of Hankow. This, of course, would cut off the flow of munitions into China from Hong Kong.

Much went on during October which I haven't time to chronicle here; there were many talks with Craigie, with whom I have con-sistently kept in closest touch, and several important talks at the Foreign Office, besides the usual flood of protests against the bomb-ing and other interference with American property in China. When the day eventually comes to settle these hundreds of claims, there will be work aplenty. The Nyhus case, wherein an American mission was bombed by Japanese planes, far from any Chinese military ob-jective as far as we know, the youngest daughter, Phoebe, killed and her mother and sister wounded, made me even more sick at heart than usual, while firsthand accounts, supported by photographs, of the barbaric behavior of the Japanese troops fill me with impotent anger. If we were not surrounded here in Tokyo with gentle Japa-nese who deplore these things as much as we do—even more, per-haps, because it concerns their own country and their own honor—I should find it very difficult to remain at this post. Once in a while I do break loose and openly express my feelings, to a few of my Japanese friends. I am sure they think I am being fed with Chinese propaganda and exaggerated tales because they themselves have no access to the facts. Foreign magazines, such as the *Reader's Digest,* are carefully stripped by the censors of all offensive articles before delivery, if delivery takes place at all. Until they themselves go abroad, or talk with Japanese returned from abroad, they have no sources whatever from which to learn the truth. And the truth is sickening.

PRESENTING THE PRESIDENT'S BILL OF PARTICULARS TO JAPAN

(Record of oral statement left with Prince Konoye)

October 3, 1938

I am calling on Your Excellency Prince Konoye as Minister for Foreign Affairs in order briefly to discuss a subject in which the President of the United States is directly interested.

Well knowing how busy is Your Excellency I do not wish to bother you with too many details and I shall therefore confine myself to discussing this subject on general lines and include such details as are necessary in the form of a note to be delivered later at the Foreign Office.

The subject to which I refer has to do with the relations between Japan and the United States with special consideration of the situation of American interests in China.

I have had many conferences on this general subject with former Ministers, especially Mr. Hirota and General Ugaki, who have repeatedly given me precise and definite assurances that American interests in China would be respected and that the principle of the Open Door and equal opportunity would be steadily maintained.

The American Government to its regret is constrained to observe that violation of American rights and interests, including violation of the principle of the Open Door, has nevertheless persisted.

In the light of the situation which I am now reviewing, the President of the United States asks that the Japanese Government implement its assurances already given with regard to the maintenance of the Open Door and to noninterference with American rights by taking prompt and effective measures to rectify the situation which I am about to explain.

On April 12, 1938, I asked the Foreign Minister for assurances that the Japanese Government would not countenance financial measures discriminating against American trade in North China; although the Foreign Minister stated that the Japanese Government would continue to support the principle of the Open Door, no specific reply has yet been made to my representations.

The American Government now learns that the Japanese authorities have in effect established an exchange control at Tsingtao, exercising discretionary authority to prohibit exports unless export bills are sold to the Yokohama Specie Bank, the bank refusing to purchase these export bills except at a rate far lower than the open market rate at Tientsin and Shanghai.

A somewhat similar situation prevails at Chefoo.

Reports continue to reach the American Government that a comprehensive system of exchange control will soon be established throughout North China.

The exacting, either directly or indirectly, by the Japanese authorities of control of exchange in North China would place those authorities in a position to thwart equality of opportunity or free competition between Japan and the United States in that area, in view of the fact that control of foreign exchange transactions gives control of trade and commercial enterprises.

In such a situation imports from and exports to the United States, as well as the choice of dealers in North China, would be entirely subjected to the dispensation of the Japanese authorities.

The American Government has already pointed out to the Japanese Government that alterations of the Chinese customs tariff by the regimes functioning in those portions of China occupied by the Japanese and for which the Japanese Government has formally assured its support are arbitrary and illegal assumptions of authority, the responsibility for which the Japanese Government cannot escape.

It is hardly necessary to state that there can be no Open Door in China so long as the ultimate authority to regulate, tax, or prohibit trade is exercised, directly or indirectly, by the authorities of one "foreign" power in furtherance of the interests of that power.

It would appear to be self-evident that a fundamental prerequisite of a condition of equality of opportunity or Open Door in China is the absence in the economic life of that country of preferences or monopolistic rights operating directly or indirectly in favor of any foreign country or its nationals.

On July 4 I spoke to the Foreign Minister of the desire of the American Government that there be avoided such restrictions and obstacles to American trade as might result from the setting up of special companies and monopolies in China. The Minister was so good as to state that the Open Door in China would be maintained and that the American Government might rest assured that the Japanese Government would fully respect the principle of equal opportunity.

American nationals and their interests have suffered serious losses in the Far East, arising from causes directly attributable to the present conflict between Japan and China, and even under the most favorable conditions an early rehabilitation-of American trade with China cannot be expected.

The American Government therefore finds it all the more difficult to reconcile itself to a situation in which American nationals must contend with continuing unwarranted interference with their rights at the hands of the Japanese authorities in China and with Japanese actions and policies which operate to deprive American trade of equality of opportunity in China.

In its treatment of Japanese nationals and their trade and enterprise the American Government has been guided not only by the letter and spirit of the Japanese-American Commercial Treaty of 1911, but by those fundamental principles of international law and order which have formed the basis of its policy in regard to all peoples and their interests; and Japanese commerce and enterprise have continued to enjoy in the United States equality of opportunity.

Your Excellency cannot fail to recognize the existence of a great and growing disparity between the treatment accorded American nationals and their trade and enterprise by Japanese authorities in China and Japan and the treatment accorded Japanese nationals and their trade and enterprise by the Government of the United States in areas within its jurisdiction.

In the light of the situation herein reviewed, the President asks that the Japanese Government implement certain assurances which it has already given. It is requested by the President that, with a view to the maintenance of the Open Door and to noninterference with American rights, the Japanese Government take prompt and effective measures to cause:

(1) The discontinuance of discriminatory exchange control and of other measures imposed in areas in China under Japanese control which operate either directly or indirectly to discriminate against American trade and enterprise;

(2) The discontinuance of any monopoly or of any preference which would deprive American nationals of the right of undertaking any legitimate trade or industry in China or of any arrangement which might purport to establish in favor of Japanese interests any general superiority of rights with regard to commercial or economic development in any region of China; and

(3) The discontinuance of interference by Japanese authorities

in China with American property and other rights, including such forms of interference as censorship of American mail and telegrams and restrictions upon residence and travel by Americans and upon American trade and shipping.

There are many other cases involving restrictions or violations of American rights in China which I do not have the time today to go into. However, I desire specifically to mention such cases as obstructions which are being placed by the Japanese military authorities in the way of the travel of American citizens in the interior of China; of the censorship of and interference with American mail and telegrams at Shanghai; the establishment of the Central China Telecommunications for the avowed purpose of controlling communications in Central China; and the organization of a Japanese controlled steamship company to monopolize water transportation in the Shanghai area.

I earnestly appeal to Your Excellency to bring your important influence to bear toward the solution of these many problems in the interests of Japanese-American relations, which must depend in large measure upon the faithful observance by Japan of the assurances frequently and categorically expressed.

JAPAN SHUTS THE OPEN DOOR

December 5, 1938

November saw no improvement in our relations with Japan; quite the contrary. Whereas we had previously received assurances from every succeeding Foreign Minister that the Open Door and equal opportunity in China would be maintained and that American rights and interests would be respected, there came on November 3, a sudden reversal of policy. I should not call it so much a reversal of policy in fact as in policy of official utterance. When Hirota and Ugaki and Prince Konoye, the last as late as October 3, successively and consistently gave me categorical assurances with regard to the Open Door, they were honestly or not honestly trying to reconcile the irreconcilable. Their slogan was: "Have patience and all will be well."

Arita says that these assurances were not given in bad faith; his predecessors had merely tried without success to reconcile principle with actualities, whereas he himself, realizing that this was impossible, proposed to call a spade a spade. He therefore declined to confirm the assurances previously given. His attitude as expressed to me, and publicly by the Government, was no longer "Have patience"; it was now in effect: "A new situation has arisen in East Asia; Japan must, for her own strategic and economic safety, control certain sources of raw material in China and certain industrial opportunities. Those particular things you foreigners can no longer enjoy. But there will be plenty of other things left over, in matters of trade and economic and financial opportunities, in which respect the Open Door will be kept well open. Please note that your trade with Manchuria has increased by leaps and bounds since the establishment of Manchukuo."

That, as I see it, is the policy of the Japanese Government expressed in a nutshell. But it is not at all the policy of the extremists in the Government, the business world, and the Army. They want and intend to crowd foreign interests and foreign trade out of China completely and to make of China an exclusive mart and economic and industrial stamping ground for Japan alone. These are the people who have no conception of the practical working of economic laws and who fail to perceive that without foreign co-operation and foreign capital Japan cannot even begin to reconstruct and develop the vast industrial and commercial potentialities which China offers. They will see it eventually, to their cost and sorrow.

One more little point might be included in that nutshell: Munich, and the fall of Canton and Hankow to Japanese troops, had intervened.

The Japanese press constantly charges America and other foreign countries with failing to grasp and understand "the new order in East Asia." When Arita himself complained to me that the American press is so dull of perception in this respect and fails to understand the assurances given that Japan has no intention (wholly) to close the Open Door to foreign trade in China (this was on December 26), I replied that not only the American press but the American Government and public and I myself found it very difficult to appraise his assurances when every official utterance of the Japanese Government was so circumscribed with qualifying phrases as to leave the real intentions of the Japanese Government quite nebulous.

As a concrete illustration I referred him merely to two paragraphs of a document which he had handed to me in which there occurred at least five qualifying words or phrases in connection with the industrial and commercial opportunities which were to be left open to foreign countries, such as "certain industries," "within the scope of the established plans," "as a rule," "any special discrimination," "undue discrimination," et cetera. I said that we were naturally more interested in results than in expressions of intention, especially when these expressions were so hemmed around with qualifications as to afford complete latitude in the Japanese interpretation thereof. The Minister saw the absurdity of this situation and laughed outright, asking me if he might copy down the phrases which I had underlined in his own memorandum.

That is roughly the situation that faces us today. How on earth were we to appraise the Prime Minister's official statement: "Japan does not reject co-operation with other powers, neither intends to damage the interests of third powers. If such nations *understand the true intention of Japan* and *adopt policies suitable for the new conditions,* Japan does not hesitate to co-operate with them for the sake of peace in the Orient." What are Japan's intentions? What policies are suitable for the new conditions? Official pronouncements of that kind are simply puerile.

Meanwhile there were buzzings as to possible financial help to Chiang Kai-shek from American and British sources, and discussions as to possible economic measures against Japan. As to the latter, no matter how much I might personally like to see retaliation for the things that Japan is doing to us and to our interests in the Far East, I have consistently recommended against such measures unless we are prepared to see them through to their logical conclusion, and that might mean war, for sanctions are always a potential incentive to ultimate war. The British, at least some British, believe that Anglo-American economic sanctions would bring Japan to her knees in short order. I disagree with that thesis. I know Japan and the Japanese pretty well. They are a hardy race, accustomed throughout their history to catastrophe and disaster; theirs is the "do or die" spirit, more deeply ingrained than in almost any other people. They would pull in their belts another notch and continue. They can live on rice and, if necessary, fight on rice. The deprival of oil, rubber, and other necessities of war might cramp their style, once their considerable supplies had given out, but it would take a long time to bring about capitulation, I think. Foreign support to Chiang Kai-shek is another matter altogether, and this does not need to be done officially, no matter what official blessings might accompany the unofficial act.

Thus lay the land up to the end of November.

THE YEAR OF ARMAGEDDON BEGINS

January 31, 1939

Seldom in modern history has a year commenced under more inauspicious circumstances than has 1939, for the totalitarian states on the one hand and the democracies on the other are rapidly lining up in battle array for what may well become another Armageddon. It will be a critical year and I cannot see that optimism is justified.

The cabinet crisis foreseen in December came to a head on January 4; Prince Konoye resigned and Baron Hiranuma, President of the Privy Council, formed a new cabinet, the only important changes apart from the Prime Minister being the dropping of Ikeda as Minister of Finance and Admiral Suetsugu as Home Minister. After a good deal of exploration we have come to the conclusion that the crisis centered about Suetsugu, whose extremist views in advocating the creation of a single national party and drastic measures along totalitarian lines had made him absolutely unacceptable to the Diet, and that it was not politically practicable simply to drop him alone. Ikeda's retirement may be explained by the inevitable Japanese policy of compromise; to drop the extremist it became necessary at the same time to drop the pronounced liberal.

Apart from the Suetsugu factor, it is well known that Prince Konoye, whose health is never very strong, has long wanted to divest himself of the burden; until Hankow and Canton were taken he could not risk the adverse psychological effect of such a crisis, but now, with the favorable progress of the hostilities in China, it was felt that the change could be made without serious repercussions. Another version of the affair is that there had been a definite letdown in the feeling and attitude of the public toward the China conflict and that a change in leadership was required to raise the pitch of popular enthusiasm; in short, that a "lift" was needed. Hiranuma says that he will carry on the same general policies. He has always been classed as an extreme nationalist, but they say that his attitude has mellowed with age, and that while possessing the confidence of the extremists, he will not necessarily follow an extreme policy. It is even thought that he will try to conciliate the democracies. Arita, who remains, gives assurance that this will be the case. But I look for no marked change, either way, in that respect just now.

THE AMERICAN AMBASSADOR AND THE AMBASSADOR
FROM MANCHUKUO EXCHANGE CALLS

February 23, 1939

Believe it or not, Mr. Ripley, I received today the official call of the Manchukuo Ambassador, by appointment, and I officially returned the call, also by appointment, five days later, in top hat, morning coat, and everything. No, gentle reader, the United States has not thereby recognized the noble state of Manchukuo. The Dean of the Diplomatic Corps has simply recognized, as is his duty, an ambassador duly accredited to the Japanese Court, and it is the Japanese Court, not the Dean, who determines the members of the Diplomatic Corps in good and official standing. Mr. Yuan was very affable, in Chinese of course, duly interpreted by Mr. Wu, but he had nothing on the Dean in point of affability. The weather and the beauties of Tokyo were discussed with the utmost thoroughness, but the real crux of the conversation only came when we got on the subject of hunting the long-haired Manchurian tiger. Then the fur really flew. Be it said, however, that no notes or cards or any other formal documents have passed or will pass between the two missions except over the inscribed title "Dean of the Diplomatic Corps," of, by, and for the Corps and not of, by, or for the Government or people of the United States of America.

AMBASSADOR SAITO'S ASHES CREATE A
DIPLOMATIC PROBLEM

April 3, 1939

Hitler unmasked. The international highwayman no longer deludes the trusting public by assurances that he was taking back only what belonged to him (the German minorities) and that he had no further territorial ambitions in Europe; the mask is off and at the point of his gun he appropriates all of Czechoslovakia, at whose birth we assisted at Versailles. Hungary already in effect a vassal; Rumania on the ragged edge; Memel taken; Poland menaced; Lithuania, Denmark, Holland, Belgium waiting for the juggernaut. And how about a port on the Adriatic? Isn't that, too, merely a question of time? No, I can't believe that Mussolini can be happy. But now at last the old British lion seems to be stirring uneasily in his serene drowsiness and at the very end of the month there was actually an indication of bristling with a slight growl or two. Don't touch that bone (Poland).

In the meantime I am deep in one of the most difficult problems presented since coming to Japan, namely the arrangement of the program attendant upon the arrival in Japan of the U.S.S. *Astoria,* bearing the ashes of the late Ambassador Saito.*

When the proposal of our Government to take this unprecedented step (unprecedented, so far as I am aware, because Saito was no longer in office when he died) was presented by me to the Japanese Government and gratefully accepted, I was merely informed that the *Astoria* would remain in Yokohama for nine days, from April 17 to 26. The reaction here was immediately and inevitably political. The Japanese interpreted the gesture as of deep political significance, and a tremendous reaction, both emotional and political, immediately took place. Not only did the Government and people of Japan assume that a new leaf had been turned in Japanese-American relations and a wave of friendliness for the United States swept over the country, but there promptly developed a determination to express Japan's gratitude in a concrete way. A program of entertainment, dinners, luncheons, receptions, radio broadcasts, garden parties, sight-seeing tours was elaborated.

At this point, on March 26 to be exact, we received from the Department the first cautionary word to go slow. This caution apparently arose from a press dispatch published in America that the Embassy had accepted twenty pearl necklaces for the wives of the officers of the *Astoria*. What happened was this. A jeweler from Osaka came up to Tokyo and handed the necklaces to Captain Bemis, our Naval Attaché, saying that he desired in this way to express his emotion at the generous action of the American Government; that he only wished he were able to give six hundred necklaces for every member of the *Astoria*'s crew. In Japan it is very difficult to refuse such a gift point-blank without giving serious offense, and as the donor had to return at once to Osaka, Captain Bemis said he would keep the necklaces temporarily in his safe until Captain Turner of the *Astoria* could be consulted, there being no naval regulation prohibiting the acceptance of such gifts.

But Bemis did not accept the necklaces; he made it clear that he was merely according them temporary custody. We did not believe that Captain Turner would accept them and it was felt that the necklaces could be returned quietly, after his arrival, with less em-

* See photographs Nos. 17 and 18.

barrassment than by peremptory rejection. We had no reason to believe that publicity would result. But the jeweler gave the story to the press, thereby clearly indicating that whatever might be his sentiment, he was using the proposed gift to publicize himself and his firm. We then promptly sent one of the naval language officers to Osaka to return the necklaces, which he did, and that part of the episode was over.

But then another difficulty arose. So intense and widespread had become the feeling in Japan of friendliness and gratitude to the United States that a monster public mass meeting to express these sentiments began to take shape. A committee of 117 prominent members of the Diet and others was formed under the chairmanship of old Count Kaneko (who is surrounded with a sort of traditional aura of being America's best friend in Japan, although I know by bitter experience in 1932 that fundamentally he is anything but friendly) and plans went ahead for a tremendous blowout of national anthems, waving flags, regimented students, and a blast of oratory, to be followed by demonstrations of judo and other Japanese warlike sports and later, in the afternoon, a big track meet or baseball game with the *Astoria*'s crew. I realized at once that such a gathering would certainly not accord with our Government's wish to avoid publicity and demonstration or with its conception of the *Astoria*'s mission, and that this sort of ballyhoo would intensely irritate the American people, whose reaction would be: "Show us your appreciation in acts, not words."

So I put my foot in the door as quickly as possible, while fully realizing that this new situation must be handled with finesse and that the Japanese must be provided with some kind of cushion on which to loose their pent-up emotion. Otherwise only annoyance and bitterness would be created, and once again the constructive effects of our gesture would be imperiled. Many telephone talks and conferences resulted and I was at least able to delay the visit of the committee to Hayama to apprise Count Kaneko of the plans.

In one midnight conference with Yoshizawa at the Embassy, in which Dooman participated, I provisionally accepted a compromise solution of the problem by which a quiet athletic meet would take place, with only a single speech by Kaneko and a brief reply by Captain Turner. The next morning, a Sunday, by routing several sleepy people out of bed before their normal hour, I arranged a meeting of the committee at the Embassy and talked to them about the solemnity of the occasion, the importance of avoiding anything in the nature of a demonstration, and the essential desideratum of obviating the kind of publicity which would lead the American Government and people to feel that their act of courtesy was being misinterpreted. This meeting was held after I had passed a sleepless night trying to think the problem through and had been up since 5. The members, at least some of them, were clearly impressed by my presentation; Uyehara, one of the ablest lawyers in Japan, saw the point clearly and gave me assurances that another meeting of the committee would be called, my views explained, a modified plan proposed and presented to me before further action were taken. This prompt action at least caused the committee to delay in going down to Hayama early Sunday morning to apprise Count Kaneko of the plans, and it was for that reason that I had dug them out of bed.

This was the situation today, April 3. Tomorrow I shall try to see Sawada, chairman of the Japanese reception committee, to put the whole problem before him, personally and "off the record," and it will require, I fear, some very plain speaking to head off the movement. I am becoming more than ever convinced that even "a quiet athletic meet with a single speech," or any mass meeting of any kind, would defeat our intentions. Flags, national anthems, parades would be the order of the day and the details would appear in the American press, conveying an impression of political ballyhoo. I want to stave this whole thing off if it can possibly be done without risk of grave irritation here. At the very least it will have to be reduced to the utmost simplicity—no waving of flags, no students' parades, no speeches save that of Count Kaneko and Captain Turner's brief reply, and I shall have to be given explicit assurances on these points if I am to permit the officers and men of the *Astoria* to attend. The matter is of prime importance; I want only good results to accrue from our Government's gesture in sending Saito's ashes home on an American cruiser—good results both in Japan and at home—and in this I am between the devil and the deep sea. It is not an easy problem. But it seems to me that the least the Japanese can do to show appreciation of our gesture is to receive it in the spirit in which it was made, and in no other spirit.

AMBASSADOR SAITO'S ASHES ARRIVE IN JAPAN
April 17, 1939

The big day, and a day which neither Alice nor I shall ever for-

get, for it was replete with impressiveness and deep emotion. I
placed our flag at half-mast. The *Astoria* arrived with the ashes of
the late Ambassador Saito and at 1:30 the ceremony of receiving
the ashes was carried out at the Yamashita Pier at Yokohama. On
the dot of the hour set, the launch put off from the *Astoria,* accompanied by minute guns from the *Astoria* and the Japanese cruiser
near by. (Alice had gone to see Mrs. Saito yesterday; she is a wonderful person, and we intensely admired the splendid way in which
she bore up with grace and dignity throughout these two trying
days.)

When the American sailors carried the little Japanese shrine containing the urn and ashes ashore, we all formed a procession and
marched to the larger shrine erected on the pier where, in a brief,
dignified, and most impressive exchange of speeches, Sawada, chairman of the reception committee, accepted the ashes from Captain
Turner of the *Astoria.* Then we all went into the shrine and bowed
in turn and the funeral procession formed and marched through the
streets of Yokohama, deeply lined with people, to the funeral train
drawn up on another pier, the guard of honor being composed both
of American and Japanese sailors and a Japanese band playing the
Chopin funeral march.

The President's wreath was carried first, then the Foreign Minister's, and then mine, the American ones, of course, in the hands of
the American sailors. The American community was represented, at
my instance, by Bishop Reifsnider, Dick Andrews, and Dr. Iglehart,
three of the oldest residents in Japan. Captain Bemis acted as my
aide. The solemnity of the occasion and the absolute precision of
every move in the carefully prepared program were tremendously
impressive.

Alice and I went in the funeral train to Tokyo, where the Foreign
Minister and other high officials were gathered in the station. The
Japanese then followed the hearse to the Saito home for a private
service, but we thought it best not to invade the privacy of the home
and left the cortege at that point. It is interesting that a bottle of
Old Parr whisky, Saito's favorite brand, was prominently displayed
on the altar and is clearly evident in the photographs, and that
three of his favorite cigarettes were burned in the incense burners.
To Americans this might seem profane, but from the Japanese point
of view nothing could be more pious or consistent. In the Shinto
rites, food for the departed is placed on the altar and if the departed liked whisky, let him have it by all means.

Alice and I, together with the Bemises and the Boyces, our Consul in Yokohama, dined quietly with Captain Turner on the *Astoria.*

The President sent his messages to Hitler and Mussolini. I felt like cabling him: "I am prouder than ever before to be an American." The message may or may not be helpful, but I feel that America's moral influence should be exerted to the fullest extent in this crisis. If we could have done it in 1914, the World War might have been avoided. It may conceivably avoid war now. The handwriting is on the wall for Hitler to read, if he can read. But I doubt it.

April 18, 1939

I half-masted our flag again. The funeral service in the big Hongwanji Temple was more impressive than anything that had gone before. All the highest people in Japan were there. First, the High Priest chanted the Buddhist rites, then, in turn, Arita, myself, and Hotta (Saito's friend and contemporary) went up to the shrine and read our respective addresses. Arita's was wonderfully phrased and he himself was deeply moved so that his voice shook (as, in fact, did mine). He ended:

> With the spring coming, everything on earth is being refreshed. But you are no more. I cannot hear you answer even if I speak to you. I cannot see you even if I try to look at you. I am indeed filled with sorrow. What a sorrow. I respectfully beseech you to accept my message.

There followed the burning of incense by everyone in turn, first Saito's eldest daughter, a child of thirteen, as his legal heir, then his mother and widow and the other daughter, Arita, Alice and myself, and so down the line. We did not go to the cemetery, feeling again that this would be intruding on the family's privacy. Iwanaga, Mrs. Saito's uncle, took some of the ashes to bury on the family estate. So ended the most impressive funeral I have ever witnessed. The solemnity, dignity, and precision of the whole ceremony from the moment of the *Astoria*'s arrival were unforgettable.

Captain Turner and his staff called.

Our dinner for Captain Turner. Alice, the only lady present, was hostess and she helped me greatly. Debuchi said afterward that my asking the Minister of War was a "master stroke." It was an eleventh-hour inspiration on my part. Probably never before have the Foreign Minister, the Imperial Household Minister, the War Minister, and the Navy Minister been present at the same time in any foreign house in Japan.

Alice had arranged a delicious dinner with terrapin; my best wines were trotted out, and it was really as nice a dinner as could be staged anywhere. Everyone was in the best of humor. I proposed the health of the Emperor and Arita responded with a health to the President; it was the only function during the entertainment of the *Astoria,* I think, at which there were no speeches! To the Japanese a formal dinner without speeches is unthinkable, but the American Embassy is American soil and I am dictator for that one evening. But we did have to surrender to the photographer, for the pressure there was too great; there was no use in antagonizing the press. Anyway, the Embassy looked perfectly beautiful, with gorgeous sprays of cherry blossoms on the tables in the loggia and small chrysanthemums on the dinner tables, of which there were two of eighteen places each. We had a right to be proud of the Embassy and indeed of the whole shindy which went off like clockwork and with no official stiffness whatever. Of course, as usual, Alice deserves the credit. I said to Arita that I supposed it must seem rather unusual in Japan for the lady of the house to be present at a stag dinner, but he said that on the contrary it was often done. At our sedate age, it's a good custom.

April 19, 1939

Luncheon given by the Foreign Minister to Captain Turner and his officers. After lunch we sat on the lawn and exchanged stories, which enabled the press to publish an excellent picture of Arita, Turner, and myself headed "Japanese-American Smiles."

In the evening a big dinner given by the Navy Minister, Admiral Yonai, at the Navy Club at which some superb pictures of Fuji, the temple of Nikko, and so on were presented for the captain, the wardroom, and the warrant officers' mess on the *Astoria.* The one for the wardroom was promptly hung in the place of honor and was there when the captain gave his farewell dinner on the 25th. After dinner at the Navy Club there was some excellent juggling by pretty girls and then some lovely Japanese dancing. Navy officers are always better mixers than Army men, probably because they have traveled abroad, and the spirit at this dinner was splendid.

After dinner Admiral Yonai took Dooman aside (the Minister doesn't speak English very fluently) and asked him to tell me that my concern about the possibility of Japan's becoming involved in Europe had come to his attention and that he wished to tell me that I need have no further concern because "Japanese policy has been decided. The element in Japan which desires Fascism for Japan and the consequent linking up with Germany and Italy had been 'suppressed.'" Japan, the Minister said, while co-operating for the maintenance of friendly relations with both the democracies and the authoritarian states, must stand apart from either group, her own ideology being different from both of them.

Yoshizawa, to whom this talk was repeated, said that the decision to stay out of an alliance with Germany and Italy must have just been taken because he had not known of it. The Minister's statement to me might be taken as a definite indication that Japan intended to avoid embroilment in European troubles, and he knew that the Navy had held the balance of power in this important question, but we must not assume that there would be no strengthening of the Anti-Comintern Pact.

In further conversation with Admiral Yonai he said that the need for restoring good relations with the United States was being keenly felt. On his being informed that our difficulties, such, for instance, as the bombing of our property in China, could readily be eliminated, he replied that he knew all about this and that effective steps would be taken to correct these attacks, which were now being investigated.

The Minister then turned to the question of naval limitation and expressed regret that such limitation is not feasible at the present time, but navies are "dangerous toys"; the progressive increase in naval requirements could lead only to bankruptcy or a general explosion and someday an agreement must be reached. "There must be disarmament," he repeatedly said.

This was one of the most important and significant conversations that we have had, and I regard it as marking a new trend, indeed a milestone, in Japanese-American relations, for Yonai can be trusted.

JAPAN STEERS AWAY FROM THE AXIS

May 15, 1939

The high light of the first half of May until we sailed on leave of absence was the effort to keep Japan from tying up in a general alliance with Germany and Italy. Up to our departure this effort was successful and I was given categorical official assurances that there would be no general alliance, although there would be some arrangement by way of strengthening the Anti-Comintern Pact with applicability only to Soviet Russia. But I know very well that the pressure on the Government will continue, and if Great Britain concludes an alliance with Soviet Russia it is not beyond the bounds of possibility that either the Government will be forced into a totalitarian alliance or will fall, Hiranuma to be succeeded possibly by General Minami, Marquis Kido, or Navy Minister Yonai. But the appointment of Yonai would still mean no totalitarian alliance.

I think that the present political situation in Japan is full of dynamite and that further assassinations are possible, if not likely. The country is sick of the hostilities in China, with no outlook for peace, and wants concrete results which do not appear to be maturing. This does not at all mean that Japan is weakening; on the contrary, there is every evidence of determination to see the whole thing through, and there is very little evidence of any financial or economic crisis in the near future. But there is plenty of dissatisfaction with the failure to achieve final results and to get the "China Incident" over with. The people are restive.

The line that I have taken in talking with Japanese high and low—and I have plenty of evidence that my arguments have penetrated to the top—is this: if a general war breaks out in Europe it is almost inevitable that the United States will be unable to stay out of it; things would be bound to happen which would inflame the American people, and history has shown that the American people are among the most inflammable people in the world. In such a case the pacifists and isolationists would be in the forefront of those supporting war—at least, the great majority would be. If Germany were to bomb London and Paris and kill a great many civilians, that alone would stir the American people to the depths. And then, even if Germany and Italy had overrun Europe in the first few weeks of the war, the determination and unlimited resources of the United States would with mathematical certainty have won in the long run, as they did in 1918. If Japan were then tied up in the German camp in a general military alliance, it would be almost impossible for the United States to remain at peace with Japan.

It therefore behooves Japan to look into the future and decide where her friendship ought in her own interests to be placed. Japanese-American relations are temporarily strained owing to difficulties arising out of the campaign in China, but these difficulties should eventually be overcome and Japan should look at the long haul rather than at the immediate present. From every point of view—economic, financial, commercial, sentimental—the United States can be a better friend to Japan, if Japan plays the game with us, than any other country in the world. A Japanese-American war would be the height of stupidity from every point of view. In the meantime, what can Germany and Italy do for Japan? What concrete results are to be gained from their friendship in the long run? These considerations are worth weighing now, before it is too late.

These arguments, as I have said, appear to have been widely discussed and weighed. I have reason to believe that they reached the Emperor, and several highly placed people have encouraged the line I was taking. Some, including the Navy Minister on his own initiative, spoke of my "anxiety" and said that I need worry no more as things were going to turn out the way I wanted them to do.

So we leave Japan for these few months of furlough feeling that, whatever the final result, at least nothing has been left undone to steer Japanese-American relations into healthy channels, which, after all, is my job.

A five-month furlough in the United States interrupts the diary at this point.

5

ONE WORLD: TWO WARS

(October 10, 1939–December 8, 1941)

THE OPENING months of the war in Europe gave
all Japanese an uneasy time. Those who did not
fear Germany feared Russia. Hope for any understanding with the United States dwindled,
though efforts to patch up an understanding
took on a new lease of life. But with the fall of
France the die was cast. Relations with the
United States had gone from bad to worse.
Britain appeared to be on the verge of defeat.
French Indo-China and the Dutch East Indies
lay defenseless to the south, while a neutral but
feverishly arming Russia looked with increasing
concern to the east. If only to get the jump on
the Germans, the Japanese determined to concentrate for a while on southward expansion. At
the end of September, 1940, Japan entered the
Axis as a full-fledged partner. This move had
two main purposes. One was to promote southward expansion. The other was to serve notice
on the United States that war between America
and Germany would also lead to war between
America and Japan. The United States refused
to be intimidated and continued its firm stand
against aggression in the Far East. War between
the two countries thus, at the end, became inevitable, and Japan struck at Pearl Harbor.

October 10, 1939

On the job once more and quite ready for it. I feel very fit and keen to get going again.

The voyage on the *Tatsuta Maru* was, according to the captain, the smoothest he had ever encountered on the Pacific, and during the last several days the sea was like a quiet lake.

The Embassy looked more lovely than ever and of course was chockablock with gorgeous gifts of flowers. The faithful staff were at the door, beaming their welcome. The very first thing Alice did was to telephone to Madame de Romer, the Polish Ambassadress, to ask to come to see her; she said she had been seeing nobody but would receive Alice and was visibly touched. I did the same to the Polish Ambassador and said that I wanted to come to see him before any of the other colleagues.

THE POLISH AMBASSADOR FINDS JAPAN ANTI-GERMAN

October 12, 1939

Having told Mr. de Romer, the Polish Ambassador, that I wished to call on him before any of the other colleagues, I went to see him this morning and endeavored to express my feelings. He was obviously touched. He said that the action of our Government in recognizing the new Polish Government had helped him very much here, because the Japanese, owing to their difficult relations with Soviet Russia, were doubtful what to do, but as soon as we had acted he was able to persuade them to continue to recognize him without more ado.

The Ambassador said that the Japanese still remembered my feeling before leaving for America last spring that if war should break out in Europe the United States would almost certainly become involved and they wondered whether I still felt the same way about it. I replied that my visit to the United States had opened my eyes to the intense and almost universal determination to stay out of the war, a very different attitude from that obtaining in 1917, and while many unpredictable things might happen, I now felt that the

287

chances of our staying out were immeasurably increased. Mr. de Romer said he thought that my arguments advanced to many influential Japanese last spring had had a marked effect in keeping Japan out of a military alliance with Germany. The Japanese were now more than ever eager for friendship with the United States. He said that except for a comparatively small group the Japanese are now intensely anti-German.

THE "HORSE'S MOUTH" SPEECH

October 15, 1939

Worked all day on my forthcoming speech before the America-Japan Society. During weeks of quiet thought at our home in the hills of New Hampshire I had determined to make this speech, and fortunately both the President and the Department had approved the idea. It is a ticklish business. The Far Eastern Division had made an original draft which I amplified in Washington and then retouched almost daily during the voyage over. But now I find that the present cabinet and its backers, Hiranuma and Prince Konoye, are apparently genuinely anxious to improve relations with the United States and that it would be very shortsighted to embarrass them by the publication of the sort of speech that we had drafted. I am now convinced that much more can be accomplished in informal talks with groups and individuals. So I must sail between Scylla and Charybdis, not minimizing the resentment of the American Government and people against the actions of the Japanese Army in China but avoiding so far as possible the dynamite and any "bill of particulars" which would be going to the public over the heads of the Japanese Government.

I am well aware that our own Government would deeply resent anything of that kind on the part of the Japanese Ambassador in Washington. The tone of my speech will be important. What are needed now are "brass tacks"—an appeal to stop the bombings, indignities, trade restrictions, and other concrete interferences with American rights. The high principles will, however, not be overlooked. As the draft stands now, the staff consider it a well-balanced speech and I think it is. There will be some unpleasant reverberations, but there is precious little in the speech to which exception could properly be taken. We shall see. Fortunately the Department had sent me a telegram, eminently wise, suggesting that I might find trends in Japan which would render the original draft inadvisable and that it would not be well to injure thereby such personal influence as I possess. Although it was I myself who originally suggested the speech, that telegram gave me a great sense of relief.

"STRAIGHT FROM THE HORSE'S MOUTH"

(From an Address Before the America-Japan Society, October 19, 1939)

We have a phrase in English "straight from the horse's mouth." I never knew why the particular animal chosen was a horse, especially as most horses are generally not very communicative. But the meaning is clear enough. What I shall say in Japan in the ensuing months comes "straight from the horse's mouth" in that it will accurately represent and interpret some of the current thoughts of the American Government and people with regard to Japan and the Far East. I had the privilege of also conferring repeatedly with the President and with the Secretary of State during my stay at home.

Before I left for America last May a Japanese friend of mine begged me to tell my friends in America the situation in Japanese-American relations as he conceived it. It ran somewhat as follows:

American rights and interests in China are suffering some minor and unimportant inconveniences in China as a result of Japanese military operations; the Japanese military take every possible precaution to avoid inconvenience to American interests; reports published in the United States in regard to damage to American interests by the Japanese in China are intentionally exaggerated in order to inflame the American people against Japan; in large measure those activities of the Japanese to which Americans object are the result of differences in customs, differences in language, and a legalistic attitude which has been adopted by the United States; the attitude of the Government of the United States in regard to impairment of American rights and interests in the Japanese-occupied areas of China is in large part due to internal political conditions in the United States; in the near future the situation in the occupied areas of China will be so improved that the United States will no longer have any cause for complaint. That was the point of view of my Japanese friend.

Alas, the truth is far otherwise. The facts, as they exist, are accurately known by the American Government. They are likewise known by the American people, and in the interests of the future relations between Japan and the United States those facts must be faced. Only through consideration of those facts can the present attitude of the American Government and people toward Japan be understood; only through consideration of those facts, and through constructive steps to alter those facts, can Japanese-American relations be improved. Those relations *must* be improved.

Having said all this I do not propose today to deal in detail with the causations which have brought about that feeling in my country. This is not the occasion to enter any "bill of particulars." Those facts, those difficulties between our nations, are matters for consideration by the two Governments; indeed, some of them are matters which I have been discussing with the Japanese Government during the past two years, and I shall continue to approach these matters. But I believe that the broad outline of those facts and difficulties are known to you. Some of these difficulties are serious.

Now, many of you who are listening to me may well be thinking: "There are two sides to every picture; we in Japan also have our public opinion to consider." Granted. In America, as I have already said, I did my best to show various angles of the Japanese point of view. But here in Japan I shall try to show the American point of view. Without careful consideration of both points of view we can get nowhere in building up good relations. I wish you could realize how intensely I wish for that most desirable end and how deeply I desire, by pure objectivity, to contribute to a successful outcome. Let me therefore try to remove a few utterly fallacious conceptions of the American attitude as I think they exist in Japan today.

One of these fallacies is that the American approach to affairs in East Asia is bound by a purely "legalistic" attitude, a conception which widely prevails in this country today. What is meant by a "legalistic" attitude? If we mean respect for treaties, official commitments, international law, yes; that respect is and always will be one of the cardinal principles of American policy. But the very term "a legalistic attitude," as it has often been used in my hearing in Japan, seems to imply a position where one cannot see the woods for the trees, where one's vision of higher and broader concepts is stultified. Let me therefore touch briefly on a few of the cardinal principles of American policy and objectives, molded to meet the requirements of modern life, which, it is true, are fundamentally based upon but which seem to me far to transcend any purely "legalistic" approach to world affairs.

The American people aspire to relations of peace with every country and between all countries. We have no monopoly on this desire for peace, but we have a very definite conviction that the sort of peace which, throughout history, has been merely an interlude between wars is not an environment in which world civilization can be stably developed or, perhaps, can even be preserved. We believe that international peace is dependent on what our Secretary of State has characterized as "orderly processes" in international dealing.

The American people desire to respect the sovereign rights of other people and to have their own sovereign rights equally respected. We have found by experience that the successful approach to the resolving of international disputes lies not so much in merely abstaining from the use of force as in abstaining from any thought of the use, immediately or eventually, of the methods of force. Let cynics look about them and contemplate the consequences of resort to menacing demands as a process in the conduct of international relations! Is it being purely "legalistic" to put to wise and practical use the finer instincts common to all mankind?

The American people believe that the day is past when wars can be confined in their effects to the combatant nations. When national economies were based upon agriculture and handicraft, nations were to a large extent self-sufficient; they lived primarily on the things which they themselves grew or produced. That is not the case today. Nations are now increasingly dependent on others both for commodities which they do not produce themselves and for the disposal of the things which they produce in excess. The highly complex system of exchange of goods has been evolved by reason of each nation's being able to extract from the ground or to manufacture certain commodities more efficiently or economically than others. Each contributes to the common good the fruits of its handiwork and the bounties of nature.

It is this system of exchange which has not only raised the standard of living everywhere but has made it possible for two or even three persons to live in comfort where but one had lived in discomfort under a simple self-contained economy. Not only the benefits of our advanced civilization but the very existence of most of us depend on maintaining in equilibrium a delicately balanced and complex world economy. Wars are not only destructive of the wealth, both human and material, of combatants, but they disturb the fine adjustments of world economy. Conflict between nations is therefore a matter of concern to all the other nations. Is there then any stultification through "legalistic" concepts when we practice ourselves and urge upon others the resolving of international disputes by orderly

processes, even if it were only in the interests of world economy?
How, except on the basis of law and order, can these various concepts in international dealing be secured?

The American people believe in equality of commercial opportunity. There is probably no nation which has not at one time or
other invoked it. Even Japan, where American insistence on the
Open Door is cited as the supreme manifestation of what is characterized as a "legalistic" American attitude—even Japan, I say—has
insisted upon and has received the benefits of the Open Door in
areas other than China, where, we are told, the principle is inapplicable except in a truncated and emasculated form. That highly
complicated system of world economy of which I have just spoken
is postulated upon the ability of nations to buy and sell where they
please under conditions of free competition—conditions which cannot exist in areas where pre-emptive rights are claimed and asserted
on behalf of nationals of one particular country.

I need hardly say that the thoughts which I have just expressed
are of universal applicability.

Another common fallacy which I am constrained to mention is
the charge that the American Government and people do not
understand "the new order in East Asia." Forgive me if I very respectfully take issue with that conception. The American Government and people understand what is meant by the "new order in
East Asia" precisely as clearly as it is understood in Japan. The "new
order in East Asia" has been officially defined in Japan as an order
of security, stability, and progress. The American Government and
people earnestly desire security, stability, and progress not only for
themselves but for all other nations in every quarter of the world.
But the new order in East Asia has appeared to include, among
other things, depriving Americans of their long-established rights
in China, and to this the American people are opposed.

There's the story. It is probable that many of you are not aware
of the increasing extent to which the people of the United States
resent the methods which the Japanese armed forces are employing
in China today and what appear to be their objectives. In saying
this, I do not wish for one moment to imply that the American
people have forgotten the long-time friendship which has existed
between the people of my country and the people of Japan. But the
American people have been profoundly shocked over the widespread use of bombing in China, not only on grounds of humanity
but also on grounds of the direct menace to American lives and

property accompanied by the loss of American life and the crippling of American citizens; they regard with growing seriousness the violation of and interference with American rights by the Japanese armed forces in China in disregard of treaties and agreements entered into by the United States and Japan and treaties and agreements entered into by several nations, including Japan. The American people know that those treaties and agreements were entered into voluntarily by Japan and that the provisions of those treaties and agreements constituted a practical arrangement for safeguarding—for the benefit of all—the correlated principles of national sovereignty and of equality of economic opportunity.

The principle of equality of economic opportunity is one to which, over a long period and on many occasions, Japan has given definite approval and upon which Japan has frequently insisted. Not only are the American people perturbed over their being arbitrarily deprived of long-established rights, including those of equal opportunity and fair treatment, but they feel that the present trend in the Far East, if continued, will be destructive of the hopes which they sincerely cherish of the development of an orderly world. American rights and interests in China are being impaired or destroyed by the policies and actions of the Japanese authorities in China. American property is being damaged or destroyed; American nationals are being endangered and subjected to indignities. If I felt in a position to set forth all the facts in detail today, you would, without any question, appreciate the soundness and full justification of the American attitude. Perhaps you will also understand why I wish today to exercise restraint.

In short, the American people, from all the thoroughly reliable evidence that comes to them, have good reason to believe that an effort is being made to establish control, in Japan's own interest, of large areas on the continent of Asia and to impose upon those areas a system of closed economy. It is this thought, added to the effect of the bombings, the indignities, the manifold interference with American rights, that accounts for the attitude of the American people toward Japan today. For my part I will say this. It is my belief, and the belief of the American Government and people, that the many things injurious to the United States which have been done and are being done by Japanese agencies are *wholly needless*. We believe that real security and stability in the Far East could be attained without running counter to any American rights whatsoever.

I have tried to give an accurate interpretation of American public opinion, most carefully studied and analyzed by me while at home. The traditional friendship between our two nations is far too precious a thing to be either inadvertently or deliberately impaired. It seems to me logical that from every point of view—economic, financial, commercial, in the interests of business, travel, science, culture, and sentiment—Japan and the United States forever should be mutually considerate friends. In the family of nations, as between and among brothers, there arise inevitable controversies, but again and again the United States has demonstrated its practical sympathy and desire to be helpful toward Japan in difficult times and moments, its admiration of Japan's achievements, its earnest desire for mutually helpful relations.

Please do not misconstrue or misinterpret the attitude which has prompted me to speak in the utmost frankness today. I am moved first of all by love of my own country and my devotion to its interest; but I am also moved by very deep affection for Japan and my sincere conviction that the real interests, the fundamental and abiding interests, of both countries call for harmony of thought and action in our relationships. Those who know my sentiments for Japan, developed in happy contacts during the seven years in which I have lived here among you, will realize, I am sure, that my words and my actions are those of a true friend.

One Japanese newspaper queried, on my return from America, whether I had concealed in my bosom a dagger or a dove. Let me answer that query. I have nothing concealed in my bosom except the desire to work with all my mind, with all my heart, and with all my strength for Japanese-American friendship.

Today I have stated certain facts, straightforwardly and objectively. But I am also making a plea for sympathetic understanding in the interests of the old, enduring friendship between our two great nations. In a world of chaos I plead for stability, now and in the long future, in a relationship which, *if it can be preserved,* can bring only good to Japan and to the United States of America.

THE BACKGROUND OF A HISTORIC ADDRESS

October 19, 1939

The background of the speech is described in the following memorandum which I gave to Dooman, Creswell, and Smith-Hutton after my return to Tokyo:

During my stay in the United States American public opinion was steadily hardening against Japan. The denunciation of the Treaty of 1911 was almost universally approved and there is an almost universal demand for an embargo against Japan next winter. The present attitude of the administration is that we will not allow American interests to be crowded out of China. If Japan retaliates against an American embargo, there is every probability that our Government will counter-retaliate in some form or other.

I have pointed out that once started on a policy of sanctions we must see them through and that such a policy may conceivably lead to eventual war. There is, however, no sign whatever of weakness in the administration's attitude now or in the attitude of the public. The President and the Secretary of State seem determined to support our position in the Far East. The fall naval maneuvers are to take place in Hawaiian waters. There has been talk of landing further American marines in Shanghai, but such a step, just before I left Washington, was held in abeyance. There can be little doubt, however, that if the Japanese military in China continue their depredations against Americans and American interests, and if they progressively take measures to drive them out of China, our Government will take retaliatory measures regardless of the eventual outcome, and the administration will be supported by the great majority of the American public. Very little is now heard of the wisdom of folding our tents and withdrawing gracefully from a possibly untenable position. Our position in the Far East is regarded as an important factor in our position in world affairs at large and not at all as an isolated problem.

Having in mind this attitude of the American Government and people, we must reach the inevitable conclusion that the time for exclusive reliance on the good will and efforts of the Japanese Government, as contrasted with the Japanese military, is past. Hitherto we in the Embassy have aimed to follow, as far as reasonable, a policy of avoiding words or actions which might tend to irritate the military. In view of the determined attitude of the American Government and people, I believe that more is now to be gained by discreetly conveying this present attitude to the Japanese Government and people in order to offset the prevailing feeling in Japan (at least prevailing before my departure in May) that in the last analysis the United States will back down. I do not now think that we will back down, and I believe that the efforts of the Embassy should now be directed toward letting that fact gradually penetrate to the Japanese consciousness. Only danger, and no good, can come from leaving the Japanese under a misapprehension on that score. But those efforts of the Embassy will have to be carried out with discretion.

During the past summer the Department of State was seriously considering writing another strong note to Japan, but Mr. Dooman advised against it and I supported him, on the ground that such a note would do no practical good and would merely anger the military, and that the record of our position was already complete. I did, however, take the position that something should be done to bring before the Japanese people the facts regarding the depredations against Americans and American interests by the Japanese military in China.

Those facts, so far as I am aware, are not generally known even by influential Japanese, who are therefore inclined to regard American opposition to Japan and Japanese policy, and to "the new order in East Asia," as arbitrarily based on what they consider to be obsolete legal technicalities on the one hand and a traditional sympathy for China on the other. If any movement is to be started by influential Japanese to restrain the military in their efforts to force American interests out of China (I have in mind, for instance, the members of the Privy Council, who presumably are influential), those Japanese must first become aware of the determined attitude of the American Government and public and the facts on which that attitude is based. As long as misapprehension on those points continues to exist, we can hardly expect constructive steps to be taken to improve our relations. It is, of course, questionable whether any constructive steps or effective steps can be taken to curb the military, but we must not let that desideratum go by default.

There must be no tone of threat in our attitude. To threaten the Japanese is merely to increase their own determination. The attitude of the American Government and people must be presented merely as a patent fact which exists and should therefore be given full weight in formulating Japanese policy.

It therefore seemed to me, and the President and the Department concurred, that in my initial address to the America-Japan Society on returning to Tokyo, an effort should be made to get across to the Japanese the real feeling in the United States and the facts on which that feeling is based. The fact that I shall merely be reporting my observations in the United States during the past four months will lend particular force to this opportunity, and I believe that full advantage should be taken of it. Later speeches will not have this advantage. My thought is to present, in as friendly a manner as possible, the points which the Department had intended to include in its proposed but eventually abandoned note. The America-Japan Society is about the only forum that we possess. My speech would be fairly widely discussed and if published at least in the *Japan Advertiser* would come to the attention of a considerable element of influential Japanese both in the Government and out of it. Any complaint that I was going to the Japanese public over the heads of the Japanese Government could be met by the fact that prominent Japanese have in times past used the Society to present the Japanese point of view (cf. Viscount Ishii's speech at the initial dinner after our arrival in Japan in 1932) and that I can properly claim an equal privilege.

After the speech was made, some of the American newspaper correspondents were using such terms as "dumfounded," "astounded," etc., in describing the reaction of the audience. As a matter of fact, only Thompson of the United Press was present and he scooped all the others, who had expected the usual diplomatic platitudes, but Morin of the A.P. and Hugh Byas very quickly began to receive calls from New York for voluminous reports. The Japanese press reacted just as I had expected, some of the papers accusing me of arrogance, impertinence, and surprising lack of diplomatic propriety. The general trend was that in spite of what I said, the American people simply don't know the facts and have construed a few unintentional "accidents" into wholesale depredations. Also that we still don't understand the "New Order in East Asia." But a few of the papers, notably the *Yomiuri,* which in the beginning had castigated me personally for arrogance, eventually were courageous enough to intimate in veiled language that there might be some merit in the American point of view and that it should be carefully examined. Such attitudes here are generally regarded as sheer heresy, but they showed that the inoculation was "taking."

SOME JAPANESE SIT UP AND TAKE NOTICE

October 25, 1939

One of my liberal Japanese friends has told me that ever since my "epoch-making" speech he had been discussing it with the highest officials, notably the Prime Minister, the Foreign Minister, Yuasa, one of the Emperor's close advisers, and Count Makino, all of whom had been studying the speech in detail. He said that he had talked for between an hour and a half and two hours with each of them. The speech, he said, had made a very deep impression; I had started the ball rolling at precisely the right moment, and now the people mentioned, plus the War Minister, General Hata, and General Yanagawa, who is heading the China Board, would form a team to keep it rolling in the right direction.

He said that some doubt is felt with regard to solving the problem of the New Order in East Asia versus the Nine-Power Treaty but there is a genuine determination to take steps to clear the atmosphere with a view to improving public opinion in the United States and to demonstrate Japan's desire for good relations. He said he believed that General Nishio, who had been sent to China to unify the command and to stop the constant bickerings between the military in the north and the military in the south, is likewise sympathetic to such a program. The time had come to stop the laissez-faire policy of letting America and Japan simply argue back and forth across the Pacific without constructive action in Japan and that my speech had turned the trick. He said that there was a general consensus among the high personages he had talked with that my more than two hundred notes of protest, which had lain dormant in the Foreign Office or had been answered with empty assurances of favorable action, should be constructively dealt with; that Admiral Nomura, the new Foreign Minister, would send for me soon and was ready to listen in sympathetic vein to anything I might say. He said that I must also have a talk with the Prime Minister, who would be equally ready to listen.

TWO CRITICAL MONTHS

November 1, 1939

While the text of my speech was promptly given to the American news agencies, I did not give it to the Japanese press, in spite of the advice of a prominent Japanese to do so, because I wanted the Foreign Office to know that I had observed this minimum of discretion in not going over the heads of the Japanese Government in that respect, and we so informed Yoshizawa, who was present, together with Kishi and Mitani of the Foreign Office, and heard the address delivered. I was banking on a public demand for publication of the text and, sure enough, two days later the Foreign Office itself asked me to release the text to the local press and it was promptly done. This was perhaps a small point, but such points loom large in Japan and it was duly noted.

The next two months, in my opinion, are going to be the most critical in the history of American-Japanese relations. Unless we can get concrete results *promptly* and not only negative but also positive steps to show the American people that Japan desires and intends to respect the interests and rights of the United States in China, the pressure for an embargo against Japan next winter is going to be great and Congress may demand it. By negative steps I mean cessation of the bombings, indignities, and other flagrant interferences with American rights; by positive steps I mean something like the opening of the Yangtze to foreign trade as concrete evidence to present to the American public. That thesis I am presenting to all with whom I talk and shall continue to do so unreservedly. This is not a threat but the statement of an objective fact. If and when we impose an embargo we must expect to see American-Japanese relations go steadily downhill; it will then be too late for any possible hope of improvement, and that is why the coming months will be critical.

AMERICA'S ALTERNATIVES IN ITS RELATIONS TOWARD JAPAN

December 1, 1939

A Japanese recently remarked that what Japan most needs at present is a statesman of the caliber of Prince Ito. No such figure, alas, has emerged nor is likely to emerge, and through lack of strong statesmanship Japan is bound to suffer. The Government is weak and is "floundering." Yet to control and unify the heterogeneous forces in Japan today would require a statesman of almost superhuman ability.

The crux of Japanese-American relations lies in the fact that while the Government is prone to give us soothing assurances, no individual or group in Japan is strong enough to bring about the full implementation of those assurances. There is little doubt that the great majority of Japanese, both in the Government and out of it, who know anything about foreign relationships want good relations with the United States, but they have yet to grasp securely the power of directing policy and taking measures in the effective way which alone can bring about good relations. International relations cannot thrive on mere pious expressions of intention. I have told them this, and am steadily continuing so to tell them, but it does little good. The outlook for the future relations between the United States and Japan does not now appear to be bright.

It is this outlook that now requires our most careful study and concern.

Two Main Desiderata

Before proceeding further with these observations, I wish to make clear the following points: my functions as American Ambassador to Japan, as I conceive them, and therefore the functions of the Embassy, involve two fundamental duties: first, the maximum protection and promotion of American interests in this field; second, the maintenance and furtherance of good relations between the United States and Japan. Even if and when these duties are found to be in conflict, we are not relieved of either responsibility. Our efforts must be to endeavor to align, so far as may be possible, these two main desiderata. Our analyses and recommendations must keep both of these primary purposes constantly in view. It then of course devolves upon the administration rather than upon the Embassy, in the light of larger policy, to determine the course to be followed by our Government.

In shaping the future course of the United States in the Far East our Government, I believe, should have in mind two distinct considerations. First and foremost, the fundamental principles of our international policy, which are based upon our own respect for legal commitments and our expectations of a similar respect on the part of other countries. Second, a sense of realism which takes cognizance of the existence of objective facts. When principle clashes with realism and when no one can be found to align them, then the question inevitably presents itself: to what extent, if at all, can we or should we seek adjustment by compromise? Should we ever compromise between principle and realism? We have now attained the desired maximum of our own national entity as well as adequate national strength. International morality, including respect for legal commitments and permanent abandonment of force as an instrument of national policy, has become for us at once a watchword and a religion.

The United States is solemnly (to use that somewhat overworked Wilsonian term) committed to uphold the principles of the Nine-Power Treaty, primarily to uphold the territorial and administrative integrity of China and the Open Door. Therein lies the point of principle.

On the other side of the picture, nothing in international affairs can be more mathematically certain (if anything in international affairs is ever certain) than that Japan is not going to respect the territorial and administrative integrity of China, now or in future, has not the slightest intention of doing so, and could be brought to do so only by complete defeat. Observance in practice of the Open Door is and will continue to be a matter of degree governed by expediency, not by principle. Herein lies the point of realism.

Can Japan Be Defeated?

Given the situation now existing in Europe, *there does not now appear on the horizon* the possibility of such a defeat being inflicted by any nation or by any set of circumstances, military, social, economic, or financial. There may be temporary setbacks or a stalemate in the military field or even, over a course of time, under increasing Chinese pressure, what the military experts call "strategic withdrawal to previously prepared positions"—in other words, withdrawal into North China, the control of which was the primary purpose of the so-called "China Incident"; there may be financial and economic difficulties and depressions; a pulling in of the belt; perhaps serious hardships; there may be increasing social unrest at home; but of an overwhelming debacle there is little present outlook.

I have already drawn attention to the beginning of an inflationary movement in this country, and I shall later discuss the further development of this movement as reflected in slower absorption of government bonds, a large increase in the paper currency, and mounting commodity prices, along with far-reaching measures designed to control prices. Attempts to control the supply and demand of rice are causing wide agrarian unrest. It is my opinion, however, that even if worse came to worst there is realization that Japan has irrevocably committed herself to the continental adventure and is determined to see it through. The majority opinion in the Embassy, which I myself share, does not believe that an American embargo, even if it covered all American exportation and importation to and from Japan, would bring about such a debacle as would cause the Japanese to relinquish their program in China.

Statisticians have proved to their own satisfaction, and will continue so to prove, that Japan can be defeated by economic pressure from without. But the statisticians generally fail to include psychological factors in their estimates. Japan is a nation of hardy warriors, still inculcated with the samurai do-or-die spirit which has by tradition and inheritance become ingrained in the race. The Japanese throughout their history have faced periodic cataclysms brought about by nature and by man: earthquakes, hurricanes, floods, epidemics, the blighting of crops, and almost constant wars within and without the country. By long experience they are inured to hardships and they are inured to regimentation. Every former difficulty has been overcome. Estimates based on statistics alone may well mislead.

"The New Order in East Asia"

During the months since my return from the United States I have carefully and thoroughly studied opinion in Japan, including opinion in the Government, the Army, the influential elements in civil life, the business world, and the masses, and on one issue that opinion can definitely be said to be unanimous: the so-called "new order in East Asia" has come to stay. That term is open to wide interpretation, but the minimum conception of the term envisages permanent Japanese control of Manchuria, Inner Mongolia, and North China. In the Army and among certain elements of the Government and the public the conception is very much broader; those elements would exert Japanese control throughout all of China, or as much of China as can now or in future be grasped and held, including the treaty ports and the international settlements and concessions. Control in Manchuria is already crystallized through the puppet state of "Manchukuo"; control in Inner Mongolia is a problem for the future. It is hoped and expected here that control of North and Central China will be exercised by setting up the two regimes under Wang Keh-min and Wang Ching-wei. These plans, of course, envisage long-term and probably permanent Japanese garrisons to compel subserviency to Japanese interests. It would be difficult to find any Japanese who visualizes "the new order in East Asia" as less far-reaching than the foregoing minimum conception.

The pill will be most carefully sugar-coated, and the Japanese are past masters at sugar-coating their desiderata and intentions. They say, and many of them actually believe, that all this is being done to bring permanent peace to China in the interests of the Chinese themselves; theirs is a "holy war." They also say, and many of them believe, that it is being done to prevent the spread of Communism into Japan proper, thereby casting aspersions, it would seem, on the generally accepted ability of the Japanese police to control and eradicate "dangerous thoughts" within the country. They will tell you, and they do tell you, that once the Wang Ching-wei regime is fully established and peace once more reigns among the bellicose Chinese who are themselves incapable of maintaining peace, why then American interests will be fully respected, the Open Door and equal opportunity will flourish in the land, and everything will be serene. Only a little patience is needed, they say, until all this lovely dream gets stabilized, as it is quite certain to do. We need not be misled by these assertions.

We ourselves can epitomize Japan's fundamental desiderata perhaps better than many Japanese can. They desire:

(1) Strategic protection against a future attack by Soviet Russia, particularly an attack on Manchuria.

(2) Economic security through control of the raw materials in China which Japan herself does not adequately possess. Japan is economically vulnerable.

(3) Eradication of both anti-Japanese and Communistic activities and propaganda in China, especially in North China.

The Japanese extremists desire much more, but the foregoing desiderata represent the fundamental and minimum purposes of Japanese aggression beginning with the Manchurian campaign in 1931.

To await the hoped-for discrediting in Japan of the Japanese Army and the Japanese military system is to await the millennium. The Japanese Army is no protuberance like the tail of a dog which might be cut off to prevent the tail from wagging the dog: it is inextricably bound up with the fabric of the entire nation; its ramifications are far too deep for any effective amputation, or any effective withering through discredit. Certainly there are plenty of Japanese who dislike the Army's methods; there is plenty of restiveness at the wholesale impressment of the able-bodied young men to fight in China, of the death and crippling of many, and of the restrictions and handicaps in everyday life entailed by the expenses of the campaign. But that the Army can be discredited in the eyes of the people to a degree where its power and prestige will become so effectively undermined as to deprive the Army of its control or at least of its preponderant influence in shaping national policy is an hypothesis which, I believe, no one intimately conversant with Japan

and the Japanese would for a moment entertain. It is reluctantly felt
that the entertaining of such a hypothesis is unfortunately but unquestionably a case of the wish being father to the thought. Should
any *coup d'état* occur in Japan through social upheaval, there is
little doubt that it would immediately lead to a ruthless military
dictatorship.

So here we find ourselves squarely faced with a problem which,
from all present indications, is to be permanently with us: the problem of principle versus realism. What are we going to do about it?

First of all, I do not think that our Government can, or should,
or will compromise with principle. It is unthinkable to me, and presumably unthinkable to the administration and to the great majority of the American people, that in this day and age we should do
so. We need not do so. Unless or until the provisions of the Nine-
Power Treaty are modified by "orderly processes" we should and
must respect and honor our own commitments under that agreement. . . .

Is an Isolated Japan Desirable?

The argument is often advanced that Japan should and can be
brought to terms through isolation. The corollary is furthermore
advanced that unless isolated and reduced by economic and financial attrition to the rank of a second- or third-class power, it is only
a question of time before Japan continues her continental and overseas expansion, involving the Philippines, the Netherlands East Indies, and other Western possessions in the Far East; that the time
to restrain her expansion is now.

With regard to this thesis, I raise the following considerations.
The resort to methods calculated to bring about the isolation of
delinquent nations must presuppose in the final analysis the use of
force. Sanctions commenced but not carried through bring in their
wake a loss of prestige and influence to the nation declaring them.
Sanctions carried through to the end may lead to war. This statement seems to me to be axiomatic and hardly open to controversy.
In my view, the use of force, except in defense of a nation's sovereignty, can only constitute an admission of a lack, first of good
will and, second, of resourceful, imaginative, constructive statesmanship. To those who hold, with regard to the specific situation with
which we are dealing, that it is not enough for good will and statesmanship to exist only on one side, my rejoinder would be that these

factors exist also in Japan, albeit in latent form until now, and that one of the functions of diplomacy is to bring those factors into full vigor. Shidehara diplomacy has existed; it can exist again.

There will be time enough to speak of sanctions when the resources of diplomacy shall have been exhausted. At the moment of this writing, those resources have not yet been exhausted. By nature not a defeatist, I believe that those resources may yet win the day.

THREE CONVERSATIONS WITH FOREIGN MINISTER NOMURA

December 4, 1939

The Foreign Minister, Admiral Nomura, asked me to call on him in his official residence at 2:30 today. Having been closeted with the Prime Minister, he came fifteen minutes late, very apologetic for the delay. The interview lasted for one hour and a half.

The Minister said that he was glad to resume our talks, the last of which had occurred on November 4, and that he was sorry for the delay in continuing them. He said that he had carefully studied the statements which I had made at our last meeting as well as the documents left with him. He considered very valuable the suggestions which I have made to him with regard to the importance of furnishing direct evidence of the intention of the Japanese authorities to put an end to the bombings of American property, the insults to American citizens, and the encroachments on American commercial activities in China which must be removed. Admiral Nomura realizes that the impression exists in the United States that these various acts have been deliberate and that there is an intention on the part of the Japanese authorities to expel American interests from China. He wanted to give me categorical assurances that such an impression is a misunderstanding and contrary to fact. Military operations on an unprecedentedly gigantic scale over extensive areas are going on in China and all of the incidents and cases of which we have complained have been accidents. The Japanese forces have been ordered to pay every possible attention in their power to protect and respect American property and citizens in China. The Minister said that he had discussed this matter with his competent colleagues in the cabinet and he could tell me as a fact that the personnel of the military commands in China has been so arranged as to ensure this protection and respect.

Admiral Nomura went on to say that such limitations to the commercial activities of Americans in China as have occurred are a result of the military operations, including control of the occupied areas, such operations not being consonant with the peaceful enjoyment of ordinary commercial rights. These limitations are, however, exceptional and temporary and our rights will be restored when peace comes. It will only lead to misunderstanding and confusion to generalize and to forecast future conditions on the basis of these temporary circumstances.

At this point I mentioned some of the different ways in which American commercial rights and interests were being injured, including the setting up of monopolies which ruined the business of various American interests. It seemed to me difficult to explain these monopolies and other restrictions as due to military necessity. The Minister said that in wartime it became necessary to control commodities and that the monopolies and other handicaps could be explained on this basis. I countered, however, with the observation that many of these measures gave the American Government and people the impression that they were intended to be permanent and that I would welcome concrete evidence to the contrary.

Admiral Nomura repeated the assurances given me by his predecessors that the Japanese forces in China have not the slightest intention to drive out American interests and that they have the strictest orders to the contrary. He said that our commercial problems in China should be dealt with both in Tokyo and in the field and he requested that American officials in the field should keep in close touch with local Japanese officials.

Admiral Nomura said that the cases both of bombings of American property and insults to American citizens were decreasing. In Pakhoi and Nanning, for instance, he has heard of no damage to any American property in that area. Constructive measures were also being taken to facilitate American commerce, as in the case of shipments of wood oil from Hankow and of lace and drawnwork from Swatow. The Minister was thus in a position, he said, to point out that possible measures were being taken in line with the valuable suggestions which I had made at our last meeting. He appreciated my honest desire to improve relations and by way of reciprocating this attitude he was now studying with the proper authorities such measures as could properly be taken.

Admiral Nomura expressed the regret that while he and I were making joint efforts to improve relations these efforts were being injured by the sometimes too-liberal expressions of opinion by important people in the United States, including statements with regard to a possible embargo against Japan.

At this point I called his attention to the freedom of the American press and of public discussion. I said that experience had taught us that measures to control the utterances of the press or of individuals often defeated their own object by causing an intensification of those utterances. I added that the public statements of individuals outside the Government, even though those individuals might be in close touch with the Government, did not necessarily represent the Government's views. The Minister smilingly observed that the same situation, especially with regard to the press, obtained also in Japan.

The Minister then said that he desired to present certain figures to meet some of my representations in our last conference and my concrete proposals for the settlement of pending questions. He said that the list of cases which I had presented to him had been carefully analyzed and a résumé drawn up on the basis of available documents. He thereupon handed me an informal document in Japanese which he thought I would probably wish to have translated and he read to me the following résumé:

A. Representations acknowledged or answered   179
B. Representations not acknowledged or answered   203
    (1) No acknowledgment or reply required   22
    (2) Not acknowledged but the contents dealt
        with by communication to the appropriate
        officials in China   27
    (3) Not answered but settled locally or dealt
        with   8
    (4) Investigations still going on but not yet
        answered   110
    (5) Miscellaneous   36

Admiral Nomura expressed regret that some of our representations had not been acknowledged or answered, owing to clerical oversight, but he assured me that all of our representations were receiving attention and that the competent officials were seeking solutions.

Some cases had been settled or were about to be settled, and they amounted to thirty-nine in all. In these cases the investigations had been completed and the Japanese officials were in touch with our own officials in Shanghai, trying to find solutions. The Minister said that Mr. Yoshizawa would explain either to Mr. Dooman or to me the details of the informal document which he had handed to me and would also be glad at all times to discuss pending questions. He said he thought it would be well for us to have periodical and frequent talks with Mr. Yoshizawa and he recommended that the officials of the Foreign Office and the Embassy constitute themselves as a sort of permanent committee to deal with these pending matters. Thus, speedy settlement of these questions could be made or agreement reached as to how to solve them and this should lead to more stable relations between Japan and the United States.

The Minister alluded to the press reports that there are over six hundred cases awaiting solution. Such incorrect reports mislead the public and injure our relations. He thought it would be useful to publish the actual facts and suggested that Mr. Yoshizawa get in touch with us with that end in view.

The Minister then said he would now like to talk "off the record." With regard to our treaty of commerce and navigation he said that "even if the treaty expires, I hope that relations may be maintained in a normal way and that there will be no cause for the people of both countries to get excited about." Japan's trade with the United States represents a very large percentage of Japan's entire trade, and if commerce with the United States should be impaired Japan would obviously have to seek other commercial channels.

As this seemed to me to contain an implied threat and as I felt it might also be interpreted as an indirect move to open negotiations for a new treaty or for a *modus vivendi,* I read to the Minister a close paraphrase of Secretary Hull's remarks to the Japanese Ambassador on November 24, emphasizing the considerations contained in the last paragraph to the effect that the American Government did not feel it incumbent upon itself to take the initiative in proposing practical measures for removing the obstacles for friendly relations between the two countries.

I then took up with the Minister the following matters:

1. Further attack on August 1 on the Lutheran Brethren Mission at Tungpeh, Honan (Nyhus case).

2. Interference with the property of the Catholic Mission at Sinsiang.

3. I read to the Minister the pertinent parts of Peiping's telegram of October 20 with regard to mob attacks on the Free Methodist Mission at Chenliu.

4. I asked the Minister to give his personal attention and interest to a subject discussed by Mr. Crocker with Mr. Suzuki concerning

the setting up in the Embassy of a radio receiving set in order that we might obtain direct information and news bulletins from our Government in Washington. I said that such sets existed in most of our important Foreign Service establishments, Japan being one of the main exceptions; that it was in the interest of both our countries that we should maintain close and rapid communication with Washington, and that while I did not wish to ask permission for establishing such a set in the Embassy (because this was a diplomatic right which we could properly exercise without permission), nevertheless I would prefer to obtain the definite approval of the Foreign Office before proceeding.

5. I told the Minister of the facts concerning the Tucker case and of the widespread interest which the case had aroused in the United States. I said that I had received many telegrams from important people at home expressing interest in the case and that our Government also took an official interest in it. I said that Mr. Tucker had been released from prison after some six weeks in jail but that he was to be tried within the next two weeks for what I understood was an alleged indiscretion in passing out certain literature not approved in Japan; that the final result of the case would undoubtedly be published in the United States and might have an important effect on the American public as well as on Mr. Tucker's friends. I added that, not wishing to interfere with the normal process of Japanese justice, I had made no formal representations in the case but I wished the Minister to know of the general interest, including official interest, evoked in the United States by the case. The Minister said that it would be very difficult even for him to interfere in this case, which was in the hands of the Department of Justice, and he felt certain that Mr. Tucker would receive full justice.

The following press release was agreed upon: "The Minister for Foreign Affairs and the American Ambassador today continued their talks covering the general field of Japanese-American relations in a mutually constructive spirit."

December 18, 1939

Admiral Nomura asked me to call on him today at the Foreign Office and in a conversation which lasted one hour and a half he read to me, through Mr. Iguchi as interpreter, and then handed to me the *pro memoria* that I at once conveyed to the Department.

The Minister informed me definitely that the Japanese Government intends to open the Yangtze River to general navigation as

far as Nanking "in about two months." The Minister added that
for the time being certain restrictions would probably have to be
imposed on such navigation owing to the military operations in
China.

The Minister definitely proposed a *modus vivendi* to carry on
Japanese-American commercial relations after the expiration of the
present treaty of commerce and navigation and expressed the hope
that, as little time is now left before the expiration of the treaty,
negotiations for a new treaty could commence shortly, if possible
before Christmas. I replied that I had no instructions with regard
to this matter and asked if the Minister desired me to communicate
this to my Government as a definite proposal from him. He replied
in the affirmative.

The Minister also touched on the following points:

1. Our problems were divided by the Minister into "positive" and
"negative" categories. I replied that between our two countries
there exist certain differences of opinion involving matters of fundamental principle, which as the Minister conceived them might
not fall within either of the above-mentioned categories.

2. In my conversation with the Minister on November 4 I do not
recall mentioning the possibility of bringing about in the United
States "a speedy" reversal of public opinion.

3. After Nomura had completed his statement and I had expressed my own appreciation of the Japanese Government's efforts
to improve relations between our two countries, I conveyed to him,
informally and fully, as under my Government's instructions, the
reaction of the Department to the statements made to me by the
Minister on December 4. This included the observation of the Department that it feels that the efforts of the authorities of Japan
thus far have little more than "touched the fringe of the problem."

4. With regard to the two "companies" and monopolies Nomura
said that it had become necessary to set up "economic blocs" among
Manchukuo, Japan, and China in order to overcome difficulties
in questions of national defense. But he declared that Japan has
no intention of excluding other countries and is "quite ready to
welcome foreign capital." When I asked the Minister "On a nondiscriminatory basis?", he replied merely that foreign participation
would be welcome in those enterprises.

5. The Minister observed that with regard to currency questions
they "had to finance the Army" but that these discriminations

"when the fighting stops and a Government of China is set up will be modified."

6. The Minister said, "off the record," at the end of our conversation that we must prevent, in the interests of both our countries, the war in Europe from spreading to the Far East and that Japanese-American conciliation will be a powerful factor in avoiding such a contingency.

December 22, 1939

In an interview with the Minister for Foreign Affairs this evening I conveyed to him orally the two separate statements substantially as set forth in two paragraphs from the State Department, dated yesterday. I also quoted the Department's instruction of December 18, which I handed to the Minister in the form of a *pro memoria*.

Admiral Nomura replied orally in Japanese and the interpreter later handed me the following translation of his remarks:

"The fact that the American Government has decided to take measures to facilitate normal commercial relations even after the termination of the effectiveness of the Japan-America commercial treaty and Your Excellency's efforts in this direction are greatly appreciated. However, the question of the commercial treaty is not limited to the commercial relations between the two countries but does, rather, in many ways relate to the general relations between our two countries. For example, even if commercial relations are maintained on a nearly normal basis without specific agreement, it is impossible to forecast day-to-day conditions in such relations. This is an uncertain prospect. In view of these considerations and looking to the improvement of relations between the United States and Japan from the broad viewpoint, I earnestly request that Your Excellency's Government give very careful consideration to the question of concluding a *modus vivendi*.

"I may inform Your Excellency that, as Mr. Yoshizawa, Chief of the American Bureau, has already communicated to Mr. Dooman, Counselor of Your Excellency's Embassy, the Japanese Government after careful study of the question from the above viewpoint has prepared a draft *modus vivendi* and has telegraphed this draft to Ambassador Horinouchi in Washington; and has informed him that he may submit the draft plan to the State Department in Washington at a propitious moment during his conversation there."

In our subsequent conversation I repeatedly made clear that Japan now had to give concrete implementation of its assurances that American rights and legitimate interests in China will be respected on a nondiscriminatory basis.

The following press release was mutually agreed upon in substance and definite assurances were given me that no publicity beyond this release would be given out by the Foreign Office:

"The Minister for Foreign Affairs and the American Ambassador this afternoon continued their conversations with regard to matters of interest to the two countries. Both the Minister and the Ambassador indicated a mutually helpful attitude toward a solution of the problems under discussion. Progress was made. The conversations will be continued."

ADMIRAL YONAI HEADS A NEW JAPANESE CABINET

January 14, 1940

The cabinet resigned and Admiral Yonai formed a new cabinet with Arita as Foreign Minister and my old friend Fujihara as Minister of Commerce and Industry. Yonai was the man who put the blocks to a military alliance with Germany last spring; I got to know him at the time of the visit of the *Astoria* with Saito's remains; he dined at our Embassy and I dined with him at the big Navy dinner, after which he told me that I need have no further anxiety about an alliance with Germany.

ARITA RETURNS TO JAPANESE FOREIGN OFFICE

January 18, 1940

Arita received the ambassadors individually, on assuming office in succession to Admiral Nomura. He told me that he had instructed Horinouchi to call on Mr. Hull to arrange the status of "treaty merchants" after the expiration of the treaty and he hoped that I would support the matter in order to avoid injury to the nationals of both countries. I merely reported the statement of fact. The Department knows my views. Later the Department cabled that the Japanese Counselor who called on Hornbeck, Horinouchi being ill, was told that the conversations regarding the treaty status should be carried on in Tokyo, so I shall now probably be called by Arita and can only cable his proposals back to Washington. This is something like a game of battledore and shuttlecock, but I think the Department is wise in concentrating the conversations in one place. I spoke to Arita briefly and informally of the unfortunate publicity in Tokyo which had misled the public into believing that I had given Admiral Nomura assurances that a treatyless situation would not arise. Now, however, the situation is being presented by the press in its proper perspective.

AN ANGLO-JAPANESE INCIDENT PUTS THE AMERICAN AMBASSADOR IN THE SHADE

January 23, 1940

The incident in which a British cruiser stopped the *Asama Maru* and took off twenty-one Germans, said to be liable to naval service in Germany, promises to cause a first-class scandal, especially due to the fact that the incident occurred almost in sight of the Japanese coast. One Japanese paper says that "the soul of Japan has been polluted," and when Sir Robert Craigie pointed out in a public statement that there have been more than 191 cases of visit and search by Japanese warships of British vessels off Hong Kong, the Japanese press rose in its wrath and, after charging the Ambassador with impertinence for publishing any explanatory statement at all, shrieked with fury at the idea of comparing noble Japan with a mere colony like Hong Kong. The emotional patriotism and chauvinism of the entire country have been let loose.

Incidentally, when I called for Craigie today to take him to the American Club luncheon, he smilingly apologized for having for the moment crowded me out of the limelight. I replied that he was more than welcome to the limelight and begged him to stay right where he is and to leave me peacefully in the shadow.

APPROVAL FROM F. D. R.

February 14, 1940

The pouch came in tonight. I had sent personally to the President the preamble to my November diary, written and dated December 1, with regard to the policy that I felt should be pursued toward Japan, saying that "I am reluctant to inflict you with a lot of reading material but I guess that your practiced eye can get the pith of any document in short order." F. D. R. wrote me a very pleasant reply, adding: "I am delighted with your handling of delicate tasks in a difficult situation. My kindest regards to Mrs. Grew. Yours in common effort," etc.

MORE SIGNS OF HESITATION IN JAPAN

April 10, 1940

The Diet ran its course and faded out. Wang Ching-wei opened shop and I wonder how long it will take for him to fade out too. The fundamental essentials for stability and permanency, apart from Japanese bayonets, appear to be lacking, and unless Japan is willing and able to keep a very considerable number of bayonets in that part of the world for a long time to come, it does not now appear that Mr. Wang will continue to feel quite sure of his footing. Predictions as to future developments are just as futile as they usually are in the Far East because of the many imponderable factors in the situation, but we can at least say that the futility of the China campaign, in its larger aspects, is steadily coming home to the great majority of thinking Japanese.

The foregoing assertion is based on many observations and many talks with important Japanese. A very small proportion of these observations and talks are covered in the diary, but just as health diagnoses are based on symptoms, I find peculiarly symptomatic a recent conversation with a well-known and influential Japanese publicist who in recent years has periodically indulged in published broadcasts of defiance against the United States and Great Britain in vitriolic terms and enunciating Japanese chauvinism at its worst. In two long talks of several hours this Japanese made *inter alia* two astonishing statements. One statement was that he had carefully examined all of Mr. Hull's published utterances since the beginning of the China campaign and had reached the conclusion that Mr. Hull was profoundly right in everything that he has said and that Japan is wrong. The fact that the Japanese under reference is a substantial and hardheaded type is sufficient to disprove the thought that he might have been using soft soap for ulterior motives. The second thing he said is even more significant, namely that, in his carefully considered opinion, the China Incident can never be solved until Japan makes up her mind: (1) to deal directly with Chiang Kai-shek; (2) to permit the interference (I think he meant mediation) of third interested powers, and (3) to define the "new order in East Asia." For a nationalistically minded Japanese to say this to the American Ambassador was, I submit, highly symptomatic.

Time, I believe, will play into our hands if we allow nature to take its course unhindered by us. By hindrances I mean steps in the nature of sanctions. What I have felt—and preached—for a long time, I feel still more certainly now. Today I have been talking separately with two Americans, Brooks Emeny, author of *The Strategy of Raw Materials,* and Jimmie Young, whose recent imprisonment, trial, and conviction for allegedly spreading false rumors about the Japanese Army might well have adversely affected his objective views concerning Japan. Each of these men, separately, agreed completely and genuinely with my thesis.

One of them, Emeny, recently asked a prominent Japanese what he thought would happen if the United States declared a legal embargo against Japan. The Japanese replied that the result would depend somewhat on the way it was done. If the step were taken in a way that would injure Japan's "face," retaliation would occur regardless of the outcome. It is difficult to see how a legal embargo could be imposed without injuring Japanese face because, even if it were labeled ostensibly for the purpose of conserving American resources, the Japanese would know better simply because a punitive embargo has so long been threatened, and things would almost certainly happen here which might well render Japanese-American relations precarious.

Many American writers and speakers discount the possibility of Japan's declaring war on the United States under any circumstances, especially while the former has her hands full in China, but what those speakers and writers do not understand is the potential intensity of Japanese nationalistic fanaticism, represented by important elements in the Army as well as the civilian population, which not only could and would halt in its tracks the efforts of the present Government and the liberal-minded elements in the country to steer a course of conciliating the United States but also could and probably would take steps which could subject Japanese-American relations to a serious if not dangerous strain. If war comes between the two countries it will probably not come through plans carefully weighed and calculated by either side in advance but through spontaneous combustion arising from an act or acts of an inflammatory nature. The American people do not want war with anyone; certain prominent Americans discount the possibility of war and they tell the people that there is no risk of war. The voices raised against this thesis include a few far-seeing men like Walter Lippmann but the others appear to have almost a clear field.

General Abe, the former Prime Minister who has been appointed envoy to the Wang Ching-wei regime and is to proceed to Nanking on April 15, is going ostensibly to negotiate with Wang Ching-wei

a basis for Japanese recognition and a treaty, but his real negotiations will be with the Japanese military authorities on the spot, and
it remains to be seen how much he can secure of the Konoye program in principle and in practice. The future as regards Japanese-
American relations will depend in large degree on the outcome of
these negotiations.

The next few months may be important, perhaps even critical,
but that is a trite observation which I make periodically. I do not
yet know whether I ought to go on leave to the United States this
spring or not. If there appears a real opportunity for constructive
work here I shall not go. On the other hand, there is little more
that I can say to the Japanese Government; our position has been
made abundantly clear; we can only await results. It may be that I
can do more useful work at home and, furthermore, gain in wisdom
by listening more closely to the voice of our Government and people
as I did last summer, with profit. I shall talk to Arita and see what
he has to offer and shall again consult Washington toward the end
of April or the beginning of May.

ARITA ENDS THE CONVERSATIONS NOMURA BEGAN

April 26, 1940

When Mr. Arita came to the Embassy this evening I asked
whether he desired our conversation to be formal or informal. He
replied, "Entirely informal." He then said he wished to apologize
for having failed to carry out his intention expressed to me when
he took office last January, to continue the conversations begun with
me by his predecessor, Admiral Nomura. After studying the situation he had come to the conclusion that because of the wide discrepancy in the views of our two countries in matters of principle a
continuance of the conversations looking toward the negotiation of
a new commercial treaty at this juncture would be futile.

I agreed with Mr. Arita that important discrepancies in questions of
principle existed in the views of our two Governments, but I added
that more acute phases of the difficulties between the United States
and Japan centered in the continued and recently aggravated interference on the part of the Japanese armed forces with American
rights and interests in China which I felt should be obviated before
the problems involving questions of principle could successfully be
solved. At this point I showed to the Minister and read the headings
of a statement of more than twenty typewritten pages covering the

instances of renewed bombings, personal indignities, et cetera, which have occurred since the first of this year, as well as a great number of instances of current interference with American business, trade, and commerce through monopolistic measures and exchange control, and import and export control restrictions in China.

I said that I had become greatly discouraged by this recrudescence of bombings and other acute cases of interference with American rights and by the absence of visible effort to implement the assurances continually given us with regard to the intention of the Japanese Government to ensure in practice the principle of equal opportunity and respect for American commercial and other interests in China. The Minister replied that Mr. Tani had informed him of my recent representations concerning the bombings and the difficulties at the barriers in Tientsin, and that he was doing his best to ameliorate these conditions. He hoped that the barriers in Tientsin would soon be raised. At least some of our complaints regarding monopolistic measures and exchange control and import and export restrictions would be solved when the hostilities in China were terminated. The Minister referred to his efforts to settle claims for damages in China which, even though the results might not be entirely satisfactory to the claimants, nevertheless represented an effort made in good faith to meet these claims. I acknowledged these efforts but added that thus far they had barely touched the fringe of the whole problem.

The Minister then spoke of the rumors of my return to the United States on leave of absence. I replied that the question of leave of absence arose annually and that my plans for this year were not yet settled but that frankly, after waiting in vain for the last several months for some evidence of implementation of the assurances given me with regard to an improvement in the situation of American rights and interests in China and seeing only a recrudescence and intensification of interference with those rights and interests, I was becoming doubtful of my ability to accomplish constructive work here and felt that personal contact with my Government at this time might be more helpful than remaining in Tokyo. I said that I had already made the position and attitude of my Government perfectly clear to the Japanese Government and that we were now waiting patiently but apparently futilely for results.

The Minister said that he hoped that I would not leave Japan at this juncture because the Japanese public, which at present is very much disturbed at the worsening of Japanese-American relations, would interpret my departure as a partial rupture of relations and that the public reaction might be "very serious." I replied that I would consider the matter in the light of the Minister's views and would let him know of my decision shortly. If I should decide to abandon my leave of absence I hoped that the decision would prove to be justified through a positive improvement in the situation of American interests in China.

A desultory discussion of the war in Europe followed. In spite of some acrid comments, the conversation, which lasted approximately one hour, was conducted in friendly vein and tone. I ended on the note that statesmanship must look to the long future rather than to the immediate present and that the reasons for Japanese-American friendship are fundamental and must win out in the long run simply because, in the long run, Japan cannot get along without the friendship of the United States.

JAPAN AND THE NETHERLANDS INDIES

May 1, 1940

The future status of the Netherlands East Indies, in case Holland should be invaded by Germany, has become an important issue. The official statement of Arita on April 15 that Japan could not view with equanimity any alteration in the *status quo* of the islands was inspired, we have reason to believe, by reports in various European neutral capitals that the United States was contemplating taking the islands under our protection in such circumstances, and we also have reason to believe that it was a German who circulated these reports. Arita's statement led to a counterstatement by Mr. Hull that we also are interested in the fate of the islands. Arita remarked ruefully to an informant that when he made his statement he had no idea that the American Government would interpret it as an indication that Japan herself intended to "protect" the islands. At any rate, the exchange of pleasantries has served to put our own Government squarely on record in this important issue.

"PUT ME DOWN AS AN ORIGINAL WILLKIE MAN"

June 10, 1940

It is still too early to foresee who the Republican presidential nominee will be. My own choice would unquestionably be Wendell Willkie and some time ago when I read his first speech and a description of his background, personality, and character I told Alice that he would eventually emerge and that she could put me down as an original Willkie man. He hasn't emerged yet, but I think he will. I hope and believe that Roosevelt will run again and be re-elected because he recognizes and is dealing effectively with the outstanding issue in our national interests today, namely the paramount importance of getting ready to meet the coming Nazi penetration—I do not say invasion—yet—of the Western Hemisphere. That issue transcends all domestic problems, and my guess is that if Roosevelt is re-elected he will promptly veer to the right so far as domestic affairs are concerned and lay all emphasis on preparedness. But if Roosevelt for some unknown reason does not run again, or if, contrary to indications, he should fail of re-election, then I should like to see Willkie as our next President. He seems to me, from this distance, to have honesty, strength, and experience, clear vision and executive ability, and above all a clear conception of our national problems in their perspective, and I base this judgment on the very few but not the less significant utterances of his that I have read. From now on we must base all our future calculations on the hypothetical loss of the British fleet. Roosevelt appreciates that fact and from what I know of Willkie's outlook I guess that he does too.

June 18, 1940

The diary has fallen back lately. We are already past the middle of June, and with the appalling developments that are going on in the world I have little stomach to sit down and record our trivial doings and interests here. When history comes to be pieced out, however, even the trivial pieces in the puzzle picture will fall into place, so with reluctance I shall try to keep up the continuity of this inadequate sketch. Events in Europe are bound to exert an important, possibly a drastic, influence in the Far East and are likely to lead to developments of far-reaching consequence. I am profoundly thankful that I didn't leave the job at this perhaps crucial period.

A JAPANESE FUNERAL RECALLS THE OTHER JAPAN

June 11, 1940

The Buddhist funeral rites for Prince Tokugawa today were intensely impressive, as all such ceremonies are in Japan. Alice and Dooman and I and the Thai Minister were the only foreigners visible at the intimate service, which lasted for nearly two hours, from 1 till 3 o'clock, the other diplomats and the crowd merely filing by after 3 o'clock to burn incense at the altar. After eight years in Japan I had the feeling today of being not outsiders but an intimate part of that group, almost as if the gathering were of old family friends in Boston and not in Tokyo. We knew well a great many of the Japanese and their wives who were sitting around us, members of the outstanding families and clans. The Tokugawas, Konoyes, Matsudairas, Matsukatas might have been Saltonstalls and Sedgwicks and Peabodys. We knew their positions, their influence and reputations, their personalities, and their interrelationships as well as those of a similar group in Boston. And we felt too that they regarded us as a sort of part of them.

This may sound a little snobbish, but that is not the idea at all. It would be just the same as if we called them Okubos and Suzukis and Hayashis in Tokyo and Smiths, Joneses, and Robinsons at home. The simple fact is that we no longer feel like outsiders in such a group and that the solemnity of honoring the memory of a friend who had gone and the deep significance of the Buddhist ritual in close association with other Japanese friends were just as significant and solemn and intimate as if the ritual had been the Christian service for the burial of the dead and the place Emanuel Church in Boston.

GERMANY'S VICTORIES MAKE JAPANESE-AMERICAN RELATIONS TAIL-SPIN

July 2, 1940

The political turmoil in Japan recorded in May has not relaxed; rather has it assumed increased intensity. The German victories, the collapse of France, and the generally predicted defeat of England are having their logical repercussions and effects here, particularly in the Army and of course among the extremists and the pro-Axis elements. The military—blusteringly—and the Government—in somewhat more moderate language—are demanding the complete cessation of the flow of war materials into China from Indo-China, Hong Kong, and Burma, as well as the removal of British troops from the International Settlement in Shanghai. Meanwhile they are demanding that the Netherlands East Indies guarantee a free flow of commodities desired by Japan regardless of the normal quotas and needs of other countries, as well as co-operation with Japan in matters of immigration and industrial exploitation in the islands.

The implication is that all of these various demands must be met —or else. Whether, in the event that all of these demands are not satisfactorily met, Japan will adopt strong-arm methods remains to be seen. The Japanese Government is moving slowly and carefully, but the extremists are increasingly vociferous and anything can happen, including the early fall of the cabinet either peacefully or through a *coup d'état* as in the "February 26 Incident." The public is increasingly anti-British and to a large extent anti-American. If and when the cabinet falls there is talk of Prince Konoye succeeding, but we do not think that he is ready to take over the reins of government. Our guess is Baron Hiranuma. The former is said to be busy organizing his single-party system.

My private conversations with Arita on June 10, 19, 24, and 28 have led to no concrete results, but they have at least served to keep the door open between our two Governments, which was their primary purpose. By meeting at the private houses of mutual friends we have largely avoided publicity, although rumors of the talks have of course leaked and at least one newspaper mentioned the fact that they were going on.

It is obvious that we cannot expect very much from a mere debating match between the Foreign Minister and myself, although we hear from a reliable source that the Prime Minister, Admiral Yonai, was annoyed with Arita for not giving me more encouragement. American-Japanese relations have got into a vicious circle. On the one hand, we ourselves take the position that there are three main obstacles to an improvement in our relations, namely (1) Japan's use of force as an instrument of national policy; (2) Japan's failure to respect treaty commitments, and (3) Japan's multifarious interferences with American rights and interests in China. On the other hand, Japan takes the position that these various obstacles cannot be removed as long as the hostilities in China are in progress, and that even after the termination of hostilities, only some but not all of our grounds for complaint can be removed. Furthermore, she takes the position that the absence of a commercial treaty between the United States and Japan is in itself an important obstacle to an improvement in our relations. The vicious circle is complete, and how to break it is a puzzle which taxes imagination.

FIRST CONVERSATION WITH FOREIGN
MINISTER MATSUOKA

July 26, 1940

The new Minister for Foreign Affairs, Yosuke Matsuoka, today received the diplomatic chiefs of mission individually in the usual purely formal reception. Instead of the customary five minutes he detained me in conversation for the better part of half an hour.

The Minister said at the outset that he had not yet had sufficient opportunity to formulate policy but he wished to say that when the press asked him what his policy was going to be as compared with the Hirota policy and the Arita policy and that of other ministers, he replied that they need look for no so-called Matsuoka policy but only for the policy of Japan.

The Minister then asked me to convey to Secretary Hull, for whom he expresses the highest respect and admiration, the assurance that he has always attached great importance to Japanese-American relations. Mr. Matsuoka said that he had always been a very frank talker and that in our contacts he might frequently say things which could be regarded as undiplomatic but he believed that much was to be gained by frank and direct speaking. He then referred to an article which he had written some time ago stating that if the United States and Japan ever have to fight each other they should know precisely the causes and reasons for which they were fighting and that if war comes, it should not develop, as in so many other cases in history, through misunderstanding. I said for my part that I also had no use for old-school diplomacy, that I also believed in straightforward talk, and that I believed the Minister and I would both profit by basing our relations on such an understanding. I thought that we might rule out the word "war."

Mr. Matsuoka then said that history is based largely on the operation of blind forces which in a rapidly moving world cannot always be controlled. I admitted that blind forces have played their part in history but I added that one of the primary duties of diplomacy and statesmanship is to direct those forces into healthy channels and that I hoped before long to explore with him the present state of American-Japanese relations in the confident belief that he and I approaching the subject in the right spirit would accomplish a great deal in giving helpful directive to the blind forces which he had in mind.

I then asked Mr. Matsuoka if he would care to read the informal record of my last talk with his predecessor, Mr. Arita, in which I had presented various points of view of the American Government, and I hoped that this record might afford a useful basis for our next conversation. The Minister said that he would be very glad to read the record, which he accepted and put in his pocket.

MATSUOKA TO ROOSEVELT

July 26, 1940

In the course of my first official meeting today with the new Imperial Japanese Foreign Minister, Mr. Yosuke Matsuoka, His Excellency asked me to transmit a personal message from him to President Roosevelt of the following tenor.

While passing through the United States several years ago following his departure from Geneva, Mr. Matsuoka, although at that time he held no official position other than that of Member of Parliament, had called upon Mr. Roosevelt at the White House in order to pay his respects and as a friendly gesture because of previous association with him. Mr. Matsuoka asked me now to express privately to the President that he shared his lifelong hope and interest in the preservation of world peace. He added, however, that he had come to understand that since the world is constantly evolving, changing, and growing, peace cannot be safeguarded by adhering to the *status quo*. The League of Nations failed, he said, because its member states had not had the courage to implement Article 19 of the Covenant, which provides for adjustments to meet such evolution and changed circumstances. A new order must come into being in the world, and the peace of the world must have as its foundation our adaptation to the development and change.

PRESIDENT ROOSEVELT REPLIES TO
FOREIGN MINISTER MATSUOKA

August 3, 1940

President Roosevelt made the following informal comments on the private message sent him by Mr. Matsuoka, and I transmitted them orally:

The assurance given by Mr. Matsuoka of his interest in maintaining world peace and his wish to preserve it, as well as the frankness with which his views were expressed concerning the necessity for adaptation to the growth of the world and world change in the interest of realizing world peace, are a source of gratification. Replying to Mr. Matsuoka in the same spirit and with the same frankness, a genuine and durable world peace, in our opinion, cannot be achieved by other than orderly processes and by dealing fairly and justly, both of which entail respect for the rights of all concerned, and which allow all nations to attain their legitimate aspirations. Every nation, including the American and the Japanese, naturally and rightly, has its aspirations for progress and security. Changes which are effected to these ends and by these means are healthful and are viewed with satisfaction by the United States. The fact that there exists among Japanese and American leaders a zeal for the preservation of world peace provides an opportunity, taking for granted mutual good will and sincerity, for exploration of a constructive nature in the direction of advancing relations between the peoples and Governments of Japan and the United States.

JAPAN GOES HELL-BENT TOWARD THE AXIS

August 1, 1940

It would be overstating the case to claim that during the life of the Yonai cabinet we had been able to erect any structure in American-Japanese relations, but we had at least laid a fairly useful foundation upon which some sort of structure might have been built had that Government continued in office. A typhoon could hardly have more effectively wrecked a foundation than the change of cabinet—with all that change implies—now appears to have accomplished. For at first sight the Konoye Government, interpreting popular and especially military demand, gives every indication of going hell-bent toward the Axis and the establishment of the New Order in East Asia, and of riding roughshod over the rights and interests, and the principles and policies, of the United States and Great Britain.

Those Japanese, especially in the Army, who favor such a policy —and we must now reluctantly accept the patent fact that they are vastly in the majority—see in the present world situation a "golden opportunity" to pursue their expansionist desires unhampered by the allegedly hamstrung democracies. France is out of the picture; Holland could do no more than put up a nominal defense of the East Indies in the face of Japanese naval and military power; Great Britain's hands are tied by the European war, her fleet fully occupied in the West; while the United States, in the opinion of these expansionists, dares not get embroiled with Japan while a potentially dangerous Hitler talks of eventually conquering the Western Hemisphere. The German military machine and system and their brilliant successes have gone to the Japanese head like strong wine.

That is the new setup. How it will perform in actual practice remains to be seen. In all probability Prince Konoye, reflecting the presumable attitude of the Emperor and the elder statesmen, will exert reasonable control over the "wild men" and will endeavor to move slowly and with some degree of caution, at least until it becomes clear whether Great Britain is going to win or lose the war. But in the meantime the "wild men," aided and abetted by certain elements of the press, are already engineering incidents calculated to incite public opinion against the United States and Great Britain and magnifying those incidents by incorrectly reporting and interpreting the facts, and if we judge by previous anti-American and anti-British campaigns in times past, there is good reason to believe that this movement may well become progressively intense. Generally such anti-American and anti-British campaigns have been waged separately and at different periods, with the idea of driving the two democracies apart, but now we, the British and ourselves, are regarded as in much the same boat and will probably receive much the same treatment.

Among the photostats of interesting clippings from the American press received from the Department in the last pouch I note that with one exception these editorials and articles oppose a policy of "appeasing" Japan, and that the single exception is an editorial in the New York *Daily News,* whose arguments are presented by the "China Information Service" merely as a target to shoot at. It is therefore amply clear, if these clippings represent a fair cross section of the American press and of American opinion, that not many voices are being heard in favor of trying to "appease" Japan. The feeling appears from these clippings to be nearly unanimously the other way.

"Appeasement" has acquired since Munich a connotation which should forever bar the word from the vocabulary of good statesmanship. The attitude for which it stands is one from which I utterly and conclusively disassociate myself. That term connotes defeatism. The recommendations which I have made at various times during the past three years were calculated—if acted upon— to avoid need or occasion for the use of "appeasement" in any phase of our relations with Japan. The point which has possibly been overlooked by those who share the views described in these clippings is that, in the situation now existing, "appeasement" would be as distasteful to Japan as it would be to the United States. Our series of telegrams on Japanese press comment has not overlooked emphatic statements to the effect that Japan will not respond to proposals for adjustment of relations which the United States may make on grounds of expediency or other considerations growing out of the impact on the United States of the military situation in Europe. I have before me an editorial which, commenting on the question put by Sir Robert Craigie to Mr. Matsuoka whether Great Britain can expect to improve her relations with Japan, states:

"We know that British desires for improved relations with Japan are inspired only by British military defeats in Europe and we cannot expect that approaches in such circumstances to Japan for improvement of relations will be entertained."

After reading these clippings, which I assume are a fair cross section of the American papers, I have the impression that the American press and therefore the American public do not differentiate between "appeasement" and that form of adjustment of mutual problems which should not be beyond the wit and good will of man to bring about consistently with our honor, our interests, and our obligation to third countries.

MATSUOKA AND STEINHARDT GET TOGETHER

August 24, 1940

For the first time since I came to Japan eight years ago, a Foreign Minister has called me directly on the telephone! It was Matsuoka, just to thank me for the dinner last night, which he said he had enjoyed enormously, and also to say that he had greatly enjoyed his talk with Laurence Steinhardt, our Ambassador to Russia, this morning. Matsuoka after last night's dinner said that he would welcome a further talk and asked Steinhardt to come to see him this morning. They talked for an hour and a quarter and of course Steinhardt told me everything. He particularly refused to discuss Japanese-American relations, as he said that that was my bailiwick on which he did not wish to presume. The talk was mainly about Soviet Russia. Perhaps Matsuoka, in telephoning me, merely wanted to make it clear that he was saying nothing behind my back.

Another interesting item is that Matsuoka sent his private secretary to my private secretary to say that he was sending an English-speaking Japanese to accompany Steinhardt all the way to Peiping and then to the Siberian frontier, just to make sure that he would have no difficulties with detectives and customs people en route. But what is more interesting is that at our next meeting Matsuoka said that he had told his private secretary to say to my private secretary that if at any moment Steinhardt should feel that the purpose of this Japanese was to spy on him, he was to send said Japanese packing back to Tokyo. And what is most interesting of all is that Matsuoka's private secretary refrained from delivering that particular message. Evidently he felt that he must censor his chief's indiscreet remarks!

JAPAN'S "NEW STRUCTURE" RISES FAST

September 1, 1940

August was a month of building up the "new structure" in Japan under the Konoye Government and of more or less marking time in foreign affairs while awaiting the result of the "Battle of Britain"—upon which many things everywhere seem to be waiting.

The "new structure" is going ahead fast and Japan is rapidly becoming a regimented nation, although in its main outlines this regimentation cannot be said to be either Fascism or Nazism. It is very far from either. There is to be no single political party, as in Italy and Germany, but rather an absence of all parties, the whole country being held together in individual loyalty to the Emperor. While there are as yet no concentration camps, the police and the gendarmes are busy cracking down hard on all who violate the principles of the "new structure," which involves an economical way of life and a general frowning upon most forms of lightheartedness, bright colors, fun, sport, and general gaiety, so much loved by the Japanese, and, of course, "dangerous thoughts." I fear that the traditional Japanese smile will become less and less evident. Every day the press announces some new restriction, some important, some trivial, and their cumulative effect is imposing.

We are preparing a dispatch in which some of these restrictions will be listed. They run all the way from announcements in matters of foods and dress and behavior to one perfectly serious statement that concubines may no longer have telephones. What a blow to the Romeos! Several of the golf clubs have announced that hereafter there shall be no tournaments for trophies, no caddies, no weekday playing, no players under the age of twenty, no arriving at the courses in automobiles, no wearing of knickerbockers in trains or trams, and that all silver trophies possessed by members shall be turned in to be melted up for the good of the nation. It is furthermore emphasized in the announcement that golf is to be played hereafter only for the purpose of building up physical stamina. Again, what a blow to a golfer's paradise, as I have often called Japan. Gambling in all forms is likewise frowned upon. Music is still permitted, but the radio is more than ever inclined to blare martial airs and patriotic songs, which, with the Japanese nasal method of singing, are too horrible to tolerate. Alas, alas, what a life!

American-Japanese relations are marking time. In a recent instruction I saw indications that our Government may be getting ready to show its teeth, an instruction which I highly applauded. Outright invasion of French Indo-China has been held in check in spite of military pressure, but if it should become evident that Germany is going to win the "Battle of Britain" I would look for an early move not only on Indo-China but likewise on Hong Kong and probably, eventually, the Netherlands East Indies. I assume that an attempted invasion of the Netherlands Indies would inevitably bring us into a frontal clash with Japan, but I do not think that this is likely to happen just now, first because I have never for a moment doubted and do not now doubt Great Britain's ability to win the war in the end, and second because the Konoye Government will probably take a long time attempting peaceful penetration into the Indies through pressure diplomacy before embarking on the hazards of an outright invasion. That is, if the Government can control the Army and Navy. If their control is too strong I look for further assassinations in due course, for the Japanese Government, with all its totalitarianism and regimentation, will never be able to control the military and the fanatics as they are controlled in Germany and Italy.

From my three or four talks with the new Foreign Minister, Matsuoka, I have the impression of a loose talker but of a man who is patently straightforward and sincere according to his lights. I think that he genuinely wants to bring about better relations with the United States and will do what he finds it possible to do in that direction. But what he may find it possible to do remains to be seen and we can only judge from facts and actions. At any rate, he is the first Foreign Minister that I have known in Japan with whom one can talk "off the record" with entire frankness. Arita's habitual "caution" is not evident in Matsuoka, and when I compare him with the sphinx Count Uchida, I see the exemplification of the extremes of diplomatic technique.

Prince Konoye I regard as a man of weak physique, poor health, and weak will, who was most reluctantly catapulted into his present position owing to his family name and tradition and by the force of irresistible circumstances. He has a mighty job on his hands and it will be intensely interesting to see what he can do with it.

That, roughly, is the setup at the end of August.

A WARNING THAT JAPAN FAILED TO HEED

September 2, 1940

One of my liberal Japanese friends says that he has just seen Count Kaneko * at Hayama and that although the old gentleman is still suffering from kidney trouble and skin disease he intends to come to Tokyo soon for a meeting of the Privy Council and will call on me then to thank me for my visit last summer. I told my friend that I would gladly call on Count Kaneko myself if this would save his strength.

My friend said that Count Kaneko has heard rumors that American businessmen are not disposed to conduct business with Japan at present. He assumed that this report is not true but that General Haraguchi is going over to the United States to find out what the trouble is. I told my friend, and asked him to repeat it to Count Kaneko, that the depredations of the Japanese military people in China against American business and other interests are steadily getting worse rather than better, and that the general situation which I explained to Count Kaneko through my friend last spring shows the reverse of any improvement. I sketched out this situation in some detail and told him that American trade and business in China which have been built up through generations are being effectively stopped by Japanese monopolies, exchange restrictions, and other totally illegal methods because the Japanese want to control the whole business field economically, financially, and politically. My friend expressed astonishment and said that Kaneko had no comprehension of this situation. I asked him to repeat to Count Kaneko everything that I had said.

I then talked at length of the utter shortsightedness of the present

* Elder statesman; former friend of Theodore Roosevelt.

Japanese program, not only with regard to its dependency on the Axis, which would render Japan nothing but the tail of a kite, but with regard to the proposed economic bloc in East Asia. I said a good deal about the unwisdom of trusting Hitler in anything and told him why Germany would never countenance a Japanese victory in China. I furthermore told him why the Germans were doing everything in their power to embroil Japan with Great Britain and the United States. I said that as a genuine friend of Japan I deplored her future outlook and feared that if she followed her present course she would eventually emerge no longer a great power. All the dictates of wisdom pointed to a course of developing friendship with the United States if only from the practical, commercial, economic, and financial points of view. But just as long as Japan continued to interfere with our rights and proper interests in this part of the world, any improvement in our relations was impossible.

My Japanese friend was visibly impressed and said that he would return at once to Hayama to report my views to Count Kaneko. I hope that the old gentleman will spill some of them at the next meeting of the Privy Council. He knows that I am speaking as a friend of Japan, and indeed it would be very difficult to say the things I do say if that were not a fact and generally known as a fact. I feel very strongly that Japan is headed straight for the rocks if she persists in her present policy.

MATSUOKA EXPLAINS JAPAN'S ULTIMATUM
ON INDO-CHINA

September 20, 1940

An appointment was made with Mr. Matsuoka on the afternoon of September 20, after the Department's telegram of September 19 had been received and decoded, and I precisely acted upon the instructions of the Department.

Mr. Matsuoka said that apart from some minor changes, the particulars of which were not mentioned, it was true that an ultimatum had been presented to the Governor General of Indo-China by General Nishihara. Matsuoka then explained the situation to be as follows:

On August 30, the French Ambassador, under instructions of the French Government, and the Japanese Government had signed an agreement in Tokyo. The agreement provided, *inter alia,* for the movement of troops of Japan through Indo-China and the temporary use of airports. The Governor General of Indo-China was on September 6 ready to sign an agreement which would have implemented the agreement signed in Tokyo on August 30, but he refused for reasons not evident to the authorities of Japan and obstructed the implementation of the agreement signed in Tokyo. The Japanese Government felt obliged, although with reluctance, to ask the French Government whether the actions of the Governor General were subject to control by the French Government, since the Governor General continued to be unco-operative, and whether on the basis of the agreement signed in Tokyo the French Government was exhibiting good faith. The French Government said that it was, and since the Governor General was evidently not acting in good faith and since the Japanese authorities were aware that to foreign consuls stationed in Indo-China the Governor had boasted that he was using obstructive tactics, the Japanese felt it necessary to present their ultimatum.

Matsuoka said that the purpose of the measures was to enable Japanese forces to attack Chiang Kai-shek and to bring peace to China. As soon as hostilities have ceased, he added, the Japanese forces will be withdrawn at once; the integrity and sovereignty of Indo-China will be accorded full respect, and as a consequence there will be no interference in East Asia with the *status quo*. The Minister said that he, Prince Konoye, and other Government members represented a minority opinion in Japan and that it was their determination that Japan should not oppress, exploit, or interfere with other countries' integrity. He said that a struggle was taking place against extreme elements within the country on this issue. My interruption at this point was to the effect that the agreement with France included clauses pertaining to commerce and economics in Indo-China. Matsuoka did not deny my statement but assured me that no exploitation would occur.

The terms of agreement between France and Japan signed on August 30 were confidential, said the Minister, and their divulgence by either of the signatories would nullify them. He said he could confidentially tell me, however, that France had broached the subject first and had requested a renewal of guarantees pertaining to France and Japan. This was negotiated at approximately the same time that the Anglo-Japanese Alliance was concluded. He did not recall the exact date but said that the agreement was in effect and registered with the League of Nations. (This presumably is the agreement of June 10, 1907, between France and Japan.) I then interrupted Matsuoka to ask what country's encroachments France desired guarantees against. Mr. Matsuoka said that this was a moot question. He then went on to say that Japan had asked permission to move forces across Indo-China and to be given temporary use of airports as "compensation" for complying with the French request. This information was given me in confidence, he emphasized, and its accuracy would of necessity be denied if any publicity followed.

The Minister talked lengthily, but in spite of this and in spite of his illogical reasoning I reported the meaning of his remarks to the Department with all possible precision. The Minister upon the conclusion of his remarks left at once to fulfill another engagement and I had time only to say that if Japanese troops moved into Indo-China my Government would regard it emphatically as an infringe- ment of the *status quo* which the Japanese Government had already pledged to preserve, and that a further statement of the attitude of my Government must await further consideration of my report.

JAPAN BECOMES A FULL-FLEDGED AXIS PARTNER

October 1, 1940

September has been one of the most momentous periods in Japa- nese history and in American-Japanese relations. The alliance be- tween Germany, Italy, and Japan became a potential consequence of the trend of Japanese policy from the moment of the establish- ment of the Konoye Government, but the pact itself came to a head with unexpected swiftness. A veil of secrecy had been drawn over the proceedings, which were carried on principally by Herr von Stahmer, a special German emissary, in Tokyo, and although specu- lation was of course rife, very few people in Tokyo had any idea that the negotiations would evolve so rapidly. Even some of the American press men thought up to five o'clock on the afternoon of the signature that the pact was to be signed in Tokyo, not Berlin, and some of my colleagues pooh-poohed the possibility of such an alliance up to the very day of its conclusion.

In spite of the fact that we were all groping more or less in the dark, the thought of such an alliance was reported by us on the basis of press comment as far back as August 3, and on September 20 I cabled that according to a reputable source, the Emperor, at a three-hour conference the previous day, in the presence of the entire cabinet and the highest military and naval authorities, had given his sanction to the conclusion of a defensive alliance with Germany.

This information, however, could not be confirmed or elaborated and we were sure of nothing until the last moment.

The pact was signed in Berlin on September 27, and on the 29th, after trying to consider the event from every angle, my thoughts were running along the following lines:

Clearly the primary aim of the alliance is against the United States. The advantage of the pact to Germany and Italy, through stimulating American apprehensions in the area of the Pacific, is obvious, but less obvious are the advantages accruing to Japan. In fact, disproportionate benefits would appear to be involved unless there are secret clauses having reference to one or more of the following points: (a) in French Indo-China and the Netherlands East Indies, control or exploitation by Japan to receive support; (b) mediation by Germany in the China conflict through intervention in Chungking; (c) Japan's anxieties in the north to be set at rest through Soviet Russian co-operation.

As to point (a), Japan can presumably be guaranteed a clear field in French Indo-China through Germany's control of the Government at Vichy, while pressure might well be brought to bear on Batavia through the ruthless use by Germany of her leverage in the Netherlands, and I feel that one of the most dangerous potentialities of the alliance is this latter consideration. Adverting to point (b), effective pressure on Chiang Kai-shek could presumably be brought to bear only in the event of co-operation by Soviet Russia. With regard to point (c), the situation is far from clear. A colleague was yesterday told by the Soviet Ambassador without hesitation that the terms of the pact had been unknown to him in advance, but on the other hand speculation as to an eventual Soviet-Japanese pact of nonaggression is rife.

In strict confidence a Japanese who is known to be sympathetic to the United States and Great Britain said, after the announcement of the pact, that the visit of an American naval force to Singapore would be the most effective countermove that could be made by the democracies and such a step would undoubtedly carry weight in giving pause to the extremists in Japan. The same purpose might be served, however, if Great Britain were to announce her willingness to allow vessels of the American Navy to avail themselves of that base.

Clearly, by the conclusion of this pact, Japan has embarked upon a tremendous gamble on Great Britain's defeat by Germany. While talking off the record and informally in a recent meeting with the

Foreign Minister, I expressed the opinion that Japan is headed straight for the rocks in pursuing her present course; that whatever may be the final result of the war in Europe, Japan, by tying up with Germany, would become merely the tail to a kite; that Germany, whatever her promises, could not and would not furnish effective support to Japan, and that by sacrificing for an economically unsound bloc in East Asia a free flow of world trade and commerce, the future financial and economic outlook of this country seemed to me to be utterly hopeless. Mr. Matsuoka did not contest my observations but merely said that all this was a matter of individual view.

Another important event, from my point of view, was the sending to Washington in September of what I can only call my "green light" telegram, perhaps the most significant message sent to Washington in all the eight years of my mission to Japan. The record will show in future that up until the fall of the Yonai cabinet in July, my recommendations have consistently been of the "red light" variety, advocating not "appeasement" but constructive statesmanship through conciliatory methods and the avoidance of coercive measures. In the face of progressive Japanese depredations against American rights and interests, especially in China, it had become more and more difficult to talk of conciliation, yet I knew that outright sanctions would set Japanese-American relations on a downward curve from which they might not be resurrected, and so long as there was any possibility of setting the pendulum swinging toward the democracies and away from the totalitarians, I felt that our efforts should continue to be applied in that direction. To relinquish those efforts seemed to me to spell defeatism. . . .

I think there have been no recommendations from this mission which, in the light of afterevents, I would now have altered, although it is easy to be wise after the event. Diplomacy has been defeated by trends and forces, both at home and abroad, utterly beyond its control.

After the fall of the Yonai cabinet and the setting up of the so called "new structure" under Konoye and Matsuoka, some six weeks or more were spent in observation and cogitation and now I summarize in the diary my diagnosis of the situation, as follows:

The views of Mr. A. T. Steele, China correspondent of the *Chicago Daily News,* regarding the situation in Japan have been carefully studied and in my opinion are well grounded. Nevertheless, his basic views that the sanest and safest naval policy for the United

States is firmness and that in the United States a tendency is to over-emphasize the risks involved in a firm policy are of such grave scope as to merit the most painstaking and considered analytical comment.

I am keeping constantly in view, while setting forth the current trend of my observations in this general connection, the fact that the formulation of American policy toward Japan must rest upon the more comprehensive point of view of the administration in Washington as well as upon many factors possibly not apparent to this mission.

There is no doubt, whatever the intentions of the present Government in Japan may be, that the military and other extremist elements here view the situation which now exists throughout the world as an ideal occasion to put their aspirations for expansion into execution. The victories of Germany have intoxicated them like strong wine. Their belief in the downfall of Britain has until recently been implicit. They have had complete faith in a rapid victory for Germany, and they believe it would be wise to consolidate the position in Greater East Asia of Japan while Germany is still acquiescent and before the ultimately expected strengthening of Germany's power at sea might preclude far-flung domination of the Orient by Japan. Although they have been carefully observing our attitude, these elements have minimized any opposition of an effective nature by the United States. The capability of sounder heads, both in the Government and outside of it, to keep these elements under control has been and remains dubious.

At present, nevertheless, I perceive a slow cooling of the sudden optimism which was manifested when the new Government assumed office. The Government, Army, Navy, and the people of Japan are now beginning to perceive that Great Britain may not be defeated by Germany after all—a possibility which I have plainly stressed again and again to the Japanese with whom I have come in contact —and, in addition to that gradual realization, they have seen our country and Great Britain drawing together more and more closely in undertakings for their mutual defense, as, for example, in the acquisition of naval bases by the United States in the British territories in the Atlantic Ocean, as well as in our assistance to the British Navy by transferring to it fifty destroyers. Reports are reaching them of American haste to construct a two-ocean Navy; of a possible strengthening of American Pacific naval bases; and even of our ultimate use of Singapore.

These reports and developments are producing on Japanese consciousness the effect that might be expected. Their tendency, on the one hand, is to accentuate the possible danger which confronts Japan from ultimate positive action by the combined strength of Great Britain and the United States, or by the United States acting alone. The peril of joint Anglo-American defensive measures has been understood in Japan for a long time, as is witnessed by Japan's efforts to refrain from antagonizing the United States and Great Britain at the same time. They furnish, on the other hand, telling reasons for those groups in Japan which desire to obtain political and economic security by acquiring sources of raw materials and markets entirely under Japanese domination. The Japanese are commencing to wonder whether, even were Germany victorious, a new risk to their program of expansion both in China and in the South Seas would not thereby be created. In the meantime, the attitude and policy which the Soviet Union may adopt in the future remain an unknown factor in their deliberations.

The various factors outlined above are beginning to make the Japanese hesitate. Especially in the Dutch East Indies, diplomatic negotiations under pressure will continue. However, a modicum of caution is indicated by the fact that, even for a time, Tokyo was able to prevent the military from executing their plans for a precipitate invasion of Indo-China, which, I feel certain, was in part, at least, due to our attitude. It appears probable that what is described by Mr. Steele as Japan's policy of nibbling is apt to be continued until the situation throughout the world, and more especially the position of the United States, have received clarification.

The opinion has been expressed that were sanctions to be imposed by us, they would have the effect of setting relations between Japan and the United States on a downward trend. Our recently initiated program of national defense, it is true, at present justifies steps not necessarily coming within the purview of out-and-out sanctions. We must keep in mind, however, the likelihood that export embargoes of a drastic nature on products so important as petroleum—which are known to be possessed in abundance by the United States—would be viewed by the Government and people of Japan as imperfectly disguised sanctions, which might, and probably would, cause some sort of retaliatory steps. The hazards seen by Mr. Steele as greatly overemphasized in the United States will be controlled less by the studied deliberations of the Japanese Government than by the reckless and headstrong temperament of the Army and Navy, should they lay at the door of the United States responsibility for the wrecking of their plans for expansion. This retaliation might assume the shape of measures by the Government to counter our export embargoes, but there would be a still greater probability of some sudden move by the Army or Navy taken unbeknownst the Government or without its prior authorization. These hazards are imponderable and not susceptible of being weighed accurately at any given juncture. To deny that they exist, however, or to proceed to formulate policy and adopt steps without giving these possible risks full weight and deciding as to the wisdom of confronting them squarely, would be shortsighted.

I am carefully bearing in mind, in the following observations, the two basic purposes of my mission to Japan, i.e., the promotion and protection of American interests, and the preservation of good relations between our two countries. In the event of conflict between the two objectives mentioned, the greater emphasis to be laid upon the former or the latter is a question of high policy not within my competence. It is my sole purpose to clarify the chief factors in the situation as viewed from this mission. I now take up the risks entailed in a policy of drift, having set forth with care those inherent in a strong policy.

It is impossible to discuss the direct question of relations between the United States and Japan or to place the matter in its proper perspective without viewing it as an integral part of the world problem, which offers in brief the following angles:

(a) Our own country and Britain are the leaders of a large group of English-speaking nations in various parts of the world. These nations stand for a manner of living which is today threatened in an appalling fashion by a group of countries—Germany, Japan, and Italy—whose declared objective is to force their will, upon nations conquered, by force of arms. Diplomatic methods are in general ineffective in endeavoring to treat with such nations. On occasions diplomacy may delay, but it cannot adequately block their onslaught. Only force or a readiness to show that force will be employed can stop those nations from realizing their objectives. At the present time Japan must be placed among the predatory nations. It has put aside all sense of morals or ethics and has become avowedly and shamelessly opportunistic, endeavoring on every occasion to exploit the weakness of other nations to its own profit. Its southward expansion policy constitutes a definite menace to the Pacific interests of the United States as well as a vital threat to the position of the British Empire in the Orient.

(*b*) It may be admitted that the security of the United States has rested to a certain extent upon the British fleet, which in its turn has had its support, and can only have its support, from the British Empire.

(*c*) If we view it as our interest to render support to the British Empire in this period which is vital to it (and it is my emphatic conception that such is the case), it behooves us by every means to keep conditions in the Pacific *in statu quo* at least until the issue of the European war has been decided. This cannot be done, in my view, nor can our interests any longer receive their full and proper protection, merely by expressing our disapproval and carefully placing it on record. Japan, it is apparent, has been restrained from dealing more highhandedly with the interests of the United States only by respect for the potential power of our country. With equal clearness it follows that to the extent to which Japan has disregarded our rights, it has done so in precise proportion to the measure of its conviction that the use of that power would not be allowed by the American people. If that conviction is once undermined, it may be that the effectiveness of diplomacy will again return.

(*d*) If, by a firm policy, we can maintain conditions in the Pacific *in statu quo* until such time as Britain may be successful in the European war, Japan will be confronted with a situation which will render it impossible for the present outlook of opportunism to remain dominant. At that time it might be feasible to set about a readjustment of the entire problem of the Pacific to the permanent benefit both of the United States and of Japan—on a just basis. Until the time when a thoroughgoing regeneration of outlook takes place in Japan, only a show of force, coupled with the intention to utilize it if necessary, can effectively conduce to the attainment of such an outcome, as well as to the future security of the United States.

In view therefore of actual conditions here in Japan, and the present outlook, it is my belief that the time has arrived when a continuance of the use of patience and restraint by the United States may and probably will tend to render relations between the United States and Japan increasingly uncertain. I cherish the hope that, if the Japanese Government and people can be brought to believe that they are overplaying their hand, eventually the pendulum will swing the other way, at which time it will be possible to reconstruct good relations between our country and Japan. To me the alternative appears hopeless.

My heart is heavy as I close the diary for September. This is not the Japan which I have known in times past.

SOME JAPANESE HAVE DOUBTS ABOUT THEIR AXIS PARTNERSHIP

October 2, 1940

Any certain estimate of public reaction in Japan to the Tripartite Pact with Germany and Italy is difficult for two reasons: (a) the present strict censorship of the press and control of public utterances, and (b) the fact that our reliable and important Japanese channels of information are in general no longer available, partly because the contacts of Japanese with the American and British Embassies are likely to bring trouble from the police, and partly because most of our Japanese friends appear to have given up all hope of improving relations with the United States. (We know that several of our erstwhile Japanese friends, including women, are on a black list and are being most carefully watched, and close friends who used to see us constantly now are afraid to be seen with Americans at all. One Japanese friend who got a little tight recently told me the whole sad story.) The privately and forcibly expressed opinions of Japanese businessmen, whose interests have been wrecked by the new orientation away from the United States and Great Britain, to which their interests were geared and who deplore the "new structure" and especially the alliance with the Axis, must not be taken as a fair criterion of public opinion as a whole.

Nevertheless, in the case of a large element of public opinion, including, we believe, the Navy and even certain circles in the Army and the Government, there is a marked absence of enthusiasm over the pact. We know that the Prime Minister was dead against the alliance and was simply defeated before the Emperor by the forceful aggressiveness of the War and Foreign Ministers, although the Emperor himself was far from happy about it. There has been no demonstration in the way of lantern parades, flag processions, the decoration of the city, and so forth, which, in the case of the Anti-Comintern Pact in 1937 indicated at least some degree of spontaneous enthusiasm. Indeed the *Hochi* naïvely wrote: "Something must be done to set the people's blood to boiling. The Tripartite Pact is a stirring march for Japan, not an elegy"! And the fact that the Emperor thought it necessary to issue an Imperial Rescript, for the first time since Japan withdrew from the League of Nations in

1934, was significant. That, of course, promptly killed all open expressions of opposition.

As for repetition in the Japanese press of American comment, the papers have very carefully avoided publishing any of the strong editorials from the foremost American papers and have emphasized, often in bold type, the published conciliatory utterances of such men as Hamilton Fish, Roy Howard, Arthur Krock, Cornelius Whitney, and others, while certain passages of a conciliatory tone in Sumner Welles' speech in Cleveland were taken out of their context. The alleged desire of America for "appeasement" was writ large in the Japanese press and that is precisely the impression conveyed to the Japanese public.

With regard to future Japanese tactics, we must guard against the flood of suppositions and opinions based on pure speculation that come to us and we must wait and watch developments. The widely mooted conclusion of a nonaggression pact with Soviet Russia would of course greatly affect the situation. I look with a degree of anxiety on the forthcoming German military mission to Japan, under the terms of the pact, because quite apart from technical assistance and material, the members will undoubtedly carry on intense propaganda, especially among the Japanese military, to drive them into hastening the southward advance and into war with the United States if possible.

When asked by some of my colleagues what Japan was to gain from the alliance, the Vice-Foreign Minister, Mr. Ohashi, has said that the pact is aimed directly against the United States, which ever since the Immigration Act of 1924 and the Manchurian Incident has hampered Japan's necessary expansion; that world totalitarianism will take the place of Anglo-Saxonism, which is bankrupt and will be wiped out, and that Japan had to ally herself with the other camp which is not intransigently set on preserving the *status quo*. He said almost the same to me.

MATSUOKA EXPLAINS WHY JAPAN JOINED THE AXIS

October 5, 1940

The Foreign Minister handed to me a statement in Japanese, entitled "A Statement to the United States concerning the Three-Power Alliance," to the general effect that the pact is aimed at no particular country (although Ohashi said to some of my colleagues that it was aimed directly at the United States) and that there will be no trouble between the two countries if America understands the New Order in East Asia. Our Embassy's translation of the original document follows:

A Statement to the United States Concerning the Three-Power Alliance

The recent Three-Power Alliance is not aimed at any particular country. If Japan, Germany, and Italy unite, the probability of being attacked by another country is decreased, the spreading of world disorder may be prevented, and in this sense the alliance contributes to world peace. By this treaty Japan has further clarified its intention to establish a new order in Greater East Asia including the South Seas.

The construction of a new order in East Asia means the construction of a new order under which Japan establishes the relationship of common existence and mutual prosperity with the peoples of each and every land in Greater East Asia, that is East Asia including the South Seas. In a position of equality with every other country, Japan may freely carry on enterprises, trade, and emigration in and to each and every land in Greater East Asia and thereby be enabled to solve its population problem. This does not mean these areas are to be exploited and conquered, nor does it mean these areas are to be closed to the trade and enterprise of other countries. Japan has long tried to solve its population problem through emigration, trade, and enterprises abroad, but the various countries of Europe and America have nullified Japan's reasonable and peaceful efforts concerning its population problem since those countries have turned back Japanese immigrants to their great territories and have obstructed trade and enterprise.

In the Greater East Asia sphere of mutual prosperity, the endeavor is being made to abolish such unnatural restrictions on the free activities of mankind. It is expected that this endeavor will be accomplished in so far as possible through peaceful means and with the least possible undesirable change in the *status quo*.

Japan's policy toward China forms an important part of the above endeavor. However, owing to the lack of understanding on the part of some Chinese people and to the attitude taken by England and the United States in not recognizing Manchukuo, which gave rise to Chiang Kai-shek's hope of recovering Manchukuo, an unfortunate clash of arms broke out. This clash is in fact war and therefore it is impossible for the Japanese Army during its activities to avoid affecting rights and interests of the powers in China. This is particularly true when such rights and interests hinder the prosecution of Japan's war against China. Accordingly, if the effects upon these rights and interests are to be brought to an end, it is most desirable to encourage and promote peace between Japan and China. This fact notwithstanding, the powers are not only checking Japan's actions through legalistic arguments and treaty pronouncements which have become inapplicable because of changed conditions, but are also oppressing Japan through such means as restrictions on the exportation of important commodities to Japan and at the same time are giving positive aid to Japan's enemy, the Chiang Kai-shek regime. These actions spring from hidden motives to keep the Orient under conditions of disorder as long as possible and to consume Japan's national strength. We must believe that these actions are not for the love of peace and are not for the purpose of protecting rights and interests. Japan concluded a defensive alliance with Germany and Italy for no other purpose than to resist such pressure from the powers, and there is not the slightest intention to proceed to attack another country. If the United States understands the aforementioned conditions and circumstances and Japan's intentions with regard to the establishment of a new order in East Asia, there will be no change whatever in the relationship between Japan and the United States following the conclusion of the treaty. Japan is determined to settle all pending questions and to promote and foster friendship with the United States.

This is the first time, so far as I am aware, that the Japanese Government has committed to writing some of the points that frequently arise in my conversations with Japanese officials of the present regime, and it is going very much farther than any previous Japanese regime ever went in calling a spade a spade. Certain salient points are to be noted:

(a) The "New Order" now embraces Greater East Asia *including the South Seas.*

(b) Within this great sphere, Japan "may freely carry on enterprise, trade, and emigration" but this, they say, doesn't mean conquest or exploitation or that these areas are to be closed to the trade and enterprise of other nations.

Various thoughts immediately arise in this connection. Are enterprise and emigration to be forced on the Netherlands East Indies, for instance, and if so, how can that be done without conquest? It is against the policy of the Indies to permit either enterprise or mass immigration by Japan. There is a very small, if any, difference between enterprise and exploitation.

If Japan once gets a foothold in those areas, the other nations will have a swell chance of "free trade and enterprise" if the Japanese remain true to form.

(c) The statement is directly aimed at our Immigration Act and at our quotas, established to stem the overwhelming tide of cheap Japanese goods entering the United States, as well as at our moral embargoes and our licensing system under the national-preparedness program.

There is no answer to these charges except that Japan in our position would have done precisely the same things.

(d) Japan will endeavor to carry out her program with "*the least possible change* in the *status quo*."

(e) The China Incident broke out *because* England and the United States refused to recognize Manchukuo and owing to the lack of understanding on the part of some Chinese people.

The first point above is an entirely new thought which I have never seen recorded before. As for the Chinese, they must indeed be dull of comprehension.

(f) Legalistic arguments—obsolete treaty pronouncements—oppression of Japan through embargoes—support of Chiang Kai-shek.

Nothing new there.

(g) "These actions spring from hidden motives to keep the Orient under conditions of disorder as long as possible and to consume Japan's national strength. We must believe that these actions are not for the love of peace and are not for the purpose of protecting rights and interests."

There are no hidden motives. Quite simply, we want Chiang Kai-shek to win because he legally and rightfully represents China. Furthermore, whatever might happen to our rights and interests after Chiang's victory, we know very well that it could be no worse than what is happening to them now under Japanese domination. As for consuming Japan's national strength, there will never be peace in the Far East unless or until the Japanese military become discredited, and that can come only when the military strength of Japan has been heavily weakened.

MATSUOKA TALKS FOR TWO HOURS AND A QUARTER

October 5, 1940

I called on Foreign Minister Matsuoka today at his invitation, and we talked, for the most part informally and off the record, for two and a quarter hours. As usual Mr. Matsuoka did about ninety-five per cent of the talking because his continuous monologues can be broken only by forceful intrusion. Although from time to time he brings up points of marked interest, his volubility flows on by the hour with little or no punctuation, and his discourses are therefore difficult to chronicle.

On this occasion Mr. Matsuoka's main thesis was that the present world situation results logically from the clash between tradition and the machine age. Only once during the conversation were heated words evoked, and those came from me when the Minister attempted to justify, on the ground of imperative necessity, national expansion by war, especially in the case of Germany. I had, as I pointed out, personally known the old Germany when within its own boundaries it was a happy, contented country, progressive and prosperous. The action of Germany's present leaders in grinding her weaker neighbors into the dust to satisfy their own megalomaniac ambitions could not possibly be condoned on the ground of necessity: to try to do so was utterly preposterous. In the case of Japan, I personally appreciated her economic needs. Japan's relations with the United States have not, however, been brought to their present deplorable pass by the reasonable urge of those needs, but rather by the employment of methods of force in following that urge instead of the methods envisaged in Mr. Hull's logical and practical plans for following orderly processes in the solution of economic troubles. At that point Mr. Matsuoka characterized the Anglo-Saxon countries as smugly convinced that they are right in everything they do and intransigently unwilling ever to acknowledge themselves in the wrong. On that point I said that I had never yet found a Japanese willing to acknowledge the patent fact that Japan had violated the provisions of the Nine-Power Treaty, to which Mr. Matsuoka to my surprise said that he was perfectly willing to admit that fact to me but he added naïvely that of course he could not do so politically as he had been urged to do before the League of Nations.

The Minister said that he had retired from public affairs for a long time and had thrice refused posts in the last Konoye cabinet, but that he had finally been led by his intensive pondering on the sorry state of his country to urge Prine Konoye to emerge again, as he felt that Konoye was the only person who could rescue Japan from impending revolution and chaos. Konoye was no longer the vacillating politician of his former premiership but an entirely different person, inflexibly determined to save his country, where even now revolution threatens. In answer to my question as to what kind of revolution he feared, Mr. Matsuoka replied, "political, economic, and social revolution," and expressed his feeling that the danger was by no means past. He then discussed at some length the vacillation and weakness of the former Minister for Foreign Affairs.

Mr. Matsuoka said that now the alliance with Germany and Italy was consummated and off his mind, he intends to get to work immediately and do all that he can to clear up the accumulation of American complaints which I had presented to him. It had been a *sine qua non* of his taking office that he was to direct Japan's foreign relations, and he says he does not propose to let the military, particularly the hotheaded younger officers, dictate to him.

In the course of his talk the Minister said that Japan has no intention of driving the interests of other nations out of East Asia, but welcomes their co-operation in the development of the New Order. I immediately took him up on this point and said I was delighted to hear him say what he had. As I had clearly indicated in former talks, however, the fact of the matter is that many legitimate American interests built up through generations have already been driven out of Japan, and that the process goes on apace. Mr. Matsuoka's reply was, as usual, that as soon as the hostilities in China are terminated and Chiang Kai-shek is defeated, these questions will be solved. He also expressed his usual appeal that the United States should cease giving aid to Chiang. Also as usual, I repeated the American position relating to that question.

When I was just about to leave, the Minister earnestly requested me to urge that my Government impose no further embargoes against Japan. He said that such embargoes "would not seriously handicap us" but would intensely anger the Japanese people. He added that the thought of war between Japan and the United States made him shudder. (I believe that Mr. Matsuoka is right as to the immediate effect of such embargoes as contrasted with their long-term effect.)

JAPAN FEARS AMERICAN INITIATIVE

October 9, 1940

For the first time in many weeks I went out to Kasumigaseki today to play in the semiannual American Club golf tournament, about seventy minutes from Tokyo, and of course the Foreign Office took just this occasion to call me back in a hurry. The chancery said that I would be back by 6 o'clock, but Ohashi replied that this was not soon enough—he wanted to see me at once. Fortunately the message did not reach me until I stepped off the last green and even then I took my time, finally arriving at the Vice-Minister's official residence at 5:35. There was no reason whatever for hurry except that the Foreign Minister clearly had the jitters over the action of our Government in "ordering" American citizens in the Far East to evacuate, and also over press reports that the American Government had decided to declare a total embargo against Japan, and Matsuoka had told Ohashi to summon me immediately.

With regard to an embargo I said that I had no information, and with regard to the evacuation I said that our Government had issued no "order" but only a suggestion as a precautionary measure. When Ohashi spoke of our "embargo" on iron and steel scrap I told him exactly what Mr. Hull had said to Horinouchi on that subject—to the effect that it was a purely domestic measure in accordance with our preparedness program, and that Japan, in view of her constant violation of our interests in the Far East, was hardly in a position to protest on that point. Fortunately the Department's telegram reporting that conversation had come in just before my interview, showing how helpful such reports can be.

Ohashi spoke of Japan's desire for peace with the United States and the fact that she has no thought of attacking America, to which I replied that we are like-minded toward Japan and that the American people, as Mr. Ohashi is aware, are strongly peace-minded. Nevertheless, the recent inflammatory utterances of the highest Japanese statesmen have led the American Government and people to have doubts of Japan's real intentions, and those utterances have brought about in my country precisely the reaction which might have been expected. I spoke also of the inevitable effect of those statements on our program of preparedness.

This conversation and the urgency with which I had been summoned convey the clear impression that Mr. Matsuoka is disturbed by the course of developments in the United States to which the recent provocative statements by members of the Japanese government have given rise. It bears out what I said in suggesting that at a given moment our Government should consider the evacuation of Americans in the Far East—that the move would have a powerful effect on Japanese consciousness.

WHAT HIROHITO AND KONOYE REALLY THOUGHT ABOUT THE TRIPARTITE PACT

October 22, 1940

I was told today on excellent authority that both the Emperor and Prince Konoye were dead against the Tripartite Alliance but that it was brought to the Emperor's attention that he might not survive a refusal and that he said to Konoye: "Well, you and I will have to stand or fall together." This came indirectly from a member of the Imperial family. There is constantly talk of the fall of Konoye and his replacement by a military dictator, a sort of revival of the old shogunate, but this obviously represents extremist views and now that the alliance has been concluded, Konoye may weather the storm, for a time.

AN AMERICAN EDITOR, NOW SERVING TIME FOR PRO-JAPANESE ACTIVITIES, CALLS AT THE AMERICAN EMBASSY

October 24, 1940

In view of the statements in the Japanese press reported to have been made by Mr. Walker Matheson, publisher of the *Living Age* and a member of the editorial board of *Current History,* I asked Mr. Matheson to call at the Embassy today. I told him that from earliest childhood I remembered having sometimes climbed on the big table in the nall of our family house and still remember finding on it a pile of the issues of a single magazine. It was the only one we could afford in those days, the *Living Age,* and out of sentiment I myself had later subscribed to it for many years. I introduced the subject in this way in order to show to Mr. Matheson that I was interested in his periodical and therefore naturally interested in its publisher, and with this background I felt that I could without any misunderstanding frankly approach the matter which I had in mind.

During the past eight years I had worked steadily to improve Japanese-American relations, but these relations had unfortunately now assumed a state of great tenseness and that especially during the present period the utterances of American citizens were very carefully scanned by the Japanese in order to appraise the attitude of the American Government and people toward Japan. At this difficult moment Mr. Matheson had come to Japan and had made statements to the Japanese press which, when carefully examined, conveyed the impression (1) that the American people were in general ignorant of the Far East, (2) that the policy and recent measures of the American Government were predicated upon the domestic political situation and their effect on the coming election, and (3) that the American people were not in accordance with that policy and those measures.

I said to Mr. Matheson that in the United States we highly prized the privilege of free press and free speech, but that when an American citizen comes abroad especially at a time of political tension it is distinctly disloyal and unpatriotic to convey to a foreign people adverse criticism of his own Government and its policy and measures. I said that Mr. Matheson's reported utterances were aimed directly against the work that I was trying to do here and tended to undo that work by creating an impression precisely contrary to the impression which I myself had been trying to convey. Such utterances could therefore be most harmful to American interests. I fully recognized the fact that visitors were often incorrectly quoted in the Japanese press, but I had heard no denial of the accuracy of Mr. Matheson's utterances as reported. I appealed to him as a loyal American to give out no further statements of that nature.

Mr. Matheson did not deny the accuracy of the reports. He said that he had come to Japan to familiarize himself with conditions in the Far East and that he had not wished to talk to the press but that it had been very difficult to avoid the importunities of the newspapermen who approached him. He said that he recognized the justice of my attitude, that he was extremely sorry for what he had done, that he had not fully appreciated the considerations which I had set forth to him, and that he would make no further public statements in future.

SECOND THOUGHTS ON JAPAN'S ADHERENCE
TO THE AXIS

November 1, 1940

In the light of fast-moving developments I scarcely dare read back in the diary nowadays because of its many inconsistencies which show it up for the patchwork sort of day-to-day scribbling it is. At least it shows our thoughts and our information, some of it reliable and some of it wholly unreliable, at any given moment—the moment of writing. It shows how often we are groping and fumbling in the dark. Less and less are we able to know what is going on behind the scenes, simply because many of our reliable contacts are no longer available and also because, even behind the scenes, the right hand often doesn't know what the left hand is doing. It is painful now to see that even as late as August I wrote that the Japanese Government was getting fed up with the Germans in their efforts to embroil Japan with the United States.

Many members of the Government, and probably the majority of Japanese out of the Government, were decidedly fed up. Yet a month later the Japanese had let the Germans draw them into the Tripartite Alliance for the specific purpose on the part of the Germans of getting Japan and the United States into eventual war. The pro-Axis Shiratori faction had won. The opinion was also expressed that Matsuoka genuinely desired to bring about better relations with the United States and that he would do what he found it possible to do in that direction. Yes, he certainly desires better relations with the United States, but he desires them on the basis of our first giving up our rightful stake in the Far East. On that basis we can enjoy a most agreeable friendship. When the Konoye Government came in, with Matsuoka and Ohashi and Shiratori on board, we were given an undeveloped photograph negative, the general type of which we knew in advance but not the precise outline of the picture that would appear. Now the negative is pretty well developed, the picture is taking shape, and it is not the sort of picture to afford complacency with regard to the future relations between Japan and the United States.

Now that the Tripartite Alliance has been concluded, we can no longer regard and treat with Japan as an individual nation. She has become a member of a team, and our attitude toward Japan must be our attitude toward the team as a whole.

Meanwhile something is getting rottener in the state of Denmark. The "new structure" is not sitting well, and a growing dissatisfaction is brewing. Even the War Minister himself announced the other day that the new structure need not be interpreted as taking all the joy out of life; he apparently sees the way things are going. There is much bickering and divided counsels and much talk that Konoye, who is hardly more than a figurehead, cannot last. The pendulum in Japan is always swinging; the moderates say that it will soon swing back toward normal, but I fear not. I fear that it must swing still farther toward the extreme, and that if Konoye falls, either through resignation or through a *coup d'état*, he is likely to be succeeded by a military dictatorship, even by a sort of revival of the shogunate.

As for American-Japanese relations, we now await the election and what may happen after the election. The Japanese are waiting too. For once, we have them guessing. They are wondering whether they still occupy the driver's seat, and are beginning to doubt it.

ADMIRAL NOMURA APPOINTED JAPANESE
AMBASSADOR TO WASHINGTON

November 7, 1940

At the Soviet reception today to celebrate their national holiday, Matsuoka told me that he was going to have another try at Admiral Nomura tonight to persuade him to go to Washington as Ambassador and he thought he would be successful.

November 8, 1940

Matsuoka telephoned me that he had been successful with Admiral Nomura last night and that the Emperor had approved the appointment as Ambassador to Washington. I cabled Washington that Nomura, as a man of high personal character who through long association had my esteem and respect and as a former Foreign Minister was believed to be fundamentally friendly to the United States, should be personally acceptable to the American Government. Incidentally, Matsuoka has on more than one occasion said to me that of course he himself was the ideal man to go to Washington but that he couldn't be spared from Tokyo. So Nomura is clearly second-string!

MATSUOKA ON ROOSEVELT AND NOMURA

November 10, 1940

A considerable part of my two-hour talk today with the Minister for Foreign Affairs was taken up with my presentation of a number of miscellaneous cases.

The Minister said that he had invited me to come to his private residence for a cup of tea without any specific purpose but merely so that we might keep in touch through periodic informal talks and to tell me of his constant efforts to obviate our grounds of complaint arising from Japanese interference with our rights and interests in China.

Mr. Matsuoka first asked me to convey to the President in one of my telegrams his hearty personal congratulations on the President's re-election.

The Minister said that Admiral Nomura had twice refused the Embassy in Washington because he did not wish to be placed in the position of giving assurances to the American Government when those assurances might later be invalidated through the fall of the cabinet and the appointment of a new Foreign Minister who might not support Mr. Matsuoka's views. The Minister said that his determination to persuade Admiral Nomura to accept the post and his final success in overcoming the Admiral's reluctance were eloquent testimony of his own attitude toward the United States.

The Minister said that it was almost impossible for him to read all the correspondence between the Embassy and the Foreign Office. His day's work sometimes extended to more than twenty hours, but in spite of that he had told his highest subordinate officials that he would not stand for bureaucratic replies to our representations and that he wanted the complete facts in every case so that he could give me, at least orally, a true picture of the Japanese position. This he proposed to do. He said that he recognized the absurdity, for instance, of making the new regime in China rather than the Japanese Government responsible for various developments. He wished to correct such an attitude on the part of the Foreign Office.

In connection with future developments I told the Minister that the United States would be impressed less by official statements than by acts and facts.

I also expressed my surprise when Mr. Ohashi had said to me that the Foreign Office received very little material from the Japanese Embassy in Washington reporting American press comment, whereas I was in the habit of telegraphing to Washington full daily reports of comment in the Japanese press. I expressed the view that especially at this time it was most important that the Japanese Government should know what the American press, and therefore the American public, was thinking and saying.

THE JAPANESE EMPIRE CELEBRATES
ITS 2600TH BIRTHDAY

November 10, 1940

Today was the first of two days of celebrating the 2600th anniversary of the founding of the Japanese Empire, and fortunately the weather smiled on Japan during both days, which were sunny and crisply cold. The first was the day of ceremonial greetings, and the second the day of celebration. For several months squads of men and schoolgirls have been working in the big plaza opposite to the palace, leveling it off, setting up decorative poles, laying out an enormous number of flowers, and finally building a big pavilion and rows of seats in front of it for about 50,000 people. They were the only people, all specially invited, who could witness the ceremonies because no one was allowed on the roofs or in the windows of the big office buildings in Marinouchi which would have afforded observation spots for many more thousands. No one may look down upon the Emperor, and I noticed how completely vacant those roofs and windows were.

On both days the Emperor and Empress, most of the Imperial princes and princesses (excepting Chichibu, who has been seriously ill with pneumonia), and all the highest officials in the country were present. Prince Konoye was master of ceremonies and read the speech to the Throne and led the banzais.

November 11, 1940

At the national celebration today we were seated at tables, whereas yesterday we had no chairs and were obliged to stand throughout, a little over an hour, which wasn't so bad. Today a Japanese meal was served with sake and everything, but we were expected to take it home in a *furoshiki,* or big silk napkin, given us for the purpose, instead of eating it on the premises, and of course we turned it over to our servants to whom it is always a tremendous privilege to eat "Imperial food." There were also a ceremonial dance and a lot of chorus singing of patriotic songs and band music. Prince Takamatsu made the welcoming speech in Japanese to the Emperor and then I had to speak for the Diplomatic Corps.

It was quite an ordeal to walk sedately in front of all the guests in the pavilion and then in front of the 50,000 people below in complete silence, then to face the Emperor, bow, get out spectacles and manuscript, read, bow, replace manuscript and spectacles, bow again, turn backward, and pace solemnly back to my place, but it went off all right and since I made a point of reading slowly and of carefully enunciating every word, the amplifiers enabled everyone in the crowd to hear perfectly, as I was told afterward. Even Mitzi and the other Embassy servants clustered around our radio and heard every word, the speeches being broadcast throughout Japan. The Emperor, who had preserved an almost rigid expression throughout the rest of the program, nodded at each of my points and nodded vigorously when at the end the hope was expressed that Japan would contribute to the general culture and well-being of mankind. Arsène-Henry, the French Ambassador, came to see me the next day on purpose to tell me that he had watched the Emperor's face and was convinced that his nods of approval were given to impress the Government and the highest officials of the Empire with his own desire for peace. Arsène-Henry was so impressed with this that he cabled his Government about it as an important political indication. Even the official Court release to the press announced that "His Majesty seemed greatly pleased" with the speech. Anyway, it was a relief to have it over. Am not yet sufficiently brazen not to find such jobs an ordeal.

Incidentally, the Department was responsible for the text of the speech. I had taken the precaution, in these days of political tensity, of cabling my original text, which the Department shortened and simplified, and it was very good, dignified without any slopping over. They left me full latitude to change it but I made no changes.

Today I called Matsuoka on the telephone and asked if he were coming to the Tokyo Club, at 6, to drink a toast to the 2600th anniversary. He said that he didn't know about it and I said: "Well, if you do come, we might have another little chat." He replied: "I'll be there." He came in at 6:45 and after greeting the few members who were left, he and I adjourned to a private room and had a long talk. It is a great advantage to be able to call Matsuoka on the telephone directly at any time, according to his own suggestion, a practice which has certainly never been welcomed by any previous Foreign Minister.

MATSUOKA AS THE MAN BEHIND THE TRIPARTITE PACT

November 18, 1940

The vernacular press is full of a story that the United States, Great Britain, and Thailand have concluded a secret military alliance, and one paper alleges that America has made a loan to Thailand of ten million dollars. It looks very much as if the Japanese were beginning to cook up an excuse, according to their usual methods, for bringing some sort of pressure, military or diplomatic, on Thailand for the use of air bases and other facilities which could be used for an eventual extension of their southward advance. I expect that we shall see developments along those lines.

With regard to the conclusion of the Tripartite Alliance, we have had to swim out gradually from the welter of speculation and inaccurate reports that come to us from many sides, but I think it is now fairly clear that in spite of the original story that the hands of Prince Konoye and Matsuoka were forced by the extremists, reluctantly on their part, it was Matsuoka himself who put it through, bringing Konoye along with him. We are told on very good authority that other cabinet ministers were not consulted until the end and knew little or nothing about it. I now have it straight from a person closely in touch with the Imperial Court that the Emperor was most reluctant to approve the pact and was finally led to do so only when Matsuoka gave the Emperor his studied conviction that war with the United States would be inevitable if the alliance with the Axis were not concluded. Judging from Matsuoka's subsequent statements I think that this version rings true.

JAPAN LOOKS SOUTH

November 25, 1940

Prince Saionji, the last surviving Genro, died last night. In view of his distinction and his high place in the life of Japan I placed the Embassy flag at half-mast besides telegraphing our condolences to the heir, Mr. Hachiro Saionji, and to Baron Harada, his private secretary.

There are indications that the Japanese Government has made some sort of peace offer to Chiang Kai-shek, it is believed at German instigation, and that if the offer is not accepted, Wang Ching-wei will be formally recognized. There is little doubt that Japanese interest is shifting more and more toward the southward advance, the first main objective being control of Indo-China. Some three divisions are believed to be concentrated in Hainan to be used if and when developments in the war in Europe and the attitude of the United States appear to warrant.

THE FUTILITY OF A JAPANESE GOOD-WILL MISSION TO AMERICA

December 7, 1940

A series of conferences with a prominent member of the Japan Economic Federation acting as a go-between for a prominent Japanese whom I shall refer to as "Mr. Y." led to some correspondence with the Department and a brief attempt on my part to analyze the present political situation. Mr. Y. wants to go to the United States with some big idea or plan which he believes would bring about an immediate improvement in American-Japanese relations. My guess is that his plan, which has not been divulged to us, is the usual one to get the United States to mediate for peace with Chiang Kai-shek.

I discouraged Mr. Y.'s proposal for a good many reasons, but later he modified his approach and said that he would go to the United States not on any so-called good-will mission and not to conduct propaganda but merely to learn the views of the American public vis-à-vis Japan so that he might report this firsthand information to the highest statesmen in Japan with whom we know that he has close contacts and influence. I therefore told the Department that I thought it might be worth while to let him come, of course in a purely private capacity, and this recommendation was accepted subject to certain conditions. The Japanese, even most of the highest officials in the Government, are amazingly ill-informed of American public opinion and I am all in favor of anything that will enlighten them.

In this connection I gave photostats of some of the more impressive editorials from outstanding American newspapers, including Walter Lippmann's article of October 8, to our go-between to suggest to Mr. Y. that he show them to his contacts. Later I was informed that those editorials had been translated to several of the higher officials who had expressed astonishment at their lack of information regarding the American attitude. This, I think, is thoroughly healthy procedure.

My analysis may be summarized as follows:

Mr. Y.'s attitude and his wish to go to the United States represent the almost despairing cry of those in Japan who realize the dangerous policies now being followed by the Government and the ultimate disaster to which those policies may lead. Yet his attitude in believing that his "plan" would immediately improve our relations indicates a basic misconception of the position of the American Government and people. He and his associates cannot understand that we are not to be swayed by mere expediency and that our position is based upon principles deeply embedded in the American creed.

It is to be questioned whether any great number of Japanese are temperamentally capable of grasping those basic facts. In their conception there is little comprehension or logic, for their views have been shaped over a long period of time by their controlled and chauvinistic press. They interpret our policy as a blind adherence to allegedly obsolete legalistic concepts, a selfish determination to obstruct Japan's reasonable expansion, and an arbitrary resistance to any alteration in the *status quo*.

These Japanese continually maintain that just beneath the surface there exists a great body of moderate opinion in Japan ready to emerge and to wrest control from the extremists if supported by some practical gesture of friendship from the United States, and they find it hard to understand why the American people feel that it is now up to Japan to take the initiative in any such gesture.

It is true that a large element of such moderate opinion exists in Japan, but unfortunately that element is just as powerless and inarticulate now as ever. The Konoye Government, which for a time was very shaky, has been considerably strengthened by the inclusion of Baron Hiranuma and by the publicly expressed support of the Ministers of War and Navy. From present circumstances we believe that when the present Government is overturned there is every likelihood that it will be followed by other Governments with the same determination to follow the course already mapped out, namely to secure for Japan the position in "greater East Asia including the South Seas" to which she considers herself entitled as a result of her growth as a first-class power in the modern world, territorially and economically restricted as she is.

As for Japanese-American relations, ever since the partial withdrawal of Americans from the Far East there has been a shift in the control of those relations. The effect is now being felt in Japan of the firm and unhurried but inexorable trend of American policy which has been given effect in the progressive steps taken since the abrogation of the Treaty of 1911. The reaction in Japan to the Tripartite Alliance and to the provocative statements of the highest Japanese statesmen immediately thereafter has been one of dismay. It is now perceived that the intended intimidation of the American people did not work out as planned, of which concrete evidence has been given by the American loan to the Chinese National Government immediately following Japan's recognition of Wang Ching-wei.

Matters have now come to a pass where the Japanese realize that something must be done to prevent the worst from happening, yet they are far from ready to consider the basic reorientation of policy which alone could serve to improve relations with the United States. It would be utterly unthinkable for any leader or group of leaders in Japan at present to advocate withdrawal from China and abandonment of their dreams of southward advance. Thus a vicious circle is established in American-Japanese relations. Admiral Nomura's appointment to Washington may represent the last effort of those now in control in Japan to save those relations from disastrous deterioration, but it would be futile to hope that the new Ambassador could undertake any revolutionary move to meet the views of the United States.

In this connection I repeated what had been said in my telegram of September 12, to wit, that while inevitable risks will be involved in a policy of firmness, nevertheless future dangers of far-greater magnitude would result from a policy of laissez faire.

"THE AXIS POWERS ARE NOT GOING TO WIN THIS WAR"

January 1, 1941

Another year has faded into history, a grim and cruel year, yet a year that has brought out in some parts of the world the finest qualities in human nature, heroism, gallantry, self-sacrifice, determination to fight, and to die if need be, for the highest principles—freedom, tolerance, right. I have never for a moment lost faith in Britain's ultimate victory—a faith that was surely not justified by facts during the dark days of last summer, had we known those facts at the time —but the best New Year's message that could come to us was in the President's radio talk on December 29: "I believe that the Axis powers are not going to win this war. I base that belief on the latest and best information."

With all our desire to keep America out of war and at peace with all nations, especially with Japan, it would be the height of folly to allow ourselves to be lulled into a feeling of false security. Japan, not we, is on the war path, and that path is not a whit the less dangerous to our own future welfare because it is camouflaged in such righteous-sounding terms as the "New Order in Greater East Asia including the South Seas" and the "Greater East Asia Co-Prosperity Sphere." If those Americans who counsel appeasement could read even a few of the articles by leading Japanese in the current Japanese magazines wherein their real desires and intentions are given expression, our peace-minded fellow countrymen would realize the utter hopelessness of a policy of appeasement. The time for that has passed. And to those well-intentioned fellow countrymen who might charge me with a destructive rather than a constructive outlook, I would say that only through the discrediting of the Japanese extremists by the failure of their plans can we hope to see peace in East Asia. Unarrested, the cancer will progressively invade everything within reach until its malignant control can perhaps never be checked. But if the cancer is arrested and rendered impotent in its earlier stages, we may yet see Japan return to healthy ways, when constructive instead of destructive forces may again control. Then, as I wrote to the President, we may approach a resumption of normal relations with Japan and a constructive readjustment of the whole Pacific problem.

Britain's victory in Europe would of course alter and render infinitely simpler our present problem out here, but it may become open to question whether we can afford to await a British victory and whether we should allow Japan to dig in throughout the areas where she now visualizes far-flung control. That question, I think, will depend upon the tempo of the Japanese advance. In the meantime let us keep our powder dry and be ready—for anything.

The turning point in the war seems to me to have come. If it was not the entry of Greece it was surely the President's address of December 29. We heard it on the radio; I have read it five times and know it almost by heart, and of course am making every effort to get it to the attention of influential Japanese because only carefully chosen excerpts were published in the vernacular press. It was a tremendous speech, and if I had had the slightest doubt as to the wisdom of

Roosevelt's re-election (which I did not have), this speech would effectually have removed any such doubt. To those of our fellow countrymen who want to get into bed and pull the covers over their heads, it is an invincible clarification and an unanswerable warning.

On December 14 I wrote the following letter to the President:

DEAR FRANK:

. . . About Japan and all her works. It seems to me to be increasingly clear that we are bound to have a showdown someday, and the principal question at issue is whether it is to our advantage to have that showdown sooner or to have it later.

The chief factors in the problem would seem, from this angle, to be:

(1) Whether and when Britain is likely to win the European war;

(2) Whether our getting into war with Japan would so handicap our help to Britain in Europe as to make the difference to Britain between victory and defeat;

(3) To what extent our own policy in the Far East must be timed with our preparedness program and with respect to the relative strength of the American and the Japanese navies now and later.

Those are questions which, with our limited information here, I am not qualified even approximately to answer.

From the Tokyo angle we see the picture roughly as follows:

After eight years of effort to build up something permanently constructive in American-Japanese relations, I find that diplomacy has been defeated by trends and forces utterly beyond its control, and that our work has been swept away as if by a typhoon, with little or nothing remaining to show for it. Japan has become openly and unashamedly one of the predatory nations and part of a system which aims to wreck about everything that the United States stands for. Only insuperable obstacles will now prevent the Japanese from digging in permanently in China and from pushing the southward advance, with economic control as a preliminary to political domination in the areas marked down. Economic obstacles, such as may arise from American embargoes, will seriously handicap Japan in the long run, but meanwhile they tend to push the Japanese onward in a forlorn hope of making themselves economically self-sufficient.

History has shown that the pendulum in Japan is always swinging between extremist and moderate policies, but as things stand today we believe that the pendulum is more likely to swing still further toward extremes than to reverse its direction. Konoye, and especially Matsuoka, will fall in due course, but *under present circumstances* no Japanese leader or group of leaders could reverse the expansionist program and hope to survive.

Our own policy of unhurried but of inexorable determination in meeting every Japanese step with some step of our own has been eminently wise, and that policy has sunk deep into Japanese consciousness. But while important elements among 'he Japanese people deplore the course which their leaders are taking, those elements are nevertheless inarticulate and powerless and are likely to remain so. Meanwhile the Germans here are working overtime to push Japan into war with us. I have told Matsuoka point-blank that his country is heading for disaster. He has at least seen that his efforts to intimidate us have fallen flat and have had an effect precisely the reverse of that intended.

It therefore appears that sooner or later, unless we are prepared, with General Hugh Johnson, to withdraw bag and baggage from the entire sphere of "Greater East Asia including the South Seas" (which God forbid), we are bound eventually to come to a head-on clash with Japan.

A progressively firm policy on our part will entail inevitable risks—especially risks of sudden uncalculated strokes, such as the sinking of the *Panay*, which might inflame the American people —but in my opinion those risks are less in degree than the fargreater future dangers which we would face if we were to follow a policy of *laissez faire*.

In other words, the risks of not taking positive measures to maintain our future security are likely to be much greater than the risks of taking positive measures as the southward advance proceeds. So far as I am aware, the great majority of the American people are in a mood for vigorous action The principal point at issue, as I see it, is not whether we must call a halt to the Japanese program, but when.

It is important constantly to bear in mind the fact that if we take measures "short of war" with no real intention to carry those measures to their final conclusion if necessary, such lack of intention will be all too obvious to the Japanese, who will proceed undeterred, and even with greater incentive, on their way. Only if they become certain that we mean to fight if called upon to do so will our preliminary measures stand some chance of proving effective and of removing the necessity for war—the old story of Sir Edward Grey in 1914.

If by such action we can bring about the eventual discrediting

of Japan's present leaders, a regeneration of thought may ultimately take shape in this country, permitting the resumption
of normal relations with us and leading to a readjustment of the
whole Pacific problem.

In a nutshell that is about the way I regard the present and
future situation. No doubt you have seen some of my telegrams
which have tried to paint the picture as clearly as has been possible at this post where we have to fumble and grope for accurate information, simply because among the Japanese themselves the right hand often doesn't know what the left hand is
doing. Their so-called "new structure" is in an awful mess and
the bickering and controversy that go on within the Government itself are past belief. Every new totalitarian step is clothed
in some righteous-sounding slogan. This, indeed, is not the
Japan that we have known and loved.

. . . You are playing a masterly hand in our foreign affairs and
I am profoundly thankful that the country is not to be deprived of your clear vision, determination, and splendid courage in piloting the old ship of state.

THE PRESIDENT SUMS UP THE FAR EASTERN CRISIS

The President replied:

The White House
Washington
January 21, 1941

DEAR JOE:

I have given careful consideration to your letter of December 14.

First, I want to say how helpful it is to have your over-all estimates and reflections—based as they are upon a rare combination of
firsthand observation, long experience with our Japanese relations,
and masterly judgment. I find myself in decided agreement with
your conclusions.

I also want you to know how much I appreciate your kind words
of congratulation on my re-election and your expression of confidence in my conduct of our foreign affairs.

As to your very natural request for an indication of my views as
to certain aspects of our future attitude toward developments in the
Far East, I believe that the fundamental proposition is that we must
recognize that the hostilities in Europe, in Africa, and in Asia are
all parts of a single world conflict. We must, consequently, recognize
that our interests are menaced both in Europe and in the Far East.

We are engaged in the task of defending our way of life and our vital national interests wherever they are seriously endangered. Our strategy of self-defense must be a global strategy which takes account of every front and takes advantage of every opportunity to contribute to our total security.

You suggest as one of the chief factors in the problem of our attitude toward Japan the question whether our getting into war with Japan would so handicap our help to Britain in Europe as to make the difference to Britain between victory and defeat. In this connection it seems to me that we must consider whether, if Japan should gain possession of the region of the Netherlands East Indies and the Malay Peninsula, the chances of England's winning in her struggle with Germany would not be decreased thereby. The British Isles, the British in those isles, have been able to exist and to defend themselves not only because they have prepared strong local defenses but also because as the heart and the nerve center of the British Empire they have been able to draw upon vast resources for their sustenance and to bring into operation against their enemies economic, military, and naval pressures on a world-wide scale. They live by importing goods from all parts of the world and by utilizing large overseas financial resources. They are defended not only by measures of defense carried out locally but also by distant and widespread economic, military, and naval activities which both contribute to the maintenance of their supplies, deny certain sources of supply to their enemies, and prevent those enemies from concentrating the full force of their armed power against the heart and the nerve center of the Empire.

The British need assistance along the lines of our generally established policies at many points, assistance which in the case of the Far East is certainly well within the realm of "possibility" so far as the capacity of the United States is concerned. Their defense strategy must in the nature of things be global. Our strategy of giving them assistance toward ensuring our own security must envisage both sending of supplies to England and helping to prevent a closing of channels of communication to and from various parts of the world, so that other important sources of supply will not be denied to the British and be added to the assets of the other side.

You also suggest as chief factors in the problem the questions whether and when Britain is likely to win the European war. As I have indicated above, the conflict is world-wide, not merely a European war. I firmly believe, as I have recently declared publicly, that the British, with our help, will be victorious in this conflict. The conflict may well be long and we must bear in mind that when England is victorious she may not have left the strength that would be needed to bring about a rearrangement of such territorial changes in the western and southern Pacific as might occur during the course of the conflict if Japan is not kept within bounds. I judge from the remarks which appear at the bottom of page 4 and at the top of page 5 of your letter that you, too, attach due importance to this aspect of the problem.

I am giving you my thoughts at this length because the problems which we face are so vast and so interrelated that any attempt even to state them compels one to think in terms of five continents and seven seas. In conclusion, I must emphasize that, our problem being one of defense, we cannot lay down hard-and-fast plans. As each new development occurs we must, in the light of the circumstances then existing, decide when and where and how we can most effectively marshal and make use of our resources.

With warmest regards,

As ever

FRANKLIN D. ROOSEVELT

GENERAL HARAGUCHI'S HOLIDAY GREETINGS

January 1, 1941

The following somewhat baffled but not the less inspired attempt of the Christian General Haraguchi to express his sentiments on his Christmas and New Year card is worthy of something more than mere derision:

> Grant all your hopes a singing breeze.
> Happy harbor safe to win;
> Quick upon un-troubled seas
> May your ships sail in!

SEASON'S GREETINGS

Merry Crystal America Mass
and
Happy Prosperous New Year.

H. J. Haraguchi.
Thanks giving for Unity
We the people, eternal people!

United immortal Childs America, who stand with Virgin Liberty at almighty foundation of Mt. Freedom. They play the musics and beautiful developed arts through speed communications and transportations and all understand the words of God. He gathered gems words with passion for unity and put on the hands of Universities Machines, shine above them as they are almighty stars in the heaven. We thanks to them, come to stand on the diamond step, ready to serve our country behind their God . . . inspite of Athenians give hemlock and Roman nailed. They meet at high light, a spiritual national unity with faiths and courage, we believe in them, can march shoulder to shoulder, of different creeds, races and nationalities. They have revealed its splendor, and inspired its passionate devotion to Childs America. Manifested in them, glory to God highest in heaven and peace to men of good will on earth everlasting.

ROOSEVELT VERSUS LINDBERGH

January 2, 1941

I have been giving to as many friends as possible not only the complete text of the President's radio address of December 29, 1940, but also the editorial comments from prominent American papers which have appeared in our daily radio bulletin. I also got Wills to publish the whole speech in the *Japan News Week,* which goes to some 3,200 subscribers in Japan, including high officials, business firms, and teachers, as well as selling 1,200 copies on the newsstands. Sumitomo alone takes 100 copies to distribute among the staff. Thus the highlights of the speech will penetrate to at least some important circles who will note the passages deleted in the vernacular press.

Thus, the comments in the vernacular press on the President's address, include such items as this from *Chugai:* "In view of the opposition to war participation by Lindbergh and others, Roosevelt's broadcast can be regarded as merely a private opinion not necessarily representative of the American people." Opposition and isolationist utterances by well-known Americans are always prominently displayed here but seldom anything on the other side of the story. So, of course, the Japanese public gets an unbalanced and distorted impression.

GERMANY WORKS FOR A JAPANESE-AMERICAN BREAK

January 3, 1941

Information from a certain source brought out the already well-known fact that the Germans here are doing everything possible to prevent Admiral Nomura from going to Washington and to bring about a partial or complete break in diplomatic relations with the United States, and that they are also about to intensify their efforts to embroil the two countries and to propel the southward advance. The following points were suggested as worthy of impression on the Japanese authorities:

1. If Japan follows the German urgings she will become involved, to her great disadvantage and probably without ultimate profit, in useless expenditures and risks.

2. If Japan enters the war on the side of the Axis she will either be defeated or, if her Axis partners should win, she will never be allowed by her partners to hold what she temporarily may have gained.

3. The opposition of the entire world to the Axis is steadily growing and crystallizing, while a Nazi and Fascist victory is daily becoming less probable.

4. If Japan allows herself to be misled by Nazi blandishments and to become involved in new military adventures, she is likely to alienate countries which do not wish to injure Japan but which have the power to do so if Japan forces them to act against her in self-defense. Japan has infinitely more to gain and less to lose by refusing to allow herself to be so misled.

5. That her Axis partners can render effective military support to Japan is not believed to be the case.

6. Japan may well pause to consider the tremendous risks without compensating advantage which she would be assuming were she to enter the war with the Axis or openly to assault or imperil important American or British interests, or interests important to those countries.

I told the Department, by the way, that we are well aware of the efforts of the Germans to embroil Japan with us and that I have been continually impressing the foregoing points on my Japanese contacts, including the Foreign Minister. Also that I am making every effort to get the full text of the President's speech of December 29 to the attention of influential quarters.

THE JAPANESE PRESS WARNS OF WAR
WITH AMERICA

January 7, 1941

A long editorial in today's *Kokumin* warns the Japanese people that war between Japan and the United States will be necessary because of the collapse of Great Britain, and America's entrance into the hostilities is expected to occur sometime this year. These events, it is said, will shift the major scene of hostilities from Europe to the Pacific, with Japan and the United States as the "main forces of the belligerents." The editorial refers to the recent remarks of War Minister Tojo and to the messages exchanged between Matsuoka and Ribbentrop, quoting Ribbentrop as stating that Britain will be "wiped out by autumn of this year at the latest" and declares that the Axis powers have had ample provocation from the United States to declare war against that country.

CLASH WITH MATSUOKA

January 18, 1941

At the farewell luncheon given by Matsuoka for Admiral Nomura today I was talking with them both and was expressing the hope that the Admiral would be able to exert his influence (I didn't say where the influence was to be exerted) to improve American-Japanese relations. Matsuoka remarked: "They certainly couldn't be worse," and turned away.

At the luncheon Matsuoka also practically threatened the United States with war, and I immediately replied to the following effect: "The Minister too has lived long enough in the United States to know that the American people are fundamentally peace-minded and furthermore that they stand for justice and equity. He also knows that the American people are firmly determined on certain matters among which, on the one hand, are their obligations and, on the other hand, their rights. Their profoundest wish is to see peace, prosperity, security, stability, and happiness assured to all nations. In the present state of world affairs we must inevitably realize that what counts in international relationships today is the concrete evidence of facts and actions, regardless of the persuasive garb in which such facts and actions may be dressed. Let us say of nations as of men: 'By their fruits ye shall know them.'"

THE ONLY VIRTUE IN THE NOMURA APPOINTMENT

January 20, 1941

In the numerous times that I have met Admiral Nomura on the round of farewell parties given for him, even though I sat with him for half an hour on the sofa tonight, he has not said a single word to me about the prospects of his job or of his observations during his recent visit to China. He is clearly not at home in speaking English. I can hardly picture him in a group of hard-boiled American Senators or Congressmen or newspapermen or officials holding up his end in a discussion. Yet Bishop Baker, visiting Methodist bishop, told me that he had had a long talk with the Admiral in the latter's home and that he had been impressed by his choice of language and familiarity with long words. In any case, language is not what counts now or what will count in the immediate future. The only potential usefulness I can see in Admiral Nomura's appointment lies in the hope that he will honestly report to his Government what the American Government and people are thinking, writing, and saying.

JAPANESE COURTESY

January 25, 1941

"Chip" Bohlen * arrived from Moscow today. He had wired from Tsuruga that he would arrive in Tokyo at a certain hour "if still alive." It was a pretty grim trip from Vladivostok and poor Bohlen had to take to bed with a feverish cold on arrival. He said that the manners of the Japanese officials in Tsuruga and of the staff on the ship were appalling; whenever he held out his passport or other papers they were rudely snatched out of his hand, and the service on shipboard was practically nonexistent. This was Bohlen's first glimpse of Japan and the so-called courteous race that inhabit it. Wiley's †️ initial experience in Japan will also be remembered, how on crossing the frontier from Russia he was rudely elbowed off the sidewalk by Japanese soldiers. The other day in Tokyo station I was queuing up to go through the ticket barrier when a Japanese thought that he had the right of way and strong-armed me out of the line with a heavy push. Luckily I counted ten before hitting him, and then discretion overcame valor. There are roughnecks in every country,

* Served as President Roosevelt's Russian interpreter at Teheran conference.
† American Minister to Latvia and Estonia.

but in Japan just now they seem to predominate. One's blood boils but there's nothing to be done about it.

It is interesting to note that when recently someone on the U.S.S. *Mindanao* was seen to take a photograph of a Japanese warship, the Japanese naval authorities in Canton made a big row about it and demanded an apology and the surrender of the film. The matter finally came up to Admiral Hart, who sent back word through Rear Admiral Glassford to Admiral Shimada, Commander in Chief of Japanese naval forces in Chinese waters, that he (Admiral Hart) "was amazed that the Japanese naval authorities in Canton should make any such demands and that he personally had witnessed the photographing of his own flagship by persons on Japanese men-of-war, notably the *Idzumo,* and that he had never dreamed of protesting such action." The Japanese demands were promptly dropped. Old Shimada has a little common sense, evidently.

FIRST RUMORS OF A SURPRISE ATTACK ON PEARL HARBOR

January 27, 1941

There is a lot of talk around town to the effect that the Japanese, in case of a break with the United States, are planning to go all out in a surprise mass attack on Pearl Harbor. Of course I informed our Government.

WARMONGERING AMERICA THROUGH JAPANESE EYES

January 31, 1941

"Considering relations with Great Britain, and in connection with the Pacific question, State Secretary Hull of the American Government has intimated that should Japan make any proposal America would be ready to consider it. This intimation is an insolent expression which is worthy to be spat upon. What country is it which is aggravating the situation to disturb the peace of the Pacific? America, without doubt. Advocating the Monroe Doctrine and emphasizing the peace of the world, it is America which has played the part of a kindler in the European disturbance. Not stopping there and then, it is busily hatching heinous schemes to extend the war to the Pacific. Should Japan make a proposal it would be for instant withdrawal of the American fleet from the Pacific."

Keijo Nippo (Korean Japanese-language daily newspaper)

JAPANESE-AMERICAN RELATIONS NEVER
LOOKED DARKER

February 1, 1941

One of my colleagues in Tokyo recently characterized the present situation in Japan as one of "unstable equilibrium." We can fully subscribe to the instability, but as to the equilibrium, that seems to be hardly the right word, and if the tilt is really held in balance, that balance is not obvious to the naked eye. It is true that the moderates are steadily working to maintain that balance, especially behind closed doors in the current sessions of the Diet, where committee meetings are being held *in camera* in order to avoid public censuring of the Government's policy. We know that Arita has been interpellating the Foreign Minister for days on end; we know that Hirota has said that Matsuoka is following a foreign policy "fatal to Japan"; we know, according to several prominent members of the Diet, that assurances have quietly been given by the Government that a policy aimed to avoid a clash with the United States will be followed.

Yet in practice the southward advance is being pushed with all energy by the military; their stranglehold on Indo-China, in contravention of the agreement with Vichy, continues with ever-increasing intensity, while Japan's insistence on mediating the Thailand-Indo-China dispute and, according to reports, on being paid for such mediation by the acquisition of naval bases in Camranh Bay is patent evidence of her firm intention to acquire jumping-off facilities for an eventual attack on Singapore. "Equilibrium" between the moderates and extremists seems hardly the right word. The latter are firmly in the saddle, and in practice there is ample evidence that they intend to push rapidly ahead, obviously stimulated by the Nazis, either in the belief that the United States will remain quiescent or, if we do not remain quiescent, discounting the results of American intervention. The outlook for the future of the relations between Japan and the United States has never been darker.

JAPAN'S NIBBLING CONTINUES

February 7, 1941

The following recent developments, both factual and reported, are concrete indications of the rapid progress Japan is making in her southward advance policy:

(a) Rumors that a Japanese force had landed at Songhkla, a Thai base close to the northern frontier of the Malay States, the presence of Japanese naval vessels in Camranh Bay, and the presence in the Gulf of Siam of one or more Japanese cruisers, a seaplane tender, and destroyers.

(b) Japan's military encroachments in Indo-China, exemplified in Japanese control of the Saigon airport, and mediation in the Thai-Indo-China dispute. It is reported that Japan expects to be granted the use of naval bases for having mediated the dispute.

Just as Japan has seized Hainan, Waichow, the Spratley Islands, and northern Indo-China in the course of the past two years, so Japan continues to carry out its nibbling policy, as foreshadowed by the Embassy. This policy, which consists of tentative thrusts and sallies in the desired direction followed by periods of inaction when the results and effects of the steps taken are felt out, is now being pursued with increased vigor due to Nazi stimulation.

Japan has already attained a position in southeastern Asia whence an investment or attack upon Singapore and the supplying of Axis ships in the Indian Ocean are possible with some added preparation. It is likely that such a move against Singapore is planned to synchronize with the expected German attempt to land in England. Apparently the conservative elements in the Army and Navy counsel delaying any action against Singapore until the European situation is favorable, and yet it must be remembered that the reckless do-or-die spirit of the military extremists may force the issue before Great Britain or the United States could or would intervene.

The Department's unofficial memorandum dated December 4, 1940, describing the vital role of Singapore in the defense of the British Isles, may be accepted as final and fundamental. Great Britain is in no position today, and presumably will not be in the near future, to part with important naval units for the defense of Singapore. In conformity with our admitted policy of aiding Britain, we must see to it that this strategically important base does not become the possession of a hostile power.

It is supposedly upon hopes of eventual American assistance that the morale of the Netherlands East Indies, the Chinese National Government, and of the British in the Far East is based. With great pressure being brought to bear on the Dutch in Batavia and with the British facing the possibility of sudden and sharp pressure, the moral is clear that an ounce of prevention is worth a pound of cure. Without the determined efforts of the Dutch, it is doubtful whether the East Indies and Singapore could be defended. The taking of Singapore by a hostile power would necessarily have grave repercussions upon Chinese morale as well as upon Britain's position in the Near East and in the eastern Mediterranean.

This Embassy is in no position to determine what action the United States should take or at what moment such action should be taken, for these are matters of high strategic policy. We recommend avoiding any halfway measure, which would not only be ineffective but would also entail all the possible undesirable results. As I have said in the past, we are faced with a momentous question, which is not whether we should check Japan's southward advance, but when. There are inevitable risks of war entailed in a concentration of American naval units in the Far East and it would be difficult to estimate the gravity of those risks, but at all events the United States should not undertake them unless prepared for war. Yet we believe that to allow the Japanese to advance indefinitely unchecked would be to court far-greater future dangers than if we were to call a halt to its southward advance in time. The Japanese, in our opinion, are relying on the passiveness of our country. We believe that if definite action is to be taken, it may have to be taken before long.

A typical report comes from Kunming describing the bombing of the American Catholic Mission at Poyang, in Kiangsi, on November 15: "One Japanese plane dived to approximately 300 feet and released bomb on its church, although the compound was marked with two large American flags, all the buildings being marked with white crosses and the visibility excellent. This plane later returned to survey the damage and to machine-gun the compound. The Mission states that there are no military establishments within a mile of the compound." Another unavoidable mistake; excuse it, please.

THE INSIDE STORY OF MATSUOKA'S MEDIATION OFFER

February 21, 1941

A report came to me today, from a source whose reliability I cannot confirm, to the effect that a movement is on foot by an important group in Japan, including influential Army officers, to stage a *coup d'état* and to overthrow the Government, by assassinations,

by methods similar to those of the February 26 Incident. This group
believes that the Government is leading Japan straight toward war
with the United States, a war in which Japan would certainly be
defeated in the long run. The names of the principal people who
are, allegedly, to assume the Government if the revolution succeeds
were given me, but I shall not put them down here. While there is
no way of checking the accuracy of this report, I know of the dissatisfaction with Konoye and Matsuoka, and knowing also the way
things go in Japan, the report is not at all unplausible.

Plenty of dust has been stirred up by Matsuoka's reported offer to
Mr. Eden to mediate for peace in the European conflict; the press
abroad was full of it and questions were asked in the House of Commons. My original guess as to how the thing happened eventually
proved correct and Matsuoka told me the whole story on February
26. It appears that in the face of criticism of Japan's action in mediating in the Thailand-Indo-China dispute, Matsuoka wrote a memorandum to Eden, through Shigemitsu in London, in which, in the
course of a long exposition, he said:

> Lastly, the Minister for Foreign Affairs [Mr. Matsuoka] would
> like to make it clear that Japan, deeply concerned as she is
> with an early restoration of peace, is fully prepared to act as a
> mediator or to take whatever action calculated to recover nor-
> mal conditions, not only in Greater East Asia but anywhere the
> world over.

What actually happened was that Ishii, deputy spokesman of the
Information Bureau, ran across this memorandum in the Foreign
Office and gave out certain parts of it to the press, in precisely the
same way that Amau had given out one of Hirota's instructions to
the Minister in China in the celebrated "Amau Statement," and
in both cases the publicity was given without the prior knowledge
or approval of the Minister. Matsuoka told me that he had been
very angry with Ishii and had issued to him "a severe warning" but
that of course Ishii's face had to be saved in public. However, the
harm had been done and it was considerable. Matsuoka said that
the British had used it to imply that Germany was in bad straits
and needed peace, which was the last thing he had intended to convey. At this point in our talk he got much stirred up and his eyes
became bloodshot with suppressed anger.

GOLF AS A DIPLOMATIC BAROMETER

February 22, 1941

In a group at the French Embassy on one of their Friday "at homes" Baron Fain, Counselor of the French Embassy, asked how my golf was going. I said: "Why is it, my dear Baron, that whenever a colleague or a Japanese opens a talk with me, instead of commenting on the weather he almost always asks about my golf?" "Why, Mr. Ambassador," replied Fain, "your golf is the thermometer which measures the temperature in the Diplomatic Corps. If a week goes by without your playing golf, the fact is cabled to every chancellery the world over, for the situation is then indeed critical!" I said: "Well, call me up tomorrow night and I'll tell you in strict confidence whether I was able to get my now once-a-week Saturday-afternoon game."

REFLECTIONS ON A TALK WITH MATSUOKA

February 26, 1941

In the course of a discussion of the Thailand-Indo-China dispute, Foreign Minister Matsuoka went out of his way to accuse the British Government of taking measures in the Far East which were a direct incitement to Japan and which rendered very difficult an improvement in the situation. He referred in this connection to the reported mining of Singapore and the dispatch of Australian troops to the Malaya-Thailand border.

I said that it seemed to me extraordinary that the Japanese should interpret and characterize obviously defensive measures as measures of offense. As I had said to the Minister at the America-Japan Society luncheon, we must inevitably be guided by "facts and actions," and the facts and actions relating to Japan's southward advance certainly offered concrete cause for serious anxiety not only on the part of Great Britain but of ourselves. Having occupied in succession Waichow, Hainan, the Spratley Islands, and other areas, the Japanese military were now pouring troops into Indo-China and, according to our information, had occupied the airport in Saigon and engaged in naval activities in those regions. These steps, together with the public utterances of many Japanese statesmen, generals, and admirals concerning Japanese intentions to the southward, had created a situation which could hardly be regarded with equanimity either by the United States or Great

Britain since they threatened not only our interests but our possessions.

Mr. Matsuoka replied that Japan was not the only country that gave voice to inflammatory utterances and in this connection he mentioned the names of certain Americans. He denied that the airfield at Saigon had been occupied, murmured something about Tongking, and said that the Japanese troops in Indo-China were there in strict accordance with the terms of the official agreement with the Vichy Government. I said that according to our own information these troops were very much in excess of the number originally stipulated, but the Minister replied that this was merely a question of replacement.

After we finished our talk, I wrote thirteen separate memorandums on the subjects touched upon and even they were not enough to cover all he said. One emerges from such a conversation with one's head feeling like a whirlpool, for the Minister's volubility is surpassed in my experience only by that of Foreign Minister Tewfik Ruschdi Bey in the old days in Turkey—and that was all in French. Fortunately, I acquired the knack of remembering the points in such a talk from experience as Under Secretary of State, when it was sometimes necessary to receive six or eight foreign diplomats in rapid succession and with no time to dictate the memorandums until afterward, and every memorandum had to be complete because to have forgotten any single point might then have had serious results.

THE ROUGHNECK JAPANESE AT HOME

February 28, 1941

The roughneck Japanese are not rough only with foreigners but with their own people as well, and the papers have recently reported that jostling, disorder, and actual fighting are occurring in the waiting lines before the movie houses. When Mr. Kita, Director of the National Life Guidance Department of the Imperial Rule Assistance Association (how's that for a title!), was asked for his view, he is reported to have said: "I should say that it resulted from lack of training on the part of the crowd. Pleasure-seeking, as long as it is limited to once or twice a month for relaxation from hard daily work, is quite all right, but even those whose pleasure-seeking is justified have no right to push and elbow one another at the entrance of a theater." The manager of the movie house said: "This shows how heatedly the general public is seeking amusements." The fact is that amusements, and in fact all the joy of life, are now so restricted that people are getting ugly. It is natural. The German slogan should in Japan be altered to *Kraft durch Unfreude*.

A JAPANESE STATESMAN UNBENDS

March 20, 1941

Diplomatic dinner at the official residence of the Vice-Foreign Minister and Mrs. Ohashi. Ohashi was affable, almost genial, and seems to have mellowed personally since he took office. Anyway, Alice kept him in gales of laughter during dinner. After dinner Ohashi talked with me for a long time and very interestingly— about education in Japan, the classics, and the faults of their educational system, which taught the young to memorize continually without using their minds in a discriminating way; on this subject he was very outspoken. Then he got onto the subject of the President's recent speech and said he had been scratching his head in an attempt to understand what the President had in mind when he referred to dictatorships in the Far East; certainly the President couldn't have been referring to Japan because, with her many faults, Japan at least was not under a dictatorship; and then he had got it; why, of course, he was referring to Chiang Kai-shek, the perfect dictator. As for America supporting the democracies, he couldn't imagine any country less democratic than Chiang Kai-shek's China.

He spoke of Admiral Nomura's talks with the President and Mr. Hull and had been glad that both sides had agreed that a Japanese-American war would be an absurdity. He inveighed against the bad treatment of foreigners in Japan. He talked with surprising interest and with a good deal of humor, and was perfectly willing to discuss the faults of his own country—although perhaps not all her faults! What we had anticipated as a grim and ghastly evening proved to be quite the contrary.

A BRIEF CASE HISTORY OF JAPANESE
SELF-DECEPTION

March 26, 1941

To what extent the intelligent Japanese are guilty of intellectual dishonesty, or to what extent they arrive at honest convictions from the propaganda with which they are fed, is always to me an open question. Since they are not allowed to know the facts, perhaps we can give them the benefit of the doubt, yet it is a little difficult to understand how an intelligent and scholarly man like the President of Waseda University, which has long stood for liberalism, can write such stuff as the following:

> As stressed in the Konoye statement made some time ago, Japan's purpose in the present conflict is not a petty territorial acquisition. . . . It is rather to safeguard China's independence, and, respecting her sovereignty, to establish a New Order in East Asia. In order to fulfill this noble mission, Japan has had to venture the greatest war in history. . . . Where in the world can another example of a battle fought with such a lofty ideal be found? This may truly be termed a Sacred War. . . . The countries that are most strongly insisting upon the maintenance of the "Open Door policy" and the principle of "equal opportunity" in the world today are the least willing to put into practice what they are advocating. Can international justice be established while such inconsistency prevails?

Yet some of them have a sense of humor in spite of all, and the following item recently appeared in the *Japan Times and Advertiser:*

> Because Britain has occupied Danish Iceland illegally the German Government has denounced it and applied the submarine blockade thereto. That should teach the British not to take over other people's territory without due process of law.

The hide of the Germans is far too thick ever to see the irony intended. A certain Japanese once remarked about the Germans: "What do they think we are? Vassals?" And the other day he told me he thought that the touchiness of the Germans springs from a marked inferiority complex. That from a Japanese is good.

On another occasion the same newspaper published a phrase from one of Hitler's speeches—"the *Herrenvolk,* the master race"—as "the hairy horde, the monster ape." I don't believe that the printer's devil could have been responsible for that one.

TRIBUTE TO WILLKIE

March 30, 1941

In the bitter controversy in the United States over the Lend-Lease Act and over the question of the degree to which we should aid

Britain, having in mind the risk of ourselves getting into the war, I fear that the intensity of feeling sometimes obscures objective think-ing. For instance, an intelligent friend at home writes:

> If a man or woman sincerely and enthusiastically believes that a course of action is really best for the country, it is wicked to keep silent for any personal reasons whatsoever.

Yet in another place the same friend writes:

> He [Willkie] seems to have lost his head completely, has be-come a publicity hound and a political adventurer. As —— says, *"He does not understand the game* and permits himself to be exploited by the administration."

The underlining is mine. What game? The game of partisan politics while the world is burning and America at the crossroads? Is it beyond the bounds of reason that Willkie just possibly may be an honest man, intellectually and otherwise, and that it would be "wicked to keep silent . . . if a man or woman sincerely and enthusi-astically believes that a course of action is really best for the country"?

Yes, we have a two-party system. A healthy opposition by the minority is part and parcel of that system. But does that mean that in national issues of vital importance to the country no member of the opposition, especially an outstanding member, shall support the administration in any policy which that member sincerely be-lieves is right?

I ask these questions because, in what seems to me to be an in-consistency in the two passages quoted above, the basic thought about Willkie is that "he does not understand the game." Alas, there must be something wrong with my own intellectual equipment or else in my appraisal of a man and his motives. Ever since last spring, when I first read some of Willkie's speeches (and my opinions were recorded in the diary at that time), I have believed him to be an honest man, intellectually and politically honest. I know very well that he has moved pretty far afield from some of his campaign speeches, but my conception of an intellectually honest man is not of one who fears to modify previously expressed views in the face of modified circumstances, broader observation, and maturer thought.

So far as Willkie is concerned, that seems to be the crux of the matter—whether he is or is not intellectually honest. If he is merely seeking publicity—"a publicity hound and a political adventurer"

—then my estimate of his character is all wet and I retire from the
debate. But if he is, as I firmly believe, honest to the core, would it
not then be wicked for him to keep silent or to oppose a course of
action which he thinks is really best for the country? Should he not
vigorously support that course of action, as he has done? My own
feeling is that Willkie grows steadily in stature and will in future
play a prominent part in the political life of our country.

JAPAN'S SOUTHWARD ADVANCE MARKS TIME

April 10, 1941

March was a month of marking time in the Far East. The
Thailand-Indo-China "mediation" came to a head, practically in
the form of a Japanese ultimatum to the French, who had to sign on
the dotted line. They knew that Indo-China was not strong enough
to resist Japanese incursion and believed that it was better to give
up a part than to have it all taken away, which would probably
have been the case if they had tried to thwart Japan. Incidentally
we know that the chief Thai delegate remarked afterward that the
settlement dictated by Japan was "devoid of all common sense." The
net result seems to be that Japan gets a stranglehold on Indo-China
and at least a semistranglehold on Thailand for use at such time in
the future as it suits the purpose of the Japanese to prepare to
attack Malaya, Burma, or Singapore. The southward advance is,
however, marking time pending developments in Europe, and while
the Japanese have at least one eye cocked toward the United States.

Meanwhile Matsuoka has gone on his historic visit to Europe.
He is known to have remarked that Ribbentrop is supposed to be
the biggest liar in Europe and that he wanted to find out if this
were true. As for Moscow, we are told on the best authority that in
his one-hour meeting with Stalin, Matsuoka lectured on Japanese
ideology for precisely fifty-eight minutes, concluding his lecture with
the amazing statement that while the Japanese were not Communists politically or economically, nevertheless a close parallel existed between Communism and Japanese family life; Stalin is said
thereupon to have remarked that he saw no reason why Russia and
Japan could not be friends in spite of differences in ideology and
left the room.

I would give a lot to know whether Matsuoka managed with
equal success to hold the floor in his talks with Hitler; it would
take a superman to outtalk Matsuoka, but maybe Hitler is a super-

man. Matsuoka is reported to have said to the German press, in effect, that all the world's troubles were due to Anglo-Saxon machinations, and I dare say that he did say just that. But if I know anything about the Germans they will have overplayed their hand with him and with their usual technique of cajolery and threats they may well have weakened rather than strengthened the Axis ties. About that, we shall see in due course. At any rate. Mr. Matsuoka could hardly have picked a worse moment for his visit, for on his arrival in Berlin the Nazi celebration of getting Yugoslavia into the Axis had turned to complete discomfiture, while on the very day of his arrival in Rome, or thereabouts, the serious Italian defeat in the naval battle of Matapan was announced. The appearance of a black cat could hardly have been more untimely than Matsuoka's arrival in the two capitals.

The domestic situation in Japan, both politically and economically, was steadily growing worse and dissatisfaction with Konoye and his cabinet was growing. This dissatisfaction led, in the early days of April, to a revamping of the cabinet with the inclusion of Ogura, Admiral Toyoda, and General Suzuki. Ogura is the head of the great business firm of Sumitomo and, incidentally, President of the America-Japan Society of the Kwansai (Osaka). Toyoda is sound and sensible. I know both of them, Ogura very well and Toyoda fairly well. Hiranuma is no doubt responsible for these changes and is, we believe, directing affairs behind the scenes, lending strength to Prince Konoye's weakness. The result should be healthy and we may expect to see a restraining influence on the hothead extremists. In fact, we begin to see symptoms of at least a slight cooling of pro-Axis sentiment.

But in the last analysis, as I have continually said, future developments will depend in large measure on the result of affairs in Europe, particularly the Battle of Britain.

With great reluctance and disappointment I have given up all thought of taking leave of absence this spring. This is no time for vacations while the world burns, and since these coming months may well be critical in Europe they may bring equally critical developments in the Far East. It would be very easy to persuade myself that other hands could run the Embassy adequately during the comparatively brief period necessary to enable me to accept an important academic invitation in the United States in June and that during that period nothing of importance might happen. But, on the other hand, something of importance *might* happen when only the Ambassador could exert influence. It nearly breaks my heart because, in the quiet watches of the night, I have sometimes dared to let myself hope that such an academic invitation might someday be extended, and now that it has been extended I can't accept it. The old New England conscience wins.

RUMORS OF A JAPANESE ATTACK ON SINGAPORE GO THE ROUNDS

April 15, 1941

During my absence in Kawana a report was circulating in Tokyo that Japan intended to attack Singapore within a few days, even before Matsuoka's return. It became so persistent that some of the correspondents cabled it home and since the diplomats were all worked up about it, the Embassy had to cable the report to Washington. The rumor lasted for some three days, from the 12th to the 15th, but on the 15th Dooman met Ohashi at lunch and received from him a categorical denial "with great vigor." At Ohashi's suggestion we put Hill of the A.P. up to asking the question of Ko Ishii, who said, "I can absolutely flatly deny that Japan intends to send Army or Navy forces against or to Singapore," and he added that Japan's intentions in the south are entirely peaceful and exclusively economic as recently stated by Prince Konoye. He characterized the reports as the "work of warmongers." At least one of the sources of the rumor was General Ishihara, retired because he had published an article advocating a Japanese attack on Singapore.

THE RUSSO-JAPANESE NONAGGRESSION PACT

April 17, 1941

As for the pact with Soviet Russia the press as a whole tends to regard it with guarded approval rather than with enthusiasm and points out that it is merely a first step in the direction of stabilizing Japan's relations with that country. There are indications that the complete confidence which would impel a southward advance is not yet felt with regard to the northern neighbor.

By and large there seems to be considerable opposition to Japan's pushing the southward advance by force. The Government is carefully watching developments in Europe and their effect on American policy, but it must be admitted that there have been noticeable repercussions in Japan in a direction favorable to the pro-Axis elements as a result of the unfortunate trend of military operations in the eastern Mediterranean during the past fortnight.

Yesterday the Government issued the following confidential instructions to the Japanese press in commenting on the treaty with Russia:

(1) The press is not to convey the impression that Japan is not enthusiastic over the conclusion of the pact;

(2) The opposition of certain anti-Soviet circles in Japan is not to be mentioned;

(3) Nothing is to be said with regard to the weaknesses of Soviet Russia which led to the conclusion of the treaty;

(4) The conditional provisions respectively exchanged by the two countries are not to be touched on.

These instructions are, of course, very significant; they speak for themselves.

I learned on good authority and so reported to the Department that German fifth columnists are steadily increasing in Japan and are causing real concern. It is said that growing activity on the part of members of the Gestapo is noticeable and that these gentry are reporting to the Japanese police the names of Japanese whom they believe to be harboring anti-Axis sentiments.

BACKGROUND ON THE SOVIET-JAPANESE PACT

April 22, 1941

I have already written, in the March diary, of Matsuoka's first talk with Stalin on the former's way to Berlin and how he lectured Stalin on Japanese ideology for fifty-eight minutes out of the sixty-minute interview, maintaining that there is a close parallel between Communism and Japanese family life. On returning from Berlin, Matsuoka told Steinhardt that he had little hope of concluding a treaty with Stalin because he was not willing, and the Japanese public would not stand for the concessions which the Russians were asking for a nonaggression pact. But then at the last minute it appears that Stalin suddenly suggested a neutrality pact, which was signed in a few minutes, with no concessions (unless there were secret concessions) on the part of Japan. Nobody, apparently, was more surprised than Matsuoka.

In my analysis of the results of the neutrality pact, in the absence of information as to any secret commitments or understandings, I have come to the following conclusions:

(a) Due to the fact that Japan, at least publicly, was not obliged to pay a price for the pact, it represented a great personal success for Matsuoka;

(b) Instead of defining the policies and obligations of the respective signatories, the treaty was apparently concluded chiefly for the effect which each party believed it would exert on the other party and on third parties (on Germany, from the Soviet point of view, and on the United States and Great Britain, from the Japanese point of view);

(c) The treaty should tend to help rather than to thwart a conclusion of the conflict in China, regardless of any reservations on the part of the Soviets with regard to China or any subtleties in phraseology;

(d) With respect to Japan's relations with Soviet Russia, the treaty will tend to balance the one-sided nature of the Tripartite Alliance, especially considering the somewhat formalistic Japanese mind;

(e) The pact will tend to stimulate and support the Japanese extremists who advocate a vigorous prosecution of the southward advance because it guarantees Soviet neutrality in case Japan gets into war with a third country (i.e., the United States).

During Matsuoka's talks with Steinhardt, who gave a luncheon for him, the following points emerged, and I have no hesitation in setting them down because Matsuoka, if he has time when he returns, will tell me everything that he told Steinhardt:

(1) No commitments were made by Matsuoka in either Berlin or Rome.

(2) The chief purpose of Japan in entering the Tripartite Alliance was to preserve peace—a theme upon which Matsuoka constantly harps both in public and in private.

(3) Japan would be obliged to go to war with the United States only if we should declare war on Germany, but that Japan would of course confer with Germany first.

(4) Matsuoka does not believe that Germany will declare war on the United States, but if that should happen he hopes that Japan will be given time to make her position clear before we make any move in the Pacific.

(5) Japan will strictly carry out her obligations to the Axis.

(6) Matsuoka had been told by both Hitler and Ribbentrop that they did not want war with the United States.

(7) They had also suggested that anti-American agitation in Japan be stopped.

(8) All three of them had expressed a wish for peace but they saw no possibility of peace until England had capitulated.

(9) Hitler had created a personally favorable impression on Matsuoka, who characterized him as a genius. He had been reasonable and calm in all their talks and had shown none of the excitable characteristics generally attributed to him.

(10) Ribbentrop admired the fight that Britain was putting up and realized that she was stronger now, from the point of view of defense, than when the war began. He expressed the opinion that the British Empire should not be destroyed.

(11) Hitler would invade Britain only under necessity and fully expected to win through aviation and the submarine.

(12) Matsuoka did not believe that Britain could drive a wedge between Germany and Italy, the latter being largely under German control while mutual personal admiration existed between Hitler and Mussolini. But the Germans had been instructed not to "look down or talk down" to the Italians. Mussolini showed no discouragement over his recent reverses and was sure that he would shortly stage a "comeback."

(13) Owing to the excessive demands of the Soviets, Matsuoka had made little progress in talking with Molotov.

(14) Japan had the choice of coming to an agreement with Moscow or becoming embroiled with the Soviet Union.

(15) Matsuoka earnestly desired an end of the war in China and felt that this could be brought about if the President would tell Chiang Kai-shek that if he refused to accept reasonable and fair peace terms, American aid would cease. Nevertheless, the Japanese would not accept mediation and peace could be effected only through direct negotiation between the two nations.

(16) Unless the Soviet Union substantially reduced its delivery of supplies to Germany, the Germans would not invade Russia, although they were fully prepared to do so. He thought that it was for the purpose of frightening the Soviets into continuing supplies that the Germans had given out rumors of a possible attack.

(17) Matsuoka hoped that the President and Mr. Hull would have confidence in him.

Steinhardt later took the precaution of reading the foregoing

points to Matsuoka, who confirmed them as an accurate record of
what he had said.

WILL GERMANY ATTACK RUSSIA?

April 22, 1941

Whether a German attack on Soviet Russia to acquire the gran-
aries of the Ukraine and the oil of the Caucasus will take place
soon is an open question. I think that eventually it is almost inevitable. Meanwhile the Germans will circulate rumors that such an
attack is imminent, with a view to intimidating the Russians into
increasing their delivery of supplies and perhaps into forcing the
Soviets into the Axis. The Germans maintain that an invasion of
Soviet Russia would be little more than a skirmish. Perhaps they
are right; but the Russians are unpredictable. They certainly
cleaned up the Japanese at Nomonhan, but perhaps that was not a
fair test.

MATSUOKA REPORTS TO THE BLACK
DRAGON SOCIETY

April 25, 1941

We learn that immediately after the return of Matsuoka from
Moscow the anti-Fascist and anti-Communist Black Dragon Society
sent a delegation to call on him in order to ascertain the extent of
the agreement which he had signed with the Russians. According to
our reliable informant the most categorical assurances were given by
Matsuoka that no secret clauses were contained in the agreement
and that neither Japan nor the Soviet Government gave any oral
commitment of any nature. They did not discuss the reduction of
their respective military forces in Siberia and Manchuria.

Matsuoka said that after all the facts had been studied and after all
elements of the situation had been carefully weighed without bias,
Japan's policy had been decided upon. This policy, while steadfastly holding in view the great ambition of finally bringing about
on earth the condition envisaged in the Japanese term *Hakko Ichiu,*
was aimed at fulfilling Japan's conception of that term, namely a
universal peace under which there would be no conquest, no oppression, and no exploitation of any peoples. Once that policy was
determined, Matsuoka said, it would be carried out resolutely but
with complete circumspection, having in mind every detail of

changing circumstances. (Altered circumstances! That is the loop-
hole which Japan always leaves herself. She will scrupulously abide
by all her commitments—until, in Japan's opinion, altered circumstances have rendered such commitments obsolete.)

MATSUOKA OVERPLAYS HIS HAND

May 2, 1941

Matsuoka returned from his visits to Berlin, Rome, and Moscow
on the crest of the wave, and his achievement of the neutrality
treaty with Soviet Russia plus the recent German military successes
in the Balkans and Libya has momentarily consolidated his stock
with the public. It is generally believed that his ambition is to become Prime Minister (God help Japan if he does) and that he will
exploit his diplomatic successes to promote his personal interests.

But we learn on the best of authority that he is sailing very close
to the wind. It is known that in his speech at the big public meeting
to welcome him on his return he made several thinly veiled allusions critical of his cabinet colleagues. He indirectly charged them
with willfully causing the breakdown in the system of commodity
distribution, and he implied treasonable action in clipping the
wings of the Imperial Rule Assistance Association by mentioning
the name of the one man in Japanese history, in the Middle Ages,
Ashikaga Takauji, who is execrated for having attempted to usurp
the throne.

Furthermore, it appears that when he reported to Prince Konoye
on his return, both the Prime Minister and the cabinet were very
angry on learning that in concluding the Neutrality Pact he had
given the Soviets a certain undertaking on his own responsibility
without the cabinet's authorization. It is not possible to ascertain
just what that undertaking was, because anyone who told us would
be liable to prosecution under the new National Secrets Law, but it
is not unlikely that it had to do with the number of troops on the
Siberian border.

It is not likely that Matsuoka will be replaced in the immediate
future, because his stock with the public is too high, but he is not
liked and is regarded as a dangerous element in the Government,
especially in risking war with the United States, and we understand
that Prince Konoye and the cabinet will under no circumstances
allow him to visit Washington as he wishes to do.

VISIT TO THE DOWAGER EMPRESS

May 10, 1941

Not having been in touch with the Dowager Empress since we came to Japan nine years ago, Alice on her own initiative asked for an audience, which was arranged through Mrs. Matsudaira and then through Viscount Matsudaira, Grand Master of Ceremonies, and took place on the 9th. The ostensible purpose of the audience was in order to express congratulations on the engagement of the Empress' son, the youngest brother of the Emperor, Prince Mikasa, as well as the engagement of her granddaughter, the Emperor's eldest daughter, to young Prince Higashikuni, and the audience was granted to Alice only as Doyenne because to receive her as Ambassadress would set a precedent for a series of other requests, and it was an unusual step, anyway. But Alice has always admired the Dowager Empress and really wanted to get in touch with her again.

As things turned out, the audience was delightful and very warm. They sat down and chatted for half an hour, the interpretation being through Alice's friend, Madam Yamanaka, lady-in-waiting, and she also saw old Nishimura, who has aged terribly since his wife's death. The Empress, Alice said, seemed to know more about her than anyone except myself. She thanked Alice for the fashion books (*Vogue*, etc.) and the jazz records which Alice sends regularly to Princess Chichibu, and when Alice regretted that her gifts were so frivolous, the Empress said she must not scorn jazz records because they were played to Prince Chichibu during his illness in Hayama and he greatly enjoyed them.

She mentioned the fact that Princess Chichibu had dined with her the evening before and had spoken of the records and also of the flowers which Alice had sent her on her young brother's death. The Empress also knew of Alice's interest in the deaf-and-dumb school and thanked her for what she had done. Alice was amazed that the Empress knew so much about her, and being somewhat embarrassed by her thanks she told several amusing anecdotes and had the Empress laughing heartily, which at least must have been a pleasant relief from the strict etiquette of the Court. The Empress also asked in detail about all our children and grandchildren.

Alice had brought some of the delicious oranges, lemons, and grapefruit which Walter Dillingham had sent us from California and we later learned that the Dowager Empress sent some of them over to the Emperor and Empress. The Dowager Empress gave Alice a magnificent bunch of orchids from the palace gardens and later Mrs. Yamanaka told Mrs. Hagiwara that the audience had been "a great success" and had given Her Majesty great pleasure, and that it was the first time in history that she had, with her own hand, presented a foreign ambassadress with flowers. The Dowager Empress said she hoped that there would soon come a time when all the ladies of different countries would be assembled there once more to admire the flowers, and she affectionately held Alice's hand a long time when the latter said good-by and curtsied herself out of the room.

I write of this meeting in such detail because it seemed to me significant of the eagerness of the Imperial family for good relations with the United States, and it will help because the story of it will go the rounds from the Emperor down, although we ourselves shall take the utmost care in mentioning it to nobody.

AN APPARENT CLEAVAGE IN JAPANESE FOREIGN POLICY

May 15, 1941

Sent a long telegram to Washington reporting and commenting on the apparent cleavage between Honda, Japan's Ambassador to Nanking, and Foreign Minister Matsuoka on the subject of China. Honda advocates strengthening the Wang Ching-wei regime and an all-out effort to create in the areas under the control of the Nanking Government a condition which can be presented to the Japanese people as a "settlement" of the China Incident. The press was instructed to play up the news of military operations in China and for the next several weeks the Japanese newspapers were full of reports of tremendous Japanese victories and the annihilation of one Chinese army after another, which didn't quite click with reports from the other side of the fence. I said to the Department that Honda's views concerning a new trend in Japan's policy in China might more properly have emanated from the Prime Minister or the Foreign Minister. Foreign diplomatic circles therefore saw in them a significant indication of divided councils within the Japanese Government.

May 16, 1941

The apparent cleavage set forth above was given further substance by remarks made by Matsuoka to the French Ambassador and related to me by Arsène-Henry himself. Matsuoka, it appears,

considered himself largely instrumental in bringing about Wang
Ching-wei's flight from Chungking and he therefore felt obliged
to support Wang in every possible way. However, in view of Wang's
attitude toward Japan, Matsuoka felt that Wang had no further
claim on him for support and that in his opinion Chiang Kai-shek
was the only person who could now carry out any settlement with
Japan. No third-party nationals or Chinese had been authorized
to make any approach to Chiang, but he, Matsuoka, was ready at
some auspicious moment to permit somebody enjoying the confidence of both sides to approach Chiang with some proposal satisfactory to Japan.

A CHAPTER IN UNORTHODOX DIPLOMACY:
FEATURING FOREIGN MINISTER MATSUOKA

May 27, 1941

As a chapter in not quite orthodox diplomacy the expressed attitude of the Minister for Foreign Affairs, Mr. Matsuoka, toward the
Tripartite Pact of September 27, 1940, and its bearing on the question of war between Japan and the United States in case war should
occur between the United States and Germany are interesting.

Witness the circumstances which gave rise to my oral and written
exchanges with Mr. Matsuoka. After an absence of some six weeks
in Europe the Japanese Foreign Minister returns to Tokyo; I immediately write requesting an appointment at the Minister's convenience; he keeps me (and other foreign ambassadors) waiting for
some three weeks and finally receives me officially at the Foreign
Office. In the course of the conversation the Minister expresses the
opinion that the "manly, decent, and reasonable" thing for the
United States to do would be to declare war openly on Germany
since our attitude toward Germany is provocative. He adds that
Hitler has been very patient and generous in not declaring war on
the United States but that Hitler's patience and restraint cannot
be expected to endure indefinitely. On my taking exception to the
Minister's remarks he withdraws the implication that the United
States is guilty of unmanly, indecent, and unreasonable conduct, and
he later writes me that owing to his inadequate knowledge of English he inadvertently used the word "decent" whereas he meant
"discreet."

The Minister thereupon makes perfectly clear his interpretation
of the Tripartite Pact to the effect that if the United States should

convoy its ships to England and if Germany should sink such ships, and if war with Germany should result, he, Mr. Matsuoka, would regard the United States as an aggressor in the sense of Article 3 of the pact, and it is his belief that war would thereupon ensue between Japan and the United States. He adds that this is only his own opinion and that there would have to be deliberation not only with his colleagues in the Japanese Government but with Japan's allies, in which deliberation Japan would have but one out of three votes. (In this connection it is interesting to note that when Germany attacked Greece this spring, Mr. Matsuoka, according to the Greek Minister here, informed Mr. Politis that Japan herself would determine her obligations under the Tripartite Pact, that her decision *would be guided by common sense,* and that Mr. Matsuoka thought that it was quite clear what the decision would be. Nothing was then said of Japan having but one out of three votes.)

I express my surprise at the Minister's interpretation of Japan's obligations under Article 3 of the pact which provides for mutual assistance between the allies only if one of them is attacked by another power, and my astonishment that Japan could thus surrender her future freedom of action and could entrust her future destiny to deliberations in which she would enjoy but one out of three votes. I set forth the attitude of the United States toward the freedom of the seas and the determination of the United States to sail those seas at will and to take all necessary measures of self-defense.

In reply to Mr. Matsuoka's first letter of May 14 I write on May 15 to thank him while at the same time expressing regret at the "grave and far-reaching implications" of his remarks in our conversation on the previous day. On the 17th Mr. Matsuoka writes me a long letter, marked "Entirely Private," emphasizing the fact that while he knows how to be "correct" as Foreign Minister, such an attitude on his part would not be conducive to better understanding between us, and that he often forgets that he is a Foreign Minister and is seldom conscious of that position. He expresses his honest hate of the so-called correct attitudes taken by many diplomats, which "hardly get us anywhere"; he acknowledges that he often indulges in thoughts in terms of one thousand or two or even three thousand years, and if this strikes me as a sign of insanity, he cannot help it as he is made that way.

The expressions which he had used in our talk on May 14, he says, would not have been uttered as Foreign Minister and those words have no place in our official relations; he had confided them to me as a world citizen and he had always regarded me as something more than an Ambassador, namely a human being to whom he might reveal his deeper thoughts and ideas. He, however, still writes of Germany's patience in the face of American provocation and of the terrible Armageddon with which civilization will be faced if the United States is drawn into the European war by attacking or being attacked, and he regards that latter point as "rather immaterial." He furthermore does not know what I mean by the phrase in my letter "grave and far-reaching implications" and believes that there must have been some misunderstanding because he cannot recall any remarks of his own upon which I could have placed such an interpretation. He suggests a further meeting in a day or two.

The Minister receives me at his private residence on May 19. We have tea and then stroll in his garden, both smoking pipes in entire informality, and chatting freely. He at once expresses his astonishment that Mr. Hull had sent for Admiral Nomura, the Japanese Ambassador in Washington, and had told him that Mr. Matsuoka had sought to "intimidate" me in our conversation on the 14th. The Minister denies that he had any intention of intimidating me or that he had intimidated me, and he furthermore expresses surprise that I had reported our conversation to my Government because he was speaking to me as Mr. Grew and not as the American Ambassador. I tell the Minister that in my report I had used the term "bellicose" as applying to the tone and substance of what he had said to me and I thereupon repeat the pertinent remarks which he had made to me which I had been led to characterize as having "grave and far-reaching implications." The Minister does not question the accuracy of my report but says smilingly that while his words may have been bellicose, his heart and thoughts are peaceful.

I make clear to the Minister the fact that one of my primary duties in Japan is to ascertain correctly and to report to my Government the policy of the Japanese Government, just as Admiral Nomura is doing the same thing in Washington with respect to the policy of the American Government, and that he, the Minister for Foreign Affairs, is the only official channel through which I can learn that policy. When, therefore, he discusses policy with me even as Mr. Grew and not as the American Ambassador, I am still in duty bound to report his views to my Government because he speaks for the Japanese Government. The Minister disagrees on this subject of reporting but he still confirms his views as expressed to me on May 14.

In the course of the two-hour conversation I speak of America's inalienable right of self-defense and of the applications of international law to the freedom of the seas and I express the view that if Japan really desires peace with the United States our own measures of self-defense could not possibly be interpreted as acts of aggression. I also read to the Minister the entire text of Mr. Hull's address of April 24 before the American Society of International Law. Mr. Matsuoka listens carefully, nodding his head in comprehension of each point; he calls it a very fine and clear presentation of the American point of view but observes that there are other viewpoints and that it seems to him that we Americans are unable to put ourselves in the place of the other parties concerned. I reply that we must be guided by facts and actions which have rendered the position and attitudes of the other parties perfectly clear.

The foregoing is merely a discursive account of some of the principal points which emerged in the two conversations and exchange of letters with Mr. Matsuoka. While reluctant to take advantage of remarks and private letters addressed to me as an American friend rather than as an American Ambassador, I am firmly of the opinion that all of these exchanges, however unorthodox, which arose from my first interview with the Foreign Minister at the Foreign Office after his long absence from Japan, can only be regarded in an official light. The question as to whether the expressed views of Mr. Matsuoka represent the views of the Japanese Government as a whole is perhaps another story.

In this general connection it may not be out of place to add that my personal relations with Mr. Matsuoka are of the best, that I rate him among my personal friends in Japan, that I enjoy his directness, or at least his ostensible directness, in our contacts, and that our discussions, even when unduly strong expressions are used and sometimes expressions of a nature which require me to take emphatic official exception, are conducted with a minimum of heat, and sometimes a freedom of give-and-take surprising in exchanges between a Foreign Minister and an Ambassador. Expressions which might be interpreted as openly insulting to one's own country, such, for instance, as his use of the phrase "the manly, decent, and reasonable thing to do," are uttered with an unstudied naïveté and a willingness to withdraw such utterances if challenged that leave no rancor afterward.

On the point of Mr. Matsuoka's intellectual and political honesty I am reluctant to express a doubt. In the political maneuvering that constantly goes on in Tokyo he is sometimes quoted as saying one thing in one quarter while making a totally divergent statement in another quarter. He talks so flowingly and freely, by the hour if time affords, that it is inconceivable that he should never make conflicting statements. I, however, incline to the opinion that in his talks with me he follows the carefully studied policy of painting the darkest picture of what will happen if the United States gets into war against Germany, probably in the mistaken belief that such tactics may serve to exert a restraining influence on American policy.

Soon after Mr. Matsuoka took office he indicated that his platform would be that the United States could and should be intimidated into adopting an attitude of complete isolation with regard to both the Far East and Europe. That platform was implemented by the Three-Power Alliance, which action not only failed to have the desired effect but was one of the major factors in stimulating the trend of American opinion away from isolationism. It would seem that, despite the egregious failure of that attempt, Mr. Matsuoka would prefer to persist in a course fraught with the gravest dangers than to chart a new course which would constitute admission on his part that he had completely misread the character and temper of the American people, and which would inevitably make his position as Foreign Minister untenable.

GERMANY PRESSES FOR A JAPANESE ATTACK ON THE NETHERLANDS INDIES

June 10, 1941

A member of the Diet, friendly to us but afraid to come to the Embassy owing to his well-known American sympathies, today sent me a message that Matsuoka was under very strong pressure both by the German Embassy and from certain Japanese extremists to take strong action against the Netherlands East Indies, which have now replied to the Japanese demands in a dignified and reasonable note that politely refuses to give up their shirt to Japan or to any other country. It appears that the Germans are pressing on the ground that the United States is in no condition to fight a war in both the Atlantic and Pacific. As for the Japanese extremists, they want to acquire the Indies before the war ends in German victory, since they fear German designs on the islands.

My informant tells me that Japanese cultural and other societies are much more deeply penetrated by Nazis than is generally known and that they are trying to force Matsuoka's hand by stirring up popular feeling against the Netherlands East Indies. There is also a belief in Government circles that an important part of the American fleet has been moved from the Pacific to the Atlantic, and that belief is of course having its obvious effect here.

In commenting on this information I told the Department that I could not with any assurance appraise the risk of a Japanese descent on the East Indies at the present time. As long as the campaign in China is still unsettled, a Japanese attack on the Indies, from the tactical viewpoint, would seem to involve the gravest dangers. On the other side of the picture, we must remember that Mr. Matsuoka is very much in the pocket of the Axis and amenable to pressure from Germany. He also commands a large and important following in Japan. In everything that he does and says he disregards and discounts forceful steps by the United States to curb his country's expansionist ambitions. It would, in fact, be shortsighted to underestimate the strength of the influence of the Japanese extremists both in military and political circles.

JAPAN'S INTERNAL SITUATION ON THE EVE OF THE RUSSO-GERMAN WAR

June 19, 1941

According to rumors persisting in Tokyo, there exists within the cabinet a divergence of views with regard to matters of high policy, and in spite of Japan's public commitment to the Tripartite Pact there has recently become apparent an attitude of strong resistance to totalitarianism, particularly the Nazi type. The "standstill" atmosphere now prevailing in Tokyo may be ascribed partly to the foregoing consideration and partly to the question of trends in the policy of the United States and possible future German moves with regard to Soviet Russia, as well as to other developments in the international field.

Certain indications of this conflict of opinion in Japan may be found of interest. One notable reflection of it is to be found in the exceedingly moderate character of the Japanese reply to the Netherlands East Indies.

According to information imparted at a recent meeting of the Co-operative Council of the Imperial Rule Assistance Association, during discussions by the delegates, the text of the address which Mr. Matsuoka had delivered at the meeting at Hibaya Hall on May

28 had been suppressed. On that occasion the Foreign Minister had vigorously defended the totalitarian system of the Nazis; he added that the economic structure of Japan was far inferior to that of Germany and he charged the Japanese Government leaders and Japanese businessmen with a lack of sense of responsibility and general incompetence. It is probable that the foregoing reasons and also the extremely Hitleresque tone of the speech caused the Home Ministry to prohibit circulation of the 200,000 copies of the pamphlet printed from the complete text furnished by Mr. Matsuoka himself.

It is understood that the Minister of Justice, General Yanagawa, has caused the arrest of 440 subordinate government officials during the past few months on the ground that the expression of their totalitarian views had rendered them amenable to the provisions of the Thought Control Law, which specifies penalties for persons who advocate the overthrow of the capitalist system. We now learn that the direct cause of the resignation on June 11 of Mr. Ishiguro, Minister of Agriculture, was the recent imprisonment of the Director of the Agricultural Policy Bureau of the Ministry of Agriculture for appropriating official funds to be used for totalitarian propaganda.

On June 17 it was announced by the press that there would be set up within the cabinet a new Bureau for Thought Control and that the suppression of dangerous thoughts held by government officials would be one of its primary objectives.

An indication of dissatisfaction with Japan's policy and of opposition to the trend toward the Nazi and Fascist ideologies was revealed in a very enlightening way by the speeches of delegates to the Co-operative Council of the Imperial Rule Assistance Association. At that meeting it was admitted by various speakers that important pro-American and pro-British elements existed within Japan and it was urged by at least one speaker that Japan should not imitate the Nazi totalitarian system.

The lack of unity in the nation is strongly suggested by the foregoing indications as well as by careful expressions of criticism in newspaper editorials. That the diplomatic policy of Japan has not been finally settled and that a sudden change in orientation is not impossible are implied by the foregoing indications.

GERMANY ATTACKS RUSSIA: FIRST IMPRESSIONS

June 22, 1941

News of the war between Germany and Soviet Russia came today. We had long expected it but I was surprised at its suddenness, believing that it would break somewhat later. From the beginning of the war in Europe I have ventured only two certain predictions—one, that Great Britain would not be defeated and, two, that Germany and Soviet Russia would eventually be fighting against each other. One prophecy has materialized; the other will materialize in due course.

This news seems to prove two things: first, that the Germans have abandoned the intention of trying to invade England this summer and, second, that the Germans are getting hard up for supplies, primarily oil. I don't know, nor do any of us know with certainty, the potential fighting ability of the Soviet Army.

JAPAN'S QUANDARY IN THE RUSSO-GERMAN WAR

June 23, 1941

Japan is in a quandary as a result of the German-Soviet war; she is pledged to the Axis and also pledged to neutrality vis-à-vis Soviet Russia; what policy will she now follow? One highly placed Japanese said that he thought Japan would sit on the fence until the combatants had fought it out and then step in and pick up the pieces. At any rate, Tokyo is humming (and continued to hum for many days) with almost continual cabinet meetings, conferences among high military and naval officers and conferences with the Emperor. We don't yet know just what is coming out of it all, but this is the time, if ever, for Japan to adopt a new orientation of conciliation with the United States, which might well be possible if Japan would take certain steps of constructive statesmanship. It is a moment pregnant with possibilities for a new turn in the road.

How this situation must chafe General Araki and his tribe, who have consistently held that Japan can never feel safe until she has taken Vladivostok and the Maritime Provinces. I have reason to believe that one high Japanese statesman, a former Prime Minister, intends to charge Matsuoka with having brought Japan into the following situation through his policies:

1. With regard to Germany, Japan's hands are tied through the Axis Pact;

2. With regard to Soviet Russia, Japan's hands are tied through the neutrality treaty;

3. The China conflict is no nearer settlement;

4. Negotiations with the Netherlands East Indies have failed to produce the results which the public, through official propaganda, have long been led to expect;

5. The relations of Japan with the United States have materially and steadily grown worse.

It must be remembered that when Germany, after the conclusion of the Anti-Comintern Pact, doubled-crossed Japan by signing a nonaggression pact with Soviet Russia, the then Hiranuma-Arita cabinet resigned by way of accepting full responsibility. The thought is being expressed that the Konoye-Matsuoka cabinet ought to do the same thing now, or at least that Matsuoka himself ought to get out.

JAPAN ADOPTS A WATCHFUL WAITING POLICY TOWARD RUSSIA

June 26, 1941

We learn that on June 24 the Soviet Ambassador did ask the Foreign Minister as to Japan's attitude in the Soviet-German war and was told that the policy of Japan had not yet been formulated. This policy, said Matsuoka, would be largely influenced by a determination as to where the responsibility for the outbreak of war lay, and he added that the fundamental policy of Japan was based on the Axis. Japan must therefore determine whether Soviet-Japanese relations could now be brought into line with this fundamental policy of Japan.

It is clear that when Japan joined the Axis, it was done on the assumption that the close association of Germany with Soviet Russia would continue and that this basic pro-Axis policy has been destroyed by the outbreak of the Soviet-German war. At least in theory. We shall see.

JAPAN DENIES DESIGNS ON RUSSIA

July 5, 1941

Received today a communication sent by the Secretary at the specific request of the President to convey to the Prime Minister an expression of hope that there was no truth in the reports that Japan intended to attack Soviet Russia, upsetting the hopes of the American Government, which it understood were shared by Japan, that peace in the Pacific area might be rendered more secure and strengthened, and the President said that he would deeply appreciate an assurance from Prince Konoye to that effect.

I immediately wrote a letter to the Prime Minister which was sent to his private residence by safe hand, asking if I could see him to deliver a message from the President and saying that I would be glad to meet him at any suggested place in order to avoid publicity. His private secretary, Ushiba, called on me shortly thereafter and said that the Prime Minister would be glad to see me but he feared publicity if I should come to his residence and suggested that we might meet on some golf course. It happened, however, to be a Sunday when all the courses were crowded and the next day was to be a holiday, so that Prince Konoye thought it would be difficult to meet until Tuesday or Wednesday. I said that as the matter was very urgent I could not delay but that in order to spare the Premier any embarrassment I would send the President's message through Ushiba himself and I thereupon communicated it to him, saying that I would remain in the Embassy all day awaiting a reply. The reply came in the evening, thanking me for the message and saying that Prince Konoye's answer would be given me as soon as possible by the Foreign Minister after he had returned from Gotemba.

Mr. Ushiba in delivering this reply expressed his regret at its incomplete nature but said that there was no precedent in Japan for a Prime Minister to deal directly with foreign ambassadors in foreign affairs. I politely but with emphasis asked Mr. Ushiba to point out to Prince Konoye as from me that it would be erroneous to assume that I had on purpose gone over the head of the Foreign Minister, and that my procedure was directly in line with the discussions which Admiral Nomura had conducted directly with President Roosevelt in Washington and indeed that the President had told Admiral Nomura that he would be happy to see him at any time. I made quite clear to Mr. Ushiba my regret that Prince Konoye had not felt able to reply directly to the message.

I said to the Department that I did not interpret Prince Konoye's attitude as in any way implying a rebuff. It was simply a question of the strength of precedent and tradition in Japan, and I well remember that when Bill Castle came on his special mission to Japan for the specific purpose of putting through the Naval Treaty he did not try for direct access to the then Prime Minister but dealt only with the Minister for Foreign Affairs in spite of the prime importance of the issue.

To carry this incident to its conclusion, it is here recorded that Matsuoka sent for me on July 8 and gave me the Prime Minister's reply for delivery to the President, to the effect that the Japanese Government had not so far considered the possibility of going to war with Soviet Russia, and he also handed to me a statement which he had made to the Soviet Ambassador on July 2 to more or less the same effect but adding that future developments would largely decide Japan's future policy. I asked Matsuoka what kind of future developments he had in mind, to which he replied that a good many possible developments came into the picture, such, for instance, as whether Soviet Russia should conclude an alliance with Great Britain or whether an attempt should be made by the United States to send war supplies to Soviet Russia through Vladivostok for use against Japan's ally, Germany. Matsuoka said that he was under great pressure by powerful elements in Japan to go to war with Soviet Russia and that the hand of the extremists would be greatly strengthened and his own sincere efforts to preserve peace would be rendered much more difficult than at present if such provocation should be given. Matsuoka said that he had appealed both to Stalin and to Molotov not to render more difficult his own present very difficult position.

As the result of this long conversation with Matsuoka, I said to the Department that I should find it very difficult to believe that at this time Japan had decided to go to war with Soviet Russia.

Incidentally, in the reply handed to me, the Minister could not resist the temptation of asking whether it was really the intention of the President and the American Government to intervene in the European war. On July 11, I received the Department's reply asking me to tell the Foreign Minister, among other things, that whatever action we might take would be of a purely defensive character and that Mr. Hitler could best furnish information on this point by revealing his future contemplated steps of aggression.

The ball, however, was not allowed to stop there because on July 17 Ohashi called me to the Foreign Office and handed me an oral statement from the Foreign Minister stating that the Japanese Government was not disposed to enter into a debate over the points raised in our reply but that it could not pass unnoticed any suggestion that we or any other Government could invoke without limit the so-called right of self-defense, nor could it agree to the indictment of Germany implied in our communication nor in the claim of our Government that any country which suggested that the United States should desist from its policy of self-defense would in fact be ranging itself on the side of aggressor nations whose aims were to conquer the whole world.

As Matsuoka, who was then ostensibly confined to his bed by illness, had resigned on the previous evening and as his successor took over very shortly thereafter, the foregoing communication was in all probability his last gasp as Foreign Minister and its vitriolic nature was quite in keeping with Matsuoka's bellicose attitude toward the United States during the greater part of our association over the past year. He died, politically, true to form, and his final communication terminated an interesting period in the intensely interesting diplomacy of these times.

PRESIDENT ROOSEVELT ASKS PREMIER KONOYE TO DENY REPORTS OF IMPENDING RUSSO-JAPANESE WAR

Message sent by the Secretary of State at the specific request of the President for delivery to His Excellency the Prime Minister of Japan, Prince Fumimaro Konoye, dated July 4, 1941

From a variety of sources reports are reaching the Government of the United States that it is the intention of the Japanese Government to enter upon hostilities against the Soviet Union.

As is well known to the Japanese Government, the maintenance and preservation of peace in the area of the Pacific have been the earnest desire of the American Government, which has contributed its greatest efforts to the achievement of that high purpose.

From statements made in recent months by the Japanese Ambassador in Washington, Admiral Nomura, to the Secretary of State, Mr. Hull, in the course of conversation between them, as well as from the utterances of responsible Japanese officials, the Government of the United States has derived the hope that it was also the desire of the Government of Japan to maintain and preserve peace in the area of the Pacific. The reports which are now reaching the American Government are so completely contrary to those statements and utterances that the Government of the United States finds it very difficult to believe in the truth of those reports.

Should Japan enter upon a course of military aggression and conquest it stands to reason that such action would render illusory the cherished hope of the American Government, which it understood was shared by the Japanese Government, that peace in the Pacific area, far from being further upset, might now indeed be strengthened and made more secure.

It is the earnest hope of the Government of the United States that the reports of Japan's decision to enter upon hostilities against the Soviet Union are not based upon fact, and an assurance to that effect from His Excellency the Prime Minister of Japan would be deeply appreciated by the Government of the United States.

Message in reply sent by His Imperial Japanese Majesty's Minister for Foreign Affairs at the request of the Prime Minister for delivery to the President of the United States of America, dated July 7, Showa 16 (1941) [Translation]

At a time like this all sorts of rumors are abundantly bred not only in Japan but in all countries.

It is hardly necessary to state that the prevention of the European war from spreading to the regions of Greater East Asia and the maintenance and preservation of peace in the area of the Pacific have always been the sincere and genuine desire of the Japanese Government, which have consistently contributed their earnest efforts toward achieving that high purpose.

The Japanese Government wish to state, in reply to the last paragraph of the message, that they have not so far considered the possibility of joining the hostilities against the Soviet Union. The position of the Japanese Government vis-à-vis the Soviet-Axis war was made clear in the Oral Statement of July 2, 1941, of H.I.M.'s Foreign Minister to the Soviet Ambassador in Tokyo. One can do no better than attach hereto a copy of this Oral Statement for the President's perusal in order to bring home the course of policy Japan has been compelled to pursue in the present circumstances. Of course, it is understood that the American Government will treat it as strictly confidential.

Incidentally, the Japanese Government would like to avail themselves of this opportunity for definitely ascertaining whether it is really the intention of the President or the American Government to intervene in the European war, as they are naturally and very deeply concerned at the prospect, disturbed as they sincerely are, by reports reaching them from a variety of sources.

JAPAN TAKES STOCK OF GERMANY'S
ATTACK ON RUSSIA

July 6, 1941

I feel that we now have sufficient evidence to justify an appraisal of the position and policy of the Japanese Government as reformulated by the Imperial Conference on July 2, an appraisal which, although necessarily somewhat speculative, would still indicate the general trend of my views.

The serious disturbance, if not an internal crisis, which occurred in Tokyo during the ten days of conferences and deliberations by Japanese policy-formulating elements and groups in Japan brought about by the German attack on Soviet Russia is becoming clear from the evidence which reaches us. So far as we can gauge the situation, it has come to a more or less open conflict between Matsuoka and Baron Hiranuma. Sensational reports are going around town and it is even said that Baron Hiranuma, in his position as Home Minister, has threatened to arrest several prominent people in the extremist camp but that he has desisted owing to warnings that he would be assassinated if he should try to do so. (From what I know of Hiranuma this story does not ring true.) It may at least be said that these rumors, whether there is anything in them or not, probably reflect an acute cleavage of opinion among the leaders in Japan, and we believe that a positive and dynamic policy which would create new involvements and commitments is unlikely just now in the absence of a unanimous or clearly dominant school of thought.

In the process of settling the last World War Japan secured for herself a place among the great powers which gave her considerable self-satisfaction and it was not fully appreciated until Japan's invasion of Manchuria came before the League of Nations to what extent she had become involved in purely European problems of no vital concern to her. Following Japan's withdrawal from the League in 1932 it will be remembered that Japan at that time announced her intention to liquidate her European commitments and to confine herself to East Asia, and after the outbreak of the present war she officially confirmed that policy and labeled it "a free and independent policy." This policy was followed with some show of determination for eight years, but it was sharply reversed when Japan concluded the Tripartite Alliance, which again involved her in European affairs, and an increasing realization had been developing for some time before the German attack on Soviet Russia that Japan, in allying herself with Germany and Italy, had assumed certain avoidable risks.

There is a great difference between the German and Japanese conceptions of the German bloc and the Japanese bloc, and especially of the secondary place which Japan is expected to take in the new scheme. Japan, in fact, has begun to take notice of Germany's desire for a privileged position in China regardless of the New Order in East Asia and she has begun to wonder whether she can afford to rely on German promises and whether, if Germany should be victorious in the war, all will be well for Japan. Matsuoka has repeatedly been challenged to refute the evidence of Germany's deliberate deception of Japan in attacking Soviet Russia in the face of the advice which Hitler is alleged to have given Matsuoka in Berlin that Japan should improve Soviet-Japanese relations by concluding a pact with the Soviet Union. I would not go so far as to say that there has been a complete collapse of Japanese confidence in German good faith, but I do not think that that confidence is today sufficiently robust to justify any initiatives tending to serve German interests more closely than the interests of Japan herself.

I therefore believe that in the light of the German-Soviet war no reformulation of Japanese policy would have been possible without considering the three factors hereinbefore mentioned, namely (1) the lack of a united opinion in Japan, (2) the desire to restrict the risks of involvement in the European war so far as possible in the light of Japan's accepted commitments, and (3) a decreasing confidence in the good faith of Germany.

It is being said by foreign observers in Tokyo that the Imperial Conference has decided before attacking the Maritime Provinces to sit on the fence and watch the general trend of the German-Soviet war, and in the meantime to push the southwest advance. In this plan the first step is alleged to be aimed at Indo-China, with the purpose of acquiring bases on Camranh Bay and elsewhere but to proceed gradually and step by step in order to avoid an open conflict with the United States. The view is also expressed that this alleged decision to push the southward advance is actually aimed at Germany so that Japan may consolidate her position to the southward before Germany is in a position to interfere with Japanese ambitions after attaining full victory in the war.

It is generally held that what Germany most wants Japan to do is to take steps which will tend to divert America's attention from

Europe and that she is not pressing Japan to intervene in Soviet Russia. If these are actually the desires of Germany, it would seem that the above-described plan attributed to the Imperial Conference would fairly well coincide therewith.

On the other hand, the "momentous decision" which the Imperial Conference is alleged to have taken may well be a determination to follow a policy of watchful waiting in the hope of a collapse in the Soviet Union. Several points tend to support this estimate, namely (1) Prince Konoye's statement to Menken of Paramount Pictures that Japan will honor its commitments both to Germany and to Soviet Russia, (2) Mr. Matsuoka's statement to the Soviet Ambassador, and (3) the Foreign Minister's statement to ——— on July 4. In connection with the last point, the impression which Matsuoka wished to convey to ———, namely that unanimity of opinion prevails in Japan and that the confidence among the members of the Tripartite Pact remains unimpaired, is so palpably contrary to the truth that we must take the Minister's statement with reserve.

JAPAN'S MOBILIZATION EFFORTS GO INTO HIGH GEAR

July 12, 1941

According to persistent rumors in Tokyo certain categories of reservists are being called up by the military authorities, but these measures do not appear to constitute more than precautionary steps natural in the present situation.

This was one of the early indications of the large mobilization movement which was continued during the next several weeks, and reports soon began to come in from Kobe, Dairen, Mukden, and Harbin that the flow of troops seemed to be largely in the direction of Manchuria. We learned that men from thirty-five to forty-two years were being called on one or two days' notice and that in one electric-line company alone fifty motormen were taken within a week. We ourselves lost our second cook. Osaka reported that the annual tennis tournament and other athletic contests scheduled for this week have all been canceled as they would require space for many students traveling in the trains which are needed for other reasons. Osaka also reported that considerable gloom and an atmosphere of increasing tensity were evident and that there was a general conviction that something is about to happen which can only be guessed at.

This movement became so intense that no foreigners were allowed to pass through the Inland Sea or to travel on trains which would necessitate their crossing the ferry between Shimonoseki and Fusan, an interference with normal traffic which caused the greatest hardship to Americans who wished to get to Shanghai to sail for the United States on a certain date. It was only at the beginning of August, however, that this situation became critical through the taking off of all Japanese ships sailing to the United States and the difficulty, and in most cases the impossibility, of even getting to Shanghai.

A BRITISH FRIEND WRITES
FROM THE HEART

July 24, 1941

Part of a long letter received from a British friend who spent the past two or three years in Tokyo is worth quoting because it is rather beautifully expressed and it indicates a fact that I have long known, namely that many Englishmen, even those who seem inarticulate, have in their natures a marked degree of sentiment and appreciation which their constitutional British inhibitions generally prevent their revealing. I believe that it may be largely due to his intimate association with Americans during his stay in Japan that this man has so effectively broken through those inhibitions and can express himself so openly. I went down to the station to see him off.

I cannot let Thursday pass, and be gone forever, without putting on record how very deeply I appreciate your coming to see me off at the station.

Not only do I look on it as due to your friendship, which I value so highly, but as to the honor which I felt, that our beloved Doyen should take the trouble to come all that way just for a few minutes; particularly with all you had to do, before leaving that day for Karuizawa, just as others were leaving for Chusenji.

You came despite all that, only to join with others in a last good-by and godspeed to me no doubt, but it was one of those small things which keep alive the flame of love, devotion, and respect, which some have no power even to kindle.

It was very hard leaving you, and all the others, together with whom I have had such a wonderfully happy time. I rejoice that I am going back at last, to join my dear wife and those who are left at home; but friendships made, as I have been blessed with, are not lightly thrown aside and cannot be broken, even for a time, without the greatest regrets and sorrow.

I trust, however, that the days are yet to come when all is over, and through whatever bunkers I may have to hack my way, with "blood, tears, and sweat," that some of us at least will be spared to meet again somewhere, to renew these past immeasurably happy days.

This vision for me, however, will never be completed, if I do not find myself once again as your partner, on the first tee—somewhere. . . .

Never again will I experience two and a half years of life among a circle of friends of all nationalities most of whom are guarding their tongues against their neighbors.

My life in the future will be bounded by a circle of friends (the most remarkable in the world) one meets in the compass of a warship; friends whose hundreds of minds must burn with a single flame, a single thought, a single aim.

To light that flame will be my work. Among those friends, the value of devotion and respect and unswerving loyalty, which is so essential to great achievements in every walk of life, has to be put to the highest tests of human endurance—in hours of battle.

To you, Mr. Grew, I owe a debt of gratitude which I can never repay.

You have added to my store, and I have had before me in Tokyo, a shining example and ideal, of how that flame can be lit and can be kept alive, whereby there is no ideal which cannot be attained, or any battle which cannot but be won.

And so, with my sincerest wishes to Mrs. Grew, and with my highest respect, and gratitude for your friendship, may I say with all sincerity and affection, my dear Mr. Grew,

Au Revoir,

VICHY YIELDS THE INDO-CHINA BASES TO JAPAN

July 25, 1941

We now learn that the official spokesman in Vichy announced on the 24th that a request had been presented by Japan to occupy bases at strategic points in Indo-China; he said that negotiations were going on both at Vichy and Hanoi and that there had been no ultimatum from Japan nor any German pressure. He added that arrangements would be made within the scope of the Franco-Japanese agreement of August 30, 1940, and that no inconvenience in temporarily extending the military agreement with Japan was seen so long as there was to be no change in French sovereignty over Indo-China and so long as no territorial demands were made by Japan.

When a correspondent asked the Vichy spokesman whether such a decision would not be inconsistent with the announced policy of France to defend her empire against all powers, he replied that the French Government had been obliged to come to this decision as the result of events in Syria. Replying to a question as to whether the assistance of the United States in preserving the *status quo* in Indo-China had been requested by France, the spokesman was evidently primed for the question because he said at once that France had not bothered to make any further request to the United States at this time since no satisfaction had been received when American assistance in Indo-China had been asked by France in 1940. In this case the spokesman did not take refuge in his usual procedure of saying that he must consult his superiors when some delicate point is brought up.

FOREIGN MINISTER TOYODA EXPLAINS WHY JAPAN DECIDED TO PROTECT INDO-CHINA

July 25, 1941

The new Minister for Foreign Affairs, Admiral Toyoda, today received the diplomatic chiefs of mission individually. In opening our conversation he said that his appointment as Minister for Foreign Affairs had come as a great surprise and that as he was an amateur at diplomacy he would count upon my assistance. He then said that the Tripartite Alliance stands and that Japanese policy is based upon that pact. He made no further reference to policy.

For my part I said that I had been working for nine years to build up something permanently constructive in American-Japanese relations and that I hoped for the Minister's collaboration in continuing those efforts. I said that an improvement in our relations was not only important to the United States but that Japan has everything to gain from such an improvement. But I added that we must remember friendship is not a one-way street.

The Minister thanked me for what I had said and assured me of his collaboration. He said that as soon as he had finished receiving the chiefs of mission today he would like to have a longer talk with me.

Our second meeting came at 9:30 the same evening when I called on the new Minister for Foreign Affairs at his request. He said that at noon the following day the Japanese Government would issue an official statement of the agreement reached with the Vichy Government concerning Japan's proposed movement into Indo-China but that in view of the concern of the United States he wished to explain to me in advance the reasons and intentions of such movement. Admiral Toyoda thereupon handed to me a document in Japanese accompanied by an unofficial English translation.

After reading the document I said that I would transmit it promptly to my Government but that in the meantime I could best reply to certain points contained therein by conveying to the Minister the statement issued to the press by the Acting Secretary of State yesterday. I thereupon read to the Minister such portions of the Acting Secretary's statement as were picked up on the radio today and said that I would send to him tomorrow the complete text.

In further discussion I emphasized and elaborated certain pertinent points in Mr. Welles' statement. I spoke of the utter fallacy of the charge of "encirclement" and of the concept that Japan was acting for the "safety and protection of Indo-China." I said that I was glad to take note of, the phrase in the Japanese statement that "Japan has no intention at all of making the southern part of Indo-China a base of armed advancement against adjoining areas" but that my Government and I myself had met with so many bitter disappointments during the past several years in the illusory nature of promises and assurances conveyed to me by former Japanese Ministers that we were now unavoidably obliged to rely on facts and actions rather than upon words. The Minister did not attempt to refute this statement but he earnestly begged me to believe him.

As the conversation continued, I spoke in detail of the successive steps of the Japanese southward advance, culminating for the present in the proposed occupation of bases in southern Indo-China and the consequent endangering of the safety of other areas in the Pacific, including the Philippine Islands, and I elaborated the practical and logical reasons for our concern in the safety of Singapore and the Netherlands East Indies, which were definitely threatened by this advance.

The Minister did not try to refute my argument except to repeat the peaceful intentions of the proposed Japanese move into Indo-China and to take issue with our use of the term "occupation" in connection therewith since Japan had no territorial ambitions. I replied that the term "occupation" connoted no question of time.

In closing our conversation the Minister earnestly appealed to me to use my best efforts to convey to my Government Japan's peaceful intentions and the great importance of avoiding at this critical moment measures which would provoke the Japanese people and render difficult the efforts to improve the relations between Japan and the United States. He said that he would convey to Admiral Nomura the substance of our conversation.

OUR FREEZING ORDER APPLIED TO JAPAN AND CHINA

Following is the text of a statement, bearing the date July 26, released to the press by the White House at 8 P.M., July 25, 1941.

In view of the unlimited national emergency declared by the President he has today issued an executive order freezing Japanese assets in the United States in the same manner in which assets of various European countries were frozen on June 14, 1941. This measure in effect brings all financial and import and export trade transactions in which Japanese interests are involved under the control of the Government and imposes criminal penalties for violation of the order. This executive order, just as the order of June 14, 1941, is designed among other things to prevent the use of the financial facilities of the United States and trade between Japan and the United States in ways harmful to national defense and American interests, to prevent the liquidation in the United States of assets obtained by duress or conquest and to curb subversive activities in the United States.

At the specific request of Generalissimo Chiang Kai-shek and for the purpose of helping the Chinese Government, the President has at the same time extended the freezing control to Chinese assets in the United States. The administration of the licensing system with respect to Chinese assets will be conducted with a view to strengthening the foreign trade and exchange position of the Chinese Government. The inclusion of China in the executive order in accordance with the wishes of the Chinese Government is a continuation of this Government's policy of assisting China.

We learn through what is regarded as an entirely reliable source that soon after the constitution of the new cabinet in Japan the German Ambassador called on the Foreign Minister and asked him to convey a message to the Premier to the effect that (1) Germany's campaign in Russia will have been successfully finished in August, (2) Great Britain will be invaded by Germany in September, and (3) a complete German victory will terminate the war before winter. Under these circumstances Japan is advised to remain loyal to the Axis pact.

The same informant says that the dropping of Matsuoka was desired by Germany not only because he was responsible for the neutrality treaty with Soviet Russia but because he talked too much. It is also stated that Japan's invasion of Soviet Russia, rather than continuation of the southward advance, is desired by Germany.

WHY JAPAN'S NEW FOREIGN MINISTER COULD NOT SLEEP

July 26, 1941

At the request of the Minister for Foreign Affairs I called on him again today and we discussed at length the situation which had come about as a result of the establishment by Japan of bases in southern Indo-China and the reported action of the American Government in freezing Japanese assets in the United States. In view of our complete divergence of opinion upon the subject under discussion, there could be no meeting of minds between the Minister and myself, and our conversation consisted largely of a reiteration of the views brought out in my conversation with him last night.

The report of the Acting Secretary's conversation with the Japanese Ambassador had been received immediately prior to this interview. I therefore conveyed its substance to Admiral Toyoda so that he might know exactly what the Acting Secretary had said to Admiral Nomura. The Minister for Foreign Affairs was particularly anxious to ascertain the exact words in which the Acting Secretary said he could not see that any basis now remained for continuing the Washington conversations. The Minister asked me to interpret the Acting Secretary's statement. I told him we could only accept the statement at its face value. The Minister gave obvious indications of being profoundly concerned at the rupture of the Washington conversations. As I have ground for believing that the Emperor had received him just before our interview, it seems to me likely that he was reflecting the concern of the Emperor.

Admiral Toyoda told me that he particularly regretted the Acting Secretary's remark to the Japanese Ambassador regarding German pressure on the French Government and told me that the Japanese negotiations with the French Government in regard to Indo-China had been carried on without any pressure from any outside source.

As with the British Ambassador, Admiral Toyoda endeavored to draw a comparison between Japanese action toward Indo-China and the measures undertaken by England in Syria, but in reply I emphasized the complete dissimilarity of the two cases.

Admiral Toyoda continually reiterated the view that the present deplorable situation between the United States and Japan was due solely to a misunderstanding on the part of the United States of Japan's real purposes, to which I replied that Japanese officials and the Japanese press had exploited this entirely unfounded allegation *ad nauseam* for many years. I recapitulated a number of bitter lessons which we had learned from experience as a result of the assurances and promises of previous Japanese governments in regard to the true aims of Japan. I made it clear why finally it had become impossible for the Government and the people of the United States to give credence to Japanese pledges and explanations of Japan's "true intentions."

The Minister inquired with every indication of concern whether the United States Government intended to adopt further retaliatory measures in addition to the freezing of Japanese assets in the United States, to which I replied that I had received no information in the premises.

Admiral Toyoda told me that he had hardly slept at all during recent nights. He appeared greatly discouraged at the turn of events and especially distressed that the present situation should have arisen at the very time of his assumption of the post of Minister for Foreign Affairs. I reviewed in detail my endeavors over many years, with particular reference to my efforts with the Yonai cabinet, to place Japanese-American relations on a sound and enduring basis and referred in this connection to Admiral Nomura's work in that direction in Washington recently.

After stating that I was reluctant to end our talk in an atmosphere of defeatism, I emphatically urged him to use his best efforts to prevent the further deterioration of relations between the United States and Japan, such as would inevitably occur if Japan made any more aggressive moves in the Pacific area.

Several friends in Tokyo have asked me why Admiral Toyoda accepted the portfolio of Foreign Affairs if he was aware of the impending Japanese action in French Indo-China and foresaw the consequences which he would be forced to face. In my personal opinion Admiral Toyoda shared the apparent belief of most Japanese officials that the United States would not resort to measures of retaliation; hence, the action of the United States in freezing Japanese assets in retaliation for the Japanese move into Indo-China caught them unaware. Whether this mistaken view of American policy arises from the inability of Japanese officials in the United States correctly to gauge American public opinion or whether they have been unable in their reports to convince the Japanese Government in this respect, I do not know. At all times in my dealings with the Japanese Government I have endeavored to the best of my ability to correct this erroneous view. I am, however, entirely convinced that the Japanese surprise and serious concern over recent developments are genuine and also that the bitter resentment which has been aroused here by the action of the American Government is real.

A FLICKER OF HOPE FOR JAPANESE-AMERICAN PEACE

July 27, 1941

This Sunday morning there came an exceedingly important telegram from the Acting Secretary reporting an equally important proposal which the President had made to Admiral Nomura with a view to settling the whole situation in the Far East and avoiding the rapid deterioration of Japanese-American relations as the direct result of Japan's aggressive policies and measures in this part of the world. I shall not at present record the details of this proposal in view of their ultraconfidential nature, but they offer to Japan a reasonable way out of her own alleged difficulties and the alleged encirclement measures of the A B C D powers which she maintains are threatening her own security.

On reading that telegram I thanked my stars that I had remained in Tokyo and had not gone to Karuizawa because it seemed to me of the utmost importance that I should immediately not only make sure that Admiral Toyoda had clearly understood the full purport of the proposal but that I should also exert every ounce of my own influence to secure its acceptance. I said once before in the diary that I had not gone home this summer because a moment might come when such influence could be exerted and this seemed to me to be precisely the sort of juncture which I then had in mind. I therefore immediately telephoned to the Foreign Minister at his private house and asked for an appointment although it was a Sunday morning. I saw him at 11:30 at his official residence and in a long talk made on my own initiative and responsibility the strongest appeal of which I was capable and perhaps the strongest representations that I have ever made.

I told the Department what I had done and said that although I had exceeded all authority I felt after careful thought that three considerations justified my step: (1) the prime importance that Admiral Toyoda should completely and accurately understand the President's proposal, (2) the importance of the time element, which made it impossible for me to ask for authority from Washington in advance, and (3) my belief that the President would wish nothing to be left undone to ensure that maximum consideration should be given to his proposal and that the Japanese Government should fully recognize its far-reaching and enlightened import because upon its rejection or acceptance might depend the future peace of the Pacific. To my astonishment Admiral Toyoda said that he had not received the President's proposal, communicated to Admiral Nomura three days ago, on the 24th, and Toyoda confirmed this after leaving me for some five minutes obviously to telephone to the Foreign Office. Two days later we learned from Terasaki, Director of the American Bureau of the Foreign Office, that on the day of his conversation with the President Admiral Nomura had sent only a very brief telegram to Tokyo and that after my talk with Toyoda he had immediately instructed Nomura to submit a comprehensive report without delay.

Two days later I received a very pleasant message from Sumner Welles stating that he regarded my action at this time as of the greatest assistance and value and that both the President and he himself had approved of what I had done. I can't say that I am over-optimistic as to favorable results, but I told Admiral Toyoda in our talk that he was now presented with an opportunity to take a step of the highest statesmanship and with a way of solving the appalling situation which faced him at the outset of his ministry; I said in fact that he now had an opportunity to go down in history as one of Japan's greatest statesmen. Whether Japan accepts or not, the President's step places the United States in an unassailable position from the point of view of history and someday history will record this step in full. If the Japanese fail to avail themselves of it, their own position in history will not be enviable. On the 30th I sent another telegram to the Department making some further suggestions on the foregoing subject.

In my recent conversations with Admiral Toyoda it seems to me significant that the only thing which really stirred him up were the allusions which I made to the belief existing in our country that German pressure is responsible for Japan's present policies, and in each case the Minister emphatically denied that Germany now exerts any influence in Japan whatsoever. One of my colleagues, incidentally, had previously told me that Matsuoka himself had confirmed to him the story that he had telegraphed to von Ribbentrop to ask if there were any basis for the reports that Germany was about to attack Soviet Russia, that he had received from von Ribbentrop a categorical denial, and that forty-eight hours later Germany's invasion of Soviet Russia had occurred. Once again it is abundantly clear that the Japanese are getting fed up with the Germans, who have obviously, as usual, overplayed their hand.

JAPAN AND AMERICA COME WITHIN
EIGHT YARDS OF WAR

July 31, 1941

In the midst of the Indo-China crisis the Japanese, with what seems to me the utmost stupidity, allowed one of their Navy aviators to drop a bomb on the *Tutuila* at Chungking, risking the very development which I had told Matsuoka was giving me more concern than any other issue since I had come to Japan. By the grace of heaven the bomb missed the *Tutuila* by about eight yards, although the ship was damaged and another bomb again came dangerously near our Embassy. Fatalities were escaped only by a miracle. It seems to me utterly inconceivable that the incident was accidental: three American officials saw the thing from a hill immediately overlooking the ship; the weather was ideal; and the bomber on approaching the city at an altitude of about 15,000 feet dropped out of formation and changed its course to a line directly over the *Tutuila* and the Embassy. It was the unanimous opinion of the American officials that the bombing was a deliberate attack on the Embassy area and the *Tutuila* which missed its targets only by the fraction of a second.

Before I could do anything about it, the Acting Vice-Minister for Foreign Affairs, Yamamoto, called on me at the Chancery at 11 o'clock and expressed the deep regret of the Japanese Government. Later I was told that the Foreign Minister himself intended to call on me at the Embassy at 2 o'clock; the appointment was later changed to 2:30 and finally a message came that the Foreign Minister was then with the Prime Minister and that Admiral Toyoda would be glad to have me come to see him at 2:45, which I did. I am unaware of the reason for the Minister's change of plans. At any rate, he also expressed regrets and assured me that the incident was purely accidental, with which I openly disagreed with him.

Later Admiral Nomura told Sumner Welles confidentially that in order to avoid such incidents in the future, the Japanese would cease from attacking Chungking from the air, and the incident was called closed.* Once again the Japanese have been playing with fire.

Incidentally, the American correspondents were prevented by the censor from sending their stories to the United States either by telephone or telegraph, and in several conferences with a high Japanese official during the day I reminded him that at the time of the *Panay* incident it was Hirota's immediate call on me at the chancery and the fact that I had got this on the wires to the United States through the American press correspondents within five minutes that had largely served to calm American public opinion. It therefore seemed to me of the utmost importance that the correspondents should now be immediately allowed to get their messages through in order to report Yamamoto's call on me and his immediate expressions of regret. My official friend worked hard, but a series of misunderstandings with the censors intervened and it was not until late in the afternoon, probably too late to catch the early editions of the morning papers in the eastern part of the United States, that he was able to clear the wires. Some of the correspondents got their messages through during a five-minute interval when the censors opened the lines, but they immediately closed them thereafter and one agency man had been unable to get off his message. However, the Japanese officials had worked so efficiently that although the beam had been turned to South America they turned back on the United States for a few minutes around four o'clock to let the representative of the American news agency send his report.

SOME INSIDE INFORMATION ON SOME INSIDE JAPANESE WEAKNESSES

August 7, 1941

Some exceedingly interesting observations were recently made in conversation with a member of my staff by a certain Japanese whom

* Further attacks on Chungking were nevertheless made within a few days.

I know very well and whose position and unquestioned honesty render it certain that he knows whereof he speaks. The following points emerged:

The staff of the Japanese Embassy in Washington is painfully weak and although Admiral Nomura is himself a very competent man he has no advisers of first-class ability. In Tokyo, although many of the younger officials in the Government are now strongly anti-American, a stabilizing influence is exerted by Prince Konoye, in whom lies the only hope for adjusting American-Japanese relations.

Prince Konoye knows that I would like to talk with him oftener, just as the President does with Admiral Nomura, but it is the fear of leakages and publicity which has prevented such interviews. It was indicated that any reports which our Embassy might send to Washington would of course become known to the Japanese authorities, although our informant said that he understood that we did have "one confidential code" (highly significant, but I feel perfectly safe in the use of the one confidential code referred to).

A Japanese informant in Berlin had recently telephoned that it was nonsensical for the Japanese to think that the German offensive in Soviet Russia was not meeting with full success. The attack, on the contrary, was proceeding precisely according to plan and the Japanese in Berlin wondered why Japan was delaying in attacking Soviet Russia. The gentleman at the Tokyo end of the wire merely said that it was his turn to say "nonsense."

From the point of view of the United States and Great Britain the most dangerous cabinet that could be formed in Japan would be one in which Matsuoka would combine the positions of Prime Minister and Foreign Minister. Our informant confirmed our own interpretation of the recent cabinet change and he said that neither the Germans nor General Oshima, the Japanese Ambassador in Berlin, were pleased with the change and that Oshima had sent practically no telegrams since the new cabinet had been installed.

It was my informant's belief that Admiral Toyoda believed that further conversations with me might be very helpful at this time and that an opportunity to develop closer contact with me would be welcomed.

THE ROOSEVELT-CHURCHILL ATLANTIC MEETING
SEEN FROM JAPAN

August 14, 1941

We learned today of the historic meeting of Roosevelt and Churchill somewhere in the Atlantic and of the eight-point declaration concerning the war and peace aims of the United States and Great Britain, announced in the *Japan Times and Advertiser* under small one-column headlines, whereas the recent German war bulletin was spread across three or four columns. Opponents of the administration will of course see in this declaration all sorts of commitments involving the United States in European affairs, but whatever happens in future I believe that history will regard this meeting and the results thereof as one of the most enlightened steps ever taken since the announcement of President Wilson's Fourteen Points.

Human nature may not change very much over the years but at least it learns something through hard experience, and I venture to believe that the politicians will never again be allowed to wreck such a far-seeing program as Roosevelt and Churchill have now announced. It will take a long time, perhaps a very long time, before such a program can be carried out in effect, but its announcement at this time seems to me to be an act of the highest statesmanship; and with all the ranting that we may now expect from the Axis in reply, it is going to take a lot of wind out of the Axis sails and nip in the bud any peace overtures which in due course Mr. Hitler may contemplate. I am happier today than I have been for a long time and, as always, inordinately proud of our country and what it is doing.

ADMIRAL TOYODA'S PEACE OFFER

August 18, 1941

The Foreign Minister asked me to call this afternoon and we had the longest conversation that I have ever had with any Foreign Minister anywhere. It lasted for two and a half hours and the boys in the Code Room finished encoding my report at 5:35 A.M., while I myself was on the job until long after midnight.

Apropos this conversation, it was a fearfully hot day, and as I wrote down his remarks, it was drip, drip, drip, so after the first hour Admiral Toyoda ordered cold drinks and cold wet towels to swab off with. He made a gesture to take off his coat and looked at me smilingly and questioningly. Of course I nodded, so we both took off our coats, rolled up our sleeves, and again pitched in to the work. The Minister speaks English moderately well and understands whatever I say without interpretation, but he always has Inagaki, of the American Bureau of the Foreign Office, present to interpret his own remarks after he gets to the "on-the-record" stage.

Today the talk was so important that I wrote down everything he said, about a dozen pages of foolscap, and I almost had writer's cramp at the end. He is a sympathetic and very human type and I think I like him more than any other Foreign Minister I have ever dealt with. Our personal relationship is very friendly. Today, while we were swabbing off with the cold towels, I said: "Admiral, you have often stood on the bridge of a battleship and have seen bad storms which lasted for several days, but ever since you took over the bridge of the Foreign Office you have undergone one long, continuous storm without any rest. You and I will have to pour some oil on those angry waves." The Minister laughed heartily and I guess he will relate that remark in cabinet, but he missed the opportunity to say: "All right, but if you stop sending us the oil, what are we going to do about it?"

Our conversation began at 4 o'clock this afternoon and in an oral statement which took two hours and a half to be delivered, interpreted from Japanese into English and transcribed by me, Admiral Toyoda set forth a proposal of prime importance for solving the present critical situation between Japan and the United States. He pointed out the supreme importance of avoiding any leakage, especially, he said, to the Germans or Italians, and he hoped that in my report to Washington no risk would be incurred of my telegram being read by others. I said that the telegram would be sent in a code which I hoped and believed was unbreakable: I said that so far as I was concerned the only persons who would be informed of the proposal would be Mr. Dooman and my confidential secretary, Miss Arnold, who would transcribe the conversation. The Minister seemed to be entirely satisfied with these assurances. . . .

The Minister commenced by stating that this was to be a long and strictly confidential talk on a very important matter in which he asked for my co-operation. He said that he would speak to me frankly as a naval officer and not as a career diplomat. I replied that I myself had no use for Old World diplomacy and was accustomed to speaking also with the utmost frankness and straight from the shoulder. What follows is a paraphrase of the summary of Admiral Toyoda's remarks:

1. The stationing of Japanese forces in Indo-China, resulting from the protocol for the joint defense of Indo-China, was a peaceful and protective step taken for the purpose of solving the China affair. It was an independent step taken on Japan's own initiative and no German or any other pressure had been exerted.

2. In spite of the foregoing assurances conveyed to me and also to Admiral Nomura, the United States had assumed that this was the exercise of armed force at the instigation of Germany and had taken an economic step (our freezing order) which had brought our countries very near to a complete severance of economic relations and had left a big black spot on the long history of peaceful relations between the United States and Japan.

3. The Japanese people, said the Minister, share his view and public opinion has become extremely excited, but the Government has done all in its power to repress this excitement by prohibiting posters, public gatherings, and hostile press comment.

4. The reply of the Japanese Government to the President's proposal of July 24 was sent immediately to Washington, and when Secretary Hull returned to Washington on August 6 Ambassador Nomura had handed him the reply. This reply had been drafted after careful and complete study and with a view to meeting as far as possible the intentions of the American Government.

5. The Japanese reply contains important proposals which would bind both Governments; Japanese forces in Indo-China would be immediately withdrawn when the China affair is settled; it contains three points binding each party.

6. Nevertheless, the President's proposal was an independent one dealing exclusively with the joint-defense measure of Indo-China. The Japanese reply was also accordingly restricted to that subject and was to be dealt with independently of the general adjustment of relations which had been discussed between Secretary Hull and Admiral Nomura.

7. On August 8 Admiral Nomura had received from Secretary Hull the American reply to the Japanese proposal reiterating the substance of the President's proposal of July 24, and Admiral Toyoda regretted that the American reply seemed to attach too little importance to the profound consideration given by the Japanese Government to the President's proposal.

8. In other words, the American proposal, it seems, suggested the withdrawal of Japanese forces from Indo-China as a prerequisite, although the Japanese Government had definitely affirmed its intention

to withdraw immediately after the China affair had been settled because the China affair is the obstacle to peace in the Far East.

9. If the United States really desires peace in the Far East the
Japanese Government hopes that it will give full consideration to
the Japanese Government's declaration and will co-operate for the
settlement of the China affair, which is the obstacle to peace in the
Far East.

10. As the Ambassador is fully aware, both the present and the
last cabinet of Prince Konoye have had the sincerest wish to adjust
relations with the United States and it is the Minister's firm conviction that there is no room for doubt that this wish has been equally
shared by President Roosevelt and Secretary Hull.

11. Admiral Toyoda fears that the breakdown of peace between
the two countries would not only be an extremely miserable matter
in itself; Japan and the United States, as the last two countries
which hold the key for maintaining world peace in the present
state of the world, would make a bad situation still worse by failing
to practice statesmanship. This would leave the blackest spot on
human history, and future historians would find themselves unable
to understand the nature of the breakdown. Finally, if we as statesmen allow such a situation to arise it will mean that we have failed
in our responsibilities to both peoples.

12. The Minister believes that both Japan and the United States
must do their duty as saviors of the world in the present crisis.
Therefore they must consider their problems in a calm and friendly
atmosphere on an equal basis as between two great powers facing
the Pacific Ocean. The Minister further believes that the two countries can adjust their relations in that spirit.

13. The Minister cannot but recognize the fact that in spite of
the points just mentioned the present relations between the United
States and Japan have become extremely strained as a result of misunderstanding between the two countries and sinister designs by
third powers, and if nothing is done to improve matters the situation can become most critical.

14. The Minister believes that the only way to surmount this
crisis is to have responsible people of both countries meet face to
face and express their true intentions toward each other, with a view
to remedying the present situation and discovering ways and means
to aid mankind and promote the peace of the world.

15. In other words, the Minister thinks that it would be most
opportune if the leaders of both countries, animated by the above-

mentioned desires, could talk most frankly in order to settle American-Japanese relations in the aforesaid spirit and also from a broad-minded point of view. He therefore expressed his conviction that it would be highly desirable that Prince Konoye should proceed to Honolulu and talk personally with President Roosevelt if the President would consent. Moreover, Toyoda had instructed Ambassador Nomura about this matter on August 7. He intended that Admiral Nomura should personally see President Roosevelt on his return to Washington.

16. According to news reports the President returned to Washington yesterday. It is the seriousness of the matter that prompts the Minister to make this statement to me and he wishes to ask for my co-operation.

17. The Minister firmly believes that I will give him my co-operation when he remembers my ever-continuing, sincere effort for the improvement of American-Japanese friendly relations during the past nine long years.

18. Needless to say, the Premier's going abroad would have no precedent in Japanese history. Nevertheless, the Prime Minister, Prince Konoye, has firmly resolved to meet the President, notwithstanding the fact that he is fully aware of the objections in certain parts of this country. This determination of Prince Konoye is nothing but the expression of his strongest desire to save the civilization of the world from ruin as well as to maintain peace in the Pacific by making every effort in his power. The Minister firmly believes that the President will also be in harmony with this thought and will give his consent to the proposal of the Japanese Government.

19. It is firmly believed that in the conversations between the Prime Minister and the President it will be possible to reach a just and equitable agreement on the general question of Japanese-American relations from the broad-minded point of view as a result of the expressions of the highest degree of statesmanship of both leaders, Japan not being necessarily bound by her reply to the President's proposal of July 24 made through Admiral Nomura on August 6. In this connection the Minister wishes to call my attention to the fact that it is absolutely necessary to avoid arousing misunderstanding or giving an impression both inside and outside this country that the Japanese Government has entered into negotiation with the American Government as a result of American pressure. Based upon this point of view, the Minister deems it desirable that various measures of economic pressure against Japan be immedi-

ately stopped or highly moderated and the Japanese Government is, of course, ready to reciprocate at once in this respect. The Minister wishes to draw the attention of the American Government to this point.

20. The foregoing is the substance of the highly serious and absolutely secret proposal for which the Minister especially asked me to visit him today. In view of its importance and delicate nature he does not need to ask me to keep this only to myself, as it is not difficult to imagine what would occur if it should leak out. This is the reason why he has so far been instructing only Admiral Nomura to discuss and to dispose of the matter in the United States, but in order to make this proposal realized he has most frankly expressed his opinion to me so that he may have my helpful co-operation, and, if there should be any question concerning this proposal, he will be very glad to talk it over with me.

In the early part of the Minister's oral statement, before he had come to the proposed meeting in Honolulu, I spoke of Japan's progressive southward advance. I pointed out that in spite of all peaceful assurances, the American Government could only be guided by facts and actions taken by Japan and not by words. I noted also that whereas in previous conversation the Minister had ascribed the Japanese move into Indo-China as brought about by the threatened encirclement by other powers including the United States and Great Britain he now ascribed it exclusively to the settling of the China affair. To these comments the Minister made no reply.

I furthermore repeated to him the statement which the Under Secretary had made to the Japanese Ambassador on July 23 to the effect that Mr. Hull could not see that any basis was now offered for continuing the conversations which had been carried on in Washington between the Secretary and Admiral Nomura. I also spoke of Mr. Hull's statement to Admiral Nomura on August 8 to the effect that in the view of the American Government the proposal handed by the Japanese Ambassador to the Secretary of State on August 6 failed in responsiveness to the proposal advanced by the President on July 24.

CHINESE UNREST REPORTED IN MANCHURIA

August 20, 1941

From a reliable source we learn that serious unrest is spreading rapidly among the Chinese throughout Manchuria. This is the re-

sult of economic hardship, the conscription by brutal methods of
workers from all occupations, including vitally needed coal miners,
in order to erect frontier fortifications, the expectation of eventual
war with Soviet Russia, and increasing hatred of the Japanese.
Guerrilla bands are increasing and are ravaging the country for
food supplies and the effects on peace and order are already considerable. This movement is expected to assume revolutionary proportions if war with Russia occurs. Even the Manchukuo troops,
being infected with the same unrest, are planning to mutiny at the
first opportunity and the Japanese are aware of all this.

August 22, 1941

From Dairen comes a report that from many sources information
in recent weeks has been coming to the Consulate reporting evidence of growing discontent on the part of local Japanese at the
international and economic policies of the Government in Tokyo.
Many of these people are so disgusted with the increasing burden
of taxation and regimentation that they are trying to evade such
taxes and restrictions in a way that they would have considered
unpatriotic a year ago, and the local reservists are often showing
great reluctance to be inducted into active service. Extreme pessimism is being expressed over the impossible military and financial
tasks to which the country is being led by the policies of the
Government, and several cases of suicide have been reported. There
can be no doubt that the morale and patriotism of the local Japanese people have appreciably declined during the past year and
that many people, including officials, are unsympathetic to the
present policies of the Government.

THE OIL EMBARGO AND FINANCIAL FREEZING
HAVE THEIR EFFECTS ON JAPAN

August 29, 1941

Mr. Terasaki, the Director of the American Bureau, telephoned
me this afternoon shortly before three o'clock to tell me that although the Foreign Minister had asked me to call upon him at three
o'clock this afternoon, a recent development had made the Minister fear the publicity that might follow such a visit. He therefore
requested Mr. Terasaki to deliver the Foreign Minister's message to
me on his behalf. Mr. Terasaki accordingly called at the Embassy
and on behalf of the Minister conveyed to me for my information

the text of the communication from the Japanese Prime Minister to the President which had been delivered by Admiral Nomura in Washington on August 28.

Mr. Terasaki's visit was substituted for my call on the Foreign Minister because the Japanese press had learned from Washington that a message from the Japanese Prime Minister had been delivered to the President and the news had reached Japan in such a form that it was impossible for the Government to conceal from the Japanese public the fact of such a message.

Mr. Terasaki, speaking on behalf of the Foreign Minister, dwelt on the unfortunate effect of the publicity which had been given to this matter in Washington.* Although the reports had not disclosed the contents of the Prime Minister's message to the President, they did reveal to the Japanese public and to the pro-Axis and extremist elements that Prince Konoye had taken the initiative in what was obviously a conciliatory move at a time when indignation was high in Japan as a result of the progressive steps recently taken by the American Government. These steps included the initial order freezing Japanese assets in the United States, the announcement that American tankers bearing oil to the Soviet Union had departed from Californian ports, and the decision to send a military mission headed by General Magruder to Chiang Kai-shek. Mr. Terasaki pointed out that the publicity given to the Prime Minister's message is consequently of direct advantage to the extremists and pro-Axis elements in this country. It has not only rendered further moves in the direction of conciliation very difficult but has in addition immeasurably augmented the possibility of an attempt on the life of Prince Konoye. He added that the Chief of Police this afternoon had indicated the increased risk to the Prime Minister's life.

Mr. Terasaki conveyed an appeal to me from Admiral Toyoda that I ask my Government to take the following three steps. Unless these are taken, the Foreign Minister feared that Prince Konoye would meet with serious obstacles in his efforts to bring about an understanding between the United States and Japan:

(1) The meeting between the two responsible heads of the American and Japanese Governments should take place without delay. Delay would afford those elements who oppose any attempt to conciliate the United States an opportunity to organize their adherents and

* It was Admiral Nomura himself who announced to the American press on emerging from the White House that he had just delivered to the President a message from the Prime Minister of Japan.

to spread the idea to the Japanese public that Prince Konoye is yielding to American pressure and, in seeking to reach an understanding with the United States in the teeth of what is publicly regarded as provocative American measures, is exposing Japan to humiliation.

(2) The United States Government should postpone the sending of tankers to the Soviet Union at least pending the outcome of the proposed meeting between the President and the Japanese Prime Minister. Mr. Terasaki told me that the Foreign Minister felt that the dangerous temper of public opinion on the question of the tankers could not be exaggerated. He added in this connection that according to information reaching Japanese authorities five American tankers destined for Vladivostok have already passed through Tsugaru or Soya Straits.

(3) The American Government, pending the proposed meeting between the heads of the two Governments, should suspend the order freezing Japanese assets in the United States.

Mr. Terasaki, again speaking for the Minister, emphasized to me that the Japanese Government has dealt in complete frankness with the American Government and has assured us that upon the settlement of the China Incident Japanese troops at present in French Indo-China would be withdrawn; that the Japanese troops in Indo-China would make no further move in that area; and that Japan would observe the treaty of neutrality with the Soviet Union so long as that country adhered equally to the letter and spirit of the same treaty. He explained that these were the maximum assurances and commitments which the Japanese Government was in a position to assume at the present time. Since the Japanese Government has gone the limit in giving these assurances, the Foreign Minister believes that the American Government for its part should make a maximum effort, along the lines of the three points outlined above, in order to assist the Prime Minister in the course which he is pursuing, a course which is now fraught with extreme difficulties and dangers as a result of the Washington publicity.

Mr. Terasaki told me that the Foreign Minister was appealing to me in an endeavor to have the situation confronting the Prime Minister fully explained to the President and the Secretary and to request that the United States Government approach the suggested concessions not from a legalistic but from a psychological point of view.

When Mr. Terasaki concluded the foregoing outline I acquainted him first of all with the substance of the first section of the Department's telegram of August 28, which had just been received, setting forth the Secretary's views upon the objections raised by the Japanese Government to the shipment of oil to the Soviet Union. I took occasion to emphasize the logical and compelling force of the position adopted by the Secretary on this matter. In order that there might be no misunderstanding in regard to the accuracy of the Japanese Ambassador's reports of his recent conversations in Washington, I communicated orally to Mr. Terasaki the substance of the Department's telegrams reporting these conversations.

In touching on the question of the reciprocal freezing regulations now in force I emphasized once more to Mr. Terasaki the disparity between the very liberal administration of the freezing regulations in the United States in respect to Japanese nationals and the exacting and harsh treatment meted out to American citizens and interests in Japan. Mr. Terasaki in reply merely reiterated that the Foreign Minister's request had been that such questions be dealt with from the point of view of their psychological effect in Japan, since at this period of intense crisis in relations between our two countries the psychological effect was an especially strong one. I then drew Mr. Terasaki's attention to the mounting anti-American attitude of the Japanese press, to which Mr. Terasaki replied that he could tell me in strictest confidence that certain members of the Cabinet Information Board, which was charged with matters relating to publicity, are distinctly pro-Axis in their sentiments and that the Japanese Government is encountering real difficulties in handling this question.

In discussing with Mr. Terasaki the three points, outlined above, raised by the Foreign Minister, I left him under no illusion that the United States Government would find it possible to agree to either of the preposterous requests contained in points (2) or (3) above.

DINNER WITH PRINCE KONOYE

September 6, 1941

This evening the Prime Minister invited me to dine at a private house of a friend. Only Mr. Dooman and Mr. Ushiba, the Prime Minister's private secretary, were also present. The conversation lasted for three hours and we presented with entire frankness the fundamental views of our two countries. The Prime Minister requested that his statements be transmitted personally to the President in the belief that they might amplify and clarify the approach through diplomatic channels which he had made in Washington through Admiral Nomura.

Prince Konoye, and consequently the Government of Japan, conclusively and wholeheartedly agree with the four principles enunciated by the Secretary of State as a basis for the rehabilitation of relations between the United States and Japan.*

Prince Konoye recognizes that the responsibility is his for the present regrettable state of relations between our two countries but, with appropriate modesty as to his personal capabilities, he likewise recognizes that only he can cause the desired rehabilitation to come about. In the event of failure on his part, no succeeding Prime Minister, at least during his own lifetime, could achieve the results desired. Prince Konoye is therefore determined to spare no effort, despite all elements and factors opposing him, to crown his present endeavors with success.

The Prime Minister hopes that as a result of the commitments which the Japanese Government is prepared to assume as communicated to me by Admiral Toyoda, a rational basis has been established for a meeting between the President and himself. The Prime Minister, however, is cognizant of the fact that certain points may need clarification and more precise formulation, and he is confident that the divergencies in view can be reconciled to our mutual satisfaction, particularly by reason of the favorable disposition on the part of Japanese naval and military leaders who have not only subscribed to his proposal but who will also be represented at the suggested meeting. The Prime Minister stated that both the Ministers of War and of the Navy have given their full agreement to his proposals to the United States.

The reports which the Prime Minister has received from the Japanese Ambassador concerning the latter's conversations with the President and the Secretary have led the Prime Minister to think that the administration in Washington entertains serious doubts as to the strength of the present cabinet and that the administration is not certain that in the event that the cabinet

---

* (1) Respect for the territorial integrity and the sovereignty of each and all nations;

(2) Support of the principle of noninterference in the internal affairs of other countries;

(3) Support of the principle of equality, including equality of commercial opportunity;

(4) Nondisturbance of the *status quo* in the Pacific except as the *status quo* may be altered by peaceful means.

should adopt a peaceful program, it could successfully resist the attacks of opposing elements. Prince Konoye told me that from the inception of the informal talks in Washington he had received the strongest concurrence from the responsible chiefs of both the Army and the Navy. Only today he had conferred with the Minister of War, who had promised to send a full general to accompany the Prime Minister to the meeting with the President; the Minister of the Navy had agreed that a full admiral should accompany the Prime Minister. Prince Konoye added in confidence that he expected that the representative of the Navy would probably be Admiral Yoshida, a former Minister of the Navy. In addition the Premier would be accompanied by the Vice-Chiefs of Staff of the Army and the Navy and other high-ranking officers of the armed services who are in entire accord with his aims. He admitted that there are certain elements within the armed forces who do not approve his policies, but he voiced the conviction that since he had the full support of the responsible chiefs of the Army and Navy it would be possible for him to put down and control any opposition which might develop among those elements.

Prince Konoye repeatedly stressed the view that time is of the essence. It might take half a year to a year to work out all the details of the complete settlement and since resentment is daily mounting in Japan over the economic pressure being exerted by other countries, he could not guarantee to put into effect any such program of settlement six months or a year from now. He does, however, guarantee that at the present time he can carry with him the Japanese people to the goal which he has selected and that should difficulties be encountered in working out the details of the commitments which he may assume, these difficulties can be overcome satisfactorily because of the determined intention of his Government to see to it that its present efforts are fully successful.

In the course of our discussion I outlined in general terms the bitter lessons of the past to our Government as the result of the failure of the Japanese Government to honor the promises given to me by former Japanese Ministers for Foreign Affairs apparently in all sincerity, as a result of which the Government of the United States had at long last concluded that it must place its reliance on actions and facts and not on Japanese promises or assurances. The Prime Minister did not attempt to refute this statement but stressed the fact that his Government now wished to bring about a thoroughgoing reconstruction of American-Japanese relations and he assured me that any commitments which he would undertake would bear no resemblance to the "irresponsible" assurances which we had received in the past and that such commitments if given would be observed. The Prime Minister concluded his presentation of this point by giving me to understand that given the will the way can be found.

Prince Konoye stated that should the President desire to communicate any kind of suggestion to him personally and confidentially he would be glad to arrange subsequent secret meetings with me, but he expressed the earnest hope that in view of the present internal situation in Japan the projected meeting with the President could be arranged with the least possible delay. Prince Konoye feels confident that all problems and questions at issue can be disposed of to our mutual satisfaction during the meeting with the President, and he ended our conversation with the statement that he is determined to bring to a successful conclusion the proposed reconstruction of relations with the United States regardless of cost or personal risk.

THE EMBASSY COUNSELOR TALKS WITH KONOYE'S PRIVATE SECRETARY

September 18, 1941

Eugene Dooman, our Counselor at the Embassy, today submitted this report of his conversation with Tomohiko Ushiba, private secretary to the Japanese Premier, Prince Konoye:

> Mr. Ushiba called me on the telephone yesterday afternoon at my house, asking whether he could call on me immediately. I told Mr. Ushiba that I had gone to bed with a cold, but that if he wished to risk the chances of an infection I would be glad to see him for a short while. Mr. Ushiba arrived at about five o'clock and stayed until shortly before seven.
>
> Mr. Ushiba asked whether the Ambassador had received any comment from Washington on his report of the meeting which recently took place between the Ambassador and the Prime Minister. I replied that the Secretary of State had telegraphed in appreciative terms concerning the attitude and views of Prince Konoye, but that a paper which Admiral Nomura had handed in to the State Department on September 4 had so confused matters that the Ambassador had not felt that he had sufficient material to warrant his asking for a further meeting with the Prime Minister.

Mr. Ushiba said that the cabinet had been completely upset by the information which Mr. Grew gave Admiral Toyoda on September 10 with regard to the action of Admiral Nomura. He said that Admiral Nomura had received from Prince Konoye a draft which was responsive to the American draft of June 21, but that in view of the cabinet crisis in Japan, Admiral Nomura had not handed in that document. He had instead written a brief letter to the Secretary of State which was not in any way helpful. Mr. Ushiba gathered that the Nomura paper of September 4 was not the draft received from Tokyo, for the reason that one of the basic ideas of the Japanese Government has been right along to have recourse to the good offices of the President in opening up a path between Japan and China—and apparently Admiral Nomura's paper of September 4 made no reference to the good offices of the President.

I then explained to Mr. Ushiba the combination of circumstances which had led to difficulty in Washington in understanding precisely what the position of the Japanese Government was, say as of September 4. I hoped that we were succeeding in untangling the crossed wires, but the loss of a week or more in straightening matters out was due in no part to any action of ours.

Mr. Ushiba remarked with surprising candor that he did not blame our government in any way for wanting to know precisely what the aims and objectives of the Japanese are before committing itself to such a dramatic move as that of a meeting between the heads of government of the United States and Japan. After all, the crux of the problem was China. He felt that the Japanese Government had shown very clearly that it proposed to maintain the principle of the Open Door in China, but that it had failed thus far to indicate clearly the terms which it would propose to China for settlement of the China conflict. Months had dragged on in conversations in Washington, and the Secretary of State had all along shown very clearly that he did not intend to commit the American Government in any decision until he knew in advance what the Japanese peace terms were and was satisfied that those terms were in conformity with the principles which he advocated for the regulating of relations between nations.

Mr. Ushiba suggested that our government should ask the Japanese Government to disclose those terms, as he could assure me that his government would immediately respond to any such request. I said that I was unable to follow him in those observations: as Mr. Ushiba had himself suggested, we had long expressed desire to know the character of the Japanese peace terms; in our draft of June 21, Section III, we had inserted a phrase which was designed to indicate that the Japanese Government would have communicated those terms to the American Government before any approach was to be made by the President to the Chinese Government. I had therefore assumed that failure on our part to be apprised of the Japanese peace terms was caused by refusal on the part of the Japanese Government to disclose them to us.

Mr. Ushiba said that he did not know precisely how the present situation arose, but that he could assure me that the Japanese Government would be only too glad to communicate the terms to the President and to have the President show them to the Chinese and other interested Governments. After some discussion, it seemed desirable that the initiative with regard to communication to us of the peace terms come from the Japanese side. Mr. Ushiba would suggest to Prince Konoye that he communicate the terms to Mr. Grew as further evidence of the good faith of the Japanese Government and of its eagerness to enter into formal negotiations with the American Government. It was also agreed that if Prince Konoye should feel that some further initiative should come from the American side, Mr. Grew—if he felt that he was in a position to do so—would express to Prince Konoye desire to be apprised of the character of the Japanese peace terms.

We then discussed the question of the attitude of the United States and Japan respectively toward the European war. Mr. Ushiba said that it was impossible for Japan to give to the United States a prior undertaking that it would interpret as a defensive act any action on the part of the United States against Germany which might lead to war between the United States and Germany. He thought that the formula which had been communicated by Admiral Toyoda to Mr. Grew was about as far as the Japanese Government could go prior to the proposed meeting. He added, however, that an understanding had been reached among the various influential elements in Japan which would enable Prince Konoye to give orally and directly to the President an assurance with regard to the attitude of Japan which, he felt sure, would be entirely satisfactory to the President.

Another matter which troubled him very much in this connection was precisely in what terms the Japanese Government would explain to Germany any understanding which might be reached with the United States on this point. I remarked that the United States, which was committed to supporting the principle of the sanctity of treaties, could not well request Japan to betray its treaty commitments. It seemed to me, however, that there was a very definite difference between the Treaty of Alliance, with its rights and obligations, and the formulation of policies by the concerned allies. It followed as a matter of course that allies pursued policies which served their common end, but there was no obligation arising out of the Three-Power Alliance which required Japan to follow policies which would serve exclusively the ends of Germany. Could not, therefore, Japan inform Germany that Japan had undertaken to pursue policies conformable to those of the United States, although Japan was prepared to fulfill its obligations under Article III of the treaty? Technically the Alliance is a defensive alliance; and it is clear from the rescript issued by the Emperor at the time of the signing of the Alliance that it was then considered by the Japanese Government as an instrument for peace. Mr. Matsuoka informed certain of the Ambassadors in Tokyo upon his return from Moscow that, in the event of a war occurring between Germany and the United States, Japan would consult its allies with regard to the antecedent circumstances, and that he felt confident that the Japanese Government would decide, in almost every conceivable instance, to enter the war on the side of Germany.

Mr. Ushiba expressed amazement. He said that he knew that Mr. Matsuoka had interpreted Article III of the Alliance in a sense which was entirely contrary to Prince Konoye's interpretation, but that he did not know that he (Mr. Matsuoka) had disclosed his interpretation to representatives of foreign governments. Apropos, he said that Mr. Matsuoka had told the Prime Minister that Mr. Grew had reported to Washington that the last cabinet change was due to American pressure on Japan. I told Mr. Ushiba that we had reported nothing of the sort. I said that I could tell him in confidence that we had reported that the cabinet change was due chiefly to two causes: first, the German attack on Soviet Russia, which upset Japanese expectation, when signing the Alliance, that peace would be maintained between Germany and Russia; and, second, the conflict of interpretations by the Prime Minister and Mr. Matsuoka with regard to the scope and significance of the Triple Alliance. Mr. Ushiba said that we had been entirely correct.

The concluding portions of the conversation were devoted largely to Mr. Ushiba's stressing the importance of the American Government's returning a favorable reply to the Japanese proposal as soon as possible. Mr. Ushiba reverted again and again to the approach of the 27th of September, the first anniversary of the signing of the Alliance.

JAPAN'S PEACE OFFER TO CHINA

September 22, 1941

I called on Foreign Minister Toyoda this afternoon at his request. After reading from a document in Japanese which was then translated into English, he made substantially the following oral statement:

1. The suggestion that the President meet with Prince Konoye was contained by implication in the message received by the President from the Prime Minister.

2. The Japanese Government had intended that the proposed meeting should discuss the questions at issue between the two countries requiring agreement, and that subsequently through normal diplomatic channels the details for executing the understanding reached at the meeting should be worked out. The Government of the United States, however, had adopted the view that the problems which had emerged from the preliminary and informal conversations should be agreed on in advance of the meeting.

3. The Foreign Minister had explained that in his statement made to me on September 4 he had replied to all of the questions raised by the Government of the United States and that his statement of September 4 had widened rather than reduced the field of the negotiations which the Japanese Government is willing to cover.

4. The Foreign Minister then gave me the basic terms of peace which Japan is prepared to offer China, to be communicated to the Secretary of State. The Minister emphasized that these terms should not be regarded as a new proposal but as related and supplementary to his statement to me of September 4 when he confirmed that the Japanese Government still desired to seek the good offices of the President in bringing the conflict with China to an end.

5. Admiral Toyoda told me that great internal changes had occurred during the past month as a result of the publicity that the suggested meeting between the President and the Japanese Prime Minister had received abroad and as a result of the published reports and references on radio broadcasts abroad in regard to the conversations in progress between Japan and the United States. Thanks to the efforts of the Japanese Government, public opinion in Japan and the Japanese press in the main are not aware of the developments referred to above, but the publicity abroad is known to certain groups in Japan and has increased the activities of those

elements in Japan who are opposed to an understanding with the United States.

6. The Government of Japan will attempt to guard against any incidents or special occurrences in connection with the anniversary on September 27 of Japan's adherence to the Axis and will allow this anniversary to be celebrated by private organizations. However, should a considerable lapse of time occur following the anniversary without any sign as to the attitude of the United States, the groups referred to above who are against an understanding with the United States and who are informed of the Japanese-American conversations might find it possible to inflame public opinion in Japan and thus make it very difficult for these talks to continue.

7. Admiral Toyoda pointed out that the Japanese Government is still awaiting the American answer to the various points set forth by him in his statement of September 4. He expressed his belief that in that statement the Japanese Government had with complete frankness revealed to the American Government its intentions and desires.

In reply to the Minister's question whether any further information had been received from Washington, I conveyed to him the substance of the Department's cable of September 20, which had been decoded immediately before my call on the Minister. Admiral Toyoda was especially struck by the Secretary's remark to the Japanese Ambassador that the Government of the United States fully shared the desire of the Japanese Government to hasten matters. The Minister expressed the thought that although the desire of the United States Government to confer with other governments in regard to the suggested agreement was clearly recognized, the element of delay which would be involved in such consultations might have a most unfortunate effect.

With reference to the lack of concern felt by the Japanese Ambassador in Washington regarding the anniversary on September 27 of Japan's adherence to the Axis, Admiral Toyoda expressed the view that Admiral Nomura was not in close enough touch with the situation in Japan to perceive the dangers. I told the Minister that I was surprised that he had not conveyed to the Japanese Ambassador in Washington his own concern on this point.

With reference to the terms of peace between Japan and China, I told the Minister that I wished to avoid any comment until the Government of the United States had had a chance to examine these terms but that for purposes of clarification I would like to know the exact meaning of the words "existing agreements and usages" mentioned in point three. The Minister in reply stated that these words must be understood as written; however, he referred in this connection to the presence in China of American marines merely by way of an illustration of the phrase in question.

I promised the Minister that I would immediately communicate to the Secretary his statement given above; likewise the proposed terms of peace between Japan and China which he had handed to me. But I added that in view of the communications between the Governments of Japan and the United States I could not be optimistic that a decision on these important matters could be reached before the 27th of September.

Text of basic Japanese terms of peace with China, handed to the American Ambassador by the Japanese Minister for Foreign Affairs on September 22, 1941

1. Neighborly friendship.
2. Respect for sovereignty and territorial integrity.
3. Co-operative defense between Japan and China.

Co-operation between Japan and China for the purposes of preventing Communistic and other subversive activities which may constitute a menace to the security of both countries and of maintaining the public order in China.

Stationing of Japanese troops and naval forces in certain areas in the Chinese territory for a necessary period for the purposes referred to above and in accordance with the existing agreements and usages.

4. Withdrawal of Japanese armed forces.

The Japanese armed forces which have been dispatched to China for carrying out the China affair will be withdrawn from China upon the settlement of the said affair, excepting those troops which come under point 3.

5. Economic co-operation.

(a) There shall be economic co-operation between Japan and China, having the development and utilization of essential materials for national defense in China as its principal objective.

(b) The preceding paragraph does not mean to restrict any economic activities by third powers in China so long as they are pursued on an equitable basis.

6. Fusion of the Chiang Kai-shek regime and the Wang Ching-wei Government.

7. No annexation.

8. No indemnities.

9. Recognition of Manchukuo.

JAPAN'S TERMS FOR A ROOSEVELT-KONOYE CONFERENCE, RESTATED

September 25, 1941

Mr. Terasaki called at his own request this afternoon and delivered to me in substance the following oral statement:

Admiral Toyoda had frequently and in detail advised me that the present attitude of the Government of Japan is one of awaiting from moment to moment a response from the Government of the United States to the Japanese Government's proposal for a meeting between the American President and the Japanese Prime Minister. Because of the press of time and due to Admiral Toyoda's absence from the Foreign Office, the Director of the American Bureau had upon his own initiative called upon me for two purposes. First, he wanted to ask whether any information regarding the above-mentioned proposal had been received by me from my Government; second, he had a document to transmit to me.

The document constitutes a response on the part of the Japanese Government to the substance and the formulae of the draft statement of the American Government dated June 21 as well as an explanation of the proposal which the Minister for Foreign Affairs handed to me on September 4. It contains no new proposal. The document was prepared mainly for use as a convenient reference, presenting in one document the Japanese position, as set forth in the Foreign Minister's proposal of September 4 and in his several explanatory statements. The instrument is not to be considered as a formal document, such, for instance, as a treaty; the text is to be regarded as "entirely flexible." It is therefore open to any revision which the Government of the United States may propose, but any modification of the document's substance will not be agreeable to the Japanese Government.

THE AMBASSADOR IN JAPAN REPORTS TO THE
SECRETARY OF STATE

(Substance)

(Paraphrase of original text prepared by Department of State)

September 29, 1941

In regard to the preliminary conversations taking place at Washington and Tokyo, the Ambassador points out that a review of telegraphic correspondence on this subject since last spring reveals the Japanese Government's efforts, increasing steadily and intensified lately, to arrange a meeting between Prince Konoye and President Roosevelt without further delay. While admitting his role to be chiefly that of a transmitting agent in these conversations, the Ambassador naturally wishes to aid in any constructive way, particularly by endeavoring to appraise accurately for the President and the Secretary of State the Japanese factors and conditions having direct or indirect bearing on the subject and also by trying to bring the Japanese Government to adopt measures and policies such as the United States Government deems to be essential for a mutual understanding or agreement between Japan and the United States. Since the fall of Admiral Yonai's cabinet in July of 1940, American diplomacy in Japan has been in eclipse temporarily through force of circumstances. However, when the Konoye-Toyoda regime began last July, American diplomacy obtained a very active new lease of life. The Ambassador expresses his earnest hope therefore that so propitious a period be not permitted to slip by without a new foundation having been laid with enough stability to warrant a reasonable amount of confidence that the structure to be erected gradually and progressively thereon can and will endure.

The Ambassador recalls his statements in the past that in Japan the pendulum always swings between moderate and extremist policies; that it was not then possible under the existing circumstances for any Japanese leader or group to reverse the program of expansion and expect to survive; that the permanent digging in by Japanese in China and the pushing of the Japanese advance to the south could be prevented only by insuperable obstacles. The Ambassador recalls likewise his views that the risks of taking positive measures to maintain United States security in the future were likely to be far smaller than the risks of not taking such measures; that only respect for potential power of the United States has deterred Japan from taking more liberties with American interests; and that Japan's program of forcible expansion could be brought to a halt only by a show of force and by a demonstration of American willingness to use this force if necessary. The Ambassador recalls also his statement that if Japan's leadership could be discredited eventually by such American action, there might take shape in Japan ultimately a regeneration of thought which would allow Japan to resume formal relations with the United States, leading to a readjustment of the entire problem of the Pacific.

The Ambassador suggests that the United States has been following very wisely precisely this policy which, furthered by other developments in the world, has helped to discredit Japanese leadership, notably that of former Foreign Minister Matsuoka. The Ambassador cites as world developments arousing a positive reaction from the United States the conclusion by Japan of the Tripartite Alliance and Japan's recognition of the Wang Ching-wei regime at Nanking, which preceded Germany's attack on the Soviet Union. Germany's action upset the basis for the Tripartite Pact, Japan having joined the Italo-German Axis in order to obtain security against Russia and thereby to avoid the peril of being caught between the Soviet Union and the United States. At the present time Japan is attempting to correct this miscalculation by getting out of an extremely dangerous position. The Ambassador recalls his reports to the Department to the effect that Japanese foreign policies are inevitably changed by the impact of events abroad and that liberal elements in Japan might come to the top in due course as a result of the trend of events. He considers that such a time has arrived. He sees a good chance of Japan's falling into line if a program can be followed of world reconstruction as forecast by the declaration of President Roosevelt and Prime Minister Churchill. American policy—of forbearance, patient argumentation, efforts at persuasion, followed for many years, plus a manifest determination of the United States to take positive measures when called for—plus the impact of world developments upon Japan, has rendered Japan's political soil hospitable to the sowing of new seeds which, the Ambassador feels, if planted carefully and nourished, may bring about the anticipated regeneration of Japanese thought and a complete readjustment of relations between Japan and the United States.

Certain quarters have advanced the thought—and no doubt it is prominently in the mind of the United States Government—that at this juncture an agreement between Japan and the United States will serve merely as a breathing spell to Japan. During such a breathing spell, Japan, having successfully untangled itself with American aid from the China conflict, will recoup and strengthen its forces in order to resume at the next favorable opportunity its expansionist program. This thought cannot be gainsaid with certainty. The same school of thought also holds that Japan will be forced to relinquish its expansionist program because of the deterioration of Japanese domestic economy and because of the threat of financial, economic, and social collapse due to a progressive intensifying of economic measures by the United States, Great Britain, and the Netherlands against Japan. The Ambassador adds that should this thesis be accepted as reasonably sound, the position will confront the United States of choosing one of two methods to approach its objective, namely, either the method of progressive economic strangulation or the method of constructive conciliation, not so-called appeasement.

The Ambassador sees the second method as the definite choice of the United States Government following the beginning of the Washington preliminary conversations and President Roosevelt's acceptance in principle of the Japanese Prime Minister's proposed meeting. Indeed, the Ambassador remarks, the United States has never departed from its readiness to negotiate on any issues with Japan despite the fact that Japan already had embarked at that time on its expansion-by-force program. He feels that, from the viewpoint of far-seeing statesmanship, the wisdom of the American choice seems to be beyond cavil. Should failure greet the constructive, conciliatory method of approach now or later, there will always be available the other method, the application of progressive economic sanctions. In the opinion of the Ambassador, whether the trend of American relations with Japan is for better or for worse, the United States obviously will have to remain for a long time to come in a state of preparedness. The thought that eventual British victory in the world war will solve automatically many problems may, meanwhile, afford whatever degree of encouragement is justified.

The Ambassador, while admitting that risks will inevitably be involved no matter what course is pursued toward Japan, offers his carefully studied belief that there would be substantial hope at the very least of preventing the Far Eastern situation from becoming worse and perhaps of ensuring definitely constructive results, if an agreement along the lines of the preliminary discussions were brought to a head by the proposed meeting of the heads of two Governments. The Ambassador mentions his previous expressions of opinion that the principal point at issue between the United States and Japan is not whether the former must call a halt to the expansionist program of the latter, but when. He raises the questions whether the United States is not now given the opportunity to halt Japan's program without war, or an immediate risk of war, and further whether, through failure to use the present opportunity, the United States will not face a greatly increased risk of war. The Ambassador states his firm belief in an affirmative answer to these two questions.

Certain quarters hold the view that it is altogether improbable under existing circumstances that counteraction will be deliberately taken by Japan in response to any American action likely to be taken in the Pacific which would bring about war with the United States. The Ambassador states his inability to agree that war may not supervene following actions, whether irrational or deliberate, by elements either in Japan or in the United States tending so to inflame public opinion in the other country concerned as to make war unavoidable. He recalls in this regard the cases of the *Maine* and the *Panay*.

The Ambassador stresses the importance of understanding Japanese psychology, fundamentally unlike that of any Western nation. Japanese reactions to any particular set of circumstances cannot be measured, nor can Japanese actions be predicted by any Western measuring rod. This fact is hardly surprising in the case of a country so recently feudalistic. The Ambassador conceives his chief duty to be an attempt to interpret accurately Japanese psychology, and he states that he has aimed to do this in his numerous reports during the last several months and years to the Department. Keeping this thought constantly before him, the Ambassador ventures at the risk of repetition to advance the considerations set forth below.

Should the United States expect or await agreement by the Japanese Government, in the present preliminary conversations, to clear-cut commitments which will satisfy the United States Government both as to principle and as to concrete detail, almost certainly the conversations will drag along indefinitely and unproductively until the Konoye cabinet and its supporting elements desiring rapprochement with the United States will come to the conclusion that the outlook for an agreement is hopeless and that the United States Government is only playing for time. If the abnormal sensitiveness of Japan and the abnormal effects of loss of face are considered, in such a situation Japanese reaction may and probably will be serious. This will result in the Konoye Government's being discredited and in a revulsion to anti-American feeling, and this may and probably will lead to unbridled acts. The eventual cost of these will not be reckoned, and their nature is likely to inflame Americans, while reprisal and counterreprisal measures will bring about a situation in which it will be difficult to avoid war. The logical outcome of this will be the downfall of the Konoye cabinet and the formation of a military dictatorship which will lack either the disposition or the temperament to avoid colliding head-on with the United States. There is a question that such a situation may prove to be more serious even than the failure to produce an entirely satisfactory agreement through the proposed meeting between President Roosevelt and Prince Konoye, should it take place as planned. Worded otherwise, the question remains whether it will not prove to be a less serious case for the negotiations undertaken in good faith to fail of complete success than for the United States to demonstrate its unwillingness to enter any such negotiations.

The Ambassador continues by stating that he has been emphatically told on numerous occasions—and such declarations he considers must be accepted at their face value—that prior to the proposed Roosevelt-Konoye meeting and formal negotiations it is impossible for the Japanese Government to define its future assurances and commitments more specifically than hitherto stated. The Ambassador explains that one reason for this Japanese position, as given him very confidentially, is that former Foreign Minister Matsuoka, after his retirement in July, recounted in complete detail to the German Ambassador in Japan the course of the Washington conversations up to that time. Because many supporters of Matsuoka remain in the Tokyo Foreign Office, the fear has been expressed that these men will not scruple to reveal to both the Germans and the Japanese extremists any information which would render the present cabinet's position untenable.

Although certain basic principles have been accepted provisionally by the Japanese Government, the definitions and formulae of Japan's future objectives and policy, as advanced so far during the preliminary conversations, and the statements supplementary to those definitions, are so abstract or equivocal and are open to such wide interpretation that they rather create confusion than clarify commitments which the Japanese Government is ready to undertake. The Ambassador states that at the same time he has been told that Prince Konoye is in a position in direct negotiations with President Roosevelt to offer him assurances which, because of their far-reaching character, will not fail to satisfy the United States. The truth of this statement cannot be determined by the Ambassador, who, however, points out that, in regard specifically to Japan's Axis relations, the Japanese Government, though refusing consistently to give an undertaking that it will overtly renounce its alliance membership, actually has shown a readiness to reduce Japan's alliance adherence to a dead letter by its indication of willingness to enter formally into negotiations with the United States. The Ambassador therefore does not consider unlikely the possibility of Prince Konoye's being in a position to give President Roosevelt directly a more explicit and satisfactory engagement than has already been vouchsafed in the course of the preliminary conversations.

In the opinion of the Ambassador, on the basis of the above observations which he has every reason to regard as sound, American objectives will not be reached by insisting or continuing to insist during the preliminary conversations that Japan provide the sort of clear-cut, specific commitments which appear in any final, formal convention or treaty. Unless a reasonable amount of confidence is placed by the United States in the professed sincerity of intention and good faith of Prince Konoye and his supporters to mold Japan's future policy upon the basic principles they are ready to accept and then to adopt measures which gradually but loyally implement those principles, with it understood that the United States will implement is own commitments *pari passu* with the steps which Japan takes, the Ambassador does not believe that a new orientation can be successfully created in Japan to lead to a general improving of Japanese-American relations and to the hope that ultimate war may be avoided in the Pacific. The sole way to discredit the Japanese military machine and Army is through wholesale military defeat, and the Ambassador sees no present prospect of this. The only alternative (and the only wise one in the view of the Ambassador) is an attempt to produce a regeneration of Japanese thought and outlook through constructive conciliation, along the lines of American efforts at present. The Ambassador inquires whether the better part of wisdom and of statesmanship is not to bring such efforts to a head before the force of their initial impetus is lost, leaving it impossible to overcome an opposition which the Ambassador thinks will mount inevitably and steadily in Japan.

In submitting the foregoing discussion, the Ambassador does so in all deference to the much broader field of view of President Roosevelt and Secretary Hull and in full awareness that the Ambassador's approach to the matter is limited to the viewpoint of the American Embassy in Japan.

THE BACKGROUND OF THE FINAL JAPANESE-AMERICAN CONVERSATIONS

September 30, 1941

At the end of September it seems somewhat ostrichlike to continue to guard in the strictest secrecy the fact that so-called preliminary conversations between the United States and Japan have been going on since early last spring because that fact has now been published all over the world, and the fact that Prince Konoye has proposed to meet the President "somewhere in the Pacific" but actually on American soil is generally known in military and political circles in Japan. Such things cannot be kept secret, at least in Japan, for too many people have been told about it. But we ourselves have guarded these facts in the strictest secrecy; the Department's telegrams on that subject have been available only to Dooman and myself, and my own telegrams are marked for the Secretary and Under Secretary only.

So far as I can gather, Admiral Nomura has not handled his end of the line particularly adeptly, for on many occasions he has delayed in carrying out his instructions and on at least one occasion he appears to have thrown a monkey wrench into the works by presenting on his own initiative a new draft agreement which Washington felt had set things back rather than moved them forward, and several weeks were lost before it was understood that this document had not been drawn up in Tokyo and was not known to Tokyo, and it had to be withdrawn. Admiral Toyoda wanted to transfer the conversations to Tokyo, owing, as he said, to difficulties in language, but while the Department agreed that parallel talks might be held here, they quite properly wanted the main conversations to continue in Washington in view of the President's direct concern in the matter. So many of the conversations are now duplicated, in Washington and Tokyo, and cabled back and forth, thus at least ensuring a check on accuracy and completeness. The President and Mr. Hull, or sometimes Welles, Hornbeck, Hamilton, or Ballantine, talk with Admiral Nomura or his assistant, Wakasugi, in Washington, while Dooman and I talk with Prince Konoye or Admiral Toyoda or Terasaki in Tokyo.

The background of these conversations is quite simple when reduced to simple facts: the Japanese found that Matsuoka (with, of course, the support of Prince Konoye and most of the military people) had led them to back the wrong horse in entering the Tripartite Alliance; the Nazis were, just as I have constantly predicted, overplaying their hand in Japan; and when the United States and Great Britain clamped down with their respective economic sanctions as a result of the Japanese move into southern Indo-China, the Japanese Government began at last to see the handwriting on the wall and to realize not only that they had nothing to gain from the Tripartite Pact, whether Germany should win or lose, but that their own economic system could not stand the strain of Anglo-Dutch-American economic pressure.

The conversations actually began long before all this came to pass. A group of influential Japanese persuaded most of the then cabinet that a rapprochement with the United States was highly desirable, and although Matsuoka himself opposed the movement strenuously for a long time, he was finally induced to withdraw his active opposition, even though he was still telling me that if we should go to war with Germany we would certainly have war with Japan on the basis of his own interpretation of Article 3 of the pact. But when Germany attacked Soviet Russia, contrary to all assurances given to Matsuoka by Berlin, his egregious miscalculation forced him out of the Government, and the new setup, with Admiral Toyoda at the helm of the Foreign Office, soon intensified the drive for an agreement with the United States.

Prince Konoye bore the heavy responsibility for having brought the country to its present pass, but since Matsuoka was made the scapegoat, the Premier stayed on and was evidently far from reluctant to support and abet the new orientation of policy. Japan was rapidly drifting toward war with the United States and Great Britain, and we know that the Emperor had long ago told his ministers that whatever policy they pursued, they must on no account get Japan into war with either of those countries. I think there can be no doubt that the Emperor was never very happy about the Tripartite Pact and was persuaded to approve it only in the light of misrepresentations by Matsuoka that Japan was about to be strangled economically by the democracies and that Germany's victory over Great Britain was certain, and also in the light of the great preponderance of public opinion, especially military opinion, at that time in favor of the totalitarian powers, carefully developed by Government propaganda.

Anyway, with the new setup, both Prince Konoye and Admiral Toyoda started all-out for a quick agreement with the United States, professing to be willing to meet all our wishes and to bring the preliminary conversations to a head in formal negotiations to be conducted by the Prime Minister himself at a proposed meeting with the President on American soil. So far as I am aware, the first suggestion for such a meeting was broached by the Japanese in one of their early drafts submitted in April, it being then proposed that a conference between American and Japanese delegates should be held at Honolulu, to be opened by President Roosevelt and Prince Konoye, as soon as possible after an understanding had been reached in the preliminary conversations.* The plan was, however, communicated to me as a definite proposal by the Japanese Government by the Foreign Minister in our long two-and-a-half-hour conversation on August 18 and, according to our records, was conveyed to the President by Admiral Nomura on August 23. For a Prime Minister of Japan thus to shatter all precedent and tradition in this land of subservience to precedent and tradition, and to wish to come hat in hand, so to speak, to meet the President of the United States on American soil, is a gauge of the determination of the Government to undo the vast harm already accomplished in alienating our powerful and progressively angry country.

Just now, at the end of September, the conversations have been making little apparent progress and the desired goal is by no means in sight even though the Japanese Government professes to believe that it has already met our desiderata all along the line. It has not done so, simply because the mentality of the Japanese is such that it cannot bring itself to express the commitments, which it claims it is prepared to undertake, in concise, unambiguous language. They present formulae in phraseology which leave the points at issue open to the widest interpretation, befogging rather than clarifying those issues, and then express surprise that we do not accept those formulae hook, bait, and sinker and proceed to arrange for an immediate meeting between the responsible heads of the two Governments. Prince Konoye's warship is ready waiting to take him to

---

* This proposal was made in a purely unofficial document which was not confirmed by the Japanese Government.

Honolulu or Alaska * or any other place designated by the President, and his staff of the highest military, naval, and civil officers is chosen and rarin' to go.

Meanwhile I have tried my level best to paint to our Government an accurate picture of the situation in Japan. A telegram of fifteen pages, one of the longest that I've ever sent, went forward on September 29. It aimed to give a clear and, I am convinced, an accurate presentation of the situation in Japan with regard to the current conversations, but I made it clear that I was looking at the subject from the point of view of this Embassy and that my discussion was sent with all deference to the far wider field of view of the President and Mr. Hull. They have to reckon with American public opinion, which seems to be steadily growing in favor of stronger measures against Japan, and also, of course, they must consider the world situation as a whole, of which the Far East is only one segment although closely bound up with everything else.

I have just had occasion to reread some of my past letters and telegrams in which I had indicated that the time for conciliation had *then* gone by and advocated a strong policy in our dealings with Japan. I still believe in every word that I then wrote when I pointed out that the present efforts of the Japanese Government to bring about a new orientation in policy, involving conciliation with the United States, is due in part to the fact that our Government had most wisely followed precisely the policy which I have advocated. Those recommendations of mine wound up with the statement: "If by such action we can bring about the eventual discrediting of Japan's leaders, a regeneration of thought may ultimately take shape in this country, permitting the resumption of normal relations with us and leading to a readjustment of the whole Pacific problem." Matsuoka's discrediting and downfall were due primarily to his miscalculations in connection with Germany's attack on Soviet Russia, but it was the strong policy of the United States—that of meeting every Japanese aggressive step with a step of our own—that led indirectly to his fall. I believe that the opportunity now presents itself to bring about a regeneration of thought in

* After the outbreak of war a rumor was current in the United States that the proposed meeting between President Roosevelt and Prince Konoye was to take place on a Japanese battleship and that the intention of the Japanese was to kidnap the President. This theory was of course devoid of foundation. Prince Konoye's proposal was that the meeting should take place on American soil, in Honolulu or Alaska, or any other place that the President might suggest.

Japan, the resumption of normal relations with the United States, and a readjustment of the whole Pacific problem. This will not be easy to accomplish—it will depend in large measure on just how near the end of her rope Japan finds herself economically as a result of our own economic steps—but it is by no means impossible if we continue to play our cards with wisdom.

It is not appeasement that I now advocate, but "constructive conciliation." That word "constructive" is important. It connotes building, and no one is going to be foolish enough to try to build any structure, if it is to be a permanent structure, on an insecure foundation. The purpose of the exploratory conversations with Japan has been to try to find such a foundation, and in laying such a foundation there can be no compromise with the fundamental principles on which American policy is based. In the second place, it is due to our following the strong policy advocated that we have created a situation where constructive conciliation may be possible.

In facing these difficult and highly complicated problems, let us not forget that diplomacy is essentially our first line of national defense, while our Navy is but the second line and our Army, let us hope, the third line. If the first line, diplomacy, is successful, those other lines will never have to be brought into action, even although that first line is immeasurably strengthened by the mere presence of those other lines, the reserves behind the front. It is the first line, diplomacy, that must bear the responsibility for avoiding the necessity of ever using those reserves, and it is in that light that I look on my duties here in Japan. What the eventual outcome will be, I do not know; nobody knows; but defeatism is not within my philosophy.

JAPAN'S HOPES FOR PEACE STILL RISE

October 1, 1941

A Japanese friend of high standing took me aside and said that he had learned from his close contacts in the Black Dragon Society that political circles in Tokyo now know of the Prime Minister's proposal to meet the President of the United States on American soil and that this proposal is generally approved, even among the military, in view of the absolute necessity of arriving at a settlement with the United States because of the economic situation. Delegations representing important political groups are said to have met with the Prime Minister and to have given him assurance that his endeavors to attain an agreement with the United States will be supported by the Japanese nation as a whole. Although these groups apparently feel that the American position has already been met by the Japanese Government, they also declare that, since if the conference is held it would be unthinkable for Prince Konoye to return to Japan from a mission which had ended in failure, the American terms would perforce have to be accepted by the Prime Minister. Importance is attached by the above-mentioned groups to the following facts: namely, that close police surveillance is now being exercised over German elements in Japan; that on the anniversary of the conclusion of the Tripartite Pact the Prime Minister purposely absented himself from Tokyo; and that the celebration of the anniversary was observed to a minimum degree.

ONLY PRINCE KONOYE CAN SAVE THE PEACE

October 3, 1941

Another Japanese tells me that unless our current conversations should come to a successful head soon, they would undoubtedly be wrecked by the growing opposition of extremist and pro-Axis elements in Japan, and that in such a case the Konoye cabinet would probably fall and no other Japanese statesman than Prince Konoye could succeed in coming to an understanding with the United States. I listened politely and then told him that I was in constant touch with the Japanese Government through the Foreign Minister, who naturally was keeping me informed of all these considerations, and that naturally I was constantly conveying to my Government an accurate picture and appraisal of conditions in Japan.

MUKDEN'S WHITE RUSSIANS MOBILIZE FOR JAPAN

October 6, 1941

On October 3 all Mukden White Russians were summoned to a mass meeting by the police, where they were told that all members of their community, male and female, between eighteen and thirty-five must at once procure uniforms in a style specified; that very shortly they would be given physical training and that they must hold themselves ready for service of a nature to be specified later. They were then addressed by an officer of the special service section of the Japanese Army who told them that within sixty days an emergency situation would exist in Manchuria and that they must expect loyally to serve the state. The American Consul at Mukden said that he would endeavor to offer some interpretative comment on this extraordinary action within a few days.

DOOMAN SEES USHIBA AGAIN

October 7, 1941

Today, our Embassy Counselor, Eugene Dooman, met again with Prince Konoye's private secretary, Tomohiko Ushiba, and submitted the following report which I quote *verbatim:*

In reply to a request by telephone yesterday from Mr. Ushiba, I suggested that he breakfast with me this morning at my house. Mr. Ushiba arrived promptly at the appointed time. Owing to the presence of the servant during the meal, that part of our conversation which needs to be recorded was brief and was substantially as follows:

Mr. Ushiba said that the Prime Minister's position had been made difficult by the failure of the preliminary conversations with the United States to make any progress. Prince Konoye was at a loss to know what further he could do, the opposition had now something concrete to use in their attacks on the cabinet, and the future looked dark. He said that, unless we fully appreciated the circumstances in which his chief had assumed responsibility for initiating these conversations, we would not be able to understand the full implications of the situation. The Army was anxious to bring the conflict with China to an end but it would never take the responsibility for initiating a liquidation of the conflict. When Prince Konoye had taken that responsibility, the Army gave him full and unqualified support, and if his high hopes are not fulfilled he will have to "assume responsibility," and there would be no one who would have the courage to take the risks which the Prince has taken or with sufficient prestige and political position to gain the support of the Army in any undertaking so vital to the nation as settlement of the China conflict by process of negotiation.

Mr. Ushiba went on to say that pessimism in Japanese official quarters had been strengthened by failure on the part of the American Government to lay any of its cards on the table. It was true that the American Government had given a full presentation of its principles, but it had not precisely specified what it wanted the Japanese Government to undertake. Although several months had elapsed since the conversations began, the apparently great care being taken by the American

Government not to give the Japanese any specifications was extremely discouraging. Since the receipt of the last American memorandum (October 2) an increasing number of persons in Japanese Government circles were of the opinion that Japan had fallen into a trap, the argument running somewhat as follows—the United States never had any intention of coming to any agreement with Japan; it has now got from Japan an exposition of Japanese policies and objectives; those policies and objectives are not in line with American policies and objectives; and there is therefore justification for refusing to make an agreement with Japan and for continuing to maintain an attitude of quasi-hostility against Japan.

I told Mr. Ushiba that there was no basis for any such conjecture. I recalled that the memorandum of October 2 referred to the reaction of the American public to reports that conversations with Japan were taking place and that the statement was made that, although the American Government was no less eager than the Japanese Government to have brought about settlement of Pacific problems, public opinion in the United States was such as to render necessary a meeting of minds on certain fundamental points prior to the opening of formal negotiations.

Mr. Ushiba asked whether we had received the actual text of the memorandum. The summary (which I had allowed him to read on October 4) shown to him by me was businesslike and objective in tone, but the actual memorandum was, he said, "extremely disagreeable." It was argumentative and preceptive, it was quite uncompromising, and it contained no suggestion or indication calculated to be helpful to the Japanese Government toward meeting the desires of the American Government. Citing the reference to attitudes toward the European war, he put the rhetorical question, Why was there not provided some indication of the kind of undertaking the Japanese Government was expected to give?

In conclusion, Mr. Ushiba expressed the thought that the only thing left for the Japanese Government was to ask the American Government to give specifications with regard to the character of the undertakings which Japan was desired to give, and that if a clear-cut reply was not forthcoming to bring the conversations to an end.*

---

* For a clear conception of the position of the Government of the United States in the situation dealt with in the diary from the Tokyo angle, it is important to study the memorandum of May 19, 1942, prepared in the Department of State and published in *Foreign Relations of the United States, Japan: 1931–1941*, page 325.

Meanwhile, I had called upon the Foreign Minister at his request this morning. He began by informing me that the text of the memorandum handed to the Japanese Ambassador on October 2 by the Secretary of State had been received and was being carefully studied. In reply to the Minister's question whether I could make any comments on the memorandum I said that until I had had an opportunity to study the full text, the Embassy having received a résumé only, I would prefer to make no observations.

Admiral Toyoda then told me that he was informed of my private meeting with the Prime Minister on September 6 and was aware that I had communicated to President Roosevelt through the Secretary of State, as a "personal and private message," the substance of Prince Konoye's statements to me at that meeting. The Foreign Minister said he wanted me clearly to understand that he harbored no objection to my contact with Prince Konoye; rather he was desirous that by such meetings between the Prime Minister and myself a helpful exchange of views might be effected. Admiral Toyoda stated that the private records of the Prime Minister with regard to the September 6 meeting revealed that, although Prince Konoye had "in principle" accepted the four points which the Secretary of State had continuously stressed, the Prime Minister had indicated that some adjustment would be required in the matter of applying the four points to actual conditions. However, a statement that the Prime Minister "fully subscribed" to the four points was contained in the memorandum given to the Japanese Ambassador on October 2. Admiral Nomura had therefore, in view of this disparity in the records, been instructed to inform the Secretary of State that the phrase "in principle" should replace the words "fully subscribed" in attributing to the Prime Minister the statement, which had been made privately.

The Foreign Minister declared that the statements made to me by the Prime Minister on September 6 were of a purely private and informal nature and were intended merely to acquaint me with the personal views of an individual who held an important position in the molding of the decisions and policies of the Government of Japan. The thought of authorizing me to communicate the substance of his observations as a personal message to the President had only occurred to Prince Konoye during the course of our meeting. Accordingly there had been no expectation, said Admiral Toyoda, that there would be incorporated into a public document, which had to be circulated among various Japanese Government officials who had no knowledge of my meeting with Prince Konoye, any statement made to me by the Prime Minister under these circumstances. Thus, since an attribution of views to the Prime Minister had appeared in an official document of the United States Government, it had been deemed necessary, in view of the absence of previous comparison between the Foreign Minister and myself of notes relating to what might have been stated by Prince Konoye at the time of his meeting with me on September 6, to clarify the Japanese record of the Prime Minister's statement. (There is no doubt whatsoever that the observations of the Prime Minister, which were made in Japanese and translated by Dooman to me, were correctly and accurately set forth in my telegram reporting my meeting with Prince Konoye. The Prime Minister doubtless is referring to his remark made subsequently that "he is convinced that divergences of view can be satisfactorily met" and that he "realizes that certain points may require elucidation and precision."

Admiral Toyoda stated at this point that he hoped to be able to comment following the completion of his examination of the Secretary's memorandum of October 2, and in the meantime he felt that it would be helpful if discussion of items arising from what he termed "technical procedure" could be avoided. He had in mind such differences of understanding as that relating to Prince Konoye's statement of September 6, and to certain material delivered to the Department by the Japanese Ambassador which either had no official standing or was incomplete as in the case of the Ambassador's draft statement of September 4. Admiral Toyoda believed that any efforts to clear up details of this character arising out of questions of technical procedure would only tend to complicate the discussions, but once some real progress had been made he would be prepared to take up such questions.

The Foreign Minister said that in so far as the Secretary's memorandum of October 2 was concerned, he would like to make one brief comment, namely, that it was his impression that the Government of the United States wished the Japanese Government to revert at once and unqualifiedly to the *status quo* which prevailed four years ago. Since that time Japan had been involved in warfare on a large scale demanding hardships and sacrifices of the people of Japan, who had been led to support such trials as a patriotic duty. The Japanese Government was willing and prepared to return to the situation prevailing four years ago but it was essential that the Government of the United States should understand that to undo virtually at a moment's notice the work of the past four years is an undertaking of tremendous scope and one entailing basic adjustments.

Admiral Toyoda then inquired whether unofficially and privately I felt able to offer an opinion on the position of the United States Government as outlined in the Secretary's memorandum of October 2. In reply I told him that it was the desire of the United States Government to establish conditions in the Far East on a sure and enduring foundation and that no lasting arrangements could be made except on such a basis. I told him that my personal reaction to the Secretary's memorandum of October 2 was that the American Government was endeavoring to assure itself that Japan would genuinely and fully observe those principles without which no sure basis for a lasting peace in the Pacific area could be achieved.

October 8, 1941

By a special dispensation from the Foreign Office I was able today for the first time since the freezing order to deposit a salary check in the National City Bank and to draw cash to pay some of our bills and household accounts, including the Mampei Hotel bill in Karuizawa. But the staff cannot yet get money. We are, however, nearing an agreement. The British had this whole thing settled by mutual agreement within a few days of the freezing order, but with us there have been a succession of delays.

Radio news from London tonight reports a story in the London *Daily Mail* that at a dinner last night I had expressed the belief that an agreement would be reached between the United States and Japan. In the course of an informal and off-the-record talk to the annual meeting of the American Association, composed exclusively of American citizens, to which I requested that no publicity be given, I repeated what Secretary Hull had said in press conference on September 13 with regard to the exploratory talks and added: "We would like to see a happy adjustment of relations, severely strained during these past years, but such an adjustment depends on the settling of many issues, and those issues in turn depend on many factors which greatly complicate our efforts and subject our exertions to great difficulties. I cannot tell you what the eventual outcome will be; I do not know; nobody knows."

Later in the talk I said: "I have never believed that our two countries would come to a break; I do not think so now. Let us have the faith that can move mountains and perhaps we shall be successful in moving those veritable mountains. I think we shall in the end succeed."

The talk dealt in detail with Japan's policy and actions during the past several years which have brought our relations to their present pass. Reference was also made to the view of the American Government that the foundation for any international building must rest on certain basic principles in international dealing and that with those principles there can be no compromise.

FROZEN CREDITS BRING JAPAN CLOSE TO BANKRUPTCY

October 9, 1941

According to information received by a member of my staff from what is regarded as a very reliable source, the amount of foreign exchange available to the Japanese Government now is approximately 20,000 reichsmarks and under the circumstances the Japanese Government will be unable to avoid defaulting on contracts calling for foreign exchange on maturity. The freezing regulations which were put into effect by the United States, Great Britain, and the Netherlands East Indies have completely cut off any exchange transactions in the currencies of those countries and in addition have greatly reduced transactions in the currencies of South American countries. According to this informant, his own contracts involve foreign exchange totaling approximately five million Swedish kronen and during recent months Japanese purchases of Swedish goods have been primarily financed through Berlin, presumably through German advanced credits.

The Japanese have been informed recently by the Germans that these credits are now frozen and are to be used only to finance the purchase of German goods. According to our informant it is possible that this action by the Germans was taken in anticipation of Japan's withdrawal from the Axis. According to another source it is believed that since Sweden is heavily indebted to Germany for armaments, the Germans are now demanding in return from Sweden goods instead of Swedish kronen. Reports are current here that Japan is now eighty million marks in debt to Germany.

In actual fact Japan is now in virtually the same embarrassing position from the point of view of international finance as are designated foreigners in this country.

ADMIRAL TOYODA AGAIN TRIES TO SPEED
THE ROOSEVELT-KONOYE MEETING

October 10, 1941

The Minister for Foreign Affairs asked me to call this afternoon.

He began by saying that although he had given careful study to the Secretary's memorandum of October 2 he had encountered some difficulty in seizing the point of the memorandum. He had, how-ever, come to the conclusion that the three questions concerning which the American and Japanese Governments held divergent views were as follows: (1) the maintenance of Japanese armed forces in China, (2) the respective attitude of the United States and Japan in regard to the war in Europe, and (3) equal opportunity in China. The Minister added that on October 3 he had instructed the Japanese Ambassador in Washington to ask the Secretary whether the United States Government would set forth in precise terms the obligations which the United States Government wished the Japanese Government to undertake with reference to the three questions mentioned above. Having heard nothing from the Japanese Ambassador, he had again on October 6 instructed Admiral Nomura to approach the Secretary in the above sense. On October 9 the Japanese Ambassador had telegraphed the Foreign Minister that he had seen the Secretary on that date but that the Ambassador was unable to provide the information which had been requested by the Foreign Minister. Admiral Toyoda added that a week of very valuable time had been wasted in an endeavor to elicit through the Japanese Ambassador information which, had it been received, would have measurably accelerated the present conversations. The Foreign Minister had today sent further instructions to Admiral Nomura to continue his efforts to obtain the desired information, but at the same time, in order to prevent further delay, he was requesting that I ask my Government to provide the desired information in reply to the following statement:

> The Government of Japan has submitted to the Government of the United States with reference to certain questions proposals which are apparently not satisfactory to the Government of the United States. Will the American Government now set forth to the Japanese Government for its consideration the undertakings to be assumed by the Japanese Government which would be satisfactory to the American Government?

At this point in the conversation I took occasion to reply to the criticism in the Japanese press concerning the absence of progress in the present conversations, by stressing to Admiral Toyoda that the American Government in the determination and execution of its policy continuously considers and gives due worth to the development and state of American public opinion. Admiral Toyoda remarked that public opinion even in Japan could not be disregarded but that it would be a comparatively easy matter to control Japanese public opinion provided, as a result of the suggested meeting between Prince Konoye and the President, some agreement were arrived at. The Minister gave me his assurances that the Japanese Government would find it possible to make commitments of a far-reaching character at such a meeting but that under present conditions the full extent of the undertakings which the Japanese Government was willing to assume could not be set forth prior to the meeting. He reiterated his concern lest the Government be unable to control extremist groups in Japan if matters remain in their present undetermined conditions.

The Minister having at the beginning of the conversation expressed his appreciation of the message which I had sent him yesterday concerning the reported plan to send additional Japanese forces into French Indo-China, I reverted to this point and strongly emphasized to him that the dispatch of Japanese reinforcements to Indo-China at this juncture while the conversations were in progress between our two Governments would create a very delicate situation and in my opinion could not but seriously and adversely affect these conversations. I told the Foreign Minister that the arrival of additional Japanese forces in Indo-China at this time, in the light of recent activities of the Japanese authorities in Indo-China to which I had already drawn his attention, such as threats to take over the telegraph, post, and customs, and the demands for additional air bases, would inevitably give rise to the most serious suspicions in regard to Japan's aims in respect to French Indo-China. The Minister replied that he was giving most careful study to my private and informal message on the subject and had already conferred with the Minister of War and hoped to be able to give me a reply in a few days. He added that he had also discussed with the War Minister the activities of the Japanese authorities in Indo-China to which I had drawn his attention and had asked the Minister to take immediate steps to remedy the situation.

The Minister for Foreign Affairs then told me that since he had the impression that the Japanese Ambassador in Washington was apparently very fatigued, serious consideration was being given to the question of sending to Washington a diplomat of wide experience to assist the Ambassador in carrying on the present conversations. Admiral Toyoda said he had in mind a high-ranking diplomatic official with the personal rank of Ambassador, but he had not yet approached the official in question and was therefore uncertain as to whether he would agree to undertake to accept the mission. It would be of great assistance to the Minister to ascertain whether the Government of the United States, in the event that it was decided to send the official in question to Washington, would be prepared to make available a reservation for him on the airplane from Manila to San Francisco. Admiral Toyoda said that the official in question would not be accredited to the Government of the United States but would be temporarily and unofficially attached to the Japanese Embassy in Washington. I told the Foreign Minister that I would transmit his inquiry to my Government.

In concluding the conversation, the Minister several times stressed to me, in view of the importance of the time factor, the necessity of expediting the progress of the conversations.

THE KONOYE CABINET FALLS

October 16, 1941

The Konoye cabinet fell at five o'clock this afternoon, the official announcement having been given out at 8:15. We were in my study, a dozen or more men, after a farewell dinner for Jack Curtis, when the Brazilian Ambassador called up to tell me the news which he had just heard. Everyone, including myself, was surprised, for although I knew that the failure of progress in the American-Japanese conversations would almost certainly bring about Konoye's fall sooner or later, I had not looked for it so soon.

EXCHANGE OF LETTERS WITH PRINCE KONOYE

October 17, 1941

Prince Konoye this morning sent me the following personal letter:

16th October, 1941

MY DEAR AMBASSADOR,

It is with great regret and disappointment that my colleagues and I have had to resign owing to the internal political situation, which I may be able to explain to you sometime in the future.

I feel certain, however, that the cabinet which is to succeed mine will exert its utmost in continuing to a successful conclusion the conversations which we have been carrying on up till today. It is my earnest hope, therefore, that you and your Government will not be too disappointed or discouraged either by the change of cabinet or by the mere appearance or impression of the new cabinet. I assure you that I will do all in my power in assisting the new cabinet to attain the high purpose which mine has endeavored to accomplish so hard without success.

May I take this opportunity to express my heartfelt gratitude for your most friendly co-operation which I have been fortunate to enjoy and also to convey to you my sincere wish that you will give the same privilege to whoever succeeds me.

With kindest personal regards, I am

Sincerely yours,

F. KONOYE

I replied:

October 17, 1941
MY DEAR PRIME MINISTER:
Your friendly letter of October 16 is very deeply appreciated and I hasten to thank you heartily for your generous expressions and for the encouragement which you have given me in your confidence that the coming cabinet will make every effort to continue to a successful conclusion the conversations carried on between our two Governments. It gives me keen gratification to know that you yourself will assist the new cabinet in attaining the high purpose for which you and your colleagues have striven, and I need hardly assure you that your successor may count fully on my own earnest co-operation in a continuance of the mutual efforts of our respective Governments to achieve a successful outcome.

Please permit me to express the hope that you yourself, if you are about to lay down for a time the cares of your high office, will now find some degree of welcome relaxation and respite after your long, arduous, and most distinguished official service to your country.

With expressions of my highest respect and cordial personal regards, I am, my dear Prince Konoye,

Sincerely yours,

JOSEPH C. GREW

At the same time Prince Konoye's private secretary, Ushiba, called on Dooman and conveyed through him to me from Prince Konoye a very interesting explanation of the circumstances which had led to the fall of the cabinet and the successful efforts of the Prime Minister to ensure the appointment of a successor who would continue the conversations with the United States. The circumstances were extraordinarily dramatic and constitute what may in future be regarded as one of the really big moments in Japanese history. What all this may lead to is still in the lap of the gods.

We cabled at 10 A.M. that General Umedzu, now Commander of the Kwantung Army, was a likely candidate for Prime Minister, but at 5 P.M. we reported the selection of General Tojo, former Minister of War, who will hold the posts of Prime Minister, War Minister, and Home Minister. Tojo was one of the original five members of the Konoye cabinet last spring who supported the opening of conversations with the United States in the face of the opposition of Matsuoka. This is important.

We understand that Fritz Wiedemann, former German Consul General in San Francisco and a confidant of Hitler, is on his way to Japan. We later learned that Wiedemann will probably go as Consul General in Tientsin, where he will supervise the Orientgruppe of the German military espionage network, his own specialties being sabotage and terrorism, for which he has large secret funds. It is believed that he will direct from Tientsin the espionage-Gestapo organization in the Far East, having under his orders Meisinger, now in Shanghai, and Hueber, now in Bangkok. The main objective of this Orientgruppe is believed to be India and Burma, and it is intended to act as the advance guard of a Far Eastern pincer movement designed to threaten India together with the other pincer represented by the German advance into western Asia. Hitler is understood to attach great importance to India as the goal of all the best conquerors since Alexander the Great.

A TOUCH OF WILD WEST IN THE
AMERICAN EMBASSY

October 19, 1941

I put aside this Sunday for a careful review of all material concerning the American-Japanese preliminary conversations since they commenced last spring, making a written résumé of important points. A graph of the movements in the progress and regress of the conversations would show extraordinary fluctuations. Lately the movement has been one of regress. I want to have the whole story at my finger tips in case Togo, the new Minister for Foreign Affairs, approaches the subject when we meet.

I feel somewhat "wild West" these days, having carried a gun for the past month or more, especially since the attack on Prince Konoye on September 18, when four men armed with daggers and short swords jumped on the running board of his car as he was leaving his private residence and tried to get at him. The doors were fortunately locked, however, and the assassins were quickly overpowered by the plain-clothes men at the residence. During September 27, the anniversary of the conclusion of the Tripartite Pact, I expected anything. Cam Forbes was once on the death list of one of the so-called patriotic societies when some assassinations were carried out in 1931 or 1932, but he happened to be away from Tokyo on that occasion, and I know that my own name is included on some of their present lists. The guard at the entrance to the Embassy has been materially strengthened, on the initiative of the police, and a guardhouse erected near the entrance to the chancery, but it would be a very simple thing for a few dagger wielders to climb over some part of our very extensive wall at night and get into the Embassy by breaking a window. I don't like heroics but have no intention of letting a group of those roughnecks carve me up without a reasonable attempt at repartee.

In one of my conversations with a Japanese official he took my hand and put it over his heart. I thought he meant to convey the idea that his heart was in the right place but it felt like a very hard heart and I soon grasped the idea that the hardness wasn't his heart at all but a very businesslike gun. Many Japanese are just as much in danger from the military extremists as are we.

ANALYSIS OF THE TOJO GOVERNMENT

October 20, 1941

Since the American press and radio are almost universally interpreting the present government as a preliminary move leading to an attack on Russia or to some other positive action which will inevitably bring about hostilities between Japan and the United States, I am setting forth certain factors, some based on fact and others on valid assumption, which indicate that the opinion which appears to have been accepted by the American public in regard to the meaning of the change of government in Japan may not be an accurate appraisal of the situation viewed in perspective.

We are informed by a confidant of Prince Konoye that the latter decided to resign and in so doing to ensure that the Prime Minister who succeeded him would be an official who would attempt to pursue the policy inaugurated by the previous government of reconstructing relations with the United States and bringing about a settlement of the China affair.

We believed that should our exploratory conversations break down or the expected formal negotiations fail, Prince Konoye would be forced to retire and his government be succeeded by a military dictatorship and not by a civilian government. In view of the fact that the conversations have not been broken off, the conditions to which the above prognostication was related have not obtained. We think that a reasonable motive for the resignation of the previous government was Prince Konoye's belief that the conversations with the United States would make more rapid progress if our Government were dealing with a Prime Minister whose power was based on a commanding position in and on support of the Army, which is the controlling force in matters affecting policy, rather than with a go-between. Despite the fact that, as anticipated, the Konoye Government was succeeded not by a civilian but by a military man, indications of a willingness on the part of the Tojo Government to proceed with the conversations in the light of the circumstances outlined in the preceding paragraph would imply that it is premature to stigmatize the Tojo Government as a military dictatorship committed to the furtherance of policies which might be expected to bring about armed conflict with the United States.

It is important to note that General Tojo, as distinguished from previous Japanese military Prime Ministers, is not a retired officer but is a full general in the active service. Thus the Japanese Army for the first time in recent years has openly assumed responsibility for the policies and conduct of government in Japan, which it had previously steadfastly declined to accept. It would be logical, therefore, to expect that General Tojo, in retaining his active rank in the Army, will as a result be in a position to exercise a larger degree of control over Army extremist groups.

I am informed by a member of my staff who was acquainted in Moscow with Mr. Togo, the new Foreign Minister, and who has on several occasions in recent months met Mr. Togo's wife and daughter here in Tokyo, that the new Foreign Minister while Ambassador to

Moscow was held in high regard by the Soviet Government as the most acceptable representative from Japan who had been sent to Moscow in recent years. It was reliably reported that the Soviet Government was frankly disappointed over his recall in the autumn of 1940 in view of Mr. Togo's successful conduct of the conversations for the conclusion of a political treaty which had been proceeding in Moscow between Japan and the Soviet Union, and the Soviet Government extended to him unusual courtesies on the occasion of his departure from Moscow. Mr. Togo, it will also be remembered, was among those Japanese diplomats removed from active office by Matsuoka last year for the reason, it is believed, that he was not in favor of the extreme foreign policy pursued by Matsuoka.

The official Japanese agency Domei has just released a statement to the effect that the Tojo Government will inaugurate no new policies since the Government of Prince Konoye has already laid down the basic national policy of Japan.

NOTE ON VICE-MINISTER NISHI

October 22, 1941

The press announced today the appointment as Vice-Minister for Foreign Affairs of Haruhiko Nishi, who for several years has specialized in Soviet-Japanese relations, having been twice assigned to Moscow. He was there with Togo, who no doubt selected him owing to their personal relations, so we now have in the two key positions in the Foreign Office men who have had firsthand experience in Soviet affairs and are regarded as friendly to the Soviet Union. Nishi, whom I know and like, is regarded as an honest and trustworthy man with no great intellectual attainments or outstanding ability. He succeeds Amau.

"COMPROMISE, COMPROMISE, COMPROMISE"

October 24, 1941

A Japanese friend made some suggestions about the American-Japanese conversations. He wants us to make a joint declaration with Japan stating that we have no intention of "infiltrating" into Indo-China, and, as usual, he said that compromise would be necessary if we were to make progress. I was pretty severe in replying, pointing out that there was no room for compromise and explaining the absurdity of issuing such a joint declaration as he suggested. I gave him a copy of my long letter to —— of September 1, to read, mark, learn, and inwardly digest. My friend, much as I like him, is difficult to debate with, for he keeps coming back to his original point no matter what one says—compromise, compromise, compromise.

HOW THE EMPEROR INTERVENED

October 25, 1941

A reliable Japanese informant tells me that just prior to the fall of the Konoye cabinet a conference of the leading members of the Privy Council and of the Japanese armed forces had been summoned by the Emperor, who inquired if they were prepared to pursue a policy which would guarantee that there would be no war with the United States. The representatives of the Army and Navy who attended this conference did not reply to the Emperor's question, whereupon the latter, with a reference to the progressive policy pursued by the Emperor Meiji, his grandfather, in an unprecedented action ordered the armed forces to obey his wishes. The Emperor's definite stand necessitated the selection of a Prime Minister who would be in a position effectively to control the Army, hence the appointment of General Tojo, who, while remaining in the Army active list, is committed to a policy of attempting to conclude successfully the current Japanese-American conversations.

The informant emphasized to me that the recent anti-American tone of the Japanese press and the extreme views expressed by pro-Axis and certain other elements gave no real indication of the desire of Japanese of all classes and in particular of the present political leaders that in some way or other an adjustment of relations with the United States must be brought about. He added in this connection that Mr. Togo, the new Foreign Minister, had accepted his appointment with the specific aim of endeavoring to pursue the current conversations to a successful end and it had been understood that should he fail in this he would resign his post.

The belief is current among Japanese leaders that the principal difficulty in the way of an understanding with the United States is the question of the removal of Japanese armed forces from China and Indo-China, but these same leaders are confident that, provided Japan is not placed in an impossible position by the insistence on the part of the United States that all Japanese troops in these areas be withdrawn at once, such a removal can and will be successfully effected.

The informant, who is in contact with the highest circles, went on to say that for the first time in ten years the situation at present and the existing political setup in Japan offer a possibility of a reorientation of Japanese policy and action.

WORDSWORTH'S ENGLAND—AND CHURCHILL'S

October 27, 1941

One hundred and thirty-five years ago, when England, after the fall of Prussia, stood alone against Europe dominated by Napoleon, Wordsworth wrote:

> *Another year! Another deadly blow!*
> *Another mighty Empire overthrown!*
> *And we are left, or shall be left, alone;*
> *The last that dare to struggle with the Foe,*
> *'Tis well! From this day forward we shall know*
> *That in ourselves our safety must be sought;*
> *That by our own right hands it must be wrought;*
> *That we must stand unpropped, or be laid low.*

According to *Punch,* the same mood was expressed in 1940 in unpoetic language by two salts, looking over the Channel to the still-smoking northern French ports, one of whom says: "Well, now we're alone." "Yes," replies the other, "the whole bloody 400,000,000 of us."

GERMAN REACTIONS TO THE TOJO CABINET

October 29, 1941

The following items gathered by members of another country's mission to Tokyo are believed to be a fairly accurate account of the reactions of the German community here to the present situation.

The Germans are not enthusiastic about the new cabinet, which disappointed the hopes of a definitely interventionist Government which they had formed on the resignation of Prince Konoye. Their feelings were cooled still further by the arrest of two Germans immediately the new cabinet had taken office.

In the event of war between the U. S. and Germany, the local

Germans from the Ambassador down are uncertain of Japan's reactions. They regard the Japanese as untrustworthy opportunists.

The Germans are at present working primarily for a Japanese attack on the Soviet. Prominent members of the German business community here were recently summoned to the German Embassy and were told that their salaries would continue in spite of the inactivity of their businesses, on the understanding that they regard themselves as agents of the German Government. Their particular instructions were to start a whispering campaign among the Japanese directed both against the American-Japanese discussions and against Russia on the lines that now is Japan's best opportunity to attack her. This line is believed to reflect (a) the anxiety of the German High Command to finish with Russia quickly, particularly in view of the difficulties of providing clothing for the German Army throughout the winter campaign, and (b) Hitler's personal wish to divert Japan's attention from the Netherlands East Indies, which he wants for himself (though the latter factor, without the former, might well be offset by Germany's wish to encourage Japan's southward expansion in order to embroil her with the democracies).

At the same time warlike preparations continue among the German community. Apart from certain shipping activities the German Military Attaché has organized premilitary training courses at the Deutsches Haus in Tokyo, where all Germans of military age must attend once a week. The rumor is that the Germans intend to form a Freikorps to fight with the Japanese Army in the event of Japan entering the war.

Although still generally confident in victory, the local Germans are anxious over certain aspects of the present situation, e.g., the losses in Russia, shortage of food in Germany, the possibility of American intervention, and especially the murders and executions in France, which have left on them a profound impression that all is not well in the New Europe.

A source which has been reliable in the past has given us the following information:

> Elaborate plans for a joint Army and Navy occupation of Thailand are complete. These plans are modeled on the German attack on Belgium and Holland. They call for a simultaneous occupation of all airfields, ports, and strategic centers by air-borne troops and parachutists. Two hundred and fifty transport planes are assembled in Taiwan and Hainan or are readily available to begin this operation when ordered.

FOREIGN MINISTER TOGO RECEIVES

October 30, 1941

The new Foreign Minister, Togo, received the ambassadors individually today at 3 P.M., the diplomatic ministers to be received tomorrow. At the Minister's official residence they separated the sheep from the goats in different waiting rooms, the British allies in one, the German allies in another, and the neutrals in a third. I, although Dean and the first to come, was shown into a tiny anteroom, the big salon where we usually gather no doubt being reserved for the Axis. I saw Arsène-Henry, directly after me in seniority, drive up but he did not come into my room; I wonder just what category they put him in. Craigie didn't come because he had asked to see the Minister urgently yesterday, but I suppose we would have been classed together.

On entering the Minister's room I encountered the usual solid array of press cameras and movies and we posed for several minutes, but then they were shooed out because they are only allowed to take the Dean, and as usual the *Advertiser* next morning carried a big picture of us on its front page, which could not have been wholly gratifying to their dear ally, General Ott.

What a difference between Admiral Toyoda and Togo, the former cheery and very friendly and always with a little exchange of pleasantries before getting down to business, the latter grim, unsmiling, and ultrareserved. He speaks English well enough but talks so low that few can understand him and I not at all, so I'm glad that he is using an interpreter. Kase sits beside me on the sofa and speaks very distinctly and in perfect English, so nothing will be lost. But I shall miss my really pleasant association with Admiral Toyoda, regardless of our negative results; he was a type that one enjoyed doing business with, however disagreeable that business might be.

During the course of our conference, Mr. Togo remarked that the relations between the United States and Japan, which had not been very good when he formerly was in the Foreign Office several years ago, had since then progressively worsened to the present situation, which, if this deterioration were not terminated, was fraught with the gravest dangers. Referring to the informal conversations which had been carried on since last spring between the Japanese and the American Governments, the Minister declared his desire that the conversations be continued and without delay be successfully brought to a conclusion. He requested my co-operation in accomplishing this objective.

Mr. Togo said that in order to make progress, the United States should face certain realities and facts. He thereupon cited the stationing in China of Japanese armed forces. Other nations, he said, at present maintained troops in certain areas of China; for instance, the Soviet soldiery stationed in Outer Mongolia. The Minister made no further allusion to the preliminary conversations but stated that he hoped to have subsequent talks with me in due time.

After assuring the Minister of my desire to co-operate with him, I described the wish of our Secretary of State that the conversations should be carried on in Washington because of the President's close and active interest in them. However, as parallel talks in Tokyo were often helpful in that they afforded an opportunity for rendering more complete and more precise the reported views of the United States Government, I had on certain occasions in the past conveyed to the Minister for Foreign Affairs the substance of the conversations in Washington which were reported me directly from the Secretary of State. I then gave Mr. Togo a paraphrase of the Department's telegram reporting the Under Secretary's conversation with Mr. Wakasugi on October 24.

I told Mr. Togo that, as it was of course impossible for the Foreign Minister personally to read all the correspondence directed by the American Embassy to the Foreign Office, I had followed the practice of bringing separate letters of special importance to the direct attention of Admiral Toyoda, with the latter's approval. Mr. Togo approved of my continuing the same practice with him, and the interview ended.

As I was leaving, Mr. Kase told me that he had been designated Chief of the First Section of the American Bureau of the Ministry of Foreign Affairs and that he would be happy to serve as a direct avenue of communication between the Foreign Minister and myself whenever I might desire. In thanking Mr. Kase I recalled our former pleasant association and told him I was glad once again to find him in the role of interpreter during my conversations with the Foreign Minister.

THE AMBASSADOR IN JAPAN REPORTS TO THE
SECRETARY OF STATE

(Substance)

(Paraphrase of original text prepared by the Department of State)

Tokyo, November 3, 1941

The Ambassador reports for Secretary Hull and Under Secretary Welles as follows:

He cites a leading article from the Tokyo *Nichi Nichi* of November 1 (reported in telegram No. 1729 of that date), adding that a banner headline declaring "Empire Approaches Its Greatest Crisis" introduced a dispatch from New York with a summary of a statement the Japanese Embassy reportedly gave to *The New York Times* regarding the need of ending the United States-Japanese economic war. Both the article and the *Nichi Nichi* editorial are believed to be close reflections of Japanese sentiments at present.

The Ambassador refers to his various telegraphic reports during several months past analyzing the factors affecting policy in Japan and says he has nothing to add thereto nor any substantial revision to make thereof. In his opinion, a conclusive estimate may be had of Japan's position through the application to the existing situation and the immediate future of the following points:

(*a*) It is not possible for Japan to dissociate either Japan or the conflict with China from the war in Europe and its fluctuations.

(*b*) In Japan political thought ranges from medieval to liberal ideas and public opinion is thus a variable quantity. The impact of events and conditions beyond Japan may determine at any given time which school of thought shall predominate. (In the democracies, on the other hand, owing to a homogeneous body of principles which influence and direct foreign policy and because methods instead of principles are more likely to cause differences of opinion, public opinion is formed differently.) For example, in Japan the pro-Axis elements gained power following last year's German victories in Western Europe; then Japanese doubt of ultimate German victory was created by Germany's failure to invade the British Isles, this factor helping to reinforce the moderate elements; and finally Germany's attack on the Soviet Union upset the expectation of continued Russo-German peace and made the Japanese realize that those who took Japan into the Tripartite Alliance had misled Japan.

(c) An attempt to correct the error of 1940 may be found in the efforts to adjust Japanese relations with the United States and thereby to lead the way to conclusion of peace with China, made by Prince Konoye and promised by the Tojo cabinet. If this attempt fails, and if success continues to favor German arms, a final, closer Axis alignment may be expected.

(d) The Embassy in Japan has never been convinced by the theory that Japan's collapse as a militaristic power would shortly result from the depletion and the eventual exhaustion of Japan's financial and economic resources, as propounded by many leading American economists. Such forecasts were unconsciously based upon the assumption that a dominant consideration would be Japan's retention of the capitalistic system. The outcome they predicted has not transpired, although it is true that the greater part of Japan's commerce has been lost, Japanese industrial production has been drastically curtailed, and Japan's national resources have been depleted. Instead, there has been a drastic prosecution of the process to integrate Japan's national economy, lacking which there might well have occurred the predicted collapse of Japan. What has happened to date therefore does not support the view that continuation of trade embargoes and imposition of a blockade (proposed by some) can best avert war in the Far East.

The Ambassador mentions his telegram No. 827, September 12, 1940 (which reported the "golden opportunity" seen by Japanese Army circles for expansion as a consequence of German triumphs in Europe). He sent this telegram under circumstances and at a time when it appeared unwise and futile for the United States to adopt conciliatory measures. The strong policy recommended in the telegram was subsequently adopted by the United States. This policy, together with the impact of world political events upon Japan, brought the Japanese Government to the point of seeking conciliation with the United States. If these efforts fail, the Ambassador foresees a probable swing of the pendulum in Japan once more back to the former Japanese position or even farther. This would lead to what he has described as an all-out, do-or-die attempt, actually risking national hara-kiri to make Japan impervious to economic embargoes abroad rather than to yield to foreign pressure. It is realized by observers who feel Japanese national temper and psychology from day to day that, beyond peradventure, this contingency not only is possible but is probable.

If the fiber and temper of the Japanese people are kept in mind, the view that war probably would be averted, though there might be some risk of war, by progressively imposing drastic economic measures is an uncertain and dangerous hypothesis upon which to base considered United States policy and measures. War would not be averted by such a course if it is taken, in the opinion of the Embassy. However, each view is only opinion, and, accordingly, to postulate the correctness of either one and to erect a definitive policy thereon would, in the belief of the Embassy, be contrary to American national interests. It would mean putting the cart before the horse. The primary point to be decided apparently involves the question whether war with Japan is justified by American national objectives, policies, and needs in the case of failure of the first line of national defense, namely, diplomacy, since it would be possible only on the basis of such a decision for the Roosevelt administration to follow a course which would be divested as much as possible of elements of uncertainty, speculation, and opinion. The Ambassador does not doubt that such a decision, irrevocable as it might well prove to be, already has been debated fully and adopted, because the sands are running fast.

The Ambassador emphasizes that, in the above discussion of this grave, momentous subject, he is out of touch with the intentions and thoughts of the administration thereon, and he does not at all mean to imply that Washington is pursuing an undeliberated policy. Nor does he intend to advocate for a single moment any "appeasement" of Japan by the United States or recession in the slightest degree by the United States Government from the fundamental principles laid down as a basis for the conduct and adjustment of international relations, American relations with Japan included. There should be no compromise with principles, though methods may be flexible. The Ambassador's purpose is only to ensure against the United States becoming involved in war with Japan because of any possible misconception of Japan's capacity to rush headlong into a suicidal struggle with the United States. While national sanity dictates against such action, Japanese sanity cannot be measured by American standards of logic.

The Ambassador sees no need for much anxiety respecting the bellicose tone and substance at present of the Japanese press (which in the past several years has attacked the United States intensely in recurrent waves), but he points out the shortsightedness of underestimating Japan's obvious preparations to implement an alternative program in the event the peace program fails. He adds that similarly it would be shortsighted for American policy to be based upon the belief that Japanese preparations are no more than saber rattling, merely intended to give moral support to the high pressure diplomacy of Japan. Action by Japan which might render unavoidable an armed conflict with the United States may come with dangerous and dramatic suddenness.

NATIONAL HARA-KIRI NOT ONLY POSSIBLE BUT PROBABLE

November 4, 1941

My thoughts with regard to the general situation in Japan, and as bearing upon American-Japanese relations, were expressed in my telegram of November 3. If war should occur, I hope that history will not overlook that telegram and especially the statement that it our peace efforts should fail, Japan may go all-out in a do-or-die effort to render herself invulnerable to foreign economic pressure, even to the extent of committing national hara-kiri, and that those of us who are in direct touch with the atmosphere from day to day realize that this is not only possible *but probable;* that Japan's standards of logic or reason cannot be gauged by any Western measuring rod; that it would be hazardous to base our national policy on the belief, held in certain quarters, that our economic pressure will not drive Japan to war; that we would be lacking in perspicacity if we were to disregard or underestimate Japan's preparations for war in case its alternative program for peace should fail or if we were to regard these preparations merely as bluff designed to reinforce Japan's diplomacy; and that war between Japan and the United States may come *with dangerous and dramatic suddenness.* That important telegram is on the record for all time.

KURUSU PREPARES TO LEAVE FOR WASHINGTON

November 4, 1941

Kase came at 12:10 with a message from the Foreign Minister that he wanted to send Kurusu to Washington to help Admiral Nomura with the conversations but that the American clipper was scheduled to leave Hong Kong tomorrow morning and that unless he could go on that plane it would be too late to wait a fortnight for the next one because, "for technical reasons," he must be in Washington by the 13th. Before the Diet meeting on the 15th, of course. If the clipper could not be held up for two days to permit Kurusu to fly to Hong Kong, the only alternative would be for Kurusu to fly to Saipan and to take a destroyer over to Guam, to catch the plane there. I knew very well that our Government would not welcome the latter plan.

Dooman telephoned to Max Hamilton in Washington, and the latter must have done some pretty snappy work because within a few hours Hamilton telephoned back that it was all arranged for the clipper to delay its departure from Hong Kong from the 5th till the 7th. I immediately called Togo on the telephone and he seemed very much pleased.

Kurusu came in at 9 P.M. to see me before leaving early tomorrow morning. He said that he was astonished when Togo broached the mission to him only yesterday afternoon. Since then he had been studying the papers relating to the conversations and he realized that he had a difficult problem. He said that he was going merely to bring a fresh point of view to the conversations and to leave no stone unturned to reach an agreement. He gave no impression that he was taking any specific proposal in his pocket. He wants to take Yuki of the American Bureau of the Foreign Office as secretary if an extra seat on the clipper can be found for him.

Kurusu, who used to be Chief of the Commercial Bureau of the Foreign Office at the time when the long negotiations with the oil companies were going on, was last Ambassador in Rome and then in Berlin, and he it was who signed the Tripartite Pact, but I have no reason to believe that he is any more friendly to the Nazis than to us. His wife is American and his daughter, Jaye, was a great friend of Elsie's. We had a long and very frank talk, and he met my remarks about our position without heat and with a reasonable and objective presentation of Japan's position, going back to the days of the Shidehara diplomacy and the reasons for its failure and the fact that it had been interpreted by the Chinese as a display of weakness.

THE JAPANESE PRESS THROWS A MONKEY WRENCH

November 5, 1941

The *Japan Times and Advertiser* came out with a nasty editorial today attacking the United States and listing seven points which the United States, on its own initiative, should adopt as a program to make "restitution" to Japan, as follows:

1. Stoppage of all military and economic aid to Chungking by all foreign states. Cessation of propaganda by military missions which now try to keep Chungking fighting Japan or in a state of civil disturbance.

2. Leave China completely free to deal with Japan and therefore end hostilities and establish economic co-operation. America could advise Chungking to make its peace with Japan.

3. Stop encirclement of Japan by military, naval, and air bases and by erection of economic barriers. Proceed no further with military naval movements in the western Pacific under the pretext of defense.

4. Acknowledge Japan's Co-Prosperity Sphere and leadership of the western Pacific, letting Manchuria, China, Indo-China, Thailand, the Netherlands Indies and other states and protectorates establish their own political and economic relations with Japan without interference of any kind.

5. Take the obviously necessary course recognizing Manchukuo if it desires. A state exists, headed by the Emperor, which nobody will change. Common political sense, let alone statesmanship, dictates such diplomatic recognition.

6. Stop immediately and unconditionally the freezing of Japan's and China's assets in America, Britain, the Netherlands Indies, and wherever that provocative measure has been applied.

7. Restore trade treaties, abolish all restrictions on shipping and commerce, undo everything wrongfully done in the name of peace but with the design of war, whether economic or military.

The American correspondents were informed in advance last night about midnight and they rushed to their offices and, I understand, cabled the whole editorial textually to the United States, where it very likely made the front pages of the newspapers. If anything could render utterly hopeless the prospect of our coming to an understanding with Japan, this editorial, from a newspaper known to be the organ of the Japanese Foreign Office, would appear to do it, and my guess is that the American people will not be sympathetic to further efforts toward conciliation. This sort of stuff is as stupid as it is discouraging. It certainly affords no help to Kurusu if it hasn't wrecked his mission in advance.

Nothing could better illustrate the childishness of the Japanese: they want and need an understanding with the United States and yet, even while efforts are going on to reach such an understanding,

they continue to fill their press with hostile articles which tend to render an understanding impossible. It is done partly, of course, for domestic consumption, to show what patriots they are, but it is also done with the idea of intimidating the United States, especially the isolationists and pacifists in the United States, with a view to forcing our Government to come to terms with Japan on Japan's terms. Considering that the utterances of our isolationists are splashed across the front pages of the Japanese press under big head-lines, it is no wonder that the Japanese people believe that they represent the majority of American public opinion. As usual Japan follows her ally, Germany, in totally misjudging foreign psychology, particularly Anglo-Saxon psychology.

I have about given up hope of the Washington conversations' making any progress, but if the door can be kept open and a complete breakdown avoided, it may be that we can tide things over until the inevitable crack in Germany and the German Army begins, and then the problem will gradually solve itself. That is about the best we can hope for now.

On October 31 the *Japan Times and Advertiser* published another nasty editorial stating as categorical fact that in return for the Lend-Lease aid to Chungking, the United States had demanded what amounts to a "mortgage" on the Chinese Republic; specifically: (1) the exclusive rights to maintain and utilize four unnamed naval bases in China, to be retained in the postwar period, and (2) the adoption by China of economic measures, such as removal of trade restrictions, nondiscriminatory use of raw materials, et cetera, which would result in the virtual economic domination of China by the United States. The editorial states that these "demands" which were presented at pistol point by the Magruder mission have been accepted in principle by the Chungking Government as a basis for discussion.

After pointing out that the Chungking Government is not China and contrasting these alleged "demands" on the part of the United States with the "co-operative" and "reciprocal" nature of Japan's program in respect to China, the editorial concludes: "Now it can be seen that the Lend-Lease aid to Chungking was not to help 'poor China' but to expand rich America."

I said to the Department that while I had in general found it wise and expedient to ignore such inaccurate and malicious attacks in the Japanese press, I felt that the charges in this particular editorial were too important to let go by and I asked if the Department would approve of my issuing a statement of denial. The Department replied that it appreciated the restraint I had shown in ignoring such false statements and attacks on the United States but in this particular case it authorized the issuance of a denial. Accordingly I wrote the following letter, which was published in the *Japan Times and Advertiser* on November 5 under the heading "U. S. Embassy Denies Report":

To THE EDITOR:

While it is not the usual practice of the American Embassy in Tokyo to take public cognizance of inaccuracies appearing in the press with regard to the policies and actions of the United States, the Embassy is constrained, under present circumstances, to depart from that practice in respect of certain specific charges put forward in the editorial of the October 31 issue of the *Japan Times and Advertiser*.

It was alleged therein that the United States had presented at Chungking certain demands which, if accepted, would create a mortgage on China, these demands, specifically, being: first, exclusive rights to maintain and utilize four unnamed naval bases in China to be retained in the postwar period, and, second, the adoption by China of certain economic measures which would result in the virtual economic domination of China by the United States.

The American Embassy is authorized to say that these charges are without foundation in fact and are, therefore, wholly imaginary.

TOGO AND SHIGEMITSU LISTEN TO REASON

November 7, 1941

At the Soviet Embassy reception today, to celebrate their national holiday (they are the only diplomatic mission which now holds such receptions), I took occasion to make the strongest representations to every Japanese to whom I talked with regard to the *Times and Advertiser* editorial, mentioned above, listing seven points as a program for American "restitution" to Japan, and to point out what serious harm the editorial had done, especially at the moment of sending Kurusu to the United States to try to bring the current conversations to a successful conclusion. I spoke of the utter stupidity of creating such a hostile atmosphere here and such an unfortunate impression on the American public at a moment when constructive, not destructive, results were desired. I made it clear that it was not my intention to presume to interfere with the Japanese press but only to point out factually the inevitable effects in my country when such editorials, assumed to represent the views of the Japanese Government since the *Times and Advertiser* is known to be controlled by the Foreign Office, were reprinted in the United States.

Togo, the Foreign Minister, appeared to know nothing about the editorial and was sure that it had not been inspired by the Foreign Office, but he undertook to look into it and a few moments later he called Toshi Go, editor of the paper, over to him and told him what I had said. I also spoke to Toshi Go, who said that he alone was responsible for the editorial and had written it himself as indicating Japan's maximum demands which would undoubtedly be far beyond what the Government would ask for in the conversations. I told him that he could have no conception of the harm that he had done. Somebody else told me that Go had published the editorial as a protest against the secrecy under which the conversations were being held.

Shigemitsu,* with whom I talked, was thoroughly sympathetic and said that he would do his best to stop this sort of thing, while Matsumoto, head of Domei, promised me that there would be an immediate change in the tone and substance of the Japanese press, and he was as good as his word because the tone did immediately change for the better. I think I succeeded in stirring them all up considerably, so the gathering at the Soviet party was distinctly useful.

The next time I called on Togo I repeated these representations and he replied that while the Foreign Office had exerted no control over the *Times and Advertiser* up to the present, it was jolly well going to exert such control from now on. The editorial may or may not have been dictated by the Foreign Office, regardless of what Toshi Go said. One informant said that it had been so dictated, but if so, I think it was probably done by some subordinate official and without the knowledge of the Minister, who, I am convinced, knew nothing about it.

Perhaps I may have overemphasized the effect of the editorial on the American public, but my guess is that it made the front pages of the papers at home, as the radio commentators talked a good deal about it.

* Former Japanese Ambassador to London, who replaced Togo as Foreign Minister in April, 1943.

While on the subject of publicity I find pertinent and very interesting the same situation obtaining when James Gallatin (whose fascinating diary I am reading for the second time) was doing his best to bring England and the United States to peace prior to the Treaty of Ghent. He writes from London under date of April 21, 1814, to William H. Crawford, Secretary of War:

They [the English people] eagerly wish "the punishment of America." They do not even suspect that we had any just cause for war, and ascribe it solely to a premeditated concert with Bonaparte at a time when we thought him triumphant and their cause desperate. That such opinions should be almost universally entertained here by the great body of the people is not at all astonishing. To produce such an effect, and thereby render the American war popular, the Ministerial powers have had nothing more to do than to transcribe American Federal speeches and newspapers. If Pickering, Quincy, Strong, Hanson, &c. have not brought a majority of the American people to their side they have at least fully succeeded here, and had no difficulty in convincing all that part of the English community which derives its information from political journals that we had no cause of complaint [in the War of 1812] and acted only as allies of Bonaparte.

If we substitute for Pickering, Quincy, Strong, Hanson, et cetera, the names of some of our isolationists, the analogy is clear, for it is the speeches of those gentlemen that are splashed across the front pages of the Japanese press, and the Japanese people naturally assume that they represent the great majority of American public sentiment.

The President said today that the Government of the United States is giving consideration to the question of withdrawal of the American marine detachments now maintained ashore in China at Peiping, Tientsin, and Shanghai.

· WHY JAPAN WOULD PREFER WATCHFUL
WAITING TO WAR AGAINST RUSSIA

November 7, 1941

With reference to a possible Japanese attack on the Soviet Far East, although its true program in this respect is obviously not known, it can only be said that since the formation of the Tojo Government there have been no indications which would justify the belief that an attack on the Soviet Union forms one of the imme-

diate intentions of that Government. Such inconclusive indications
as have recently been apparent point rather toward an effort on the
part of the Tojo Government to maintain normal relations with the
Soviet Government and possibly efforts through negotiations to take
advantage of the present position of the Soviet Union in order to
secure for Japan certain desiderata especially in relation to Soviet
policy toward China. Some clue in regard to the immediate intentions of Japan in this respect may be found in the fact that both the
new Minister and Vice-Minister for Foreign Affairs have personally
had experience in constructive dealings with the Soviet Government.

It has been noted that since the formation of the new Government the press has been in general more circumspect and objective
toward the Soviet-German war. On October 31 the *Nichi Nichi* referred in its leading editorial to certain unsettled aspects of Soviet-
Japanese relations and observed that the continued Soviet attitude
of support to Chiang Kai-shek despite the existence of the Japanese-
Soviet neutrality pact was an impediment to improvement in relations between the two countries, and in this connection urged the
new Foreign Minister to take advantage of the present opportunity
to adjust these unsettled questions. In addition the *Japan Times
and Advertiser,* which is generally considered to be the mouthpiece
of the Japanese Foreign Office, in commenting editorially during
the past two weeks on the German-Soviet war has in general tended
to stress the view that even if all of European Russia, including
Moscow and Leningrad, fall into the hands of the Germans there
will be no collapse of the Soviet regime since the Soviet Government has at its disposal sufficient men, material resources, and industrial bases to continue the war, with British and American
assistance, from Siberia.

While clearly any signs that the disintegration of the Soviet
regime was imminent would immediately transform the situation,
the indications are that Japan for the near future at least will continue its previous attitude of watchful waiting along the Soviet Far
Eastern frontiers. The best available estimates of the number of
Japanese troops in Manchuria vary from half a million to eight
hundred thousand. This force, while ample to take advantage of
any disintegration in Siberia following a collapse of the Soviet system, is not regarded by competent military observers as sufficient to
carry out a full-fledged attack on Siberia so long as the Soviet Far
Eastern forces are intact.

With reference to the foregoing, it is yet too early to estimate the possible effect on Soviet-Japanese relations of the sinking of the *Kehi Maru* allegedly by a Soviet mine, although up to the present there is no indication in the press of any desire to exploit this accident and Japanese reaction has so far been confined to a protest to the Soviet Ambassador here. This disaster took place following a number of Japanese complaints concerning the presence of Soviet floating mines in waters adjacent to Japan.

JAPAN'S PRESS PIPES DOWN

November 8, 1941

In view of the unrestrained tone of the Japanese press during the past week in its numerous articles devoted to discussion of the United States and foreign policy, it is significant that the flow of invective appears suddenly to have ceased, judging by this morning's newspapers. Aside from one relatively mild editorial in the *Miyako* regarding the Kurusu mission and Japanese-American conversations, the papers confine their comment to subjects which, from our point of view, are quite innocuous.

CHURCHILL PLEDGES WAR WITHIN THE HOUR

November 11, 1941

Churchill has come out with the statement that "if the United States should be involved in a war with Japan, a British declaration of war would follow within the hour." It does one's heart good to hear such an unqualified statement by the British Prime Minister, leaving nothing whatever to Japan's imagination.

"WHEN DOGS ARE FRIGHTENED, THEY BARK"

November 13, 1941

The editorial in this week's *Japan Times Weekly* begins with the sentence: "In many ways the political and economic program now under way between Japan and French Indo-China furnishes a cross section of Japan's idea of a co-prosperity sphere." Knowing what is going on in Indo-China today and the methods by which Japan obtained her present stranglehold on that country, it is refreshing to have so clear-cut an acknowledgment of just what Japan's program is.

The naïveté of the Japanese is really amazing. They love high-sounding formulas and slogans to cover whatever they want and intend to do, with the idea of imparting to their plans the most perfect righteousness, lulling even themselves into the belief that their acts are wholly righteous. Thus "The New Order in Greater East Asia" and "The East Asia Co-Prosperity Sphere" and their "immutable" policies. A Japanese friend said to me the other day: "The trouble with you Anglo-Saxons is that you regard and deal with the Japanese as grown-up people, whereas the Japanese are but children and should be treated like children. An encouraging word or gesture immediately inspires confidence. The Germans understand this psychology of the Japanese and they have played upon it with marked success." I might add, parenthetically, that if this is true, it is the first time in my experience that the Germans have understood any foreign psychology.

That same friend, in reply to my observations about the immense harm being done by the hostile utterances of the Japanese press and many Japanese writers and speakers, said: "When dogs are frightened, they bark, and the more they are frightened, the louder they bark. Just now, the Japanese, even the military people, are frightened. Don't pay any attention to the Japanese press."

I had to say to my friend that when so important a paper as the *Nichi Nichi* comes out with an article charging that the United States acts "like a prostitute, whispering on dark corners," as that paper did the other day, it is a little difficult for an American and for the American people not to pay any attention to it.

TOJO ADDRESSES THE JAPANESE DIET

November 16, 1941

This morning I attended the ceremonial opening of the Diet in the presence of the Emperor, taking Turner and Fearey of our Embassy with me. The Axis diplomats were there in force and a few neutrals, but Craigie did not come. The Canadian and Australian representatives did come after consulting me; I knew that my absence would be noticed and saw no reason to leave the field to the Axis or to convey the impression that I regarded the situation with the United States as critical, especially in the presence of the Emperor. Although we all met in the big reception room and, as usual, I shook hands with Ott, the German Ambassador, and Indelli, the Italian Ambassador, we were for the first time separated in the dip-

lomatic box, the Turk, the Thai, and myself taking seats on the
left, while the German and Italian moved to the right, carefully
directed by Okubo, Master of Ceremonies. Okubo has an eagle eye
in chaperoning the Diplomatic Corps: he sent one man packing because he wore a short jacket instead of the required morning coat,
and he also discovered and ousted another, who is not on the diplomatic list but came to interpret for his chief.

The next day, when the Prime Minister and Foreign Minister
made their speeches, four members of our staff were in the diplomatic box and at the end of Tojo's address, Smith-Hutton, our
Naval Attaché, leaned over to Benninghoff, one of our secretaries,
and whispered: "Well, he didn't declare war, anyway." The *Asahi*
commented:

> Four staff members of the American Embassy first appeared at
> the seats reserved for foreign guests in the House of Peers,
> where the Premier made his first administrative speech. At the
> close of the Prime Minister's speech thundering applause re-
> sounded throughout the House of Peers, where normally even
> excellent speeches fail to receive a clapping of hands. The four
> staff members of the American Embassy suddenly went into a
> huddle and conversed with each other. And then they all
> strongly shook their heads, although no one knows what they
> meant by this conduct. All others in the visitors' gallery looked
> at them with fixed attention.

The speeches were chiefly for domestic consumption, but they
won't make a good impression in our country, particularly Togo's
three points for reaching an understanding with the United States,
as follows:

1. Third powers will refrain from obstructing a successful conclusion of the China affair, which Japan has in view. '

2. The countries surrounding our Empire will not only refrain
from presenting a direct military menace to our Empire, but will
nullify such measures of a hostile character as economic blockade
and restore normal economic relations with Japan.

3. Utmost efforts will be exerted to prevent the extension of the
European war and the spread of the disturbances into East Asia.

Thus Japan's "immutable" policy.

IT'S UP TO AMERICA TO KEEP THE PEACE

November 18, 1941

The editorial in this morning's *Japan Times and Advertiser* contains the paragraph:

> The outstanding issues between Japan and America, as Ambassador Grew said, may be counted by the hundred. But what seems most important at this juncture is that the American Government should realize the all-importance of imparting to Japan a sense of security. The formidable cordon of naval and air bases which America has developed round Japan in concert with Britain, the Netherlands East Indies, Australia, and Chungking constitutes a direct threat against the Japanese Empire. As long as this strategic situation persists, Japan can have little assurance of security or safety. If America desires no war in this part of the world, it should realize that it holds in its own hands the key to the solution of the whole situation.

Typical of the viewpoint here. It is always we who threaten; it is always we who are the potential aggressor, never Japan. Thus does the United States wholly "misunderstand" Japan's peaceful intentions in developing the New Order and the Co-Prosperity Sphere, and thus do we render an adjustment of relations impossible by "encircling" (a word so loved by the Nazis) innocent and unoffending Nippon.

SECOND THOUGHTS ON PRINCE KONOYE

November 21, 1941

Have often thought about my letter to Prince Konoye, in reply to his letter informing me of the fall of his cabinet, and especially my allusion to the distinguished service which he had rendered his country. Some people might quibble at that statement, on the ground that he had led his country into all sorts of difficulties, including the Axis alliance. I grant all that, but I put it down more to the nefarious influence of Matsuoka than to Konoye himself, who had his own military people and the extremists to deal with.

The chief reason why I mentioned his outstanding service was the fact that he alone tried to reverse the engine, and tried hard and courageously, even risking his life and having a very close call as it was. Whatever mistakes he made in directing Japan's policy, he had the sense and the courage to recognize those mistakes and to try to start his country on a new orientation of friendship with the United

States. If only for that, I think he deserves some degree of good will. With the invasion of Indo-China staring us in the face during the Washington conversations, it is difficult for anyone not living in Japan and understanding the forces and stresses loose in this misguided country to appreciate what Konoye was up against, but I do, and hence that allusion in my letter. I would not change it if I had the letter to write again.

KURUSU: MISSION EMBARRASSES GERMANY

November 20, 1941

Thanksgiving Day. The service at the American Union Church was put ahead to 10:30 so that we could attend the Esin-Tek wedding at 12. Craigie, Officer, Politis, Madame Forthomme, among other foreigners, attended, for they wished to show their gratitude to our country, and I am glad that Dr. Axling gave a very fine and inspiring address, but it was longer than expected and Craigie and we ourselves had to leave before the service was over. I read the President's Proclamation, as usual.

An interesting telegram from Berlin says that the Japanese Embassy in Berlin has been embarrassed by the sending of Kurusu to Washington and resents it, Ambassador Oshima insisting to the Germans that no matter what happens in Washington, Japan fully intends to carry on her southward advance. It is said that, in Oshima's opinion, the United States will do nothing at present to stop a Japanese attack on the Dutch East Indies or on the Burma Road and that the situation is more favorable now than it will be later.

It is possible that these views of Oshima reflect the efforts of the Nazis to impress Japanese circles in Berlin with the conclusive character of the German victories in Russia, but it is likewise probable that Oshima knows very well that any real alteration of Japanese policy toward moderation would render his own position difficult both in Berlin and in Tokyo. General Oshima is of the Shiratori school of thought and a dyed-in-the-wool pro-Nazi.

THE AMERICAN TEN-POINT OFFER REACHES JAPAN

November 29, 1941

Our Government has handed to the Japanese a ten-point draft proposal for adjusting the whole situation in the Far East. It is a broad-gauge, objective, and statesmanlike document, offering to Japan practically everything that she has ostensibly been fighting for if she will simply stop her aggressive policy. By adopting such a program she would be offered free access to needed raw materials, free trade and commerce, financial co-operation and support, withdrawal of the freezing orders, and an opportunity to negotiate a new treaty of commerce with us. If she wants a political and economic stranglehold on the countries of East Asia (euphemistically called the New Order in East Asia and the East Asia Co-Prosperity Sphere)—which most of her extremists do want—and if she pursues her southward advance by force, she will soon be at war with all of the A B C D powers and will unquestionably be defeated and reduced to the status of a third-rate power. But if she plays her cards wisely, she can obtain without further fighting all of the desiderata for which she allegedly started fighting—strategic, economic, financial, and social security.

Japanese public opinion can always be molded, in a comparatively short time, and the clever move of the Government now would be to persuade the public that the Government, in the Washington conversations, had won a great diplomatic victory by achieving, without further force of arms, the securities or "freedoms" for which she had been fighting.

For the next two or three days I went regularly to the Tokyo Club and talked along the foregoing lines to several prominent Japanese, and I was later told that my observations, which were carefully labeled as purely personal and unofficial, had been brought to the attention of Togo, Prince Konoye, Matsudaira, Marquis Kido, et cetera. It may have helped, although most of the men to whom I talked were very pessimistic as a result of our draft proposal, with which most of them appeared to be familiar. My hope is that my remarks got through to the Emperor. They were very forcibly expressed.

In the meantime, however, the Japanese were pouring more troops and supplies into southern Indo-China and giving every indication of an intention to invade Thailand. Also, at this critical juncture, the Prime Minister took the occasion of the celebration of the anniversary of the Anti-Comintern Pact to make a speech in which he said that the United States and Britain were putting the peoples of East Asia against each other in order to grasp hegemony in the Far East and that "for the honor and pride of mankind, we must purge this sort of practice from East Asia with a vengeance."

The President interrupted his brief visit to Warm Springs, Georgia, to hurry back to Washington, and I have little doubt that Tojo's bellicose speech was at least one reason for the hurry. The speech, at this critical moment, was utterly stupid; of course, it was chiefly for domestic consumption but it clearly represented the belief of most Japanese that the United States can be intimidated by a sufficient amount of saber rattling; and if the Government really wants to remain at peace with us, it seems to be the height of stupidity to continue to inflame domestic public opinion against us. Once again I am impressed with the truth of the remark of a Japanese friend that when dogs are frightened, they bark, and the more they are frightened, the louder they bark; and also that the Japanese are really children and should be treated as children. The Prime Minister's speech seems to me to be utterly childish. Where is the much-vaunted Japanese statesmanship of olden days?

JAPAN'S PESSIMISTIC REACTION TO THE AMERICAN PROPOSALS

December 1, 1941

During the past several days I have talked with a number of prominent Japanese, some of whom have been in direct touch with the Foreign Minister, and most of them appeared to be already familiar with the substance of our Government's recent ten-point draft proposal. While desirous of continuing the Washington conversations, they all reflect a pessimistic reaction, perceiving the difficulties of bridging over the positions of the two countries and emphasizing what they seem to regard as the unconciliatory "tone" of our proposal.

In all of my talks I have stressed my personal opinion that our draft is a proposal of the highest statesmanship, envisaging an objective and broad-gauge plan, because it offers to Japan in effect the very things for which she says that she has been fighting, as well as a peaceful and logical way of achieving without further fighting her constantly publicized desiderata. At the same time I have expressed in no uncertain terms my surprise that at this critical juncture the Prime Minister should have seen fit to deliver an address which can only be regarded as bellicose in tone and substance, and I have made clear the deplorable and serious reaction which that speech will surely have created in the United States and on the American Government and people.

I have also said that the Japanese Government is now in a position to mold public opinion to the conception that the Government has won a diplomatic victory in the conversations (if face must be saved) by securing without further fighting the chief purposes for which she ostensibly took up arms in the beginning.

The papers tonight report that the cabinet today decided to continue the conversations in spite of the difficulties of reaching an adjustment.

I saw one of my old Japanese friends at the Tokyo Club tonight; he looked gray and worn and he told me that the cabinet had decided to break off the conversations. I said that in that case I feared that everything was over and that I would soon be leaving Japan. Soon afterward, however, the press announced that the conversations would be continued. But my friend seemed crushed.

TOGO IS DISAPPOINTED

December 3, 1941

Attended the funeral of the Dowager Princess Kaya, with all the ceremonial rites customary at Imperial funerals. It was very cold and since we could not wear coats I had put on two sets of underclothes and a sweater. Found myself next to the German Ambassador when standing in line waiting for the hearse. I merely asked after Frau Ott and he replied that she was in Kobe. I led the Diplomatic Corps to the altar to place the *sakaki* branches, and then went out just behind the Prime Minister, General Tojo. Foreign Minister Togo said to me, while we were awaiting our cars: "I am very much disappointed." I replied: "Let us continue the conversations in any case." Admiral Shimada, the Navy Minister, greeted me cordially.

"WASHINGTON HAS DELIVERED AN ULTIMATUM TO US"

December 5, 1941

Yesterday I received in his own handwriting a letter from a prominent Japanese who is closely in touch with Government circles here. This letter reads in part as follows: "The situation is very regrettable. You know how I feel and I may understand your feelings. Permit me to set forth frankly to you what is now in my mind.

I have had conversations with friends and after examining their feelings I have come to the conclusion that they believe, with no knowledge of the actual contents of the American document of November 26, that Washington has delivered an ultimatum to us. Such is the regrettable psychology of our people that in my opinion the only way out at the present time is for the United States to accept as a possible basis for a *modus vivendi* the Japanese proposals and later on work out a final agreement in line with the American proposal. I am emboldened to write to you by my hope that matters will end happily."

In my opinion the above letter is a fair sample of public opinion in Japan at the present time.

MORE JAPANESE SUSPICIONS THAT AMERICA STALLS FOR TIME

December 6, 1941

According to a Japanese informant of known reliability, neither the Prime Minister nor any member of the cabinet had seen the text of General Tojo's speech of November 30 in advance and it is believed that it was written by some person in the Imperial Rule Assistance Association. The address was read by proxy, as is often done in Japan, and it is pointed out that the substance and tone of the speech are different from all General Tojo's previous addresses.

It is secretly reported that according to news from a fairly reliable informant, although unconfirmed, the Nazi terrorist organization, directed by Wiedemann, is making a desperate effort to sabotage the Washington conversations, and that three German agents of this organization carried out the recent bombing attacks on an American-owned oil-storage tank and on the American Consulate at Saigon, in order to create the impression on the Americans that the Japanese had inspired the attack. The chief purpose of this organization is to work against American interests in the Far East and its activities will probably soon be intensified.

ROOSEVELT APPEALS TO HIROHITO

December 7, 1941

Today the radio announced that the President had sent a message to the Emperor of Japan but gave no information as to its substance or the channel of transmission. Late in the evening, however, a short triple-priority telegram came from Mr. Hull saying that a telegram was then being encoded containing a message from the President which I was to communicate to the Emperor at the earliest possible moment. I immediately asked Dooman to come to the Embassy and telephone to Tomoda, Togo's secretary, to make an urgent appointment with the Minister for me around midnight; that is, Dooman telephoned as soon as the message itself had arrived and was being decoded. That telegram had been received at the Japanese telegraph office at noon, as indicated thereon, but in spite of its urgency was not delivered until 10:30 P.M. The two telegrams had been sent from the Department December 6 at 8 P.M. and 9 P.M. respectively. Tomoda seemed upset at my asking for an appointment so late and he asked Dooman if the matter was so urgent that it couldn't wait till tomorrow. Dooman's impression the next day was that Tomoda could not possibly have then known of the impending outbreak of war.

Tomoda, however, made the appointment and Benninghoff kindly drove me to the Minister's official residence at 12:15 A.M., our own chauffeurs having long gone home. Togo saw me immediately and I requested an audience with the Emperor in order to present the President's message, which I then read aloud and handed a copy to Togo. The Department had left to my discretion the appropriate method of communication and I felt it important to give it the maximum weight by asking to see the Emperor myself —and to make sure that it got to him personally. Togo at first said that he would study the document, but when I asked if that meant some doubt as to whether he would ask for an audience for me, he replied that he would present the matter to the Throne. He made some further remarks about the Washington conversations, but when I said that I had not yet received a report of the conversation of December 5 and that it would merely complicate matters if I should undertake to repeat his comments to the Department, he said that it was not necessary. I left him at about 12:30 A.M.

The Secretary's instructions and the President's message to the Emperor were as follows:

TRIPLE PRIORITY

818, December 6, 9 P.M.

Confidential

Please communicate at the earliest possible moment in such manner as you deem most appropriate a message to the Emperor from the President reading as follows:

"His Imperial Majesty the Emperor of Japan:

"Almost a century ago the President of the United States addressed to the Emperor of Japan a message extending an offer of friendship of the people of the United States to the people of Japan. That offer was accepted and in the long period of unbroken peace and friendship which has followed, our respective nations, through the virtues of their peoples and the wisdom of their rulers, have prospered and have substantially helped humanity.

"Only in situations of extraordinary importance to our two countries need I address to Your Majesty messages on matters of state. I feel I should now so address you because of the deep and far-reaching emergency which appears to be in formation.

"Developments are occurring in the Pacific area which threaten to deprive each of our nations and all humanity of the beneficial influence of the long peace between our two countries. Those developments contain tragic possibilities.

"The people of the United States, believing in peace and in the right of nations to live and let live, have eagerly watched the conversations between our two Governments during these past months. We have hoped for a termination of the present conflict between Japan and China. We have hoped that a peace of the Pacific could be consummated in such a way that nationalities of many diverse peoples could exist side by side without fear of invasion; that unbearable burdens of armaments could be lifted for them all; and that all peoples would resume commerce without discrimination against or in favor of any nation.

"I am certain that it will be clear to Your Majesty, as it is to me, that in seeking these great objectives both Japan and the United States should agree to eliminate any form of military threat. This seems essential to the attainment of the high objectives.

"More than a year ago Your Majesty's Government concluded an agreement with the Vichy Government by which five or six thousand Japanese troops were permitted to enter northern French Indo-China for the protection of Japanese troops which were operating against China further north. And this spring and summer the Vichy Government permitted further Japanese military forces to enter into southern French Indo-China for the common defense of French Indo-China. I think I am correct in saying that no attack has been made upon Indo-China nor that any has been contemplated.

"During the past few weeks it has become clear to the world that Japanese military, naval, and air forces have been sent to southern Indo-China in such large numbers as to create a reasonable doubt on the part of other nations that this continuing concentration in Indo-China is not defensive in its character.

"Because these continuing concentrations in Indo-China have reached such large proportions and because they extend now to the southeast and the southwest corners of that peninsula it is only reasonable that the people of the Philippines, of the hundreds of islands of the East Indies, of Malaya, and of Thailand itself are asking themselves whether these forces of Japan are preparing or intending to make attack in one or more of these many directions.

"I am sure that Your Majesty will understand that the fear of all these peoples is a legitimate fear inasmuch as it involves their peace and their national existence. I am sure that Your Majesty will understand why the people of the United States in such large numbers look askance at the establishment of military, naval, and air bases manned and equipped so greatly as to constitute armed forces capable of measures of offense.

"It is clear that a continuance of such a situation is unthinkable.

"None of the peoples whom I have spoken of above can sit either indefinitely or permanently on a keg of dynamite.

"There is absolutely no thought on the part of the United States of invading Indo-China if every Japanese soldier or sailor were to be withdrawn therefrom.

"I think that we can obtain the same assurance from the Governments of the East Indies, the Governments of Malaya, and the Government of Thailand. I would even undertake to ask for the same assurance on the part of the Government of China. Thus a withdrawal of the Japanese forces from Indo-China would result in the assurance of peace throughout the whole of the south Pacific area.

"I address myself to Your Majesty so that Your Majesty may, as I am doing, give thought in this definite emergency to ways of dispelling the dark clouds. I am confident that both of us, for the sake of the peoples not only of our own great countries but for the sake of humanity in neighboring territories, have a sacred duty to restore traditional amity and prevent further death and destruction in the world.

"FRANKLIN D. ROOSEVELT."

The press here is being informed simply that the President is sending a message to the Emperor.

HULL.

6

ONE WORLD: ONE WAR

(December 8, 1941–May 31, 1942)

JAPAN'S ATTACK on the United States bypassed our first line of national defense—diplomacy— and launched a military offensive without the usual preliminary declaration of hostilities. In consequence, the staff of the American Embassy at Tokyo and all our other officials in the Japanese sphere of influence found themselves isolated from a series of events that shook the world and brought the United States into a global, total war. The Philippines, Wake, and Guam; Hong Kong, Malaya, and Singapore; the Netherlands Indies and Burma, all fell to Japan during the winter and early spring of 1941–42. By the end of May, when arrangements were finally made for the United States and Japan to exchange their diplomats, the Japanese had not only reached the limits of their expansion for the year; they had suffered in the Coral Sea their first defeat and had experienced one bombing of Tokyo. America was passing through its darkest months since the Civil War, yet already the tide of battle had begun to show signs of turning.

WAR

December 8, 1941

At 7 A.M. I was awakened by a telephone call from Kase, who asked me to come to see the Minister as soon as possible. He said that he had been trying to telephone to me ever since 5 A.M. but could not get through. I hurriedly dressed and got to the official residence at about 7:30. Kase was cordial; Togo grim and formal. He made a brief statement which is contained in my report to the Department and then handed to me a memorandum of thirteen pages, dated December 8, which he said had been communicated by Admiral Nomura to the Secretary today, breaking off the conversations. The final paragraph read:

> The Japanese Government regrets to have to notify hereby the American Government that, in view of the attitude of the American Government, it cannot but consider that it is impossible to reach an agreement through further negotiations.

Togo said that he had seen the Emperor (at 3 A.M., I understand), and that the memorandum constituted the Emperor's reply to the President's message. He then made a little speech thanking me for my co-operation during the conversations and came downstairs to see me off at the door. Not a word was said about Pearl Harbor.

On returning to the Embassy I shaved and breakfasted and then sent off my report to the Department, but it probably did not get through. Shortly afterward we heard that Imperial Headquarters had announced that Japan was in armed conflict with the United States and Great Britain. This was contained in a *Yomiuri* statement issued early this morning. At first it was difficult to believe, although it had all the earmarks of officialdom, and later in the morning Ohno, of the Foreign Office, called on Crocker and read to him, his hands trembling, the official announcement that armed conflict had commenced.

Soon afterward the Embassy's gates were closed and we were told that no one could go in or out. Masuo, a clerk in the Foreign Office, was assigned as a liaison officer and to act as a channel between us and the Foreign Office. We were told that no cipher telegrams could be sent and all telegrams must be submitted to the Foreign Office for approval. Sir Robert Craigie came to see me and was stopped by the police at the gate; he dismounted from his car and said who he was, but the police grabbed him by the arms; he shook them off, however, and found an officer to let him in. We had a last talk with mutual expressions of appreciation of our co-operation, which, he said, had been one of the few bright spots during his years in Japan. Mrs. Tillitse, wife of the Danish Minister, also came to see Alice and had difficulty in getting home but finally was able to do so with the aid of a plain-clothes detective. Our last callers early in the morning were Politis, the Greek Minister, and Mrs. de Vigo, wife of the Spanish Minister, who saw Alice.

A group of Japanese radio experts came and went through the chancery and the apartment houses with a fine-tooth comb, taking away all short-wave radio sets. They were very polite but very thorough, but when they came to the residence they took my word for the fact that I had only two radio sets and removed them without searching the other rooms. They were all exceedingly courteous and apologized for the trouble caused, especially Ohno of the Foreign Office, who accompanied them.

The moment we knew that the news of war had been confirmed I gave orders to burn all our codes and confidential correspondence.

Word had meanwhile been passed around that everyone should stay on the compound for his own protection. A telegram *en clair* was prepared for the Department stating that the entire Embassy staff was safe and well, but it was held as it was discovered on checking up that Randall Jones was not accounted for. It developed that, it being his day off, he had gone to Yokohama and had not yet returned. After some anxious moments we were greatly relieved and somewhat surprised to see Jones walking across the compound. It seems that, having heard the news at Yokohama, he took the first train back, without incident, and took a taxi in a perfectly normal manner from Shimbashi Station to the Embassy. Upon arrival he found the Embassy gates locked and ingress and egress both barred. As he was standing uncertain, trying to decide what to do, he was approached by a plain-clothes policeman who pointed to the adjoining compound where the Naval Attaché lives and suggested that he go there and climb into the Embassy compound by the ladder which has been kept against the wall in the Smith-Huttons' garden for a number of years. He took the advice and thus returned safe and sound.

Part of the diary kept by our Counselor, Eugene Dooman, covering the day's events should be included for the record at this point:

My houseboy calls me every morning at 7:30. This morning,
however, he called me shortly before that time to say that Mr.
Max Hill, correspondent of the Associated Press, was on the
telephone. I heard Mr. Hill say: "I shall have to ask the police
whether I can speak to you." I could faintly hear Mr. Hill's
voice at the other end of the phone talking with some Japanese
and I realized that Mr. Hill's remark was intended to convey a
message. After a considerable pause, his maid came to the
phone and said that Mr. Hill had been obliged to leave the
house. I replied that I understood perfectly.

I thereupon called Mr. Benninghoff on the telephone and
asked him to go immediately to Mr. Hill's house to ascertain
what had happened as I very much feared he had been arrested
by the police. At about 8:30 Mr. Benninghoff came to my house
and said that he had just returned from seeing Mr. Hill. He
reported that Mr. Hill was under arrest at his house, and that
he was having breakfast before leaving for the metropolitan
police station, where he was to be put under examination. Mr.
Dynant, the junior correspondent of the Associated Press, and
Mr. Robert Bellaire, correspondent of the United Press, were
also at Mr. Hill's house, but Mr. Benninghoff reported that
they were not permitted by the police to communicate with
Mr. Hill. The last two named correspondents were apparently
not under arrest. Mr. Bellaire had found a moment to tell Mr.
Benninghoff that the Imperial Headquarters had announced
that the Japanese fleet had already come into touch with the
American and British fleets somewhere in the southwestern
Pacific. Mr. Bellaire added also that he had heard that Japanese airplanes had bombed Honolulu this morning early. Mr.
Benninghoff had breakfast with me and then rushed home to
bathe and get ready for the day.

The Japanese have profited by the German methods of *Blitzkrieg*,
a dastardly thing to do while the conversations had not yet broken
down. I do not yet know the precise timing, but it seems to me very
doubtful if Admiral Nomura had informed Mr. Hull of the breakdown of the conversations before Hawaii was bombed and the war
started. If the Japanese had confined themselves to the Far East and
had attacked only the Philippines, there would have been pacifists
and isolationists at home who would have said that we have no
business in the Far East anyway, but once they attacked Hawaii

it was certain that the American people would rise up in a solid unit of fury. Senator Wheeler was quoted on the radio as saying that the United States must "lick hell out of the Japanese." This may be easier said than done; it may take a very long time and we may get some serious knocks before our full power is able to register. But in the long run, Japan's defeat is absolutely certain, for the American people, once aroused, won't let go. With the United States, Britain, Australia, the Netherlands East Indies, and perhaps Soviet Russia, as well as China, eventually out against her, she will have her hands full before very long.

I am glad to have gone on record in a recent telegram to the effect that Japan would be perfectly capable of an all-out, do-or-die attempt to render herself impervious to foreign economic pressure even if it meant national hara-kiri, and that we should be ready for any step of "dangerous and dramatic suddenness." That is now precisely what has happened.

Fortunately, all of our staff, including the noncommissioned staff, were in the compound when ingress and egress were forbidden, except Jones, who was in Yokohama and got safely in. I had already forbidden anyone of our staff to leave the compound even before we were locked in. Rumors are flying around of a difficult domestic situation; even that martial law has been declared in Tokyo, but that I doubt. But there are probably demonstrations going on against us, and Makinson, our First Secretary and Consul General, reports seeing from the windows of the chancery a group of some two hundred Japanese, headed by a large swastika flag, coming toward the Embassy. They apparently never got to it, however.

Max Hamilton telephoned to me from Washington today; I could hear him perfectly but he appeared to have difficulty in understanding me. He said that the Department was considering to whom we should confide our interests in Japan and asked for my views. I mentioned the Argentine and Brazil, although I thought that the latter might come into the war. The British have turned their interests over to the Argentines. Later I sent a telegram mentioning also Switzerland, Spain, and Portugal among the neutrals but don't know if the telegram got through. I said that we had informally suggested to the Foreign Office that the *Tatuta Maru* should continue her voyage to the United States to pick up the Japanese Embassy and Consulates, and that the Japanese might place another vessel at our disposal, but of course we made no commitment as I didn't know what the attitude of the administration might be.

There are a lot of Americans and diplomats on the *Tatuta,* so I suppose we would not wish to interrupt her trip. But perhaps she has already turned back to Japan, anyway. Hamilton expressed a very kind message from all in the Department.

At 6:45 in the evening we had the entire staffs of the Embassy and Consulate in for cocktails, about sixty people. Dooman made a very nice little speech about Alice and myself which moved us very much. Miss Coles, Dooman, Williams, Crocker, Bohlen, Turner, Benninghoff, Cooper, and Espy have all moved in to the Embassy, since they live outside the compound, and we have found beds for all and they will take most of their meals with us. Those who have apartments in the apartment houses are giving shakedowns to anyone who needs a bed or a mattress on the floor. We are a well-united and co-operative group, and a congenial one, which is very helpful at times like these. Everyone was pretty well exhausted tonight, the first day of war with Japan, the only country, so far as I know, that ever declared war on us.

Of course when I saw Togo in the early morning of the 8th he must already have known of the outbreak of war, but he said nothing about it. If any indication was given at all, it was in his gesture when he came into the room and slapped down on the table the Japanese reply to our recent draft proposal, as much as to say that this was final. But his manner was, as usual, wholly imperturbable, and on rising after our talk he made a pleasant little speech of thanks for my co-operation. On leaving his official residence I had not the slightest feeling that a break had occurred, except for a break in the conversations. Togo must have sensed that I had no suspicions whatever as to what had occurred. The conversations had broken down once before, when the Japanese went into Indo-China, yet they were later resumed. The surprise of the *Blitzkrieg* was complete so far as we in the Embassy were concerned, except for my prognostication on November 3 that war might come "with dangerous and dramatic suddenness."

It is significant that the Department's 818, December 6, 9 P.M., communicating the President's message to the Emperor, was actually received at the central telegraph office in Tokyo at noon on the 7th but was not delivered until 10:30 that evening. The notation in Japanese on the telegram made this clear.

PRISONERS OF JAPAN

December 9, 1941

The Superintendent General of the Metropolitan Police, Tsukio Tomeoka, called on me this morning with an aide and interpreter, although Turner did the interpreting, and said that he wished to do everything possible for our comfort and convenience. He was very affable. The subsequent actions and attitude of the police, who treated us in every respect as prisoners, if not as criminal prisoners, invading at will the chancery, the apartment houses, and even the Embassy residence and making every difficulty in our getting food and clothing from outside, were no doubt due to orders from subordinate officers and to the utter stupidity of the police guard in interpreting their instructions without the slightest effort to undersand our position, and I doubt if the Superintendent himself had any knowledge of what was going on.

Ohta, of the European Section of the Foreign Office, also called. He said that Kase, of the American Bureau of the Foreign Office, was to have come today but unfortunately he was very busy. Ohta said that he had just called at the British Embassy to see what could be done to ease the position there, and that he would be glad to receive any suggestions Dooman might make for the improvement of the situation at this Embassy. Dooman called in Benninghoff and together they gave Ohta a long list of matters which had to be dealt with. Among them were included the question of supplying us with fresh foodstuffs, the lack of co-ordination among the Japanese officials here, and the supply of fuel oil. Ohta said that he would take all of these matters under consideration. After Benninghoff left, Ohta referred to the telephone conversation which Dooman had had with Tomoda on Sunday night. Dooman asked Ohta whether the Foreign Minister, in expressing reluctance to stay up very late to receive me, was trying to avoid having to meet me in person again after the beginning of the hostilities. Ohta burst out spontaneously and with considerable feeling, "Not at all. The Foreign Minister knew nothing about the attack on Hawaii until early the next morning." Without pressing the point too far, it seems clear that His Imperial Majesty's Minister for Foreign Affairs had no prior knowledge that an act of war was to be committed by the Japanese forces.

For a while, the Smith-Huttons were able to live in their house just outside the compound and to provide room and board for some sixteen persons, entering the compound by a ladder over the wall (the celebrated ladder used during the February 26 Incident) and they were thus able to bring us newspapers. The police knew of the ladder and at first raised no objections. But then one of our consuls sent for his Chinese servant to come in over the wall, without consulting Dooman or any of the rest of us; the servant, with an armful of eggs, stumbled in the dark directly into the reflection pool and raised such a row that the police came running. This brought about an investigation: the ladder was removed and the Smith-Huttons with all their guests were obliged to come into the compound permanently, sixteen extra persons to bed and feed, necessitating beds being set up in the chancery offices, although we took in the three Smith-Huttons at the residence as well as Dooman, Williams, Crocker, Bohlen, Turner, Benninghoff, and Miss Coles, Alice's secretary. We also kept daily table for fourteen, inviting other members of the staff and clerks in rotation.

For the record I give below the text of the communication handed to Crocker by Ohno, Chief of the Second Section of the American Bureau of the Foreign Office, on the morning of the 8th. We prepared a telegram reporting this document to the Department and handed it to the Foreign Office representative, Masuo, and were later told that it had been sent, but there is no assurance that it ever got through

No. 136—Strictly Confidential—Investigation V.

Ministry of Foreign Affairs,
Tokyo, December 8, 1941

Excellency:

I have the honor to inform Your Excellency that there has arisen a state of war between Your Excellency's country and Japan beginning today.

I avail myself of this opportunity to renew to Your Excellency the assurances of my highest consideration.

SHIGENORI TOGO
Minister of Foreign Affairs

His Excellency
Joseph Clark Grew,
Ambassador Extraordinary and Plenipotentiary of the
United States of America at Tokyo.

When he had finished reading, Crocker said: "This is a very tragic moment," to which Ohno replied: "It is; and my duty is most distasteful."

Ohno then proceeded to read a translation of the following statement prepared by the Japanese authorities concerning the Embassy and its functions:

The following statement was read by Mr. Ohno to Mr. Crocker at 11 A.M., December 8, 1941:

1. That functions of the Embassy and the Consulates will be suspended as of today.

2. That members of the Embassy and Consulates be accorded protection and living facilities in accordance with international usages.

3. That in order to secure protection and facilities aforementioned it is recommended that all the members of the Embassy be congregated in the Embassy compound.

4. That communication with the outside, including telephone and telegraph, be suspended. In case anyone desires to go out, permission must be obtained from the Gaimusho through the officer who will be posted in front of the Embassy, Liaison Officer Mr. Masuo. He has come here with me.

5. As soon as a country representing your interests is nominated, contact between your Embassy and representatives of the said country will be allowed as is necessary for the purpose of representing your interests.

6. That due attention is being paid to protecting the citizens of the United States.

7. That all wireless transmitting sets be surrendered at once.

8. That all short-wave wireless receiving sets, private as well as official, the use of which will no more be acquiesced, be handed over.

9. That *en clair* telegrams informing your Government of having been notified of a state of war will be allowed through the liaison officer.

TRIBUTE TO JAPANESE EMPLOYEES OF
THE EMBASSY

December 12, 1941

The conduct of our Japanese employees has been beyond all praise. All of them expressed desire to stay with us until our departure, but as they are not permitted to leave the premises or to communicate with their families and to return while under employment of the American Government, we have been forced to discharge those whose services are not essential. We assume that all of them will eventually have to be discharged. A substantial number of persons will be continuously needed to prevent deterioration of the buildings and grounds and to maintain machinery and equipment, and we expect that arrangements can be made by the mission eventually representing American interests to engage our Japanese.

I urgently requested of the Department that in the meantime I be authorized to assure our Japanese employees, whose loyalty and sense of responsibility under the most difficult conditions have been extraordinary, that our Government will adequately compensate those discharged and will arrange to continue the employment of the older men during the war. The chief messenger has been with us for about forty years, and many others have been employed for ten years or more.

GRACE UNDER PRESSURE

December 13, 1941

The staff wished to have a dance this Saturday evening in the community rooms at the chancery but while wishing to take every practicable and proper step to keep up their morale, I vetoed the idea of a dance, because I thought it unwise at this serious time to convey to the police, who were then swarming in the compound, the assumption that we in the Embassy were taking the situation flippantly. I knew that there was not the slightest harm in the dancing itself but, unfortunately, the mere idea of dancing always conveys an assumption of gaiety, and our thoughts are anything but gay just now. Every other step for entertainment and for keeping up morale I approved.

Thus the community room, arranged and ably managed by Ruth Kelley, became known as "The Lido," and it afforded a pleasant gathering place for the staff, with an open fire, big comfortable easy chairs, a piano and gramophone for music, and tables for bridge and poker, mah-jongg, and chess, as well as books and magazines. Meanwhile at the residence Alice had bridge nearly every afternoon after luncheon.

Furthermore, Commander Stone, our Assistant Naval Attaché, laid out a cleverly constructed golf course in the lower compound, for chip shots and putts, which gave us opportunity for exercise and amusement. It was duly opened with ceremony and a tournament, won by Bohlen. The course was christened "The Greater East Asia Black Sulphur Springs Championship Golf Course," the latter allu-

sion being to a report that Japanese in Washington were interned
at White Sulphur Springs.

THE SWISS TAKE CHARGE

December 14, 1941

The Swiss Minister, Mr. Gorgé, was informed by his Government on the 9th that he was to take charge of American interests
in Japan, and he promptly wrote to the Foreign Minister, but it
was not until last night, the 13th, that he was permitted to visit
me, which he did this morning. We saw his car at the gate, but
it was not allowed by the police to enter, so he had to go to the
Foreign Office to have instructions telephoned to the police, one
indication among many of the almost total lack of co-ordination
between the Foreign Office and the police.

When finally the gates were opened and the Minister drove in,
Dooman was forbidden by the police to speak to him, but Dooman
quickly sent word to the staff, who came down to the courtyard
and loudly applauded as the Minister descended from his car. The
police were much irritated and tried to stop the ovation, which
increased rather than diminished, and nothing could be done
about it. Dooman put his finger to his lips, indicating to the
Minister that he could not speak, and Mr. Gorgé was then escorted
by a large escort of police up to the residence, one in front, one
at each elbow, and one or two behind. The theory that we were
prisoners and to be treated as criminal prisoners was clearly the
attitude of the police from the very beginning, and when, after
nearly three weeks, the Minister's representations resulted in their
being ousted from the compound and told to relax their severity,
they were clearly irritated and tried to take it out on us in various
petty ways. They had lost face.

Up to that time, namely during the first three weeks, the police
swarmed in the compound, entered the chancery and private
apartments of the staff at will, peered through the windows of the
residence, and in one case a policeman stepped into our salon
to watch the packing, although he withdrew when requested to
do so. Guard boxes were erected, and once, when I went down
to the chancery with a parcel under my arm, I saw a policeman
making an entry in his notebook. Thus was civilized international
diplomatic usage totally ignored. The police took various petty
obstructive measures which might have been extremely serious if

we had not had the good fortune to receive a large consignment of canned foodstuffs from the United Groceries in San Francisco just before our internment. In order to conserve the trivial amount of heating oil allowed us, we very nearly froze.

At first Dooman was not allowed to join my conference with the Minister, but he shortly broke through this obstruction and thereafter was always present. The Minister came every two or three days and we soon appreciated our good fortune in having as our representative a forceful man with a businesslike sense of organization and of our rights under diplomatic usage. He made notes of every complaint and made representations to Sato or Nishi with eventually marked success. Former Foreign Minister Sato was placed at the head of a committee to deal with our problems, but he was timid and unwilling to make decisions and was a great disappointment. Nishi, the Vice-Minister, was far more co-operative and understanding. Never was the segregation and divided control between the Foreign Office and the police more acutely exemplified.

THE JAPANESE PETTY OFFICIAL IN ACTION

December 16, 1941 (*From Dooman's Diary.*)

A fairly uneventful day. There was, however, one incident worth recording because it is so revealing of the Japanese indecision, uncertainty, and childishness. For two days now our Officer of the Day, with a desk in the hall of the chancery, has been working out very well indeed and has contributed at once to a general sense of orderliness and discipline, besides furnishing a most useful information center, messenger service, and so forth. As we can spare enough fuel only to have the heat on for two hours out of every twenty-four it is essential that the front door be kept closed and there is a large sign in English and in Japanese to that effect. One of the duties of the O.D. is to remind persons who thoughtlessly leave it open to go back and close it. During the course of the day a uniformed Japanese policeman with sword clanking at his side flung the door open and strode across the lobby toward the office of Masuo, the liaison man from the Japanese Foreign Office. The O.D. spoke up politely and asked the policeman please to close the door. He stopped in his tracks and after perceptible hesitation went back and closed it. We thought nothing of it at the time but our minds went back to the incident when some six hours later, about ten P.M., the Embassy translator, Fujimoto, came to me in some agitation and said that the head police officer sent him to tell me that we must abolish the institution of O.D. and have the desk removed, on the grounds that the Embassy's functions had been suspended by order of the Japanese Government and that therefore no officer could perform any duties or exercise any authority! It is perfectly clear that the policeman who was asked to close the door had been taken aback by the request but that at the time he was not able to think fast enough to decide to refuse to accede to it; so he closed the door. However, having then gone to his office, he began to brood upon it and the idea slowly grew in his mind that he was being ordered around by an officer of the Embassy and that this was not to be tolerated. His mind probably turned also to the notice on the bulletin board in which we set forth among the duties of the O.D. that of "supervision over the policing of the building." To anyone familiar with the American military idiom the word "policing" means merely the business of cleaning and tidying up. But undoubtedly the Japanese felt that we were conferring upon the O.D. the authority to supervise the Japanese police, an intolerable insult. There is also the strong likelihood that by ten P.M. the policeman had acquired a reasonable alcoholic glow and so, after some six hours of communing with himself, and, no doubt, with his outraged colleagues, he made a great decision to do away with the institution of O.D. But he did not act through the proper channel, that is, through the Foreign Office liaison man and a written communication addressed to the Ambassador. This would have required an irrevocable decision and an assumption of authority which he was unwilling to take. So he indulged in the typical Japanese trick of trying to bring about the removal of the O.D. by running a bluff, just to see if it would work.

However that may be, Ned Crocker told Fujimoto to say in reply that nothing could be done until the Ambassador was consulted, and we proposed to ignore the matter and await developments. Crocker did, however, remove the sign on the bulletin board and had it rewritten, changing the word "policing" to "cleaning" and rephrasing it so that there would be nothing in it to which the Japanese could possibly take exception.

In the end the O.D. remained.

CHRISTMAS EVE AND CHRISTMAS DAY

December 24 and 25, 1941

Christmas Eve was memorable. For dinner Gene Dooman contributed a Virginia sugar-cured ham which he had been storing up for some special occasion, while Ned Crocker brought two bottles of delicious Berncastler Doktor, 1933. Jane and Hank Smith-Hutton, Miss Coles, Williams, Turner, Benninghoff, Bohlen, and Creswell were also there. With the champagne I proposed two toasts on the part of Alice and myself: first, to our commissioned and noncommissioned staffs with an expression of our deep sense of their splendid organization, initiative, thoughtfulness, and general helpfulness at this difficult time which we would certainly never forget, and, second, to the wives at home who, we hoped, would find happy reunion with their husbands before long, God bless them. Dooman made a touching reply.

Flowers had been coming in from several friends and a beautiful letter and remembrance from Yolande Arsène-Henry, wife of the French Ambassador, to Alice, and before dinner Mrs. Nishi, wife of the Vice-Foreign Minister, sent Alice two turkeys, which was Nishi's way of expressing his personal friendliness, a greatly appreciated gesture. Also flowers for Alice and myself from the entire staff, and what a staff it is!

But the real event of the day was after dinner when almost the whole staff, some thirty or forty, came up the hill and serenaded us in the Embassy with Christmas hymns and carols. First they sang *Adeste Fideles* in the hall and then moved slowly into the loggia, singing *Heilige Nacht*. It was a spontaneous action, for they had practiced only once, but the singing was truly beautiful under Benninghoff's direction. Alice and I were both greatly moved; she broke down, poor dear, and I had to hold myself in. They continued to sing for some time, finally moving slowly off, again singing *Holy Night* pianissimo as they went out, and again *Oh Come, All Ye Faithful* as they went down the hill. That was an evening we shall always remember. Later the staff continued to sing and play the piano in the community room at the chancery and I am sure that the evening afforded a healthy outlet for their pent-up emotions and for those whose morale is being put to a hard test.

Christmas Day

A clear, crisp, sunny day, springlike in the sun at noon. Alice's knee, which had gone back on her for a few days, was better and she enjoyed our usual walk up and down on the lawn, accompanied by our dogs, Sasha and Micky. For the first time during our eighteen days of incarceration several copies of the *Japan Times and Advertiser* were delivered, and while the reading of it was not particularly cheery, we take the Japanese reports of military and naval successes with several grains of salt. I still confidently count on the eventual crack in Germany, and once the German Army begins to disintegrate, it will be the beginning of the end, for with Germany out of the picture and the entire naval and air forces of the United States and Great Britain, which will steadily increase in power, available to attack Japan, even the cocky and truculent Japanese can hardly fail to see their ultimate doom writ large. This is, of course, wishful thinking, but it is based on my intimate knowledge of the German character. What happened in 1918 will in all probability happen again, and Hitler's miscalculation in attacking Soviet Russia will prove to be his downfall. May history substantiate this prognostication.

The very fact of our present situation and the community spirit called forth by that situation resulted in a celebration of Christmas, as of Christmas Eve, never experienced in all our years in Tokyo. Miss Arnold and her mess group, including Mrs. Skouland, Miss Gardiner, Mrs. Playfair, Captains Johnson and Stuart, came up to the residence for cocktails and then we had an admirable Christmas dinner at 1, with Mrs. Nishi's turkeys and with Ned Crocker's plum puddings swimming in burning brandy. Presents were exchanged and I managed through a friendly policeman, who appears to have gone all over town in search of them, to get two lovely potted orchids for Alice.

At four o'clock our servants, Shimoda, Fukaya, Funayama, and Kato, were informed that their families had been allowed to come into the compound and there was a joyful meeting in front of the chancery which moved us very much. They had not been allowed to talk with their families since our internment.

Then came the Christmas tree in the community room. We had two trees, one at the residence and this one in the chancery, Gene Dooman having given orders to cut down the trees which grew along the wall of the lower compound and were obstructing the light in front of other houses, and both were well decorated with our leftover things from other years. First Dave Thomasson, one of our vice-consuls, and I played the piano; then the Christmas hymns and carols were sung by everyone, and finally Captain Gould appeared as Santa Claus and gave presents to everybody with clever and amusing verses read to each. He did it exceedingly well and it was a very successful party.

Thus ended a Christmas celebration that will always remain vividly in our memory.

EXCHANGE OF DIPLOMATS ARRANGED

December 30, 1941

The Swiss Minister today told us that the Japanese Government has accepted our proposal for an exchange in Lourenço Marques and is now translating into French its note with regard to details, which the Minister said he would promptly cable to Washington through Berne. So at last things seem to be moving. At Dooman's wise suggestion I called a meeting of the staff and told them the news, which called forth loud applause; it will help their morale. The suggestion for a direct exchange between Yokohama and San Francisco has been discarded by the Japanese Foreign Office (which had been toying with the idea on its own initiative) because the Japanese Army and Navy have categorically refused to consider allowing an American ship to come into Japanese waters.

I turned over to the Minister the large metal trunk containing the archives of the Décanat, which he was to deliver to Arsène-Henry, the new Dean, *after* the archives had been examined by Kiuchi at the Foreign Office to be sure that we were not slipping other papers out to the French Ambassador. A Japanese official had to drive with Gorgé to the Foreign Office. Thus are the police measures for our segregation raised to the nth degree.

The Axis diplomats are not very keen about having the French Ambassador as Dean and would prefer the Brazilian Ambassador, who comes next in seniority, and it remains to be seen whether Arsène-Henry will be able to get away with it.

SOME JAPANESE FRIENDS REMAIN TRUE

December 31, 1941

A Japanese friend came to see me. He said that he could not bring himself to come sooner owing to the intensity of his feeling of sorrow at the outbreak of war between our two countries. He brought me very friendly messages and two letters from Japanese friends. He said that the severity of our initial treatment by the police during the first two weeks of our internment was due to the total unexpectedness of the war; no plans had been made for such an emergency and there was therefore at the beginning a complete lack of co-ordination among the authorities. I said that the improvement was now noticeable but our treatment was still that of criminal prisoners and in no way corresponded to the very considerate and lenient treatment of the Japanese Ambassador in Washington and his diplomatic and consular staffs.

The two letters were as follows:

Tokyo, December 17, 1941

DEAR MR. AND MRS. GREW:

No one could have foreseen this tragic end of our long-standing friendly relations, although so many unfortunate events occurred in recent years. I well remember that you always tell me that to promote the friendship of our two countries is your lifework. I know also how hard you worked to prevent the breaking up of the talk in Washington even till the very last moment. It is a very sad thing that even your unfatigued efforts could not save the peace. But you can rest assured that we will never forget your friendship to our country and to us. Before ending my letter I must add one thing. Whenever I told the progress of our talk in Washington to my wife at her sick bedside during the last summer, she always tried to strain her weakening nerves not to have escaped any words from her ears. She is happy not to have witnessed in her lifetime this tragic end of our good relations.

Please accept my gratitude for your personal friendship and kindness to me and to my family, and I beg to remain,

Yours most sincerely,

Tokyo, December 30, 1941

DEAR MR. GREW:

It is with a sense of great grief that I write you this letter. In spite of our sincere and sustained endeavors to avert the rupture of our relations, the awful eventuality has at last come. I do not want to say much on the causes and circumstances that have led to this war; I only wish that the present struggle may prove but a brief episode in the long annals of our relations, which I hope will be quickly restored.

You and Mrs. Grew have won numerous friends among my compatriots by your able and admirable work extending over nine long years. As you well know, it is not the habit of our people to forget their friends easily, especially when they are so highly esteemed as you are, and I assure you that there are many of us who tender their deep sympathy to you in your great difficulty.

Perhaps it is unnecessary for me to say that I consider it a great privilege to have enjoyed your genial and generous friendship. I look forward keenly to the happy day when we shall once again co-operate heartily for the advancement of the relations of our two countries.

As I have been transferred, I am leaving for my new post within a few days' time. I wish Mrs. Grew and your good self a happy new year and safe voyage home.

Yours very sincerely,

The New Year's Eve buffet supper at the chancery. At 11:59 the lights went out and everyone sang *Auld Lang Syne*. When the lights came on, Captain Gould was in the midst of the circle dressed as Father Time; he made a little speech and *Auld Lang Syne* was sung again, everyone holding hands. But Alice and I had left at about 10:30 and we did not wait up for the New Year. We did not feel in a mood to wait up for anything.

THE NEW YEAR BEGINS

January 1, 1942

A bright, clear, crisp day. Went down this morning to the chancery to wish the members of the staff a happy New Year and to speak to the Japanese police, Sergeant Kiyokawa and his nine officers, who were responsible for our protection at the residence. Kiyokawa was the officer who had been with us at the time of the February 26 Incident in 1936 and who had driven around with me for some time thereafter. He reminded me of that time when I had given him a silver cigarette case. Kiyokawa said that this was a war between states and not between individuals.

The Swiss Minister came, just before going to the New Year's reception at Court, which, I observed, would be somewhat smaller than usual so far as the Diplomatic Corps was concerned. Gorgé told us that while the Japanese had accepted our proposal that the transfer of personnel take place at Lourenço Marques, some of them were toying with the idea of Tahiti, which would entail far shorter voyages. Gorgé said he would pass the suggestion on to Washington as coming from Japanese sources. The Foreign Office has written him a note which detailed proposals for the exchange, a copy of which he gave us.

HOLE IN ONE

January 4, 1942

Made my first hole in one on our Embassy golf course. The course is 422 yards long, nine holes, with small putting greens and everything. One of the shots goes over or around one of the apartment houses and those who elect the straight over-the-roof shot run risks, but only one window has been broken so far. The fish in the reflection pool are having a lovely time—if they like old golf balls.

There are always from ten to fourteen at our table for every meal and our group is fortunately a congenial one. The clerks and other members of the staff who do not mess with us regularly come up in rotation for a meal, and thus we keep in touch. Alice goes frequently to the chancery to visit the commissariat or the community room, as well as to the individual apartments.

"WE KEEP BUSY"

January 9, 1942

About one-half of the Foreign Office was burned in a big fire during the night. It appears that some of the records concerning our eventual evacuation were destroyed, and although the Swiss Minister will furnish extra copies of his own notes, I fear that this may delay matters beyond the delay already encountered. We are, however, fairly comfortable, except for the intense cold of the house due to necessary economy in fuel (the heating is never turned on until late afternoon). The days pass quickly. I work in the morning from breakfast until 11:30; then golf for an hour or so in order to get a little exercise and fresh air; early to bed. Plenty of time for good reading. I have just finished Cronin's *The Keys of the Kingdom,* an admirable book.

EXCHANGE

January 16, 1942

The Swiss Minister brought the Japanese reply to our Government's proposal relating to the exchange of personnel at Lourenço Marques. The place of exchange has been accepted but there are various discrepancies in the two proposals, discussed in a memorandum prepared by Bohlen. I called a meeting of the entire staff and told them of the progress made in the negotiations, once

again expressing my admiration of their maintenance of a high
morale and of their splendid community spirit which is beyond
all praise.

January 18, 1942

At Alice's suggestion a number of us met in the music room at
the chancery this Sunday morning and sang a number of favorite
hymns, Jones at the piano and Benninghoff conducting. Marion
Arnold's lovely voice was delightful to hear.

Our free time affords an opportunity for much good reading.
Have just finished, for the second time, John Masefield's *Bird of
Dawning*, one of the greatest epics of the sea ever written—a book
which nobody should pass by. Also have finished the second volume
of the life of Balfour by Mrs. Dugdale, and am now reading the
life of Elihu Root, by Professor Jessup. Root had much to do in
handling Far Eastern questions with Theodore Roosevelt and his
comments and actions are intensely interesting at this particular
time.

January 19, 1942

The Swiss Minister and Madame Gorgé, who was finally allowed
to visit Alice, came this morning, and the ladies talked for some
two hours. Meanwhile many of our Japanese friends and others
are sending flowers and fruit, twenty-two in all, and others tried
but failed to get permission. Several of the colleagues have also
sent flowers.

January 20, 1942

The vainglorious boasting of the Japanese papers is disgusting
reading these days. I am taking home two complete sets of the
Japan Times and Advertiser from December 8, one for the Department and one for myself.

January 22, 1942

Beat Stone one-up in our golf tournament but was quickly
eliminated by Bob Fearey shortly thereafter. Benninghoff won
the badminton tournament in a thrilling final from Lamm. There
are also going on tournaments in bridge, chess, and checkers. We
keep busy.

Am very proud of Bob Fearey, my private secretary, a grandson of
Bishop Lawrence of Massachusetts, who has measured up admirably.

In the absence of laundry facilities, each member of the staff has been doing his or her own washing, and the lower part of the compound looks like a back yard with the washed clothes and bedding hung out to dry. But Fearey discovered an old washing machine in our garret and he now does the washing for the entire staff twice a day, assisted by Rustad. He is also air-raid warden for his apartment house as well as director of athletics and he also takes his turn as Officer of the Day as well as officer in charge of policing the chancery. Incidentally he is an electrician, radio expert, and air pilot, having taken more than five hundred parachute jumps. He did all this during his summer vacations at Harvard. A keen, efficient, and public-spirited young man who should go far.

January 24, 1942

General Pabst, the Netherlands Minister, died today at St. Luke's from heart trouble. He was by far the senior diplomat in Japan, having been Minister since 1923 and Military Attaché even before that. He, with Craigie and Romer, was one of my most intimate colleagues. He was a typical hardheaded Dutchman but personally agreeable and congenial, and I shall always look back on him as one of my few most highly valued friends in Japan. I am greatly depressed at his sudden death, but for him it is a happy release, for he had, I believe, no close family bonds, being a bachelor, and the developments brought about by the war must have been a profound sorrow.

January 25, 1942

Sunday hymns again, which will now become a fixture. These gatherings are rather inspiring. The days pass rapidly and the intervals between Sundays seem short. We are never for a moment bored, at least I am not, and I doubt if many of the others are, especially those who have some scholarly work to keep them interested.

Dooman is busy writing a very interesting book throwing sidelights on Townsend Harris' mission to Japan, derived from Japanese documents to which he was given access by Count Hotta, the tennis player who is a descendant of one of the high Japanese officials, equivalent to the Foreign Minister, in Harris' time. It is intensely interesting to see how closely the psychology of Japanese officialdom, especially of the police, compared with that which we in the Embassy are facing today.

The only members of the staff I am really sorry for are those few who have no scholarly interests and little or no incentive to take up a course of profitable reading. Most of them are busy enough with the daily duties of the chancery and the compound, including even duties of the swabbing and cleaning gang which undertakes the job of our departed charwomen in rotation every morning. But certain members of the staff, I fear, depend too much upon pure sociability, and to those who are thus dependent, there must come moments of boredom.

FUNERAL SERVICE FOR GENERAL PABST

January 29, 1942

The Swiss Minister again. He generally has a number of questions to discuss but he comes every few days in any case, just to keep in touch. We could not possibly have a better person looking after our interests; he has a keen perception of the situation and a business-man's approach, forceful while exercising great care not to compromise his usefulness by any improprieties or unorthodox procedure. At the same time his assistant, Hausheer, who also comes constantly, is equally businesslike. Their attitude reminds me closely of that of the Swiss Chargé d'Affaires in Washington in 1917 and 1918 who had charge of German interests and who used to come to see me at the Department, as Chief of the Western European Division, almost daily with a long list of questions to be discussed.

Today was the funeral service for General Pabst at St. Luke's chapel. The Japanese Government had arranged that one member from each enemy diplomatic mission might attend, and for the first time in fifty-two days I emerged from our Embassy compound, accompanied by Masuo of the Foreign Office and Sergeant Kiyokawa. I entered St. Luke's by a side entrance, hung with mourning curtains, and was shown immediately into the chapel without an opportunity to speak to anyone. I wanted to slip into a rear pew, but Kishi, who was ushering, greeted me affectionately and showed me to the aisle seat in the second pew on the right. In the first pew on the right were Bagge, the Swedish Minister, representing Dutch interests, and the Dutch Chargé d'Affaires and Madame Reuchlin and other members of the Dutch Legation. In our pew were other members of the Dutch Legation and Sir Robert and Lady Craigie, and behind us were the Belgian Ambassador and Madame Forthomme, the Peruvian, Colombian, Greek, and other representatives of countries now at war with Japan or which had broken relations with Japan.

On the left, in the first pew, were Nishi, Vice-Foreign Minister, Hirota, Sato, and Shidehara, who came in late and who had aged noticeably, as he was walking with a cane and was very shaky. Behind them were the Arsène-Henrys, he as Dean of the Diplomatic Corps, and behind them many others, including the Tillitses, the Gorgés, the Chilean Minister, the Argentine Chargé d'Affaires, and all the other nonenemy diplomats. Also a great many Japanese. The service was all in Japanese save for the address given by a Dutch clergyman in Dutch and then in English. At the end a Dutchman came to the organ and played the Dutch national anthem.

Bagge and the Reuchlins left first; then I was immediately shown out, as, I suppose, were all the enemies so that they would not meet the others. I shook hands with Bagge and the Reuchlins and immediately went down to the car. Just before leaving, the Craigies appeared and I had just a word with them, merely an exchange of amenities and "See you on the boat." I would have liked to stop for a chat, but the police had indicated that any talk, especially between Craigie and myself, would greatly embarrass them, so I abstained. Alice did not go to the funeral, although invited by the Foreign Office to do so, and we heard afterward from Japanese friends, indirectly, that her sense of delicacy was understood and appreciated.

SINGAPORE FALLS

February 15, 1942

Singapore, now Shonan, fell. The new name combines the thought of the Showa era and the southward advance. This is a heavy blow, but I look on it as only a temporary blow. The Japanese will have to withdraw eventually from all of their ill-gotten gains; their home islands are vulnerable; their fleet and limited merchant marine will inevitably suffer from attrition, and the day will come when we shall be in a position to blockade Japan effectively, cutting off the homeland from all of their gains to the south. Failing a decisive naval battle or the entry of Russia or the collapse of Germany, it may take a long time, but we shall never let go until the task is completed.

February 16, 1942

The Swiss Minister brought us a copy of the latest note from our Government concerning evacuation. It had been sent through Spanish channels and, being dated February 5 in Washington, there had been long delay. It appears that Ohta in the Foreign Office had had it for five days before Satoh, who is in charge of the subject, knew of its arrival. Gorgé is very much chagrined that the negotiations were taken out of his hands, or at least that he was not informed of the note through Berne. It appears that the Japanese asked our Government to centralize the negotiations through Spanish channels, but Satoh told Gorgé that this was untrue. The usual lack of co-ordination in the Gaimusho, I suspect.

The lack of directness in the Japanese processes of thought and negotiation is well illustrated in the fact that it has taken the Swiss Minister over two months, with hours and hours of inconclusive conference, to arrange finally for him to sell our automobiles, wine, and so on to other diplomatic colleagues.

Today the Japanese are busily celebrating the fall of Singapore, and a big procession came to demonstrate in front of our Embassy and probably also in front of the British Embassy. Major Babcock, Assistant Military Attaché, went out on the balcony and waved to the demonstrators. The demonstrators waved back with their handkerchiefs, laughing genially, and in spite of the efforts of their leaders to stop their friendly gestures, the whole thing broke up in laughter and they went away still laughing.

In spite of all the war propaganda, there does not seem to exist any fundamental hatred of the United States among the people. We learn, too, from various sources that in spite of Japan's initial successes in the war, people are asking themselves whether, in view of the unlimited resources of America, Japan can ever really win.

JAPAN MUST BE OVERWHELMINGLY BEATEN

February 17, 1942

I called a meeting of the entire staff today and told them of the progress made in the negotiations for our evacuation. I also spoke of my absolute certainty that in spite of the present dark days our country would without question win in the end, and I read to them the following passage from my diary:

> We are returning to our country to take whatever part we may properly be called upon or find opportunity to take toward contributing to the certain ultimate victory of the United States in this war of the nations, and with the firm conviction that in spite of initial successes by the Axis powers, a terrible reckoning

in the eventual defeat of those powers is as mathematically certain as is the law of gravity. For her own good, for the future safety and welfare of the United States, and for the future security and welfare of world civilization, Japan must be overwhelmingly beaten, for only thus, under present circumstances, can her armed forces, her military machine and system, be wholly discredited and liquidated, and the Japanese nation be turned permanently into paths of peace. However long this process may take, however much it may involve American "blood, sweat, and tears," there must be no relinquishing of this essential task until it is finally and effectively completed. There is not room in the Pacific area for a peaceful America and a swashbuckling Japan.

TENTH ANNIVERSARY AS AMBASSADOR TO JAPAN

February 19, 1942

Appointed to Japan ten years ago today. They have been an interesting ten years, and despite the final failure of my mission I would not now willingly have given up that experience even in the light of events.

The Lessons of History

History is properly based upon facts and upon such contemporary comments as may tend to clarify those facts. Yet a study of history is futile unless, from the lessons of history, mankind derives constructive guidance in the art of statesmanship. The rapidly accelerating progress in certain phases of civilization, notably in science, economics, communication, and transit, has rendered national isolation an anachronism. The nations of the world have become so closely integrated and knitted together that, as frequently stated by our Government in recent years, any war between any two or more nations disturbs a delicately balanced world economy and is, therefore, of concern to all other nations. For that reason our Government has consistently manifested its concern in situations in various parts of the world which threatened to, or did in fact, lead to war.

The right to intervene morally or physically in such situations carries with it, however, a corollary in the way of an obligation: we cannot logically on the one hand exercise the right of intervention, morally or physically, in situations between other nations which might lead to war on the ground that our national interests are affected thereby, while on the other hand manifesting indifference to the conditions creating such situations. It is a fact and not a theory that the nations are today interdependent: in a world so closely integrated as it is today, the policies and actions of every nation carry consequences which reach the world's five continents and seven seas. We cannot permit nations to seize and pre-empt by processes of conquest areas whose resources should be available to all. Nevertheless, so long as any nation follows policies designed exclusively for the protection and furtherance of its own interests and is not solicitous to assist in resolving the problems of other nations whose well-being is equally necessary for the operation of a world economy such as we have today, just so long will the progress of civilization and the welfare of mankind be retarded through unnecessary and futile wars.

In the world of today and tomorrow, no nation can afford simply to "mind its own business," for the problems of its neighbors, all its neighbors, must inevitably become an important part of its business, and sound statesmanship must recognize that the practical logic of "splendid isolationism," or bloc isolationism, has gone forever. And so long as we, in our future diplomatic, political, and legislative policies and actions, fail to perceive the lessons of history and the lost opportunities of the past, just so long shall we as a nation continue to overlook opportunities to employ our limitless strength, both material and moral, toward the development of civilization and of the welfare of our own country and people without the dissipation of lives and wealth in useless wars.

PURE HIGHWAY ROBBERY

February 21, 1942

The Swiss Minister came again today and told us that the matter of selling our cars, wine, et cetera, has now been entirely reopened because the Ministry of Finance insists on the Swiss Minister putting the proceeds into an account at the Yokohama Specie Bank separate from his account for official expenses. From that account we would be allowed to draw cash for our current expenses while here, but as soon as we have left, the money would be frozen and the Minister would not be allowed to use it for official expenses, crediting us with our individual proceeds in Washington. That, as the Minister pointed out to Kiuchi, is tantamount to confiscation. I shall certainly not sell my cars or wine under such conditions and

I asked the Minister to let the whole matter ride for the present, merely reporting the facts to Washington.

This is pure highway robbery. The Ministry of Finance, the Home Office, and the War Office are determined to decide every question over the head of the Foreign Office and with no consideration of international usage. The Foreign Office, they say, has been given the opportunity to conduct the country's foreign affairs and has failed, and it has lost so much face that it must now be crowded out of the picture. One Japanese diplomat's wife told Gorgé that her husband was depressed and wanted to get out, because he was placed in the position of being authorized to give the Minister certain assurances and then was obliged to withdraw those assurances owing to a change of decision in some other ministry. The Finance Ministry, for instance, has taken the position that the Ministry and not the Swiss Minister has custody of the effects of the Embassy and of its officers and will decide all matters of the disposition of such effects. This, of course, is absurd, and Gorgé quite properly pointed out to Kiuchi that in such a case the members of the Embassy would have no legal rights of protection as they could not have recourse to the Japanese courts of law. Yet all kinds of arbitrary decisions are taken by the other ministries without consulting the Foreign Office on points of international law or usage.

Another point is that the police in Yokohama will not allow the Swiss delegate to visit one of the civilian internment camps, and they want two representatives of the civilians to meet the Swiss delegate at the police office. That, of course, is contrary to all international usage, and it implies that something is wrong with the camp. The civilian delegates would of course be warned by the police not to complain lest matters be made harsher for them. No such prohibitions arose in Germany during the last war, and we used to visit the civilian camp at Ruhleben at least every week. In other parts of Japan the Swiss were allowed to talk to the prisoners quite alone and without the presence of any police official. There seems to be no co-ordiation, and each official takes such arbitrary decisions as he sees fit.

WASHINGTON'S BIRTHDAY

February 22, 1942

Washington's Birthday and Sunday. At the end of the hymns we sang the *Battle Hymn of the Republic* and then the national anthem, and at 11:30 we had the entire staff at the Embassy, where I proposed a toast to the President.

THE DEFEAT OF JAPAN IS CERTAIN

February 28, 1942

With Japan steadily expanding her conquests and with so little to show on the credit side of the ledger up to the present, it is difficult to foresee the certain eventual victory of the Allies and Japan's final defeat. Yet of that final defeat I have not the slightest doubt. As I have said, that defeat seems to me as mathematically certain as the law of gravity.

Prophecies unsupported by facts are perhaps idle daydreams, but I visualize the eventual outcome somewhat as follows. Germany will eventually crack, either through economic dissolution, especially through lack of oil, or through revolution, possibly commencing in the occupied countries. I know the breed by long experience: blatant bullies while on top, craven and whining defeatists when the tables are turned. The strain in Germany in matters of food and raw materials must be steadily increasing. Once the Army fails to show continued victories, whether in Russia or elsewhere, the dissolution will rapidly progress. Morale will go to pieces and the end will then be in sight. The casualty lists from the Russian campaign will have their due effect, and the time will come, perhaps very soon, when Goebbels' propaganda lies will no longer serve to bolster morale and moral disintegration will be rapid. When Churchill recently said that victory may come sooner than expected, an unusually optimistic statement from him because he has always painted the darker side of the picture, I dare say that he had the foregoing situation in mind and that he may very likely possess evidence of the impending crack in the German Army or people.

Once Germany is out of the picture, Italy will of course immediately have to follow suit. That will leave Japan with the prospect of facing alone the combined sea and air forces of the United States and Great Britain, with the probable addition of Soviet Russia. If Soviet Russia should then come in—and it is difficult to see how she could afford to pass up the opportunity to acquire lost territory and to render herself permanently invulnerable against Japan—the problem would be immensely simplified, because, with the allied sea and air forces based on Vladivostok, Japan proper could be rapidly blockaded, her cities bombed, her shipping destroyed, and her life lines and contacts with her outlying forces completely severed. Occupation of Japan might even eventually be feasible.

But even if Soviet Russia should remain neutral and should await the final Anglo-American victory before settling her own problems with Japan, there could be no doubt that the combined American and British fleets, totally freed from the Atlantic, would be able to reoccupy at least some of the bases within striking distance of Japan, whence their submarines and planes could intercept shipping and still blockade the islands.

Indeed, with Germany out of the picture, the Japanese Government could hardly fail to perceive the inevitable outcome, and with a view to saving her cities and avoiding the total destruction of her merchant marine, if only by gradual attrition, her capitulation might well take place after the downfall of the Axis. But we shall have to guard against a premature peace.

To return to Europe, the moment the crack in Germany begins to appear I shall expect a general rising among the people of the occupied countries, including the French. Turkey may well come into the war at that time, while Rumania is more than likely to desert the Axis and attack Hungary for the purpose of acquiring Transylvania. Italy, too, would fade rapidly from the scene.

All this is, of course, painting the future picture in its brightest colors, but the hypothesis does not seem to me to be too far-fetched. And even if the end should not come so quickly as we might hope, nevertheless, with the downfall of the Axis, processes would immediately be set in motion which could not fail in the end to lead to total victory for our country.

YANKEE REMINISCENCE

March 10, 1942

Father's centenary. He was born March 10, 1842. I proposed at dinner a toast to his memory and made a little speech with a few reminiscences. One anecdote was of my grandfather Grew who, on his deathbed, was worried by some problem, and just before he died he managed to get it out: coming into Boston from Hyde Park in the morning (I think it was New Year's Day and that he was going to deliver his usual presents of books) he had forgotten his purse and had borrowed five cents from the conductor on the train to pay his horse-car fare; he wanted before he died to be sure that the debt would be paid. It was.

MORE EMBASSY NOTES, SOCIAL AND OTHERWISE

March 24, 1942

Went to the dentist, Dr. Kotani, as a tooth broke and an inset came out. Had a little talk with Houstoun-Boswall and the Kennedys of the British Embassy, who were there; we call the dentist's the social club of Tokyo, as one generally meets some colleagues.

Fujimoto, one of our translators, a full American citizen without dual nationality, was today actually kidnaped from the Embassy by the police and arrested, charged with some breach of Japanese law about which we are ignorant. The last seen of him was when he accompanied a policeman to the gate, no doubt having been told that someone wanted to see him, and once outside he was quietly taken away. His wife and young son are in the Embassy. His family wanted him to remain in Japan, but he decided that he wished to return with us to his home in the United States. Subsequently he wrote his wife that he had decided to remain in Japan, but we have little doubt that pressure was brought to bear on him by the police. The Swiss Minister has made strong representations but so far without avail. The Foreign Office says that it is awaiting a report from the Minister of Justice. This is just one more of the outrages inflicted on us by the Japanese police.

ONE AMERICAN-BORN JAPANESE WHO CHOSE JAPAN

March 25, 1942

Dooman's birthday. We had a cake at tea and drank his health. I made a little speech to the effect that no man could wish for a more effective chief of staff, and that no group could have had a better executive officer whose constant thought was for our welfare, both as a group and individually. He told me afterward that he was too much moved to make more than a perfunctory reply.

Here is another entry from Dooman's diary telling about the American-born Japanese who chose Japan:

> Yesterday evening shortly before six o'clock Benninghoff reported to me that Fujimoto, the translator, had disappeared. Fujimoto was born in the United States and had dual nationality until a few years ago, when he returned to the United States and divested himself of Japanese nationality. He came back to Japan and has since been a member of the Embassy staff.

According to Benninghoff, Fujimoto was last seen at about 10:30 in the morning. Although his wife had noticed his absence, she was not particularly alarmed until about three o'clock in the afternoon, when she reported to Benninghoff that she had not been able to find her husband. Benninghoff and Turner then made a thorough search of the buildings and grounds, but to no effect. Benninghoff thereupon went to Kyokawa, the officer in charge of the police detachment at the Embassy. He found Kyokawa working on some papers, and he asked him whether he knew where Fujimoto was. Kyokawa continued writing without looking up and asked: "Isn't he here?" Benninghoff then described the efforts to find Fujimoto and said that it was obvious that Fujimoto was not in the compound. Kyokawa all this time continued to work on his papers and did not look up. If anyone in the compound had left the compound without Kyokawa's knowledge, one could be certain that Kyokawa would be extremely excited, but he showed himself wholly unconcerned over the disappearance of Fujimoto. It was apparent to Benninghoff that Kyokawa was cognizant of the matter.

Upon receiving this report from Benninghoff I immediately went to Kyokawa and asked him whether he knew anything at all about the disappearance of Fujimoto. Kyokawa looked me straight in the eye and said he knew nothing at all about it, but that he would call up the metropolitan police station and make inquiries. He went into the next room where the telephone is and I heard him through the door say over the telephone that I was making inquiries about the Fujimoto case and he asked what position he should take. Kyokawa returned shortly thereafter and said that he was going to the police station and would inquire about the Fujimoto case. I asked Kyokawa to telephone to the Swiss Minister at once and ask that the Swiss Minister come and call upon the Ambassador. Kyokawa then turned quite ugly, said that he was under no obligation to "obey my instructions," and he walked off.

After dinner the Ambassador gave me a note asking the Swiss Minister to call the first thing this morning and I took the note to the policeman on duty and asked whether he would allow the note to be taken at once to the Swiss Minister. The officer called up the metropolitan police station on the telephone, and then reported to me that the note could not be sent out until this morning.

As soon as Kyokawa arrived this morning, I asked him what he had to say about the Fujimoto case. Kyokawa said that all he could tell me at that moment was that Fujimoto had been arrested. I told Kyokawa that I knew perfectly well yesterday evening when he denied all knowledge of the matter that he was fully cognizant of it and was probably instrumental in bringing about the seizure of Fujimoto. Kyokawa admitted that, but he said that he had been angered by my threatening attitude. He calmed down after a while and I was able to extract considerable information out of him. It appears that Fujimoto's mother has been bitterly opposed to Fujimoto's return to the United States, and that some grave charge has been lodged by some member of his family against Fujimoto in order to provide a pretext for his detention.

March 27, 1942

I gave out the prizes for the Greater East Asia Bridge Marathon. Smith-Hutton won the first prize, Makinson the second, and Parkes the consolation or booby prize.

Mrs. Tillitse, wife of the Danish Minister, wrote Alice that Kishi had finally managed to arrange for us to play golf outside and that he hoped to play with me himself. I told the staff of my attitude and then wrote a letter to Mrs. Tillitse. I understand that the British, Canadians, and Australians have played once but that Craigie refused to go.

GOLF REFUSED AND WHY

Embassy of the
United States of America
Tokyo, March 29, 1942

DEAR MRS. TILLITSE:

Alice has told me of Mr. Kishi's efforts to arrange for us to play golf and the fact that his efforts appear to have been finally successful. I sincerely appreciate what he has done, and I shall be very grateful if you or the Minister will find occasion to tell him so from me. Kishi has always been one of my highly valued friends in Japan and nothing can ever change my feeling of personal friendship and affection for him. That feeling will endure permanently no matter what has happened or what may happen in future. His thoughtfulness and kindness in trying to arrange the golf are typical of his constant desire to be helpful to others, a characteristic which no one has appreciated more than I during the ten years that I have known him, and I hope that some day in future we may meet in happier circumstances and continue our friendship as before.

Unfortunately, there are a number of reasons why I cannot accept the invitation to play golf, and I think that in view of Mr. Kishi's efforts it is only right that he should know these reasons. The Swiss Minister made similar efforts long ago, but I told him at the beginning that I would definitely not accept such an invitation and I asked him to desist. As a matter of fact, the manager of one golf club told the Minister that it would be embarrassing to the members if we were to come there, and I certainly would not wish to place myself in that position in any club. The embarrassment would be mutual.

But there are even more fundamental reasons why I could not accept such an invitation. Nearly four months have gone by, during which we were not permitted to leave our Embassy except for medical reasons. Now, just as the date for our evacuation is approaching, the authorities deign to permit us to go to some golf links—perhaps once, perhaps twice—I do not know. The assumption is logical that this is now being done for the purpose of putting a more favorable light on the record of our internment, and knowing the way in which the Japanese propaganda office functions, I have little doubt that were I to accept such an invitation, full publicity would be given to it as an indication of our considerate treatment during this entire period. Yet our treatment has been very far from considerate, and at the beginning it was contrary to all concepts of international usage. We were treated not only as prisoners but as criminal prisoners, and throughout our internment we have been subjected to repeated indignities and humiliations by the police. I will not bore you with a recitation of these things, but it will be difficult ever to forget them in future.

Quite apart from our treatment in the Embassy, the intensity of my own feeling is undoubtedly shared by the American people to an inexpressible degree.

With regard to the members of my staff, I have put the matter as follows: I do not wish them to accept this invitation as a matter of sport or entertainment, but if they feel that they need the excursion for reasons of physical or moral health, I have no objection to their playing among themselves. Some of my staff, especially those who, unlike myself, have been separated from their wives and families during this bitter experience, are really suffering from the effects of the long confinement; they want and need to get out into the open spaces, and I fully sympathize with that need. I do not know whether they will accept the invitation or not, but they have my full permission to do so.

In view of Mr. Kishi's very kind attitude and efforts, I think it is only fair to him that he should fully understand my own attitude, and I believe that it would be proper to let him read this letter.

With our warmest affectionate regards to you and the Minister,

Always cordially yours,

March 28, 1942

Swiss Minister. When he came to the Embassy gate today it was partially closed and the police merely stood with folded arms, scowling at Gorgé, and made no move to open the gate or even to ask the chauffeur to open it himself. The Minister then drove to the Foreign Office and told Kiuchi of the incident; Kiuchi said, "*Mais c'est très grave.*" He telephoned to the police headquarters, but Gorgé insisted on a Foreign Office official accompanying him. The police maintained the same attitude even in the presence of the official and the chauffeur had to get out and open the gate himself. I am glad that the official saw it. This may be due merely to the attitude of one policeman, but it is more likely a studied insult, either because they think that the Minister comes too often or because they are angry at our protest in the Fujimoto case. Gorgé was, of course, very angry and nettled, as it was a direct insult to him. Just one more indignity, and we in the Embassy are powerless.

March 30, 1942

Kase came to see me with a piece of lamb and some oranges from a high Japanese official and friend. I talked to Kase of the Fujimoto case and other indignities inflicted on us by the police, hoping that he would repeat my remarks to Togo.

Dr. Amano, the wife, came to the Embassy and gave us all our first inoculations for typhoid and paratyphoid.

March 31, 1942

The Swiss Minister. The Japanese Government has proposed to our Government that we leave for Lourenço Marques on or about April 25, via Shanghai, Saigon, and probably Singapore, arriving there on May 20. The ship will accommodate about 1100 passengers, and as there will be about 500 officials, that will leave room for approximately 600 nonofficials, which Gorgé suggests might be divided roughly to include the 100 nonofficials in Indo-China and Thailand and 250 each from Japan and China. The Japanese hope

that the American evacuation ship will arrive at Lourenço Marques
at the same time.

PLANS FOR DEPARTURE STILL MISFIRE

April 1, 1942

I called a meeting of the full staff today and told them of the
Japanese proposal for our evacuation from Japan on or about April
25, the Japanese evacuation ship to stop at Shanghai and Saigon to
pick up other evacuees and to arrive at Lourenço Marques about
May 20. This communication gave great encouragement to all and
everyone's spirits rose immediately. The proposal, alas, did not go
through.

April 5, 1942

We held an Easter service in the chancery, with several of the
Easter hymns and music by Jones, piano, Tiso and Mrs. Playfair,
violins, and Miss Williams, flute. I also read the lesson from St.
John. We had been asked by the police if we wished to have some
American clergyman come in to hold the service, but we declined,
preferring an informal gathering. The Catholics were taken to Mass
in one of the Catholic churches.

April 8, 1942

The Swiss Minister. It now looks as if we should not get away
until the middle of May at earliest. It is amusing to remember how,
in December, Alice remarked that we had better conserve our fire-
wood because we might be here until February and how everyone had
laughed at the joke. I lost ten dollars to Ned Crocker in a bet that
we should be away before St. Valentine's Day, and I believe that he
cleaned up in several other monthly bets.

JIMMIE DOOLITTLE RAIDS TOKYO

April 18, 1942

The Swiss Minister came again, and just as he was leaving before
lunch we heard a lot of planes overhead and saw five or six large
fires burning in different directions with great volumes of smoke. At
first we thought that it was only maneuvers but soon became aware
that it was the first big raid on Japan by American bombers which
are reported to have attacked first in the Hokkaido and then, in

turn, Tokyo, Yokosuka, Nagoya, and Kobe. We saw one of them, apparently losing altitude and flying very low, just over the tops of the buildings to the west, and at first we feared that it had crashed but then realized that it was intentionally following these tactics in order to avoid the dives of pursuit planes and the antiaircraft fire. To the east we saw a plane with a whole line of black puffs of smoke, indicating antiaircraft explosions, just on its tail; it didn't look like a bomber and we are inclined to believe that the Japanese batteries lost their heads and fired on their own pursuit planes.

All this was very exciting, but at the time it was hard to believe that it was more than a realistic practice by Japanese planes. The Japanese press claimed that nine enemy planes had crashed, but we doubt if any were lost since, if even one had crashed on land, the papers would have been full of triumphant pictures of the wreck. They appeared too large to have come from an aircraft carrier, and they may have been flying from the Aleutian Islands to the new air bases in China. We were all very happy and proud in the Embassy, and the British told us later that they drank toasts all day to the American fliers.

AFTER BATAAN AND THE CORAL SEA

May 26, 1942

Japanese propaganda is so childish that it merely becomes amusing. After the fall of Bataan the *Nichi Nichi* published on April 15 (evening edition) a photograph of the alleged entrance to the captured base, but the big painted sign says: U.S. Navy Vase, Mariveles, spelled with a *V*. The next day the *Times and Advertiser* published the same picture, but obviously recognized the error because they had scratched out the *V* and roughly substituted a *B*, the erasure being quite obvious. Of course the Japanese painted that sign themselves to prove to the public what they had captured.

In the *Miyako* and other vernacular papers on May 26 there are published photographs of the Coral Sea Battle, one picture showing the wake of a ship apparently leading up to a spout of spray and smoke which is labeled in the paper as marking the sinking of an American warship. But on another page of the paper another picture, clearly taken from the same spot but shifted a little more to the right, shows an American aircraft carrier going in the other direction *away* from the explosion, and it is clearly her wake that shows in the first picture!

WE PREPARE TO DEPART

May 29, 1942

Called a meeting of the staff to announce the good news of our prospective departure on June 18. There was great enthusiasm.

May 31, 1942

Memorial Day meeting at the residence; we sang *My Country, 'Tis of Thee, The Battle Hymn of the Republic,* and *The Star-Spangled Banner,* and I spoke. Everyone was there, 63 of us.

MEMORIAL DAY ADDRESS: "OUR NATIVE LAND"

For many years, according to the traditions of Memorial Day, we have annually on May 30 decorated in the cemetery in Yokohama the graves of the American soldiers, sailors, and civilians who are buried in Japan, and our Naval Attaché has annually placed a wreath on the water off Yokohama in memory of those who died at sea. These ceremonies, carried out with simple reverence, were symbolic of the American spirit: we do not, we cannot ever forget those who gave their lives for our country, whether in the heat of combat or in carrying out other duties aimed to create conditions in which combat might never occur. The American soldiers, sailors, and civilians who are buried in Japan were fortunately in the latter category. Who shall say whether it is the warriors in battle or those who work for peace before war intervenes that best serve their country? Many an American has lived and died abroad without fanfare, yet who labored loyally, unselfishly, and patriotically for what he considered to be the highest concept of his nation's good. But when war comes, when freedom and righteousness and law and order are confronted with lawlessness and disorder and slavery and the predatory instincts of primeval man, then:

> *Though love repine and reason chafe,*
> *There came a voice without reply:*
> *'Tis man's perdition to be safe*
> *When for the truth he ought to die!*

During these months of our internment, we have regularly held these Sunday meetings for the singing of hymns. Those of us who have attended those meetings must have felt their spontaneity, the reverent spirit in which they were conducted, and the inspiration which we have derived from them. Without the formality of church services we have, in the words of the psalm and in our own way, "worshiped God in the beauty of holiness," simply but from the heart. These Sunday gatherings, I believe, have served to brighten the flame of our Christian faith during moments of discouragement; they have taken us momentarily away from a war-torn world; they have brought us together. This year we cannot in practice hold the traditional ceremonies of decorating the graves on Memorial Day, but we have set aside this Sunday meeting of ours to remember in mind and spirit those who gave their lives for our country, and so that we may hold their memory perpetually warm.

I have mentioned the occasional moments of discouragement which must have come to all of us during these past difficult months. So far as I am concerned, such moments of discouragement have been but temporary. I have not an iota of doubt of our ultimate victory in this war of the nations. Call it a blind faith if you will. We cannot sit down and prove it as we would solve a mathematical problem. There are too many imponderable factors. Cold logic may ascribe that faith merely to wishful thinking. But there is more to it than that. Let us call it a fundamental instinctive conviction, based on many palpable factors, which to me is just as satisfying as mathematical proof, and if I can pass on to you even a tithe of that conviction and faith to add to your own, it is yours.

Now at last we are going home. I have spoken of these past months as difficult ones. They have been difficult, in some respects terribly difficult, in varying degrees and for various reasons in the case of each of us. To those who have been separated from their families our sympathy and understanding have been complete if inexpressible. I myself, during these past months, have had plenty of time to survey the ruins of a life's work, as an architect might regard, after earthquake and fire, the ruins of a great building which he had conceived and had endeavored to erect, pier by pier and stone by stone, with a solidity that might permanently withstand the elements. That castle, alas, has crumbled about us. It is not a happy vision.

Some of us, no doubt, will in the future look back upon this experience since last December as a nightmare. Yet to me it will never be a nightmare, simply because it has been the most inspiring experience in a longish public life full of vivid experiences. Here was a group of many different elements, heterogeneous elements if you will, with varying interests, characters, and predilections. Human nature is always human nature, and there were inevitable possibilities, if not probabilities, that this little group of ours would fail to stand the strain of the daily and hourly close association of our confinement over this long period. I leave it to you, each of you, to determine whether or not it has stood that strain. My own impression is that no similar group in the same circumstances could ever have stood the strain so well. The community spirit, the desire to share with the others what each could contribute, the co-operation and mutual helpfulness, the abnegation of self in so preponderant a number of cases, and, above all, the cheerfulness and humor that have pervaded our group in its restricted life, restricted both in space and activity, have given me a feeling of the deepest pride that I shall retain as long as I live, just as I shall always retain a close affection for you all. The spirit that has pervaded this group and that has resulted in this splendid co-operative atmosphere is fundamentally and intrinsically American. It is one of the instinctive traits that have made our country great, the trait of community spirit and mutual helpfulness. And as we look back in future on this experience, I believe we shall realize that far from being a period of stagnation, each one of us has gained something, each one of us has developed traits of character that may have needed development, each one of us has perhaps grown a little in stature. "And if I drink oblivion of a day," wrote Meredith, "so shorten I the stature of my soul." There has been no oblivion during this period, but rather work and care for the greatest good of the greatest number. That is the cause of my feeling of inspiration. I venture to hope that you all feel the same way about it, and that that same magnificent community spirit will carry us all the way home, right up to our landing on the soil of our beloved country.

Now we are going home to take whatever part we may find or be called upon to take in the great effort of our country. Please share my abundant faith, if you can, that that effort will not be in vain. We shall need the courage of our faith, and we shall continually need, in working with our fellow Americans at home, the same close co-operative spirit of which we have learned something during these months of our association here. "Faith, hope, and charity" is a pretty solid basis for the guidance of mankind, but I have always felt, and I feel it now more than ever, that a better connotation of the essential intention of that scriptural phrase can be expressed by the words "Faith, courage, and love." Those words give us a sound bearing for our future navigation, for both faith and hope need to be supported by courage if they are to be something more alive and vibrant than a mere pious platitude, and for their application in everyday life— so that our co-operative spirit shall be equally alive and vibrant— they need to be reinforced by what our hymn *America the Beautiful* refers to as our "brotherhood . . . from sea to shining sea."

Throughout the greater part of my life I have followed two little personal traditions. The first began in early youth and I carried it into our family, and when our children began to grow up and we returned from time to time to our country from abroad, we used to take those four little girls of ours to the bow of the liner just as we passed the Statue of Liberty in New York Harbor, and together we recited those burning lines of Scott which Edward Everett Hale, who in fact married us, had used so poignantly in his book *The Man Without a Country:*

> *Breathes there the man, with soul so dead,*
> *Who never to himself hath said:*
> *"This is my own, my native land";*
> *Whose heart hath ne'er within him burn'd*
> *As home his footsteps he hath turn'd*
> *From wandering on a foreign strand?*
> *If such there breathe, go mark him well;*
> *For him no minstrel raptures swell;*
> *High though his titles, proud his fame,*
> *Boundless his wealth as wish can claim,*
> *Despite his titles, power, and pelf,*
> *The wretch concentered all in self,*
> *Living, shall forfeit fair renown,*
> *And, doubly dying, shall go down*
> *To the vile dust, from whence he sprung,*
> *Unwept, unhonor'd, and unsung.*

The other little tradition of which I speak is to repeat every Memorial Day the Gettysburg Address, and today I should like to take this moment, while with you all, to do so, for I know of nothing ever written in the English language that can surpass it in the sheer beauty and inspiration of its diction. No doubt you know how it was prepared and delivered. The weary and harassed President made his rough notes for the address on the back of an old envelope while going down to Gettysburg in the train, and that night, while in the hotel, he put the speech into shape. At the meeting on the battlefield the next day, November 19, 1863, he was preceded by one of the foremost speakers of our country, who indulged at great length in the then customary flight of oratory. And when Lincoln, gaunt and ungainly, arose, spoke for but two or three minutes and then sat down, the audience was amazed and bitterly disappointed that on such an occasion they should have been deprived of the long bursts of grandiloquence to which they were accustomed and which they had eagerly awaited. The anticlimax after the preceding oration and the almost total absence of applause were pitiable. Even Lincoln himself believed that the address had been a woeful failure. It was only later, when the address was read and the majestic beauty and dignity of its words had penetrated, that the world found it was the richer for one of the greatest and most inspiring literary masterpieces of all time. How apt are those historic words on this Memorial Day, nearly eighty years later, must overwhelmingly impress us all.

Fourscore and seven years ago our fathers brought forth on this continent a new nation, conceived in liberty and dedicated to the proposition that all men are created equal.

Now we are engaged in a great civil war, testing whether that nation or any nation so conceived and so dedicated can long endure. We are met on a great battlefield of that war. We have come to dedicate a portion of that field as a final resting place of those who here gave their lives that this nation might live. It is altogether fitting and proper that we should do this.

But, in a larger sense, we cannot dedicate—we cannot consecrate—we cannot hallow—this ground. The brave men, living and dead, who struggled here, have consecrated it, far above our poor power to add or detract. The world will little note, nor long remember, what we say here, but it can never forget what they did here. It is for us the living, rather, to be dedicated here to the unfinished work which they who fought here have thus far so nobly advanced. It is rather for us to be here dedicated to the great task remaining before us—that from these honored dead we take increased devotion to that cause for which they gave the last full measure of devotion—that we here highly resolve that these dead shall not have died in vain —that this nation, under God, shall have a new birth of freedom—and that government of the people, by the people, for the people shall not perish from the earth.

Postscript to the American People

Radio Address delivered over the CBS network, August 30, 1942

FIRST OF ALL, I should like to say how deeply we have been moved, my associates and myself, who have just returned on the exchange ship *Gripsholm,* by the many greetings of friends and the great volume of messages of welcome which have come to us from all over the country. The welcome given us has warmed our hearts, and it is one that we can never forget, nor can we ever forget the really inexpressible joy of coming home after the difficult months and moments through which we have passed in Japan and Japanese-occupied territories. It may be impossible to answer all those messages individually. Please let me express now to all who hear me our most grateful thanks for them.

Never before has my native land looked to me so beautiful. Never before has a home-coming meant so much. I think you will realize a little of what it meant to us when I tell you of those last seven days at anchor off Yokohama before our evacuation vessel finally sailed from Japanese waters. We were awaiting the completion of the negotiations for our exchange, not knowing whether those negotiations would be successful and whether, if they were unsuccessful, we might not all be returned to our imprisonment in Japan. Among us were many Americans—missionaries, teachers, newspaper correspondents, businessmen—who had spent the preceding six months in solitary confinement in small, bitterly cold prison cells, inadequately clothed and inadequately fed and at times subjected to the most cruel and barbaric tortures. I will not go into the nature of those tortures, which were many, except to mention an incident on the *Gripsholm* when three elderly Americans, one of them over seventy years old, gave me a demonstration of the water cure which had repeatedly been inflicted upon them. We went up to the bow of the ship early in the morning where a friend posed as the subject of the torture. He was tied up with his knees drawn up to his chin, his neck being attached to his knees and his hands securely bound behind him so that the cords in the actual torture had penetrated deep under the skin. He was then rolled over with his face up and

water was poured into his nose and mouth. It was a realistic performance, but only from the oral description of those men could I
visualize what the actual torture must have been. Six large buckets
of water were used by the Japanese police, so that the subject in
every case lost consciousness and then was brought back to consciousness merely to have the same thing repeated. One of those
elderly missionaries was given the water cure six separate times in
order to make him divulge information which he was supposed to
have acquired as an alleged spy.

Nearly all of the American missionaries, teachers, newspaper correspondents, and businessmen were regarded as potential spies. The
stupidity of those Japanese police was only surpassed by their utter
cruelty. That same American told me that once while he was lying
tied on the ground a Japanese had ground his boot sole into his
face and then had brutally kicked him, smashing a rib. When he
was finally untied, he could barely stand and he said he feared that
a rib had been broken. One of the Japanese police asked where the
broken rib was and began to feel his body. As the Japanese came
to the broken bone he said, "Is that the place?" and when the man
answered "Yes," the policeman hauled off with his fist and hit that
broken rib as hard as he could. In another case, a well-known
American has been seriously maimed as a result of the gangrene
which was caused by the ill-treatment he received in his prison cell.
I had known him in years gone by and seldom have I had so great
a shock as when I saw him on the ship, a mere shadow of his former
self. There were many, many other cases.

I had heard indirectly of the horrible atrocities perpetrated in
the rape of Nanking and of the fearful things done in Hong Kong
when soldiers who had been taken as prisoners of war were bayoneted to death. But on shipboard we had direct evidence, for the
dying shrieks of those soldiers were heard by a woman, a fellow
passenger of ours, who herself told me the terrible story. This was
no secondhand evidence, but the reports of reliable firsthand witnesses and, in the case of the torture, the firsthand evidence of
those who had suffered the tortures themselves.

Do you wonder that during those seven days of waiting in the
harbor of Yokohama several of those people told me that if the
negotiations for our exchange failed they would commit suicide
rather than return to their imprisonment in Japan? I know that
they would have done so.

And then came one of the greatest of all moments. I awoke at

1:00 A.M., on June 25, sensing that something was happening. I looked out of the porthole and saw a piece of wood slowly moving past in the water. Another piece of wood moved faster. We were at last under way, slowly accelerating until the ship was finally speeding at full steam, away from Yokohama, away from Japan, pointing homeward. Ah, what a moment that was, even though we had 18,000 miles to cover and seventy days in all before we should pass the Statue of Liberty in New York Harbor and repeat to ourselves, with tears pouring down many a face,

> *Breathes there the man with soul so dead*
> *Who never to himself hath said,*
> *This is my own, my native land?*

I shall have something to say tonight about the Japanese military machine which brought on this war and against which we are fighting today. But before turning to that subject, there is something else which I cannot leave unsaid. I have lived for ten years in Japan. I have had many friends in Japan, some of whom I admired, respected, and loved. They are not the people who brought on this war. As patriots they will fight for their Emperor and country, to the last ditch if necessary, but they did not want this war and it was not they who began it. Even during our imprisonment in Tokyo many of those friends used to contrive to send us gifts, in spite of the usual obstruction of the police who wished to cut us off completely from the outside world. They were not the usual gifts of flowers but gifts of food, sometimes a piece of meat, which was the most precious gift they could confer because they themselves could seldom get meat. For ten years I have broken bread in their houses and they in mine. They were personally loyal to me to the end.

But there is the other side to the picture, the ugly side of cruelty, brutality, and utter bestiality, the ruthlessness and rapaciousness of the Japanese military machine which brought on this war. That Japanese military machine and military caste and military system must be utterly crushed, their credit and predominance must be utterly broken, for the future safety and welfare of the United States and of the United Nations, and for the future safety and welfare of civilization and humanity. Let us put it in a nutshell: there is not sufficient room in the area of the Pacific Ocean for a peaceful America, for any and all of the peace-loving United Nations, and a swashbuckling Japan.

And now, before closing, I should like to tell you something about the Japanese military machine against which we are fighting today. That machine has been trained and perfected through many years, for it has always had in view, even before the invasion of Manchuria in 1931, the prospect of eventually sweeping not only to the north against Russia, but to the west and south in order to control what the Japanese have latterly termed "The Co-Prosperity Sphere of Greater East Asia including the South Seas." It need hardly be said that the phrase "Co-Prosperity Sphere" denoted in fact the intention to exert Japanese control, politically, economically —absolutely—over all those far-flung territories.

In 1931 came their invasion of Manchuria. In 1937 came their invasion of China south of the wall, and while their Army eventually floundered in China, due to the magnificent fighting spirit of Chiang Kai-shek, his courageous armies, and his determined people, nevertheless the warfare which then ensued proved a practical training for the Japanese soldiers and sailors, who tirelessly developed and perfected the tactics which they subsequently used in their landings and conquests to the south.

The idea should not for a moment be entertained that the failure of the Japanese forces in China has discouraged the Japanese people. It has instead served to steel them for still greater sacrifices and to prepare them better for the war of deadly purpose to conquer upon which they have finally embarked. As the realization came home to them of the need for greater and greater efforts, they accepted the inevitable war-footing reorganization of the country's life with characteristic calmness and determination.

Probably no other factor has contributed more heavily to the preliminary victories achieved by the Japanese in this war than the offensive spirit which permeates all of the armed forces of the Empire. This spirit, recognized by competent military men as the most vital intangible factor in achieving victory, has been nourished and perpetuated since the foundation of the modern Japanese Army. The Japanese High Command has counted heavily upon the advantages this would give them over less aggressive enemies. They have put great store in what they consider to be the white man's flabbiness. They look upon us Americans as constitutional weaklings, demanding our daily comforts and unwilling to make the sacrifices demanded for victory in a war against a military machine which has prepared and trained itself in Spartan simplicity and the hardness and toughness demanded by war. They attach great importance to the former disunity in the United States over the war issue and they still count on an appreciable interval before an aroused nation can find itself and develop a fighting spirit of its own. By that time, they feel, Japan will be in complete control of all East Asia. When they struck, they made no provision for failure; they left no road open for retreat. They struck with all the force and power at their command. And they will continue to fight in the same manner until they are utterly crushed.

We shall crush that machine and caste and system in due course, but if we Americans think that, collectively and individually, we can continue to lead our normal lives, leaving the spirit of self-sacrifice to our soldiers and sailors, letting the intensification of our production program take care of itself, we shall unquestionably risk the danger of a stalemate in this war of ours with Japan. I say this in the light of my ten years' experience in Japan, my knowledge of the power of the Japanese Army and Navy and of the hardness and fighting spirit of the Japanese. I feel it my bounden duty to say this to my fellow countrymen. I know my own country even better than I know Japan and I have not the slightest shadow of doubt of our eventual victory. But I do not wish to see the period of our blood, sweat, and tears *indefinitely and unnecessarily prolonged.* That period will be prolonged only if our people fail to realize the truth of what I have just said, that we are up against a powerful fighting machine, a people whose morale cannot and will not be broken even by successive defeats, who will certainly not be broken by economic hardships, a people who individually and collectively will gladly sacrifice their lives for their Emperor and their nation, and who can be brought to earth only by physical defeat, by being ejected physically from the areas which they have temporarily conquered or by a progressive attrition of their naval power and merchant marine which will finally result in cutting off their homeland from all connection with and access to those outlying areas—by complete defeat in battle.

I need say no more. I have told you the truth as I see it from long experience and observation. I have come home with my associates in the Far East to join our war effort with yours and I realize, perhaps better than anyone else, that nothing less than the exertion of our maximum capacities, individually and collectively, in a war of offense will bring our beloved country safely through these deep waters to the longed-for haven of a victorious peace.

We are fighting this war for the preservation of righteousness,

law, and order, but above all for the preservation of the freedoms
which have been conferred upon us by the glorious heritage of our
American citizenship, and for these same freedoms in other countries of the United Nations, and while we are fighting against the
forces of evil, lawlessness, and disorder in the world, we are primarily fighting to prevent the enslavement which actually threatens
to be imposed upon us if we fail. I am convinced that this is not an
overstatement. Surely ours is a cause worth sacrificing for and living for and dying for if necessary. "Though love repine and reason
chafe, there came a voice without reply; 'tis man's perdition to be
safe, when for the truth he ought to die."

List of Prominent Japanese Officials and Foreign Diplomatic Chiefs of Mission Accredited to Japan

Dates in parentheses indicate time of taking office.

1932 (June)

PRIME MINISTER: Admiral Viscount
Makoto Saito (May 23, 1932)
MINISTER FOR FOREIGN AFFAIRS:
Makoto Saito (May 23, 1932)
Count Yasuya Uchida (July 6, 1932)
VICE-MINISTER FOR FOREIGN AFFAIRS:
Mr. Hachiro Arita (May 23, 1932)

CABINET MEMBERS:

WAR: Lieutenant General Sadao Araki
(May 26, 1932)
NAVY: Admiral Keisuke Okada
(May 26, 1932)
FINANCE: Mr. Korekiyo Takahashi
(May 26, 1932)
COMMERCE AND INDUSTRY: Baron
Kumakichi Nakajima (May 26, 1932)

AMBASSADORS:

BELGIUM: Baron Albert de Bassompierre
(Sept. 15, 1921)
U.S.S.R.: Mr. Alexander Troyanovsky
(Feb. 1, 1928)
GERMANY: Dr. Ernst Arthur Voretzsch
(Jan. 22, 1929)
ITALY: Mr. Giovanni Cesare Majoni
(June 17, 1930)
FRANCE: Count Damien de Martel
(July 7, 1930)
BRAZIL: Mr. Sylvino Gurgel do Amaral
(June 8, 1931)
GREAT BRITAIN: Sir Francis Lindley
(July 8, 1931)
UNITED STATES OF AMERICA:
Mr. Joseph C. Grew

MINISTERS:

NETHERLANDS: General J. C. Pabst
(July 7, 1923)
POLAND: Mr. Zdzislaw Okecki
(June 13, 1928)
SWITZERLAND: Mr. Emile Traversini
(Oct. 26, 1928)

CHILE: Mr. Enrique Gallarde Nieto
(Oct. 31, 1928)
SWEDEN: Dr. J. E. Hultman
(April 12, 1929)
CANADA: Hon. Herbert Marler
(Sept. 18, 1929)
MEXICO: Dr. Miguel Alonzo-Romero
(Nov. 25, 1929)
NORWAY: Mr. Ludwig Caesar Aubert
(March 22, 1930)
PORTUGAL: Mr. Justino de Montalvao
(Sept. 17, 1930)
CUBA: Mr. Orestes Ferrara
(May 28, 1931)
CHINA: General Tsiang Tso-ping
(Oct. 5, 1931)
ARGENTINA: Dr. Rodolfo Freyre
(Dec. 24, 1931)
PERSIA: Mr. Hassan Ali Hedayat
(Feb. 25, 1932)
SPAIN: Mr. Santiago Mendez de Vigo
(April 25, 1932)
CZECHOSLOVAKIA:
Mr. Frantisek Havlicek (May 6, 1932)

CHARGÉS D'AFFAIRES:

RUMANIA: Mr. Georges Stoïcesco
(July 18, 1929)
FINLAND: Mr. George Winckelmann
(April 22, 1930)
TURKEY: Mr. Nebil Bey
(Dec. 22, 1931)

AMERICAN EMBASSY:

COUNSELOR: Mr. Edwin L. Neville
MILITARY ATTACHÉ: Lieutenant-Colonel
James G. McIlroy
NAVAL ATTACHÉ:
Captain Isaac C. Johnson
COMMERCIAL ATTACHÉ:
Mr. Halleck A. Butts
FIRST SECRETARY: Mr. Erle R. Dickover
THIRD SECRETARIES: Mr. William T.
Turner, Mr. S. Walter Washington
CONSUL GENERAL: Mr. Arthur Garrels

1933 (January 1)

PRIME MINISTER: Admiral Viscount
Makoto Saito (May 23, 1932)
MINISTER FOR FOREIGN AFFAIRS:
Count Yasuya Uchida (July 6, 1932)
VICE-MINISTER FOR FOREIGN AFFAIRS:
Hachiro Arita (May 23, 1932)

CABINET MEMBERS:

WAR: Lieutenant General Sadao Araki
(May 26, 1932)
NAVY: Admiral Keisuke Okada
(May 26, 1932)
FINANCE: Mr. Korekiyo Takahashi
(May 26, 1932)
COMMERCE AND INDUSTRY: Baron
Kumakichi Nakajima (May 26, 1932)

AMBASSADORS:

BELGIUM: Baron Albert de Bassompierre
(Sept. 15, 1921)
U.S.S.R.: Mr. Alexander Troyanovsky
(Feb. 1, 1928)
GERMANY: Dr. Ernst Arthur Voretzsch
(Jan. 22, 1929)
ITALY: Mr. Giovanni Cesare Majoni
(June 17, 1930)
FRANCE: Count Damien de Martel
(July 7, 1930)
BRAZIL: Mr. Sylvino Gurgel do Amaral
(June 8, 1931)
GREAT BRITAIN: Sir Francis Lindley
(July 8, 1931)
UNITED STATES OF AMERICA:
Mr. Joseph C. Grew (June 14, 1932)

MINISTERS:

NETHERLANDS: General J. C. Pabst
(July 7, 1923)
POLAND: Mr. Zdzislaw Okecki
(June 13, 1928)
SWITZERLAND: Mr. Emile Traversini
(Oct. 26, 1928)
CHILE: Mr. Enrique Gallarde Nieto
(Oct. 31, 1928)
SWEDEN: Dr. J. E. Hultman
(April 12, 1929)
CANADA: Hon. Herbert Marler
(Sept. 18, 1929)
MEXICO: Dr. Miguel Alonzo-Romero
(Nov. 25, 1929)
NORWAY: Mr. Ludwig Caesar Aubert
(March 22, 1930)
PORTUGAL: Mr. Justino de Montalvao
(Sept. 17, 1930)
CUBA: Mr. Orestes Ferrara
(May 28, 1931)

CHINA: General Tsiang Tso-ping
(Oct. 5, 1931)
ARGENTINA: Dr. Rodolfo Freyre
(Dec. 24, 1931)
PERSIA: Mr. Hassan Ali Hedayat
(Feb. 25, 1932)
SPAIN: Mr. Santiago Mendez de Vigo
(April 25, 1932)
CZECHOSLOVAKIA:
Mr. Frantisek Havlicek (May 6, 1932)
SIAM: General Phya Indra Vijit
(Oct. 6, 1932)

CHARGÉS D'AFFAIRES:

RUMANIA: Mr. Georges Stoïcesco
(July 18, 1929)
FINLAND: Mr. George Winckelmann
(April 22, 1930)
TURKEY: Mr. Nebil Bey
(Dec. 22, 1931)

AMERICAN EMBASSY:

COUNSELOR: Mr. Edwin L. Neville
MILITARY ATTACHÉ: Lieutenant-Colonel
James G. McIlroy
NAVAL ATTACHÉ:
Captain Isaac C. Johnson
COMMERCIAL ATTACHÉ:
Mr. Halleck A. Butts
FIRST SECRETARY: Mr. Erle R. Dickover
SECOND SECRETARY:
Mr. William T. Turner
THIRD SECRETARY:
Mr. S. Walter Washington
CONSUL GENERAL: Mr. Arthur Garrels

1934 (January 1)

PRIME MINISTER: Admiral Viscount
Makoto Saito (May 23, 1932)
MINISTER FOR FOREIGN AFFAIRS:
Mr. Koki Hirota (Sept. 14, 1933)
VICE-MINISTER FOR FOREIGN AFFAIRS: Mr.
Mamoru Shigemitsu (May 16, 1933)

CABINET MEMBERS:

WAR: Lieutenant General Sadao Araki
(May 26, 1932)
NAVY: Admiral Mineo Osumi
(Jan. 9, 1933)
FINANCE: Mr. Korekiyo Takahashi
(May 26, 1932)
COMMERCE AND INDUSTRY: Baron
Kumakichi Nakajima (May 26, 1932)

AMBASSADORS:

BELGIUM: Baron Albert de Bassompierre
(Sept. 15, 1921)

BRAZIL: Mr. Sylvino Gurgel do Amaral
(June 8, 1931)
GREAT BRITAIN: Sir Francis Lindley
(July 8, 1931)
UNITED STATES OF AMERICA:
Mr. Joseph C. Grew (June 14, 1932)
U.S.S.R.: Mr. Constantin Yurenev
(March 20, 1933)
ITALY: Mr. Giacinto Auriti
(July 10, 1933)
FRANCE: Mr. Fernand Pila
(Nov. 30, 1933)
GERMANY: Dr. Herbert von Dirksen
(Dec. 27, 1933)

MINISTERS:

NETHERLANDS: General J. C. Pabst
(July 7, 1923)
SWEDEN: Dr. J. E. Hultman
(April 12, 1929)
CANADA: Hon. Herbert Marler
(Sept. 18, 1929)
MEXICO: Dr. Miguel Alonzo-Romero
(Nov. 25, 1929)
NORWAY: Mr. Ludwig Caesar Aubert
(March 22, 1930)
CHINA: General Tsiang Tso-ping
(Oct. 5, 1931)
ARGENTINA: Dr. Rodolfo Freyre
(Dec. 24, 1931)
PERSIA: Mr. Hassan Ali Hedayat
(Feb. 25, 1932)
SPAIN: Mr. Santiago Mendez de Vigo
(April 25, 1932)
CZECHOSLOVAKIA:
Mr. Frantisek Havlicek (May 6, 1932)
SIAM: General Phya Indra Vijit
(Oct. 6, 1932)
MANCHUKUO: Mr. M. W. S. Tinge
(May 18, 1933)
FINLAND: Mr. Hugo Valvanne
(Oct. 5, 1933)
POLAND: Mr. Michael Moscicki
(Oct. 5, 1933)
AFGHANISTAN: Mr. Habibullah Tarzi
(Oct. 18, 1933)

CHARGÉS D'AFFAIRES:

RUMANIA: Mr. Georges Stoïcesco
(July 18, 1929)
TURKEY: Mr. Nebil Bey
(Dec. 22, 1931)

AMERICAN EMBASSY:

COUNSELOR: Mr. Edwin L. Neville
MILITARY ATTACHÉ:
Major William C. Crane

NAVAL ATTACHÉ:
Captain Fred F. Rogers
COMMERCIAL ATTACHÉ:
Mr. Frank S. Williams
FIRST SECRETARY: Mr. Erle R. Dickover
SECOND SECRETARY:
Mr. Edward S. Crocker
THIRD SECRETARIES: Mr. William T.
Turner, Mr. Morris N. Hughes,
Mr. George D. Andrews
CONSUL GENERAL: Mr. Arthur Garrels

1935 (January 1)

PRIME MINISTER:
Admiral Keisuke Okada (July 4, 1934)
MINISTER FOR FOREIGN AFFAIRS:
Mr. Koki Hirota (Sept. 14, 1933)
VICE-MINISTER FOR FOREIGN AFFAIRS: Mr.
Mamoru Shigemitsu (May 6, 1933)

CABINET MEMBERS:

WAR: General Senjuro Hayashi
(Jan. 21, 1934)
NAVY: Admiral Mineo Osumi
(Jan. 9, 1933)
FINANCE: Mr. Sadamobu Fujii
(July 5, 1934)
Mr. Takahashi (Nov. 27, 1934)
COMMERCE AND INDUSTRY:
Mr. Chuji Machida (July 5, 1934)

AMBASSADORS:

BELGIUM: Baron Albert de Bassompierre
(Sept. 15, 1921)
UNITED STATES OF AMERICA:
Mr. Joseph C. Grew (June 14, 1932)
U.S.S.R.: Mr. Constantin Yurenev
(March 20, 1933)
ITALY: Mr. Giacinto Auriti
(July 10, 1933)
FRANCE: Mr. Fernand Pila
(Nov. 30, 1933)
GERMANY: Dr. Herbert von Dirksen
(Dec. 27, 1933)
GREAT BRITAIN: Sir Robert Clive
(June 28, 1934)
BRAZIL: Mr. Carlos Martins Sousa
(Sept. 17, 1934)

MINISTERS:

NETHERLANDS: General J. C. Pabst
(July 7, 1923)
SWEDEN: Dr. J. E. Hultman
(April 12, 1929)
CANADA: Hon. Herbert Marler
(Sept. 18, 1929)

MEXICO: Dr. Miguel Alonzo-Romero
(Nov. 25, 1929)
NORWAY: Mr. Ludwig Caesar Aubert
(March 22, 1930)
CHINA: General Tsiang Tso-ping
(Oct. 5, 1931)
SPAIN: Mr. Santiago Mendez de Vigo
(April 25, 1932)
CZECHOSLOVAKIA:
Mr. Frantisek Havlicek (May 6, 1932)
MANCHUKUO: Mr. M. W. S. Tinge
(May 18, 1933)
FINLAND: Mr. Hugo Valvanne
(Oct. 5, 1933)
POLAND: Mr. Michael Moscicki
(Oct. 5, 1933)
AFGHANISTAN: Mr. Habibullah Tarzi
(Oct. 19, 1933)
COLOMBIA: Dr. Domingo Esguerra
(April 28, 1934)
SIAM: Mr. Phra Raksha
(June 18, 1934)
PORTUGAL: Mr. Thomaz Ribeiro de
Mello (July 2, 1934)
PERSIA: Mr. Mirza Bagher Azimi
(Oct. 18, 1934)

CHARGÉS D'AFFAIRES:
RUMANIA: Mr. Georges Stoïcesco
(July 18, 1929)
TURKEY: Mr. Nebil Bey
(Dec. 22, 1931)

AMERICAN EMBASSY:
COUNSELOR: Mr. Edwin L. Neville
MILITARY ATTACHÉ:
Major William C. Crane
NAVAL ATTACHÉ:
Captain Fred F. Rogers
COMMERCIAL ATTACHÉ:
Mr. Frank S. Williams
FIRST SECRETARY: Mr. Erle R. Dickover
SECOND SECRETARY:
Mr. Edward S. Crocker
THIRD SECRETARIES: Mr. William T.
Turner, Mr. Morris N. Hughes,
Mr. George D. Andrews
CONSUL GENERAL: Mr. Arthur Garrels

1936 (January 1)
PRIME MINISTER:
Admiral Keisuke Okada (July 4, 1934)
MINISTER FOR FOREIGN AFFAIRS:
Mr. Koki Hirota (Sept. 14, 1933)
VICE-MINISTER FOR FOREIGN AFFAIRS: Mr.
Mamoru Shigemitsu (May 6, 1933)

CABINET MEMBERS:
WAR: General Yoshiyaki Kuwashima
(Sept. 4, 1935)
NAVY: Admiral Mineo Osumi
(Jan. 9, 1933)
FINANCE: Mr. Sadanobu Fujii
(July 5, 1935)
COMMERCE AND INDUSTRY:
Mr. Chuji Machida (July 5, 1934)

AMBASSADORS:
BELGIUM: Baron Albert de Bassompierre
(Sept. 15, 1921)
UNITED STATES OF AMERICA:
Mr. Joseph C. Grew (June 14, 1932)
U.S.S.R.: Mr. Constantin Yurenev
(March 20, 1933)
ITALY: Mr. Giacinto Auriti
(July 10, 1933)
FRANCE: Mr. Fernand Pila
(Nov. 30, 1933)
GERMANY: Dr. Herbert von Dirksen
(Dec. 27, 1933)
GREAT BRITAIN: Sir Robert Clive
(June 28, 1934)
CHINA: General Tsiang Tso-ping
(June 20, 1935)
MANCHUKUO: Mr. Hsieh Chieh-shih
(July 4, 1935)

MINISTERS:
NETHERLANDS: General J. C. Pabst
(July 7, 1923)
SWEDEN: Dr. J. E. Hultman
(April 12, 1929)
CANADA: Hon. Sir Herbert Marler
(Sept. 18, 1929)
SPAIN: Mr. Santiago Mendez de Vigo
(April 25, 1932)
CZECHOSLOVAKIA:
Mr. Frantisek Havlicek (May 5, 1932)
FINLAND: Mr. Hugo Valvanne
(Oct. 5, 1933)
POLAND: Mr. Michael Moscicki
(Oct. 5, 1933)
AFGHANISTAN: Mr. Habibullah Tarzi
(Oct. 19, 1933)
COLOMBIA: Dr. Domingo Esguerra
(April 28, 1934)
SIAM: Mr. Phra Raksha
(June 18, 1934)
PORTUGAL: Dr. Thomaz Ribeiro de
Mello (July 2, 1934)
IRAN: Mr. Mirza Bagher Azimi
(Oct. 18, 1934)
SWITZERLAND: Mr. Walter Thurnheer
(Feb. 7, 1935)

MEXICO: General Francisco J. Aguilar
(March 14, 1935)
ARGENTINA: Mr. Eduardo Racedo
(Nov. 28, 1935)

CHARGÉS D'AFFAIRES:
RUMANIA: Mr. Georges Stoïcesco
(July 18, 1929)
TURKEY: Mr. Nebil Bey
(Dec. 22, 1931)

AMERICAN EMBASSY:
COUNSELOR: Mr. Edwin L. Neville
MILITARY ATTACHÉ:
Lieutenant-Colonel William C. Crane
NAVAL ATTACHÉ: Captain Fred F. Rogers
COMMERCIAL ATTACHÉ:
Mr. Frank S. Williams
FIRST SECRETARY: Mr. Erle R. Dickover
SECOND SECRETARIES: Mr. Edward S.
Crocker, Mr. Cabot Coville
THIRD SECRETARIES: Mr. Morris N.
Hughes, Mr. George Andrews
CONSUL GENERAL: Mr. Arthur Garrels

1937 (January 1)
PRIME MINISTER: Mr. Koki Hirota
(March 19, 1936)
MINISTER FOR FOREIGN AFFAIRS:
Mr. Koki Hirota (March 19, 1936)
Mr. Hachiro Arita (April 2, 1936)
VICE-MINISTER FOR FOREIGN AFFAIRS: Mr.
Kensuke Horinouchi (April 1, 1936)

CABINET MEMBERS:
WAR: General Count Juichi Terauchi
(March 9, 1936)
NAVY: Admiral Osami Nagano
(March 9, 1936)
FINANCE: Mr. Eiichi Baba
(March 9, 1936)
COMMERCE AND INDUSTRY: Mr. Chikukei
Nakajima (March 9, 1936)

AMBASSADORS:
BELGIUM: Baron Albert de Bassompierre
(Sept. 15, 1921)
UNITED STATES OF AMERICA:
Mr. Joseph C. Grew (June 14, 1932)
U.S.S.R.: Mr. Constantin Yurenev
(March 20, 1933)
ITALY: Mr. Giacinto Auriti
(July 10, 1933)
GERMANY: Dr. Herbert von Dirksen
(Dec. 27, 1933)
GREAT BRITAIN: Sir Robert Clive
(June 28, 1934)

MANCHUKUO: Mr. Hsieh Chieh-shih
(July 4, 1935)
BRAZIL: Mr. Pedro Leao Velloso
(Dec. 24, 1935)
TURKEY: Mr. R. Husrey Gerede
(March 23, 1936)
CHINA: Mr. Hsu Shih-ying
(April 6, 1936)
FRANCE: Mr. Albert Kammerer
(July 2, 1936)

MINISTERS:
NETHERLANDS: General J. C. Pabst
(July 7, 1923)
SWEDEN: Dr. J. E. Hultman
(April 12, 1929)
SPAIN: Mr. Santiago Mendez de Vigo
(April 25, 1932)
CZECHOSLOVAKIA:
Mr. Frantisek Havlicek (May 5, 1932)
FINLAND: Mr. Hugo Valvanne
(Oct. 5, 1933)
POLAND: Mr. Michael Moscicki
(Oct. 5, 1933)
AFGHANISTAN: Mr. Habibullah Tarzi
(Oct. 19, 1933)
COLOMBIA: Dr. Domingo Esguerra
(April 28, 1934)
SIAM: Mr. Phra Raksha
(June 18, 1934)
PORTUGAL: Dr. Thomaz Ribeiro de
Mello (July 2, 1934)
IRAN: Mr. Mirza Bagher Azimi
(Oct. 18, 1934)
SWITZERLAND: Mr. Walter Thurnheer
(Feb. 7, 1935)
MEXICO: General Francisco J. Aguilar
(March 14, 1935)
ARGENTINA: Mr. Eduardo Racedo
(Nov. 28, 1935)
DENMARK: Baron Rudolph Bertouch-
Lehn (Dec. 19, 1935)
RUMANIA: Mr. Georges Stoïcesco
(April 14, 1936)
CHILE: Mr. Martin Figueroa
(May 14, 1936)
NORWAY: Mr. Finn Koren
(May 28, 1936)
CANADA: Hon. R. Randolph Bruce
(Nov. 7, 1936)
PERU: Dr. Ricardo Rivera Schreiber
(Dec. 18, 1936)

AMERICAN EMBASSY:
COUNSELOR: Mr. Edwin L. Neville
(absent)
MILITARY ATTACHÉ:
Lieutenant-Colonel William C. Crane

NAVAL ATTACHÉ: Captain Harold Bemis
COMMERCIAL ATTACHÉ:
Mr. Frank S. Williams
FIRST SECRETARIES: Mr. Erle R. Dickover,
Mr. Joseph F. McGurk
SECOND SECRETARIES: Mr. Edward S.
Crocker, Mr. Cabot Coville
THIRD SECRETARY:
Mr. George D. Andrews
CONSUL GENERAL: Mr. Arthur Garrels

1938 (January 1)
PRIME MINISTER:
General Senjuro Hayashi
(Feb. 2, 1937)
Prince Fumimaro Konoye
(June 4, 1937)
MINISTER FOR FOREIGN AFFAIRS:
General Senjuro Hayashi
(Feb. 2, 1937)
Mr. Naotake Sato (March 1, 1937)
Mr. Koki Hirota (June 4, 1937)
VICE-MINISTER FOR FOREIGN AFFAIRS: Mr.
Kensuke Horinouchi (April 1, 1936)

CABINET MEMBERS:
WAR: General Kotaro Nakamura
(Feb. 2, 1937)
NAVY: Admiral Mitsumasa Yonai
(Feb. 2, 1937)
FINANCE: Mr. Toyotaro Yuki
(Feb. 2, 1937)
Mr. Okinobu Kaya (June 3, 1937)
COMMERCE AND INDUSTRY:
Admiral Takuo Godo (Feb. 2, 1937)
Mr. Sheinji Yoshino (June 3, 1937)

AMBASSADORS:
BELGIUM: Baron Albert de Bassompierre
(Sept. 15, 1921)
UNITED STATES OF AMERICA:
Mr. Joseph C. Grew (June 14, 1932)
ITALY: Mr. Giacinto Auriti
(July 10, 1933)
BRAZIL: Mr. Pedro Leao Velloso
(Dec. 24, 1935)
TURKEY: Mr. Husrey Gerede
(March 23, 1936)
FRANCE: Mr. Charles Arsène-Henry
(March 12, 1937)
MANCHUKUO: Mr. Yuan Chen-tse
(July 2, 1937)
U.S.S.R.: Mr. Mikhail Slavoutski
(Sept. 2, 1937)
GREAT BRITAIN: Hon. Sir Robert Craigie
(Sept. 11, 1937)
POLAND: Mr. Thaddée de Romer
(Nov. 2, 1937)

GERMANY: General Eugen Ott
(April 28, 1938)

MINISTERS:
NETHERLANDS: General J. C. Pabst
(July 7, 1923)
CZECHOSLOVAKIA:
Mr. Frantisek Havlicek (May 6, 1932)
FINLAND: Mr. Hugo Valvanne
(Oct. 5, 1933)
AFGHANISTAN: Mr. Habibullah Tarzi
(Oct. 19, 1933)
PORTUGAL: Dr. Thomaz Ribeiro de
Mello (July 2, 1934)
SWITZERLAND: Mr. Walter Thurnheer
(Feb. 7, 1935)
MEXICO: General Francisco Aguilar
(March 14, 1935)
ARGENTINA: Mr. Eduardo Racedo
(Nov. 28, 1935)
DENMARK: Baron Rudolph Bertouch-
Lehn (Dec. 19, 1935)
RUMANIA: Mr. Georges Stoïcesco
(April 14, 1936)
CHILE: Mr. Martin Figueroa
(May 14, 1936)
NORWAY: Mr. Finn Koren
(May 28, 1936)
CANADA: Hon. R. Randolph Bruce
(Nov. 6, 1936)
SWEDEN: Mr. Widar Bagge
(March 12, 1937)
SIAM: Mr. Phya Sri Sena (Nov. 11, 1937)

AMERICAN EMBASSY:
COUNSELOR: Mr. Eugene H. Dooman
MILITARY ATTACHÉ: Lieutenant-Colonel
Harry I. Creswell
NAVAL ATTACHÉ: Captain Harold Bemis
COMMERCIAL ATTACHÉ:
Mr. Frank S. Williams
FIRST SECRETARY: Mr. Joseph C. McGurk
SECOND SECRETARIES: Mr. Edward S.
Crocker, Mr. Cabot Colville
Mr. George D. Andrews
CONSUL GENERAL: Mr. Charles Cameron

1939 (January 1)
PRIME MINISTER: Prince Fumimaro
Konoye (June 4, 1937)
MINISTER FOR FOREIGN AFFAIRS:
Mr. Koki Hirota (June 4, 1937)
General Ugaki (May 26, 1938)
Mr. Hachiro Arita (Oct. 29, 1938)
VICE-MINISTER FOR FOREIGN AFFAIRS: Mr.
Kensuke Horinouchi (April 1, 1936)
Mr. Renzo Sawada (Dec. 1, 1938)

CABINET MEMBERS:
WAR: General Gen Sugiyama
(December, 1937)
General Seishiro Itagaki
(May 26, 1938)
NAVY: Admiral Mitsumasa Yonai
(Feb. 2, 1937)
FINANCE: Mr. Seishin Ikeda
(May 26, 1938)
COMMERCE AND INDUSTRY: Mr. Seishin
Ikeda (May 26, 1938)

AMBASSADORS:
BELGIUM: Baron Albert de Bassompierre
(Sept. 15, 1921)
UNITED STATES OF AMERICA:
Mr. Joseph C. Grew (June 14, 1932)
ITALY: Mr. Giacinto Auriti
(July 10, 1933)
BRAZIL: Mr. Pedro Leao Velloso
(Dec. 24, 1935)
TURKEY: Mr. Husrey Gerede
(March 23, 1936)
FRANCE: Mr. Charles Arsène-Henry
(March 12, 1937)
MANCHUKUO: Mr. Yuan Chen-tse
(July 2, 1937)
GREAT BRITAIN: Hon. Sir Robert Craigie
(Sept. 11, 1937)
POLAND: Mr. Thaddée de Romer
(Nov. 2, 1937)
GERMANY: General Eugen Ott
(April 28, 1938)

MINISTERS:
NETHERLANDS: General J. C. Pabst
(July 7, 1923)
CZECHOSLOVAKIA: Mr. Frantisek Havlicek
(May 6, 1932)
FINLAND: Mr. Hugo Valvanne
(Oct. 5, 1933)
AFGHANISTAN: Mr. Habibullah Tarzi
(Oct. 19, 1933)
SWITZERLAND: Mr. Walter Thurnheer
(Feb. 7, 1935)
ARGENTINA: Mr. Eduardo Racedo
(Nov. 28, 1935)
DENMARK: Baron Rudolph Bertouch-
Lehn (Dec. 19, 1935)
RUMANIA: Mr. Georges Stoïcesco
(April 14, 1936)
CHILE: Mr. Martin Figueroa
(May 14, 1936)
NORWAY: Mr. Finn Koren (May 28, 1936)
SWEDEN: Mr. Widar Bagge
(March 12, 1937)
SIAM: Mr. Phya Sri Sena (Nov. 11, 1937)
EGYPT: Mr. Abdel Wahab Bey
(Jan. 17, 1938)

PERU: Dr. Ricardo Rivera Schreiber
(Sept. 8, 1938)
PORTUGAL: Mr. Joaquim Pedroso
(Sept. 8, 1938)
SPAIN: Mr. Santiago Mendez de Vigo
(Oct. 6, 1938)

AMERICAN EMBASSY:
COUNSELOR: Mr. Eugene H. Dooman
MILITARY ATTACHÉ:
Lieutenant-Colonel Harry I. Creswell
NAVAL ATTACHÉ:
Captain Harold M. Bemis
COMMERCIAL ATTACHÉ:
Mr. Frank S. Williams
FIRST SECRETARIES: Mr. Joseph F.
McGurk, Mr. Edward S. Crocker
SECOND SECRETARY: Mr. Cabot Coville
THIRD SECRETARIES: Mr. Frank A.
Schuler, Mr. Max W. Schmidt
CONSUL GENERAL: Mr. Charles Cameron

1940 (January 1)
PRIME MINISTER:
Baron Kiichiro Hiranuma
(January 4, 1939)
General Nobuyaki Abe
(August 30, 1939)
MINISTER FOR FOREIGN AFFAIRS:
Mr. Hachiro Arita (Oct. 28, 1938)
General Nobuyaki Abe
(August 30, 1939)
Admiral Kichisaburo Nomura
(Sept. 25, 1939)
VICE-MINISTER FOR FOREIGN AFFAIRS:
Mr. Renzo Sawada (Dec. 1, 1938)
Mr. Masayuki Tani (Aug. 30, 1939)

CABINET MEMBERS:
WAR: General Shuroku Hata
(August 30, 1939)
NAVY: Vice-Admiral Zengo Yoshida
(August 30, 1939)
FINANCE: Mr. Kazuo Aoki
(August 30, 1939)
COMMERCE AND INDUSTRY:
Mr. Takuo Godo (August 30, 1939)

AMBASSADORS:
UNITED STATES OF AMERICA:
Mr. Joseph C. Grew (June 14, 1932)
ITALY: Mr. Giacinto Auriti
(July 10, 1933)
FRANCE: Mr. Charles Arsène-Henry
(March 12, 1937)
MANCHUKUO: Mr. Yuan Chen-tse
(July 2, 1937)
GREAT BRITAIN: Hon. Sir Robert Craigie
(Sept. 11, 1937)

POLAND: Mr. Thaddee de Romer
(Nov. 2, 1937)
GERMANY: General Eugen Ott
(April 28, 1938)
BRAZIL: Mr. Frederico de Castello-
Branco Clark (April 10, 1939)
BELGIUM: Mr. Pierre Forthomme
(Nov. 6, 1939)
U. S. S. R.: Mr. Constantin Smetanin
(Nov. 20, 1939)
TURKEY: Mr. Ferid Tek (Dec. 14, 1939)

MINISTERS:

NETHERLANDS: General J. C. Pabst
(July 7, 1923)
SWEDEN: Mr. Widar Bagge
(March 12, 1937)
THAILAND: Mr. Phya Sri Sena
(Nov. 11, 1937)
PERU: Dr. Ricardo Rivera Schreiber
(Sept. 8, 1938)
SPAIN: Mr. Santiago Mendez de Vigo
(Oct. 6, 1938)
COLOMBIA: Mr. Alfredo Michelsen
(Feb. 24, 1939)
ARGENTINA: Dr. Rodolfo Moreno
(April 7, 1939)
MEXICO: Mr. Primo Villa Michel
(April 7, 1939)
DENMARK: Mr. Lars P. Tillitse
(April 10, 1939)
GREECE: Mr. Athanase G. Politis
(April 24, 1939)
AFGHANISTAN: Zul Facar Khan
(June 12, 1939)
RUMANIA: Mr. Georges Parachivesco
(June 12, 1939)
FINLAND: Dr. Charles Gustave Idman
(Nov. 6, 1939)
CHILE: Mr. Armando Labra Carvajal
(Nov. 30, 1939)
HUNGARY: Mr. Georges de Ghika
(Dec. 21, 1939)

AMERICAN EMBASSY:

COUNSELOR: Mr. Eugene H. Dooman
MILITARY ATTACHÉ:
Lieutenant-Colonel Harry I. Creswell
NAVAL ATTACHÉ:
Lieutenant-Commander Henri H.
Smith-Hutton
COMMERCIAL ATTACHÉ: Mr. Frank S.
Williams
FIRST SECRETARIES: Mr. Edward S.
Crocker, Mr. Stuart E. Grummon
SECOND SECRETARY:
Mr. William T. Turner
THIRD SECRETARIES: Mr. Frank A.
Schuler, Mr. Max W. Schmidt,
Mr. James Espy
CONSUL GENERAL: Mr. Charles Cameron

1941 (January 1)

PRIME MINISTER:
General Nobuyuki Abe
(Aug. 30, 1939)
Admiral Mitsumasa Yonai
(Jan. 16, 1940)
Prince Fumimaro Konoye
(July 22, 1940)
MINISTER FOR FOREIGN AFFAIRS:
Admiral Kichisaburo Nomura
(Sept. 25, 1939)
Mr. Hachiro Arita (Jan. 16, 1940)
Mr. Yosuke Matsuoka (July 22, 1940)
VICE-MINISTER FOR FOREIGN AFFAIRS:
Mr. Masayuki Tani (Aug. 30, 1939)
Mr. Chuichi Ohashi (Aug. 19, 1940)

CABINET MEMBERS:

WAR: Lieutenant General Hideki Tojo
(July 22, 1940)
NAVY: Admiral Koshiro Oikawa
(Sept. 5, 1940)
FINANCE: Mr. Isao Kawata
(July 22, 1940)
COMMERCE AND INDUSTRY:
Mr. Ichizo Kobayashi (July 22, 1940)

AMBASSADORS:

UNITED STATES OF AMERICA:
Mr. Joseph C. Grew (June 14, 1932)
FRANCE: Mr. Charles Arsène-Henry
(March 12, 1937)
GREAT BRITAIN: Sir Robert Craigie
(Sept. 11, 1937)
POLAND: Mr. Thaddée de Romer
(Nov. 2, 1937)
GERMANY: General Eugen Ott
(April 28, 1937)
BRAZIL: Mr. Frederico de Castello-
Branco Clark (April 10, 1939)
BELGIUM: Mr. Pierre Forthomme
(Nov. 6, 1939)
U. S. S. R.: Mr. Constantin Smetanin
(Nov. 20, 1939)
TURKEY: Mr. Ferid Tek (Dec. 14, 1939)
ITALY: Mr. Mario Indelli (July 20, 1940)
MANCHUKUO: Mr. Li Shao-keng
(Dec. 24, 1940)

MINISTERS:

NETHERLANDS: General J. C. Pabst
(July 7, 1923)
SWEDEN: Mr. Widar Bagge
(March 12, 1937)
THAILAND: Mr. Phya Sri Sena
(Nov. 11, 1937)
PERU: Dr. Ricardo Rivera Schreiber
(Sept. 8, 1938)
SPAIN: Mr. Santiago Mendez de Vigo
(Oct. 6, 1938)

COLOMBIA: Mr. Alfredo Michelsen
(Feb. 24, 1939)
ARGENTINA: Dr. Rodolfo Moreno
(April 7, 1939)
MEXICO: Mr. Primo Villa Michel (April 7, 1939)
DENMARK: Mr. Lars P. Tillitse
(April 10, 1939)
GREECE: Mr. Athanase G. Politis
(April 24, 1939)
AFGHANISTAN: Zul Facar Khan
(June 12, 1939)
FINLAND: Dr. Charles G. Idman
(Nov. 6, 1939)
CHILE: Mr. Armando L. Carvajal
(Nov. 30, 1939)
HUNGARY: Mr. Georges de Ghika
(Dec. 21, 1939)
SWITZERLAND: Mr. Camille Gorgé
(March 5, 1940)
PORTUGAL: Dr. Luiz Esteves Fernandes
(March 29, 1940)
AUSTRALIA: The Hon. Sir John G.
Latham (Dec. 24, 1940)

AMERICAN EMBASSY:
COUNSELOR: Mr. Eugene H. Dooman
MILITARY ATTACHÉ: Lieutenant-Colonel
Harry I. Creswell
NAVAL ATTACHÉ: Lieutenant-
Commander Henri H. Smith-Hutton
COMMERCIAL ATTACHÉ:
Mr. Frank S. Williams
FIRST SECRETARIES: Mr. George A.
Makinson, Mr. Edward S. Crocker,
Mr. Stuart E. Grummon
SECOND SECRETARY:
Mr. William T. Turner
THIRD SECRETARIES: Mr. Max W.
Schmidt, Mr. John K. Emmerson,
Mr. Charles A. Cooper, Mr. James
Espy

1942 (January 1)
PRIME MINISTER:
Prince Fumimaro Konoye
(July 22, 1940) 2d Cabinet
Prince Fumimaro Konoye
(July 18, 1941) 3d Cabinet
General Hideki Tojo
(October 18, 1941)
MINISTER FOR FOREIGN AFFAIRS:
Mr. Yosuke Matsuoka (July 22, 1940)
Admiral Teijiro Toyoda
(July 18, 1941)
Mr. Shigenori Togo (Oct. 18, 1941)

VICE-MINISTER FOR FOREIGN AFFAIRS:
Mr. Chuichi Ohashi (Aug. 19, 1940)
Mr. Eiji Amau (Aug. 15, 1941)
Mr. Haruhiko Nishi (Oct. 21, 1941)

CABINET MEMBERS:
WAR: General Hideki Tojo
(concurrently Prime Minister)
(Oct. 18, 1941)
NAVY: Admiral Shigetaro Shimada
(Oct. 18, 1941)
FINANCE: Mr. Okinobu Kaya
(Oct. 18, 1941)
COMMERCE AND INDUSTRY:
Mr. Nobusuke Kishi (Oct. 18, 1941)

AMBASSADORS:
UNITED STATES OF AMERICA:
Mr. Joseph C. Grew (June 14, 1932)
FRANCE: Mr. Charles Arsène-Henry
(March 12, 1937)
GREAT BRITAIN: Sir Robert Craigie
(Sept. 11, 1937)
GERMANY: General Eugen Ott
(April 28, 1938)
BRAZIL: Mr. Frederico de Castello-
Branco Clark (April 10, 1939)
BELGIUM: Mr. Pierre Forthomme
(Nov. 6, 1939)
U. S. S. R.: Mr. Constantin Smetanin
(Nov. 20, 1939)
TURKEY: Mr. Ferid Tek (Dec. 14, 1939)
ITALY: Mr. Mario Indelli (July 20, 1940)
MANCHUKUO: Mr. Li Shao-keng
(Dec. 24, 1940)
THAILAND: Mr. Phya Sri Sena
(Oct. 2, 1941)
CHINA: Mr. Hsu Liang (Nov. 27, 1941)

MINISTERS:
NETHERLANDS: General J. C. Pabst
(July 7, 1923)
SWEDEN: Mr. Widar Bagge
(March 12, 1937)
PERU: Dr. Ricardo Rivera Schreiber
(Sept. 8, 1938)
SPAIN: Mr. Santiago Mendez de Vigo
(Oct. 6, 1938)
COLOMBIA: Mr. Alfredo Michelsen
(Feb. 24, 1939)
DENMARK: Mr. Lars P. Tillitse
(April 10, 1939)
GREECE: Mr. Athanase G. Politis
(April 24, 1939)
AFGHANISTAN: Zul Facar Khan
(June 12, 1939)
FINLAND: Dr. Charles Gustave Idman
(Nov. 6, 1939)
CHILE: Mr. Armando Labra Carvajal
(Nov. 30, 1939)

SWITZERLAND: Mr. Camille Gorgé
(March 5, 1940)
PORTUGAL: Dr. Luiz Esteves Fernandes
(March 29, 1940)
AUSTRALIA:
The Hon. Sir John G. Latham
(Dec. 24, 1940)
PANAMA: Mr. Angelo Ferrari
(March 13, 1941)
IRAN: Mr. Abolghassem Nadjm
(March 13, 1941)
RUMANIA: General Georges Bagulesco
(April 28, 1941)
HUNGARY: Mr. Nicolas de Vegh
(June 11, 1941)
MEXICO: General José Luis Amezcua
(Sept. 18, 1941)

AMERICAN EMBASSY:
COUNSELOR: Mr. Eugene H. Dooman
MILITARY ATTACHÉ: Lieutenant-Colonel
Harry I. Creswell
NAVAL ATTACHÉ: Lieutenant-
Commander Henri H. Smith-Hutton
COMMERCIAL ATTACHÉ:
Mr. Frank S. Williams
FIRST SECRETARIES: Mr. George A.
Makinson, Mr. Edward S. Crocker
SECOND SECRETARIES: Mr. William T.
Turner, Mr. Charles E. Bohlen,
Mr. H. Merrell Benninghoff
THIRD SECRETARIES: Mr. John K.
Emmerson, Mr. Charles A. Cooper,
Mr. James Espy

INDEX

ABOUT THE AUTHOR

Joseph Clark Grew served as American Ambassador to Japan from February, 1932, until the attack on Pearl Harbor. He was born in Boston, Massachusetts, in 1880, and attended Groton and Harvard, graduating two years before President Roosevelt. After traveling in Europe and the East, he was made clerk to the American Consul General at Cairo in 1904. Since then he has made diplomacy his life-work. Before the last war, he served in Mexico, Russia, Austria-Hungary, and Germany. He was counselor to our Embassy in Berlin during the last war and Chargé d'Affaires at Vienna when the break came. In 1918 he became acting head of the Western European division of the State Department. He took part in the peace negotiations at Paris and also represented the United States during the negotiations with Turkey at Lausanne in 1922. He has served as Minister to Denmark and to Switzerland, as Under Secretary of State, and as Ambassador to Turkey. From Turkey he went to Japan. Mr. Grew is married and is the father of three daughters. He is now special assistant to the Secretary of State. One year after the attack on Pearl Harbor a collection of his speeches to the American people appeared under the title Report from Tokyo. Ten Years in Japan *consists of entirely different and new material.*